ELEMENTARY AND SECONDARY EDUCATION ACT, AS AMENDED BY THE EVERY STUDENT SUCCEEDS ACT - ACCOUNTABILITY AND STATE PLANS (US DEPARTMENT OF EDUCATION REGULATION) (ED) (2018 EDITION)

Updated as of May 29, 2018

THE LAW LIBRARY

TABLE OF CONTENTS

AGENCY

Office of Elementary and Secondary Education, Department of Education.

ACTION

Final regulations.

SUMMARY

The Secretary amends the regulations implementing programs under title I of the Elementary and Secondary Education Act of 1965 (ESEA) to implement changes to the ESEA by the Every Student Succeeds Act (ESSA) enacted on December 10, 2015. The Secretary also updates the current ESEA general regulations to include requirements for the submission of State plans under ESEA programs, including optional consolidated State plans.

DATES

These regulations are effective January 30, 2017.

FOR FURTHER INFORMATION CONTACT

Meredith Miller, U.S. Department of Education, 400 Maryland Avenue SW., room 3C106, Washington, DC 20202-2800.

Telephone: (202) 401-8368 or by email: Meredith.Miller@ed.gov.

If you use a telecommunications device for the deaf (TDD) or a text telephone (TTY), call the Federal Relay Service (FRS), toll free, at 1-800-877-8339.

SUPPLEMENTARY INFORMATION

Executive Summary

Purpose of This Regulatory Action: On December 10, 2015, President Barack Obama signed the ESSA into law. The ESSA reauthorizes the ESEA, which provides Federal funds to improve elementary and secondary education in the Nation's public schools. The ESSA builds on ESEA's legacy as a civil rights law and seeks to ensure that every child, regardless of race, income, background, or where they live has the opportunity to obtain a high-quality education. Through the reauthorization, the ESSA made significant changes to the ESEA for the first time since the ESEA was reauthorized through the No Child Left Behind Act of 2001 (NCLB), including significant changes to title I.

In particular, the ESSA significantly modified the accountability requirements of the ESEA. Whereas the ESEA, as amended by the NCLB, required a State educational agency (SEA) to hold schools accountable based solely on results on statewide assessments and one other academic indicator, the ESEA, as amended by the ESSA, requires each SEA to have an accountability system that is State-determined and based on multiple indicators, including, but not limited to, at least one indicator of school quality or student success and, at a State's discretion, an indicator of student growth. The ESSA also significantly modified the requirements for differentiating among schools and the basis on which schools must be identified for further comprehensive or targeted support and improvement. Additionally, the ESSA no longer requires a particular sequence of escalating interventions in title I schools that are identified and continue to fail to make adequate yearly progress (AYP). Instead, it gives SEAs and local educational agencies (LEAs) discretion to determine the evidence-based interventions that are appropriate to address the needs of identified schools.

In addition to modifying the ESEA requirements for State accountability systems, the ESSA also modified and expanded upon the ESEA requirements for State and LEA report cards. The ESSA continues to require that report cards be concise, presented in an understandable and uniform format, and, to the extent practicable, in a language that parents can understand, but now also requires that they be developed in consultation with parents and that they be widely accessible to the public. The ESSA also requires that report cards include additional information that was not required to be included on report cards under the ESEA, as amended by the NCLB, such as information regarding per-pupil expenditures of Federal, State, and local funds; the number and percentage of students enrolled in preschool programs; where available, the rate at which high school graduates enroll in postsecondary education programs; information regarding the number and percentage of English learners achieving English language proficiency (ELP), and certain data collected through the Civil Rights Data Collection (CRDC). In addition, the ESSA requires that report cards include certain information for subgroups of students for which information was not previously required to be reported, including homeless students, students in foster care, and students with a parent who is a member of the Armed Forces.

Further, the ESEA, as amended by the ESSA, authorizes an SEA to submit, if it so chooses, a consolidated State plan or consolidated State application for covered programs, and authorizes the Secretary to establish, for each covered program, the descriptions, information, assurances, and other material required to be included in a consolidated State plan or consolidated State application.

On May 31, 2016, the Secretary published a notice of proposed rulemaking (NPRM) for the title I, part A program and general ESEA regulations in the Federal Register (81 FR 34539). We issue these regulations to provide clarity and support to SEAs, LEAs, and schools as they implement the ESEA, as amended by the ESSA—particularly, the ESEA requirements regarding accountability systems, State and LEA report cards, and consolidated State plans—and to ensure that key requirements in title I of the ESEA, as amended by the ESSA, are implemented consistent with the purpose of the law: "to provide all children significant opportunity to receive a fair, equitable, and high-quality education, and to close educational achievement gaps."

Summary of the Major Provisions of This Regulatory Action: The following is a summary of the major substantive changes in these final regulations from the regulations proposed in the NPRM. The rationale for each of these changes is discussed in the Analysis of Comments and Changes section of this document.

- Section 200.12 has been revised to clarify that if an authorized public chartering agency, consistent with State charter school law, acts to decline to renew or to revoke a charter for a particular charter school, the decision of the agency to do so supersedes any notification from the State that the school must implement a comprehensive or targeted support and improvement plan under §§ 200.21 or 200.22.

- The Department made a number of changes to § 200.13, which describes a State's long-term goals and measurements of interim progress for achievement, graduation rates, and progress toward ELP for English learners:

—Section 200.13(a) is revised to clarify that long-term goals and measurements of interim progress for academic achievement must measure the percentage of students attaining grade-level proficiency on the State's annual assessments in reading/language arts and mathematics based on the State's academic achievement standards under section 1111(b)(1) of the ESEA, as amended by the ESSA, including alternate academic achievement standards for students with the most significant cognitive disabilities as defined by the State under section 1111(b)(1)(E) of the ESEA.

—Section 200.13(c) requires States to establish long-term goals and measurements of interim progress for increases in the percentage of English learners making annual progress toward attaining ELP using a uniform procedure, applied to all English learners in a consistent manner, that establishes applicable timelines for English learners sharing particular characteristics to attain ELP after a student's identification and student-level targets within that timeline. The final rule is revised to require each State, in its State plan, to describe how it sets research-based, student-level targets; a rationale for a State-determined maximum number of years in its uniform procedure; and the applicable timelines over which English learners sharing particular characteristics are expected to attain ELP.

- In § 200.14, which describes the requirements related to the five indicators—Academic Achievement, Academic Progress, Graduation Rate, Progress in Achieving English Language Proficiency, and School Quality or Student Success—within the statewide accountability system, the final regulations include the following significant changes:

—Section 200.14(b)(1)(i) and (ii) is reorganized and revised to clarify that the Academic Achievement indicator (1) must include a grade-level proficiency measure based on the State's academic achievement standards under section 1111(b)(1) of the ESEA, including alternate academic achievement standards for students with the most significant cognitive disabilities as defined by the State under section 1111(b)(1)(E) of the ESEA; (2) may include measures of student performance below or above the proficient level (e.g., in an achievement index), so long as a school receives less credit for the performance of a student who is not yet proficient than for the performance of a student who is proficient, and the credit a school receives for the performance of a more advanced student does not fully compensate for the performance of a student that is not yet proficient; and (3) does not require State assessments in reading/language arts and mathematics that are "equally measured."

—Section 200.14(b)(1) and (3) is revised to ensure that the Academic Achievement and Graduation Rate indicators are based on the corresponding long-term goals under § 200.13.

—Section 200.14(c)(4) is revised to remove the requirement that a given measure may be used no more than once across the accountability indicators.

—Section 200.14(d) is revised to clarify that States must demonstrate that measures in the Academic Progress and School Quality or Student Success indicators are supported by research that high performance or improvement on such measures is likely to increase student learning (e.g., grade point average, credit accumulation, or performance in advanced coursework), or—for measures at the high school level—graduation rates, postsecondary enrollment, postsecondary persistence or completion, or career readiness.

- Section 200.15, which describes the requirements related to participation in statewide assessments and the annual measurement of achievement, is revised as follows:

—Section 200.15(a) is revised to clarify the distinction between the statutory requirement for States to administer assessments to all students and the statutory requirement for States to measure, for accountability purposes, whether at least 95 percent of all students and of each subgroup of students participated in State assessments.

—Section 200.15(b)(2)(iv) is revised so that a State may develop and use a State-determined action or set of actions that is sufficiently rigorous to improve the school's participation rate in order to factor the statutory requirement for 95 percent participation on statewide assessments into its accountability system, rather than requiring such actions to be equally rigorous and result in a similar outcome as other possible options.

- In § 200.16, which describes the requirements related to inclusion of subgroups of students, the final regulations include the following significant changes:

—Section 200.16(b) is revised to permit a student previously identified as a child with a disability to be included in the children with disabilities subgroup for up to two years following the year in which the student exits special education services, for the limited purpose of measuring indicators that use results from required State assessments under section 1111(b)(2)(B)(v)(I) of the ESEA, as amended by the ESSA. A State choosing to include former children with disabilities for these indicators must include all such students, for the same period of time, and must also include all such students in determining whether the subgroup meets the State's n-size for purposes of calculating any such indicator.

—Section 200.16(c)(1) is revised to allow former English learners to be included in the English learner subgroup for up to four years following the year in which the student achieves English language proficiency consistent with the standardized, statewide exit procedures, when measuring any indicator under § 200.14(b) that uses data from required assessments under section 1111(b)(2)(B)(v)(I) of the ESEA, as amended by the ESSA.

- Section 200.17 is revised to clarify that if a State proposes to use an n-size above 30 students, the justification it provides in its State plan must include data on the number and percentage of schools that will not be held accountable for the performance of each subgroup of students described in § 200.16(a) compared to such data if the State had selected an n-size of 30.

- Within section 200.18, the Department made the following substantial revisions from the NPRM, primarily to better align requirements for differentiation in § 200.18 with requirements for identification of schools in § 200.19:

—Section 200.18 is renamed to clarify all of the components within annual meaningful differentiation of schools: "performance levels, data dashboards, summative determinations, and indicator weighting."

—Section 200.18(a)(2)-(3) describes the requirements for each State to describe a school's level of performance on each accountability indicator, from among three performance levels that are distinct, aligned to a State's long-term goals, and clear and understandable to the public. The final rule clarifies that the levels must also be discrete, indicating that reporting on a continuous measure (e.g., scale scores) would not meet the requirement, and that a data "dashboard" is an example of a way for a State to report performance levels for a school.

—Section 200.18(a)(4) specifies that a State must provide each school with a single summative "determination," from among at least three categories, based on all of the accountability indicators. We are revising the final regulation to clarify that a State may either use (1) determinations that include the two categories of schools required to be identified in § 200.19 (i.e., schools identified for comprehensive support and improvement and targeted support and improvement) and a third category of unidentified schools, or (2) determinations distinct from the categories of schools described in § 200.19. We are also revising § 200.18(a)(4) to clarify that the summative determination must meaningfully differentiate between schools based on differing performance on the indicators and provide information on a school's overall performance in a clear and understandable manner on annual report cards.

—Section 200.18(a)(6) is revised to clarify that annual meaningful differentiation must inform the State's methodology to identify schools under § 200.19, including identification of consistently underperforming subgroups of students.

—Section 200.18(c)(3) is revised to require each State to demonstrate that a school with a consistently underperforming subgroup will receive a lower summative determination than it would have otherwise received if the school had no consistently underperforming subgroups.

—Section 200.18(d)(1)(ii) is revised to require each State to demonstrate in its State plan that schools that are low-performing on indicators afforded "substantial" weight are more likely to be identified under § 200.19.

—Section 200.18(d)(1)(iii) incorporates provisions from the proposed State plan regulations to clarify that a State may develop and propose to use alternate methods for differentiation and identification under §§ 200.18-200.19 in order to ensure all public schools are included, such as schools in which no grades are assessed, schools with variant grade configurations, small schools, newly opened schools, and schools designed to serve special populations of students (e.g., newcomer English learners, students receiving alternative programming in alternative educational settings, and students living in local institutions for neglected or delinquent children, including juvenile justice facilities).

- The Department made several changes to § 200.19, primarily for clarification or to align requirements with other sections of the regulations:

—Section 200.19(a)(1) is revised to clarify that each State must identify the lowest performing five percent of all title I schools, not five percent of title I schools at each grade span, and to make conforming changes based on the significant changes under § 200.18.

—Section 200.19(a)(3) is revised to allow each State to determine how long a school with a low-performing subgroup identified for targeted support and improvement that also must receive additional targeted support under § 200.19(b)(2) may implement a targeted support plan before the State must determine that such a school has not met the State's exit criteria and must, if it receives title I funds, be identified for comprehensive support and improvement. A corresponding change is made to § 200.22(f)(2).

—Section 200.19(b)(2) is revised to clarify that a State must use the same process to identify schools with individual subgroups performing at or below the performance of all students in the lowest-performing five percent of title I schools as it uses to identify the lowest-performing five percent of title I schools for comprehensive support and improvement.

—Section 200.19(c)(1) is revised to allow a State, in order to identify schools with one or more consistently underperforming subgroups, to consider a school's performance among each subgroup of students in the school over more than two years, if the State demonstrates that a longer timeframe will better support low-performing subgroups of students to make significant progress in achieving long-term goals and measurements of interim progress in order to close statewide proficiency and graduation rate gaps, consistent with section 1111(c)(4)(A)(i)(III) of the ESEA, as amended by the ESSA, and § 200.13.

—Section 200.19(c)(3)(i) is revised to ensure that when a State chooses a definition for consistently underperforming subgroups that considers a subgroup's performance on the State's measurements of interim progress or State-designed long-term goals, the SEA also considers a schools' performance on the indicators for which goals and measurements of interim progress are not required, consistent with the requirement that the State's definition be based on all indicators.

—Section 200.19(c)(3) is revised to remove options for a State to define a consistently underperforming subgroup of students based on indicator performance levels, a single measure within an indicator, or performance gaps between the subgroup and State averages as described in proposed § 200.19(c)(3)(ii)-(iv).

—Section 200.19(d)(1)(i)-(ii) is revised to allow a State to delay identification of schools for comprehensive support and improvement and schools with a low-performing subgroup for targeted support and improvement that also must receive additional targeted support until no later than the beginning of the 2018-2019 school year.

—Section 200.19(d)(1)(iii) is revised to allow a State to delay identification of schools with consistently underperforming subgroups for targeted support and improvement until no later than the beginning of the 2019-2020 school year.

—Section 200.19(d)(2) is revised to clarify that for each year in which a State must identify schools for comprehensive or targeted support and improvement, it must do so using data from the preceding school year, except that the State may use adjusted cohort graduation rate data from the year immediately prior to the preceding school year.

- The Department made revisions to § 200.20 for clarity, including:

—Section 200.20(a) is revised to use consistent terminology for how States can produce averaged results by combining data across both school years and grades within a school and to clarify that a State combining data must sum the total number of students in each subgroup of students described in § 200.16(a)(2) across all school years when calculating a school's performance on each indicator under § 200.14 and determining whether the subgroup meets the State's minimum number of students described in § 200.17(a)(1).

—Section 200.20(a) is revised to clarify the limited purposes in the accountability system for which States may average school-level data across school years.

- Within sections §§ 200.21 and 200.22, Comprehensive Support and Improvement and Targeted

10

Support and Improvement, the Department made the following substantial revisions from the NPRM, primarily to strengthen and clarify the requirements for school improvement:

—Section 200.21(c)(4) is revised to require that an LEA, in conducting a school-level needs assessment for each school within the LEA identified for comprehensive support and improvement, consider a school's unmet needs, including with respect to students, school leadership and instruction staff, quality of the instructional program, family and community involvement, school climate, and distribution of resources.

—Section 200.21(d)(1) is revised to clarify that for LEAs affected by section 8538 of the ESEA, the LEA must develop school improvement plans in partnership with Indian tribes, among other required stakeholders.

—Section 200.21(d)(1), and similar requirements in §§ 200.15(c)(1)(i) and 200.22(c)(1), is revised to encourage the involvement of students, as appropriate, in developing school improvement plans.

—Section 200.21(d)(3) is revised to clarify examples of interventions that an LEA may consider implementing in an identified school and to clarify optional State authorities for State-approved lists of interventions or State-determined interventions, further described in § 200.23(c).

—Section 200.21(d)(3)(vi) is revised to clarify that differentiated improvement activities that utilize evidence-based interventions may be used in high schools that primarily serve students returning to education or who, based on their grade or age, are significantly off track to accumulate sufficient academic credits to meet State high school graduation requirements.

—Sections 200.21(d)(4) and 200.22(c)(7)(i) are revised to require that LEAs, in identifying and addressing resource inequities in schools identified for comprehensive support and improvement, or schools with a low-performing subgroup identified for targeted support and improvement that also must receive additional targeted support, respectively, must review access to advanced coursework, access to full-day kindergarten programs and preschool programs, and access to specialized instructional support personnel.

—Consistent with the revisions to § 200.21(d)(3)(vi), § 200.21(g) is revised to clarify State discretion to exclude very small high schools from developing and implementing a support and improvement plan if such schools are identified as a low graduation rate high school under § 200.19(a)(2).

—Sections 200.21(f) and 200.22(f) are revised to require that each SEA make its State-established exit criteria publicly available.

- The Department has revised § 200.23 as follows:

—Section 200.23(a) is revised to clarify that in periodically reviewing resources available for each LEA in the State serving a significant number or percentage of schools identified for comprehensive or targeted support and improvement, the State must consider each of the resources in its review that is listed in § 200.21(d)(4)(i)(A)-(E) and consider resources in such LEAs as compared to all other LEAs in the State and in schools in those LEAs as compared to all other schools in the State.

—Section 200.23(c)(1) is revised to list examples of additional actions a State may take to initiate improvement at the LEA level, or, consistent with State charter school law, in an authorized public chartering agency, that serves a significant number or percentage of schools identified for comprehensive support and improvement and that are not meeting exit criteria or a significant number or percentage of schools in targeted support and improvement.

—Section 200.23(c)(1) is revised to clarify that any action to revoke or non-renew a school's charter must be taken in coordination with the applicable authorized public chartering agency and be consistent with both State charter school law and the terms of the school's charter.

—Section 200.23(c)(3) is revised to clarify the distinction between this provision and a related provision in § 200.23(c)(2). The final regulations give States flexibility to establish evidence-based interventions for use by LEAs and schools identified for support and improvement either by creating lists of State-approved, evidence-based interventions for use in any identified school, or by developing their own alternative evidence-based interventions that may be used specifically in comprehensive support and improvement schools.

- The Department has made the following significant changes to § 200.24, which describes requirements for school improvement funding under section 1003 of the ESEA:

—Section § 200.24(c)(2)(ii) is revised to clarify that a State may award a grant of less than the minimum award size if the State determines that a smaller amount is appropriate based on the school's enrollment, identified needs, selected evidence-based interventions, and other relevant factors described in the LEA's application.

—Section 200.24(c)(4)(iii)(A) is revised to require that a State consider, in determining strongest commitment, both the proposed use of evidence-based interventions that are supported by the strongest level of evidence available, and whether the evidence-based interventions are sufficient to support the school in making progress toward meeting the applicable exit criteria under §§ 200.21 or 200.22.

- The Department revised § 200.30 for clarity, including as follows:

—Section 200.30(e) is revised to provide for a State to delay inclusion of per-pupil expenditure data on its report card until no later than June 30 following the December 31 deadline for reporting all other information required under section 1111(h) of the ESEA, as amended by the ESSA.

—Section 200.30(e)(3)(ii) is revised to clarify that a State requesting a one-time, one-year extension of the December 31 deadline for disseminating report cards must submit a plan and timeline for how it will meet the December 31 deadline for report cards that include information from the 2018-2019 school year.

—Section 200.30(f)(1)(iv) clarifies that students in the subgroup of "student with a parent who is a member of the Armed Forces" includes students whose parents are on full-time National Guard duty. Further, § 200.30(f)(1)(iv)(C) defines full-time National Guard duty.

- The Department revised § 200.31 for clarity, including as follows:

—Section 200.31(b)(3) removes the page limit requirement on the LEA overview for each school served by the LEA.

—Section 200.31(e) is revised to provide for an LEA to delay inclusion of per-pupil expenditure data until no later than June 30 following the December 31 deadline for reporting all other information required under section 1111(h) of the ESEA, as amended by the ESSA.

- The Department revised § 200.34, which provides the requirements on how to calculate the adjusted cohort graduation rate, including the following significant changes:

—Section 200.34(a)(3)(iii) is revised to clarify the requirements for removing a student entering a prison or juvenile justice facility from a sending school's cohort.

—Section 200.34(a)(5) is added to clarify that a State must include students with the most significant cognitive disabilities who receive a State-defined alternate diploma in the calculation of the adjusted cohort graduation rate in the year in which they exit, and describes how they should be treated in the numerator and the denominator.

—Section 200.34(c)(2) is revised to clarify that a diploma based on meeting a student's Individualized Education Program (IEP) goals is considered a lesser credential.

—Section 200.34(d)(2) is revised to remove language limiting an extended-year graduation rate to seven years.

—Section 200.34(e)(2) is added to describe the criteria a State must use to include students in the following subgroups in the graduation rate calculation: English Learners, children with disabilities, children who are homeless, and children who are in foster care.

—Section 200.34(e)(f) has been removed and revised requirements have been placed in § 200.34(a)(5).

- The Department has revised § 200.35 for clarity, including:

—Section 200.35(a) and (b) has been revised to clarify that State and LEA report cards must report the total current expenditures that were not reported in school-level per-pupil expenditure figures.

—Section 200.35(a) and (b) has been revised to clarify that State and LEA report cards must, when reporting per-pupil expenditures, include with State and local funds all Federal funds intended to replace local tax revenues.

—Section 200.35(c)(2) has been revised to clarify the denominator used for purposes of calculating per-pupil expenditures must be the same figure as reported to the National Center for Education Statistics (NCES) on or about October 1.

- The Department made a number of changes to § 299.13, which provides an overview of the State plan requirements.

—Section 299.13(c)(ii) is revised to require that an SEA ensures that LEAs will collaborate with local child welfare agencies to develop and implement clear written procedures that ensure children in foster care receive transportation to and from their school of origin when in their best interest.

—Section 299.13(c)(iii) was moved from proposed § 299.18(c) to require an SEA to assure that it will publish and update specific educator equity information and data regarding ineffective, out-of-field, and inexperienced teachers.

—Section 299.13(d)(3) is revised to allow an SEA to request a 3 year extension, rather than the 2 year extension originally proposed, to calculate statewide rates of educator equity data using school-level data when meeting the requirements of § 299.18(c)(3)(i).

- The Department made the following changes in § 299.14, which describes the framework and the requirements when submitting a consolidated State plan:

—Section 299.14(c) was added to include consolidated State plan assurances on coordination of federal programs, challenging academic standards and assessments, State support and improvement for low-performing schools, participation for private school children and teachers, and appropriate identification of children with disabilities. With the exception of the assurance regarding participation for private school children and teachers, the required assurances were previously required descriptions in the proposed consolidated State plan requirements, with revisions made in order to reduce unnecessary burden on each SEA.

- The Department made the following changes in § 299.15, which describes the requirements related to consultation on the consolidated State plan:

—Section 299.15 is revised to include two additional stakeholder groups with whom an SEA must consult in developing its consolidated State plan—representatives of private school students and early childhood educators and leaders—and to clarify that the stakeholder groups listed in § 299.15(a) represent the minimum stakeholder groups with whom an SEA is expected to consult.

—Section 299.15 is further revised such that § 299.15(b) no longer includes the proposed requirement that each SEA describe its plans for coordinating across Federal educational laws. Section 299.15(b) now includes the performance management requirements which only require an SEA to describe its performance management system once, and not for each component of its consolidated State plan.

- The Department made a number of changes to § 299.16, which describes the requirements related to challenging academic assessments, including:

—The final regulations do not require a State that elects to submit a consolidated State plan to provide evidence in such plan related to challenging academic content standards and aligned academic achievement standards, alternate academic achievement standards, as applicable, or ELP standards but rather, in § 299.14(c)(2), requires the SEA to assure that it will meet the statutory requirements. Specifically, the assurance in § 299.14(c)(2) clarifies that a State that elects to submit a consolidated State plan will meet the statutory requirements in section 1111(b)(1)(A)-(F) and 1111(b)(2) of the Act, including requirements related to alternate academic achievement standards and alternate assessments for students with the most significant cognitive disabilities and ELP standards and assessments.

—The final regulations do not require an SEA that elects to submit a consolidated State plan to provide evidence in such plan related to a State's academic assessments, including providing the names of such assessments and evidence that such assessments meet the requirements under section 1111(b)(2) of the ESEA and applicable regulations. Rather, the SEA must provide an assurance under § 299.14(c)(2) that it will meet the statutory requirements related to a State's academic assessments.

—Proposed § 299.16(b)(7) has been removed, and the Department will not require an SEA to describe in its consolidated State plan how it will use funds under section 1201 of the ESEA.

- The Department has revised some provisions in § 299.17 for clarification and alignment with revisions to other provisions in the final regulations as follows:

—Section 299.17(a) clarifies that, with respect to its State-designed long-term goals under § 200.13, an SEA must both provide its baseline, measurements of interim progress, and long-term goals, and describe how it established its long-term goals and measurements of interim progress.

—Section 299.17(b)(5)(iv) clarifies that an SEA must describe, among other elements as noted in § 299.17(b), how its methodology for differentiating all public schools in the State meets the requirements under § 200.18(c)(3) and (d)(1)(ii).

—Section 299.17(b)(8) incorporates the requirements for an SEA to describe how it includes all public schools in the State in its accountability system if it is different from the methodology described in § 299.17(b)(5), consistent with § 200.18(d)(1)(iii).

—Section 299.17(d)(2) is revised to include a description of how an SEA will provide technical assistance to each LEA in the State serving a significant number or percentage of schools identified for comprehensive or targeted support and improvement, including how it will provide technical assistance to LEAs to ensure the effective implementation of evidence-based interventions, consistent with § 200.23(b).

—Section 299.17(d)(4) is revised to require an SEA to describe how it will periodically review, identify, and, to the extent practicable, address resources available in LEAs serving a significant number or percentage of comprehensive or targeted support and improvement schools consistent with § 200.23(a).

- The Department made a number of changes in § 299.18, which provides the requirements related to supporting excellent educators as follows:

—Section 299.18(a) is amended to clarify that an SEA need only describe the State's system of certification and licensure, its strategies to improve educator preparation programs, and its strategies for professional growth and improvements for educators that addresses induction, development, compensation, and advancement if it intends to use Federal funds for these purposes.

—Section 299.18(b) is amended to remove the list of student subgroups that was provided in proposed § 299.18(b)(2).

—Section 299.18(c) is amended to clarify that an SEA must describe whether there are differences in the rates at which low-income and minority students are taught by ineffective, out-of-field, or inexperienced teachers.

—Section 299.18(c)(5) is revised to clarify that an SEA must identify likely causes of the most significant differences in the rates at which low-income and minority students are taught by ineffective, out-of-field, or inexperienced teachers.

—Section 299.18(c)(5)(ii) is revised to clarify that an SEA must prioritize strategies to address the most significant differences in the rates at which low-income and minority students are taught by ineffective, out-of-field, or inexperienced teachers.

—Section 299.18(c)(5)(iii) is revised so that an SEA must include its timeline and interim targets for eliminating any differences in the rates at which low-income and minority students are taught by ineffective, out-of-field, or inexperienced teachers.

- The Department made a number of changes in § 299.19, which provides the requirements for an SEA to describe how it will ensure a well-rounded and supportive education for all students, including the following:

—Section 299.19(a)(1) is amended to clarify that State must describe use of title IV, part A funds and funds from other included programs, including strategies to support the continuum of a student's preschool-12 education and to ensure all students have access to a well-rounded education. Such description must include how the SEA considered the academic and non-academic needs of the subgroups of students identified in § 299.19(a)(1)(iii).

—Section 299.19(a)(2) is revised to clarify that a State need only describe its strategies to support LEAs to improve school conditions for student learning, effectively use technology, and engage families, parents, and communities if the State uses title IV, part A funds or funds from one or more of the included programs for such activities.

—Section 299.19(a)(2) removes the requirement for a State to describe how it will ensure the accurate identification of English learners. Section 299.19(b)(4) retains the requirement for each SEA to describe its standardized entrance and exit procedures for English learners.

—Section 299.19(b)(3) is revised to include program-specific requirements for title I, part D that requires each SEA to provide a plan for assisting the transition of children and youth between correctional facilities and locally operated programs and a description of the program objectives and outcomes that will be used to assess the effectiveness of the program.

Please refer to the Analysis of Comments and Changes section of this preamble for a detailed discussion of the comments received and any changes made in the final regulations.

Costs and Benefits: The Department believes that the benefits of this regulatory action outweigh any associated costs to SEAs and LEAs, which may be financed with Federal grant funds. These benefits include a more flexible, less complex and costly accountability framework for the implementation of the ESEA, as amended by the ESSA, that respects State and local decision-making; the efficient and effective collection and dissemination of a wide range of education-related data that will inform State and local decision-making; and an optional, streamlined consolidated application process that will promote the comprehensive and coordinated use of Federal, State, and local resources to improve educational outcomes for all students and all subgroups of students. Please refer to the Regulatory Impact Analysis section of this document for a more detailed discussion of costs and benefits, including changes in estimated costs in response to public comment. Consistent with Executive Order 12866, the Secretary has determined that this action is economically significant and, thus, is subject to review by the Office of Management and Budget under the order.

Public Comment: In response to our invitation to comment in the NPRM, 21,609 parties submitted comments on the proposed regulations.

We discuss substantive issues under the sections of the proposed regulations to which they pertain, with the exception of a number of cross-cutting issues, which are discussed together under the heading "Cross-Cutting Issues." Generally, we do not address technical and other minor changes, or suggested changes the law does not authorize us to make under the applicable statutory authority. In addition, we do not address general comments that raised concerns not directly related to the proposed regulations or that were otherwise outside the scope of the regulations, including comments that raised concerns pertaining to particular sets of academic standards or the Department's authority to require a State to adopt a particular set of academic standards, as well as comments pertaining to the Department's regulations on statewide assessments.

Tribal Consultation: The Department held four tribal consultation sessions on April 24, April 28, May 12, and June 27, 2016, pursuant to Executive Order 13175 ("Consultation and Coordination with Indian Tribal Governments"). The purpose of these tribal consultation sessions was to solicit tribal input on the ESEA, as amended by the ESSA, including input on several changes that the ESSA made to the ESEA that directly affect Indian students and tribal communities. The Department specifically sought input on: The new grant program for Native language Immersion schools and projects; the report on Native American language medium education; and the report on responses to Indian student suicides. The Department announced the tribal consultation sessions via listserv emails and Web site postings on http://www.edtribalconsultations.org/.

During the consultation session held on June 27, 2016, which was held during the public comment period, the attendees discussed a range of topics pertaining to the ESEA, as amended by the ESSA, many of which related to provisions and titles of the law that fall outside the scope of these regulations. We do not address those comments in these regulations, but we are continuing to consider them in accordance with the Department's Tribal Consultation Policy, which is available at: http://www.edtribalconsultations.org/documents/TribalConsultationPolicyFinal2015.pdf.

A number of participants at the June 27, 2016 consultation session provided input pertaining to these regulations. For example, a number of participants expressed concerns about the consultation, or lack of consultation, conducted by States and districts with local tribes. Participants wished to be more involved in the development of State and local policies that affect Native students. A few participants expressed specific concerns that the proposed regulation regarding the minimum number of students that must be in a subgroup for that subgroup to be included in accountability determinations would not ensure that Native students were included in accountability determinations to the maximum extent possible.

The Department considered the input provided during the first three consultation sessions in developing the proposed requirements. We considered input from the June 27, 2016 tribal consultation session on the topics that are within the scope of these regulations, as part of public comments received on the NPRM. We respond to the comments from that session that are within the scope of these regulations under the sections of the proposed regulations to which they pertain.

Analysis of Comments and Changes: An analysis of the comments and changes in the regulations since publication of the NPRM follows.

Cross-Cutting Issues

Legal Authority

Comments: A number of commenters asserted that these regulations constitute an overreach by the Department because the regulations include requirements pertaining to topics on which the ESEA, as amended by the ESSA, delegates authority to States and LEAs. A number of commenters cited specific statutory provisions that are intended to limit the Department's authority to create new requirements or criteria for statewide accountability systems beyond those specifically enumerated in the ESEA, as amended by the ESSA. Some of these commenters contended that any regulatory requirement that is not specifically authorized by the statute and that establishes parameters for how States or LEAs implement the law exceeds the Department's authority and violates the statute.

Discussion: Section 410 of the General Education Provisions Act (GEPA), 20 U.S.C. § 1221e-3, authorizes the Secretary, "in order to carry out functions otherwise vested in the Secretary by law or by delegation of authority pursuant to law, . . . to make, promulgate, issue, rescind, and amend rules and regulations governing the manner of operations of, and governing the applicable programs administered by, the Department." Section 414 of the Department of Education Organization Act (DEOA) similarly authorizes the Secretary to prescribe such rules and regulations as the Secretary determines necessary or appropriate to administer and manage the functions of the Secretary or the Department. 20 U.S.C. 3474. Section 1601(a) of the ESEA, as amended by the ESSA, bolsters this general authority through an additional grant of authority for the Secretary to issue regulations under title I of the ESEA. That provision states that the Secretary "may issue . . . such regulations as are necessary to reasonably ensure that there is compliance with this title." Further, section 8302(a)(1) of the ESEA, as amended by the ESSA, authorizes the Secretary to "establish procedures and criteria" for the submission of consolidated State plans.

The provisions of these regulations are wholly consistent with the Department's rulemaking authority. In particular, section 1001 of the ESEA, as amended by the ESSA, establishes the purpose of title I of the statute, which is "to provide all children significant opportunity to receive a fair, equitable, and high-quality education, and to close educational achievement gaps." In furtherance of that goal, section 1111(a) requires any State that desires to receive a grant under title I, part A to file with the Secretary a plan that meets certain specified requirements, which may be submitted as part of a consolidated plan under section 8302 of the ESEA. Section 1111(c)(1) of the ESEA requires each State plan to describe a statewide accountability system that complies with the requirements of subsections 1111(c) and 1111(d). In addition, section 1111(h)(1) of the ESEA requires a State that receives assistance under title I, part A to prepare and disseminate widely to the public an annual State report card for the State as a whole that meets the requirements of that paragraph, and section 1111(h)(2) requires an LEA that receives assistance under title I, part A to prepare and disseminate an annual LEA report card that includes certain specified information on the agency as a whole and each school served by the agency.

The Department has determined that each of these regulations is necessary to provide clarity with respect to provisions of the law that are vague or ambiguous, or to reasonably ensure that States and LEAs implement key requirements in title I of the ESEA, as amended by the ESSA— particularly the requirements regarding accountability systems, State and LEA report cards, and consolidated State plans—consistent with the statute and with the statutory purpose of the law.

In developing these regulations, we carefully considered each of the statutory restrictions on the Department's authority, including the restrictions in section 1111(e)(1)(A) of the ESEA, as amended by the ESSA, as well as the more specific restrictions on the Department's authority to regulate particular aspects of statewide accountability systems in section 1111(e)(1)(B). We were also mindful of the fact that one of the goals of the reauthorization of the ESEA through the ESSA was to provide greater discretion and flexibility to States and LEAs than had been provided to them under the ESEA, as amended by NCLB, and have taken steps to ensure that States and LEAs have significant discretion and flexibility with respect to how they implement these regulations.

However, we disagree with the contention that any regulation that is not explicitly authorized by the statute and places any limitation on a State's or LEA's discretion either violates the specific statutory restrictions or is otherwise inconsistent with the statute. A regulation would be inconsistent with the statute if it were directly contrary to the statutory requirements, or if it would be impossible for a State or LEA to comply with both the statutory and regulatory requirements. Regulatory requirements that provide greater specificity regarding how a State must implement certain requirements are not inconsistent with the statute or the Department's rulemaking authority in any way.

We similarly disagree with the contention that any of the regulations governing statewide accountability systems add new requirements that are outside the scope of title I, part A of the ESEA, as amended by the ESSA. All of the regulatory requirements governing statewide accountability systems fall squarely within the scope of title I, part A, as those requirements implement the statutory requirements in sections 1111(c) and 1111(d) of the ESEA, as amended by the ESSA, and are specifically intended to ensure compliance with those sections. The fact that these regulations impose certain requirements for statewide accountability systems that are not specifically mentioned in those sections of the statute does not mean that those requirements fall outside the scope of title I, part A. Accordingly, the final regulations also do not violate section 1111(e) of the ESEA, as amended by the ESSA, which prohibits the Secretary from promulgating any regulations that are inconsistent with or outside the scope of title I, part A.

Moreover, given that the Secretary has general rulemaking authority, it is not necessary for the statute to specifically authorize the Secretary to issue a particular regulatory provision. Rather, the Secretary may issue any regulation governing title I that is consistent with the ESEA, as amended by the ESSA, that enables the Secretary to "carry out functions otherwise vested in the Secretary by law or by delegation of authority pursuant to law," and, with respect to regulations under title I of the ESEA, that the Secretary deems "necessary to reasonably ensure that there is compliance with" that title.

In promulgating these regulations, the Secretary has exercised his authority under GEPA, the DEOA, and under sections 1601(a) and 8302(a) of the ESEA, as amended by the ESSA, to issue regulations that are necessary to reasonably ensure that States, LEAs, and schools comply with the requirements for statewide accountability systems, consolidated State plans, and State and LEA report cards, and that they do so in a manner that advances the statutory goals.

Changes: None.

Comments: One commenter suggested that any of the Department's proposed regulations that proposed adding a requirement not expressly contained in the ESEA, as amended by the ESSA, might violate the Spending Clause of the U.S. Constitution (Article I, section 8, Clause 1), by failing to provide "clear notice" to grantees of the requirements with which they must comply by accepting title I funds.

Discussion: Congress' authority to enact the provisions in title I of the ESEA, as amended by the ESSA, governing statewide accountability systems, report cards, and State plans flows from its authority to ". . . provide for general Welfare of the United States." Article I, Section 8, Clause 1 (commonly referred to as Congress' "spending authority"). Under that authority, Congress authorized the Secretary to implement the provisions of the ESEA, as amended by the ESSA, and specifically authorized the Secretary to issue "such regulations as are necessary to reasonably ensure that there is compliance with" title I. Thus, the regulations do not conflict with Congress' authority under the Spending Clause. With respect to cases such as Arlington C. Sch. Dist. Bd. of Educ. v. Murphy, States have full notice of their responsibilities under these regulations through the rulemaking process the Department has conducted under the Administrative Procedure Act and the General Education Provisions Act to develop the regulations.

Changes: None.

Data Collection

Comments: Some commenters recommended removing § 200.17, stating that the amount of data already collected has not improved academic achievement and that the Federal government should not collect data on children. These comments were also made regarding §§ 200.20-24, 200.30-31, 299.13, and 299.19 of the proposed regulations. In addition, a number of commenters recommended retaining § 200.7 of the current regulations, which sets forth the data disaggregation and privacy requirements under the NCLB, without commenting specifically on proposed § 200.17, which would establish similar requirements under the ESSA.

Discussion: The Department believes that data collected for purposes of accountability and data reported on State and LEA report cards are important for providing parents and stakeholders the information they need to understand how schools are held accountable and how students, including each subgroup of students, are performing. Further, collecting these data is necessary to comply with the requirements of section 1111 of the ESEA, as amended by the ESSA. In addition to promoting transparency, this information is essential for identifying and closing educational achievement gaps, which is one of the primary purposes of the law. We note that there are also multiple provisions in title I of the ESEA, as amended by the ESSA, including section 1111(c)(3), (g)(2)(N), and (i), that specify privacy protections for individuals related to collection or dissemination of data consistent with section 444 of the GEPA (20 U.S.C. 1232g, commonly known as the Family Educational Rights and Privacy Act of 1974). We further note, as we stated in the NPRM, that § 200.17 retains and reorganizes the relevant requirements of current § 200.7, which would be removed and reserved, so that these requirements (related to disaggregation of data primarily for accountability purposes) are incorporated into the sections of the final regulations pertaining to accountability, instead of pertaining to assessments.

Changes: None.

Section 200.12   Single Statewide Accountability System

Comments: A number of commenters asked for clarity about the timeline under which a State will be required to implement a statewide accountability system, noting the distinction between the school year in which data are collected and the school year in which schools are differentiated and identified for support and improvement.

Discussion: While we address specific comments related to the implementation timeline for the identification of schools in the statewide accountability system in § 200.19, which begins no later than the 2018-2019 school year, in order to avoid confusion between the year in which a State collects data to calculate its indicators under § 200.14 and the year in which a State first differentiates and identifies schools under §§ 200.18 and 200.19, we have removed the reference to a specific year of implementation in § 200.12.

Changes: We revised § 200.12(a)(1) to strike "beginning no later than the 2017-2018 school year."

Comments: One commenter suggested that the Department create, through the regulatory process, an education office of the ombudsman for each State that would be an independent organization to ensure fair, objective, and transparent investigations of complaints and that would resolve data and other disputes related to key elements of statewide accountability systems, including meaningful differentiation of all public schools and identification of schools to implement comprehensive or targeted support and improvement plans.

Discussion: While we recognize that LEAs or schools may occasionally dispute accountability determinations under the ESEA, we believe that States are best positioned to determine an appropriate and timely process for resolving such disputes, which may include establishing an ombudsman's office for this purpose without the Department requiring this. We decline to change the regulations in this area.

Changes: None.

Comments: Many commenters wrote either in support of or opposition to various aspects of the proposed regulations on statewide accountability systems, which are listed in § 200.12, including indicators under § 200.14 and school improvement plans under §§ 200.21 and 200.22.

Discussion: We appreciate feedback in response to the high-level overview of statewide accountability systems in proposed § 200.12. However, we address comments on specific components of the accountability system in the sections of the proposed regulations that address these specific components.

Changes: None.

Single System

Comments: A number of commenters wrote generally about the framework for a single statewide accountability system; some supported and others opposed the creation of a single system. Commenters writing in opposition variously objected to the word "single" as not specifically authorized by the statute, described the proposed regulations as an overreach of the Department's authority, and warned that the proposal, contrary to its stated purpose, would encourage separate State and Federal accountability systems. Other commenters asserted that the requirement for a single statewide system would prevent States, LEAs, or charter schools from creating their own accountability systems, separate from the accountability system required under the ESEA, that are better tailored to local needs. Another commenter asked the Department to provide guidance on how to reconcile conflicting school improvement identifications that may result from separate State and ESEA accountability systems. Finally, one commenter recommended that the regulations permit flexibility for rural schools and districts, suggesting, for example, that rural schools be overseen in accordance with State rural school laws, similar to the provisions in the statute and § 200.12(a) for public charter schools.

Discussion: We believe that a single statewide system is necessary to meet ESEA requirements, particularly for ensuring that annual meaningful differentiation and identification of schools is fair, consistent, and transparent to the public; and to ensure that all schools are treated equitably and held to the same expectations. However, the requirement for a single statewide system in § 200.12 for Federal accountability purposes does not preclude a State, LEA, or charter school organization from establishing a separate accountability system for its own purposes, including school identification and support, should such a system be required under State or local law, or desired for other reasons.

Finally, it is not necessary for the ESEA, as amended by the ESSA, to specifically authorize the Secretary to clarify that the statewide accountability system must be a single statewide accountability system, as this regulatory requirement is being promulgated pursuant to the Secretary's rulemaking authority under GEPA, the DEOA, and section 1601(a) of the ESEA, as amended by the ESSA, and is fully consistent with section 1111(e) of the ESEA, as amended by the ESSA (see discussion of the Department's general rulemaking authority under the heading Cross-Cutting Issues). Without this clarification, the statutory provision on its own is ambiguous and could lead to inconsistent or unfair systems of annual meaningful differentiation and identification for schools. In addition, the requirement is necessary to reasonably ensure compliance with, and falls squarely within the scope of, the requirement in section 1111(c)(1) of the ESEA, as amended by the ESSA.

Changes: None.

Comments: A number of commenters suggested that the Department provide flexibility for different accountability systems for certain types of schools, particularly alternative schools, to allow for the use of measures that are better suited to describe student outcomes and school performance in alternative settings. Specifically, commenters noted a need to differentiate accountability requirements associated with the four-year adjusted cohort graduation rate to allow students in non-traditional settings to achieve high school diplomas without time constraints. However, other commenters requested that the Department maintain strong and uniform accountability measures for all schools, including those that serve students with unique and specialized needs.

Discussion: We agree that certain types of schools, such as alternative high schools, schools serving students living in local institutions for neglected or delinquent children, including juvenile justice facilities, and very small schools, may have unique concerns and, in some instances, need additional flexibility that the statewide accountability system described in § 200.12 may not be able to provide in order to adequately reflect the achievement of the student population and overall success of the school. We address this concern in response to comments under the subheading Other Requirements in Annual Meaningful Differentiation of Schools in § 200.18, which we have revised to clarify the differentiation in accountability requirements permitted for certain categories of schools that are designed to serve special populations of students.

Changes: None.

Comments: Several commenters from tribal organizations suggested that the Department revise proposed § 200.12 to require specific provisions in a State's accountability system for students instructed primarily through Native American languages. Another commenter representing tribes expressed support for a uniform statewide accountability system in § 200.12, noting that the requirements to measure student achievement are critical for the more than 90 percent of American Indian and Alaska Native students that attend public schools supported by SEAs.

Discussion: We appreciate the comments addressing unique concerns affecting American Indian and Alaska Native students. As described in § 200.12, a State's accountability system must be based on the challenging State academic standards under section 1111(b)(1) of the ESEA and academic assessments under section 1111(b)(2). To the extent that commenters requested revisions regarding requirements for State assessments, these regulations do not address the requirements associated with the specific academic assessments that a State must administer and use in its statewide accountability system; rather, such issues will be addressed through the final regulations on assessment for title I, part A. Section 200.12 provides broad parameters for State accountability systems and does not address the language of instruction used. We agree with the commenter that a single statewide accountability system is critical to maintain uniform high expectations for all students, including American Indian and Alaska Native students, and to close achievement gaps.

Changes: None.

Comments: None.

Discussion: As a technical edit, we have replaced § 200.12(b)(3) to emphasize that the State's accountability system must include all indicators in § 200.14.

Changes: We have replaced § 200.12(b)(3) with the requirement that the State's accountability system must include all indicators in § 200.14. We have subsequently renumbered proposed paragraphs (b)(3) through (b)(5) to (b)(4) through (b)(6), respectively.

Consideration of Additional Academic Subjects

Comments: Multiple commenters expressed that State accountability systems should allow for consideration of academic subjects in addition to reading/language arts and mathematics. However, several commenters also expressed support for the emphasis on academic achievement and high school graduation in the regulations, among the multiple measures of school performance that can be included in statewide accountability systems.

Discussion: Section 1111(c)(4)(A)-(B) of the ESEA, as amended by the ESSA, require each State to establish long-term goals and measurements of interim progress and an accountability indicator that are based on student academic achievement on the State's reading/language arts and mathematics assessments. Further, section 1111(c)(4)(C) requires that the Academic Achievement indicator be one that receives "substantial" weight in the system of annual meaningful differentiation of schools. However, we agree with commenters emphasizing that a well-rounded education includes subjects beyond reading/language arts and mathematics, and this is a valuable opportunity for States under the ESEA. Under the ESEA and our regulations, a State may include additional subjects in its statewide accountability system. We further address this concern in response to comments in §§ 200.13 and 200.14, which establish the requirements for the long-term goals and indicators used in the State accountability system.

Changes: None.

Goals and Measurements of Interim Progress

Comments: A few commenters requested that the Department strengthen the language in proposed § 200.12(b)(2) requiring that the State's accountability system be informed by the State's long-term goals and measurements of interim progress under § 200.13. One commenter requested that the Department clarify in the text of § 200.12 that the long-term goals and measurements of interim progress established under § 200.13 must be ambitious.

Discussion: Section 200.12 is intended to provide a high-level overview of the requirements for a single statewide accountability system; section 200.13 fully addresses the requirements for long-term goals and measurements of interim progress. In addition, we are revising § 200.14 (accountability indicators) and § 200.18 (annual meaningful differentiation of school performance) to clarify the role of goals and measurements of interim progress in the statewide accountability system. We agree with the comment that the regulations would be more precise and consistent with the requirements in § 200.13 with the addition of the word "ambitious."

Changes: We have revised § 200.12(b)(2) to clarify that a State's accountability system must be informed by ambitious long-term goals and measurements of interim progress.

Charter Schools

Comments: A number of commenters supported the requirement in § 200.12 that the statewide accountability system applies to all public elementary and secondary schools in the State, including public charter schools. Many commenters also supported the additional statutory requirement that charter schools be overseen in accordance with State charter school law. One commenter noted that including this language helps to clarify that, in general, charter schools are subject both to ESEA accountability requirements and any additional accountability expectations that State charter school authorizers may establish in accordance with State charter school law. For example, a charter authorizer may revoke or decline to renew a charter based on school performance measured against the requirements of the charter even if the State is not requiring action based on the ESEA accountability requirements.

Another commenter expressed concern that under the ESEA, as amended by NCLB, State charter school laws emphasized the use of high-stakes testing to assess school performance; this commenter requested that the final regulations support accountability for charter schools based on the same multi-measure systems required by the ESEA, as reauthorized by the ESSA, for traditional public schools.

A few commenters called for increased regulation and accountability for charter schools.

Discussion: We appreciate support from commenters stating that the regulations help to clarify the applicability of accountability requirements for charter schools under both the ESEA and State charter school laws, and we believe that it is helpful to further clarify how public charter schools are both accountable under the ESEA requirements, as well as the performance expectations established under State charter school law and the charter school's authorizer. For example, we agree with the commenter who noted that charter authorizers may still revoke or decline to renew a charter based on school performance using the authorizer's established charter review or revocation processes, even if the school is in compliance with the ESSA accountability requirements, and are revising the final regulations to specify that in the case of an authorizer that acts to revoke or non-renew a school's charter, such action supersedes the requirements to implement a comprehensive or targeted support and improvement plan under §§ 200.21 or 200.22, respectively, recognizing that State charter school laws may impose more rigorous interventions than those required by the ESEA, as amended by the ESSA. We also agree that public charter schools must be included and held accountable in the statewide accountability system using the same methodology (including the same indicators) that is used with traditional public schools to annually differentiate school performance and identify schools for support and improvement. While accountability for charter schools must be overseen in a way that is consistent with State charter school law, this does not exempt charter schools from the State's system of annual meaningful differentiation, identification of schools, and implementation of support and improvement plans. We have revised § 200.12(b)(5)-(6) to reiterate the inclusion of public charter schools in these components of the statewide accountability system, with a corresponding change to § 200.18(a).

Changes: We have revised § 200.12(c)(2) to clarify that if an authorized public chartering agency, consistent with State charter school law, acts to decline to renew or to revoke a charter for a particular charter school, the decision of the agency to do so supersedes any notification from the State that such a school must implement a comprehensive support and improvement or targeted support and improvement plan under §§ 200.21 or 200.22, respectively. We have also revised § 200.12(b)(5)-(6) to further specify that the requirements for annual meaningful differentiation and identification of all public schools include all public charter schools, and made a corresponding change to § 200.18(a).

Section 200.13   Long-term Goals and Measurements of Interim Progress

Academic Achievement

Comments: Several commenters expressed support for the requirement that States set long-term goals and measurements of interim progress for improved academic achievement based on grade-level proficiency as measured on annual State assessments in mathematics and reading/language arts.

Other commenters recommended that the Department give States flexibility to use different measures in setting long-term goals and measurements of interim progress for academic achievement, including individual student growth, metrics that account for student achievement at all levels (e.g., average scale scores, proficiency indices), or measures that give credit for students moving toward proficiency who have not yet attained grade-level proficiency. Some commenters also stated that the Department's proposed requirement to base academic achievement goals and measurements of interim progress on grade-level proficiency ignores section 1111(e)(1)(B)(iii)(I)(bb) of the ESEA, as amended by the ESSA, which prohibits the Department from prescribing States' numeric long-term goals and measurements of interim progress and is inconsistent with Congressional intent to give States flexibility in setting their goals.

Commenters also suggested that the grade-level proficiency requirement be retained, but revised to reflect that:

- grade-level proficiency must be aligned with minimum State requirements to enroll in college or enter a career; and

- achieving proficiency is the minimum goal for academic achievement, and so the phrase "at a minimum" should be added before every instance of "grade-level proficiency."

Discussion: We appreciate the support of commenters for requiring goals based on grade-level proficiency. We believe this requirement is both essential to maintain high expectations for all students and consistent with the statutory requirements in section 1111(c)(4) of the ESEA for the accountability system to be based on the State's challenging academic standards, which must include grade-level academic achievement standards and may include alternate academic achievement standards for students with the most significant cognitive disabilities, and in section 1111(c)(4)(A)(i)(I)(aa) which specifies that the long-term goals and measurements of interim progress must be measured by proficiency on the State's annual assessments, which are aligned to these achievement standards. We also note that the statutory requirements for challenging academic standards under section 1111(b)(1)(D) specify that a State's standards must align with entrance requirements for credit-bearing coursework in the system of public higher education in the State and relevant State career and technical education standards, so we do not think it is necessary to restate that in this section. We further maintain that for educators, parents, and students, but especially, parents and students, information about whether students are performing at grade-level lets them know whether their student is meeting their State's expectations for their grade.

In response to commenters who asserted that the proposed requirement violates the provision in section 1111(e)(1)(B)(iii)(I)(bb) of the ESEA, as amended by the ESSA, we note that the requirement in § 200.13(a)(1) for States to set goals for academic achievement based on grade-level proficiency is consistent with section 1111(e)(1)(B)(iii)(I)(bb) of the ESEA, as amended by the ESSA, because it does not prescribe the numeric long-term goals that a State establishes for academic achievement, or the progress that is expected for each subgroup toward those goals. Further, the Department has determined that the requirement in § 200.13(a)(1)is necessary to clarify that the reference to academic achievement as "measured by proficiency" in section 1111(c)(4)(B)(i)(I) of the ESEA, as amended by the ESSA, means academic achievement as measured by the percentage of students attaining grade-level proficiency because, without that clarification, the statutory language is vague and ambiguous; absent clarification, States may have difficulty determining whether they are complying with the requirement. Moreover, this clarification of the statutory requirement is necessary to reasonably ensure that the measure of proficiency used in the Academic Achievement indicator is consistent with the requirement in section 1111(b)(2)(B)(ii) that a State's academic assessments provide coherent and timely information about whether a student is performing "at the student's grade level." In addition, given the Department's rulemaking authority previously described in the discussion of Cross-Cutting Issues, it is not necessary for the statute to specifically authorize the Secretary to issue a particular regulatory provision.

We recognize that States may find value in accounting for students who are not yet proficient or performing above grade-level or measuring how students are performing against other measures of performance, such as student growth. We note that States can set goals for measures other than grade-level proficiency for their own purposes, if they so choose, and we further discuss in response to comments in § 200.14 how progress and performance of students who are below or above the proficient level may be included in the Academic Achievement indicator or other indicators in the accountability system and how student growth is included in the Academic Progress indicator.

Changes: None.

Comments: None.

Discussion: We have determined that the regulations could provide greater clarity regarding how States are expected to set long-term goals and measurements of interim progress for academic achievement, to reflect that those goals are measured by the percentage of students attaining grade-level proficiency.

Changes: We have revised § 200.13(a)(1) to specify that the goals and measurements of interim progress are based on the percentage of students attaining grade-level proficiency on the State's annual assessments.

Comments: Some commenters requested that the Department require States to set goals for academic subjects beyond reading/language arts and mathematics, with some asserting that what they described as the overly narrow focus on reading/language arts ignores the need for a well-rounded education, including access to arts and music education. One commenter specifically recommended that States be required to establish goals for science, while another commenter wrote that proposed § 200.13 over-emphasizes student performance on standardized tests.

Discussion: The proposed regulations are consistent with section 1111(c)(4)(A)(i)(I)(aa) of the ESEA, as amended by the ESSA, which specifies that States must establish long-term goals and interim measurements of progress for, at a minimum, academic achievement on the State's reading/language arts and mathematics assessments. The statute gives States flexibility to establish goals for other subjects if they choose, and we do not wish to limit State discretion to address their own needs and priorities in this area in the final regulations.

Changes: None.

Graduation Rates

Comments: A few commenters requested that the Department clarify what is meant by "more rigorous" in regards to the requirement that, if a State chooses to use an extended-year adjusted cohort graduation rate as part of its Graduation Rate indicator, the State must establish long-term goals for that extended-year rate that are more rigorous than those established for the four-year adjusted cohort graduation rate. In particular, two commenters requested clarification that the term "more rigorous" refers to the graduation rate and not the academic requirements for graduation (e.g., standards, levels of proficiency).

Discussion: We generally intend that the "more rigorous" goals required for extended-year cohort graduation rates be higher than those for four-year adjusted cohort graduation rates, but we decline to require this in the final regulations in recognition that States have flexibility to determine how much higher over a State-determined period of time. We also note that, consistent with the statute, our regulations for graduation rate goals address only the rates of, and not the requirements for, high school graduation.

Changes: None.

Comments: None.

Discussion: We believe the proposed regulations could provide greater clarity on the expectation that the "more rigorous" requirement applies to both the long-term goals and measurements of interim progress for any extended-year rate that the State chooses to use and are revising § 200.13(b)(2)(ii) to indicate that both long-term goals and measurements of interim progress should be higher for each extended-year rate as compared to long-term goals and measurements of interim progress for the four-year rate.

Changes: We have revised § 200.13(b)(2)(ii) so that the requirement for more rigorous expectations applies to both the long-term goals and measurements of interim progress for each extended-year graduation rate.

Comments: While a few commenters indicated support for State discretion to establish long-term goals and measurements of interim progress for both four-year and extended-year graduation rates, two commenters expressed concern that the four-year rate was over-emphasized in the proposed regulations, with a potentially negative impact on schools that focus on dropout prevention.

Discussion: We agree that it is important for States to have the flexibility within their accountability systems to give credit to schools for students who graduate from high school in more than four years, and we believe that the final regulations provide such flexibility. For example, § 200.14 allows States to measure the extended-year adjusted cohort rate as part of the Graduation Rate indicator. Further, the regulations are aligned with section 1111(c)(4)(A)(i)(bb)(AA) of the ESEA, as amended by the ESSA, which requires that States establish goals for the four-year adjusted high school graduation rate.

Changes: None.

Expected Rates of Improvement

Comments: A number of commenters supported the requirement that States establish goals to require greater rates of improvement for subgroups of students that are lower-achieving and graduate high school at lower rates. Commenters indicated that this requirement is important for equity, that it is appropriate to focus on progress for the most disadvantaged student groups, that it is important to hold schools accountable for closing achievement and opportunity gaps, and that this requirement appropriately expects teachers, principals, and other school leaders to make greater progress with historically underserved students.

However, multiple other commenters opposed this requirement, variously stating that students progress at different rates; that no subgroup should be expected to progress at a greater rate than any other student subgroup; that the requirement is too prescriptive in view of Congressional intent to allow States flexibility in establishing goals; and that it ignores section 1111(e)(1)(B)(iii)(I)(bb) of the ESEA, as amended by the ESSA, which states that nothing in the ESEA, as amended by the ESSA, authorizes the Department to prescribe the progress expected from any subgroup of students in meeting long-term goals.

Discussion: We appreciate the support of commenters for the proposed regulations on setting goals that require greater improvement from lower-performing student subgroups, which we believe are essential for clarifying and reasonably ensuring compliance with the requirement in section 1111(c)(4)(A)(i)(III) of the ESEA, as amended by the ESSA, that a State's goals for subgroups of students who are behind on academic achievement and graduation rates take into account the improvement needed to make significant progress in closing gaps on those measures. We agree with commenters that students make progress at different rates, but believe that it is appropriate, with the goal of closing achievement gaps in mind, for States to set goals to make greater progress with subgroups of students who are further behind.

Given that the requirement thus falls squarely within the Secretary's rulemaking authority under GEPA, the DEOA, and section 1601(a) of the ESEA (see discussion of the Department's rulemaking authority under the heading Cross-Cutting Issues), it is not necessary for the statute to specifically authorize the Secretary to issue this particular regulatory requirement. Moreover, the requirement does not violate section 1111(e) of the ESEA, as amended by the ESSA, because the requirement for States to set goals that require greater rates of improvement from lower-performing subgroups is within the scope of and consistent with section 1111(c)(4)(A)(i)(III) of the ESEA, as amended by the ESSA, which requires that a State's goals for subgroups of students who are behind on academic achievement and graduation rates take into account the improvement needed to make significant progress in closing gaps on those measures. It is also consistent with section 1111(e)(1)(B)(iii)(I)(bb) of the ESEA, as amended by the ESSA, because it does not prescribe the numeric long-term goals that a State establishes for academic achievement and graduation rates or the progress that is expected for each subgroup toward those goals.

Changes: None.

Comments: A few commenters requested that the Department further clarify what is meant by requiring "greater rates of improvement" for subgroups of students that are lower-achieving and subgroups of students that graduate high school at lower rates. One commenter specifically recommended that the Department add language ensuring that States take into account how much improvement would be necessary for these subgroups of students to meet long-term goals and make significant progress in closing statewide proficiency gaps.

Discussion: We recognize that there are many ways in which States could choose to provide for greater rates of improvement and therefore decline to make the requested change. Rather, we intend to issue non-regulatory guidance to support States in setting meaningful long-term goals and measurements of interim progress.

Changes: None.

English Language Proficiency

Comments: A number of commenters responded to the Department's directed question asking whether, in setting ambitious long-term goals for English learners to achieve ELP, States would be better able to support English learners if the proposed regulations included a maximum State-determined timeline and, if so, what that maximum timeline should be. Many commenters appreciated the parameters established in the proposed regulations for using a uniform procedure to create long-term goals based on English learners with similar characteristics, but felt that English learners would be better served if the proposed regulations also set a maximum State-determined timeline for English learners to achieve ELP. The majority of the commenters in favor of setting a maximum State-determined timeline supported a maximum timeline of five years for English learners to achieve ELP in order to best align with existing research. On the other hand, several commenters urged the Department not to set a limit on the maximum State-determined timeline for English learners to achieve ELP; these commenters highlighted the diversity of the English learner population as a key reason to avoid setting a uniform maximum timeline, and worried that such a timeline would create incentives for States to prematurely exit English learners from services. Some commenters further believed that limiting the maximum State-determined timeline (such as five years) would provide a disincentive for States to adopt certain types of evidence-based language instructional education programs, such as dual-language programs, in which English learners on average achieve proficiency over a longer period of time, but have been found to perform better in the academic content areas compared to English learners who participated in other types of language instructional education programs. In addition, some commenters believed that creating a limit on the maximum timeline in the regulations constitutes overreach and goes beyond any necessary requirements to comply with the statute.

Discussion: We agree with commenters who stated that the heterogeneity of the English learner population would make it difficult to set an appropriate maximum State-determined timeline that would be the same across all States for all English learners to achieve ELP. Additionally, the Department does not wish to create a disincentive for States in adopting any types of language instructional education programs that have been demonstrated to be effective through research, nor do we want to encourage States to cease providing necessary services to English learners to avoid exceeding a certain timeline. (1) Although there is a body of research on the time it takes for English learners to achieve ELP which would support a maximum State-determined timeline of five years, most research identifies a range of years over which English learners typically achieve ELP, based on a number of factors including the diverse and unique needs of the English learner population. (2) Therefore the final regulations do not establish the same maximum State-determined timeline across all States for English learners to achieve ELP, but leave that determination to States' discretion.

We believe it is appropriate for a State to retain the flexibility to adopt a uniform procedure for establishing its own maximum timeline, with applicable timelines within that maximum for each category of English learners to attain proficiency, based on selected student characteristics it chooses from the list in § 200.13(c) and research, for purposes of its long-term goals. Thus, we are revising the final regulations to require that a State set an overall maximum timeline for English learners to achieve ELP on the basis of research and describe its procedure and rationale in its State plan, in § 200.13(c)(2)-(3).

Additionally, based on the comments received in response to the directed question, we believe greater clarity is needed to explain how the State-determined maximum timeline interacts with the student-level characteristics of English learners included in § 200.13 that are used to set timelines and student-level progress targets. More specifically, the proposed regulations were not sufficiently clear that a State must create and use a consistent method for evaluating selected student-level characteristics, including the student's level of ELP at the time of a student's identification as an English learner, and, based on those characteristics, determine the appropriate timeline for the student to attain ELP within the State's overall maximum timeline. The applicable timeline for a particular category of English learners is then broken down to create targets for progress on the annual ELP assessment for that category of English learners. In this way, the State's uniform procedure is used to create student-level targets for English learners who share particular characteristics. We are revising § 200.13(c) to provide greater clarity on this process for setting timelines and student-level targets. Further, we note that both the proposed and final regulations make clear that an English learner must not be exited from English learner services or status until attaining English language proficiency, without regard to such timeline.

Further, we are revising § 200.13(c) to make a clearer distinction between the State-determined maximum timeline that informs the student-level targets (the topic on which we asked a directed question in the NPRM) and the overall timeframe for which the State establishes long-term goals. Thus, the final regulations specify that the State-level long-term goals and measurements of interim progress are based on increases in the percentage of all English learners in the State who make annual progress toward ELP (i.e., meet their student-level targets, based on the uniform procedure described previously). For example, a State's goal could be that within three years, 95 percent of English learners will make sufficient progress, based on the student-level targets, on the ELP assessment to achieve ELP within the State's expected timeline; the measurements of interim progress might be 85 percent and 90 percent in years one and two respectively. That State may have timelines that expect English learners who started at lower proficiency levels to achieve proficiency within 5-7 years, and English learners who start at more advanced levels and at younger ages achieving proficiency on shorter timelines. The State will set the ELP assessment progress targets based on research and data particular to the ELP assessment used; for those English learners at the lower levels of proficiency and younger ages, a larger score change or level change may typically be expected than for those who started at higher proficiency levels and for older students. By tailoring progress targets to categories of English learners, the State can realistically expect all English learners to show progress.

Changes: We have revised § 200.13(c) to require that: (1) States identify and describe in their State plans how they establish long-term goals and measurements of interim progress for increases in the percentage of all English learners in the State making annual progress toward attaining ELP; (2) States describe in their State plans a uniform procedure, applied to all English learners in the State in a consistent manner, to establish research-based student level targets on which their long-term goals and measurements of interim progress are based; and (3) the description includes a rationale for determining the overall maximum number of years for English learners to attain ELP in its uniform procedure for setting research-based, student-level targets, and the applicable timelines over which English learners sharing particular characteristics are expected to attain ELP within the State-determined maximum number of years. We have also revised 200.13(c)(2) to clarify that a State's uniform procedure includes three elements: The selected student characteristics, including the student's initial level of ELP; the applicable timelines (up to a State-determined maximum number of years) for English learners sharing particular characteristics to attain ELP after the student's identification; and the student-level targets that expect English learners to make annual progress toward attaining English language proficiency within the applicable timelines for such students.

Comments: Several commenters wrote in support of the particular student-level characteristics of English learners included in proposed § 200.13(c) that States would use to determine long-term goals and measurements of interim progress for English learners. These commenters expressed the view that the proposed regulations would provide States appropriate flexibility to establish long-term goals that were tailored to the diverse needs of the English learner population and that would support effective instruction for English learners by ensuring goals were meaningful and attainable for students and educators.

In addition, a number of commenters recommended including additional student-level characteristics, including disability status, the type of language instruction educational program an English learner receives, and other State-proposed characteristics that could have an impact on a student's progress in achieving ELP.

Discussion: We appreciate feedback from commenters on the list of student-level characteristics of English learners that may be taken into account in establishing long-term goals and measurements of interim progress for attaining ELP. While we recognize that research has shown that disability status can affect an English learner's ability to attain proficiency in English, and that there are cases (as noted in § 200.16(c)) where a student's type of disability directly prevents him or her from attaining proficiency in all four domains of ELP, we note that there are many types of disabilities that have minimal or no impact on an English learner's ability to attain ELP and such a determination would need to be made on an individualized basis. Given this complexity and the difficulty in setting rules that would apply consistently to determine when it is, and is not, appropriate to set different expectations for attaining ELP for an English learner with a disability, we believe it is best to address these issues in non-regulatory guidance.

Similarly, we appreciate that students enrolled in certain types of language instructional programs, including dual language programs, may take longer to attain ELP, and it was not our intent to discourage LEAs or schools from adopting such methods. However, we believe that the current list of characteristics in § 200.13 that may be considered already includes significant flexibility for States to design appropriate and achievable goals and measurements of interim progress for English learners. We believe that encouraging implementation of high-quality programs that support English learners toward acquisition of ELP is better addressed in non-regulatory guidance. (3)

Changes: None.

Comments: Many commenters wrote in support of the general parameters for setting long-term goals included in § 200.13(c), noting that they provided States with flexibility to set goals in ways that are both ambitious and attainable and recognize the diversity within the English learner subgroup. But a few commenters stated that the proposed regulations focused too much on attainment of, rather than progress toward, achieving English language proficiency, and would require States to establish goals for both progress and proficiency similar to Annual Measurable Achievement Objectives (AMAOs) under NCLB. One commenter recommended using the statutory language of "making progress in achieving" ELP, rather than "attaining." Another commenter was concerned that proposed § 200.13(c) was contrary to statutory intent in this area, and objected to imposing any additional requirements on States regarding their long-term goals and measurements of interim progress for English learners, believing such decisions should be made by States.

Discussion: We appreciate commenters' support for § 200.13(c). We also recognize that the statute uses progress towards "achieving" rather than "attaining" English language proficiency, but disagree with commenters that there is a meaningful distinction between "achieving" and "attaining" ELP. We further disagree with commenters who asserted that the proposed requirements for long-term goals for English Learners making progress in achieving ELP were too prescriptive and overly focused on attainment of ELP. We continue to believe that the parameters in § 200.13(c) are essential for ensuring that States establish meaningful long-term goals and measurements of interim progress that are appropriate for the diverse range of English learners found in every State.

Moreover, we do not agree that the requirements in § 200.13(c) would require States to establish attainment goals similar to AMAO-2 under the ESEA, as amended by the NCLB. Rather, States will set goals and measurements of interim progress based on the percentage of students attaining their student-level progress targets each year, as clarified in revised § 200.13(c)(1)-(2). There is no requirement for States to set a goal regarding the number or percentage of English learners achieving English language proficiency.

With respect to the comment that proposed § 200.13(c) was contrary to statutory intent in this area, and that any additional requirements regarding long-term goals and measurements of interim progress for English learners should be left to State discretion, as previously described in the discussion of Cross-Cutting Issues, we disagree with the argument that a regulation that sets parameters on the way a State implements its discretion under the statute is inherently inconsistent with the statute. Further, we believe the parameters established by § 200.13(c) are necessary to ensure that the goals set by States, and timelines underlying those goals, are reasonable and will help to ensure compliance with the requirement in section 1111(c)(4) that a statewide accountability system be designed to improve student academic achievement. The regulations do not dictate a specific maximum number of years for any English learner to attain proficiency, and do not dictate that a State choose particular student characteristics in setting its progress timelines, other than initial ELP level. As explained in the NPRM, (4) initial ELP level as a factor in time-to-proficiency is supported by substantial amounts of research and should help ensure fair treatment of schools with high numbers of English learners in the State accountability system.

Changes: None.

Other Topics

Comments: The Department received a variety of supportive comments on proposed § 200.13. Several commenters stated that the proposed regulations, in general, give States the authority and discretion to establish long-term goals and appreciated the flexibility afforded to States in this matter. A few commenters indicated that they appreciated that the Department emphasized holding all students to the same high standards of academic achievement. Commenters also expressed support for requiring States to:

- Set academic achievement goals for reading/language arts and mathematics separately;

- establish goals for student subgroups as well as for all students; and

- use the same multi-year timeline to set long-term goals for all student subgroups.

Discussion: We appreciate the support from commenters for these regulations. We agree that it is important for States to have flexibility to establish long-term goals and measurements of interim progress that are appropriate for their unique contexts. Further, to provide additional clarity on these requirements, we are revising § 200.13 to emphasize the required use of the same multi-year timeline to set long-term goals for all students and for each subgroup of students, except that the requirement for disaggregation of long-term goals and measurements of interim progress does not apply to goals related to ELP.

Changes: We have revised § 200.13 so that the requirement for a State to use the same multi-year timeline to achieve its long-term goals for all students and for each subgroup of students applies across all three areas in which a State must set long-term goals—achievement, graduation rates, and ELP—except that the requirement for disaggregation of long-term goals and measurements of interim progress does not apply to goals related to ELP.

Comments: A few commenters recommended that the Department adjust the language in § 200.13(a)(2)(i) to clarify what it means to apply the same standards of academic achievement to all public schools in the State, except as provided for students with the most significant cognitive disabilities. Several commenters recommended that the Department make clear that alternate academic achievement standards for students with the most significant cognitive disabilities who take an alternate assessment must be based on the same grade-level academic content standards as for all other students. One commenter suggested that the Department use the phrase "academic achievement standards" instead of "standards of academic achievement" to be more precise in meaning and consistent with the statute.

Discussion: The Department agrees that it is important for the language of the regulations to be clear regarding expectations for students with the most significant cognitive disabilities, to whom the same grade-level academic content standards apply, even though their progress may be assessed using an alternate assessment aligned with alternate academic achievement standards. However, because the statute and applicable regulations on standards and assessments address these concerns and because this provision is specifically focused on the academic achievement standards, we decline to add language regarding grade-level academic content standards in § 200.13. We agree that referencing alternate academic achievement standards, as described in section 1111(b)(1)(E) of the ESEA, as amended by the ESSA, and changing the phrase "standards of academic achievement" to "academic achievement standards" is appropriate and helpful to clarify requirements for long-term goals and measurements of interim progress as they pertain to students with the most significant cognitive disabilities.

Changes: We have revised the language in § 200.13(a)(2)(i) to be clear that the requirements for long-term goals and measurements of interim progress for academic achievement against grade-level proficiency refer to the State's academic achievement standards, as described in section 1111(b)(1) of the Act, and to make clear that the performance of students with the most significant cognitive disabilities may be assessed against alternate academic achievement standards defined by the State consistent with section 1111(b)(1)(E) of the ESEA, as amended by the ESSA.

Comments: One commenter recommended that the Department establish a minimum annual percentage increase in proficiency rates necessary to meet the requirement that long-term goals and measurements of interim progress be "ambitious." Another commenter requested that the Department establish parameters for what is meant by an interim measurement of progress, without specific suggestions for what the parameters should be.

Discussion: We agree that it will be important for States to establish meaningful and ambitious long-term goals and measurements of interim progress ambitious, but we believe the final regulations provide States with the appropriate level of discretion in this area, consistent with the statute. In addition, we intend to issue non-regulatory guidance on this topic to support States in setting meaningful long-term goals and measurements of interim progress.

Changes: None.

Comments: A few commenters requested that the Department add clarifying language to communicate that scores from assessments given in students' native languages should be included in the accountability system and publicly reported. Additional commenters suggested that the Department clarify that a State's long-term goals and measurements of interim progress should pertain, where applicable, to a Native American language of instruction for students instructed primarily through Native American languages.

Discussion: We are regulating separately on assessment requirements, but we note that the statute provides in section 1111(b)(2)(F) that States make every effort to develop student academic assessments in languages that are present to a significant extent in the student population. For assessments that are part of a State's assessment system and that are given to English learners in the student's native language for reading/language arts, mathematics, and science, the results would be included in the State's accountability system. Because this is clear under the statute, we do not believe it is necessary to add this to the regulations.

With regard to the comment about instruction through a Native American language, nothing in § 200.13 addresses the language of instruction, and thus no change is needed.

Changes: None.

Comments: One commenter requested that States be required to establish a uniform procedure for setting long-term goals and measurements of interim progress for students with disabilities, taking into account student characteristics and available research, similar to what is required of States in establishing goals for English learners toward achieving ELP under § 200.13(c). This commenter suggested that such a process would be beneficial to students with disabilities and help ensure that goals for students with disabilities are set in alignment with accountability requirements as well as a student's individualized education program (IEP).

Discussion: The Department included the requirement that States establish uniform procedures with regards to setting goals for English learners toward achieving language proficiency in order to allow differentiation of goals for categories of English learners that share similar characteristics, including initial level of ELP. We believe this is appropriate for English learners, given the varied needs and shifting composition of the particular students included in the English learner population and for whom the goal is to attain English proficiency and exit the program, but do not think it is applicable or appropriate to require States to develop such procedures for setting goals for children with disabilities who, while their educational needs also vary, are entitled to receive special education and related services for as long as determined necessary by their IEP teams in order to receive a free appropriate public education, and who therefore are not routinely exiting the subgroup. Rather than a differentiated process based on particular student characteristics, we encourage States to consider how they may set long-term goals and measurements of interim progress in ways that expect greater rates of progress, and result in closing educational achievement gaps, for low-performing subgroups, including—if applicable—children with disabilities. We intend to issue non-regulatory guidance to assist States in these efforts.

Changes: None.

Comments: One commenter recommended that the Department make clear that failing to meet a State's established measurements of interim progress and long-term goals is not a violation of the law.

Discussion: We do not believe this clarification is necessary, as neither the statute nor the final regulations suggest or imply that a failure to meet State-determined goals or measurements of interim progress would be considered a violation of the law.

Changes: None.

Comments: One commenter indicated that the emphasis on on-time graduation and grade-level proficiency is contrary to child development because some students require more time and support than others to achieve the same goal.

Discussion: We agree with the commenter that students have unique needs and require different types and levels of support and amounts of time to reach certain goals. However, we disagree that establishing goals for grade-level proficiency and high school graduation is developmentally inappropriate; such goals set high expectations for students and provide valuable information about whether students are performing on grade-level and are prepared to graduate from high school. Additionally, the regulations align to the requirements in section 1111(c)(4)(A) of the ESEA, as amended by the ESSA, that States set long-term goals and measurements of interim progress for academic achievement based on proficiency on annual assessments and for high school graduation rates.

Changes: None.

Comments: None.

Discussion: We have determined that § 200.13(a)(1) and § 200.13(b)(1) could provide greater clarity on what information States have to include in their State plans regarding their long-term goals and measurements of interim progress and have revised the regulations to make clear that States must identify and describe how they established their long-term goals and measurements of interim progress. We believe the language in the proposed regulations was vague and that without this clarification States may have difficulty determining whether they are complying with the requirement.

Changes: We have revised the language in § 200.13(a)(1) and § 200.13(b)(1) to clarify what information regarding long-term goals and measurements of interim progress a State must include in its consolidated State plan.

Section 200.14   Accountability Indicators

Comments: One commenter opposed the requirement in proposed § 200.14(a) that the same measures be used within each indicator for all schools, asserting that this requirement would unfairly penalize students in alternative schools.

Discussion: In general, we believe that statewide accountability systems must include the same measures within each indicator in order to provide fair, consistent, and transparent accountability determinations. However, as we discuss later in these final regulations, we have revised § 200.18(d)(1)(iii) to incorporate the flexibility included in proposed § 299.17 that allows States to use a different methodology for identifying for comprehensive support and improvement and targeted support and improvement schools that are designed to serve unique student populations, including alternative schools. Given that flexibility, we decline to make any changes to this requirement.

Changes: None.

Comments: Several commenters expressed appreciation for the Department's clarification in the preamble of the NRPM that States can update and modify indicators and measures over time. In particular, these commenters noted that such flexibility would allow States to include additional indicators as the research basis for such indicators matures, consistent with the proposed requirements in section 200.14(d). One commenter suggested we clarify that States may include indicators they plan to use in the future, when data is available, within their State plans so that their intentions are transparent.

Discussion: We appreciate the support we received from commenters regarding the flexibility for States to change or add measures to their accountability systems over time. As we discussed in the

NPRM, we recognize that States may want to update their accountability systems after receiving additional input or as new data become available. However, because States may not yet know which measures they would change or add to their accountability system at a later date, we do not believe it would be appropriate to require States to include a discussion of that topic in their State plans. Therefore, we decline to add such a requirement to the final regulations.

Changes: None.

Comments: A number of commenters broadly opposed the requirements in proposed § 200.14 and recommended the Department give States as much flexibility as possible in developing and implementing indicators and measures within their statewide accountability systems. Some of these commenters believe the proposed requirements reduce flexibility for States and LEAs, inconsistent with the ESEA. Other commenters asserted that the proposed requirements would limit States to a specific number of indicators, contrary to the statutory requirements.

Discussion: We agree with the commenters that States have flexibility in defining the indicators that are most appropriate for their context. However, the ESEA, as amended by the ESSA, includes specific requirements for each indicator and clearly identifies which indicators must be included in the accountability system, and these statutory requirements are reflected in the final regulations. We also note that under the statute, while States may only have a single indicator of Academic Achievement, Academic Progress, Progress in Achieving English Language Proficiency, and Graduation Rate, they may have more than one indicator of School Quality or Student Success, and neither the statute nor the proposed regulations limit the number of indicators of School Quality or Student Success States may include.

Changes: None.

Comments: Some commenters encouraged the Department to require that States report disaggregated data on the homeless student subgroup, foster student subgroup, or both, on each accountability indicator given the unique needs of students in each of those groups.

Discussion: We agree with the commenters that foster and homeless students have unique educational needs and that it may be helpful for stakeholders to have data on each group's performance on the accountability indicators. To that end, sections 1111(h)(1)(C)(ii) and 1111(h)(1)(C)(iii)(II) of the ESEA, as amended by the ESSA, require that each State report on disaggregated academic achievement and graduation rates for students identified as homeless or as a child in foster care. However, section 1111(c)(2), which identifies subgroups for the purposes of accountability, does not include such students and, thus, reporting on those subgroups is not required for the other accountability indicators. While States are certainly welcome, and even encouraged, to report separately on the performance of homeless and foster students on all of the accountability indicators, the Department declines to add such a reporting requirement.

Changes: None.

Comments: In discussing the requirement for a single summative rating in proposed § 200.18, one commenter recommended specifying that the rating be based on all accountability indicators, including the performance of all students and each subgroup of students on the State's long-term goals and measurements of interim progress.

Discussion: We agree with the commenter that it is critical for the annual meaningful differentiation of schools, as described in § 200.18, to be based on all indicators. Further, we appreciate that this suggestion highlighted a statutory requirement that was not sufficiently recognized in the proposed regulations. Under section 1111(c)(4)(B)(i) and (iii) of the ESEA, as amended by the ESSA, indicators of Academic Achievement and Graduation Rates must be based on a State's long-term goals and measurements of interim progress. Accordingly, we believe it is best to address this comment in § 200.14, rather than in § 200.18, so that we may emphasize this relationship in the requirements related to indicators, rather than the overall system of annual meaningful differentiation.

Changes: We have revised § 200.14(b)(1) and (3) to specify that the Academic Achievement and Graduation Rate indicators must be based on the long-term goals established under § 200.13.

Comments: A few commenters requested that the accountability indicators include specific provisions for students instructed primarily through Native American languages, including a disaggregated subgroup for such students, and provisions relating to inclusion of assessment scores of such students.

Discussion: We decline to add specific provisions for students instructed through a specific language medium or through a particular instructional approach. In addition, the student subgroups for the indicators are specifically required by the statute (section 1111(c)(2) of the ESEA, as amended by the ESSA), and we decline to expand those subgroups.

Changes: None.

Academic Achievement Indicator

Comments: Numerous commenters recommended clarifying the requirement in proposed § 200.14(b)(1)(i) so that it allows for a greater range of approaches in how States measure grade-level proficiency in the Academic Achievement indicator. Some commenters were concerned that the Department's interpretation of "grade-level proficiency" would mean only the percentage of students that attain a proficient score on State assessments would be recognized in the indicator, which they feel narrowly focuses States and schools on students just below or just above the State's achievement standards for proficiency. A few commenters instead recommended modifying the final regulation to affirmatively permit States to use a measure of achievement that considers student performance at multiple levels of achievement in order to measure grade-level proficiency. Some of these commenters requested flexibility for States to examine student performance at each level of achievement on the State's academic achievement standards and create an index that awards partial credit to a student who is not yet proficient and additional credit to a student who is at an advanced level. Similarly, other commenters suggested permitting States to consider a school's average scale score, rather than proficiency rates, as the measure of grade-level proficiency in the Academic Achievement indicator.

Discussion: Section 1111(c)(4)(B)(i)(I) of the ESEA, as amended by the ESSA, states that the Academic Achievement indicator must be "measured by proficiency on the annual assessments required under subsection (b)(2)(B)(v)(I)," and we agree with commenters that further clarity on this language is needed. Because proficiency must be measured by the State's annual assessments, we believe it is helpful to clarify that grade-level proficiency in § 200.14 means, at a minimum, a measure of student performance at the proficient level on the State's academic achievement standards.

We share the commenters' concerns that a focus exclusively on percent proficient could create an incentive for schools to focus too narrowly on students who are just above, or just below, the threshold for attaining proficiency and that additional ways of measuring proficiency could improve the statistical validity and reliability of a State's accountability system. For these reasons, we are revising § 200.14(b)(1)(ii) to clarify that the scores of students at other levels of achievement may be incorporated into the Academic Achievement indicator. Under the revisions to § 200.14(b)(1)(ii), a State that chooses to recognize schools for the performance of students that are below the proficient level and, at its discretion, for the performance of students that are above the proficient level within the Academic Achievement indicator must do so in a way such that (1) a school receives less credit for the score of a student that is not yet proficient than for the score of a student that has reached or exceeded proficiency, and (2) the credit a school receives for the score of an advanced student does not fully mask or compensate for the performance of a student who is not yet proficient. For example, a State may award each school 0.5 points in the achievement index for every student that scores at a level below the proficient level on the State's assessment, 1.0 points for every student that achieves a score at the proficient level, and 1.25 points for every student that scores at levels above the proficient level, but may not award 1.5 points for each of these more advanced students (as such an approach would fully compensate for the performance of a student who is not yet proficient). These safeguards allow for the scores of students at other levels of achievement to contribute toward a school's overall determination, consistent with many commenters' concerns, while minimizing the extent to which the inclusion of measures of student performance at other levels may detract from the required information in the indicator: Proficiency on the State assessments. In addition, we note that all States, including those that choose to adopt an achievement index, must report information on its State and LEA report cards under section 1111(h) of the ESEA, as amended by the ESSA, and § 200.32, disaggregated by each subgroup of students, on the number and percentage of students performing at each level of achievement; this provides another safeguard to ensure that information on proficiency on the State assessments is clear and transparent.

Because the calculation of an average scale score treats scores above the proficient level the same as scores below the proficient level, however, the use of such scores in the Academic Achievement indicator could result in an average scale score for the school above the proficient level even if a majority of the students in the school are not yet proficient. Such an outcome on the Academic Achievement indicator would not be consistent with the statutory requirement to measure students' proficiency on the State assessments, and is thus excluded from the list of additional measures that a State may incorporate in its Academic Achievement indicator under new § 200.14(b)(1)(ii).

We also note that the ESEA, as amended by the ESSA, offers ample flexibility for States to account for student progress and achievement at all levels in their statewide accountability systems, particularly by using measures of student growth in the Academic Progress indicator (for elementary and middle schools) or Academic Achievement indicator (for high schools), or in, for example, measures related to students taking and succeeding in accelerated coursework or the percentage of students scoring at advanced levels on statewide assessments as a School Quality or Student Success indicator. We strongly encourage States to consider these other ways to help recognize the work schools are doing to help low-performing students reach grade-level standards and high-performing students in maintaining excellence and support schools in increasing access to advanced pathways for all students, while maintaining the focus of the Academic Achievement indicator on grade-level proficiency based on the State assessments.

Changes: We have revised and reorganized § 200.14(b)(1)(i)-(ii) to clarify that the Academic Achievement indicator must include a measure of student performance at the proficient level against a State's academic achievement standards, and may also include measures of student performance below or above the proficient level, so long as (1) a school receives less credit for the performance of a student that is not yet proficient than for the performance of a student at or above the proficient level; and (2) the credit a school receives for the performance of a more advanced student does not fully compensate for the performance of a student who is not yet proficient.

38

Comments: A number of commenters supported the requirements in §§ 200.13 and 200.14 that require academic achievement to be measured based on grade-level proficiency, as an important check to align school accountability requirements with challenging State academic standards and to ensure all students and subgroups of students are supported in meeting rigorous academic expectations. However, several commenters generally opposed the use of student test scores in the Academic Achievement indicator, or asserted that the proposed requirements would continue an overemphasis on test-based accountability systems.

Discussion: We agree with commenters that it is important for the Academic Achievement indicator to include a measure of students' grade-level proficiency, aligned with the State's challenging academic standards, as a way to promote excellence for all students. We also believe this provision is critical to fulfill the statutory purpose of title I to close educational achievement gaps, and are revising the final regulations to make the alignment of grade-level proficiency with the State's challenging academic standards clearer.

While we recognize other commenters' concerns regarding a focus on grade-level proficiency on State assessments in the Academic Achievement indicator, we disagree that its inclusion is unwarranted. First, section 1111(c)(4) of the ESEA requires the accountability system to be based on the State's challenging academic standards, which includes challenging academic achievement standards for each grade level and subject that must be assessed and included in the accountability system. Second, section 1111(c)(4)(B)(i) specifies that the Academic Achievement indicator must be measured by proficiency on the annual assessments required by section 1111(b)(2)(B)(v)(I), which must assess student performance against the challenging academic achievement standards for the grade in which a student is enrolled, and in the case of students with the most significant cognitive disabilities, may assess performance against alternate academic achievement standards that are aligned with the State's academic content standards for the grade in which a student is enrolled. In addition, section 1111(c)(4)(C) of the ESEA requires that the Academic Achievement indicator receive "substantial" weight in the accountability system, a distinction not afforded to the indicators of School Quality or Student Success, thus demonstrating intent that the Academic Achievement indicator based on State assessments receive greater emphasis in statewide accountability systems.

Finally, there are significant opportunities for States to design multi-measure accountability systems under the law and the final regulations that emphasize student performance and growth at all levels, not just proficient and above, as well as non-test-based measures that examine whether the school is providing a high-quality and well-rounded education. For example, we encourage States to consider using measures of student growth on their annual assessments, as these measures can identify schools where students that are not yet proficient but are making significant gains over time and closing achievement gaps. States may also consider adding measures related to students taking and succeeding in accelerated coursework as a School Quality or Student Success indicator to recognize the work schools are doing with high-performing students and encourage schools to increase access to and participation in advanced pathways for all students.

Changes: We have revised and reorganized § 200.14(b)(1)(i) to clarify that a grade-level proficiency measure is based on the State's academic achievement standards under section 1111(b)(1) of the Act, including alternate academic achievement standards for students with the most significant cognitive disabilities defined by the State consistent with section 1111(b)(1)(E) of the Act.

Comments: A few commenters supported the requirement in proposed § 200.14(b)(1)(i) that a State's Academic Achievement indicator equally measure grade-level proficiency on the statewide reading/language arts and mathematics assessments required under title I of the ESEA. Other commenters opposed this requirement, with some misunderstanding it as a requirement for equivalent assessments in both subjects (despite being based on different academic standards) and others asserting that it is inconsistent with the statute, including section 1111(e)(1)(B)(iii)(IV)-(V) of the ESEA regarding the Secretary's authority to regulate on the weight of any measure or indicator or the specific methodology that States use to meaningfully differentiate and identify schools.

Discussion: We disagree with commenters that the Department lacks authority to regulate in this area, given the Secretary's rulemaking authority under GEPA, the DEOA, and section 1601(a) of the ESEA, as amended by the ESSA, and that these regulations fall squarely within the scope of section 1111(c)(4), consistent with section 1111(e) of the ESEA, as amended by the ESSA (see discussion of the Department's general rulemaking authority under the heading Cross-Cutting Issues). Moreover, these regulations are consistent with our rulemaking authority given that section 1111(c)(4) requires the statewide accountability system to be based on the challenging State academic standards for both reading/language arts and mathematics and section 1111(c)(4)(B)(i)(I) requires the indicator to measure proficiency in both subjects. However, we agree with other commenters that the proposed requirement to equally measure grade-level proficiency on State assessments in reading/language arts and mathematics was ambiguous, and that it could be misinterpreted to require these assessments to be able to be equated (e.g., by using the same scale), even though they must be based on separate academic content and achievement standards. In response, we are removing the requirement, and believe it is more appropriate to address how reading/language arts and mathematics, as measured by the State assessments, may be meaningfully considered within the Academic Achievement indicator in non-regulatory guidance.

Changes: We have revised § 200.14(b)(1) to remove the requirement for States to "equally measure" proficiency in reading/language arts and mathematics.

Comments: One commenter suggested the Department replace the slash (/) in "reading/language arts" with "or" to make the language consistent with the statutory requirements to assess students in reading or language arts.

Discussion: We appreciate the commenter's point that the ESEA, as amended by the ESSA, uses "reading or language arts" to describe the academic content standards in these subjects. We note that the prior authorizations of the ESEA, the NCLB and the Improving America's Schools Act of 1994, also used the term "reading or language arts" to describe standards in these subjects, while the corresponding regulations on such acts used the term "reading/language arts." As this is consistent with policy and practice for over two decades as a way to describe the body of content knowledge in this subject area—and we are unaware of significant confusion on this matter—we believe it is unnecessary to change "reading/language arts" in § 200.14 and other sections in the final regulations.

Changes: None.

Comments: A couple of commenters supported the requirement to calculate the Academic Achievement indicator, based on student participation in the State's annual assessments, by using the greater of 95 percent of all enrolled students or the number of students that participated in such assessments.

Discussion: We appreciate the commenters' support for the clarification in proposed § 200.14(b)(1) of the requirements for calculating the Academic Achievement indicator.

Changes: None.

Comments: In order to allow States to incorporate measures of student growth into their accountability systems, one commenter asked the Department to clarify that, consistent with the proposed requirements for high schools, an elementary or middle school could also include growth on the statewide assessments in its Academic Achievement indicator as part of a composite index and to include parameters to ensure these growth measures are meaningful and reflect student learning.

Discussion: We agree with the commenter that States should have the ability to incorporate student growth into their accountability systems, but disagree that growth measures are permissible in the Academic Achievement indicator for non-high schools. Section 1111(c)(4)(B)(i)(II) of the ESEA specifies that, for high schools, States may include a measure of student growth on State assessments as part of the Academic Achievement indicator. However, the statute specifies that for elementary and middle schools, student growth may be included in the Academic Progress indicator described in section 1111(c)(4)(B)(ii) rather than the Academic Achievement indicator. We also note that States may include a measure of student growth as part of a School Quality or Student Success indicator, consistent with the requirements in § 200.14, providing ample opportunity for States to include measures of growth in their indicators. Finally, because the use of student growth measures is optional and because section 1111(e)(1)(B)(iii)(III) limits the Department from prescribing specific metrics used to measure growth, we believe additional considerations for States in measuring student growth are best addressed in non-regulatory guidance.

Changes: None.

Academic Progress Indicator

Comments: Several commenters supported the use of growth in a State's accountability system and the flexibility provided around growth. One commenter asserted that a State should not be allowed to include growth on statewide assessments in its State's system unless or until adjustments can be made to account for factors beyond a school or teacher's control, including homelessness and poverty.

Discussion: We appreciate the commenters' support for the inclusion for growth in statewide accountability systems, but believe that States should have discretion, consistent with the statute, to develop and implement their own measures of student growth so long as those measures meet the other requirements of § 200.14, including validity, reliability, and comparability. The Department declines to restrict the growth models that States may use in order to provide States flexibility to develop a model appropriate for their State context, so long as it is consistent with the other requirements.

Changes: None.

Comments: A few commenters opposed what they described as the proposed requirement that a State's Academic Progress indicator be based on a measure of growth on the statewide assessments in reading/language arts or mathematics. These commenters noted that the statutory language does not require a growth score based on statewide assessments for the purposes of calculating the Academic Progress indicator and that the Department should not limit States to using growth based solely on test scores.

Discussion: While we appreciate the commenters' concern, the requirements do not limit States to using growth based solely on statewide assessment results. Under § 200.14(b)(2), a State may include either a measure of student growth based on annual reading/language arts and mathematics assessments or another academic measure that meets the requirements of § 200.14(c). For example, a State could measure achievement on reading/language arts or mathematics on a different assessment or could measure achievement in science on the statewide science assessment within the Academic Progress indicator. Given this existing flexibility, the Department declines to make any additional changes.

In addition, as noted earlier in these regulations, it is not necessary for the statute to specifically authorize the Secretary to issue a particular regulatory provision, given the Secretary's rulemaking authority under GEPA, the DEOA, and section 1601(a) of the ESEA, as amended by the ESSA, and that these regulations fall squarely within the scope of section 1111(c) of the ESEA, as amended by the ESSA, consistent with section 1111(e) (see discussion of the Department's general rulemaking authority under the heading Cross-Cutting Issues).

Changes: None.

Comments: One commenter encouraged the Department to require a State electing to include student growth in its Academic Progress indicator to use a valid and reliable growth model that adequately measures student growth for students with the most significant cognitive disabilities taking the alternate assessment. The commenter also asked the Department to clarify that States may not use an alternative growth measure, such as growth based on meeting IEP goals, for such students. Another commenter noted more generally that we should recognize individual growth for students with disabilities.

Discussion: We appreciate the commenters' interest in ensuring that students with the most significant cognitive disabilities taking an alternate assessment aligned with alternate academic achievement standards are appropriately included in any measure within the Academic Progress indicator. Section 200.14(a) requires that all indicators measure performance for all students and subgroups, including students with disabilities, and § 200.14(c) requires that any measure used by a State within the Academic Progress indicator be valid, reliable, and comparable, and calculated in the same way for all schools across the State. Together, these provisions require that States choose a measure that includes all students, including those who take an alternate assessment based on alternate academic achievement standards. Therefore, a State could not use statewide assessment results for some students and growth based on meeting IEP goals for other students. Given these existing parameters, we decline to add additional requirements.

Changes: None.

Comments: One commenter recommended that the Department use more general language when discussing the proposed Academic Progress indicator. The commenter suggested referring to this indicator as "Another Indicator" or "Growth or Other Academic Indicator," which the commenter believed aligned more closely with the statutory description of this indicator.

Discussion: The Department believes the term "Academic Progress" is aligned with the description of the indicator under section 1111(c)(4)(B)(ii), which requires that such an indicator measure academic performance of students in elementary and middle schools and allow for meaningful differentiation. Use of the term "Academic Progress" is also necessary to reasonably ensure a clear distinction between the Academic Achievement indicator required by section 1111(c)(4)(B)(i) and the indicator required by section 1111(c)(4)(B)(ii). It thus falls squarely within the scope of title I, part A of the ESEA, as amended by the ESSA, consistent with section 1111(e), and the Department's rulemaking authority under GEPA, the DEOA, and section 1601(a) of the ESEA, as amended by the ESSA (see discussion under the heading Cross-Cutting Issues).

Changes: None.

Graduation Rate Indicator

Comments: One commenter requested the Department clarify that the Graduation Rate indicator may include only four-year and extended-year adjusted cohort graduation rates and not other measures related to graduation, including dropout rates or completer rates. Another commenter recommended allowing alternative measures or indicators, such as a high school completion indicator, in order to recognize schools that help students complete alternate pathways in more than four years.

Discussion: Consistent with section 1111(c)(4)(B)(iii) of the ESEA, as amended by the ESSA, the Graduation Rate indicator may only include the four-year adjusted cohort graduation rate, and, at the State's discretion, any extended year adjusted cohort graduation rates the State uses, consistent with the requirements in § 200.34. Consequently, the regulations do not permit a State to include other measures related to high school completion, including dropout or completer rates or alternate diplomas based on high school equivalency, in this indicator, and we believe this is accurately reflected in § 200.14(c)(3). We note that States would have discretion to include other measures of high school completion in a School Quality or Student Success indicator, if such measures met all applicable requirements in § 200.14.

Changes: None.

Progress in Achieving English Language Proficiency Indicator

Comments: A few commenters expressed support for the provisions pertaining to the Progress in Achieving English Language Proficiency indicator in proposed § 200.14(b)(4), including the requirement that the indicator take into account a student's initial ELP level and, at a State's discretion, the allowable student-level characteristics described in § 200.13(c), consistent with the State's uniform procedure for establishing long-term goals and measurements of interim progress for ELP.

Discussion: We appreciate the commenters' support and are renumbering and revising § 200.14(b)(4)(ii) to better align with the final requirements in § 200.13 related to the State-determined timelines, including the State-determined maximum number of years, for each English learner to attain ELP after their initial identification as an English learner, which includes consideration of a student's initial level of ELP and may include additional student-level factors as described in § 200.13.

Changes: We have revised § 200.14(b)(4) to better align with the final requirements in § 200.13(c) for considering student—level characteristics of English learners and determining applicable timelines, within a State-determined maximum number of years, for each English learner to attain ELP as the basis for setting long-term goals and measurements of interim progress in setting.

Comments: Several commenters suggested that multiple measures, specifically those not based on performance on the State's annual ELP assessment, be used to calculate the Progress in Achieving English Language Proficiency indicator in order to better align with the criteria that many States use to exit students from English learner status.

Discussion: The ESEA, as amended by the ESSA, states that the Progress in Achieving English

Language Proficiency indicator must be measured by the assessments described in section 1111(b)(2)(G) (the annual ELP assessment) for all English learners in grades 3-8 and once in high school, with progress measured against the ELP assessment results from the previous grade. The Department does not have discretion to permit additional measures beyond the State's ELP assessment to be used to calculate this indicator. However, we are clarifying the final regulations to specify that a State may, at its discretion, measure the progress of English learners in additional grades toward achieving English language proficiency on the State's ELP assessment in the indicator, particularly given the large and growing number of English Learners enrolled in the early grades.

Changes: We have revised § 200.14(b)(4) to clarify that the Progress in Achieving English Language Proficiency indicator must measure English learner performance on the State's annual ELP assessment required in "at least" each of grades 3 through 8 and in grades for which English learners are assessed under section 1111(b)(2)(B)(v)(I)(bb) of the ESEA, as amended by the ESSA.

Comments: Several commenters supported the requirement that, for calculating the Progress in Achieving English Language Proficiency indicator, a State must use an objective and valid measure of progress on the State's ELP assessment. However, other commenters opposed this requirement, arguing that States should have greater flexibility when determining the best measure to determine an English learner's progress.

Discussion: The Department agrees that States should have flexibility to determine which measure of progress on the ELP assessment to use for calculating performance on the Progress in Achieving English Language Proficiency indicator. However, we believe that the requirement that any measure a State selects be objective and valid is critical to ensuring that a State's accountability system fairly and meaningfully includes the progress of English learners. We maintain that the final regulations provide sufficient flexibility to States in developing this indicator, while upholding critical parameters that will help States effectively support English learners. We therefore agree with commenters that valid and objective measures must be used in the Progress in Achieving English Language Proficiency indicator and decline to make changes.

Changes: None.

Comments: One commenter attested that proposed § 200.14(b)(4) conflicts with proposed § 200.13(c), because the former allows a State to include attainment of proficiency within the Progress in Achieving English Language Proficiency indicator, while the latter requires that a State's long-term goals and measurements of interim progress expect that all English learners attain proficiency within a State-determined period of time. Another commenter recommended that all references to attainment of ELP be struck in the final regulations.

Discussion: The Department is revising § 200.13(c) to clarify how the attainment of English language proficiency factors into a State's long-term goals and measurements of interim progress, as described in response to comments on § 200.13(c). Accordingly, we are revising § 200.14(b)(4) to better align with those requirements, such as by clarifying in § 200.14(b)(4)(ii) that the measures in this indicator must be aligned to the applicable timelines for each English learner to attain proficiency after their initial identification as an English learner, within a State-determined maximum number of years. Further, we note that the provision in § 200.14(b)(4)(iii) is permissive in that States may, but are not required to, include a measure of proficiency in setting the indicator. We also disagree that the proposed requirements inappropriately provide discretion for States to measure attainment of ELP and believe that a measure of attaining ELP, if a State chooses to include one, can be complementary to the information on progress that is required in the indicator, providing schools additional information about how they are supporting the diverse range of

English learners found in their communities. Therefore we are maintaining this discretion for States in § 200.14(b)(4)(iii).

Changes: We have revised § 200.14(b)(4)(ii) to better align with § 200.13 and clarify that the measures in this indicator must be consistent with the applicable timelines for each English learner to attain proficiency after the student's initial identification as an English learner, within the State-determined maximum number of years.

Comments: A few commenters suggested that the Department require that States aggregate the results of English learners on the ELP assessment at the school level (i.e., not at each grade level) for the purposes of meeting the State's minimum n-size and calculating performance on the Progress in Achieving English Language Proficiency indicator.

Discussion: The Department agrees with the commenters' goal to ensure that the assessment results of as many English learners as possible are included when calculating performance on the Progress in Achieving English Language Proficiency indicator. However, we do not believe that the statute allows the Department to require States to apply their minimum n-sizes at the school level. We note that States may average data across grades and school years under § 200.20(a), summing the number of students with available data in order to meet the State's minimum n-size and ensure appropriate school-level accountability for student subgroups, and we encourage States to consider this practice as a way to maximally include English learners (as described further in response to comments we received on §§ 200.17 and 200.20).

Changes: None.

Comments: One commenter did not support the reference to student growth percentiles in proposed § 200.14(b)(4)(ii) as an example of a potential measure for the Progress in Achieving English Language Proficiency indicator that would be valid and objective. The commenter attested that student growth percentiles may be an inappropriate measure for older, recently arrived English learners.

Discussion: We continue to believe that student growth percentiles are an appropriate example of a measure for the Progress in Achieving English Language Proficiency indicator and note that States have final discretion over the measure or measures selected for use in this indicator, so long as they meet all applicable statutory and regulatory requirements. However, we are revising § 200.14(b)(4)(i) to further clarify our intent that other methods of measuring progress are also permitted, so long as they assess progress toward achieving ELP for an English learner from the prior year to the current year.

Changes: We have revised § 200.14(b)(4)(i) to indicate that the objective and valid measures of progress for English learners toward ELP are based on students' current year performance on the ELP assessment as compared to the prior year.

Comments: One commenter stated that requiring the measurement of the Progress in Achieving English Language Proficiency indicator on an annual basis is inconsistent with the statute.

Discussion: Annually measuring performance on the Progress in Achieving English Language Proficiency indicator is fully consistent with section 1111(c)(4)(B) of the Act, which requires all indicators to be annually measured for all students and subgroups of students. The exception included in the statute, which may have misled the commenter, is not an exception to the requirement for annual measurement; rather, it is an exception to the requirement for disaggregation. The indicator for Progress in Achieving English Language Proficiency is based only on the English learner subgroup and is not required to be further disaggregated by the other categories of students described in § 200.16(a)(2). We have revised § 200.14(a)(1) to clarify this statutory exception to the requirement for disaggregation of indicators.

Changes: We have revised § 200.14(a)(1) and (c)(3) to specify that all indicators must be disaggregated for each subgroup, with the exception of the Progress in Achieving English Language Proficiency indicator.

Comments: One commenter recommended that the Department require that States use a measure in the Progress on Achieving English Language Proficiency indicator based on reducing the number of students who are long-term English learners in middle school and high school.

Discussion: We appreciate the commenter's suggestion, but note that requiring additional measures within this indicator for English learners, particularly those that are not inclusive of all English learners and only include the progress of a subset of English learners, would be inconsistent with section 1111(c)(4)(B)(iv) of the ESEA, as amended by the ESSA.

Changes: None.

School Quality or Student Success Indicator

Comments: Several commenters supported the inclusion of requirements for School Quality or Student Success indicators in the proposed regulations, generally expressing appreciation for a more holistic approach to accountability under the ESSA that looks at indicators beyond test scores and graduation rates. A number of commenters continued to be concerned that accountability systems at the State level were focused solely on assessment results and graduation rates, and one commenter was concerned that States were only required to include one measure beyond standardized tests.

Some commenters generally recommended that States be given broad flexibility in developing and implementing indicators of School Quality or Student Success within their new statewide accountability systems.

Discussion: We agree with commenters that the inclusion of the School Quality or Student Success indicator(s) in the statewide accountability systems required by the ESEA, as amended by the ESSA, presents an opportunity for States to develop robust, multi-measure accountability systems that help districts and schools ensure each student has access to a well-rounded education and that take into account factors other than test scores and graduation rates in differentiating school performance. Given that States must include indicators beyond academic achievement and graduation rates, we disagree with commenters who asserted that accountability systems are solely focused on these factors. We recognize that the statute requires only one School Quality or Student Success indicator, but anticipate that most States will take advantage of statutory flexibility to develop or adopt multiple indicators, particularly in view of the examples included in the statute itself.

Changes: None.

Comments: Some commenters suggested that the Department add a requirement that States hold schools accountable for providing students with access to programs that address particular needs of students, including access to arts, music, and world language programs, in order to support development of the whole child.

Discussion: We share the commenters' interest in ensuring that all students receive a well-rounded education that will prepare them for success beyond the classroom. However, the Department is statutorily prohibited from mandating curricula either directly or indirectly, as such decisions are a State and local responsibility.

Changes: None.

Comments: One commenter opposed the use of "Standard Core" measures within the School Quality or Student Success indicator because such measures lacked empirical evidence.

Discussion: While we appreciate the commenter's concern about the use of measures that lack evidence, we are not clear which measures the commenter is referencing; therefore, we cannot respond to the comment.

Changes: None.

Comments: One commenter raised specific questions about whether, if a State used a survey to collect data on its School Quality or Student Success indicator, the State must survey all students or whether the data must be reflective of all students, or only those that are full academic year students. Additionally, the commenter sought clarity about whether a State could choose to measure only some grades within a range, so long as all schools in the State had one or more of the grades to be measured. For example, the commenter wanted to know if a State could measure a School Quality or Student Success indicator for grades kindergarten, 3, and 5, instead of each grade in a kindergarten-5 school.

Discussion: We appreciate the commenter's request for clarity about implementation of the specific indicators and measures within the statewide accountability system, but believe that non-regulatory guidance is a more appropriate way to address such questions. Generally, the ESEA, as amended by the ESSA, and § 200.14 of the regulations recognize that some indicators will not include all grades in a school. For example, the Graduation Rate indicator only includes the results of students that are part of the cohort of students graduating in a given year, and the Academic Achievement indicator only includes the results of students taking assessments in specific grades (i.e., grades 3-8 and one grade in high school). Therefore, it does not seem unreasonable that an indicator of School Quality or Student Success would only include the results of a specific grade. For example, a State may choose to use as an indicator, for middle schools, the percentage of eighth grade students that have already received credit for a course such as Algebra I. To the specific question about whether States must include only those students who are full academic year students in measuring the School Quality or Student Success indicator, section 1111(c)(4)(F) of the ESEA, as amended by the ESSA, allows a State to exclude the performance of students who do not attend the same school within an LEA for at least half of a school year on the Academic Achievement, Academic Progress, Progress in Achieving English Language Proficiency, and the School Quality or Student Success indicators for accountability purposes. However, all students should be included for the purposes of reporting performance on State and LEA report cards under §§ 200.30 and 200.31.

Changes: None.

Comments: Some commenters suggested the Department require States to undertake stakeholder consultation specific to the development of meaningful indicators of School Quality or Student Success. For example, one commenter recommended the Department require States to convene summer and other out-of-school partners for input, because these stakeholders have expertise in supporting and measuring students' social-emotional development. Other commenters recommended that States be required to consult with the diverse community of professionals that contribute to student success, including instructional support staff.

Discussion: We agree with commenters that States should engage in robust and meaningful consultation with diverse stakeholders related to the development or adoption of the State's indicators of School Quality or Student Success. In fact, the Secretary issued a Dear Colleague Letter to States on June 22, 2016, to emphasize the importance of early and meaningful stakeholder engagement. (5) States should be working now with a broad array of stakeholders on formulating new statewide accountability and support systems. Additionally, under §§ 299.13 and 299.15, States are required to consult with many stakeholders, including teachers, principals, other school leaders, paraprofessionals, specialized instructional support personnel, and organizations representing such individuals, as well as community-based organizations, in the development of the State plan. One component of that plan is a description and information about which indicators the State plans to use in its statewide accountability system, including School Quality or Student Success indicators. The Department encourages States to engage stakeholders meaningfully in the development of State plans, including School Quality or Student Success indicators, and believes that existing consultation and State plan requirements provide sufficient opportunity for input on State selection of these indicators; therefore, we decline to add further requirements specific to this category of indicators to the final regulations.

Changes: None.

Comments: A number of commenters suggested the Department require States to hold schools accountable for a wide range of specific indicators of School Quality or Student Success. For example, commenters suggested that States be required to hold schools accountable for the presence of wrap-around services, access to preschool, and career and technical programs.

Other commenters suggested the Department provide additional examples of measures and indicators of School Quality or Student Success within the regulatory requirements but not require States to use specific indicators. For example, these commenters suggested that the Department highlight health-based measures, specific measures of school climate and school discipline, and measures of participation in advanced or gifted programs.

Other commenters expressed interest in examples, which could be made available either in regulation or non-regulatory guidance, of valid and reliable indicators that could measure School Quality or Student Success and support equity and excellence, as well as tools that may be used to measure performance on these indicators (e.g., existing student survey tools).

Discussion: We appreciate the strong interest of commenters in requiring or highlighting a wide range of measures that States could include in their indicators of School Quality or Student Success, as well as the recognition that States likely will need assistance in selecting high-quality indicators. However, we believe that requiring the inclusion of specific measures would be inconsistent with the statute, and we believe that non-regulatory guidance is a more appropriate vehicle for offering additional examples and tools to help States select valid, reliable, and comparable indicators of School Quality or Student Success. Therefore, we decline to include additional examples of indicators of School Quality or Student Success, beyond the list in § 200.14(b)(5), which includes only those examples provided in section 1111(c)(4)(B)(v) of the ESEA, as amended by the ESSA. We plan to issue non-regulatory guidance that will provide additional examples of indicators of School Quality or Student Success that States may choose to include in statewide accountability systems.

Changes: None.

Comments: Several commenters provided feedback or recommendations related to the examples of School Quality or Student Success indicators the Department listed in the preamble of the NPRM, with some expressing concern that the examples could preclude or discourage the use of other indicators and other commenters highlighting specific concerns or drawbacks with the examples and suggesting alternatives.

Discussion: While we appreciate the feedback provided by commenters on such examples and will consider this feedback in any future guidance on the selection and implementation of indicators of School Quality or Student Success, the examples were provided in the preamble of the NPRM and not in the regulatory requirements. Therefore, the Department declines to make any regulatory changes based on this feedback.

Changes: None.

Comments: Several commenters requested that the Department require States to define and measure school climate within specific parameters if the State chooses to use school climate as an indicator of School Quality or Student Success. For example, some commenters encouraged the Department to define positive school climate and safety and offer multiple ways of measuring data, including student surveys and through the use of school discipline data.

Discussion: We appreciate the commenters' efforts to encourage the selection and use of meaningful, high-quality, and readily available measures of school climate in States that use such measures in one or more indicators of School Quality or Student Success. We believe that decisions about which measures to include are best made at the State level and encourage States to meaningfully engage stakeholders in considering them.

Changes: None.

Comments: A few commenters wanted to ensure that, in establishing and collecting data on indicators of School Quality or Student Success, States do not collect data regarding student social emotional factors, beliefs and behaviors, or other information beyond the scope of the school's purview, or use such information for accountability purposes. Another commenter suggested the Department clarify that indicators should not require any additional assessments beyond what is already required by law in reading and math.

Discussion: We appreciate the commenters' concern that a State may establish and develop an indicator of School Quality or Student Success that will require the State to collect additional data, consistent with the statutory requirement to measure and report on this indicator. States must still meet the requirements for protecting personally identifiable information described in the statute and under § 200.17. Because States are best positioned to determine whether an additional assessment or tool is needed to determine a student's performance on its particular School Quality or Student Success indicator(s), we decline to limit State discretion in this area.

Changes: None.

Comments: Many commenters provided feedback on the proposed requirement in § 200.14(d) that any measure used within a State's indicators of Academic Progress and School Quality or Student Success be supported by research that performance or progress on such a measure is likely to increase student achievement, or at the high school level, graduation rates. Some suggested eliminating the requirement that the School Quality or Student Success indicator be supported by such research, because it would prevent States from using measures of school climate or safety, parent engagement, or other measures that they believe may not be directly linked to academic achievement. These commenters also were concerned that the requirement restricts State flexibility to choose appropriate indicators, results in a continued emphasis on test-based accountability, is contrary to the ESSA's inclusion of multiple indicators beyond assessment results, and goes beyond the authority granted to the Secretary. Another commenter noted that the statute did not include an evidence requirement for these indicators as it did other parts of the statewide accountability system. A few commenters also asserted that the proposed requirement violated sections 1111(e)(1)(B)(iii)(IV) and (V) of the ESEA, as amended by the ESSA.

Other commenters supported the proposed requirement because it ensures that measures within each indicator are likely to close educational achievement gaps, consistent with the purpose of title I of the ESEA. Of those commenters that supported the requirement, one recommended adding that the indicators should not only be linked to student achievement, but would also be appropriate for accountability purposes. Some commenters supported the requirement but recommended modifying the regulations to allow States to demonstrate that proposed measures used in indicators of School Quality or Student Success are supported by research that performance or progress on such measures is likely to increase at least one of a variety of outcomes beyond student achievement and graduation rates, including student educational outcomes, college completion, postsecondary or career success, employment or workforce outcomes, civic engagement, military readiness, student access to and participation in well-rounded education subject areas, or student learning and development. Finally, one commenter suggested that States be required to demonstrate that the indicator they select to use in middle school is linked to student achievement or graduation rates because waiting until high school to focus on indicators that are linked to graduation is too late.

Discussion: The requirement that measures used for indicators of Academic Progress and School Quality or Student Success be supported by research demonstrating a link to increased student achievement was not intended to limit such measures to those that improve State assessment results. Rather, our intention was to include a wide variety of measures of student learning such as grade point average, course completion and performance, or credit accumulation. We maintain that a requirement linking indicators of School Quality or Student Success to student outcomes is critical to fulfill the goal of title I to close educational achievement gaps and to reasonably ensure compliance with the more specific requirements in section 1111(c)(4) that the State's accountability system should improve "student academic achievement." Accordingly, this requirement falls squarely within the scope of title I, part A of the ESEA, as amended by the ESSA, consistent with section 1111(e) and is consistent with the Department's rulemaking authority under GEPA, the DEOA, and section 1601(a) of the ESEA, as amended by the ESSA.

Further, these requirements do not contravene the provisions in sections 1111(e)(1)(B)(iii)(IV)-(V) of the ESEA, as amended by the ESSA, because they do not prescribe either the weight of any measure or indicator or the specific methodology that States must use to meaningfully differentiate and identify schools.

However, we recognize that many measures may be supported by research demonstrating a positive impact on a broader array of student outcomes that are related to college and career readiness and are revising § 200.14(d) accordingly.

Changes: We have revised § 200.14(d) to provide States with additional flexibility to demonstrate that the Academic Progress and School Quality or Student Success indicators are supported by research that performance or improvement on such measures is likely to increase student learning, like grade point average, credit accumulation, or performance in advanced coursework, or, for measures within the indicators at the high school level, graduation rates, postsecondary enrollment, postsecondary persistence or completion, or career readiness.

Comments: None.

Discussion: In revising the requirement under § 200.14(d), consistent with the discussion directly above, we determined that an additional change would clarify the requirement in order to ensure States can comply with the requirements in 1111(c) of the ESEA, as amended by the ESSA, and § 200.14. In order to more closely align with the purpose of the accountability system and to meaningfully ensure that measure used within the Academic Progress and School Quality or Student Success indicators are likely to increase student learning, consistent with the previous discussion, we are clarifying that a State must demonstrate that each of these indicators is supported by research that high performance or improvement on such measures is likely to increase student learning, or for measures within indicators at the high school level, graduation rates, postsecondary enrollment, postsecondary persistence or completion, or career readiness.

Changes: We have revised § 200.19(d) to clarify that each indicator of Academic Progress and School Quality or Student Success must be supported by research that "high" performance or improvement on such measures is likely to increase student learning.

Other Indicator Requirements

Comments: A few commenters recommended that the Department include additional requirements in the final regulations related to the selection and use of accountability indicators, including requirements related to ensuring that measures are valid and reliable for the purposes for which they are being used and are developmentally appropriate. Another commenter encouraged the Department to avoid further defining comparability due to pending innovations in how comparability might be demonstrated.

One commenter offered specific guidance for the Department and States to consider in identifying or selecting research-based, non-academic, or non-cognitive School Quality or Student Success indicators.

Discussion: We appreciate the commenters' request for further clarification around the requirements for accountability indicators. We believe it will be important to carefully consider the validity, reliability, and comparability of each State's indicators within the broader context of its statewide accountability system through our State plan review process and corresponding peer review, but we decline to add new regulatory requirements in this area. We will consider this input in the context of non-regulatory guidance.

Changes: None.

Comments: Some commenters opposed the requirement in proposed § 200.14(c)(2) that States measure each indicator in the same way across all schools, except that the indicators of Academic Progress and School Quality or Student Success may vary by grade span. One commenter was concerned that this requirement dilutes local flexibility to select measures that may be more appropriate given a school's local context. Other commenters particularly appreciated the flexibility to vary certain indicators by grade span, because they believed this would allow States to use a broader array of indicators rather than only indicators that were relevant to all grades.

Discussion: While we appreciate the concern that this does not provide States with an opportunity to vary indicator measurement across schools broadly, we believe that in order to ensure indicators are comparable and that accountability determinations are fair and equitable across schools and districts, the measures within those indicators must be measured in the same way. The regulations provide States with flexibility beyond that in the statute—to vary the Academic Progress indicator across grade spans—but the Department declines to allow States to measure performance on

51

indicators differently across schools or districts, or to permit States to adopt a menu of measures from which districts can choose to use within an indicator.

Changes: None.

Comments: Several commenters strongly supported the requirement in proposed § 200.14(c)(3) that States disaggregate performance on each indicator by student subgroup, citing the need for such disaggregation for transparency in reporting, identification of schools with consistently underperforming subgroups for targeted support and improvement, and alignment with the statutory requirements for indicators. One commenter suggested clarifying that each indicator should be disaggregated by individual student subgroup and reflect actual student experience. That commenter was concerned that, as drafted, the regulations would permit a school to say, for example, that all members of a particular subgroup had access to AP courses, even if no members of that group were actually enrolled in AP courses. A number of commenters opposed the requirement and recommended the Department remove or modify this provision. In particular, many commenters were concerned that the requirement to disaggregate each indicator of Student Quality or Student Success would preclude a State from using indicators that cannot be disaggregated, such as teacher mentoring programs, educator engagement or school climate measures collected through an anonymized survey, and student access to resources such as dual enrollment programs, specific course sequences, or school counselors. Commenters were concerned about the latter because it would not adequately reflect differences among subgroups in actual participation in or use of such resources. Some commenters were concerned with the validity and reliability of these indicators at the subgroup level. One commenter suggested that a State should be required to disaggregate one indicator of School Quality or Student Success, but not each such indicator. Another commenter asked for clarification about whether the proposed regulations would require a State using a survey to collect demographic information for each participant.

Discussion: We appreciated hearing from commenters who supported the requirement to disaggregate results on each indicator, and we agree that this requirement is vitally important to ensuring equity and meeting other statutory requirements related to indicators. For too long, the performance of individual subgroups was hidden within State accountability and reporting systems, and the ESSA has maintained a focus on illuminating the performance of each subgroup by requiring in section 1111(c)(4)(B) that States measure each indicator for all students and separately for each subgroup of students. Additionally, in order to identify schools with consistently underperforming subgroups of students for targeted support and improvement, the State must consider the performance of individual subgroups based on each indicator. We understand that this requirement to disaggregate results on each indicator may limit to some degree a State's selection of indicators for its statewide accountability system, but the reasons for such disaggregation are compelling, and the ESSA requires this disaggregation. Therefore, we decline to make any changes. The only exception to this requirement, as discussed previously, is that the Progress in Achieving English Language Proficiency indicator need not be disaggregated by student subgroup because it is measured for only one subgroup: The English learner subgroup.

Changes: None.

Comments: While some commenters supported the proposed requirement in § 200.14(c)(4) that a State cannot use a measure more than once in its statewide accountability system, many commenters opposed this requirement. One commenter noted that a State may want to use the same measure but in a different way in another indicator. For example, a State might include proficiency, as measured by the ACT, in the Academic Achievement indicator, but a measure of the number of students who meet the ACT college and career readiness benchmark in three or more content areas as a measure of postsecondary readiness within the School Quality or Student

Success indicator. Other commenters noted that States may have other reasons to use a particular measure or instrument in more than one indicator. For example, States may want to use a nationally recognized assessment to measure postsecondary readiness within the State's School Quality or Student Success indicator, but also allow LEAs to use the same assessment in lieu of a State-required high school assessment for the Academic Achievement indicator, consistent with the flexibility under the ESEA, as amended by the ESSA.

Discussion: We appreciate the commenters' concern that proposed § 200.14(c)(4) could be interpreted to prevent a State from using an applicable measure across multiple indicators. In the scenario described by the commenters, the State would not be using the same measure, but rather the same instrument, within two different indicators. The Department's intention was not to preclude a State from using different measures derived from the same instrument for more than one indicator in its statewide accountability system, as described in the ACT example cited previously. Therefore, we agree that this requirement could have the unintentional effect of limiting a State's opportunity to use measures derived from the same data source across two indicators, and we are removing the requirement.

Changes: We have removed the requirement in proposed § 200.14(c)(4).

Comments: Several commenters supported the requirement in proposed § 200.14(e) that State-selected indicators of Academic Progress or School Quality or Student Success produce varied results across schools in order to meet the statutory requirement for meaningful differentiation and to ensure that indicators provide meaningful insight into a school's performance. A few commenters were opposed to the requirement because they are concerned it would unduly limit State flexibility in selecting indicators. One commenter was concerned by the Department's language in the preamble of the NPRM that indicated average daily attendance was unlikely to show variation across schools; the commenter believes attendance is important and just because schools are all doing well on an indicator should not indicate that it would be unhelpful as a component of a statewide accountability system.

Discussion: We appreciate the support for the requirement that indicators of Academic Progress and School Quality or Student Success must produce varied results across schools. Under section 1111(c)(4)(B)(ii)(II) and 1111(c)(4)(B)(v)(I)(aa) of the ESEA, respectively, States must ensure that Academic Progress and School Quality or Student Success indicators allow for meaningful differentiation in school performance. While the Department does not define the term meaningful differentiation, or how much variation an indicator must show, we believe that indicators in the State's system, consistent with the requirements of the law, must show varied results across schools in order to enable States to actually differentiate school performance. Given concerns that this requirement will overly limit State flexibility, which we believe may partly stem from a misinterpretation of the proposed language, we are revising § 200.14(e) to clarify that a State must demonstrate the measures in its Academic Progress and School Quality or Student Success indicators show variation across "schools" in the State, as the proposed language of "all schools" could be misinterpreted to require a different result on the selected measure for each school in the State, which was not the intent of this provision. Finally, while we think it unlikely, as suggested in the preamble of the NPRM, that average daily attendance would yield the varied results needed to meet this requirement, the regulations do not prohibit such a measure if a State can demonstrate otherwise.

Changes: We have revised § 200.14(e) to refer to variation in results across schools generally, rather than "all schools."

Section 200.15 Participation in Assessments and Annual Measurement of Achievement

Comments: Many commenters expressed support for the proposed regulations clarifying the actions that a State may take to ensure that all schools adhere to the 95 percent participation rate requirement on State assessments, including the 95 percent participation rate requirement for student subgroups, with one noting that this requirement was retained from NCLB. These commenters also stated that the proposed regulations are consistent with the spirit of the ESEA, as amended by the ESSA, by allowing States to determine the specific actions for schools that do not meet the 95 percent participation rate requirement while also providing flexibility for States to develop their own approaches to improving participation rates. Other commenters praised the proposed regulations for reinforcing the inclusion of all students in the State's assessment system through the 95 percent participation rate requirement. One commenter stated that the proposed regulations are critical to ensuring that States, districts, and schools take seriously the need to assess at least 95 percent of students and avoid loopholes that could undermine accountability systems. Several commenters also expressed strong support for the proposed improvement plans for schools that do not meet the 95 percent participation rate requirement, including the involvement of stakeholders such as parents and educators in developing these plans.

Discussion: We appreciate the support of these commenters for the proposed regulations on the 95 percent participation rate requirement. In reviewing the comments and proposed regulations, we have determined that the regulations could more clearly reflect the statutory requirement that each State administer academic assessments to all public school students in the State, and we are revising § 200.15(a) to better distinguish this assessment requirement from the separate accountability requirement under section 1111(c)(4)(E) of the ESEA, as amended by the ESSA. The proposed regulations focused on this requirement to annually measure, for accountability purposes, the achievement of at least 95 percent of all students and 95 percent of all students in each subgroup on reading/language arts and mathematics assessments, but did not explicitly address the requirement under section 1111(b)(2)(B)(i)(II) of the ESEA that the required assessments in reading/language arts, mathematics, and science be administered to all public school students in the State, or the requirement under section 1111(b)(2)(B)(vi)(I) of the ESEA that the State must provide for the participation of all students in such assessments. If we do not explicitly reference these requirements in the regulations, States and other stakeholders might misinterpret the regulations to mean that only 95 percent of students must be assessed on the required academic assessments, contradicting the requirements in section 1111(b)(2)(B) of the ESEA.

Changes: We have revised § 200.15(a)(1) to clarify that States are required to administer academic assessments in reading/language arts, mathematics, and science to all public school students in the State, and provide for all such students' participation in those assessments.

Comments: One commenter cited numerous benefits of ensuring high participation rates consistent with the statute and the proposed regulations, emphasizing that high-quality assessments provide essential information that can be used to inform instruction, support student learning, ensure readiness for postsecondary education, guide professional development, and target evidence-based interventions to meet the needs of students and schools. The commenter also noted that non-participation inhibits the data transparency needed to support effective monitoring and program improvement, which can have a disparate impact on students with special needs and contribute to a widening of achievement gaps. This commenter also recommended that States provide information to parents, educators, and the public regarding the consequences of non-participation in assessments under their accountability systems and include parents and other stakeholders in developing interventions and supports for schools that do not meet the 95 percent participation rate requirement.

Discussion: We appreciate and share this commenter's views on the importance of the 95 participation rate requirement. We note that the requirements for participation rate improvement plans in § 200.15(c)(1) of the final regulations include involvement by stakeholders—including principals and other school leaders, teachers, and parents—in the development of improvement plans.

Changes: None.

Comments: One commenter expressed strong support for proposed § 200.15, noting that accountability systems can be effective only when they include information on each student's performance on assessments aligned to rigorous State standards in reading/language arts and mathematics, and that there is no way to determine whether all students are meeting the long-term goals and measurements of interim progress for academic achievement required by section 1111(c)(4)(A) of the ESEA, as amended by the ESSA, without achievement data on State tests.

Discussion: We appreciate the commenter's support for the proposed regulations.

Changes: None.

Comments: Many commenters asserted that the proposed regulations on the 95 percent participation rate requirement are part of an effort to restore what they described as test-based accountability in the ESEA, as amended by the ESSA. These commenters objected to the menu of proposed actions that would be required for schools that do not meet the 95 percent participation rate requirement, describing the 95 percent requirement as an arbitrary threshold that effectively would punish schools and in turn parents for their decisions to opt out of State assessments required by the ESEA, as amended by the ESSA.

Discussion: While the ESEA, as amended by the ESSA, promotes statewide accountability systems based on multiple measures of student and school performance, the accurate and reliable measurement of student achievement on annual State assessments in reading/language arts and mathematics remains a required component of those systems. Specifically, as part of their statewide accountability systems required by the ESEA, as amended by the ESSA, States must set long-term goals and measurements of interim progress for academic achievement in reading/language arts and mathematics under section 1111(c)(4)(A)(i)(I)(aa), as measured by the assessments in these subjects required under section 1111(b)(2). Academic achievement as measured by proficiency on these assessments also is a required indicator for State systems of annual meaningful differentiation under section 1111(c)(4)(B). In support of these requirements, the law requires annual assessments in reading/language arts and mathematics to be administered to all public school students in each of grades 3-8, and at least once between grades 9 and 12, and, separately, that States hold schools accountable for assessing at least 95 percent of their students. The 95 percent threshold is specified in section 1111(c)(4)(E) of the ESEA, as amended by the ESSA, and both the Department and States are responsible for ensuring that all schools meet the 95 percent participation rate requirement. The final regulations, like the proposed regulations, are designed to assist States in fulfilling this responsibility, and ultimately provide States flexibility in determining how to factor participation rate into their accountability system.

Changes: None.

Comments: One commenter wrote that proposed § 200.15 undermines the clear intent of Congress to empower State and local educators to engage in a collaborative process for developing broader accountability systems based on multiple measures of performance.

Discussion: The proposed regulations on the 95 percent participation rate requirement are narrowly and appropriately targeted on ensuring that all schools meet that requirement, and do not in any way undermine or interfere with the authority or discretion of States to develop, or to engage in a collaborative process for developing, the broader, statewide accountability systems based on multiple measures of student and school performance that are encouraged by the ESEA, as amended by the ESSA. Further, the provisions of § 200.15 are wholly consistent with, and within the scope of, the provisions of title I, part A of the ESEA, as amended by the ESSA, as well as with the Department's rulemaking authority under GEPA, the DEOA, and section 1601(a) of the ESEA, as amended by the ESSA, (as previously described in the discussion of Cross-Cutting Issues) because they are consistent with and necessary to ensure that States fulfill their responsibilities under section 1111(c)(4)(E) of the ESEA, as amended by the ESSA. As such, they also do not violate section 1111(e) of the ESEA, as amended by the ESSA.

Changes: None.

Comments: One commenter stated that the requirements of proposed § 200.15 do not take into account current efforts by States to improve assessment participation rates or the unique circumstances that may negatively affect participation rates.

Discussion: We appreciate that many States, school districts, and schools already are engaged in efforts to increase assessment participation rates and that there are many reasons for low participation rates. However, the law requires States to factor the 95 percent participation rate requirement, for schools and subgroups of students, into their statewide accountability systems regardless of such efforts, and the proposed regulations were designed to help States implement that requirement. States may incorporate current strategies and incentives for improving participation rates that reflect local needs and circumstances into the State-determined option for factoring the 95 percent participation rate requirement into their statewide accountability systems under § 200.15(b)(2)(iv). We also note that existing State and local efforts to improve participation rates may provide a solid foundation for the school- and district-level improvement plans required by the final regulations.

Changes: None.

Comments: One commenter asserted that the proposed regulations could result in the diversion of resources from needy schools to wealthier schools due to the recent high incidence of opt outs at many wealthier schools. This commenter also stated that lower grades for typically high-performing schools due to their failure to meet the 95 percent participation rate requirement could erode support for both State accountability systems and the individuals responsible for administering those systems.

Discussion: The Department believes it is unlikely that meeting the 95 percent participation rate requirement would divert significant resources to wealthier schools; the combination of ESEA program allocation requirements and the fiscal provisions in part A of title I generally ensure that high-poverty schools continue to receive their fair share of Federal, State, and local funds. In addition, under § 200.24(a)(1), LEAs may not use section 1003 school improvement funds to serve schools identified under § 200.15(b)(2)(iii), if applicable, for targeted support and improvement due to missing the 95 percent participation rate requirement. This provision is explicitly intended to prevent the diversion of section 1003 improvement funds from schools that are identified for comprehensive or targeted support and improvement due to consistently poor student outcomes. We also note that the integrity of statewide accountability systems is at greater risk when schools—regardless of general beliefs about their quality or performance—do not meet the 95 percent participation requirement than when they receive lower performance determinations reflecting the lack of reliable data for accurately measuring performance against State-determined college- and career-ready academic standards.

Changes: None.

Required Denominator for Calculation of Academic Achievement Indicator

Comments: Several commenters objected to the provisions that require States to take specific actions for schools that fail to meet 95 percent participation rates, as well as the school and district improvement plans in proposed § 200.15(c). These commenters stated that proposed § 200.15(b)(1), which incorporates the statutory requirement that non-participants be counted as non-proficient for the purposes of annual meaningful differentiation, is sufficient penalty for failing to assess at least 95 percent of all students and all students in each subgroup.

Discussion: Section 1111(c)(4)(E) of the ESEA, as amended by the ESSA, specifies two distinct consequences for failure to meet the 95 percent participation rate requirement: (1) Counting non-participants in any school with a participation rate below 95 percent as non-proficient for purposes of calculating the Academic Achievement indicator (by ensuring that the denominator for such calculation, at a minimum, includes at least 95 percent of students enrolled in the school); and (2) factoring the requirement into statewide accountability systems. The Department disagrees with the commenters that the second statutorily specified consequence should be ignored. The final regulations, like the proposed regulations, are designed to support effective implementation of the requirement that States factor the 95 percent participation requirement into their accountability systems.

Changes: None.

Comments: Several commenters expressed concern about proposed § 200.15(b)(1), which incorporates statutory requirements related to the denominator that must be used for calculating the Academic Achievement indicator, essentially requiring non-proficient scores for most non-participants for the purpose of annual meaningful differentiation of schools. In particular, commenters suggested that this requirement would unfairly reduce school performance ratings for schools in which parents are exercising their legal rights to opt their children out of State assessments required by the ESEA, as amended by the ESSA—actions over which districts and schools have no control. One commenter asserted that proposed § 200.15(b)(1) exceeded the Department's legal authority.

Other commenters expressed support for proposed § 200.15(b)(1) and encouraged the Department to clarify in the final regulations how it must be implemented, including that students who opt out of State assessments must be part of the denominator for the Academic Achievement indicator calculation and that the only students who may be excluded from the denominator are those who were enrolled in a school for less than half of the academic year, as provided under proposed § 200.20(b).

Discussion: The final regulations retain the requirement that the denominator used for calculating the Academic Achievement indicator must include, for all students and for each subgroup of students, at least 95 percent of all such students in the grades assessed who are enrolled in the school each year. This requirement has the effect of ensuring that participation rates below 95 percent not only could have a significant impact on a school's performance on the Academic Achievement indicator but could also affect the school's overall determination in a State's accountability system. We further note that this provision is incorporated directly from the statute, specifically from the requirement in section 1111(c)(4)(E)(ii) of the ESEA, as amended by the ESSA. We appreciate that it would be helpful to provide States with assistance in implementing this requirement and plan on providing clarification in non-regulatory guidance. Finally, requiring all students that opt-out of State assessments to be counted as non-participants would be inconsistent with the statute, which would not count such students as non-participants until a school's participation rate falls below 95 percent in a given year.

Changes: None.

State Actions To Factor Participation Rate Into Statewide Accountability Systems

Comments: Numerous commenters stated that the proposed actions that States would be required to take in schools that do not test 95 percent of their students in reading/language arts and mathematics, specifically lowering the rating of such schools in statewide accountability systems or identifying them for targeted support and improvement, are not consistent with other requirements of the Act. More specifically, these commenters asserted that proposed § 200.15 conflicts with section 1111(b)(2)(K) of the ESEA, as amended by the ESSA, which states that the assessment requirements in section 1111(b) do not preempt State or local law regarding the decision of a parent to not have his or her child participate in the assessments required by Part A of title I of the ESEA, as amended by the ESSA. Some commenters further expressed the belief that the proposed regulations appear to be intended to minimize parental resistance to what they described as the overuse and misuse of standardized tests, while others emphasized that districts and schools should not be penalized for the actions of parents. A few commenters stated that by not taking into account the opt-out movement, the proposed regulations could undermine the legitimacy and public acceptance of statewide accountability systems. These commenters generally recommended that the proposed regulations on assessment participation be revised to restate statutory requirements, including the right to "opt out" of ESEA assessments, and permit States to determine how to factor the 95 percent participation requirement into their accountability systems, or that the Department not issue any regulations on meeting the 95 percent participation rate requirement.

Discussion: We recognize that section 1111(b) of the ESEA, as amended by the ESSA, protects the right of parents to withhold children from participation in State assessments in reading/language arts and mathematics. At the same time, the law requires that all students participate in annual assessments in English language arts and mathematics in each of grades 3-8, and at least once between grades 9 and 12, and that States hold schools accountable for assessing at least 95 percent of their students. Ensuring that States, LEAs, and schools have reliable, accurate assessment data on all students and all subgroups of students is essential to design meaningful accountability systems, to provide teachers and parents the information they need to improve instruction and student outcomes, and to guide States and districts in providing schools the resources, support, and assistance they need to make sure that all students graduate high school ready for college and careers.

The proposed regulations provide a menu of options for States to use to help ensure that all schools meet the statutory 95 percent participation rate requirement. We believe these options will help protect the integrity of a State's accountability system; ensure that participation rate is included in a State's accountability system in a meaningful, transparent manner; and ensure that parents and teachers get the information they need to support students. For these reasons, the final regulations retain a menu of actions from which States may select for schools that do not test at least 95 percent of their students in reading/language arts and mathematics.

Changes: None.

Comments: A number of commenters requested that the Department strengthen the State options for addressing low assessment participation rates. One commenter provided specific recommendations for more rigorous actions by States for schools that miss the 95 percent participation rate requirement. For example, this commenter suggested strengthening improvement plan consultation requirements by requiring the inclusion of at least one parent from each subgroup that does not meet the 95 percent participation rate requirement. This commenter also expressed concern that assigning a lower summative rating to a school that missed the 95 percent participation rate requirement might result in a relatively inconsequential reduction, such as from a "B+" to a "B" rating, and called for the final regulations to ensure that a State's actions lead to a meaningful reduction in the rating of such schools. The same commenter recommended that States be required to provide technical assistance aimed at helping schools explain to parents why assessment participation is important for the integrity of the State's accountability system as well as how that system is used to provide supports for students and schools. Other commenters recommended clarifying that States may take more rigorous actions in schools that do not meet the 95 percent participation rate requirement than those included in the proposed regulations.

Discussion: The Department appreciates support from commenters for strong actions to ensure that all schools meet 95 percent participation rates, but does not believe that more prescriptive requirements in this area would be consistent with the ESEA, as amended by the ESSA. We also believe that some of the recommended changes are unnecessary; for example, the requirement that participation rate improvement plans be developed in partnership with parents is likely to lead to involvement from parents from subgroups that do not meet the 95 participation requirement. Improvement plans also are likely to include efforts to explain to parents why assessment participation is important for the effective functioning of State accountability systems, including the delivery of supports for students and schools. Finally, because the proposed regulations already require States to take "at least one" of the required actions for schools that miss the 95 percent participation, we believe the regulations are clear that States may take more rigorous actions, including more rigorous State-determined actions, and that this point would be more appropriately reiterated through non-regulatory guidance.

Changes: None.

Comments: Many commenters asserted that the proposed regulations exceed the Department's authority under the ESEA, as amended by the ESSA, to determine how and the extent to which a State factors the 95 percent participation rate requirement into its system of annual meaningful differentiation of schools. In support of their contention, commenters specifically cited section 1111(e)(1)(B)(iii)(XI), which prohibits the Secretary from prescribing the way in which a State factors the 95 percent participation rate requirement into its statewide accountability system. Several commenters also noted that while the assessment participation rate was a required accountability indicator under NCLB, it was not included among the indicators required by section 1111(c)(4)(B) of the ESEA, as amended by the ESSA. These commenters also stated that there is no basis in statute for the proposed requirements for school and district improvement plans to increase participation rates, and recommended the elimination of all proposed actions that States, districts, and schools would be required to take regarding schools that fail to assess at least 95 percent of all students and students in each subgroup.

Discussion: The requirements in § 200.15(b)-(c) for State actions to factor participation rates into their accountability systems and improve assessment participation in schools and LEAs are not inconsistent with section 1111(e)(1)(B)(iii)(XI) of the ESEA, as amended by the ESSA, because they do not prescribe the way in which a State must factor the 95 percent participation requirement into its statewide accountability system. The final regulations, like the proposed regulations, provide options for how a State may factor the 95 percent participation rate requirement into its accountability system, including a State-determined option. In addition, each State has significant discretion regarding the precise manner in which it incorporates its selected option into its overall accountability system. Thus, we do not specify the way in which a State incorporates the 95 percent participation rate requirement into its accountability system.

Further, the provisions of § 200.15 are consistent with, and within the scope of, the provisions of title I, part A of the ESEA, as amended by the ESSA, as well as with the Department's rulemaking authority under GEPA, the DEOA, and Section 1601(a) of the ESEA, as amended by the ESSA (previously described in the discussion on Cross-Cutting Issues), because they are necessary to reasonably ensure that States factor participation rate into statewide accountability systems, as required in section 1111(c)(4)(E) of the ESEA, as amended by the ESSA, and comply with the statutory requirement in section 1111(1)(b)(2)(B)(i) of the ESEA, as amended by the ESSA, that a State assess all public elementary and secondary school students in the State. As such, they also do not violate section 1111(e).

Finally, the proposed participation rate improvement plans are intended to support effective State and local implementation of the statutory 95 percent participation rate requirement through a collaborative, locally determined improvement process designed to minimize the need for more heavy-handed compliance actions by State or Federal authorities. Consequently, we believe the improvement plan requirements in the final regulations also are fully appropriate and consistent with the ESEA, as amended by the ESSA.

Changes: None.

Comments: One commenter expressed support for proposed § 200.15(b)(2)(iii), which provides the option that a State may identify schools that miss the 95 percent participation rate requirement for targeted support and improvement. However, the commenter said this result should only be permitted if the identified schools are eligible to receive section 1003 school improvement funds to support implementation of their targeted support plans aimed at improving assessment participation.

Discussion: The Department declines to make this change because the number of schools that could be identified by a State for targeted support and improvement due to missing the 95 percent participation rate requirement could reduce the availability of section 1003 improvement funds for schools that are identified for comprehensive or targeted support and improvement due to consistently poor student outcomes.

Changes: None.

Comments: One commenter recommended that the regulations be revised to allow States to take into account the level of assessment participation and other factors (e.g., the number of subgroups, the size of the participation gap, the number of years missed) in determining consequences that would potentially increase over time if a school continues to miss the 95 percent participation rate threshold. Similarly, a few commenters variously recommended giving States flexibility to design multiple State-determined actions, including escalating interventions and supports that may be less rigorous than those in proposed § 200.15(b)(2). Another commenter suggested that States be permitted to vary the weight given to the 95 percent participation rate requirement, with less severe consequences if failure to meet the requirement results from parents opting their children out of State assessments required by the ESEA.

Discussion: The Department believes that the final regulations governing accountability for the 95 percent participation rate, like the proposed regulations, provide considerable flexibility for States to take into account the circumstances attending each school that fails to meet the 95 percent participation rate requirement. For example, under the final regulations, a State could assign a lower summative determination to a school that falls below the 95 percent threshold for one subgroup, while both assigning a lower determination and identifying for targeted support and improvement a school that fails to meet the 95 percent participation requirement for multiple subgroups. A State also could propose a set of State-determined actions that includes escalating interventions depending on the extent to which or how long a school has missed the 95 percent participation rate requirement. These actions, consistent with the section 1111(c)(4)(E) of the ESEA, as amended by the ESSA, must be included in the State's accountability system for meaningfully differentiating schools and identifying schools for support and improvement. In this context it is important to note that States have discretion under the final regulations to take more rigorous actions for schools that consistently fail to meet the 95 participation rate requirement or that miss the 95 percent threshold by a wide margin, or for all students or multiple subgroups of students in the school. However, we agree that States would benefit from greater flexibility to devise their own State-determined actions based on the scope and extent to which a school misses the 95 percent participation rate, and we are revising the final regulations accordingly. We further note that the required improvement plans also provide an opportunity for States and districts to take into account local circumstances, such as by varying the scope and rigor of such plans depending on the severity of the participation rate problem in a particular school.

While we agree that States should have flexibility to determine the action taken in the school based on the scope or extent to which a school fails to meet the participation rate requirement, we disagree that States should be permitted to take less rigorous actions based on the reason for a school failing to meet the 95 percent participation rate requirement. Ensuring that all schools meet this requirement is essential for the integrity of the statewide accountability systems required by the ESEA, as amended by the ESSA, and permitting interventions that are not sufficiently rigorous risks sending the message that it is acceptable to miss the 95 percent participation rate requirement in some circumstances—an outcome that would not be consistent the requirements of the ESEA, as amended by the ESSA.

Changes: We have revised § 200.15(b)(2)(iv) to specify that an State may factor the 95 percent participation rate requirement into its system of annual meaningful differentiation through a State-determined action or set of actions that is "sufficiently rigorous" to improve a school's assessment participation so that it meets the requirement and removed the requirements for the State-determined action to be "equally rigorous" and result in a similar outcome as actions described in § 200.15(b)(2)(i)-(iii).

Comments: A few commenters generally supported proposed § 200.15 with the exception of language in proposed § 200.15(b)(2)(iv) that would subject any State-determined action to approval by the Department as part of the State plan review and approval process under section 1111(a) of the Act. These commenters believe that the Department's role, consistent with their interpretation of the statute, should be limited to reviewing, and not approving, proposed State-determined actions for schools failing to meet the 95 percent participation rate requirement.

Discussion: The requirement for Department review and approval of each State plan, which must include a description of the statewide accountability system that complies with all the requirements in sections 1111(c) and (d) of the ESEA, as amended by the ESSA, including the 95 percent participation rate requirement, is specified in section 1111(a) of the ESEA, as amended by the ESSA. Limiting the Department's role to simply reviewing proposed State-determined actions for schools that fail to meet the 95 percent participation rate requirement would be inconsistent with this statutory requirement.

Changes: None.

Comments: One commenter requested that the Department provide greater clarity to States regarding what would constitute an "equally rigorous" State-determined action, consistent with proposed § 200.15(b)(2)(iv), in schools that do not meet the 95 percent participation requirement for all students and all subgroups of students. Another commenter similarly expressed concern that the term "equally rigorous" is subject to interpretation and thus could cause confusion.

Discussion: We are revising "equally rigorous" to "sufficiently rigorous" in the final regulations, as discussed previously. Given that we have removed language regarding "equally rigorous" actions, there is no need to clarify this term in the final regulations, as we believe the revisions to the final regulation will support effective review and approval of any proposed State-determined action or set of actions submitted to the Department through the State plan process under section 1111(a) of the ESEA, as amended by the ESSA. We recognize there are many ways in which States could design actions that are sufficiently rigorous to improve participation rates in schools that miss the requirement under § 200.15(a)(2) and therefore decline to limit State discretion by adding more specific requirements.

Changes: None.

Comments: One commenter expressed concern that the proposed actions for schools that miss the 95 percent participation rate requirement would not permit flexibility when technical issues, such as the failure of computer networks, affect test participation rates.

Discussion: The Department would retain authority under the final regulations to address technical or logistical anomalies related to State administration of the annual assessments required by the Act that have a negative impact on the ability of schools to meet the 95 percent participation rate requirement.

Changes: None.

Comments: One commenter expressed concern that the proposed regulations would require changes to existing methods of incorporating the participation rate into statewide accountability systems.

Discussion: We believe that the final regulations related to the 95 percent participation rate requirement, like the proposed regulations, provide sufficient flexibility and discretion for States that already have rigorous methods of incorporating assessment participation rates into their statewide accountability system to use the same or similar methods to meet the requirements of these final regulations. For example, under § 200.15(b)(2)(iv), as revised in these final regulations, a State may propose, as part of its State plan under the Act, a State-determined action or set of actions to factor the 95 percent participation rate requirement into its system of annual meaningful differentiation of schools, so long as any proposed action is sufficiently rigorous to improve participation rates in any school that fails to assess at least 95 percent of all students or 95 percent of students in each subgroup so that it will meet the requirements in § 200.15(a).

Changes: None.

Comments: One commenter recommended that the final regulations include an exception to the 95 percent participation rate requirement for States that use a small n-size, on grounds that in such cases the effective participation rate for small schools or subgroups effectively becomes 100 percent.

Discussion: The Department declines to make this change. Section 1111(c)(4)(E) of the ESEA, as amended by the ESSA, does not provide for such an exception to the 95 percent participation rate requirement.

Changes: None.

Comments: One commenter stated that the proposed regulations specifying a range of State actions to enforce the statutory 95 percent participation rate requirement are unnecessary because any school failing to meet the requirement would already be subject to State and/or Federal compliance remedies, which could include an improvement plan or other actions.

Discussion: The Department believes clear regulations and guidance that promote State and local adherence to all the requirements of the ESEA, as amended by the ESSA, better serve students, educators, and the public than compliance remedies available under applicable law and regulation. The final regulations provide a clear, uniform, and understandable framework for effective implementation of the 95 percent participation rate requirement, through collaborative efforts at the State and local levels, which will support the overall goals and purposes of statewide accountability systems under the ESEA, as amended by the ESSA, while minimizing the need for heavy-handed compliance remedies.

Changes: None.

Comments: One commenter recommended that the final regulations regarding the 95 percent participation rate requirement include flexibility to prevent schools that fail to meet the requirement from being identified for comprehensive support and improvement or targeted support and improvement if their academic performance does not support such identification.

Discussion: We believe that the menu of options in the final regulations provides sufficient flexibility and discretion to States to factor the 95 percent participation rate into their statewide accountability systems without inappropriately identifying schools for comprehensive or targeted support and improvement.

Changes: None.

Comments: One commenter recommended delaying the State actions required by proposed § 200.15 until a school has missed the 95 percent participation rate requirement for two consecutive years. This commenter asserted that such a delay would give schools time to meet the 95 percent participation rate requirement without State intervention, while ensuring that such interventions occur in schools that continue to fail to meet the requirement.

Discussion: We appreciate commenter's recommendation in response to the directed question in the NPRM aimed at soliciting additional or different ways of supporting States in ensuring that low assessment participation rates are meaningfully addressed as part of their statewide accountability systems. However, given the statutory requirement that each State administer academic assessments to all public school students in the State, we believe that falling below a 95 percent participation rate requires action as part of a State's annual system of meaningful differentiation of schools rather than what, under the commenter's proposal, would amount to little more than a warning after missing the 95 percent requirement for one year, even in cases where non-participation was widespread and significant. Waiting an additional year would jeopardize further the availability of reliable, accurate assessment data that teachers and parents need to improve instruction and student outcomes and that States, LEAs, and schools need to support timely and effective school improvement consistent with the requirements of the ESEA, as amended by the ESSA. However, consistent with the previous regulations implementing the

ESEA, as amended by the NCLB, we are revising the final regulations to permit States to average a school's participation rates over two to three years for the limited purpose of meeting the requirements of § 200.15(b)(2), as described in revisions to § 200.20(a) under the subheading Data Averaging.

Changes: None.

Participation Rate Improvement Plans

Comments: One commenter objected to the proposed requirement that all schools not meeting the 95 percent participation rate requirement develop and implement an improvement plan designed to increase assessment participation rates. In particular, the commenter believed that States should have flexibility around this requirement relating to how many times a school has missed the 95 percent participation rate requirement, the number of subgroups involved, or the size of a school (i.e., schools with small n-sizes where a school might miss the 95 percent participation requirement due to non-participation by just one or two students). Other commenters supported the proposed participation rate improvement plan requirements.

Discussion: We believe the participation rate improvement plan requirement includes much of the flexibility sought by the commenter. For example, a school that misses the 95 percent participation rate requirement by one or two students for a single subgroup may not require as rigorous or comprehensive an improvement plan as a school that has an 80 percent participation rate for the all students group. As for triggering the requirement, section 1111(b)(2)(B) of the ESEA, as amended by the ESSA, requires States to administer annual assessments in reading/language arts and mathematics to all public elementary school and secondary school students in the State and section 1111(c)(4)(E) requires States to annually measure, for accountability purposes, the achievement of not less than 95 percent of all students and all students in each subgroup of students who are enrolled in public schools. In view of these statutory requirements, we believe requiring a participation rate improvement plan for any school that misses the 95 percent participation rate in any year, for any reason is consistent with the ESEA, as amended by the ESSA.

Changes: None.

Comments: One commenter recommended that schools not meeting the 95 percent participation requirement in the ESEA, as amended by the ESSA, undertake a root cause analysis to determine the reasons for low participation rates, with an emphasis on such issues as chronic absence, suspension rates, school climate, student engagement, and parental support for testing. This commenter also recommended that, in cases where low participation rates are linked to chronic absenteeism, the final regulations should encourage States to work with public agencies and community stakeholders to remove barriers to regular school attendance.

Discussion: We agree that a root cause analysis may be a useful part of a local process to develop the participation rate improvement plans required by the final regulations for schools that miss the 95 percent participation rate requirement, and that the factors noted by the commenter could negatively affect assessment participation rates. However, we decline to further prescribe the components of the required school or district assessment rate improvement plans in recognition of the fact that the scope of such plans may vary widely depending on local context, and thus schools and LEAs should have discretion to develop plans that address local needs and circumstances.

Changes: None.

Comments: One commenter expressed appreciation for the inclusion of principals and other school leaders in the consultation requirements for the improvement plans that would be required under proposed § 200.15(c)(1), but recommended that the final regulations emphasize that such plans should be developed under the leadership of, and not just in consultation with, school principals.

Discussion: We believe that the final regulations, like the proposed regulations, provide sufficient flexibility to support strong leadership for principals in the development of participation rate improvement plans, while recognizing that in some cases other individuals or organizations (e.g., the local Parent Teacher Association) could take the lead in developing such plans.

Changes: None.

Comments: One commenter requested that the Department clarify the meaning of the term "significant number of schools" as used in proposed § 200.15(c)(2), which requires participation rate improvement plans for districts with a significant number of schools that fail to meet the 95 percent participation rate requirement.

Discussion: The Department declines to define or offer parameters around the term "significant number of schools" in the final regulations because the meaning may vary depending on local context and circumstances. For example, in a medium-size district, 5 schools could constitute a significant number, while 15 schools might not be considered a significant number of schools in a large district. However, the final regulations clarify that States may consider the number or percentage of schools failing to meet the participation rate requirement.

Changes: We have revised § 200.15(c)(2) by replacing the term "a significant number of schools" with "a significant number or percentage of schools."

Comments: One commenter recommended clarifying that locally based approaches to improving test participation may be incorporated into State accountability systems.

Discussion: We believe that § 200.15(b)(2)(iv) provides sufficient flexibility to incorporate locally based approaches to improving assessment participation rates into a State-determined option for factoring participation rates into statewide accountability systems without further elaboration in the final regulations.

Changes: None.

Comments: Two commenters recommended that the improvement plan requirement in proposed § 200.15(c)(1) for schools that miss the 95 percent participation rate requirement be expanded to cover schools that fail to assess at least 95 percent of their English learners on the ELP assessment. These commenters observed that including 100 percent of English learners in ELP assessments is increasingly difficult due to a combination of the opt-out movement and high mobility among English learners, and asserted that requiring improvement plans for schools that do not assess at least 95 percent of their English learners on the ELP assessment would help improve participation rates on that assessment. These commenters further stated that such a requirement would align accountability requirements under the ESEA, as amended by the ESSA, while holding English learner students to a standard no higher than that of all other students. Another commenter requested clarification on whether the 95 participation rate requirement applies to ELP assessments.

Discussion: The 95 percent participation rate requirement is statutorily limited to the reading/language arts and mathematics assessments required by section 1111(b)(2)(v)(I) of the

ESEA, as amended by the ESSA, and there is no basis for applying this requirement to ELP assessments. Moreover, such application, even to the extent of requiring participation rate improvement plans for schools that fail to administer ELP assessments to 95 percent of their English learner students, would send a confusing message to States, districts, and schools about the requirement under section 1111(b)(2)(G)(i) of the ESEA, as amended by the ESSA, to administer ELP assessments to all such students. In addition, any regulatory action that might be interpreted as permitting schools to administer ELP assessments to fewer than 100 percent of English learners would likely be judged inconsistent with applicable civil rights laws.

Changes: None.

Other Comments on Participation in Assessments

Comments: One commenter recommended that the Department clarify proposed § 200.15(d)(2) to specify that disciplinary actions may not be used to systematically exclude students in any subgroup of students from participating in State assessments required by the ESEA.

Discussion: The Department agrees that disciplinary actions should not be used to exclude students from participating in assessments, but declines to enumerate in the final regulations the various methods and practices that may result in systematic exclusion of students from assessment participation. Such examples are more appropriate for non-regulatory guidance. We are, however, revising the final regulations to clarify that systematic exclusion of students from the assessment system on any basis is not permitted, and that students may not be systematically excluded on State assessments any content area: Reading/language arts, mathematics, or science.

Changes: We have revised § 200.15(d)(2) to clarify that a State, LEA, or school may not systematically exclude students, including any subgroup of students described in § 200.16(a), from participating in the State assessments in reading/language arts, mathematics, and science.

Comments: One commenter urged the Department to clarify in the final regulations that proposed § 200.15(d)(3), which permits counting a student with the most significant cognitive disabilities who is assessed based on alternate academic achievement standards described in section 1111(b)(1)(E) of the ESEA, as amended by the ESSA, as a participant for purposes of meeting the 95 percent participation rate requirements only if a State has developed the guidelines required by section 1111(b)(2)(D)(ii) of the ESEA, as amended by the ESSA, and ensures that its LEAs adhere to such guidelines, applies only for the purposes of calculating the participation rate. The commenter also sought clarification that students who take the alternate assessment, but are not counted as participants for calculating the participation rate because the State has not developed appropriate guidelines for IEP teams, should be counted as participants for calculating proficiency.

Discussion: We appreciate the concerns of the commenter but believe that the recommended clarifications are more appropriately addressed in non-regulatory guidance.

Changes: None.

Comments: One commenter recommended revising the final regulations to use the 95 percent participation rate requirement to increase school-level accountability for students who drop out and to incentivize reengagement efforts. More specifically, the commenter recommended that students who do not participate in assessments, and who have not been removed from a high school cohort because there is no documentation to support their removal as outlined in § 200.34(b)(3), be included in the denominator when calculating the 95 percent assessment participation rate.

Discussion: The Department appreciates and shares the commenter's commitment to increase high school graduation rates. However, we decline to make the recommended changes because they are not consistent with the overall purpose of the 95 percent participation rate requirement. That purpose is to help ensure the highest possible rates of student participation in the assessments in reading/language art and mathematics that are used in statewide accountability systems under the ESEA, as amended by the ESSA, and not to serve as a lever or incentive to improve other student outcomes.

Changes: None.

Comments: Two commenters recommended revising proposed § 200.15 to recognize the right of Native American students receiving instruction in Native American language medium schools to opt out of State assessments in reading/language arts and mathematics that are administered in English. These commenters also requested that States be required to exclude such students from the 95 percent participation rate requirement if the State lacks an appropriate assessment in the Native American language.

Discussion: The Department declines to make these changes because the ESEA, as amended by the ESSA, does not provide for an exception to the 95 percent participation rate requirement for Native American students receiving instruction in Native American language medium schools. In addition, a policy of excluding certain students from statewide assessments would be inconsistent with the purpose of title I to close educational achievement gaps.

Changes: None.

Comments: None.

Discussion: In reviewing the proposed regulations, the Department believes it is helpful to clarify the reason recently arrived English learners may be counted as participants on the State's reading/language arts assessment if they take either the State's reading/language arts assessment or the State's English language proficiency assessment; specifically, this flexibility applies to recently arrived English learners that may be exempted from one administration of the State's reading/language arts assessment, as described in § 200.16(c)(3)(i)(A), and not to other recently arrived English learners who take the State's reading/language arts assessment in each year of their enrollment in U.S. schools. This clarification is necessary because the ESEA, as amended by the ESSA, added an additional exemption that States may consider for holding schools accountable for the performance of recently arrived English learners, which requires assessment in reading/language arts in the first year of the student's enrollment in U.S. schools as described in § 200.16(c)(3)(ii).

Changes: We have revised § 200.15(d)(4) to clarify that this provision applies to recently arrived English learners who are exempted from one administration of the State's reading/language arts assessment consistent with § 200.16(c)(3)(i)(A).

Section 200.16   Subgroups of Students

Comments: A few commenters suggested that the Department replace the word "subgroups" with the term "student groups" throughout the regulations. One commenter explained that the term subgroup is an outdated term that implies that some groups are lesser than others.

67

Discussion: We appreciate the commenters' suggestion, but believe it is beneficial to use the same terminology contained in the statute. Therefore, throughout the regulations, we refer to subgroups of students.

Changes: None.

Comments: Two commenters asked that the Department modify proposed § 200.16 to specify that a student who meets the definition of English learner in section 8101(20) of the ESEA and who is instructed primarily through a Native American language be included in the English learner subgroup for the entire time that the student is taught in a Native American language, and that such students who transfer to a school in which instruction is in English may be considered as newly-enrolled English learners.

Discussion: As the commenters note, the term "English learner" is defined in section 8101(20) of the ESEA, as amended by the ESSA. That definition includes provisions under which a student who is Native American or Alaska Native and who comes from an environment where a language other than English has had a significant impact on his/her level of English language proficiency is considered an English learner. States include students in the English learner subgroup for accountability as long as they are "English learners." Specifically, under section 3113(b) of the ESEA, as amended by the ESEA, and §§ 299.13(c)(2) and 299.19(b)(4) of the final regulations, States must establish standardized statewide entrance and exit procedures for English learners, which, as in § 299.19(b)(4) of the final regulations, require English learner exit criteria to be the same criteria used to exit students from the English learner subgroup for accountability purposes. The issue of when a student is no longer an "English learner" is not dependent on the classroom language of instruction. Because the exit procedures are not related to the language of instruction, there is no need for the specific provisions requested. In addition, we note that § 200.16(c) permits States to include in the English learner subgroup the performance of former English learners for four years, for purposes of calculating any indictor that is based on data from State assessments under section 1111(b)(2)(B)(v)(I) of the ESEA, as amended by the ESSA.

Changes: None.

Combined Subgroups of Students ("Super Subgroups")

Comments: Many commenters expressed support for what they believed was a prohibition against combined subgroups of students in the proposed regulations. One commenter suggested that § 200.16(c) be clarified to explain that a State may not combine any of the subgroups listed in § 200.16(a)(2) as an additional subgroup.

Discussion: We appreciate the support from commenters highlighting the importance of accountability for individual subgroups of students, but note that the proposed regulations did not prohibit combined subgroups entirely; rather, they require the use of specified individual subgroups of students for certain purposes in statewide accountability systems and permit the use of additional subgroups of students in its statewide accountability system, which may include combined subgroups of students. Consistent with section 1111(c)(2) of the ESEA, the regulations require that a State include certain subgroups of students, separately, when establishing long-term goals and measurements of interim progress under § 200.13, measuring the performance on each indicator under § 200.14, annually meaningfully differentiating schools under § 200.18, and identifying schools under § 200.19. These subgroups of students include economically disadvantaged students, students from each major racial and ethnic group, children with disabilities, as defined in section 8101(4) of the ESEA, and English learners, as defined in section 8101(20) of the ESEA. However, the statute does not prohibit a State from using additional subgroups in its statewide accountability system, which may include combined subgroups. We also believe it is appropriate for States to retain flexibility to include various additional subgroups, based on their contexts, so long as each required individual subgroup is also considered. Accordingly, we are not revising the regulations.

Changes: None.

Comments: A number of commenters supported the requirement that a combined subgroup cannot be used in place of considering each of the required individual subgroups. A few commenters focused on the importance of maintaining the individual subgroups included in the proposed regulations. Some commenters noted that the use of so-called "super subgroups" in school ratings can mask underperformance of some individual subgroups of students, making it more difficult to identify schools with one or more consistently underperforming subgroups of students for targeted support and improvement, making it more challenging to provide specialized supports to support improvement, and limiting information available to the public and parents. Other commenters stated that combining subgroups of students without considering individual subgroups of students is contrary to the statutory purpose of increasing transparency, improving academic achievement, and holding schools accountable for the success of each subgroup. One commenter noted that there are different funding streams for particular subgroups of students, and that retaining individual definitions of these subgroups helps to ensure accountability for use of these funds.

Some commenters highlighted that a combined subgroup can be important as an additional subgroup, as it may allow a State to include students in the statewide accountability system that would not otherwise be included. One commenter provided a State-level example to highlight how many more students are identified in a State accountability system when a combined subgroup is used in addition to individual subgroups.

A few commenters supported the use of combined subgroups for accountability and believe a State should be able to use them in place of each of the required subgroups. Other commenters suggested that holding schools accountable for individual subgroups of students could raise questions regarding the validity and reliability of statewide accountability systems. Some commenters suggested that combined subgroups should be permitted for accountability, but that individual subgroups should be maintained for reporting.

Discussion: We appreciate the wide range of views from commenters both in support of and in opposition to the requirement that each individual subgroup described in § 200.16(a)(2) must be considered in a State's accountability system, and that such subgroups cannot be replaced by a combined subgroup. We believe that the final regulations strike the appropriate balance between ensuring accountability for individual subgroups of students specified in the ESEA, as amended by the ESSA, while also providing flexibility for States to include additional subgroups, including combined subgroups, in their statewide accountability systems.

Changes: None.

Comments: One commenter opposed the requirement that all indicators in a statewide accountability system measure the performance of each subgroup of students that meets the minimum n-size because it would increase the likelihood of diverse schools missing goals or receiving lower school ratings.

Discussion: We acknowledge the commenter's concern, but believe that the ESEA, as amended by the ESSA, requires the consideration of individual subgroups for accountability purposes. Annual meaningful differentiation of school performance is addressed in greater detail in response to comments on § 200.18.

Changes: None.

Comments: One commenter suggested that the Department consider allowing the use of the combined subgroup approach for the English learners, children with disabilities, and economically disadvantaged subgroups of students, provided that each State that combines these subgroups of students reports data on each subgroup individually as well as each of the ways that these three groups of students may be combined.

Discussion: We believe that the ESEA, as amended by the ESSA, requires the consideration of these individual subgroups of students for accountability purposes, and not, as recommended by the commenter, just for reporting purposes.

Changes: None.

Comments: One commenter requested that the proposed regulations be clarified to reflect that each subgroup of students should not include any duplicated students. Another commenter suggested that the use of combined subgroups of students in place of individual subgroups of students would help address what the commenter described as the problem of including students in multiple subgroups (e.g., an economically disadvantaged student who is also a child with a disability).

Discussion: We appreciate that under both the ESEA, as amended by the ESSA, and the proposed regulations some students may be identified in more than one subgroup of students, but we believe this duplication is essential to ensure that statewide accountability systems account for and help address what often are the multiple needs of individual students for different types of academic and non-academic support. Reducing such duplication through the use of a combined subgroup could mask underperformance by individual subgroups of students and thus inhibit the provision of needed services and supports for such students.

Changes: None.

Racial and Ethnic Subgroups

Comments: One commenter supported the requirement that a State consider each major racial and ethnic subgroup separately in its statewide accountability system. A few commenters, however, objected to the proposed requirement that students from each major racial and ethnic subgroup must be considered separately for the purposes of statewide accountability systems as an overreach of the Department's authority. These commenters asserted that the absence of the word "each" in the reference to students from major racial and ethnic groups in section 1111(c)(2)(B) of the ESEA, as amended by the ESSA, should be interpreted as providing flexibility for States to use a combined subgroup of students that includes students from all racial and ethnic groups. The commenters explained that the performance of students in individual racial and ethnic subgroups can still be reported for transparency.

Discussion: We agree with the commenter who expressed support for the regulations requiring a State to consider each major racial and ethnic subgroup separately for the purposes of its statewide accountability system. We believe that this regulation reflects the best reading of the statute, and do not agree with those commenters who assert that the absence of the word "each" from section

1111(c)(2)(B) of the ESEA, as amended by the ESSA, indicates that Congress intended for students from all major racial and ethnic groups to be combined into one subgroup. Such a subgroup would be virtually, if not completely, duplicative of all students, which could not have been Congress' intent. Rather, we believe Congress' reference to "major racial and ethnic groups" was intended to refer to the fact that States have authority to determine what the major racial and ethnic groups in their State are for purposes of compliance with this requirement. As such, there is not one list of major racial and ethnic groups that Congress could have included within section 1111(c)(2) of the ESEA, as amended by the ESSA. Accordingly, we believe the regulatory clarification that "each" major racial and ethnic subgroup must be included is necessary to reasonably ensure compliance with this provision of the statute, and to ensure that States incorporate differentiated information for historically underserved subgroups of students into their accountability systems, thereby promoting educational equity. We note, further, that this interpretation of the statute is consistent with the interpretation of identical language used in prior authorizations of the ESEA.

Changes: None.

Comments: One commenter suggested that the Department require every student to be included as a member of one major racial and ethnic subgroup. The commenter indicated concern that when a student is included as a member of the "two or more races" subgroup of students the student may not be identified as a member of any one specific racial and ethnic subgroup should the "two or more races" subgroup of students not be identified by the State, which could result in the State not collecting data on all students. The commenter expressed that requiring each student to be a part of one racial and ethnic subgroup will help to ensure that subgroups of students meet the minimum n-size and can be included in a State accountability system.

Discussion: We appreciate the commenter's desire to ensure that subgroups of students accurately reflect the population of the school. Section 1111(c)(2)(B) requires a State to identify, for the purposes of including required subgroups of students in its statewide accountability system, "students from major racial and ethnic groups." This requirement places responsibility on each State to identify which racial and ethnic groups are "major" within the State. Therefore, we decline to define in the final regulations which subgroups of students must be included in a State's major racial and ethnic subgroups, as that is a State-specific determination. For the purposes of Federal data collection, the Department published final guidance in 2007 that allows individuals to select more than one race and/or ethnicity and expanded the reporting categories to include "two or more races." Accordingly, a State may choose to include two or more races as a subgroup of students for accountability purposes, if the State considers that subgroup of students to be a major one within the State. We appreciate the commenter's concern that there may be small numbers of students in certain subgroups of students, and therefore, that students in those smaller subgroups of students may not be identified in a State's statewide accountability system, and address that issue in response to comments on § 200.17 (disaggregation of data).

Changes: None.

New Subgroups

Comments: A number of commenters requested that States be required to include additional subgroups beyond those listed in proposed § 200.16, including, for example, Native American students who attend Native American Language Schools and Programs, juvenile justice-involved youth, LGBT students, students who did not attend preschool, homeless students, transient students, and migratory students.

Discussion: The individual subgroups of students currently required in statewide accountability systems by the regulations are consistent with those required by the ESEA, as amended by the ESSA. While we understand that creating additional subgroups of students may help focus needed attention of underserved students with unique academic and non-academic needs, we believe States should have discretion over the inclusion of any additional subgroups in their statewide accountability systems. Consequently, we decline to provide further regulation in this area.

Changes: None.

Comments: One commenter noted that proposed § 200.16(b)(2) included a reference to students with a disability who are covered under Section 504 of the Rehabilitation Act (Section 504) when discussing students who are English learners with a disability and raised questions regarding the inclusion of students receiving services under Acts other than the IDEA. The commenter noted that nowhere else in the proposed changes, nor historically in ED Facts data collections, have students served under Section 504 been included with the subgroup of children with disabilities, as ED Facts collects information only on students identified as children with disabilities under the IDEA. The commenter questioned whether States should expect that students with disabilities covered under Section 504 will be included in the children with disabilities subgroup for the purposes of reporting, and asked for additional clarification about whether the Department intends to require separate reporting for students with disabilities covered under Section 504.

Discussion: We appreciate the request for clarification about this provision of the proposed regulations, which applies only to the English learner subgroup of students with regard to using the State's ELP assessment within the Progress in Achieving English Language Proficiency indicator. Under the section 1111(b)(2) of the ESEA, as amended by the ESSA, assessment accommodations for all students, including English learners, extend to students with disabilities covered under the IDEA, Section 504, and students with a disability who are provided accommodations under other Acts (i.e., title II of the Americans with Disabilities Act (ADA)). To be more consistent with these statutory requirements, we are revising the final regulations on English learners with a disability to include English learners that receive services under title II of the ADA. It is possible that English learners with a disability covered under IDEA, Section 504, or title II of the ADA may have a disability for which there are no available and appropriate accommodations for one or more domains of the State's ELP assessment because the student has a disability that is directly related to that particular domain (e.g., a non-verbal English learner who because of an identified disability cannot take the speaking portion of the assessment, even with accommodations)—the students described in proposed § 200.16(b)(2). Under the final regulations, we are clarifying that this determination can be made, on an individualized basis, by the student's IEP team, the student's 504 team, or for students covered under title II of the ADA, by the individual or team designated by the LEA to make those decisions; for such an English learner, the State must include the student's performance on the ELP assessment based on the remaining domains in which it is possible to assess the student. Whether the student receives services under the IDEA or is not eligible for services under the IDEA, but receives services under Section 504 or title II of the ADA, this student's score would count for the purpose of measuring performance against the Progress in Achieving English Language Proficiency indicator.

These regulations do not create an additional subgroup for accountability or for reporting purposes on the performance of students with disabilities who receive services under Section 504 or title II of the ADA who are also English learners. Additionally, we note that under section 3121(a)(2) of the ESEA, as amended by the ESSA, an LEA must provide disaggregated data when reporting the number and percentage of English learners making progress toward ELP for English learners with disabilities. The term "English learner with a disability" is defined in the ESEA to mean an English learner who is also a child with a disability as defined under section 602 of the IDEA.

Rather than modifying the students included in the children with disabilities subgroup, the Department intended for these provisions to emphasize the importance of ensuring that there are available and appropriate accommodations for English learners who are also students with disabilities and who receive services under the IDEA, Section 504, or title II of the ADA.

Changes: We have revised § 200.16(c)(2) to clarify that the accommodations for English learners with a disability are determined on an individualized basis by the student's IEP team, 504 team, or individual or team designated by the LEA to make these decisions under title II of the ADA.

Former Children With Disabilities

Comments: A number of commenters replied to the Department's directed question asking whether the provision to allow a State to include the scores of students who were previously identified as children with disabilities under section 602(3) of the Individuals with Disabilities Education Act (IDEA), but who no longer receives special education services ("former children with disabilities"), in the children with disabilities subgroup for the limited purpose of calculating the Academic Achievement indicator, and if so, whether such students may be included in the subgroup for up to two years consistent with current title I regulations, or for a shorter period of time.

A few commenters indicated that a State should have the flexibility to include the scores of former children with disabilities for the purpose of calculating the Academic Achievement indicator for up to four years, consistent with the statutory approach for former English learners. One commenter indicated that this approach would recognize that the student population changes over time and allow schools to be rewarded for the progress they have made in supporting former children with disabilities even after they exit from special education services. Another commenter asserted that the proposed flexibility would be important as students are still often receiving specialized supports when they have recently exited from special education services. A few commenters endorsed this approach so that students in the children with disabilities subgroup would be treated the same way as students formerly in the English learner subgroup. Another commenter believed that the flexibility should be more expansive so that a State could include the scores of former children with disabilities for as long as the State determines to be appropriate. The commenter cited the example of a student with a language-based disability who is instructed in a Native American language and may overcome the disability as related to the Native American language, and then encounter the disability again when transferred to a school where the student receives instruction in English.

A number of commenters supported States having the flexibility to include the scores of former children with disabilities in the children with disabilities subgroup for the purpose of calculating the Academic Achievement indicator for up to two years. The commenters contended that this flexibility would provide appropriate incentives to exit students from special education when they no longer require services and receive credit for the progress that schools have made in supporting such students. A few commenters also noted that it would ensure that schools remain accountable for the academic progress of children with disabilities once they exit from special education services. One commenter highlighted that students who transfer from special education back to general education make up about 9.3 percent of students aged 14-21 who exit a State's special education services under IDEA and explained that allowing their scores to be counted in the children with disabilities subgroup for up to two years would allow a State to continue monitoring and better understand special education and general education student performance.

On the other hand, many commenters objected to allowing a State to include the scores of former children with disabilities in the children with disabilities subgroup for purposes of calculating the Academic Achievement indicator. Most of these commenters agreed that the last year a student should count in the subgroup of children with disabilities is the year in which the student exits from receiving special education services. These commenters emphasized the need for accountability systems to accurately reflect students who are currently receiving special education services in the subgroup of children with disabilities. One commenter suggested that this flexibility would confound the baseline data in States, while a few commenters noted that unlike with respect to former English learners, the law does not explicitly provide States with the flexibility to include former children with disabilities in the subgroup of children with disabilities. One commenter asserted that extending flexibility to former children with disabilities would exceed the Department's rulemaking authority because such flexibility is not included in statute. A few other commenters suggested that past reasons for including former children with disabilities in the subgroup of children with disabilities are irrelevant under the ESSA because of changes to the accountability requirements. One commenter indicated that including the achievement of former children with disabilities for purposes of determining the achievement of the subgroup of children with disabilities under the ESSA's accountability structure will result in a system in which former children with disabilities are included for some purposes, but not all—adding confusion to the system and undermining transparency. A few commenters objected to this flexibility, noting that while English learners are expected to gain proficiency and exit English learner status, the goal for children with disabilities is not necessarily to exit special education services. One commenter indicated that there is not sufficient data on how many States, if any, are currently using this option and another suggested it is not the methodology employed within its State.

Finally, one commenter suggested that former children with disabilities who are included in the subgroup of children with disabilities should also be counted in calculations of whether a school's subgroup of children with disabilities exceeds the State's n-size.

Discussion: We appreciate the comments in response to the directed question. We asked this question to determine whether we should maintain the flexibility that exists under § 200.20 of the current regulations. Current § 200.20 provides that in determining AYP for English learners and students with disabilities, a State may include in the English learner and students with disabilities subgroups, respectively, for up to two AYP determinations, scores of students who were previously English learners, but who have exited English learner status, and scores of students who were previously identified as a child with a disability under section 602(3) of the IDEA, but who no longer receive services.

We believe the flexibility to count the scores of former children with disabilities in the subgroup of children with disabilities for up to two years after the student exits services for the limited purpose of calculating indicators that are based on data from the required State assessments in reading/language arts and mathematics under section 1111(b)(2)(B)(v)(I) of the ESEA, as amended by the ESSA, recognizes the progress that schools and teachers make to exit students from special education and provides an incentive to continue to support such students in the initial years in which the student is transitioning back to general education. We also agree that it is critical to maintain a transparent subgroup of children with disabilities, so that the subgroup data are accurate and schools are appropriately identified for supports. To that end, the final regulations require that a State include such scores only if the scores of all former children with disabilities are included in conformance with a uniform statewide procedure. Allowing a State to select which former children with disabilities to include, for which purposes, or for how long could undermine the fairness of accountability systems across the State by encouraging the inclusion of higher-achieving former children with disabilities only, or encouraging the inclusion of higher-achieving former children with disabilities for longer periods of time than their lower-achieving peers. We note that this regulation is a limited exception as it only allows a State to include these scores for the purposes of calculating indicators that rely on State assessment data in reading/language arts and mathematics and, as noted in proposed § 200.16(d), does not extend such flexibility to other elements of the statewide accountability system or for reporting purposes.

However, we are not persuaded that either available data or current practices related to including former children with disabilities in the subgroup of children with disabilities justify extending this flexibility beyond two years, whether it be up to four years as is the case for former English learners or for a State-determined period of time as recommended by one commenter.

We do not agree that the fact that Congress specifically provided flexibility to include the scores of former English learners in the subgroup of English learners precludes the Department from offering flexibility to include the scores of former children with disabilities in the subgroup of children with disabilities. Nothing in the statute indicates that, by offering flexibility for one subgroup of students, Congress intended to prohibit similar flexibility for other subgroups of students. Providing this flexibility with respect to former children with disabilities constitutes a reasonable exercise of the Department's rulemaking authority under GEPA, the DEOA, and section 1601(a) of the ESEA, as amended by the ESSA, and does not violate section 1111(e) of the ESEA, as amended by the ESSA (see discussion of the Department's general rulemaking authority under the heading Cross-Cutting Issues), as such flexibility is necessary to reasonably ensure that each statewide accountability system is appropriately designed to improve student academic achievement and school success, in accordance with the requirements in section 1111(c)(4) of the ESEA, as amended by the ESSA.

For all of these reasons, we are revising § 200.16 to retain the flexibility provided in the current regulations for former children with disabilities. We also are revising § 200.16 to require States to count former children with disabilities who are included in the subgroup of children with disabilities for purposes of determining whether a school's subgroup of children with disabilities exceeds the State's n-size for the purposes of calculating any indicator that is based on State assessment data, in accordance with the similar treatment for former English learners.

Changes: We have revised § 200.16 by adding § 200.16(b) to allow a State to include the scores of former children with disabilities for up to two school years following the year in which the student exits from special education services for the purposes of calculating any indicator under § 200.14(b) that uses data from State assessments under section 1111(b)(2)(B)(v)(I) of the ESEA, as amended by the ESSA, including that such a student must also count toward whether the school meets the State's minimum number of students for the children with disabilities subgroup for measuring any such indicator, and that the State must develop a uniform statewide procedure for doing so that includes all such students for the same State-determined period of time. We also made conforming edits to the remaining paragraphs in § 200.16 and reorganized and renumbered them, including by adding a paragraph on limitations in § 200.16(d) to clarify the purposes for which both former English learners and children with disabilities may be included, consistent with revisions to § 200.34 on calculating four-year adjusted cohort graduation rates.

Comments: One commenter suggested that the flexibility to include former children with disabilities should extend to the Graduation Rate indicator, as well as the Academic Achievement indicator, believing that including the scores of exited students in both indicators will provide a better snapshot of school performance over time. Another commenter suggested that the flexibility to include former children with disabilities in the children with disabilities subgroup should extend across all indicators and to identification of schools for targeted support and improvement.

Discussion: We believe that revisions to § 200.34 of the final regulations addresses the commenter's concern with regard to graduation rates, because those revisions require a child with a disability to be included in the adjusted cohort graduation rate for the children with disabilities subgroup if the student was identified as part of the subgroup at any time during high school. In practice, this means that if a student exited from receiving special education services in grade 9 and graduated in four years, the student will count as a graduate for the subgroup of children with disabilities, even though the student did not receive services under IDEA for the student's final three years of high school. Further, a State may include the results of former children with disabilities in other indicators, such as Academic Progress, if the measure is based on data from the required State assessments in reading/language arts or mathematics (e.g., student growth or gap closure on these assessments). However, we do not believe further flexibility is warranted with regard to other indicators used for differentiation and identification of schools that do not utilize data from State assessments, as States already have significant discretion in selecting measures for other indicators that take into account school climate, student engagement, or other factors that are less directly related to academic achievement.

Changes: We have revised § 200.16(d) to clarify the purposes for which both former English learners and children with disabilities may be included within the applicable subgroups, consistent with revisions to § 200.34 on calculating adjusted cohort graduation rates.

Comments: One commenter suggested that the ability to include the scores of former children with disabilities should not apply to students whose parents revoke consent to the continued provision of special education services.

Discussion: We believe it would create undue confusion to create an exception for parents who revoke consent to the general rule about including the scores of former children with disabilities, especially as this provision is already limited in scope to the calculation of indicators that are based on data from State assessments required under section 1111(b)(2)(B)(v)(I) of the ESEA, as amended by the ESSA.

Changes: None.

Former English Learners

Comments: A number of commenters requested that a State be permitted to include former English learners for calculating indicators in addition to the Academic Achievement indicator. One of those commenters requested that former English learners also be included for reporting purposes.

Discussion: Section 1111(b)(3)(B) of the ESEA, as amended by the ESSA, permits inclusion of former English learners' results on the reading/language arts and mathematics assessments for up to four years for purposes of English learner subgroup accountability. These assessment results are included in the Academic Achievement indicator, as recognized in the proposed regulations, but we agree with commenters, in part, that there may be cases where other indicators should include former English learners because the indicator is also based on data from the required State assessments in reading/language arts or mathematics (e.g., a State that measures growth in reading/language arts and mathematics in grades 3-8 in its Academic Progress indicator). Further, we believe this interpretation is more consistent with the statutory provision in section 1111(b)(3)(B) of the ESEA. Thus, we are revising the final regulations to clarify that, if a State chooses to include former English learners for accountability purposes, such students may be included in any indicator under the ESEA that uses results from the State's reading/language arts and mathematics assessments. In any case where required State assessments in reading/language arts and mathematics are not included in an accountability indicator, former English learners may not be included, as expanding this flexibility to indicators that are not based on such State assessments or reporting would potentially limit subgroup accountability for current English learners in contravention of the statute. However, consistent with revisions to § 200.34, an English learner may be included for purposes of calculating the adjusted cohort graduation rate for the subgroup if the student was identified as part of the subgroup at any time during high school. In practice, if a student met the State's exit criteria for English learners in grade 11 and graduated in four years, the student could be counted as a graduate in the four-year adjusted cohort graduation rate for the English learner subgroup, even though the student did not receive language instruction services for the final year of high school. We believe that this additional flexibility partially addresses the commenters' concern with regard to the Graduation Rate indicator, but we do not believe further flexibility is warranted with regard to other indicators, as States already have significant discretion in selecting measures for other indicators that take into account student progress, school climate, student engagement, or other factors that are less directly related to academic achievement.

Changes: We renumbered and revised § 200.16(d) to clarify the purposes for which both former English learners and children with disabilities may be included within the respective subgroups, consistent with revisions to § 200.34 on calculating adjusted cohort graduation rates.

Comments: A number of commenters expressed their support for proposed § 200.16(b)(1), permitting a State to include in the Academic Achievement indicator, for up to four years, a student who has exited English learner status. One such commenter, however, noted concern that allowing former English learners to be included may mask the performance of the English learner subgroup.

Discussion: We appreciate the support for proposed § 200.16(b), as well as the concern about masking of subgroup performance. Section 1111(b)(3)(B) of the ESEA, as amended by the ESSA, gives States the discretion to include the scores of former English learners on the reading/language arts and mathematics assessments for up to four years for purposes of English learner subgroup accountability; States are not required to do so. In addition, we believe that the masking concern is mitigated by § 200.16(d), which excludes former English learners from the English learner subgroup for reporting purposes (except those directly related to reporting on the indicators where such students may be included), thus ensuring that parents and other stakeholders receive information about the performance of current English learners through the reporting requirement. Further, we note that the inclusion of former English learners, if a State chooses to do so, may increase the likelihood that schools are held accountable for the English learner subgroup, as such students must be counted toward meeting the State's minimum number of students for indicators that are based on data from State assessments in reading/language arts and mathematics. To that end, we are clarifying § 200.16(c)(1)(ii) to specify that this provision on counting former English learners towards meeting the State's minimum number of students only applies for such indicators.

Changes: We have revised the regulations in § 200.16(c)(1)(ii) to specify that former English learners are included for purposes of calculating whether a school meets the State's minimum number of students under § 200.17(a) for the English learner subgroup on any indicator under § 200.14(b) that uses data from State assessments under section 1111(b)(2)(B)(v)(I) of the ESEA, as amended by the ESSA.

Comments: One commenter asked that the Department clarify that an English learner whose parents refuse services should not be considered a former English learner for purposes of proposed § 200.16(b)(1). In addition, commenters requested clarification that an English learner who exits status during the school year would be considered an English learner—not a former English learner—in that school year.

Discussion: We agree that only students who have exited English learner status can be considered as students who have ceased to be identified as English learners; English learners whose parents have opted the student out of services are still English learners until they meet the State's exit criteria. We also agree that students who do meet the exit criteria during the school year should count as an English learner for that school year. We are therefore clarifying, in § 200.16(c), that the regulation applies only to students who have met the State's exit criteria, beginning with the year after they meet those criteria.

Changes: We have modified § 200.16(c) to clarify how to calculate the four years after a student ceases to be identified as an English learner (i.e., the four years following the year in which the student meets the statewide exit criteria, consistent with § 299.19(b)(4)).

English Learners With a Disability

Comments: A few commenters provided suggestions related to English learner students who are unable to be assessed in all four domains of language on the ELP assessment, as related to the requirement that such a student's performance be included in the Progress in Achieving English Language Proficiency indicator. Most commenters indicated support for proposed § 200.16(b)(2), which requires that if an English learner's IEP team or 504 team determines that the student is unable to be assessed in all four domains of language, the State must include the student's performance on the ELP assessment based on the remaining domains in which it is possible to assess the student. One commenter expressed hope that this exception would truly be an exception, and not apply to most English learners with disabilities. Another commenter supported the rule but suggested the addition of language indicating that the composite score for any student not assessed in the four domains of language must be valid and reliable. Additionally, a commenter suggested that the Department add language to the proposed regulations to allow accommodations for students with disabilities who have limited or no oral speech to take the speaking components of State assessments generally in ways that measure communication skills rather than only oral speech. The commenter provided specific examples of such accommodations, including using text-to-speech, sign language, and/or augmentative and assistive communication devices.

One commenter disagreed with the proposed regulation, stating that an English learner who has a disability that prevents the student from being assessed in one or more domains of language on the ELP assessment should be excluded from all calculations.

Discussion: We appreciate the support we received on this provision, as well as the nuanced issues raised by some of the commenters. We agree with the commenter indicating that this rule should be an exception and only serve the small fraction of English learners with disabilities who, because of an identified disability, cannot be assessed in one of the four domains of language. For these reasons, we are clarifying the final regulations to specify that this exception applies only in the case of an English learner with a disability that precludes assessment in one or more domains of the ELP assessment such that there are no appropriate accommodations for the affected domain(s), as determined on an individualized basis by the student's IEP team, 504 team, or individual or team designated by the LEA to make these decisions under Title II of the ADA. We disagree with the commenter who asserted that such students' scores should be completely excluded from accountability systems; the exclusion of student scores is not only contrary to the statute but can result in a lack of proper attention and services for such students.

We appreciate the concerns of the commenter who requested that we add examples of particular accommodations and discuss issues of validity and reliability with regard to composite scores that do not include performance in all four domains. While we believe this information is critical to the field, we believe that the recommended clarifications would be best addressed through non-regulatory guidance. Further, we note that specific issues regarding the statewide ELP assessment, including validity, reliability, and accommodations, are outside the scope of these regulations, as they pertain to regulations on State assessments under part A of title I.

Changes: We have revised § 200.16(c)(2) to clarify that—in the case of an English learner with a disability that precludes assessment in one or more domains of the ELP assessment such that there are no appropriate accommodations for the affected domains, as determined on an individualized basis by the student's IEP team, 504 team, or individual or team designated by the LEA to make these decisions under Title II of the ADA—States must, for purposes of measuring performance against the Progress in Achieving English Language Proficiency indicator, include such a student's performance on the ELP assessment based on the remaining domains in which it is possible to assess the student.

Recently Arrived English Learners

Comments: A number of commenters expressed support for proposed § 200.16(b)(3)-(4) with respect to including the results from recently-arrived English learners in accountability determinations. Of those, two commenters suggested extending the flexibility for inclusion of such results to three to five years.

Discussion: We appreciate the support for the regulations on recently arrived English learners. The timeframes in proposed § 200.16(b)(3) are the same as the requirements in section 1111(b)(3)(A) of the ESEA, as amended by the ESSA.

Changes: None.

Comments: Several commenters expressed concern that the requirement in proposed § 200.16(b)(3)(ii)(C), regarding growth on content assessments, effectively requires any State that decides to avail itself of that option for including recently arrived English learners in accountability to use a growth measure in its Academic Progress indicator.

Discussion: The requirements in section 1111(b)(3)(A) of the ESEA, as amended by the ESSA, permit the use of growth on content assessments in lieu of proficiency for accountability purposes in limited instances for recently arrived English learners. The commenters are correct that, under the second statutory option (section 1111(b)(3)(A)(ii)(II)(bb), and reflected in proposed § 200.16(b)(3)(ii)), in which recently arrived English learners are assessed in their first year on the reading/language arts as well as the math assessments, States are required to include a measure of student growth in the accountability system. Under the proposed regulations, a State would have been required to include the performance of such recently arrived English learners in their second year of enrollment in U.S. schools on those content assessments in a growth measure in the Academic Achievement indicator for high schools, and in the Academic Progress indicator for non-high schools. We recognize that not all States may decide to use a measure of growth in the Academic Progress indicator, and are revising § 200.16(c)(3)(ii)(C) to clarify that a State may include a measure of growth in the second year of enrollment for such an English learner in either the Academic Achievement or Academic Progress indicator to provide greater flexibility to States with regard to including growth for recently arrived English learners in elementary and middle schools.

Changes: We have revised § 200.16(c)(3)(ii)(C) to allow growth for recently arrived English learners in their second year of enrollment in elementary and middle schools to be included in either the Academic Progress indicator or the Academic Achievement indicator.

Comments: None.

Discussion: In reviewing the proposed regulations, we believe it is necessary to clarify the uniform statewide procedure for determining which assessment and accountability exception, if any, applies to an individual recently arrived English learner, for States that choose not to apply the same exception to all recently arrived English learners in the State. The proposed regulations specified that the statewide procedure must take into consideration a student's ELP level, consistent with the requirements for setting long-term goals and measurements of interim progress for English learners in § 200.13, but did not similarly specify the point in time in which a recently arrived English learner's ELP level should be examined. As the intent was to consider such a student's initial level of ELP—and make a decision about which exception would apply for each of the following two to three years—we are revising the regulations accordingly. This approach is necessary, as a State must determine which exception is appropriate during the student's first year of enrollment in the U.S. schools in order to comply with the requirements of that exception in each succeeding year.

Changes: We have revised § 200.16(c)(4)(i)(B) to clarify that, for States that choose to use a uniform statewide procedure, a recently arrived English learner's ELP level at the time of the student's identification as an English learner must be taken into account in determining whether the exception applies.

Section 200.17   Disaggregation of Data

N-Sizes for Accountability and Reporting

Comments: We received a number of comments regarding a State's determination of the minimum number of students sufficient to yield statistical and reliable information and protect student privacy, commonly known as the "minimum n-size." A number of commenters supported the proposed requirements in § 200.17(a) for information that States must submit in their State plans related to n-size, including that States submit a justification and receive approval from the Department in order to use an n-size that exceeds 30 students for accountability purposes. Multiple commenters stated that the proposal preserves State flexibility and balances the need for n-sizes to be small enough to be inclusive of all required student subgroups in the statute, but also large enough to ensure statistical reliability and to protect students' privacy. In particular, some commenters noted that requiring States to justify n-sizes above 30 will help ensure that historically disadvantaged student subgroups are not overlooked nor absent from the accountability system.

Discussion: We appreciate the support of these commenters, and agree that the requirements in § 200.17(a) are necessary and appropriate to ensure that States establish n-sizes that not only help produce valid and reliable accountability determinations, but also ensure all students and subgroups of students are meaningfully included in annual meaningful differentiation and identification of schools and in annual report cards. These provisions provide sufficient flexibility for States to determine their own n-sizes for accountability and reporting while protecting equity and the focus on educational opportunity and excellence for all students.

Changes: None.

Comments: A number of commenters disagreed with the proposed requirement for a justification to exceed a minimum n-size of 30 students and recommended eliminating this requirement in the final regulation. These commenters recommended that instead States be allowed to select, in consultation with stakeholders, an n-size they believe is appropriate without any further parameters, or that the Department move these provisions to non-regulatory guidance. Some of these commenters also objected that a requirement for States to justify their n-size exceeds the Department's statutory authority or violates the prohibition in section 1111(e)(1)(B)(iii)(VIII) of the ESEA, as amended by the ESSA, related to prescribing the minimum number of students a State uses for purposes of accountability and reporting.

Discussion: As discussed previously, we appreciate the support of many commenters for the requirement that States submit a justification for a minimum n-size exceeding 30 students for review and approval by the Department as part of the State plan process. We agree that this approach strikes the right balance toward ensuring each State's n-size meets all statutory requirements. We also believe this requirement is consistent with both the Department's rulemaking authority under GEPA, the DEOA, and section 1601(a) of the ESEA, as amended by the ESSA (as previously described in the discussion of Cross-Cutting Issues), and the specific provisions of the ESEA, as amended by the ESSA, and that it does not violate section 1111(e) of the ESEA, as amended by the ESSA. More specifically, the requirement in § 200.17(a)(2)(iii) and (3)(v) is not inconsistent with section 1111(e)(1)(B)(iii)(VIII) of the ESEA, as amended by the ESSA, because it does not prescribe a specific minimum n-size. Rather, the regulations establish a baseline expectation that a State will select an n-size of 30 or less, or otherwise submit a justification for a higher number. A State that selects an n-size that is lower than 30 has significant discretion to select any n-size below 30, so long as it meets the requirements of section 1111(c)(3) of the ESEA and § 200.17(a)(1)-(2). Further, a State retains the flexibility to establish an n-size that is higher than 30, provided it demonstrates how the higher number promotes sound, reliable accountability decisions consistent with the statutory requirements for n-size and the law's focus on accountability for subgroup performance at the school level. The requirements in §§ 200.17(a)(2)(iii) and (3)(v) fall squarely within the scope of the title I, part A of the statute and are necessary to reasonably ensure that States are able to meet the requirements of section 1111(c)(4)(C)(iii) of the ESEA, as amended by the ESSA, which requires a State to establish a system of meaningful differentiation that includes differentiation of any school in which any subgroup of students is consistently underperforming, while also meeting the requirements of section 1111(c)(3) of the ESEA.

The State-determined n-size must meet several requirements in the statute, including to support valid and reliable accountability determinations and data reporting; to protect student privacy; and to support the inclusion of each subgroup of students for purposes of measuring student progress against the State's long-term goals and indicators, annually meaningfully differentiating schools based on those indicators, identifying schools with low-performing and consistently underperforming subgroups, and providing support for improvement in those schools. We agree with commenters that stakeholder engagement is critically important in selecting an n-size that works in the context of each State; in fact, under the statute and §§ 299.13 and 299.15, States are required to conduct meaningful and timely stakeholder engagement to establish their accountability systems, including their n-size. That said, we disagree that additional parameters for a State to consider in setting its n-size are unnecessary or best discussed in non-regulatory guidance only. Setting an n-size that is statistically sound and inclusive of subgroups has been a challenge for States, and past approaches have, at times, prioritized setting a conservative n-size (e.g., 100 students) at the expense of providing meaningful subgroup accountability. Current regulations in § 200.7, which were updated in 2008, include many similar parameters as those in proposed § 200.17(a). These regulations were promulgated to provide greater transparency to the public in how n-sizes are established and establish a reasonable approach for States to balance statistical reliability and privacy with the statutory emphasis on disaggregation and subgroup accountability, consistent with the NCLB's purpose to close achievement gaps. (6) These reasons remain applicable under the ESEA, as amended by the ESSA, given that section 1111(c)(3) requires all States to select an n-size that is statistically sound and protects student privacy for all purposes under title I, including subgroup accountability and reporting. Further, since the 2008 regulations took effect, numerous States have lowered their n-sizes, including sixteen in the last two years. (7) We strongly believe that creating a process in the State plan for stakeholders to meaningfully engage in establishing a State's n-size, including by requiring a State selecting an n-size larger than 30 students to provide transparent data and clear information on the rationale and impact of its selected n-size, is essential to maintain this progress in using lower n-sizes and to support a better, and more appropriate balance between validity, reliability, student privacy, and maximum inclusion of subgroups of students.

Changes: None.

Comments: Many commenters supported proposed § 200.17(a), under which a State must justify in its State plan setting any minimum n-size above 30 students, but recommended that the threshold above which a justification for the State's proposed n-size is required be lower than 30 students. The majority of those commenters recommended that any proposed n-size above 10 students for accountability and reporting purposes (as the proposed regulations would permit a State to select a lower n-size for reporting) require a justification in the State plan; a few commenters recommended that the Department require a justification for any proposed n-size above 20. Some commenters who supported a lower number were concerned that a threshold of 30 students would provide an incentive for States that are currently using a lower n-size to raise their n-size to 30.

In support of their suggestion that we lower to 10 the threshold above which a State must provide further justification for its proposed n-size, some commenters cited research, including a 2016 Alliance for Excellent Education (8) report and a 2010 IES report (9) concluding that data based on n-sizes of 5 or 10 students may be reported reliably without revealing personally identifying information. To show how a lower number would increase subgroup accountability, some commenters provided evidence from select States on the number and percentage of students that were "added" to the accountability system or the number and percentage of schools that were newly held accountable for subgroup performance when that State lowered its n-size. Other commenters cited a general concern about including particular subgroups, such as children with disabilities, English learners, or Native American students, in the accountability system or ensuring particular schools, like rural schools, were held accountable for subgroup performance. Others who recommended a threshold of 10 pointed to the Department's proposed rule, Equity in IDEA, which suggested a minimum n-size of not more than 10 as the standard methodology to determine whether there is significant disproportionality in each State and its LEAs, based on race or ethnicity due to overrepresentation in the identification, placement, and discipline of children with disabilities. Another commenter believed that lowering the threshold to 10 would improve the ability to make cross-State comparisons based on educational data.

Finally, a few commenters challenged the research basis for the proposal of 30 as the n-size above which a justification is required—but instead of recommending a lower threshold, the commenters either requested that the final regulations provide States greater flexibility in selecting an n-size, or require States to describe how their n-size minimizes error and provides for adequate validity and reliability of school-level reporting and accountability decisions generally.

Discussion: We appreciate the support of commenters for our approach to State-determined minimum n-sizes, including requiring a justification from States for proposing to use an n-size above a certain threshold, and agree with the goal of maximizing subgroup accountability; we strongly encourage States to use the lowest possible n-size that will produce valid and statistically sound data, protect student privacy, and meaningfully include all subgroups of students—which may well be lower than 30 students in many States. However, we do not believe that the current state of practice or current research on minimum n-sizes supports requiring States to submit a justification of an n-size below 30 students for accountability purposes, although this could change in the future, as additional research is produced and as evidence from State implementation of disaggregated accountability and reporting under the ESEA is gathered. We also disagree with commenters that research suggests 30 is an inappropriate threshold altogether and preferred for States to provide a general description of how their n-size meets the statutory requirements for validity and reliability.

The Department believes that requiring additional information for an n-size above 30 students is warranted, because, based on basic statistics and research analyses, an n-size that exceeds 30 is less likely to meet the requirements in the statute, particularly those requiring States to adopt school accountability systems that reflect the performance of individual subgroups of students, and thus, requires justification as part of the State plan review and approval process. Validity and reliability are not the only statutory and regulatory requirements for a State in selecting its n-size; these criteria must be balanced with the requirement for an n-size that is small enough to provide for the inclusion of each student subgroup in school-level accountability and reporting. Not only is this critical to maintain educational equity and protect historically underserved populations of students, but it is also a clear purpose of accountability systems under section 1111(c) of the ESEA, as amended by the ESSA, as disaggregation is required when measuring student progress against the State's long-term goals and indicators and notifying schools with a consistently underperforming subgroup of students for targeted support and improvement. Thus, it is equally important for States to justify how their n-size preserves accountability for subgroups as it is for States to demonstrate validity and reliability as a result of their chosen n-size. Research demonstrates how n-sizes larger than 30 require further justification to show that subgroups of students will be included. For example, under NCLB, 79 percent of students with disabilities were included in the accountability systems of States with an n-size of 30, but only 32 percent of students with disabilities were included in States with an n-size of 40. (10) Similarly, a more recent analysis

of California's CORE school districts, (11) found that only 37 percent of African American students' math scores are reported at the school-level with an n-size of 100 students, but 88 percent of such students were included using an n-size of 20 students. For students with disabilities, the difference was larger: 25 percent of students with disabilities were reported at the school-level under an n-size of 100, while 92 percent were included with an n-size of 20. Other reports have demonstrated that an n-size of 60 can potentially exclude all students with disabilities from a State's accountability system. (12)

In addition, while there are many desirable and stable statistical properties that are attributable to an n-size of 30, because that is the sample size at which a distribution approaches normality (an assumption for strong validity for most statistical tests of inference based on the Central Limit Theorem), the subgroups of students that are included for school accountability and reporting purposes are not, technically, a sample. Because a State is required to measure the performance of all students and all students in each subgroup of students in calculating the accountability indicators for a given school, the data used for accountability are representatives of a census, or universe, of the entire school population for any given year on any given measure. While collecting data for an entire population does not mitigate all potential sources of error in the data, it does mitigate one very large one: Sampling error because the data are not representative of the school as a whole.

Accordingly, the Department does not dispute that an n-size lower than 30 students, such as 10 or 20, may also be valid, reliable, and maximally inclusive of subgroups—especially for reporting purposes—which is why we believe further justification in a State selecting such an n-size is unnecessary. In specifying 30 as the threshold, we were not only considering the current state of research, but also current practice; only eight States use an n-size for accountability greater than 30 students, (13) so we believe a threshold of 30 will not add burden to the State plan for most States and recognizes the significant progress many States have made in recent years to lower their n-sizes below 30 students. (14) We also do not believe that establishing a threshold of 30 students will encourage States currently using a lower n-size to move to a higher number; such States have established lower n-sizes in response to their own needs and circumstances, and not because of any current statutory or regulatory provision, and thus would be unlikely to revisit earlier decisions in response to a regulation that would not require such action. In sum, after examining these trends in practice and research, we believe a lower threshold would mostly result in greater burden without the desired outcome of commenters (lower n-sizes), because, based on the current the state of knowledge, many States could likely provide a solid justification for selecting an n-size between 10 and 30 students in their State plans.

We also note that § 200.17(a)(2)(iv) would permit States to use a lower n-size, such as 10, for reporting, while using a different n-size for accountability. Further, § 200.20(a) permits a State to average school-level data across grades or over time for particular accountability purposes, including calculating each indicator, so that a State choosing to take advantage of this flexibility may sum the number of students with valid data in a particular subgroup and increase the likelihood that a school meets the minimum n-size (see final § 200.20(a)(1)(A)). For example, the indicators for a school that served a total of ten English learners for each of the last three years will, if an SEA chooses to combine results over three years, be calculated as a combined average of its data from all grades and years; the LEA would have 30 students in this subgroup.

This decision to maintain a threshold of 30, above which a State must justify its proposed n-size, is independent of the different analysis and proposal accompanying the Equity in IDEA proposed regulations, which was based on the context and experience of the IDEA and not the statewide accountability systems required by the ESEA. Finally, as the ESEA provides States with discretion to develop their own challenging academic standards and aligned assessments, ambitious long-term goals and measurements of interim progress, and unique measures and indicators for differentiation of schools, it is not clear that simply setting a lower n-size would support meaningful cross-State comparisons, since even if there was additional information available at a school-level for particular subgroups, such comparisons would be meaningless across States as the underlying measures are, more often than not, unique to each State.

Changes: None.

Comments: A few commenters recommended that the Department require all States, not only those that propose n-sizes greater than 30 students, to submit data on the number and percentage of schools that would not be held accountable for the performance of particular subgroups of students based on the selected n-size.

Discussion: While the final regulations require States that request to use an n-size greater than 30 students to submit data on the number and percentage of schools that would not be held accountable for the results of students in each subgroup described in § 200.16(a)(2), requiring all States to submit this information would unnecessarily increase burden on States that select an n-size that is likely to meet the law's requirements for a threshold that is valid, reliable, and maximally inclusive of all students and each subgroup of students, as discussed previously. However, in light of these comments on the importance of comparative data on school-level accountability for subgroups, we are revising § 200.17(a)(3)(v), to provide that a State's justification of an n-size above 30 includes both data on the number and percentage of schools in the State that would not be held accountable for the results of subgroups described in § 200.16(a)(2) under its proposed n-size as well as comparative data on the number of schools that would not be held accountable for the performance of those subgroups with an n-size that is 30.

Changes: We have revised § 200.17(a)(3)(v) to clarify that a State's justification for an n-size above 30 students includes data on the number and percentage of schools that would not be held accountable for results from each subgroup based on the State's proposed n-size, compared to data on the number and percentage of schools in the State that would not be held accountable for each subgroup if the State had selected an n-size of 30 students.

Comments: Some commenters recommended that all States be required to submit data on the number and percentage of all students and subgroups described in § 200.16(a)(2) for whose results a school would not be held accountable for each indicator in the State accountability system. In addition, a few of these commenters recommended making this information available on SEA and LEA report cards in addition to the State plan.

Discussion: Proposed § 200.17(a)(3)(iv) requires all States in their State plans to submit information regarding the number and percentage of all students and students in each subgroup of students for whose results a school would not be held accountable in the State accountability system for annual meaningful differentiation under § 200.18. As annual meaningful differentiation of schools is based on all of the State's indicators, we believe that it would be unnecessarily burdensome for all States to provide an indicator-by-indicator analysis on the number and percentage of students in each subgroup that are included in the accountability system, or for States to provide this information in two places, the State plan and their report cards. We encourage States, as part of the process of meaningful and timely consultation in developing new accountability systems as described in §§ 299.13 and 299.15, to conduct any analyses, in consultation with stakeholders and technical experts, that they believe will be useful in setting an n-size that is valid, reliable, consistent with protecting student privacy, and maximally inclusive of all students and each subgroup of students. (15) We also note that States may provide additional analyses or data on their selected n-size in their State plans, or make such additional analyses and data public, if they so choose.

Changes: None.

Comments: A few commenters recommended prohibiting the use of an n-size that exceeds 30 students.

Discussion: We believe that restricting n-sizes above 30 students would be inconsistent with section 1111(e)(1)(B)(iii)(VIII) of the ESEA, which prohibits the Department from prescribing a State's n-size so long as the State-determined number meets all requirements of section 1111(c)(3).

Changes: None.

Comments: A few commenters recommended prohibiting States from using n-sizes over 10 students for reporting purposes or requiring States to use a lower n-size for reporting than for accountability purposes.

Discussion: The Department agrees that States should use an n-size that is no larger than necessary to protect student privacy for reporting purposes, especially given the importance of providing transparent and clear information on State and LEA report cards that includes disaggregated information by each subgroup. However, we decline to establish a specific threshold for reporting purposes, because States have demonstrated a commitment to using a low n-size (e.g., 10 or lower) for reporting purposes without regulations requiring them to do so. In addition, we believe that restricting n-sizes for reporting purposes above 10 students would be inconsistent with section 1111(e)(1)(B)(iii)(VIII) of the ESEA, which prohibits the Department from prescribing a State's n-size so long as the State-determined number meets all requirements of section 1111(c)(3). We also disagree with the recommendation to require a lower n-size for reporting, as this could require States that have set a similarly low n-size (e.g., 10 students) for both purposes to increase their n-size for accountability, and believe the decision to use a lower reporting n-size is best left to States.

Changes: None.

Comments: Some commenters opposed the requirement in proposed § 200.17(a)(2)(ii) that the n-size be the same for all accountability purposes, including for each indicator and for calculating participation rates on assessments, believing that the proposed requirements are overly prescriptive and unnecessary to ensure States comply with the law's requirements for establishing n-sizes. In addition, one commenter disagreed with other provisions in proposed § 200.17(a)(2), including the requirement that the State-determined n-size be the same for all students and for each subgroup of students and the option of using a lower n-size for reporting purposes.

Discussion: We disagree with the commenters that the proposed requirements in § 200.17(a)(2) are unnecessary to ensure that States set valid and reliable n-sizes consistent with the law's requirements. First, the requirement in § 200.17(a)(2)(i) for the n-size established by each State to be the same for all students and for each subgroup of students is statutory (section 1111(c)(3)(A)(i) of the ESEA, as amended by the ESSA) whenever disaggregation is required under part A of title I. Second, we believe it is critical for a State to use the same n-size for all accountability purposes, including for each indicator in the accountability system, as required under § 200.17(a)(2)(ii), in order to ensure fairness and equity in accountability decisions and the maximal inclusion of all students in all indicators (with the exception of the Progress in Achieving English Language Proficiency indicator, which applies only to English learners). For example, allowing a State to set a higher n-size for a School Quality or Student Success indicator would reduce the number of schools held accountable for student performance on these new indicators and undermine a key goal of the ESEA, as amended by the ESSA, that school performance determinations be based on broader multiple measures of student and school performance. Finally, as discussed previously, we believe that allowing a lower n-size for reporting is both reflective of current practice in numerous States, encourages States to consider ways they can report results for as many subgroups as possible, and consistent with the statutory requirements related to minimum n-size.

Changes: None.

Comments: A few commenters objected to the Department's proposal that a State explain how other components of its accountability system interact with the State's n-size to affect the statistical reliability and soundness of the State's accountability system and to ensure the maximum inclusion of all students and each subgroup. They recommended eliminating this requirement because they believe it exceeds the Department's legal authority and unnecessarily increases burden on States.

Discussion: We believe these requirements, which mirror similar requirements in current regulations regarding a State's n-size used for accountability, continue to be reasonably necessary to ensure that this key aspect of a State's accountability system—its selected n-size for accountability purposes—is consistent with one of the stated purposes of title I of the ESEA, as amended by the ESSA: To close educational achievement gaps. This purpose cannot be accomplished without subgroup accountability and, thus, it is necessary that the regulations emphasize how States can consider ways to maximize inclusion of student subgroups comprehensively, looking across the design of their accountability system. For example, averaging school-level data across grades or years for calculating the indicators, as permitted under § 200.20(a), is one tool a State can use to maximize the inclusion of subgroups, as States choosing to use this procedure combine, for any measure in an indicator, the number of students with valid data in the applicable subgroup across a whole school, or the number of students in the subgroup with valid data over up to three years. As a result, a school is much more likely to meet a State's minimum n-size for a particular subgroup because it can sum the amount of available data (across grades and across years) for the subgroup on each indicator as described in § 200.20(a)(1)(A). Further, making this information available in the State plan is necessary to reasonably ensure that the public will be able to consult on the State's n-size (consistent with section 1111(c)(3)(A)(ii) of the ESEA) and better understand how schools are being held accountable for the performance of students, including each subgroup. Accordingly, these requirements fall within the Department's rulemaking authority under GEPA and the DEOA as well as under section 1601(a) of the ESEA, as amended by the ESSA, and, as they are within the scope of section 1111(c) of the ESEA, as amended by the ESSA, they do not violate section 1111(e) of the ESEA, as amended by the ESSA (see further discussion under the heading Cross-Cutting Issues). Finally, because of the importance of n-sizes for the validity, reliability, and transparency of statewide accountability systems, the benefits of these requirements outweigh the burden on States of complying with them.

Changes: None.

Comments: Some commenters recommended that LEAs be added to the list of required stakeholders in section 1111(c)(3)(A)(ii) with whom States must collaborate in determining their n-sizes.

Discussion: LEAs are one of the stakeholders States must consult in the overall development of the State plan consistent with §§ 299.13 and 299.15, which includes the State's accountability system and determination of n-size as described in § 299.17.

Changes: None.

Comments: One commenter questioned why the proposed regulations request a justification from States that select an n-size above 30 students in § 200.17, but permit a high school with fewer than 100 students that is identified for comprehensive support and improvement due to low graduation rates to forego implementation of a comprehensive support and improvement plan under § 200.21.

Discussion: The State discretion for small high schools in § 200.21(g) is a statutory requirement in section 1111(d)(1)(C)(ii) of the ESEA, as amended by the ESSA, and is separate and unrelated to the requirements in section 1111(c)(3)(A) of the ESEA for States to establish an n-size for any purpose where disaggregated data are required under part A of title I.

Changes: None.

Comments: One commenter requested that the Department issue non-regulatory guidance in addition to § 200.17 to better support States in reporting information that can be disaggregated for the maximum number of subgroups, particular if a school or LEA does not meet the State's n-size.

Discussion: We appreciate the commenter's suggestion and agree that these best practices would be best discussed in non-regulatory guidance.

Changes: None.

Comments: None.

Discussion: In reviewing the proposed regulations, the Department believes it is necessary to clarify that if a State elects to use a lower n-size for reporting purposes than it does for accountability purposes, it must do so in a way that continues to meet the statutory requirement under section 1111(b)(3)(A)(i) and § 200.17(a)(2)(i) for the State to use the same minimum number of students for all the students group and for each subgroup of students for provisions under title I that require disaggregation. The intent of this flexibility in the proposed regulations was to permit a State, consistent with current practice, to use an n-size for reporting purposes (e.g., 6 students) that the State may feel is too low for accountability purposes but will maximize transparency and the amount of publicly reported data on subgroup performance—not to exempt the State from other critical requirements under proposed § 200.17. Because a consistent n-size for all subgroups is a statutory requirement, we believe it is important to reiterate that it applies to any n-size used for either reporting or accountability under title I of the ESEA.

Changes: We have revised § 200.17(a)(2)(iv) to clarify that a State that elects to use a lower n-size for reporting purposes must continue to meet the requirement to use the same n-size for the all students group and for each subgroup of students for purposes of reporting.

Personally Identifiable Information

Comments: Several commenters pointed out that a minimum n-size lower than 30 students has the ability to adequately protect student privacy, often citing a 2010 Institute of Education Sciences (IES) report (16) concluding that data based on n-sizes of 5 or 10 students may be reported reliably without revealing personally identifying information.

Discussion: While we recognize that suppression of data for small subgroups of students is often necessary to protect the privacy of individuals in those subgroups, we maintain that the specific n-size adopted by States is only one component of a broader methodology for protecting privacy in public reporting. In most cases, suppression of data about small subgroups must be accompanied with the application of additional statistical disclosure limitation methods (e.g., complementary suppression, blurring, top/bottom-coding) to effectively protect student privacy. Selection of a specific n-size (e.g., 5 students versus 10 students) to protect student privacy is secondary to the proper application of these additional methods.

In response to those that believe a lower threshold is appropriate, because such a lower number (e.g., 10 students) is sufficient to protect student privacy, the proposal that States justify and receive approval to use an n-size exceeding 30 students is not driven solely by privacy considerations. Privacy protections must also be considered within the larger context of selecting an n-size that meets the statutory requirements that all disaggregated data used for accountability and reporting purposes be of sufficient size to yield statistically sound information and be small enough to maximally include all students and subgroups of students.

Changes: None.

Comments: Recognizing the complexity of protecting privacy in public reporting, several commenters requested that the Department provide guidance to States and LEAs on this issue.

Discussion: The Department previously released several technical assistance resources on this subject through the Privacy Technical Assistance Center (PTAC, available at http://ptac.ed.gov), and offers further guidance and targeted technical assistance on disclosure methods through PTAC's Student Privacy Help Desk (PrivacyTA@ed.gov). The Department also intends to release additional non-regulatory guidance in the future on this subject to assist educational agencies and institutions with their reporting requirements under the ESEA, as amended by the ESSA.

Changes: None.

Comments: Several commenters questioned the Department's authority to expand privacy protections under this section to anyone other than students, as the Family Educational Rights and Privacy Act only protects personally identifiable information from students' education records and does not extend similar protections to school personnel.

Discussion: The provision in § 200.17(b) merely reiterates section 1111(i) of the ESEA, as amended by the ESSA, which prohibits the reporting of disaggregated information if it would reveal personally identifiable information about teachers, principals, or other school leaders. As § 200.17(b) reiterates this statutory requirement, it is being issued consistent with the Department's rulemaking authority under GEPA and the DEOA and under section 1601(a) of the ESEA, as amended by the ESSA, as the regulation is necessary to reasonably ensure compliance with section 1111(i) of the statute.

Changes: None.

Section 200.18   Annual Meaningful Differentiation of School Performance: Performance Levels, Data Dashboards, Summative Determinations, and Indicator Weighting

Summative Ratings

Comments: Many commenters supported the proposed regulations as consistent with the law's requirement for all States to meaningfully differentiate schools and identify schools for support and improvement, including the lowest-performing five percent of title I schools, using a methodology that is based on all of the indicators and affords certain indicators "much greater" weight. These commenters further noted that the statute, in effect, includes three summative rating categories: The two categories of schools that must implement improvement plans (i.e., comprehensive support and improvement and targeted support and improvement schools), and a third category of schools, those not identified for comprehensive or targeted support and improvement.

Some commenters recommended that the Department clarify that a State may use these classifications of schools in the statute (i.e., comprehensive support and improvement, targeted support and improvement, not identified for support and improvement) to meet the proposed requirement in § 200.18 to give all schools a summative rating from among at least three categories. These commenters recommended conforming edits throughout the regulation, including in proposed § 200.19, to refer to a State's summative "determination" or "classification," as an alternative to a "rating." Further, they suggested we clarify that a State could use a "dashboard" approach to make those determinations, although a State would also be permitted to create a separate and distinct methodology, like a numerical index.

Alternatively, several other commenters stated that the requirement for a summative rating was inconsistent with the statute, an overreach of the Department's authority, and at odds with the law's intent to provide more flexibility and create less burden for States with regard to accountability. Some of these commenters also asserted that the requirement for a summative rating violates section 1111(e)(1)(B)(iii)(V) of the ESEA, as amended by the ESSA, which provides that nothing in the ESEA, as amended by the ESSA, authorizes or permits the Secretary to prescribe the specific methodology used by States to meaningfully differentiate or identify schools under title I, part A.

Discussion: We appreciate commenters' support and agree with those who recommended clarifying that (1) the requirement for each State to provide schools with a summative rating from among at least three rating categories is consistent with the law's requirements for school identification, and (2) a State may satisfy the summative rating requirement by making these statutorily required identification determinations its summative rating for each school, as opposed to developing a separate system of ratings that uses different categories of schools for annual meaningful differentiation. Given that these determinations in the statute are one way a State may meet the requirement to provide information on a school's overall level of performance, we are revising the final regulation to clarify that the system of annual meaningful differentiation must produce a single summative "determination" for each school that "meaningfully differentiates" between schools. Because the ESEA, as amended by the ESSA, requires identification of three summative categories of schools based on all indicators—comprehensive support and improvement, targeted support and improvement, and schools that are not identified—we are further renumbering and revising § 200.18(a)(4) to note that a State's summative determinations for each school may be those three categories. We believe the final regulation, as with the proposed regulation, promotes State flexibility in designing accountability systems, so that multiple approaches may be used, with different categories, such as A-F grades, numerical scores, accreditation systems, or other school classifications. A State choosing to use one of these approaches would still be required to identify comprehensive support and improvement and targeted support and improvement schools as required under the statute.

Given the clarification in § 200.18(a)(4) that a State may meet this requirement by identifying, at a minimum, the two statutorily required categories of schools along with a third category of schools that are not identified, we believe it is clear that this regulation falls squarely within the Department's rulemaking authority under GEPA, the DEOA, and section 1601(a) of the ESEA, as amended by the ESSA, and within the scope of section 1111(c) of the ESEA, as amended by the ESSA, consistent with section 1111(e) of the ESEA, as amended by the ESSA (see further discussion of these authorities in the discussion of Cross-Cutting Issues). Moreover, each State retains significant discretion to design its methodology and determine how it will reach a single summative determination for each school. For example, one State could develop a two-dimensional matrix, with schools assigned an overall performance category based on how they fare on each dimension, while another State could design a numerical index that awards points for each indicator, with an overall score driving the summative determination, while yet another State could assign each school a determination based on the number of indicators on which the school performs at a particular level or another set of business rules. A State also has discretion to assign a single grade or number or to develop some other mechanism, including one based on a data "dashboard," for reaching a single summative determination—categories of schools like "priority" and "focus" schools that States have used under ESEA flexibility, for example, would also be permitted. (17) Given the broad flexibility available to a State for meeting this requirement, § 200.18(a)(4), as renumbered, is not inconsistent with section 1111(e)(1)(B)(iii)(V) of the ESEA, as amended by the ESSA, because it does not prescribe a particular methodology that a State must use to annually differentiate schools.

Changes: We have renumbered and revised § 200.18(a)(4) to clarify that a State must provide each school, as part of its system of meaningful differentiation, a single summative "determination," which may either be (1) a unique determination, distinct from the categories of schools described in § 200.19, or (2) a determination that includes the two categories of schools that are required to be identified in § 200.19 (i.e., schools identified for comprehensive support and improvement and schools identified for targeted support and improvement) and those that are not identified. We have also made conforming edits throughout § 200.18 and other sections of the final regulations that reference school summative determinations. In addition, we have clarified that the summative determination must "meaningfully differentiate" between schools.

Comments: We received a number of comments supporting the requirement in proposed § 200.18(b)(4) for a State's system of annual meaningful differentiation to result in a single rating, from among at least three rating categories, to describe a school's summative performance across indicators because it would increase transparency for parents and stakeholders by communicating complex data and information on school quality, across a number of metrics, through a single overall rating. These commenters generally expressed concerns that other approaches absent a summative rating, such as a data "dashboard," would make it difficult for parents to understand the overall performance of their child's school, particularly to determine how the results from the dashboard led to the school's identification for comprehensive or targeted support and improvement. Other commenters noted that summative ratings are widely used in other sectors precisely because they communicate complex information succinctly and effectively in a manner that empowers stakeholders and guides decision-making; this view is consistent with that of another commenter who cited research that suggests parents prefer summative ratings like A-F grades. (18)

Many commenters noted that a summative rating and detailed indicator-level information in a "dashboard" are not mutually exclusive, and voiced support for a summative rating requirement that, as provided for in the proposed regulations, also requires performance on each indicator to be reported, so that parents and the public have information on overall school quality in the summative rating—which would drive identification of schools—alongside more detailed information breaking down performance on each indicator—which would drive continuous improvement. A number of commenters also cited the benefits of summative ratings for school improvement efforts, asserting that such ratings support meaningful differentiation of schools, promote successful interventions by helping direct resources to schools that are most in need of support, and, as suggested by research, motivate and are associated with successful efforts to improve and achieve a higher rating. (19)

However, numerous other commenters suggested removing the requirement for a single rating, because they believe it undermines the value and transparency of an accountability system based on multiple measures—including the addition of new indicators under the ESEA, as amended by the ESSA—by reducing school performance, and any subsequent improvement efforts, to a single label. The commenters asserted parents and educators alike would find data on individual indicators more useful and straightforward than a single rating, particularly when designing improvement strategies targeted to a school's needs. Other commenters suggested that requiring a summative rating for each school would result in one-size-fits-all accountability systems that discourage innovative accountability approaches, such as data "dashboards," and demoralize educators by promoting punitive accountability systems that are focused on ranking schools against each other, which some linked with increased staff turnover. Many of these commenters associated a summative rating with a requirement to assign all schools an A-F letter grade or a single score, and noted their objections to such methodologies. One commenter requested the Department allow States to either award schools with a single, overall summative determination, or multiple determinations (i.e., one for each indicator), believing an approach that allowed for "determinations" instead of ratings would provide greater flexibility for States to choose how they communicate areas in need of improvement in a school.

Finally, a number of commenters believed the requirement for a single summative rating would create arbitrary, invalid, and unfair distinctions among schools or objected to such a requirement as inconsistent with research on school performance and improvement. (20)

Discussion: We appreciate the strong support from many commenters for the summative rating requirement we proposed as part of each State's system of annual meaningful differentiation of schools. We also acknowledge the strong objections raised by many other commenters. However, we believe some of the concerns expressed by commenters may be rooted in misconceptions about the requirement, as proposed, which we have clarified in these final regulations, as previously described.

We agree that the accountability requirements in the ESEA, as amended by the ESSA, move away from a one-size-fits-all approach by requiring multiple indicators of school success, beyond test scores and graduation rates, to play a factor in accountability decisions. However, we disagree that a summative determination will undermine these positive steps, diminish the ability of States to develop innovative models, and lead to a narrow focus on ranking schools—or on test scores or overall school grades—at the expense of other indicators. Under the regulations, States can design a number of approaches to produce an overall determination, based on all indicators, for each school—including an approach that utilizes data "dashboards," A-F school grades, a two-dimensional matrix based on the accountability indicators, or other creative mechanisms to communicate differences in overall school quality to parents and the public. These approaches must also be developed through meaningful and timely stakeholder engagement, including parents and educators, as described in §§ 299.13 and 299.15.

Moreover, we believe the requirement for a summative determination is most consistent with research on what makes an effective accountability and improvement system. For example, in addition to research cited in the NPRM, additional studies have shown the positive benefits of providing schools with a summative determination on student academic achievement. (21)

We agree with commenters that ensuring transparent, clear information on school quality for parents, educators, and the public is an essential purpose of accountability for schools under the ESEA, an opinion shared by those commenting in support of and opposition to the proposed requirement for summative ratings. Further, we agree that the increased number of required accountability indicators under the ESEA, as amended by the ESSA, provides a valuable opportunity for States to provide a more nuanced picture of school performance that includes both academic and non-academic factors. This is why our regulations would require both a summative determination and information on each indicator, which must be reported separately as described in the statute and in §§ 200.30 through 200.33 and which could be presented as part of a data "dashboard." In this way, parents, educators, and the public have a wealth of school-level information, including information disaggregated by subgroups, at their disposal—information that will be critical in supporting effective school improvement. Given that many commenters did not recognize that a data "dashboard" or other mechanism for indicator-level reporting and a summative determination were both a part of State systems of annual meaningful differentiation under § 200.18, we are revising the name of the section in the final regulations to provide greater clarity and reflect all of the components that are included. Section 200.18, "Annual Meaningful Differentiation of School Performance: Performance Levels, Data Dashboards, Summative Determinations, and Indicator Weighting" reflects our strong belief that requiring States to report information on each school's performance on the indicators separately and report a comprehensive determination for each school is both effective and reasonably necessary, consistent with the requirement for robust statewide accountability systems in the ESEA, as amended by the ESSA, to provide useful, comparable, and clear information to parents, teachers, and other stakeholders about how schools are performing. In addition, we are revising § 200.18(a)(4) to emphasize the importance of transparent information by clarifying that the purpose of the summative determination is to provide information on a school's overall performance to parents and the public "in a clear and understandable manner."

Changes: We have renamed § 200.18 in the final regulations to clarify and recognize all of the components of annual meaningful differentiation—performance levels, data dashboards, summative determinations, and indicator weighting. We have also clarified § 200.18(a)(4) to require that the summative determination provide information "in a clear and understandable manner" on a school's overall performance on annual report cards.

Comments: Several commenters wrote in opposition to the requirement for a single summative rating, believing such a requirement unfairly penalizes schools based on the makeup of students in their communities, due to the correlation between student demographics and student achievement measures, with a few commenters specifically concerned such a rating would fail to address the unique needs and circumstances of rural schools.

Discussion: We disagree that a requirement for a single summative determination, as revised in the final regulation, will unfairly differentiate schools based on the students they serve. We believe such criticisms may be rooted more in concerns with the accountability system required in the past under NCLB, which primarily considered student test scores and graduation rates, and that these concerns are significantly mitigated by changes in the accountability systems that will be implemented under the new law. Under § 200.18, States, in consultation with stakeholders, must develop a multi-indicator system for annually differentiating schools that looks beyond achievement measures to take into account a more well-rounded picture of school success. As a result, schools could be recognized for the significant progress they are making in helping low-achieving students grow academically to meet State standards, improvements in school climate or the percentage of English learners who progress toward language proficiency, and reductions in rates of chronic absence, among many other measures that could be added within one of the new accountability indicators. Because of the new discretion States have to rethink the measures they use to differentiate schools and create systems that represent their local goals and contexts, including the particular needs of rural communities, we are hopeful that States can avoid some of the pitfalls of their prior accountability systems and provide annual school determinations that are clearer and more meaningful to the parents and the public.

Changes: None.

Comments: One commenter believed that a summative rating requirement would inhibit capacity at the local level to conduct the data analysis needed to design effective school improvement strategies that will meet a school's specific needs, and suggested that we add to the regulations an option for States to submit in their State plans an alternative method (instead of a summative rating) for differentiating schools based on their performance, which would require approval from the Secretary based on a number of criteria.

Discussion: Given the revisions described previously to § 200.18(a)(4), we believe it is unnecessary to provide an alternative method for States to differentiate schools—a State may use the required categories for identification enumerated in the statute as its summative determinations, or adopt a host of other approaches to provide an overall picture of each school's performance across all of the indicators. Because this overall determination must also be presented on report cards alongside indicator-specific information (e.g., in a data "dashboard"), we disagree with the commenter that a summative determination makes it more challenging for LEA and school staff to access and analyze the data necessary to drive effective school interventions. We strongly encourage schools to consider all data from its State accountability system, in addition to local data, in designing school improvement plans, so that the plans reflect, to the fullest extent, the needs and strengths of each identified school. Further, we are regulating on the required needs assessment for schools identified for comprehensive support and improvement under § 200.21 to ensure that the school improvement process is data-driven and informed by each school's context, relevant student demographic and performance data, and the reasons the school was identified, not just an overall determination.

Changes: None.

Comments: Several commenters were concerned that aggregating performance, including performance of student subgroups, across each indicator into a single rating would make information about how well a school was serving its subgroups of students more opaque and less consequential in the overall accountability system.

Discussion: We agree with commenters that a requirement for a summative determination for each school could appear to deemphasize related statutory requirements to hold schools accountable for the performance of an individual subgroup. This concern is mitigated by the fact that summative determinations must reflect the performance of all students and subgroups in the school. Nevertheless, we are revising § 200.18(a)(6), as renumbered, to reinforce the importance of subgroup accountability, while retaining an overall summative determination. Further, we note that information on LEA and State report cards—including the overview section as described in §§ 200.30-200.31—must show student-level data related to each indicator, disaggregated by subgroup, which will help ensure that parents and the public have access to both an overall understanding of school performance, as well as detailed information broken down by subgroup.

Changes: We have renumbered and revised § 200.18(a)(6) to reiterate that the system of annual meaningful differentiation must inform the State's methodology for identifying schools for comprehensive and targeted support and improvement, including differentiation of schools with a consistently underperforming subgroup.

Comments: Two commenters suggested modifying the requirement in proposed § 200.18(b)(4) for each State to provide schools with a single rating, from among at least three rating categories, to require at least five rating categories. With only three categories, they attested, the lowest category would be reserved for schools in the lowest-performing five percent of title I schools, while the highest category would be limited to a handful of top performers—leaving the majority of schools in the middle tier and providing little differentiation.

Discussion: While we appreciate the commenters' concern that three summative categories could result in a system where many schools are grouped into a single category, we also recognize that the requirement for at least three summative categories of schools is most consistent with the statutory requirement to, based on all indicators, identify schools for comprehensive support and improvement, targeted support and improvement, or to not identify schools for either category. Further, we believe that a system with five categories of schools could also result in the majority of schools identified in a single category, depending on the State's methodology. Ultimately, the external peer review of State plans will inform whether a State has established a system for meaningfully differentiating between schools in a manner consistent with the statutory and regulatory requirements. Moreover, we believe a number of methodologies and approaches can meet these requirements, and we want to ensure States have the ability to adopt a range of methods to provide summative determinations. Nothing in the regulations prevents a State from adopting additional categories of schools, particularly if they find that three categories are not providing sufficient differentiation, but we believe States should retain that discretion to go beyond the three required categories, working with stakeholders and other partners to meets their particular needs and goals.

Changes: None.

Comments: A few commenters suggested removing the requirement in proposed § 200.18(b)(4) for each LEA report card to describe a school's summative performance as part of the description of the State's system for annual meaningful differentiation on LEA report cards under §§ 200.31 and 200.32, preferring to give States the discretion to report a school's summative rating publicly.

Discussion: We believe the overall performance of a school is among the most critical and essential information to make readily available to parents and the public on LEA report cards, alongside data on individual measures and indicators. In particular, given the role of summative determinations in identification for support and improvement under § 200.19, parents and the public need to know a school's determination in order to better understand why a school was, or was not, identified for intervention.

Changes: None.

Performance Levels on Indicators

Comments: Several commenters supported the requirement in § 200.18 for States to establish and report a performance level (from among at least three levels) for each school, for each indicator, as part of the State's system of annual meaningful differentiation of schools, because such levels would provide necessary and complementary information to a school's summative rating by recognizing areas of strengths and weakness, in addition to overall performance, and would support a more accurate and comprehensive picture of a school's impact on learning in the context of multi-measure accountability systems. As a result, they believe the requirement helps improves trust in, and the transparency of, school determinations among parents and the public and informs more effective improvement strategies targeted to the specific needs of schools and their students.

A number of other commenters, however, objected to the proposed requirements for States to report the level of performance, from among at least three levels, for each indicator on LEA report cards and use the performance levels as the basis for a school's summative rating. Some of these commenters opposed performance levels as a return to prescriptive and limiting subgroup-based accountability formulas required by the NCLB. Other commenters raised methodological objections to performance levels on indicators, asserting that such an approach is inconsistent with research and does not yield valid or reliable accountability determinations, particularly by setting arbitrary cut points, where there is no meaningful difference between schools just above, and just below, those cut points.

Several commenters called for giving States more flexibility to design their own systems for differentiating performance on indicators. Some of these commenters believe this would result in a less complicated and more user-friendly accountability system, while one commenter noted that the same policy goals behind performance levels could be reached in other ways, such as comparing performance on each indicator to State averages or similar schools. Other commenters asserted that the requirement for performance levels is inconsistent with the ESEA, as amended by the ESSA, or that it violates the prohibition in section 1111(e)(1)(B)(iii)(V) of the ESEA, as amended by the ESSA, regarding the specific methodology used by States to meaningfully differentiate or identify schools—noting that the only performance levels required under the statute are the academic achievement standards under section 1111(b)(1).

Discussion: We appreciate the support from many commenters for the requirement for States to establish performance levels on each indicator as part of the system of annual meaningful differentiation. We agree that an overall determination for a school is most useful and effective when coupled with clear information, such as would be provided by State-determined performance levels, on the underlying data, which helps contribute to a better understanding of how that data led to the school's final determination. We also believe that a clear set of performance levels provide the context parents and the public need to understand whether a school's performance is adequate, or exemplary, context that otherwise may not be evident from comparisons to district and State averages on LEA report cards.

We note, however, that performance levels are not intended to create AYP-like thresholds for individual subgroups that definitively determine school identification, which some commenters viewed as undermining the validity and reliability of schools' accountability designations in the past; rather, States must report school results on each indicator against the State-determined performance levels as part of their overall system of meaningful differentiation of schools on LEA report cards. We also note that States have discretion to develop their own criteria for performance levels, including norm-referenced approaches linked to State averages or performance quartiles— so long as the levels are consistent with attainment of the long-term goals and measurements of interim progress and clear and understandable, as demonstrated in its State plan. In addition, to help clarify the role of performance levels in providing schools with a summative determination and the distinction between this more flexible approach and AYP, we are revising § 200.18(a)(4) to indicate that the summative determination is "based on differing levels of performance on the indicators," rather than on "each indicator."

In response to commenters who stated that the requirement to establish at least three levels of performance on all indicators exceeds the Department's authority because it was not explicitly included in the statutory text, as previously discussed (see discussion of the Department's legal authority under the heading Cross-Cutting Issues), given the Department's rulemaking authority under GEPA, the DEOA, and section 1601(a) of the ESEA, as amended by the ESSA, and that the requirement falls within the scope of section 1111(c) of the ESEA, as amended by the ESSA, consistent with section 1111(e), it is not necessary for the statute to specifically authorize the Secretary to issue a particular regulatory provision. Further, the requirements in § 200.18(a)(2)-(3), as renumbered, for States to adopt and report on a school's performance, from among at least three levels of performance, on each indicator are necessary to reasonably ensure that parents and the public receive comprehensive, understandable information on school performance on LEA report cards—information that can empower parents, lead to continuous improvement of schools, and guide decision-making at the local and State levels.

By increasing transparency, performance levels help reinforce the statutory purpose of title I: "to provide all children significant opportunity to receive a fair, equitable, and high-quality education, and to close educational achievement gaps." Without such a requirement, publicly reported information on the accountability system would lack the comparative information needed to determine whether all children were receiving an equitable education and closing such gaps on a host of measures. This is because data presented on LEA report cards "must include a clear and concise description of the State's accountability system" consistent with section 1111(h)(1)(C)(i) and 1111(h)(2)(c) of the ESEA, as amended by the ESSA, yet is not (with the exception of academic assessments under section 1111(b)(2)) presented in any context, such as by reporting on the distribution of data at the State or LEA level compared to a school's results. Thus, any contextual information for parents and the public from the accountability system regarding whether schools and LEAs are living up to this purpose would be missing, absent a performance level requirement.

Additionally, these requirements are not inconsistent with section 1111(e)(1)(B)(iii)(V) because they do not prescribe a particular methodology that a State must use to annually differentiate or identify schools. States will have discretion to determine how best to meet the requirement within the overall design of their system. For example, each State will need to decide what the performance levels should be for each indicator; whether the same performance levels should be used for each indicator; how many levels are appropriate; how the levels will be incorporated into the overall system, such as whether they will be part of the basis for identifying consistently underperforming subgroups; and the particular methodology it will use to determine a level for each school.

Changes: We have revised § 200.18(a)(4) to require that a school's summative determination be based on "differing levels of performance on the indicators" rather than on the school's performance level on "each indicator."

Comments: One commenter suggested that requiring indicator performance levels to inform the summative rating could mask the performance of low-performing subgroups in the context of an overall rating, as the performance levels would not necessarily be disaggregated for each subgroup in the school. The commenter believed the proposed requirements were insufficient to ensure States comply with the statutory requirement under section 1111(c)(4)(C)(iii) for annual meaningful differentiation to include differentiation of consistently underperforming subgroups. Instead, the commenter suggested requiring a school with a consistently underperforming subgroup to receive a lower summative rating than it would have otherwise received if one of its subgroups of students was not consistently underperforming.

Discussion: We agree that the proposed regulations were not clear on the relationship between performance levels and subgroup accountability. Our intent was not to require a system of performance levels for each subgroup on each indicator, but to ensure that performance levels reflect a State's long-term goals for all students and each subgroup of students. For example, if a State sets a goal of achieving a 90 percent four-year graduation rate for all students and each subgroup of students, a school with only 70 percent of English learners and Black students graduating in four years should not receive the highest performance level for that indicator. We recognize, however, that not all indicators have a corresponding long-term goal; this provision was only intended to apply to indicators for which there is a related long-term goal (i.e., academic achievement, graduation rates, and ELP), and we are revising the final regulations for clarity so that this requirement only includes indicators where an applicable long-term goal exists. Further, we are also revising § 200.18(a)(6), as renumbered, to reinforce the overall importance of subgroup accountability by stating that the system for differentiation of schools must inform identification of consistently underperforming subgroups.

Finally, we also agree with the commenter that to ensure differentiation for consistently underperforming subgroups, as required by section 1111(c)(4)(C)(iii) of the ESEA, as amended by the ESSA, it is helpful to require any school with a consistently underperforming subgroup of students to receive a lower summative determination than it would have otherwise received, and we are revising § 200.18(c)(3) accordingly.

Changes: We have renumbered and revised § 200.18(a)(2)-(3) to further clarify the relationship between subgroup performance and the performance levels on each indicator. Section 200.18(a)(2) clarifies that the three performance levels on each indicator must be consistent with attainment of the long-term goals and measurements of interim progress, if applicable, because the State is only required to establish goals and measurements of interim progress for some indicators (i.e., Academic Achievement, Graduation Rate, and Progress in Achieving English Language Proficiency). In addition, we have renumbered and revised § 200.18(a)(6) to reiterate that the system of meaningful differentiation must inform the State's methodology for identifying schools for comprehensive and targeted support and improvement, including differentiation of schools with a consistently underperforming subgroup of students.

Finally, we have renumbered and revised § 200.18(c)(3) to require that each State, in order to meet the requirements for annual meaningful differentiation under § 200.18(a), demonstrate that any school with a consistently underperforming subgroup of students receives a lower summative determination than it otherwise would have received had no subgroups in the school been so identified.

Comments: One commenter recommended revising the requirement for each State to establish at least three levels of school performance on each indicator under proposed § 200.18(b)(2) so that binary measures would be permitted, which could distinguish between schools that met or did not meet a certain threshold, providing additional flexibility for States. Another commenter suggested clarifying that continuous measures would be permissible to meet the requirement for setting performance levels on each indicator. For example, the commenter suggested that an indicator measured on a 0-100 scale could meet the requirement, without further aggregation, because it arguably results in 101 performance levels. This comment was consistent with others that supported the adoption of data "dashboards" as the primary basis for school accountability determinations, or the increased use of scale scores or raw performance data for accountability purposes.

Discussion: While it is important to understand whether a school is meeting a particular performance expectation, such information may be incorporated into a system that includes three levels of performance, while a binary measure would not support differentiation among above-average, typical, and below-average performance. Given the statutory requirement for meaningful differentiation between schools, we believe requiring at least three performance levels on each indicator is necessary to meet this requirement. We also believe the requirement for three levels is not limiting on States, as nearly any binary measure can be expressed in three or more levels (e.g., "approaching," "meets," and "exceeding").

Similarly, the intent of the provision was to encourage State-determined performance levels that provide meaningful information on each indicator. Merely reporting that a school received 55 out of a possible score of 100 on an indicator, for example, does not include any context about whether a 55 is a typical score, or whether this is an area where the school is lagging or exceeding expectations. Thus, a continuous measure does not meet the requirement to establish at least three levels of performance for each indicator, as it would otherwise be no different than reporting raw data for each indicator; the performance levels must be "discrete." We recognize that a data "dashboard" holds potential to be a useful tool for communicating information on school quality and may be used by a State to meet this requirement, as reflected in revised § 200.18(a)(3), so long as the data on the "dashboard" is presented in context by creating bands of performance or performance thresholds, so that parents and the public have clear information on whether a school's level of performance is acceptable. The requirement for performance levels on each indicator does not prohibit the use of a data "dashboard" that shows the full scale of values for an indicator; rather, it requires States to make distinctions between schools based on the data presented in the "dashboard," such as by performance bands or quartiles.

Changes: We have renumbered and revised § 200.18(a)(2)-(3) to clarify that a State must, as part of its system of annual meaningful differentiation, include at least three distinct and discrete performance levels on each indicator, as opposed to continuous measures or scale scores, and may use a data "dashboard" on its LEA report cards for this purpose.

Comments: One commenter requested the Department require, for the Academic Achievement indicator, that a State's academic achievement standards under section 1111(b)(1) of the ESEA, include below proficient, proficient, and above proficient levels of performance.

Discussion: We appreciate the commenter's suggestions on ways to ensure that academic achievement standards are rigorous and set high expectations for all students. Although framed as a comment about performance levels, the commenter is actually requesting that the Department regulate on academic achievement standards, which require negotiated rulemaking. Consequently, the Department is not authorized to make the requested change through these final regulations.

Changes: None.

Weighting of Indicators

Comments: Numerous commenters were concerned that the proposed regulations overemphasized the role of student achievement, as measured by assessments in math and reading/language arts, in the system of annual meaningful differentiation of schools. Some of these commenters opposed the general requirements in proposed § 200.18(c)(1)-(2) to afford indicators of Academic Achievement, Academic Progress, Graduation Rates, and Progress in Achieving English Language Proficiency "substantial" weight, individually, and "much greater" weight, in the aggregate, than indicators of School Quality or Student Success. A number of commenters, however, strongly supported proposed § 200.18(c)(1)-(2), recognizing that the language regarding "substantial" and "much greater" weight was taken from section 1111(c)(4)(C) of the ESEA, as amended by the ESSA.

Discussion: We appreciate that consideration of a greater number of factors in measuring school quality can help shed light on important aspects of school performance. However, we agree with other commenters that the provisions in proposed § 200.18(c)(1)-(2) are based on the statutory requirements related to the weighting of indicators, which ensure that students' academic outcomes and progress remain a central component of accountability.

Changes: None.

Comments: A number of commenters supported the provisions in proposed § 200.18(d) for how States demonstrate they meet the requirements for weighting of indicators and recommended maintaining them in the final regulation. These commenters variously stated that the requirements (1) provide helpful clarification on the vague statutory terms "much greater" and "substantial" weight; (2) erect necessary guardrails to ensure that student academic outcomes, including for low-performing subgroups, drive the differentiation of schools and identification for support and improvement within State-determined, multi-measure accountability systems; and (3) preserve State discretion over weighting of indicators in their accountability systems by focusing on outcomes, rather than particular weighting methodologies or percentages. While many of these commenters recognized, and often appreciated, the addition of new School Quality or Student Success indicators to add nuance to the accountability system, they strongly believed that student academic outcomes should have the greatest influence on differentiation and identification of schools for support and were concerned that, absent these regulations, accountability systems would undercut the importance of student learning. In addition, many commenters stated that the requirements strike an appropriate balance, noting that States could adopt a myriad number of approaches and methodologies for weighting their accountability indicators, based on their particular goals and needs.

Numerous commenters, however, objected to these requirements, stating that they would prevent new School Quality or Student Success indicators from having a meaningful impact in statewide accountability systems, including by affecting the differentiation of school performance, identification for support and improvement, or the school improvement process. While they recognized that these indicators are not afforded "substantial" weight under the statute, they believed the proposed regulations would result in little or zero weight for these measures and an overemphasis on test-based measures. In addition, several commenters believed the requirements related to demonstrating the weighting of indicators discourage the collection of more nuanced accountability measures such as school climate or chronic absenteeism. Other commenters variously stated that the requirements for weighting would be best determined by stakeholders; result in more a complex and less transparent system for parents and the public; inhibit creative approaches to differentiating school performance and be overly prescriptive; inappropriately limit State flexibility in a manner that is inconsistent with the ESEA, as amended by the ESSA; or violate section 1111(e)(1)(B)(iii)(IV)-(V) of the ESEA, as amended by the ESSA, which provides that nothing in the statute authorizes or permits the Secretary to prescribe the weight of any measure or indicator or the specific methodology used by States to meaningfully differentiate or identify schools.

Discussion: We agree with commenters that it is vital to provide guardrails for State systems of annual meaningful differentiation that clarify and support effective implementation of the statutory requirements for certain indicators to receive "substantial" and "much greater" weight, and that these are ambiguous terms that warrant specification in regulation, given the influence of indicator weighting on how schools will be annually differentiated and identified for support and improvement. Section 1111(c)(4)(C)(ii) of the ESEA, as amended by the ESSA, requires academic indicators to have a larger role in annually differentiating schools, relative to School Quality or Student Success indicators, which in turn influences school identification. Moreover, we share the views of commenters who believe it is important for student academic outcomes, including for subgroups, to be at the heart of the accountability system in order to safeguard educational equity and excellence for all students.

In response to commenters who argued that the requirements for these demonstrations exceed the Department's authority because they are not explicitly authorized by the statute, as previously discussed (see discussion of the Department's general rulemaking authority under the heading Cross-Cutting Issues), it is not necessary for the statute to specifically authorize the Secretary to issue a particular regulatory provision, given the Secretary's rulemaking authority under GEPA, the DEOA, and section 1601(a) of the ESEA, as amended by the ESSA. Further, the requirements in § 200.18(c), as renumbered, are within the scope of, and necessary to reasonably ensure compliance with, the requirements for the weighting of indicators set forth in section 1111(c)(4)(C)(ii) of the ESEA, as amended by the ESSA, and for differentiation of schools with consistently underperforming subgroups set forth in section 1111(c)(4)(C)(iii), and therefore do not violate section 1111(e). If a school could receive the same overall determination, regardless of whether one of its subgroups was consistently underperforming or not, a State's system could not reasonably be deemed to "include differentiation of any . . . school in which any subgroup of students is consistently underperforming, as determined by the State, based on all indicators" as required by section 1111(c)(4)(C)(iii). Similarly, if a school can go unidentified for support and improvement, despite the fact that this school would have been in the bottom five percent of title I schools based on substantially weighted indicators and despite not making significant progress for all students on substantially weighted indicators, the State's system of meaningful differentiation is not providing those indicators "much greater" and "substantial" weight, as required by section 1111(c)(4)(C)(ii). In both cases, failing to meet the demonstrations in § 200.18(c) means that factors identified by the statute as requiring extra emphasis (i.e., substantially weighted indicators and consistently underperforming subgroups) received insufficient attention and did not result in "meaningful" differentiation."

Additionally, the requirements in § 200.18(c), as renumbered, for States to demonstrate how they have weighted their indicators and ensured differentiation of consistently underperforming subgroups by examining the results of the system of annual differentiation and the schools that are identified for support and improvement are consistent with section 1111(e)(1)(B)(iii)(IV)-(V) of the ESEA, as amended by the ESSA, because they do not prescribe the weight of any indicator, nor a particular methodology that a State must use to annually differentiate schools, such as an A-F grading system. There are numerous weighting schemes and processes for differentiating and identifying schools that could meet these requirements—including percentages for each indicator, business rules or other mechanisms to ensure certain schools are identified or flagged for having a consistently underperforming subgroup or low performance on "substantial" indicators, or a matrix approach where a particular combination of performance across various indicators results in identification.

We agree with many commenters that an approach that focuses on outcomes (i.e., the overall determination for the school and the schools that are identified for support and improvement), is both appropriate and necessary to ensure compliance with the requirements in section 1111(c)(4)(C)(ii)-(iii) of the ESEA that emphasize certain academic indicators and the importance of differentiating schools with underperforming groups of students, while maintaining State discretion to develop its system of meaningful differentiation. Because these demonstrations can apply to any methodology a State designs, they provide the Department a way to verify a State has met critical statutory requirements for indicator weighting and differentiation of subgroups, without stifling the new flexibility States have to adopt innovative approaches to differentiate and identify schools for support, including those that use categorical labels instead of a numerical index.

We recognize and agree that the intention of the ESSA was to create State accountability systems based on multiple measures; however, we disagree with commenters that § 200.18(c) will result in a less transparent, overly complicated, and test-driven accountability system. Under both the NCLB and ESEA flexibility waivers, States often adopted business rules or other mechanisms to ensure school identification based on their accountability systems was aligned with definitions for categories of identified schools, and we are confident that similar approaches can be used to ensure compliance with the definitions and requirements in the ESSA. Further, section 1111(h)(1) of the ESEA and §§ 200.30-200.33 require annual State and LEA report cards to include a full description of the accountability system, including the weighting of indicators, to ensure parents have a clear understanding of how differentiation and identification work in their State. Under these regulations, States ultimately have the responsibility to design accountability systems that meet the statutory requirements for weighting of indicators and as a result, may develop systems for weighting that are either straightforward or more complex. We strongly encourage States to consider the value of clarity and transparency in developing their systems, and to develop them in close consultation with stakeholders who will be regularly using the information produced by the accountability system, including parents, educators, and district-level officials, among others.

Finally, we note that School Quality or Student Success indicators must, and should, play a role in providing schools with annual determinations and identifying them for improvement and clarify that the requirements in § 200.18(c) do not prohibit School Quality or Student Success indicators from being taken into account for these purposes. Each school's overall determination under § 200.18(a)(4) must reflect all of the indicators the State uses, and we believe there are significant opportunities for States to develop new and meaningful indicators, as discussed further in response to comments on § 200.14. Because these demonstrations are simply meant to ensure that— regardless of a school's summative determination—the substantially weighted indicators receive sufficient emphasis in determining whether a school needs support and improvement, we believe the final regulations do not discourage the adoption of innovative approaches to measure school success or the collection of new indicators and that many methods (as previously described) can meet them.

Changes: None.

Comments: Numerous commenters provided feedback on both ways that a State must demonstrate it meets the statutory provisions for weighting of indicators described in proposed § 200.18(d)(1)-(2), which requires that an indicator of School Quality or Student Success may not be used to change the identity of a school that would otherwise be identified for interventions, unless such a school was also making significant progress on a substantially weighted indicator, for the same reasons they supported or opposed proposed § 200.18(d) generally, as described previously.

In addition, several commenters had specific concerns about these provisions, feeling that under proposed § 200.18(d)(1)-(2) a School Quality or Student Success indicator could only be used to penalize, rather than reward, schools in the State's system of annual meaningful differentiation. In doing so, they believed the proposed regulations eliminated a valid rationale (i.e., performance on School Quality or Student Success indicators) for differentiating between schools and undermined the reliability and validity of school identification. A few of these commenters also raised objections that the proposed demonstrations potentially conflict with exit criteria in §§ 200.21 and 200.22 by requiring improvement on test-based measures. One commenter suggested that the proposed demonstrations in § 200.18(d)(1)-(2) were unnecessary, so long as States identified the required percentage of the lowest-performing schools for comprehensive support and improvement.

Discussion: We disagree with commenters that these demonstrations are unnecessary. While States are required to identify certain schools for targeted and comprehensive support and improvement, including at least the lowest-performing five percent of title I schools, the requirements for weighting indicators are a distinct requirement under section 1111(c)(4)(C)(ii) of the ESEA, as amended by the ESSA, that must be taken into account when identifying schools, in addition to any statutory requirements regarding the categories or definitions of identified schools.

We also disagree that the proposed regulations failed to account for the positive role that School Quality or Student Success indicators can play in a State's accountability system or would lead to invalid determinations because these factors were not considered; we believe that some of these concerns may be ameliorated by further explanation and clarification of how the demonstrations will work. Under the proposed and final regulations, each school's level of performance on all indicators must be reported and factored into the school's summative determination under § 200.18(a)(2)-(4), including School Quality or Student Success indicators. Schools that do well on indicators of School Quality or Student Success should see those results reflected in both their performance level for that indicator (which may be part of a data "dashboard"), and in their overall determination (e.g., an overall numerical score or grade, a categorical label like "priority" or "focus" schools, etc.). The separate requirements in § 200.18(c)(1)-(2), as renumbered, are intended to help States demonstrate that their methods afford "much greater" weight to the academic indicators, in the aggregate, than to indicators of School Quality or Student Success not by focusing solely on school summative determinations, but by analyzing school identification for comprehensive and targeted support and improvement—this will serve as a check to ensure that, on the whole, each substantially weighted indicator is receiving appropriate emphasis in the State's accountability system and that schools struggling on these measures receive the necessary supports.

These requirements are completely distinct from exit criteria, which are described in §§ 200.21-200.22 and apply to schools that have been implementing comprehensive and targeted support and improvement plans. The demonstrations described in § 200.18(c)(1)-(2) happen earlier in the accountability process to help determine which schools should be identified and subsequently placed in support and improvement. In particular, a State would meet these demonstrations for indicator weighting by flagging any unidentified school that met two conditions: (1) The school would have been identified if only substantially weighted indicators had been considered; and (2) the school did not show significant progress from the prior year, as determined by the State, on any substantially weighted indicator. While schools are expected, under §§ 200.21-200.22, to make progress in order to exit improvement status, the progress referenced in proposed § 200.18(d)(1)-(2) could avoid entry into improvement status altogether. We believe that minor clarifications to proposed § 200.18(d)(1)-(2) can help clarify how these requirements are intended to be implemented.

Changes: We have renumbered and revised § 200.18(c)(1)-(2) to distinguish these requirements for demonstrating the weight of indicators from exit criteria that remove schools from identified status, as specified in §§ 200.21 and 200.22. We have also revised § 200.18(c)(1)-(2) to clarify that these demonstrations are intended to verify that schools that would hypothetically be identified on the basis of all indicators except School Quality or Student Success, but were excluded from identification when the State considered all indicators, have been appropriately categorized in a status other than comprehensive support and improvement or targeted support and improvement, because these schools made significant progress on the accountability indicators, including at least one that receives "substantial" weight.

Comments: Some commenters asked for additional guidance on what significant progress means, or for revisions to clarify that significant progress is determined by the State. One commenter further suggested that we strike the expectation for significant progress, and replace it with a demonstration of sufficient progress.

Discussion: We agree with commenters that it is helpful to make clear that significant progress, in the context of the demonstrations for indicator weighting required under renumbered § 200.18(c)(1)-(2), is defined by the State based on the school's performance from the prior year, and are revising the final regulations accordingly. Given that States have this discretion to define significant progress in context of their unique indicators and goals, we believe additional examples or considerations for "significant progress" are best addressed in non-regulatory guidance.

Changes: We have revised § 200.18(c)(1)-(2) to clarify that the meaning of significant progress from the prior year, as determined by the State, on a substantially weighted indicator as part of these demonstrations.

Comments: A few commenters asserted that the proposed regulations complicated the statutory requirements for "substantial" and "much greater" weight and recommended alternative approaches, such as requiring that School Quality or Student Success account for less than 50 percent of all indicators in a statewide accountability system, or that each indicator be weighted equally at 25 percent (meaning that non-School Quality or Student Success indicators would make up 75 percent of the overall rating). Finally, some commenters recommended additional guidance on the weighting of indicators, including specific percentages that might be afforded to certain indicators consistent with statutory and regulatory requirements, as well as how to demonstrate compliance with §§ 200.18(d)(1) and (2).

Discussion: We agree with commenters that further examples and discussion to clarify the requirements for weighting of indicators in § 200.18(c) would be helpful and should be addressed in any non-regulatory guidance the Department issues to support States in implementation of their accountability systems.

Because States retain the discretion to develop numerous methods for annual meaningful differentiation, including those that build on data "dashboards", use a two-dimensional matrix, or rely on categorical labels rather than a numerical index, we believe it would be inappropriate to regulate that a particular percentage for each indicator, or set of indicators, would meet the statutory requirements to afford academic indicators "substantial" and "much greater" weight, as it could imply that only numerical indices were permitted. Although we are not including any percentages in the final regulations, we also note that we disagree with commenters suggesting that "much greater" weight for academic indicators could be as little as half of the overall weight in the system of differentiation—"much greater" implies that these indicators should be afforded well over 50 percent of the weight.

Changes: None.

Comments: One commenter stated that the required demonstrations for States related to weighting of indicators could create confusion for rural or small schools where data on the "substantial" (in particular, those based on student assessment results) indicators may not be available due to n-size limitations.

Discussion: We recognize the commenter's concern that there are cases where a school may be missing a particular indicator for a number of reasons, which would complicate meeting the requirements in § 200.18(c). As discussed in greater detail below under the subheading Other Requirements in Annual Meaningful Differentiation of Schools, we are revising § 200.18(d)(1)(iii) to include a provision previously in proposed regulations for consolidated State plans that permit a State to propose a different methodology for very small schools, among other special categories of schools, in annual meaningful differentiation, which would include how indicators are weighted.

Changes: None.

Comments: Numerous commenters provided feedback to the Department on proposed § 200.18(d)(3), which would require each State to demonstrate that a school performing at the State's highest performance level on all indicators received a different summative rating than a school performing at the lowest performance level on any substantially weighted indicator, based on the performance of all students and each subgroup of students in a school, citing the same reasons they generally supported or opposed the requirements in proposed § 200.18(d) overall.

However, a number of commenters raised additional concerns that were specific to proposed § 200.18(d)(3). Several commenters felt the requirement would undermine the transparency of summative ratings, because a single low-performing subgroup could prevent a school from receiving the highest possible distinction in the State's accountability system. They further noted that the proposed demonstrations felt like a return to the top-down and prescriptive system of AYP, which the ESSA eliminated in favor of greater flexibility for States with respect to the design of accountability systems and determinations. In addition, a few commenters suggested eliminating this provision, citing their overall objection to summative ratings.

Other commenters suggested replacing this demonstration with a requirement that would emphasize differentiation of schools with consistently underperforming subgroups of students, believing that § 200.18(d)(3), as proposed, created incentives for States to establish a very small "highest" rating category (e.g., an A+ category of schools in an A-F system), so that schools could still receive a very high rating when one or two subgroups were struggling on a substantially weighted academic indicator. They recommended requiring a State to demonstrate that any school with a consistently underperforming subgroup of students, as identified under § 200.19, would be assigned a lower summative rating than it would have otherwise received as a stronger way to ensure States' systems of annual meaningful differentiation meet the statutory requirement to differentiate schools with consistently underperforming subgroups.

Discussion: We appreciate many commenters' views on the importance of upholding the statutory requirements for the academic indicators to receive "substantial" weight individually, and "much greater" weight in the aggregate, in each State's system of annual meaningful differentiation, and their recognition that this is particularly important to ensure subgroup performance is meaningfully recognized in the State's accountability system. Moreover, the statute requires the Academic Achievement, Academic Progress, Graduation Rate, and Progress in Achieving English Language Proficiency indicators to have a "much greater" role in school differentiation, compared to School Quality or Student Success indicators, and we share the views of commenters who believe that student academic outcomes, including outcomes for subgroups, must be a primary focus of the accountability system as a way to promote equity and excellence for all students.

We agree with commenters that these ends, however, would be better realized by revising the proposed regulations to require that a school with a consistently underperforming subgroup of students receive a lower summative determination than it would have otherwise received if the subgroup were not consistently underperforming, given the commenters' argument that the proposed regulations did not adequately include the statutory requirement differentiate schools with a consistently underperforming subgroup. We believe the suggestion of linking this demonstration to consistently underperforming subgroups of students better reinforces the requirement in section 1111(c)(4)(C)(iii) of the ESEA, as amended by the ESSA, for a State's system of annual meaningful differentiation to include differentiation of schools with a consistently underperforming subgroup; we agree that if a school is able to receive the same overall determination, regardless of whether a subgroup is underperforming, a State has not met this requirement. We also agree with the commenter that this approach will provide less of an incentive for States to create a very small "highest" category (an "A+" category), rather than remove schools from an exemplary category (an "A" grade) due to subgroup performance.

While we recognize commenters' concerns that this demonstration, as proposed, would undermine the transparency of school determinations or would require States to develop an AYP-like accountability system, we believe that such concerns are outweighed by the statutory requirement that consistently underperforming subgroups must be meaningfully differentiated each year and be identified for targeted support and improvement—and believe that an accountability system is not communicating school performance clearly to the public if a consistently underperforming subgroup is not reflected in a school's overall performance designation. Finally, in response to commenters that opposed this provision as proposed due to their opposition to summative ratings for schools, as the final regulation clarifies that the summative determination may be aligned to the categories required for school identification (in which case, schools with a consistently underperforming subgroup would be in targeted support and improvement), we believe the revisions to § 200.18(a)(4) address their concerns.

Changes: We have renumbered and revised § 200.18(c)(3) to require that each State, in order to meet requirements for annual meaningful differentiation under § 200.18(a) and section 1111(c)(4)(C)(iii) of the ESEA, as amended by the ESSA, demonstrate that any school with a consistently underperforming subgroup of students receives a lower summative determination than it otherwise would have received had no subgroups in the school been so identified.

Comments: A few commenters suggested replacing all three of the demonstrations related to indicator weighting with an alternative requirement that States demonstrate in their State plans how the academic indicators carry "much greater" weight than non-academic indicators, and how the State's methodology to identify schools will ensure that schools with low performance on indicators receiving "much greater" weight will be identified for improvement as a result.

Discussion: We appreciate the commenters' recognition that a State's system for weighting indicators should align with its methodology for identifying schools for comprehensive and targeted support and improvement. While we disagree that the demonstrations in § 200.18(c), as renumbered, are unnecessary (as previously described), we agree that schools performing poorly on substantially weighted indicators should be more likely to be identified for intervention, and the focus on the outcomes of the system of annual meaningful differentiation (rather than inputs) is consistent with our approach to the weighting requirements generally. To reiterate this focus on outcomes and ensure that, through its State plan, each State describes how it is meeting the underlying purpose of the requirements in § 200.18(c)(1)-(2) related to weighting, we are revising § 200.18(d)(1)(ii) to specify that the overall goal behind the requirements for weighting indicators is to ensure that schools performing poorly across the indicators receiving "much greater" weight are more likely to be identified for support and improvement under § 200.19 and to include this explanation in the State plan with the State's demonstration of how it is meeting the requirements of § 200.18(c).

Changes: We have revised § 200.18(d)(1)(ii) to require that each State describe in its State plan how it has met all of the requirements of this section, including how the State's methodology for identifying schools for comprehensive support and improvement and targeted support and improvement ensures that schools with low performance on substantially weighted indicators are more likely to be so identified.

Comments: Several commenters supported the clarification in proposed § 200.18(e)(2) that the indicators required by the statute to receive "substantial" weight (Academic Achievement, Graduation Rate, Academic Progress, and Progress in Achieving English Language Proficiency) need not be afforded the same "substantial" weight in order to meet the requirement—promoting flexibility and discretion for States in designing their accountability systems under the ESSA and weighting indicators based on State-determined priorities and goals.

Discussion: We appreciate the commenters' support for this provision.

Changes: None.

Comments: A few commenters expressed support for the requirements in proposed § 200.18(c)(3) and (e)(3) that States maintain the same relative weighting between the accountability indicators for all schools within a grade span, including for schools that are not held accountable for the Progress in Achieving English Language Proficiency indicator, as a way to maintain consistency and fairness in States' systems for differentiating schools. Other commenters, however, opposed the requirement. Some believed the requirement goes beyond the statute because the only requirements related to grade spans in section 1111(c) of the ESEA, as amended by the ESSA, are related to indicators of School Quality or Student Success. Others thought the requirement was an overly prescriptive intrusion on State discretion over the weighting of indicators, as States will be in a better position to determine a method to maintain comparable and fair expectations for all schools. A few other commenters requested that we modify the relative weighting requirement so that States may vary the weighting between indicators not only by grade span, but also based on the characteristics of students served by the school or the amount of data available for a given indicator in a school; these commenters believed, for example, that school demographics could make one indicator more relevant than other indicators, and thus deserving of greater weighting, in measuring school performance. Similarly, commenters questioned how this provision would work in small schools and in schools that serve variant grade configurations. However, another commenter believed that all schools should be held accountable for the Progress in Achieving English Language Proficiency indicator, regardless of the number of English learners in the school, to ensure that States selecting higher n-sizes do not avoid accountability for ELP.

Discussion: We appreciate that commenters want to ensure States have the ability to establish multi-indicator accountability systems that are fair for all schools and accurately capture a school's overall impact on student learning, consistent with the requirements for substantially weighing certain indicators, and agree that requiring the same relative weighting among all schools within a grade span should be maintained.

We recognize that it is challenging to have a system of annual meaningful differentiation with completely uniform weighting, given differences in school size, grade configurations, and special populations of students served. Therefore, we are revising the regulations, as discussed previously, to permit States to propose alternative approaches that are used to accommodate special kinds of schools. However, very small schools or schools with variant grade configurations that do not fit into a single grade span are the exception, not the norm; we believe it is paramount to ensure that schools are treated consistently in the system of annual meaningful differentiation given the consequential decisions (e.g., identification for comprehensive or targeted support and improvement, eligibility for school improvement funding) that flow out of this system. The statute requires a statewide, multi-indicator accountability system, and a non-uniform weighting scheme between those indicators across a State would undermine this requirement significantly. States retain significant flexibility to design the statewide weighting scheme between each grade span using their various indicators, but without uniform weighting within each grade span, the methodology for differentiating schools and identifying them for support and improvement could be unreliable from district to district, or worse, biased against particular schools or set lower expectations for certain schools, based on the population of students they serve.

Thus, it is crucial that all of the accountability indicators be afforded the same relative weights across schools within a grade span to reasonably ensure compliance with the statutory requirements in section 1111(c) regarding a statewide system of annual meaningful differentiation and identification of schools for support and improvement, including the weighting of indicators in section 1111(c)(4)(c). As such, this regulation falls squarely within the Department's rulemaking authority under GEPA, the DEOA, and section 1601(a) of the ESEA and within the scope of section 1111(c) of the ESEA, as amended by the ESSA, and therefore does not violate section 1111(e). For example, allowing the Academic Achievement indicator to matter more for subgroups that are already high achieving, and less in schools where subgroups are low-performing, would be both inconsistent with the purpose of the accountability system to improve student achievement and school success, and introduce bias into the system of differentiation. In response to commenters who noted this provision was not explicitly referenced in the statutory text, given the Secretary's rulemaking authority under GEPA, the DEOA, and section 1601(a) of the ESEA, as amended by the ESSA (see discussion of the Department's general rulemaking authority under the heading Cross-Cutting Issues), it is not necessary for the statute to specifically authorize the Secretary to issue a particular regulatory provision.

In general, because the Progress in Achieving English Language Proficiency indicator is the sole indicator that is measured for a single subgroup, we believe it is helpful to clarify that the relative weighting of indicators must be maintained when a school cannot be held accountable for this indicator due to serving a low number of English learners; as the n-size will be determined by each State, and as some schools may not serve any English learners, we cannot require all schools to be held accountable on the basis of this indicator. Since the statute creates this distinction (by creating one of the five required indicators around a single subgroup), we believe it is appropriate to include a specific exception to the relative weighting requirement based on this indicator, but to limit other exceptions to the relative weighting requirement.

Changes: None.

Comments: A few commenters suggested that the Department encourage each State to emphasize student growth or progress, over absolute achievement, when weighting its accountability indicators consistent with proposed § 200.18(c)(1)-(2), because they believe student growth more accurately reflects the impact of a school on student learning than a measure of achievement taken at a single point in time.

Discussion: We agree that student academic growth is a critical measure to include in State accountability systems, and encourage all States to incorporate both achievement and growth into the annual differentiation of schools, because a student growth measure can reveal and recognize schools with low achievement levels that nevertheless are making significant strides to close achievement gaps and thus should be celebrated, and may not need to be identified for improvement. However, we believe it is most consistent with the statute for each State, and not the Department, to determine whether using student growth is appropriate for its accountability system, and to select the weight afforded to student growth relative to other required indicators.

Changes: None.

Other Requirements in Annual Meaningful Differentiation of Schools

Comments: Several commenters suggested that § 200.18 should include additional references to stakeholder engagement, including consultation with parents, district and school leaders, educators and other instructional support staff, and community members, in developing the system of annual meaningful differentiation. One commenter suggested such engagement be expanded to include the creation of parent and community advisory boards to develop and implement the system of differentiation used in their State and LEA, while another commenter suggested schools be held accountable for how well they involve parents in key decisions and improvement efforts.

Discussion: The requirements for annual meaningful differentiation of schools in § 200.18 already are subject to requirements for timely and meaningful consultation as part of the consolidated State plan regulations, and we believe additional emphasis on stakeholder engagement here is unnecessary.

Changes: None.

Comments: A number of commenters supported the reiteration of statutory requirements in proposed § 200.18(b)(1) for the system of annual meaningful differentiation to include the performance of all students and each subgroup of students on every required accountability indicator, consistent with the requirements for inclusion of subgroups in § 200.16, for n-size in § 200.17, and for partial enrollment in § 200.20. Other commenters objected to these requirements as precluding certain indicators that could provide helpful information to differentiate between schools but could not be disaggregated for each student subgroup, such as teacher or parent surveys or whole-school program evaluations.

Discussion: Section 1111(c)(4)(B) of the ESEA, as amended by the ESSA, is clear that each indicator used in statewide accountability systems must be disaggregated by subgroup, with the exception of the Progress in Achieving English Language Proficiency indicator, which is only measured for English learners. Further, section 1111(c)(4)(C) states that meaningful differentiation of schools must be based on all indicators for all students and for each subgroup of students.

Changes: None.

Comments: A few commenters objected to the requirements in proposed § 200.18(b)(5) for the system of annual meaningful differentiation to meet requirements in § 200.15 to annually measure the achievement of at least 95 percent of all students and 95 percent of students in each subgroup on the required assessments in reading/language arts and mathematics.

Discussion: Section 1111(c)(4)(E) of the ESEA, as amended by the ESSA, requires each State to measure the achievement of at least 95 percent of students and 95 percent of students in each subgroup and factor this participation requirement into the statewide accountability system, and this provision only reiterates regulatory requirements described further in § 200.15.

Changes: None.

Comments: A number of commenters requested additional flexibility or exceptions to the requirements for annual meaningful differentiation for certain categories of schools, such as rural schools, small schools, schools that combine grade spans (e.g., a K-12 schools), and alternative schools (e.g., schools serving overage or under-credited students, other dropout recovery programs, or students with disabilities who may need more time to graduate). These commenters generally acknowledged the need to hold such schools accountable for their performance, but sought flexibility to use different indicators or methods that they believe would be more suited to the unique needs and circumstances of these schools. One commenter noted that while proposed § 299.17 would permit States to propose different methods for differentiating school performance in their consolidated State plans, it was not sufficiently clear whether this flexibility extended to school identification. Other commenters expressed concerns about creating loopholes in the accountability system for schools that serve vulnerable and historically underserved student populations.

Discussion: We appreciate the commenters' concerns with designing accountability systems that are inclusive of all schools and provide fair, consistent methods for reporting school performance and determining when additional interventions and supports are necessary. We share these goals, which is why proposed § 299.17 permitted States flexibility to develop or adopt alternative methodologies under their statewide accountability systems that address the unique needs and circumstances of many of the schools cited by commenters.

This flexibility, which is similar to past practice under NCLB, is also intended to apply to both annual meaningful differentiation and identification of schools under §§ 200.18 and 200.19, and allows a State, if it desires, to propose an alternative way for producing an annual determination for these schools (based on the same, or modified, indicators) and for identifying these schools for comprehensive or targeted support and improvement. We are revising § 200.18(d)(1)(iii) to include the list of schools for which a State may use a different methodology for accountability previously included in § 299.17, with additional clarification or examples to better explain why such schools might require this flexibility. We note, however, that this provision allows for this flexibility only where it is impossible or inappropriate to include all of the indicators a State typically uses to differentiate schools, and thus is not generally applicable to regular public schools, including most rural schools.

Changes: We have revised § 200.18(d)(1)(iii) to include clarifying language, previously in proposed § 299.17, that a State may propose a different methodology for annual meaningful differentiation—and by extension, identification for comprehensive and targeted support and improvement—for certain schools, such as: (1) Schools in which no grade level is tested on the assessments required by the ESEA under section 1111(b)(2)(B) (e.g., P-2 schools); (2) schools with variant grade configurations (e.g., K-12 schools); (3) small schools that do not meet the State's n-size on any indicator even after averaging data across schools years or grades consistent with § 200.20; (4) schools that are designed to serve special populations, such as students receiving alternative programming in alternative educational settings; students living in local institutions for neglected or delinquent children, including juvenile justice facilities; students enrolled in State public schools for the deaf or blind; and recently arrived English learners enrolled in public schools for newcomer students; and (5) newly opened schools where multiple years of data are not available consistent with procedures for averaging school-level data described in § 200.20 for at least one indicator (e.g., a high school that has not yet graduated its first cohort for students).

Comments: We received several comments from tribal organizations that recommended exempting schools from the requirement for annual meaningful differentiation in section 200.18 if they instruct students primarily in a Native American language and if the State does not provide an assessment in that Native American language; these commenters suggested such schools should be listed as "undifferentiated." However, other tribal organizations supported the proposed regulations for a single statewide accountability system, particularly because over 90 percent of American Indian and Alaska Native students attend State-funded public schools, as opposed to schools funded by the BIE or private operators. For these public school students, one commenter noted, the statewide accountability systems, including indicators that measure student achievement, are especially important.

Another tribal organization raised concerns about a lack of accountability for schools served by the Bureau of Indian Education (BIE) and requested that separate accountability measures should apply to tribally-controlled schools, and that schools located on Indian lands should be funded and monitored directly by the Department rather than by States.

Discussion: While States have some flexibility to develop alternate methods for differentiating and identifying schools, as described previously, the ESEA, as amended by the ESSA, continues to require that all public schools in each State be held accountable through a single statewide system of annual differentiation, and States may not exempt any school entirely from annual meaningful differentiation or identification. This includes schools that primarily instruct students in a Native American language.

In addition, under section 8204(c)(1) of the ESEA, as amended by the ESSA, the Secretary of the Interior must use a negotiated rulemaking process to develop regulations pertaining to standards, assessments, and accountability, consistent with section 1111, for BIE-funded schools "on a national, regional, or tribal basis, as appropriate, taking into account the unique circumstances and needs of such schools and the students served by such schools." Given the specific rulemaking process required for schools funded by the BIE, we cannot address in these regulations the role of individual schools under the BIE accountability system. We do note, however, that section 8204(c)(2) permits a tribal governing body or school board of a BIE-funded school to waive, in part or in whole, the requirements that BIE establishes and to submit a proposal to the Secretary of the Interior for alternative standards, assessments, and an accountability system, consistent with section 1111, that takes into account the unique circumstances and needs of the school or schools and students served. The Secretary of the Interior, along with the Secretary of Education, must approve those alternative standards, assessments, and accountability system unless the Secretary of Education determines that they do not meet the requirements of section 1111.

With respect to the comment about the funding and monitoring of schools located on Indian lands, to the extent that the comment is referring to State-funded public schools, State funding and oversight are matters of State law and are outside the scope of these regulations.

Changes: None.

Comments: None.

Discussion: Each State must describe in its State plan how its system of annual meaningful differentiation meets all statutory and regulatory requirements, but in proposed § 200.18, multiple paragraphs referenced information that must be included in the State plan. To provide additional clarity for States, prevent the inadvertent omission of required information in a State plan, and ensure that required information is transparent for those preparing and reviewing State plan submissions, we are revising § 200.18 to combine all requirements related to information submitted on annual meaningful differentiation in the State plan in a single paragraph.

Changes: We have revised § 200.18(d)(1), and renumbered remaining paragraphs of § 200.18 accordingly, to include, in one paragraph, all information that each State must submit in its State Plan under section 1111 of the ESEA to describe how its system of annual meaningful differentiation meets the regulations.

Comments: While many commenters supported the provisions in § 200.18 regarding annual meaningful differentiation of schools, a few commenters recommended striking § 200.18 in its entirety, out of concern that the regulations are too prescriptive, punitive, test-driven, and unnecessary to clarify the statute.

Discussion: As discussed previously, the regulations are necessary and useful to clarify the requirements for annual meaningful differentiation and weighting of indicators. Further, we believe these regulations will help States in their efforts to support students and schools, consistent with the purpose of title I: "to provide all children significant opportunity to receive a fair, equitable, and high-quality education, and to close educational achievement gaps."

Changes: None.

Section 200.19   Identification of Schools

Comments: One commenter stated that the proposed regulations lack clarity regarding the terms used for the various groups of schools that States must identify for school improvement. As an example, the commenter noted that schools identified for additional targeted support are referenced as having either a chronically low-performing subgroup or a low-performing subgroup.

Discussion: The Department has made every effort to use consistent language throughout the regulations when referring to categories of identified schools. The examples cited by the commenter actually refer to two separate categories of schools. Schools with low-performing subgroups are schools identified for targeted support and improvement that also must receive additional targeted support under section 1111(d)(2)(C) of the ESEA, as amended by the ESSA; if they do not improve over time, then they are defined as chronically low-performing subgroup schools and must be identified for comprehensive support and improvement. For greater clarity regarding the types of schools that must be identified, the Department is revising the final regulations to include the chart below, which summarizes each category of schools that States must identify to meet the requirements in section 1111(c) and 1111(d) of the ESEA, as amended by the ESSA:

Types of schools	Description 22	Statutory provision 23	Regulatory provision	Timeline for identification	Initial year of identification
Category: Comprehensive Support and Improvement					
Lowest-Performing	Lowest-performing five percent of schools in the State participating in Title I	Section 1111(c)(4)(D)(i)(I)	§ 200.19(a)(1)	At least once every three years	2018-2019.
Low High School Graduation Rate	Any public high school in the State with a four-year adjusted cohort graduation rate at or below 67 percent, or below a higher percentage selected by the State, over no more than three years	Section 1111(c)(4)(D)(i)(II)	§ 200.19(a)(2)	At least once every three years	2018-2019.
Chronically Low-Performing Subgroup	Any school participating in Title I that (a) was identified for targeted support and improvement because it had a subgroup of students performing at or below the performance of all students in the lowest-performing schools and (b) did not improve after implementing a targeted support and improvement plan over a State-determined number of years	Section 1111(c)(4)(D)(i)(III), 1111(d)(3)(A)(i)(II)	§ 200.19(a)(3)	At least once every three years	State-determined.
Category: Targeted Support and Improvement					
Consistently Underperforming Subgroup	Any school with one or more consistently underperforming subgroups	Section 1111(c)(4)(C)(iii), 1111(d)(2)(A)(i)	§ 200.19(b)(1), (c)

Annually | 2019-2020. |

| Low-Performing Subgroup | Any school in which one or more subgroups of students is performing at or below the performance of all students in the lowest-performing schools. These schools must receive additional targeted support under the law. If this type of school is a Title I school that does not improve after implementing a targeted support and improvement plan over a State-determined number of years, it becomes a school that has a chronically low-performing subgroup and is identified for comprehensive support and improvement | Section 1111(d)(2)(D) | § 200.19(b)(2) | At least once every three years | 2018-2019. |

Changes: We have revised § 200.19 to include a table that describes each category of school support and improvement, including each type of school within the category, and lists the related statutory and regulatory provisions.

Comments: Several commenters expressed concerns that the proposed regulations would not allow States to identify schools for support if they are eligible for, but do not receive, title I funds. Commenters believe this is inconsistent with current practice and would result in the identification of fewer high schools because most school districts run out of title I funds before awarding funds to high schools. A few commenters suggested that the Department allow States to identify the lowest-performing five percent of title I-eligible schools, rather than the lowest-performing five percent of title I-receiving schools. One commenter raised concerns that if a State did not identify any high schools for support and improvement because they did not receive title I funds, then high schools would not be eligible for funds under section 1003.

Discussion: We appreciate commenters' interest in ensuring that all low-performing high schools are identified and supported. However, under section 1111(c)(4)(D)(i)(I) of the ESEA, as amended by the ESSA, a State is limited to identifying only schools that receive title I funds when it identifies its lowest-performing five percent of title I schools for comprehensive support and improvement. On the other hand, States must identify any public high school with a graduation rate below 67 percent for comprehensive support and improvement and any school with subgroups that are consistently underperforming for targeted support and improvement, regardless of their title I status. Any school identified for comprehensive or targeted support and improvement that meets the definitions of those categories of schools under the statute is eligible for funds under section 1003 of the ESEA, as amended by the ESSA, regardless of whether the school receives other title I funds. Given these statutory requirements for States to identify and support high schools that do not receive title I funds, we do not believe that additional regulatory flexibility is appropriate or necessary.

Changes: None.

Comments: One commenter suggested the Department provide non-regulatory guidance on how title I funds can be used to support non-title I high schools identified for comprehensive support because they have a graduation rate less than 67 percent.

Discussion: We appreciate the commenters' suggestion and will consider this recommendation for non-regulatory guidance. As described in the previous discussion section, a school non-title I high school identified for comprehensive support because it has a graduation rate of 67 percent or less is eligible for funds under section 1003 of the ESEA, as amended by the ESSA.

Changes: None.

Comments: One commenter asked for clarity about whether a single school can be identified for comprehensive and targeted support and improvement simultaneously.

Discussion: It is possible that a school could meet the criteria to be identified for both comprehensive and targeted support and improvement. Given that the requirements for developing and implementing comprehensive and targeted support and improvement plans do not fully align, we are revising the regulations to clarify that States must identify any school that is not identified for comprehensive support and improvement under § 200.19(a), but that has a consistently underperforming subgroup or low-performing subgroup, for targeted support and improvement. We encourage States and LEAs to ensure that, for each school that is identified for comprehensive support and improvement but who has a consistently underperforming or low-performing subgroup, to ensure that the school's comprehensive improvement and support plan identifies the needs of all students and includes interventions designed to raise the achievement of all low-performing students.

Changes: We have revised § 200.19(b)(1)-(2) to clarify that any school identified for comprehensive support and improvement under § 200.19(a) need not also be identified for targeted support and improvement under § 200.19(b)(1) or (2).

Comments: One commenter suggested the Department eliminate any requirement to identify comprehensive support and improvement schools beyond those that are in the lowest-performing five percent of all title I schools in the State and any public high school in the State failing to graduate one-third or more of its students. The commenter also suggested that the Department eliminate the targeted support and improvement category.

Discussion: Section 1111(c)(4)(D) of the ESEA, as amended by the ESSA, requires that each State identify three types of schools for comprehensive support and improvement: Those that are the lowest-performing five percent of all title I schools, all public high schools failing to graduate one third or more of their students, and all title I schools with low-performing subgroups that were originally identified for targeted support and improvement but have not met the LEA-determined exit criteria after a State-determined number of years. Additionally, section 1111(d)(2)(A) requires States to identify schools with consistently underperforming subgroups for targeted support and improvement, and section 1111(d)(2)(C) requires identification of schools if a subgroup, on its own, is performing as poorly as students in the lowest-performing five percent of title I schools, i.e., a low-performing subgroup. Given these statutory requirements, the Department declines to make changes in this area.

Changes: None.

Comments: One commenter suggested that the Department add a requirement that a school identified for comprehensive support and improvement must provide support through the Native American language of instruction to those students instructed primarily in a Native American language, and provide such support through the Native American language based in the structure and features of the language itself such that it does not limit the preservation or use of the Native American language.

Discussion: We appreciate the commenter's emphasis on ensuring that interventions in comprehensive support and improvement schools align with the unique characteristics and goals of schools that provide instruction primarily in a Native American language. We believe that, in general, the concerns of the commenter would be addressed through key components of the school improvement process, such as a needs assessment and consultation requirements, both of which could emphasize the need for instructional interventions to be delivered through the specific Native American language used in the school. We encourage States and districts to work with such schools to address the required components of the school improvement process, while also maintaining the core aspects of the Native Language instructional program.

We note that it may not be necessary for some interventions developed and implemented as part of a school's comprehensive or targeted support and improvement plan (e.g., an early warning system aimed at curbing chronic absenteeism) to be delivered in a Native American language. The specific suggestion that the supports be provided to students in a particular language is beyond the scope of these regulatory provisions, which address comprehensive support and improvement for a school in general (see examples in § 200.21(d)(3)), rather than to students individually. Therefore, we decline to make the use of Native American language a blanket requirement for such interventions.

Changes: None.

Comments: One commenter requested that the Department require States to identify schools for comprehensive support and improvement every year.

Discussion: While the statute and proposed regulations provide States with the flexibility to identify schools for comprehensive support and improvement each year, section 1111(c)(4)(D)(i) of the ESEA, as amended by the ESSA, requires States to identify schools no less than once every three years. The change requested by the commenter would not be consistent with this statutory flexibility.

Changes: None.

Comments: Some commenters encouraged the Department to clarify that States may adopt or continue more rigorous systems for school and subgroup accountability than those required by the statute and regulations. For example, the commenters suggested clarifying that a State could identify all high schools with a single subgroup that has a graduation rate at or below 67 percent, rather than only schools where the all students group has a graduation rate at or below 67 percent. Additionally, one commenter suggested that the Department clarify that States can identify more than the lowest performing five percent of title I schools.

Discussion: We appreciate the commenters' interest in clarifying that States have additional flexibility to design and implement accountability systems that go beyond the minimum requirements of the ESEA, as amended by the ESSA, and corresponding regulations. For purposes of identifying schools to meet the Federal requirements for school identification and to determine eligibility for Federal funds, including school improvement funds under section 1003 of the ESEA, States must use the applicable statutory and regulatory definitions, and we believe the regulations should reflect these minimum requirements. States may go beyond these minimum requirements by identifying additional categories of schools, such as Warning Schools or Reward Schools. Likewise, they may identify for comprehensive or targeted support and improvement additional schools that do not meet the definitions for those categories of schools, but any such additional schools would not be eligible to receive Federal funds—including school improvement funds under section 1003 of the ESEA—that are specifically for schools identified for comprehensive or targeted support and improvement, as defined in the statute. We believe that further clarification on this issue is more appropriate for non-regulatory guidance.

We recognize, however, that the language in the proposed regulations stating that a State's identification of schools for comprehensive support and improvement must include "at a minimum" the three types of schools specified in the statute and regulations, and similar language regarding the two types of schools specified in the statute and regulations for targeted support and improvement, may have created some confusion as to whether a State has authority to identify additional types of schools for comprehensive and targeted support and improvement, and thereby to make such additional schools eligible for funds that are to be provided specifically to schools identified for comprehensive or targeted support and improvement. To clarify this issue, we are removing the words "at a minimum" from those paragraphs of the final regulations.

Additionally, section 1111(c)(4)(D)(i)(I) of the ESEA, as amended by the ESSA, is clear that State must identify "not less than" the lowest-performing five percent of title I schools for comprehensive support. To clarify that this permits a State to identify more than the lowest-performing five percent of title I schools (e.g., the bottom ten percent of title I schools or five percent of each of title I elementary, middle, and high schools), we have revised the regulatory language to include this statutory flexibility.

Changes: We have removed the phrase "at a minimum" from § 200.19(a) and (b). We have also revised § 200.19(a)(1) to include the phrase "not less than" in describing the lowest-performing schools identified for comprehensive support.

Lowest-Performing Schools

Comments: One commenter expressed support for the requirement to identify the lowest-performing five percent of schools, but another commenter opposed the implication of the requirement that a State could never have a system in which all schools were successful.

Discussion: The regulation requiring identification of the lowest-performing schools implements section 1111(c)(4)(D)(i)(I) of the ESEA, as amended by the ESSA, which requires that each State identify not less than its lowest-performing five percent of title I schools for comprehensive support and improvement.

Changes: None.

Comments: Several commenters raised concerns that proposed § 200.19(a)(1) would require each State to identify the lowest-performing five percent of schools at each of the elementary, middle, and high school levels for comprehensive support and improvement. Other commenters found this requirement inconsistent with section 1111(c)(4)(D)(i)(I) of the ESEA, which requires the identification of the lowest-performing five percent of title I schools in the State. One commenter specifically requested that States have flexibility to identify the lowest-performing schools across grade spans, while another commenter warned that such flexibility could result in not identifying any schools in a particular grade-level (if, for example, all of a State's elementary schools were high-performing but most middle schools were performing poorly).

Discussion: We agree with the commenters that the proposed requirements may have created confusion with respect to whether States were required to identify the lowest-performing five percent of title I schools at each of the elementary, middle, and high school levels. This was not our intent, and we are revising the final regulations to eliminate the reference to each grade span, although a State could choose to identify five percent of title I schools at each grade span. While we appreciate that a State could identify more schools in a particular grade span than another, we believe it is unlikely that a State would not identify any schools in a grade span and do not believe it is appropriate to require a State to identify schools in each grade span if it is otherwise identifying the lowest-performing five percent of all title I schools in the State.

Changes: We have revised § 200.19(a)(1) to clarify that each State must identify the lowest-performing five percent of its title I schools, without reference to particular grade spans.

Comments: Commenters raised concerns about the proposed requirement that States identify the

115

lowest-performing five percent of all title I schools in the State based on each school's summative rating among all students. Some of these commenters opposed the requirement because they generally oppose the requirement to provide each school with a summative rating and, as a result, oppose the requirement that it be used for school identification. Another commenter questioned whether summative ratings will be precise enough to separate a school at the fifth percentile from a slightly higher ranked school. Other commenters suggested specific approaches or flexibilities related to identifying the lowest-performing five percent of schools, such as using school academic proficiency rates, a combination of assessment data and other measures, such as parent and climate surveys and graduation rates, methods similar to those used to identify priority schools under ESEA flexibility, or a combination of summative ratings and factors related to school capacity and district support.

Discussion: Section 1111(c)(4)(D) of the ESEA, as amended by the ESSA, requires States to identify schools for comprehensive support and improvement based on the State's system of annual meaningful differentiation, which includes multiple indicators beyond statewide assessment results. Moreover, as required under § 200.18(a)(4), a State's system of meaningful differentiation must result in a summative determination that is based on a school's performance on all indicators, but does not include other factors, such as district capacity or commitment. Therefore, a State cannot identify a school as among its lowest-performing schools for comprehensive support and improvement based on a single indicator, such as student performance on the statewide assessments, nor incorporate into such identification factors that are not indicators in its statewide accountability system. However, as noted previously, States have the ability to identify more than five percent of title I schools if the State determines such identification is appropriate and useful to ensure additional low-performing schools receive support. Further, as noted in the discussion on § 200.18, each State retains significant discretion to design its system of meaningful differentiation and may incorporate a wide range of academic and non-academic factors in the indicators that will be used for the providing a summative determination for each school and identification of the lowest-performing 5 percent of title I schools. We are also revising § 200.18(a)(4) to allow a State to use the summative determinations discussed in the statute (i.e., comprehensive support and improvement, targeted support and improvement, not identified for support) and are making corresponding changes to § 200.19(a)(1) to incorporate this flexibility.

Changes: Consistent with the changes to § 200.18, we have revised § 200.19(a)(1) to require States to identify at least the bottom five percent of title I schools consistent with the summative determinations provided under § 200.18(a)(4).

Comments: One commenter suggested that once summative ratings were used to identify the bottom five percent of title I schools, teachers from the top five percent of schools should be sent to the bottom five percent of title I schools to help them improve.

Discussion: Under the ESEA, as amended by the ESSA, school districts are responsible for determining appropriate interventions in schools identified for comprehensive support and improvement.

Changes: None.

Comments: None.

Discussion: Under § 200.18 of the regulations, States must include the performance of all students in calculating a school's performance on each of the accountability indicators under § 200.14, as well as in calculating the school's summative determination. Therefore, it is unnecessary to refer to "all students" in § 200.19(a)(1), which requires States to identify the lowest-performing five percent of title I schools for comprehensive support and improvement.

Additionally, consistent with the existing regulations and practice across many States, § 200.20 allows a State to average school-level data across grades and across no more than three years in determining a school's performance for accountability purposes. Therefore, the Department is removing references in § 200.19(a)(1) to averaging summative determinations over no more than three years because, although States may use data that have been averaged over up to three years to calculate performance on indicators consistent with § 200.20, the determinations themselves are not averaged. For clarity, we are also removing other references to data averaging throughout § 200.19 because § 200.20 provides the full parameters under which States may average school-level data over school years and across grades.

Changes: We have revised § 200.19(a)(1) to: (1) Remove references to "all students," and (2) remove references to averaging summative ratings (now summative determinations in the final regulations) over no more than three years. We have also removed a reference from data averaging in § 200.19(c)(2).

Low High School Graduation Rate

Comments: Some commenters opposed the 67 percent graduation rate threshold for identification of high schools for comprehensive support and improvement, particularly if applied to dropout recovery high schools. Another commenter recommended identifying for comprehensive support and improvement the lowest 10 percent of high schools based on graduation rates, similar to the requirement that States identify the lowest-performing five percent of all title I schools.

Discussion: The regulations are consistent with section 1111(c)(4)(D)(i)(II) of the ESEA, as amended by the ESSA, which requires States to identify all public high schools in the State that fail to graduate one-third or more of their students. Section 200.18(d)(1)(iii), which contains provisions that were included in proposed § 299.17, allows a State to use a differentiated accountability approach for schools that serve special populations, including dropout recovery high schools.

Changes: None.

Comments: A number of commenters supported the Department's proposal to require States to consider only the four-year adjusted cohort graduation rate in identifying low graduation rate high schools for comprehensive support and improvement and to permit a State to set a threshold higher than 67 percent in identifying such schools. One commenter suggested that the Department clarify that the threshold for such determination was inclusive of schools with a graduation rate of 67 percent, rather than just schools with graduation rates below 67 percent, and that this criterion applies to all public high schools in the State, not just those that receive funds under title I of the ESEA.

Discussion: We appreciate the commenters' support for the exclusive use of the four-year adjusted cohort graduation rate in identifying low graduation rate high schools and agree that a school with a graduation rate of 67 percent must be identified, consistent with the statutory requirement that the State identify each public high school that fails to graduate one third or more of its students; we are revising the regulations to clarify this point. However, we do not believe it is necessary to further clarify that States must identify all public low graduation rate high schools, not just schools receiving title I funds, for comprehensive support and improvement, given that the statute and regulations are clear on this point.

Changes: We have revised § 200.19(a)(2) to specify that a high school with a four-year adjusted cohort graduation rate at or below 67 percent must be identified for comprehensive support and improvement.

Comments: Several commenters suggested that the regulations be modified to allow States to identify low graduation rate high schools based on the four-year adjusted cohort graduation rate, an extended-year adjusted cohort graduation rate, or a combination of these rates. Similarly, one commenter suggested that a State be allowed to use an extended-year adjusted cohort graduation rate for this purpose, provided the State sets a higher graduation rate threshold (e.g., 70 percent) for identifying schools based on an extended-year rate.

Some commenters believe that an extended-year adjusted cohort graduation rate is a more appropriate measure because it would recognize the importance of serving students who may take longer than four years to graduate. Many of these commenters suggested that the use of the four-year adjusted cohort graduation rate only to identify schools is inconsistent with the inclusion, at the State's discretion, of extended-year adjusted cohort graduation rates in the calculation of long-term goals, measurements of interim progress, and indicators under section 1111(c)(4)(A)(i)(I)(bb)(BB) and 1111(c)(4)(B)(iii)(II) of the ESEA and proposed §§ 200.13-200.14. Some of these commenters also stated that the statute's silence on the rate to be used for purposes of identifying schools should be interpreted as providing States flexibility in this area.

Commenters were particularly concerned that identifying schools based solely on the four-year adjusted cohort graduation rate would discourage schools from serving over-age or under-credited youth who may take longer than four years to graduate, is inconsistent with many States' provision of a Free Appropriate Public Education (FAPE) until a student turns 21, and would inappropriately identify alternative schools such as dropout recovery schools, schools for students in neglected or delinquent facilities, and schools for recently arrived immigrants. One commenter stated the proposed regulations were inconsistent with title IV of the ESEA, which creates a priority for charter schools to serve students at risk of dropping out or who have dropped out of school (Section 4303(g)(2)(E) of the ESEA) and with the Workforce Innovation and Opportunity Act (WIOA), which encourages schools and States to reengage out of school youth and provide a high school diploma as a preferred credential for those aged 16 to 24. Another commenter recommended that the Department allow dropout recovery schools to collect and report one-year graduation rates in place of the four-year and extended-year adjusted cohort graduation rates because using even the extended-year rate would over-identify such schools.

A few commenters noted that the Department previously recognized the need for flexibility under its 2008 title I regulations by allowing States to use a four-year adjusted cohort rate and an extended-year adjusted cohort graduation rate in calculating AYP for high schools. Other commenters suggested that a more nuanced approach that allowed a State to use an extended-year rate for certain alternative education programs would be appropriate. One commenter noted that, under the proposed regulations, nearly all of the alternative high schools in its State would be identified.

Discussion: We agree with commenters that it is vital for States, LEAs, and schools to serve students who have been traditionally underserved because of their age or lack of credits, and that programs and priorities like those in title IV of the ESEA and the WIOA are essential to support these students. However, we also seek to ensure that States identify and support high schools that fail to graduate one-third of their students, as required by section 1111(c)(4)(D)(i)(II) of the ESEA, as amended by the ESSA. The four-year adjusted cohort graduation rate is the primary measure of graduation rates within the statewide accountability system, including the Graduation Rate indicator, long-term goals, and measurements of interim progress. Therefore, identifying low graduation rate high schools using the four-year adjusted cohort graduation rate is critical to ensuring that when schools fail to graduate one-third of their students, they are identified and receive appropriate and meaningful supports so that each of their students can graduate. Indeed, using the four-year adjusted cohort graduation rate is essential to helping ensure that low graduation rate high schools are identified and receive appropriate and meaningful supports, even if a State establishes a graduation rate threshold that is higher than 67 percent.

However, we recognize that for a small subset of schools that serve unique populations of students, an extended-year rate may be a more appropriate indicator of a school's performance, and we have revised § 200.18(d)(1)(iii) to clarify that States have flexibility to develop and implement alternate accountability methods—which may include the use of extended-year graduation rates—for schools designed to serve special student populations, including alternative schools, dropout recovery programs, and schools for neglected and delinquent youth. Under this provision, a State could, for example, propose through its State plan to use a five- or six-year adjusted cohort graduation rate to determine if an alternative or dropout recovery school's graduation rate was 67 percent or less for the purposes of identifying those schools.

Given this flexibility, the Department does not believe that requiring States to use the four-year adjusted cohort graduation rate will result in the inappropriate or over-identification of schools that primarily serve special populations of students.

Further, in response to commenters who noted the statute's silence on the particular rate to use for identification of low graduation rate high schools, given the Secretary's rulemaking authority under GEPA, the DEOA, and section 1601(a) of the ESEA, as amended by the ESSA (see discussion of the Department's general rulemaking authority under the heading Cross-Cutting Issues), it is not necessary for the statute to specifically authorize the Secretary to issue a particular regulatory provision. Moreover, we do not agree that Congress' silence on which graduation rate is to be used for purposes of identifying schools precludes the Department from clarifying the requirement. To the contrary, given the specific references to extended-year rates in the statutory provisions regarding goals, measurements of interim progress, and accountability indicators, it seems clear that if Congress intended to permit States to use an extended-year rate for purposes of identifying schools, it would have specified. Accordingly, we believe that the clarification in § 200.19(a)(2) that identification of low graduation rate high schools is to be based on the four-year adjusted cohort graduation rate falls squarely within the scope of section 1111(c) of the ESEA, as amended by the ESSA, consistent with section 1111(e) and is reasonably necessary to ensure compliance with the requirements in section 1111(c)(4)(D)(i)(II) and, as such, constitutes an appropriate exercise of the Department's rulemaking authority.

Changes: None.

Comments: Some commenters suggested that the Department allow States, in identifying low graduation rate high schools, to use a non-cohort graduation rate or to include students who attain an alternate diploma in determining if a school's graduation rate was 67 percent or less. Another commenter requested that the Department allow States to include students who have met all the terms of their IEPs as graduates.

Discussion: While we understand the commenters' interest in recognizing the support schools provide to all students, regardless of whether those students receive a regular high school diploma, sections 8101(23)(A)(ii) and 8101(25)(A)(ii) of the ESEA and related regulations in § 200.34 already explicitly allow States to include students with the most significant cognitive disabilities who take an alternate assessment based on alternative academic achievement standards, meet certain other criteria, and receive an alternate diploma, in the State's adjusted cohort graduation rate or rates. The statute expressly prohibits States from including students that earn a high school equivalency diploma or other alternate diploma in the State's adjusted cohort graduation rate or rates. Therefore, we decline to allow States to use measures other than the four-year or extended-year adjusted cohort graduation rates, calculated consistently with the statutory and regulatory requirements, to identify high schools for the purposes of comprehensive support and improvement.

Changes: None.

Chronically Low-Performing Subgroup

Comments: Some commenters asserted that the Department created a third category of comprehensive support schools, those with chronically low-performing subgroups, that was not in the statute. One commenter proposed making it clear that it was up to States to include this category of schools through the development of a State plan. Another commenter noted the statute uses the term consistently underperforming subgroup, but does not refer to chronically low-performing subgroups.

One commenter suggested that the Department reconsider its definition of chronically low-performing subgroup schools and move this definition into non-regulatory guidance. The commenter is concerned that this requirement, in conjunction with other provisions in this section, will result in very high rates of identification of schools for comprehensive support and improvement.

Discussion: The chart at the beginning of this section provides a reference guide on the types of schools that must be identified for comprehensive support and improvement or targeted support and improvement under the law. With respect to "chronically low-performing subgroups," that term is not specifically used in the statute but is the term we are using in the regulations to identify a category of schools described in two sections of the ESEA. Section 1111(d)(2)(C) of the ESEA, as amended by the ESSA, requires each State to identify schools with low-performing subgroups (i.e., those with subgroups who, on their own, are performing as poorly as the lowest-performing five percent of all title I schools) for targeted support and improvement and these schools also must receive additional targeted support. Section 1111(c)(4)(D)(i)(III) then states that if these schools do not improve after implementing a targeted support and improvement plan over a number of years, they must be identified for comprehensive support and improvement. When these schools are first identified for targeted support and improvement, they are referred to in the regulations as schools with "low-performing subgroups"; however, if they do not improve over a State-determined number of years, they must be identified for comprehensive support and improvement. The Department is referring to these schools as schools with "chronically low-performing subgroups" for the sake of clarity because the statute does not provide a specific term for them and a term is needed to clarify for States their statutory obligations with respect to these schools.

Changes: None.

Comments: Several commenters opposed the proposed requirement that States identify for comprehensive support and improvement any title I school with a low-performing subgroup that has not improved after implementing a targeted support and improvement plan over no more than three years. In particular, commenters believed that the proposed requirement would force States to set a three-year timeline for the exit criteria for a school with a low-performing subgroup and would likely result in the over-identification of schools with chronically low-performing subgroups. The commenters referred to section 1111(d)(3)(A)(i)(II) of the ESEA, as amended by the ESSA, which requires States to set exit criteria for schools with low-performing subgroups and to determine the number of years by which, if such a school is a title I school that has not met the exit criteria, it must be identified for comprehensive support and improvement. One commenter suggested, in addition to modifying the regulations to reflect that the State determine the number of years before a school with a low performing subgroup be identified for comprehensive support, that States publish a list, at least once every three years, of the schools with low-performing subgroups that are identified for targeted support and improvement that also must receive additional targeted support because they have one or more low-performing subgroups that are still identified as such because they have not yet met the State's exit criteria. Another commenter stated that three years was too long to permit a school to languish as a school receiving additional targeted support before it is identified for comprehensive support, and would result in students in such schools not receiving timely support.

Discussion: Section 1111(c)(4)(D)(i)(III) requires States to identify schools with chronically low-performing subgroups for comprehensive support and improvement at least once every three years. Section 1111(d)(3)(A)(i)(II) authorizes States to establish statewide exit criteria for such schools. Under this same section, if those criteria are not satisfied in a State-determined number of years, those schools that receive title I funds must be identified for comprehensive support and improvement. The final regulations reflect these statutory requirements. Within these requirements, States still have discretion regarding the timelines and exit criteria. Thus, we encourage each State to carefully consider the various timelines for school identification it must implement to meet its statutory and regulatory obligations. Finally, we do not believe that an additional reporting requirement is necessary as States and LEAs must annually publish State and local report cards that include information about schools identified for support and improvement, including those with low-performing or chronically low-performing subgroups.

Changes: The Department has revised § 200.19(a)(3) to clarify that States determine the number of years over which a school with a low-performing subgroup identified for targeted support under § 200.19(b)(2) may implement a targeted support plan before the State must determine that the school has not met the State's exit criteria and, if it receives title I funds, identify the school for comprehensive support and improvement. We have made a corresponding change to § 200.22(f)(2).

Comments: One commenter opposed the requirement that a school be identified for comprehensive support and improvement if a single subgroup's low performance would lead to such identification. In particular, the commenter was concerned that requiring a school with a single low-performing subgroup to be identified for comprehensive support and improvement would dilute State support services and funding, diminishing support for schools with greater needs.

Discussion: The identification of schools with chronically low-performing subgroups for comprehensive support and improvement if they do not improve after implementing a targeted support and improvement plan over a State-determined number of years is required by section 1111(c)(4)(D)(i)(III) of the ESEA, as amended by the ESSA, and reflects the key focus of title I on closing educational achievement gaps.

Changes: None.

Targeted Support and Improvement, in General

Comments: One commenter suggested that the Department amend proposed § 200.19(b) to encourage States to consider third-grade reading scores as one measure that can trigger the need for targeted support.

Discussion: The Department recognizes that there are a wide range of measures that States may choose to incorporate into their systems of annual meaningful differentiation of schools, including for purposes of identifying schools for targeted support and improvement, but we believe the inclusion of any additional measures should be left to State discretion.

Changes: None.

Comments: Several commenters recommended that the Department remove proposed § 200.19(b) and allow States to determine the parameters for identifying schools for targeted support and improvement. Some of these commenters argued that the proposed regulations would result in the identification of more schools than required by the statute. One commenter was concerned that the number of schools identified within this category would overwhelm State title I staff that support school improvement, leading to inadequate support for such schools. Another commenter noted that the law requires identification of the lowest-performing five percent of title I schools, but failed to recognize the law also requires identifying schools for targeted support, and said that the proposed regulations require school identification based on subgroup status, which would result in States exceeding what the commenter believed to be a statutory limit of five percent. One commenter asserted that proposed § 200.19(b) violated section 1111(e)(1)(B)(iii)(V) of the ESEA because it specifies requirements for differentiating schools for targeted support and improvement.

Discussion: Section 1111(c)(4)(C)(iii) and section 1111(d)(2)(A) of the ESEA, as amended by the ESSA, require a State to use its method for annual meaningful differentiation, based on all indicators, to identify any public school in which one or more subgroups of students is consistently underperforming, so that the LEA for the school can ensure that the school develops a targeted support and improvement plan. Section 1111(d)(2)(D) further requires that, if a subgroup of students in a school, on its own, has performed as poorly as all students in the lowest-performing five percent of title I schools that have been identified for comprehensive support and improvement, the school must be identified for targeted support and improvement and implement additional targeted supports, as described in section 1111(d)(2)(C). Given these explicit statutory requirements regarding the schools that must be identified for targeted support and improvement, which are incorporated into § 200.19(b), we disagree with commenters who asserted that the requirements in this regulatory provision are not explicitly authorized by the statute. Further, we disagree with comments asserting that § 200.19(b) is inconsistent with section 1111(e)(1)(B)(iii)(V) of the ESEA; § 200.19(b) does not prescribe a specific methodology to meaningfully differentiate or identify schools. Rather, it simply clarifies the two types of schools that the statute requires to be identified for targeted support and improvement. States retain flexibility to determine precisely how they will identify these schools. For example, States have discretion to determine how they will identify schools with subgroups that are performing as poorly as schools that are in the lowest-performing five percent of title I schools. Although we appreciate the commenters' concerns about the limited capacity of States and LEAs to support all identified schools, because the requirements regarding which schools to identify for targeted support and improvement are statutory (section 1111(d)(2)(A) and (D) of the ESEA), we decline to make the suggested changes. However, we recognize that language in § 200.19(b)(1) allowing States to identify, at the State's discretion, schools that miss the 95 percent participation rate requirement for all students or a subgroup of students, within the category of schools with consistently underperforming subgroups identified for targeted support, conflated a statutory requirement and regulatory flexibility. While, under § 200.15(b)(2)(iii), States retain the option to identify such schools for targeted support and to require these schools to implement the requirements under § 200.22, we are removing the reference to these schools in § 200.19(b)(1) because schools with low participation rates may not necessarily meet the State's definition of consistently underperforming subgroups.

Changes: We have removed language in § 200.19(b)(1) that referred to schools identified under § 200.15(b)(2)(iii).

Low-Performing Subgroup

Comments: One commenter was concerned that the requirement to identify schools with subgroups performing as poorly as the lowest-performing five percent of title I schools would require States to generate summative ratings for individual subgroups of students. The commenter noted that under ESEA flexibility, the commenter's State identified the lowest-achieving five percent of schools solely on the basis of academic proficiency rates of the all students group. Another commenter noted that the statute refers to subgroups performing as low as the lowest-performing five percent of title I schools, but does not require that States look at the results for the all students group or use a summative rating in identifying schools.

Discussion: We understand the commenters' concern that a State may need to undertake additional analysis at the subgroup level to identify when an individual subgroup is performing as poorly as students in the lowest-performing five percent of title I schools. The statute requires that States identify schools based on its system of annual meaningful differentiation which relies on multiple measures; therefore, an approach that only considered academic proficiency rates would be inconsistent with the ESEA, as amended by the ESSA. We generally agree with the commenters that States may take different approaches to identify a school with at least one subgroup that is as low performing as the lowest-performing five percent of title I schools, but section 1111(d)(2)(C) requires that a State identify schools with low-performing subgroups based on the same methodology it uses to identify the lowest-performing five percent of title I schools. We are revising the regulations to clarify that States must use the same approach to identify schools with low-performing subgroups as they do to identify the lowest-performing five percent of all title I schools.

The regulations do not require reporting of subgroup-specific summative determinations. However, they do require a consistent approach in order to ensure that States are meeting the requirement in section 1111(d)(2)(C) of the ESEA, as amended by the ESSA, to identify each school with an individual subgroup whose performance on its own would result in the school's identification in the lowest-performing five percent of title I schools.

Changes: We have revised § 200.19(b)(2) to remove the requirement that a State compare each subgroup's performance to the summative rating (now summative determination in the final regulations) of all students in the lowest-performing five percent of title I schools in order to identify schools with low-performing subgroups. Instead, States must use the same methodology they use to identify the lowest-performing five percent of title I schools under § 200.19(a)(1) to identify schools with low-performing subgroups.

Comments: One commenter stated that the proposed regulations helped clarify the statutory requirements around identifying schools for targeted support and improvement and additional targeted support, but encouraged the Department to provide States with additional flexibility in identifying such schools. A few commenters objected to the Department's proposed definition of low-performing subgroups. They said the proposed definition ignores statutory provisions that limit this group of schools to a subset of those identified for targeted support and improvement because they also include consistently underperforming subgroups. Other commenters suggested that the requirement to separately identify schools for targeted support and improvement and additional targeted support is inconsistent with the statute. Some commenters believed that the statute does not contain the requirement for two separate sets of schools, and that the proposed requirements require separate identification on separate timelines, adding significant complexity to accountability systems.

Discussion: Section 1111(c)(4)(C)(iii) of the ESEA, as amended by the ESSA, requires each State to annually identify schools with consistently underperforming subgroups for targeted support and improvement. Separately, section 1111(d)(2)(C) requires each State to identify for targeted support and improvement schools with any subgroup of students that, on its own, would have resulted in a school's identification as one of the lowest-performing five percent of title I schools in the State that are identified for comprehensive support and improvement. These schools must receive additional targeted support under the law and are described as schools with low-performing subgroups in the regulations. We, therefore, believe that these requirements are wholly consistent with the identification requirements and methodologies specified in the ESEA, as amended by the ESSA.

Changes: None.

Comments: One commenter expressed concern that the proposed requirements for identifying schools with low-performing subgroups that receive targeted support and improvement, as well as additional targeted support, might not be appropriate for high schools, because most high schools do not receive title I funds and, therefore, the lowest-performing five percent of title I schools may not contain any high schools. The commenter recommended that, for the purpose of identifying schools with low-performing subgroups at the high school level, States be permitted to measure subgroup performance against the lowest-performing five percent of all high schools or high-poverty high schools, rather than comparing performance only to those high schools identified in the lowest-performing five percent of schools that receive title I funds.

Discussion: We appreciate the commenter's concern that there may be few high schools identified within a State's lowest-performing five percent of title I schools, but section 1111(d)(2)(C) expressly requires that a State identify for targeted support and improvement any school with a subgroup that, on its own, would have resulted in the school's identification as a school in the lowest-performing five percent of title I schools. For this reason, the Department declines to make the suggested change.

Changes: None.

Comments: One commenter was unclear about whether, in identifying schools with low-performing subgroups, the State should be comparing a subgroup's performance to the performance of the all students group on individual accountability indicators, or on the indicators collectively. The commenter suggested the Department clarify the requirements for school identification broadly, but particularly in this area.

Discussion: We appreciate the commenter's request for clarification. We are revising § 200.19(b)(2) to specify that schools with low-performing subgroups must be identified using all indicators and the same methodology the State uses to identify its lowest-performing five percent of title I schools. We will consider providing further clarification in non-regulatory guidance to support States in identifying each group of schools, consistent with applicable statutory and regulatory requirements.

Changes: We have revised § 200.19(b)(2) to clarify that schools with low-performing subgroups are identified by applying the State's methodology for identifying its lowest-performing schools to individual subgroups.

Comments: Several commenters expressed concern that the lack of a cap on the number of schools that could be identified as having low-performing subgroups that receive targeted support and improvement, as well as additional targeted support, may result in exceeding a State's capacity to support effective school improvement or hindering efforts to create robust statewide systems of support that are tailored to local needs and goals. Some commenters suggested capping the number of schools that could be identified for targeted support and improvement at five to ten percent of title I schools.

Discussion: Under the regulations, as under the statute, States have flexibility to design their systems for annual meaningful differentiation in a way that takes into account the requirement to address the needs of low-performing subgroups as well as State capacity to support meaningful and effective school improvement. Given that the ESEA, as amended by the ESSA, requires identification of all schools that fall within the various identification categories, we do not believe that providing a cap on the number or percentage of schools that are identified for targeted support and improvement, as well as additional targeted support, would be consistent with the statute.

Changes: None.

Comments: One commenter expressed concern that setting a threshold at the lowest-performing five percent of title I schools to identify schools with low-performing subgroups for targeted support and improvement that also receive additional targeted support could be detrimental to students with disabilities because it might not require a generally high-performing school to address the needs of a particular subgroup until its performance dropped to the level of the lowest-performing five percent of title I schools.

Discussion: We believe that the concerns of the commenter are addressed in significant part by the requirements that States identify any schools with a consistently underperforming subgroup and schools with a low-performing subgroup for targeted support and improvement. This requirement will help ensure that any school in which the students with disabilities subgroup is underperforming receives support even if the subgroup is not performing as poorly as the lowest-performing five percent of title I schools.

Changes: None.

Methodology To Identify Consistently Underperforming Subgroups

Comments: Many commenters supported proposed § 200.19(c)(1), which requires States to consider each subgroup's performance over no more than two years in identifying schools with consistently underperforming subgroups for targeted support and improvement, because the regulation would ensure prompt recognition of underperforming subgroups so that students in those subgroups receive timely and appropriate supports to improve student outcomes, particularly because many of these subgroups have been historically underserved. However, many commenters opposed two years as an arbitrary timeline for identifying consistently underperforming subgroups. Others stated that the Department was exceeding its legal authority, with some of these commenters pointing specifically to section 1111(e)(1)(B)(iii)(V) of the ESEA, as amended by the ESSA, which provides that nothing in the ESEA authorizes or permits the Department to prescribe the specific methodology used by States to meaningfully differentiate or identify schools under title I, part A. Some of these commenters noted that identifying schools with a single subgroup underperforming for only two years would result in the over-identification of schools, replicate the identification of schools under NCLB, and overstretch the capacity of States and districts to support identified schools. One commenter also noted that using just two years of data could increase the likelihood of misidentification because the State would not be able to ensure that the data used was valid and reliable. These commenters generally suggested that the Department remove all specific timeline considerations from the requirements.

As an alternative, one commenter suggested that a State be permitted to identify schools based on whether an individual subgroup had been low-performing on the majority of current year indicators or demonstrated low levels of performance on the same indicator over three years, consistent with the flexibility for States to average a school's data over three years under proposed § 200.20. One other commenter suggested requiring a State to consider at least three years of data in identifying schools with consistently underperforming subgroups, while another suggested allowing a State to determine its own timeline of no more than four years, consistent with other requirements to identify schools and evaluate a school's performance on relevant exit criteria after no more than four years.

Discussion: The Department appreciates support from commenters who agreed that identifying schools with consistently underperforming subgroups based on two years of data is essential to ensuring prompt recognition of, and support for, such subgroups of students. We believe that this benefit, which is consistent with the focus of title I on closing achievement gaps, outweighs the risk of over-identifying schools, particularly because a longer timeline could permit entire cohorts of low-performing students to exit a school before the school is identified for targeted support and improvement. However, we appreciate that a State may, due to the specific design of the State's accountability system, require flexibility in order to consider the performance of subgroups of students over more than two years. We, therefore, have revised the regulations to permit a State to consider student performance over more than two years, in certain circumstances. Specifically, to ensure that students in subgroups that are underperforming in schools that have not yet been identified for targeted support and improvement will receive support and that a State will meet the requirement in section 1111(c)(4)(A)(i)(III) of the ESEA, as amended by the ESSA, we are revising § 200.19(c)(1) to require that a State that proposes to use a longer timeframe demonstrate how the longer timeframe will better support low-performing subgroups of students to make significant progress in achieving long-term goals and measurements of interim progress, in order to close statewide proficiency and graduation rate gaps. In response to commenters who believe that provisions in § 200.19(c)(1) were not explicitly authorized in the statutory text, these regulations are being issued in accordance with the Secretary's rulemaking authority under GEPA, the DEOA, and section 1601(a) of the ESEA, as amended by the ESSA, and need not be specifically authorized by the statutory text. Further, issuing this requirement is a proper exercise of the Department's rulemaking authority as revised § 200.19(c)(1) falls squarely within the scope of, and is necessary to reasonably ensure compliance with section 1111(c)(4), which requires statewide accountability systems to be designed to improve student academic achievement and school success, as well as with the purpose of title I of the ESEA, to provide all children significant opportunity to receive a high-quality education and to close educational achievement gaps. For these reasons, the regulation does not violate section 1111(e) of the ESEA, as amended by the ESSA. Moreover, we do not agree that proposed or revised § 200.19(c)(1) is inconsistent with section 1111(e)(1)(B)(iii)(V) because the regulation does not require the State to use a specific methodology in identifying schools with consistently underperforming subgroups. More specifically, revised § 200.19(c)(1) permits a State to consider subgroup performance over a longer timeframe if it makes the required demonstration.

Changes: Section 200.19(c)(1) has been revised to allow a State, in order to identify schools with one or more consistently underperforming subgroups, to consider a school's performance among each subgroup of students in the school over more than two years, if the State demonstrates that a longer timeframe will better support low-performing subgroups of students to make significant progress in achieving long-term goals and measurements of interim progress in order to close statewide proficiency and graduation rate gaps, consistent with section 1111(c)(4)(A)(i)(III) of the

Act and § 200.13.

Comments: A few commenters supported the proposed definitions, including the option for a State-determined definition, of consistently underperforming subgroups under § 200.19(c)(3). Some commenters recommended removing all of the proposed definitions in § 200.19(c)(3) because the Department does not have the authority to require States to choose one of these definitions. Others suggested that the Department make it clear that the proposed definitions are optional. These commenters generally cited section 1111(c)(4)(C)(iii) of the ESEA, as amended by the ESSA, which allows a State to determine what constitutes consistent underperformance, and one commenter cited section 1111(e)(1)(B)(iii)(V) of the ESEA, as amended by the ESSA, which provides that nothing in the ESEA authorizes the Secretary to prescribe the specific methodology States use to meaningfully differentiate schools.

Discussion: The Department's regulations provide States with a number of options for identifying schools with consistently underperforming subgroups of students in a way that promotes equity and ensures compliance with one of the stated purposes of title I—to close educational achievement gaps—as well as with the requirement for accountability systems to be designed to improve student academic achievement and school success. The regulations allow a State to propose its own definition of consistently underperforming subgroups, so long as that definition considers each school's performance among each subgroup of students and is based on all the indicators used for annual meaningful differentiation, consistent with the weighting requirements for such indicators. As such, the regulation is a proper exercise of the Department's rulemaking authority (see further discussion under the heading Cross-Cutting Issues). We do not agree that § 200.19(c)(3) is inconsistent with section 1111(c)(4)(C)(iii) or 1111(e)(1)(B)(iii)(V) of the ESEA, as amended by the ESSA, because the regulation does not require the State to use a specific methodology in identifying schools with consistently underperforming subgroups.

However, in reviewing the comments, the Department has determined that some of the definitions proposed in § 200.19(c)(3) were unclear or inconsistent with the proposed requirement in § 200.19(c)(2) to consider each indicator used for annual meaningful differentiation. Accordingly, we are revising § 200.19(c)(2)-(3) for clarity to ensure that: (1) Each State's methodology to identify schools with a consistently underperforming subgroup must be based on all indicators a State uses for annual meaningful differentiation; and (2) States defining consistently underperforming subgroups on the basis of long-term goals or measurements of interim progress also consider indicators for which the State is not required to establish goals or measurements of interim progress. In this way, States defining a consistently underperforming subgroup on the basis of its long-term goals and indicators can, for example, develop a methodology that considers all goals and indicators, even if identification for targeted support and improvement is made only on the basis of a single goal or indicator.

Changes: We have revised § 200.19(c)(2)-(3) to clarify that all definitions of consistently underperforming subgroups must be based on all indicators in the accountability system, so that a State's methodology examines a school's performance across all indicators, even if a subgroup's performance against the State's measurements of interim progress and long-term goals or performance on a single indicator is sufficient to trigger identification of the school for targeted support and improvement.

Comments: Several commenters specifically opposed the options for defining consistently underperforming subgroups of students in proposed § 200.19(c)(3)(ii)-(iv), because States would be able to use a definition that includes a relative threshold for identification rather than an absolute standard and, consequently, only schools with the very lowest-performing subgroups would be identified.

Discussion: We appreciate the commenters' concern that the use of a relative measure may narrow the definition of consistently underperforming subgroups depending on the range of performance across measures within a State. Therefore, while we are retaining a State's flexibility to propose a State-determined definition, we are removing the proposed options for identifying consistently underperforming subgroups of students that included relative measures, such as the size of performance gaps between the subgroup and State averages.

Changes: We have removed the definitions in proposed § 200.19(c)(ii) through (iv) of the final regulations.

Comments: Many commenters suggested requiring all States to consider a subgroup's performance against the State's long-term goals and measurements of interim progress, as described under 200.19(c)(3)(i), in determining whether a subgroup is consistently underperforming.

Discussion: Sections 1111(c)(4)(C)(iii) and 1111(d)(2)(A) of the ESEA, as amended by the ESSA, require that States consider a subgroup's performance on all of the indicators in identifying schools with consistently underperforming subgroups for targeted support and improvement. Because only two of these indicators—the Academic Achievement indicator and the Graduation Rate indicator—must be based on a State's long term goals and measurements of interim progress, a methodology for identifying consistently underperforming subgroups that looked only at long-term goals or measurements of interim progress would not be consistent with the statute.

Changes: None.

Comments: One commenter suggested that the Department provide States with two additional options for identifying consistently underperforming subgroups: (1) Comparing a subgroup's performance against the average performance among all students, or the highest performing subgroup, in the school, and (2) comparing a subgroup's performance against the all students group, or the highest performing subgroup, in the LEA. The commenter also recommended that these additional options be used in tandem with a method based on an absolute measure, such as a subgroup's performance against a State's long-term goals and measurements of interim progress.

Discussion: We appreciate the commenter's suggestion and believe that a State could propose either of the options suggested by the commenter under final § 200.19(c)(3)(ii) so long as its proposal also met the requirements of 200.19(c)(1)-(2). A State could also propose to use one of these options in concert with a subgroup's performance against a State's long-term goals and measurements of interim progress. Because these approaches could already be proposed by a State as part of a State-determined definition of consistently underperforming subgroup, we decline to add these specific options to the regulations.

Changes: None.

Comments: While a few commenters recommended that the Department remove the requirement under proposed § 200.19(c)(2) regarding the use of indicators, other commenters asked the Department to clarify that States must consider a subgroup's performance on each indicator, including indicators of School Quality or Student Success, in determining which schools have consistently underperforming subgroups. Specifically, commenters were concerned that a State could consider performance only on a single indicator, such as Academic Achievement, but not other indicators in identifying schools with consistently underperforming subgroups.

Discussion: As previously discussed in the second summary of changes in the "Methodology to Identify Consistently Underperforming Subgroups", the Department has modified the regulations to clarify that a State must establish a definition of consistently underperforming subgroups that is based on all of the indicators, and that a school need not be underperforming on every indicator in order to be identified for targeted support and improvement. In other words, although a State's definition must examine a subgroup's performance on all indicators, a school may be identified based on having a subgroup that is underperforming on any one (or more) of those indicators. For example, although a State cannot systematically look only at each subgroup's performance on the Academic Achievement indicator to identify schools with low-performing subgroups (it must look at performance on all the indicators under § 200.14), it may identify an individual school for targeted support and improvement if a subgroup in that school is underperforming on the Academic Achievement indicator. We appreciate the commenters' concern that this requirement was not sufficiently clear in the proposed regulations.

Changes: We have revised § 200.19(c)(2)-(3) to clarify that all definitions of consistently underperforming subgroups must be based on all indicators in the accountability system, such that a State's methodology examines performance across all indicators, even if a subgroup's performance against the State's measurements of interim progress and long-term goals or low performance on a single indicator is sufficient to trigger identification of the school for targeted support and improvement.

Comments: A few commenters suggested that the Department require a State's definition of consistently underperforming subgroups to result in the identification of more schools for targeted support and improvement than the State identifies for targeted support and improvement due to low-performing subgroups.

Discussion: The statute requires each State to identify two categories of schools—those with consistently underperforming subgroups for targeted support and improvement and those with low-performing subgroups for targeted support and improvement that must also receive additional targeted support. We believe requiring one group to be larger than the other would be arbitrary and inconsistent with the requirements to identify all schools that meet the applicable definitions. Consequently, we decline to set parameters around the number of schools that must be identified in either category.

Changes: None.

Comments: One commenter suggested requiring that a State's method for identifying consistently underperforming subgroups be understandable by all stakeholders to promote transparency.

Discussion: We agree that it is important for stakeholders, including schools, educators, and parents to understand a State's methodology for identifying consistently underperforming subgroups. In its State plan and in the description of its system of annual meaningful differentiation on its State report card under § 200.30, each State must describe its methodology for identifying schools with consistently underperforming subgroups. Therefore, we decline to add an additional consultation or reporting requirement.

Changes: None.

Timeline

Comments: One commenter supported the proposed requirements in § 200.19(d)(1) that States must identify: (1) Schools for comprehensive support and improvement at least once every three years, beginning with identification for the 2017-2018 school year; (2) schools with one or more consistently underperforming subgroups for targeted support and improvement annually, beginning with identification for the 2018-2019 school year; and (3) schools with one or more low-performing subgroups for targeted support and improvement that must also receive additional targeted support when it identifies schools for comprehensive support and improvement, beginning with identification for the 2017-2018 school year. Many commenters, however, strongly opposed the proposed timelines because they would require States to use data from the 2016-2017 school year to identify schools by the beginning of the 2017-2018 school year. These commenters generally encouraged the Department to move the timeline back one year, so that States must identify schools for the first time by the beginning of the 2018-2019 school year. A handful of commenters also encouraged the Department to move the timeline for identifying schools with consistently underperforming subgroups for targeted support and improvement back one year, to the beginning of the 2019-2020 school year.

Commenters believed that the delayed timelines they proposed were necessary to allow States to engage in more robust consultation with stakeholders, to better align with the Department's intended State plan submission and review timeline, and to ensure consistency with sections 1111(c)(4)(D)(i) and 1111(d)(2)(D) of the ESEA, as amended by the ESSA. In particular, commenters were concerned that schools would be identified on the basis of results generated under States' prior accountability systems, using existing indicators with a heavy emphasis on test-based data, rather than the broader range of academic and non-academic indicators required by the ESEA, as amended by the ESSA. They suggested that the originally proposed timeline would not allow States to meaningfully establish systems—including taking the time to design new indicators to satisfy the requirements of the Student Success or School Quality indicator—and collect information on new indicators that had not previously been part of the accountability system.

Some commenters also encouraged the Department to allow States, under the proposed extended implementation timelines, to maintain their lists of identified schools from the 2016-2017 school year into the 2017-2018 school year consistent with the flexibility for the 2016-2017 school year under the ESSA transition provisions.

Discussion: We agree that extending the timelines for identification of schools for improvement would better support full and effective implementation of the statewide accountability systems, consistent with the requirements of the ESEA, as amended by the ESSA, and are revising the regulations accordingly. The Department also anticipates releasing non-regulatory guidance to support States in using the 2017-2018 school year as a transition year, and to ensure that States continue to support low-performing schools during this time.

Changes: We have revised § 200.19(d), and made conforming revisions throughout the final regulations, to allow States to: (1) Identify schools for comprehensive support and improvement no later than the beginning of the 2018-2019 school year; (2) identify schools with low-performing subgroups for targeted support and improvement that also must receive additional targeted support no later than the beginning of the 2018-2019 school year, based on data from the 2017-2018 school year, and (3) allow States to identify schools with consistently underperforming subgroups for targeted support and improvement no later than the beginning of the 2019-2020 school year. We have made also made additional clarifying edits, including renumbering and reorganizing this section, that do not change the substance of the requirements. Additionally, given revisions to the deadlines for submission of consolidated State plans, if a State chose to submit its plan in the first application window, it is possible the State may be able to begin their process for identifying schools for comprehensive and targeted support and improvement sooner than the required timeline in order to take advantage of the new multi-measure accountability systems established under the ESSA more quickly.

Comments: Some commenters supported the requirement to identify schools for comprehensive and targeted support and improvement by the beginning of the school year in order to give schools sufficient notice and planning time to implement appropriate interventions. One commenter recommended moving identification up by one week so that teachers know a school's status before school starts.

Other commenters opposed the requirement to identify schools by the beginning of each school year, primarily because they believed the requirement does not take into account State timelines for the collection, validation, and reporting of the data that will be used to identify schools. Some commenters recommended alternatives to the requirement that States identify schools by the beginning of the school year. For example, some commenters suggested requiring that schools be identified no later than one month after school starts, by the end of the first quarter of the school year, in the fall, by December 31 of each year, or on a State-determined timeline developed in consultation with stakeholders and submitted with State plans.

Some commenters opposed any specific timeline for school identification because they asserted the statute does not identify a point during the school year by which identification must occur.

Discussion: While we understand the challenges associated with making accountability decisions by the beginning of the school year, we believe that, given the time required for planning and implementing high-quality school improvement plans that include meaningful consultation with stakeholders, it is imperative that districts and schools know they have been identified for comprehensive or targeted support and improvement before the beginning of the school year. To that point, we are revising the regulation to clarify that it is preferable for State to identify schools as soon as possible, particularly so LEA and school staff have this information while they are engaged in other planning for the school year. Further, we believe that requiring identification no later than the start of the school year is necessary to reasonably ensure compliance with section 1111(d) of the ESEA, as amended by the ESSA, which requires that States develop and implement plans aimed at improving student performance. It therefore falls squarely within the scope of title I, part A of the statute, consistent with section 1111(e) of the ESEA, as amended by the ESSA, and within our rulemaking authority under GEPA, the DEOA, and section 1601(a) of the ESEA, as amended by the ESSA.

Changes: We have revised § 200.19(d)(2)(i) to clarify that a State should identify schools for comprehensive or targeted support and improvement as soon as possible, but no later than the beginning of the school year for each year in which it identifies schools.

Comments: Some commenters stated that because cohort graduation rates include students who graduate at the end of the summer following the regular school year, it would not be feasible to use graduation rate data from one school year to identify schools at the beginning of the next school year.

Discussion: We recognize that the use of the preceding year's adjusted cohort graduation rate data will be difficult given the inclusion of summer graduates. For this reason, we are revising the regulations to permit States to lag graduation rate data by one year for the purposes of school accountability, including the identification of low graduation rate high schools and calculation of the Graduation Rate indicator. Additionally, in revising these regulations, we are making additional edits to clarify and streamline the regulatory requirements for the use of preceding data in school identification.

Changes: We have revised § 200.19(d)(2) to clarify that States generally must use data from the preceding school year to identify schools for comprehensive and targeted support and improvement by the beginning of each school year, but may use data from the year immediately prior to the preceding year to calculate the Graduation Rate indicator and to identify high schools with low graduation rates for comprehensive support and improvement.

Section 200.20   Data Procedures for Annual Meaningful Differentiation and Identification of Schools

Averaging Data

Comments: None.

Discussion: The Department is concerned that the use of both the terms "combining" and "averaging" in proposed § 200.20(a) is confusing because it suggests that using data from multiple grades involves a different procedure than using data from multiple school years. Both § 200.20(a)(1) and (a)(2) enable States to include greater numbers of students and students in each subgroup in data calculations for school accountability, by adding up the total number of students in a given subgroup from the current school year and the previous two school years, and by adding the total number of students in a given subgroup across each grade in a school. For example, a State using chronic absenteeism as a School Quality or Student Success indicator and selecting to combine data across school years and grades would add the number of students in the school that missed 15 days or more in each of the past three school years, and divide that number by the total number of students in the school, summed across each of the past three years—resulting in an indicator based on averages across both school years and grades. To clarify that the data procedures for combining data across grades are the same as averaging data across grades (i.e., in both cases a State would "combine" data in order to produce an averaged result), we are revising § 200.20(a)(1) by replacing the term "averaging" with the term "combining" in each place that it appears, while maintaining the term "averaging" to describe the general concept in § 200.20(a). We are also revising § 200.20(a)(1)(A) to specifically clarify that in combining data across multiple schools years for purposes of calculating a school's performance on each indicator and determining whether a subgroup of students in a school meets the State's minimum n-size, the State's uniform procedure for combining data must sum the total number of students in each subgroup of students in a school described in § 200.16(a)(2) across all available years.

Further, as discussed in response to comments on § 200.19, we believe the proposed regulations were not sufficiently clear about which school-level data could be considered over multiple years—the measures that are included in a particular indicator used for annual meaningful differentiation, or a school's overall determination. We are revising § 200.20(a) to clarify that the indicators may be averaged over up to three school years or across all grades in a school, and that these indicators are subsequently used for differentiation and identification of schools. Further, we are revising § 200.20(a), as previously discussed in response to comments on § 200.15, to clarify that a State may average school-level data for the limited purpose of meeting the requirement in § 200.15(b)(2), and the adjusted cohort graduation rate for purposes of identifying high schools with low graduation rates. Any further clarification of these requirements will be provided in non-regulatory guidance.

Changes: We have revised § 200.20(a) to (1) be more consistent and clear in using the term "averaging" to describe generally how school-level data may be used over multiple years or school grades and "combining" to describe the procedures in § 200.20(a)(1) and (2); (2) to specify that in averaging data across years a State must sum the total number of students in each subgroup of students across all school years for purposes of calculating school performance on the indicators and whether a particular subgroup meets the State's minimum n-size; and (3) to clarify the purposes for which a State may average data across years: Calculating indicators used for annual meaningful differentiation, meeting the requirement under § 200.15(b)(2), and identifying low graduation rate high schools.

Comments: One commenter suggested that proposed § 200.20 require that the procedure used for averaging data across school years and combining data across grades be identified in LEA report cards, in addition to State report cards.

Discussion: Section 200.32(a)(3) requires each State and LEA report card to describe, as part of the description of the accountability system, the State's uniform procedure for averaging data across years or across grades consistent with § 200.20.

Changes: None.

Comments: One commenter recommended allowing States to average date used for accountability purposes for more than three school years.

Discussion: The Department's proposal gives States the flexibility to combine data across years or grades because averaging data in this manner can increase the data available to consider as part of accountability systems, both improving the reliability of accountability designations and increasing the number of subgroups in a school that meet the State's minimum n-size (e.g., because adding together up to three cohorts of students for whom there is available data potentially triples the number of students with valid data, consistent with final § 200.20(a)(1)(A)). The Department believes that averaging data over more than three school years is inconsistent with current practice and regulation, ill-aligned with the requirements for school identification under the statute (e.g., the identification of schools for comprehensive support and improvement at least once every three years), and increases the risk of inappropriately masking current-year school performance—increasing the risk that low-performing schools are not identified in a timely fashion.

Changes: None.

Comments: Commenters supported the proposed requirement that States continue to report data for a single year, without averaging, on State and LEA report cards, even if a State averages data across years. Other commenters supported the language in this section that allows States to average data across school years to meaningfully differentiate schools. Commenters noted this flexibility allows States to have more meaningful accountability determinations for smaller schools, while also minimizing the number of schools that move in or out of a particular status from year to year due to n-size limitations.

Discussion: We appreciate the commenters' support for these provisions and agree that this flexibility is an important tool for States in designing effective systems of school accountability.

Changes: None.

Comments: Some commenters felt that the ESEA, as amended by the ESSA, does not authorize the Department to regulate on data averaging and that decisions about data averaging should remain with the States. Other commenters objected to the proposed requirement that States continue to report data that is not averaged for each indicator on State and LEA report cards even if a State averages data across years for accountability purposes (§ 200.20(a)(1)(ii)(B)). The commenters asserted that reporting data that is not averaged undermines the purpose of averaging, which is to obtain a more statistically valid and reliable measure of performance than shorter timeframes such as a single year, and that States electing to average data over three years should report a rolling average for each indicator each year.

Discussion: The proposed data averaging procedures are intended to provide States with limited additional flexibility to increase the data available to consider in the accountability system, thereby improving the reliability of accountability determinations and increasing the number of subgroups in a school that meet the State's minimum n-size. These rationales are not as relevant to reporting, where the key goal is to inform parents and other stakeholders (e.g., teachers, principals or other school leaders, local administrators) of the performance of specific students rather than cohorts of students averaged over multiple years.

Further, we believe the requirement to use the same uniform data averaging procedure for all public schools is necessary to ensure that the Statewide accountability system is applied in a fair and consistent manner to all public schools in a State. Additionally, the requirement to report data for a single year, even if a State averages data for accountability purposes, is necessary to ensure compliance with the requirement in section 1111(h) of the ESEA that report cards be presented in an "understandable and uniform format." Accordingly, the parameters that the regulation places on a State's use of data averaging fall squarely within the scope of section 1111 of the ESEA, as amended by the ESSA, consistent with section 1111(e), and constitute an appropriate exercise of the Department's rulemaking authority under GEPA, the DEOA, and section 1601(a) of the ESEA (see further discussion under the heading Cross-Cutting Issues).

Changes: None.

Partial Enrollment

Comments: Some commenters objected to the use of the term "enroll" in proposed § 200.20(b) instead of "attend," which is the term used in the statute.

Discussion: The Department believes that enrollment, rather than attendance, is a better measure of determining which students a school should be held accountable for, both because schools have a responsibility to promote and ensure regular attendance and because including students in accountability systems on the basis of attendance could create an incentive to discourage low-performing students from attending school, which is contrary to the purpose of title I to provide all children significant opportunity to receive a fair, equitable, and high-quality education, and to close educational achievement gaps. For this reason, the Department declines to make changes to § 200.20(b).

Changes: None.

Comments: Commenters also objected to the requirement that students enrolled for more than half of the year be included in the calculation of school performance for accountability purposes, in part because it represents a significant change from the "full academic year" requirements under the NCLB. Other commenters sought additional flexibility for States or LEAs to use existing methods or definitions for determining what constitutes partial enrollment or to develop their own definitions; including, for example, the percentage of time a student is in the school building.

Discussion: The requirement that the performance of any student enrolled for at least half of the school year be included on each indicator in the accountability system is based on section 1111(c)(4)(F) of the ESEA, as amended by the ESSA.

Changes: None.

Comments: A few commenters supported the proposed regulations in § 200.20(b)(2)(ii) for ensuring students are included in graduation rate calculations if they exit school and were only enrolled in a high school for part of the school year. Other commenters supported adding a requirement, in order to ensure all students are included in the calculation of graduation rates, to provide each State the authority to reassign students to schools for calculating adjusted cohort graduation rates when implementing the partial attendance requirements of ESSA.

Discussion: We appreciate the support of commenters for these provisions and agree that it is critical to ensure accurate calculation of adjusted cohort graduation rates. While we disagree that the regulations should be amended to provide a State will sole responsibility to reassign students to a different cohort, we note that § 200.20(b)(2) requires that if a student who was partially enrolled exits high school without receiving a regular diploma and without transferring to another high school that grants such a diploma during the school year, the State establishes a process, described further under 200.34, that the LEA must use to assign the student to the cohort of a particular high school. In addition, § 299.13(c)(1)(A)-(B) requires each State receiving funds under part A of title I to assure in its State plan that—in applying the approach under § 200.20(b) that its LEAs include students who are enrolled in the same school for less than half of the academic year and who exit high school without a regular diploma and without transferring into another high school that grants such a diploma in the calculation of adjusted cohort graduation rates—all students are included in the denominator of the calculation either for the school in which the student was enrolled for the greatest proportion of school days while enrolled in grades 9 through 12, or for the school in which the student was most recently enrolled.

Changes: None.

Sections 200.21 and 200.22   Comprehensive and Targeted Support and Improvement

Comments: Several commenters provided general support for the clarification in the proposed regulations regarding the actions to be taken to support and improve schools identified for comprehensive and targeted support and improvement, including State and local flexibility to determine the appropriate interventions for struggling schools.

Discussion: We appreciate the general support for the regulations on comprehensive and targeted support and improvement.

Changes: None.

Comments: Several commenters opposed the requirement that a State notify each LEA with a school identified for comprehensive support and improvement no later than the beginning of the school year, with one commenter stating that the proposed timeline is unreasonable given that identified schools may use the first year for planning and need not implement improvement plans and another recommending that States instead be permitted to develop their own notification timelines as part of their State plans.

Discussion: A clear, regular timeline for identification of schools is critical to meet the needs of students, who are likely to have been poorly served for years before their schools are identified for improvement and whose risk of educational failure only increases if identification is further delayed. As previously discussed under § 200.19, we also believe that given the time required for planning and implementing high-quality school improvement plans that include meaningful consultation with stakeholders, it is imperative that districts and schools know they have been identified for support and improvement as soon as possible, but no later than the beginning of the school year. Moreover, States and LEAs have faced, and generally met, an even earlier school identification timeline for the past decade under NCLB.

Changes: For consistency with revisions to § 200.19(d)(2)(i), we are revising § 200.21(a) and § 200.22(a)(1) to clarify that a State should notify each LEA with an identified school of such a school's identification as soon as possible, but no later than the beginning of the school year.

Notice to Parents: Comprehensive and Targeted Support and Improvement

Comments: Many commenters supported the Department's proposed requirements regarding notice to the parents of students enrolled in the schools identified for comprehensive and targeted support and improvement, including an explanation of how parents can become involved in the development and implementation of the support and improvement plan.

Some commenters supported the requirements but suggested additional modifications to the proposed notice requirements, including defining "promptly" so as to specify a timeline for notifying parents (e.g., no later than 30 or 60 days following identification), extending notice requirements to cover students as well as parents, and requiring LEAs to pilot their notices (potentially in collaboration with available parent or family engagement centers) to ensure they are easily understandable by diverse parents.

Several commenters, however, stated that the proposed parental notification requirements exceeded the Department's authority under the ESEA, as amended by the ESSA, and recommended eliminating any language not in the statute or making § 200.21(b)(1)-(b)(3) permissive rather than required.

Discussion: We appreciate those comments in support of our proposed notification requirements. We decline to further define terms (e.g., "promptly") or to otherwise expand requirements related to parental notification because we believe States should have flexibility, in consultation with their LEAs, to determine a notification process that meets local needs and circumstances. At the same time, we believe the requirements in § 200.21(b)(1)-(3) are necessary to ensure that LEAs and schools, respectively, are able to comply with the requirements in section 1111(d)(1)(B) regarding the development and implementation of comprehensive support and improvement plans, and in section 1111(d)(2)(B) regarding the development and implementation of targeted support and improvement plans, "in partnership with stakeholders," including parents. Accordingly, these requirements fall squarely within the scope of section 1111(d) of the ESEA, as amended by the ESSA, consistent with section 1111(e), and within the Department's rulemaking authority under GEPA, the DEOA, and section 1601(a) of the ESEA, as amended by the ESSA (see further discussion regarding the Department's rulemaking authority under the heading Cross-Cutting Issues). We, therefore, decline to revise these notice requirements.

Changes: None.

Comments: Several commenters made suggestions regarding the content of the notice to parents required by §§ 200.21(b) and 200.22(b), including specifying any low-performing subgroup or subgroups of students that led to the school's identification, and describing available supports and interventions for students who are below expected levels in math, reading, or ELP.

Discussion: Sections 200.21(b) and 200.22(b) require the notice to include, among other requirements, the reason or reasons for the identification, including, for a school that is identified for targeted support and improvement, the specific subgroup or subgroups that led to the school's identification. However, we believe the LEA is unlikely to have information on available supports and interventions for low-performing students at the time of initial parental notification, in part because a key purpose of such notification is to involve parents, in collaboration with other stakeholders, in decisions about the supports and interventions for such students that will be included in comprehensive or targeted support and improvement plans, as applicable.

Changes: None.

Comments: A few commenters suggested a change to the requirement that parental notification of a school's identification for comprehensive or targeted support and improvement include, if applicable, the subgroup or subgroups that led to the school's identification because it could reveal personally identifiable information. These commenters recommended that the regulations cross-reference the provision in § 200.16(b) establishing a minimum subgroup size for protection of personally identifiable information.

Discussion: Section 200.16(b) requires that a school is only held accountable for subgroup performance if that subgroup meets a State-determined minimum subgroup size sufficient to yield statistically reliable information for each purpose for which disaggregated data are used, including for purposes of reporting information under section 1111(h) of the ESEA, as amended by the ESSA, or for purposes of the statewide accountability system under section 1111(c) of the ESEA, as amended by the ESSA. Consequently, any notice to parents that includes the subgroup or subgroups that led to a school's identification would not include a subgroup that did not meet the minimum subgroup size, thereby protecting personally identifiable information.

Changes: None.

Comments: Some commenters suggested specific modifications to proposed § 200.21(b)(2) regarding written and oral translation of notices to parents. In particular, rather than requiring oral translation when written translation may not be practicable, some commenters suggested requiring LEAs to secure written translations for at least the most populous language other than English in a school that is identified for support and improvement. One commenter suggested that the final regulations should require the translation of those notices consistent with the Civil Rights Act of 1964 and Executive Order 13166. Another commenter felt that the regulations should require written notice and not rely on oral translations. However, another commenter suggested that oral translations and alternate formats should be required only to the extent practicable. Several commenters suggested that the phrase "to the extent practicable" should be clarified. One commenter requested that all LEAs consider it to be practicable to translate notices into American Indian, Alaska Native, and Native Hawaiian languages. This commenter also suggested the Department provide assistance in either funding or procuring services that will allow States to enforce the translation requirements. A few commenters stated that if a notice is not translated, it should include information for how a parent can request free language assistance from the school or district.

Other commenters opposed the specific requirements regarding written and oral translation because they believe there is no statutory authority for the requirement. One commenter specifically stated that this is an issue that should be left to the States.

Discussion: The statute and regulations require that, before a comprehensive or targeted support and improvement plan is implemented in an identified school, the LEA or school, as applicable, must develop such a plan in partnership with stakeholders, including parents. In order to ensure that parents are meaningfully included in this process, §§ 200.21(b) and 200.22(b) require an LEA to provide notice to parents of the school's identification that is not only understandable and clear about why a school was identified, but also enables parents to be engaged in development and implementation of the comprehensive or targeted support and improvement plan, as required by the statute. These requirements provide greater transparency and help parents understand the need for and the process for developing a school's comprehensive or targeted support and improvement plan, so that they can meaningfully participate in school improvement activities and take an active role in supporting their child's education. Accordingly, we believe that the requirements regarding written and oral translations fall squarely within the scope of, and are necessary to ensure compliance with sections 1111(d)(1)(B) and 1111(d)(2)(B) of the ESEA, as amended by the ESSA, and therefore constitute a proper exercise of the Department's rulemaking authority under GEPA, the DEOA, and section 1601(a) of the ESEA and are consistent with section 1111(e) (see further discussion under the heading Cross-Cutting Issues).

We also disagree with commenters that we should require only written translations and not allow for oral translations, or that we should require oral translations and alternate formats only to the extent practicable. Parents with disabilities or limited English proficiency have the right to request notification in accessible formats. Whenever practicable, written translations of printed information must be provided to parents with limited English proficiency in a language they understand. However, if written translations are not practicable, it is practicable to provide information to limited English proficient parents orally in a language that they understand. This requirement is consistent with Title VI of the Civil Rights Act of 1964 (Title VI), as amended, and its implementing regulations. Under Title VI, recipients of Federal financial assistance have a responsibility to ensure meaningful access to their programs and activities by persons with limited English proficiency. It is also consistent with Department policy under Title VI and Executive Order 13166 (Improving Access to Services for Persons with Limited English Proficiency).

We decline to further define the term "to the extent practicable" under these regulations, but remind States and LEAs of their Title VI obligation to take reasonable steps to communicate the information required by the ESEA, as amended by the ESSA, to parents with limited English proficiency in a meaningful way. (24) We also remind States and LEAs of their concurrent obligations under Section 504 and title II of the ADA, which require covered entities to provide persons with disabilities with effective communication and reasonable accommodations necessary to avoid discrimination unless it would result in a fundamental alteration in the nature of a program or activity or in undue financial and administrative burdens. Nothing in ESSA or these regulations modifies those independent and separate obligations. Compliance with the ESEA, as amended by the ESSA, does not ensure compliance with Title VI, Section 504 or title II.

Changes: None.

Comments: While a small number of commenters supported the proposed accessibility requirements generally, several of the commenters expressed concern that the requirements do not sufficiently ensure that parents and other stakeholders are able to access the notices and documentation and information when it is posted on Web sites. Of the commenters expressing concern, several discussed the accessibility of parent notices provided on LEA Web sites, particularly for individuals with disabilities.

Discussion: For a detailed discussion about accessibility of Web sites, please see the discussion below in §§ 200.30 and 200.31.

Changes: None.

Comments: None.

Discussion: Proposed § 200.21(b)(3) required notice of a school's identification for comprehensive

138

support and improvement in an alternative format accessible to a parent or guardian who is an individual with a disability, upon request. The term "parent" is defined in section 8101(38) of the ESEA, as amended by the ESSA. Under this definition, a "parent" includes a legal guardian or other person standing in loco parentis (such as a grandparent or stepparent with whom the child lives, or a person who is legally responsible for the child's welfare). Including the term "guardian" in § 200.21(b)(3) is unnecessary and redundant.

Changes: We have revised § 200.21(b)(3) by removing the reference to a guardian.

Comments: One commenter suggested that a review of notices be part of Federal and State monitoring of the requirements under title I of the ESEA, as amended by the ESSA.

Discussion: The Department appreciates and will take this comment into consideration when developing plans for monitoring State and local accountability systems under the ESEA, as amended by the ESSA.

Changes: None.

Needs Assessment: Comprehensive Support and Improvement

Comments: Many commenters expressed general support for the proposed regulations in § 200.21(c) requiring that, for each identified school, an LEA conducts a needs assessment in partnership with stakeholders (including principals and other school leaders, teachers, and parents). Many of these commenters suggested the regulations would be strengthened by ensuring LEAs partner with a broader array of stakeholder groups, such as: Students, public health and health care professionals, community-based organizations, faith-based organizations, local government, institutions of higher education, businesses, and intermediary organizations. Some suggested the stakeholders engaged in this endeavor also include specific types of teachers and leaders, such as childhood educators and leaders working with children prior to school entry, career and technical educators, and specialized instructional support personnel. Several commenters expressed concern about the opportunity for limited English proficient families to fully participate in the needs assessment; one of these commenters recommended that the regulations require LEAs to provide interpretation services in order for parents to have a meaningful opportunity to participate in the process.

Discussion: We appreciate the support from commenters for the proposed needs assessment requirements. The regulations require LEAs to partner with the same stakeholders with whom they are required to partner for purposes of developing the comprehensive support and improvement plan when they conduct the needs assessment that will inform that plan—principals and other school leaders, teachers, and parents. Although we encourage LEAs to partner with a broad range of stakeholders when developing and implementing a robust needs assessment, we believe LEAS should have discretion regarding the inclusion of additional groups or individuals in this work. LEAs must provide language assistance, consistent with their obligations under title VI, in order for limited English proficient families to participate meaningfully in the needs assessment.

Changes: None.

Comments: Some commenters suggested that a comprehensive needs assessment examine other measures in addition to those described in § 200.21(c)(1)-(c)(4). For instance, many commenters recommended requiring the needs assessment to include measures of school climate (e.g., chronic absenteeism; suspension; bullying and harassment). One commenter suggested the needs assessment also include the school's existing interventions, including how they are being implemented and their effectiveness. Several commenters suggested changes specific to § 200.21(c)(4) regarding the optional examination of the school's performance on additional, locally selected indicators. One such commenter suggested adding a requirement that locally selected indicators be supported, to the extent practicable, by the strongest evidence that is available and appropriate to the identified school. One commenter recommended that States be given discretion to specify which additional local indicators should be included in the needs assessment in order promote uniform requirements for needs assessments used by LEAs. Finally, one commenter stated that the Department does not have the authority to specify the minimum elements of a needs assessment.

Discussion: The Department agrees with the commenters who indicated that the regulations should require LEAs, in partnership with stakeholders, to examine additional measures in a needs assessment. The needs assessment should examine the school's unmet needs, including the needs of students; school leadership and instructional staff; the quality of the instructional program; family and community involvement; school climate; and distribution of resources, including results of the resource inequity review. We believe these additions allow for the needs assessment to include measures of school climate and the school's existing interventions, as recommended by commenters.

We disagree, however, with commenters' suggested revisions regarding the optional use of a school's performance on additional, locally selected indictors. Section 200.21(c)(4) allows, at the LEA's discretion, examination of an identified school's performance on additional, locally selected measures that are not included in the State's system of annual meaningful differentiation and that affect school outcomes in the school. We do not want to reduce local discretion on these measures for use in the needs assessment by adding specific requirements in the areas suggested by the commenters. Consequently, we decline to regulate further in this area.

We also disagree with commenters who indicated that the Department lacks authority to specify the minimum requirements of the needs assessment. We believe these requirements are necessary to reasonably ensure that the needs assessment is meaningful and results in the development of a support and improvement plan that meets all requirements for such plans and will ultimately meet the statutory goal of improving student achievement and school success and closing academic achievement gaps. Accordingly, the regulation constitutes a proper exercise of the Department's rulemaking authority under GEPA, the DEOA, and section 1601(a) of the ESEA and falls squarely within the scope of section 1111(d), consistent with section 1111(e) (see further discussion under the heading Cross-Cutting Issues).

Changes: We have revised § 200.21(c) to require the needs assessment to include an examination of the school's unmet needs, including the unmet needs of students; school leadership and instructional staff; the quality of the instructional program; family and community involvement; school climate; and distribution of resources, including results of the resource inequity review. We have also renumbered the paragraphs in this subsection to accommodate the substantive revision.

Comments: One commenter suggested adding a needs assessment requirement for targeted support and improvement schools that would include an assessment of school climate and safety.

Discussion: The statute does not require a school identified for targeted support and improvement to conduct a needs assessment, but we encourage LEAs to consider conducting a needs assessment for such schools in order to develop an effective support and improvement plan tailored to local needs.

Changes: None.

Comments: None.

Discussion: In proposed § 200.21(c)(4), the needs assessment may examine, at the LEA's discretion, the school's performance on additional, locally selected indicators that are not included in the State's system of annual meaningful differentiation under § 200.18 and that affect student outcomes in the identified school. In order to clarify that the term "locally selected indictors" is separate and apart from the accountability indicators described in § 200.14, we have changed the term to "locally selected measures."

Changes: We have revised § 200.21(c)(5), as renumbered, to say that an LEA may examine locally selected measures.

Comprehensive and Targeted Support and Improvement Plans: In General

Comments: One commenter claimed that the Department does not have the authority to promulgate regulations that specify the minimum elements of comprehensive support and improvement support plans.

Discussion: The regulations clarify and provide additional detail regarding how an LEA must comply with the requirements in section 1111(d)(1)(B)(i)-(iv) of the ESEA, as amended by the ESSA, which establish the basic elements of a comprehensive support and improvement plan. We believe these regulatory provisions are necessary to reasonably ensure that each comprehensive support and improvement plan meets the statutory requirements for such plans and ultimately meets the statutory goal of improving student achievement and school success and closing educational achievement gaps and therefore fall squarely within the scope of title I, part A of the statute. Moreover, the regulations ensure compliance with these key statutory provisions while maintaining significant flexibility for LEAs by, for instance, offering examples of evidence-based interventions an LEA might implement but leaving the selection of appropriate interventions to LEAs. Accordingly, the regulation constitutes a proper exercise of the Department's rulemaking authority under GEPA, the DEOA, and section 1601(a) of the ESEA and does not violate section 1111(e) (see further discussion under the heading Cross-Cutting Issues).

Changes: None.

Comments: One commenter suggested that the regulations clarify that States and districts can implement comprehensive support and improvement plans that address not only a school in need of comprehensive support and improvement but also the schools that feed students into that school.

Discussion: While § 200.21(d) requires that each LEA develop and implement a comprehensive support and improvement plan only for each identified school, an LEA may choose to consider supporting schools that feed into identified schools. Given this existing flexibility, we do not believe further regulation is necessary.

Changes: None.

Comments: A few commenters suggested requiring a comprehensive support and improvement plan to address how the LEA will build sufficient teacher and leader capacity to effectively implement interventions.

Discussion: We appreciate the intentions of the commenters in recommending changes to support teachers and leaders in their implementation of comprehensive support and improvement plans but believe that further requirements in this area would not be consistent with the significant discretion afforded to schools by the ESEA, as amended by the ESSA, in the development and implementation of such plans.

Changes: None.

Comments: One commenter suggested adding new requirements for comprehensive support and improvement plans regarding the effective implementation of evidence-based interventions, while another commenter suggested recommended schools share data on the implementation of selected interventions with LEAs to support an evaluation of the intervention's impact.

Discussion: We believe § 200.21(d)-(f) already provides for a continuous improvement process that would support the effective implementation of interventions selected as part of a comprehensive support and improvement plan, including stakeholder participation, State monitoring of plan implementation, and more rigorous interventions and State support if an identified school does not meet exit criteria.

Changes: None.

Comments: One commenter suggested strengthening the requirements for monitoring schools identified for targeted improvement and support by revising § 200.22(c) so that targeted support and improvement plans include, at a minimum, annual performance and growth benchmarks. The plan should also require a demonstration of sustained improvement against benchmark goals over at least two years before a school is exited from targeted support and improvement.

Discussion: We believe §§ 200.22(c)-(e) already require a meaningful continuous improvement process for schools implementing targeted support and improvement plans, and decline to regulate further in this area.

Changes: None.

Comments: Several commenters suggested that the targeted support and improvement plans required in § 200.22(c) should include interventions designed for the specific subgroups of students identified as consistently underperforming rather than for all of the lowest-performing students. One commenter asserted that if a targeted support and improvement school has both consistently underperforming and low-performing subgroups, the students in these groups should be considered the lowest-performing students to whom interventions should be tailored.

Discussion: We appreciate the comments suggesting that the Department require targeted support and improvement plans to focus on interventions tailored to specific subgroups. We decline to make this change, however, in order to maintain consistency between these regulations and the applicable non-discrimination legal requirements. To that end, we are clarifying in § 200.22(c)(7) that the resource inequity review required for a school with low-performing subgroups must identify and address resource inequities, but not the effects of any identified inequities on the low-performing subgroups.

Changes: We have revised § 200.22(c)(7) to eliminate the requirement that the resource inequity review address the effects of identified inequities on each low-performing subgroup in the school.

Comments: Several commenters suggested revising proposed § 200.22(c)(3)(ii) regarding the school's performance on additional, locally selected indicators that are not included in the State's system of annual meaningful differentiation under § 200.18 and that affect student outcomes in the identified school. Recommended changes include requiring that, to extent practicable, locally selected indicators be supported by the strongest available evidence, distinguish between schools, predict performance, and are amenable to intervention.

Discussion: We appreciate the intentions of the commenters in recommending changes designed to strengthen the impact of locally selected measures described in § 200.22(c)(3)(ii), but believe that further requirements in this area would not be consistent with the significant discretion afforded to schools by the ESEA, as amended by the ESSA, in the development and implementation of targeted support and improvement plans.

Changes: None.

Comments: One commenter suggested adding to § 200.22(c)(3) a new requirement to consider the implementation and effectiveness of existing interventions when developing a targeted support and improvement plan.

Discussion: We appreciate the intention of the commenter in recommending changes designed to strengthen targeted support and improvement plans, but believe that further requirements in this area would not be consistent with the significant discretion afforded to schools by the ESEA, as amended by the ESSA, in the development and implementation of targeted support and improvement plans.

Changes: None.

Stakeholder Engagement: Comprehensive and Targeted Support and Improvement Plans

Comments: Many commenters expressed support for the required involvement of key stakeholders—including principals and other school leaders, teachers, and parents—in the development and implementation of comprehensive and targeted support and improvement plans, but recommended the addition of a wide range of other specified stakeholders in the final regulation, such as school psychologists, students, and community-based organizations. In addition, one commenter recommended the addition of language requiring school districts subject to section 8538 of the ESEA to consult with tribal representatives before taking action under proposed §§ 200.21 and 200.22 (as well as under proposed §§ 200.15(c), 200.19, and 200.24).

Discussion: We appreciate the support for the proposed regulations regarding stakeholder engagement in plan development and implementation. We emphasize that the list of stakeholders specified in the regulations—which mirrors the list provided in section 1111(d) of the ESEA, as amended by the ESSA—represents the minimum requirements for the stakeholders who should be engaged in plan development and implementation, and we encourage LEAs to include additional stakeholders as appropriate. We are, however, revising the final regulations in § 200.21(d)(1) to encourage the inclusion of students, as appropriate, in the development of school improvement plans. While parents must be included in the development of the plans and are effective advocates on behalf of their children, we believe that directly involving students in developing school improvement plans, particularly in the case of older students, could ensure that a school's plan represents the perspectives of those who will be most directly impacted by its implementation. We are also making this revision to similar provisions in §§ 200.15(c)(1)(i) and 200.22(c)(1).

We also agree that the tribal consultation requirement in section 8538 of the ESEA, which requires certain school districts to consult with tribal representatives before submitting a plan or application under ESEA-covered programs, applies to comprehensive support and improvement plans under § 200.21(d). We are therefore adding language to § 200.21(d)(1) to specify that, for those affected LEAs, the stakeholders with whom the LEA works to develop the plan must include Indian tribes.

The requirements of section 8538 do not apply to the needs assessments under § 200.21(c) because there is no LEA plan or application that must be submitted. However, because the needs assessment is an important part of developing a comprehensive support and improvement plan, we encourage affected LEAs to involve local tribes in the needs assessment process. The tribal consultation requirement does not apply to the other provisions requested by the commenter, either because the regulatory requirements do not apply to LEAs (proposed § 200.19 contains State requirements, not LEA plan requirements; proposed §§ 200.15(c) and 200.22 apply to school-level rather than LEA-level plans) or because the LEA application requirement is not for a covered program (proposed § 200.24 contains application requirements for school improvement funds under section 1003(a) of the ESEA, which is not a covered program).

Changes: We have revised § 200.21(d)(1) to include Indian tribes as a stakeholder for LEAs affected by section 8535 of the ESSA, as amended by the ESSA, and to include students, as appropriate. We have also revised §§ 200.15(c)(1)(i) and 200.22(c)(1) to include students, as appropriate, in the development of school improvement plans related to low participation rates and to identification for targeted support and improvement.

Comments: Comprehensive and targeted support and improvement plans (as described in §§ 200.21(d) and 200.21(c), respectively) must be developed in partnership with stakeholders. Several commenters suggested the regulations clarify what is meant by the term "partnership," including by requiring shared decision-making with families (including training for parents and family members and specific provisions ensuring the meaningful inclusion of English learner families), sustained collaboration with equitable participation by diverse stakeholders, the integration of such partnerships with LEA and school parent and family engagement policies, and participation in the plan's monitoring and refinement cycle. One commenter also requested that the Department urge LEAs to work with stakeholders to determine whether changes are needed in pre-existing plans that may have been created without stakeholder engagement.

Discussion: We appreciate the commenters' suggestions to further define how comprehensive and targeted support and improvement plans are developed and implemented in partnership with stakeholders, but we believe the requirements in §§ 200.21(d)(1) and 200.22(c)(1) largely address the concerns and suggestions made by commenters on this matter.

Changes: None.

Comments: None.

Discussion: Proposed §§ 200.21(d) and 200.22(c) stated that, in developing comprehensive support and improvement plans, each LEA must describe in the plan how early stakeholder input was solicited and taken into account in the development of the plan, including the changes made as a result of such input. It is possible that no changes are necessary as a result of that input. Therefore, for the sake of clarity, we are revising the requirement to refer to "any" changes made as a result of input.

Changes: We have revised §§ 200.21(d)(1)(i) and 200.22(c)(1)(i) to say "any changes" rather than "the changes made as a result of such input."

Evidence-Based Interventions: Comprehensive and Targeted Support and Improvement Plans

Comments: Many commenters supported the specific examples of interventions cited in § 200.21(d)(3) or suggested adding a wide range of other interventions to the final regulations. Some of these suggestions were similar to interventions already on the list, such as: Partnering with teacher preparation providers to implement year-long, clinically rich preparation programs that incorporate residents fully into instructional and school improvement efforts; expanded learning time and afterschool programs; and increased access to high-quality, developmentally-appropriate early education. Other commenters suggested additional examples not part of the current list, such as: Culturally responsive modifications to school interventions for underserved students; strategies to increase family and community engagement; and innovative instructional models that incorporate high-quality career technical education. Several commenters also recommended clarifying certain aspects of the interventions on the proposed list or revising them to reflect additional requirements or strategies.

Other commenters opposed the inclusion of certain interventions on the list, citing concerns about the research base and/or effectiveness of the examples on the list, whether they would necessarily be appropriate in all local contexts, and whether the appearance of an "approved" list in the regulations is consistent with local discretion to select appropriate interventions responding to local needs. One commenter recommended striking the list of examples in favor of simply requiring that interventions meet the definition of "evidence-based" under section 8101(21) of the ESEA, as amended by the ESSA, or revising the list to include only those interventions supported by strong, moderate, or promising evidence, since those three levels are required for any improvement plans funded by the school improvement funds authorized by Section 1003 of ESSA.

Discussion: The list of examples in § 200.21(d)(3) is intended merely to illustrate the types of interventions an LEA may choose to consider when developing a comprehensive support and improvement plan, and we recognize that there are many other interventions that an LEA could select in response to the specific needs of a particular school and community. The options available to LEAs include any of the activities and approaches recommended by the commenters, as long as they meet the requirements of § 200.21(d)(3). For these reasons, we decline to add or remove any interventions to the non-exhaustive list, though we are making clarifications to several of the interventions currently on the list.

Changes: We have revised the final regulations to clarify several of the examples of interventions in § 200.21(d)(3). For one of these interventions, strategies designed to increase diversity by attracting and retaining students from varying socioeconomic backgrounds, we added students from varying racial and ethnic backgrounds. In the strategy to replace school leadership, the example now also includes identifying a new principal who is trained for or has a record of success in low-performing schools. We clarified the language regarding the revoking or non-renewing a public charter school's charter by adding language about public charter schools working in coordination with the applicable authorized public chartering agency to revoke or non-renew a school's charter and ensuring actions are consistent with State charter law and the school's charter.

Comments: One commenter recommended including in § 200.22(c) a examples of interventions for targeted support and improvement similar to that proposed in § 200.21(d)(3) and including in that list: (1) Increasing access to effective general and special education teachers and specialized instructional support personnel or adopting incentives to recruit and retain effective general and special education teachers and specialized instructional support personnel; and, (2) adopting the use of multi-tiered systems of support to address academic and behavioral deficits, including the use of positive behavioral interventions and supports.

Discussion: The examples of interventions listed in § 200.21(d)(3) are intended, in part, to illustrate the types of broad, comprehensive reforms that address the needs of an entire school, and not the narrower, more tailored interventions generally appropriate for schools identified for targeted support and improvement. Given the large number of differentiated strategies that may be used in schools identified for targeted support and improvement, depending on the specific needs and circumstances of the lowest-performing students in such schools, we do not believe it would be helpful to create a similar illustrative list for such schools in the final regulations.

Changes: None.

Comments: Several commenters suggested adjustments to the proposed requirement in § 200.21(d)(3) and 200.22(c)(4) that comprehensive and targeted improvement and support plans include "one or more" interventions to improve student outcomes in the school that meet the definition of evidence-based under section 8101(21) of the ESEA, as amended by the ESSA. Some believe that considering the multitude of issues facing identified schools, a single intervention is insufficient to address the root cause of the overall low performance of the school. Several commenters suggested requiring more than one intervention, such as requiring two or more interventions that are evidence-based; two or more interventions for each subgroup identified; and multiple evidence-based interventions that directly and comprehensively address the particular root causes of the school's low performance, which may include interventions that vary by academic subject area or meet the differing needs of students within a single subgroup.

Discussion: While we believe that the commenters have identified important issues for LEAs and schools to consider in developing their improvement plans, we do not believe it is either appropriate or consistent with local discretion under the ESEA, as amended by the ESSA, to include additional requirements around the use of evidence-based interventions in the final regulations.

Changes: None.

Comments: One commenter suggested clarifying the term "intervention" in § 200.22(c)(4) by adding regulatory language that an intervention may include activities, strategies, programs, or practices.

Discussion: We agree that an intervention may include activities, strategies, programs, and practices, but decline to define the term further in the final regulation. However, we have provided further guidance around the use of evidence-based interventions in non-regulatory guidance. (25)

Changes: None.

Comments: One commenter recommended requiring that the intervention or interventions chosen for students instructed primarily through a Native American language that are included in comprehensive support and improvement plans are provided through the Native American language of instruction and do not limit the preservation or use of Native American languages.

Discussion: Comprehensive and targeted support and improvement plans are developed in partnership with school leaders, teachers, and parents, and we encourage stakeholders and LEAs to consider the unique needs of students in identified schools when choosing appropriate interventions. However, requiring that supports be provided to students in a particular language is beyond the scope of these regulatory provisions, which address support and improvement to a school in general (see examples in § 200.21(d)(3)), rather than to students individually.

Changes: None.

Comments: Many commenters expressed general support for the proposed requirements in §§ 200.21(d)(3)(i)-(iv) and 200.22(c)(4)(i)-(iv) regarding the selection of evidence-based interventions in comprehensive and targeted support and improvement plans. Some of these commenters also recommended a wide range of specific changes to these provisions, including, for example, additional methodological requirements for selecting and using evidence-based interventions, the use of State-established evidence-based interventions or a State-approved list of evidence-based interventions, ensuring that selected interventions respond to the needs assessment, strengthening local capacity to identify and implement evidence-based interventions, building evidence through evaluation of selected interventions, and justifying the use of non-evidence-based interventions. One commenter suggested changing the provisions to require that interventions maintain access to well-rounded education for all students, including access to, and participation in, music and the arts as well as other well-rounded education subjects supported by the ESEA, as amended by the ESSA. Another commenter recommended that the Department, with assistance from the Institute of Education Sciences, create a compendium of Federally-supported rigorous research on effectiveness of interventions.

Some commenters opposed the proposed requirements in § 200.21(d)(3)(i)-(iv) and § 200.22(c)(4)(i)-(iv) regarding the selection of evidence-based interventions, asserting that these requirements inappropriately exceed those of the ESEA, as amended by the ESSA. One commenter stated that many districts do not have the capability to meet these requirements and may have to rely on costly external consultants for this purpose. This commenter also noted that the highest three tiers of evidence in the evidence-based definition are required only for interventions funded with State-awarded school improvement grants under section 1003 of the ESEA, as amended by the ESSA.

Discussion: We appreciate the support of some commenters for the regulations regarding evidence-based interventions. While we appreciate the suggested revisions to the language in §§ 200.21(d)(3) and 200.22(c)(4), the Department believes, with one exception, that the current language is clear and declines to amend the regulations. Specifically, we are revising the provisions in proposed §§ 200.21(d)(3)(iv) and 200.22(c)(4)(iii) that stated that an intervention may be selected from a State-approved list of interventions consistent with § 200.23(c)(2) to more clearly articulate these optional State authorities. Specifically, we are revising final §§ 200.22(d)(3)(iv) and 200.22(c)(3)(iv) so that it pertains only to "exhaustive or non-exhaustive" lists of evidence-based interventions that may be established by the State and so that it references the optional State authority in § 200.23(c)(2). We are further clarifying that, in the case of a State choosing to establish an exhaustive list of evidence-based interventions under § 200.23(c)(2), the evidence-based interventions in the support and improvement plan must be selected from that list, while in the case of a State opting to establish a non-exhaustive list under § 200.23(c)(2), the evidence-based interventions may be selected from that list. We are also adding § 200.22(d)(3)(v) as a separate provision to clarify that the evidence-based intervention selected in a comprehensive support and improvement plan may be one that is determined by the State, consistent with State law, as described in section 1111(d)(1)(3)(B)(ii) of the ESEA, as amended by the ESSA, and § 200.23(c)(3). We believe these revisions help clarify how a State may utilize the authorities described in § 200.23(c)(2)-(3), and the distinctions between them. These revisions in no way alter an LEA or school's discretion to choose an evidence-based intervention from those included on a State-established list, exhaustive or otherwise.

We disagree with commenters who indicated that § 200.21(d)(3) exceeds the Department's rulemaking authority. These requirements clarify how an LEA is to comply with the new and complex statutory requirement to select and implement evidence-based interventions in schools identified for comprehensive or targeted support and improvement; without such clarification, an LEA might have difficulty meeting this requirement. Moreover, these clarifications of the statutory requirements are necessary to reasonably ensure that the selected interventions will advance the statutory goals of improving student academic achievement and school success and closing achievement gaps and therefore fall squarely within the scope of section 1111 of the ESEA, as amended by the ESSA, consistent with section 1111(e). Accordingly, these requirements constitute an appropriate exercise of the Department's rulemaking authority under GEPA, the DEOA, and section 1601(a) of the ESEA.

Changes: We have revised §§ 200.21(d)(3)(iv) and 200.22(c)(4)(iv) to more clearly articulate the distinctions between the optional State authorities for lists of State-approved interventions and State-determined interventions, as described in § 200.23(c)(2)-(3), and their impact on the evidence-based interventions used in school support and improvement plans. Specifically, in the case of an exhaustive list of interventions established by the State consistent with § 200.23(c)(2), the intervention must be selected from that list, while in the case of a State establishing a non-exhaustive list, the intervention may be selected from that list. In addition, for comprehensive support and improvement plans, § 200.21(d)(3)(v) clarifies that the intervention may be one that is determined by the State, consistent with State law, as described in section 1111(d)(1)(3)(B)(ii) of the ESEA, as amended by the ESSA, and § 200.23(c)(3).

Equity and Resource Allocation: Comprehensive and Targeted Support and Improvement Plans

Comments: A number of commenters expressed support for § 200.21(d)(4) and § 200.22(c)(7), which require comprehensive support and improvement plans and targeted support and improvement plans for schools with low-performing subgroups that also must receive additional targeted support to identify and address resource inequities by reviewing certain LEA- and school-level resources. Other commenters requested that the Department eliminate these requirements or that it simply provide illustrative examples of resources that LEAs or schools might choose to review. Some commenters also suggested that such reviews might not be permissible under State law or questioned the Department's authority to require the review of any specific resources. One commenter specifically stated that the requirements conflicted with section 8527 of the ESEA, as amended by the ESSA.

Discussion: The Department appreciates the support for the resource review provisions in the proposed regulations. We believe that specifying certain types of resources for review is essential for ensuring that the reviews are meaningful and that they enable LEAs and schools to meet the statutory requirements for comprehensive support and improvement plans and targeted support and improvement plans for schools with low-performing subgroups schools that also must receive additional targeted support to identify and address resource inequities (ESEA section 1111(d)(1)(B)(iv), 1111(d)(2)(C)). We also believe that reviewing the particular resources in §§ 200.21(d)(4) and 200.22(c)(7) falls squarely within the scope of section 1111(d) of the ESEA, as amended by the ESSA, because it is necessary to the development of support and improvement plans that advance the statutory goals of improving student academic achievement and school success and closing educational achievement gaps. Further, the regulations ensure that these statutory requirements and purposes are met while minimizing burden on LEAs and schools by focusing on key data that States already will be collecting and reporting under the ESEA, as amended by the ESSA. Accordingly, we believe §§ 200.21(d)(4) and 200.22(c)(7) are a proper exercise of the Department's rulemaking authority under GEPA, the DEOA, and section 1601(a) of the ESEA, as amended by the ESSA, and do not violate section 1111(e).

Further, we disagree that the requirement to identify and address resource inequities by reviewing certain resources violates section 8527 of the ESEA, as amended by the ESSA. That provision states that nothing in the ESEA authorizes an officer or employee of the Federal Government "to mandate, direct, or control" a State, LEA, or school's allocation of State or local resources. As the regulations require the review of certain resources in order to identify and address resource inequities but do not require that such inequities be addressed in any particular way, they in no way "mandate, direct, or control" the allocation of State or local resources.

Changes: None.

Comments: A number of commenters recommended changes to the list of resources reviewed under §§ 200.21(d)(4)(i) and 200.22(c)(7)(i), including changes in required and optional elements of an LEA- or school-level resource review. Suggested elements included, for example, access to technology, music and art, and specialized instructional support personnel. Two commenters requested that we re-designate the examples in proposed §§ 200.21(d)(4)(ii)(A)-(C) and 200.22(c)(7)(ii)(A)-(C)—access advanced coursework, preschool programs, and instructional materials and technology—as required elements of resource reviews. One commenter also suggested adding to the list of required elements data that a State is required to report under section 1111(h)(1)(C)(viii) of the ESEA, as amended by the ESSA, which includes measures of school quality such as rates of suspensions and the number and percentage of students enrolled in preschool programs and accelerated coursework.

Discussion: We recognize that, as suggested by commenters, there are numerous examples of resources that contribute to positive educational outcomes that could be included in either a required or optional list in §§ 200.21(d)(4) and 200.22(c)(7), and we note that the final regulations would permit an LEA or school to add nearly any educational resource to its review that it deems important for supporting the effective implementation of school improvement plans.

We also believe, however, that the final regulations are more likely to promote meaningful resource reviews by focusing on a discrete list of required elements while continuing to reserve significant discretion to LEAs and schools in the conduct of such reviews. For this reason, we are revising the final regulations to make access to advanced coursework as well as access to both preschool and full-day kindergarten required elements of resource reviews. We also are adding as a required element access to specialized instructional support personnel, as defined in section 8101(47) of the ESEA, as amended by the ESSA. Specialized instructional support personnel such as school counselors are an important resource for creating and maintaining a safe and positive school climate and it is essential that students in all schools, but particularly low-performing schools, have access to those resources.

Finally, we decline to add school climate or suspension rates to the list of resources for review. Although these are important aspects of a school that should be evaluated and analyzed, they are not resources that are allocated. We encourage an LEA conducting a needs assessment pursuant to § 200.21(c) to examine a school's unmet needs with respect to school climate, including by reviewing data reported under section 1111(h)(1)(C)(viii)(I) of the ESEA, as amended by the ESSA, on rates of in-school suspensions, expulsions, school-related arrests, referrals to law enforcement, chronic absenteeism, and incidences of violence, including bullying and harassment.

Changes: We have revised the language in §§ 200.21(d)(4)(i) and 200.22(c)(7)(i) to require that an LEA, or school, include as part of its resource inequity review, in addition to per-pupil-expenditures and access to ineffective teachers, access to full-day kindergarten programs and preschool programs (in the case of an elementary school) as reported annually consistent with section 1111(h)(1)(C)(viii) of the ESEA, as amended by the ESSA, advanced coursework, including accelerated coursework as reported annually consistent with section 1111(h)(1)(C)(viii) of the ESEA, as amended by the ESSA, and specialized instructional support personnel, as defined in section 8101(47) of the ESEA, as amended by the ESSA, including school counselors, school social workers, school psychologists, other qualified professional personnel, and school librarians. We have also made conforming changes to § 200.21(d)(4)(ii) and § 200.22(c)(7)(ii).

Comments: One commenter requested that the Department expand the resource inequity review requirements to apply to schools identified for targeted support and improvement due to one or more consistently underperforming subgroups.

Discussion: The Department believes that requiring resource reviews for schools identified for targeted support and improvement would not be consistent with the ESEA, as amended by the ESSA; nevertheless, we strongly encourage those schools and their LEAs to include resource reviews as part of their targeted support and improvement plans.

Changes: None.

Comments: One commenter requested that the Department require that an LEA, or school, include, with respect to the required review in §§ 200.21(d)(4)(i) and 200.22(c)(7)(i) of per-pupil-expenditures and ineffective teachers, a review of budgeting and resource allocation.

Discussion: The Department believes that requiring a review of LEA and school-level budgeting and resource allocation would be inconsistent with section 1111(d) of the ESEA, as amended by the ESSA, which specifies that resource reviews "may include" budgeting and resource allocation decisions.

Changes: None.

Comments: Several commenters supported the requirements in § 200.21(d)(4) and § 200.22(c)(7) but noted concern about the elimination of the highly-qualified teacher requirements that existed under the ESEA, as amended by NCLB.

Discussion: The ESSA eliminated the highly-qualified teacher requirements in NCLB, and we therefore decline to include them.

Changes: None.

Timeline, Plan Approval, and Public Availability: Comprehensive and Targeted Support and Improvement Plans

Comments: Many commenters supported local discretion to use the first year following identification for targeted or comprehensive support and improvement as a planning year, as described in §§ 200.21(d)(5) and 200.22(c)(5).

Discussion: The Department appreciates the strong support for the allowance of a planning year; we agree that it will facilitate the development and implementation of targeted and comprehensive support and improvement plans consistent with the requirements of the ESEA, as amended by the ESSA. To further clarify that schools may begin implementation of targeted or comprehensive support and improvement plans during the planning year, we have made revisions to the proposed requirements in §§ 200.21 and 200.22.

Changes: We have revised the language in §§ 200.21(d)(5) and 200.22(c)(5) to clarify that a school identified for comprehensive or targeted support and improvement may begin implementation of its approved plan during the planning year, or, at the latest, the first full day of the school year following the school year for which the school was identified.

Comments: One commenter suggested adding language that an LEA may identify a new principal, if applicable, during the planning year in order to encourage districts to thoughtfully plan for leadership transitions as early as possible.

Discussion: We decline to require the identification of a new principal during the planning year, the timing of which we believe is a local decision.

Changes: None.

Comments: Several commenters supported requiring LEAs, consistent with §§ 200.21(d)(6) and 200.22(d)(2), to make comprehensive and targeted support and improvement plans publicly available, including to parents consistent with the requirements for notice in § 200.21(b). Other commenters recommended additional requirements, including making a hard copy available or providing online access to the documents at the school for parents who do not have a home computer.

Discussion: We appreciate the support of commenters for our proposed regulations regarding the public availability, including to parents, of comprehensive and targeted support and improvement plans. We believe these requirements will ensure that plans are accessible to parents, including those with limited English proficiency needing language assistance. We encourage but do not require the plan be made available in a particular format (e.g., via hardcopy or online) unless that is necessary to meet the requirement for an alternative format requested by a parent who is an individual with a disability.

Changes: None.

Comments: Several commenters opposed the proposed language in § 200.21(d)(7) requiring school approval of comprehensive support and improvement plans because they believe that LEAs should retain final approval authority to ensure that all schools in the district are treated equally and that no school has veto power over an improvement plan.

Discussion: The final regulations are consistent with section 1111(d)(1)(B)(v) of the ESEA, as amended by the ESSA, which requires that a comprehensive support and improvement plan be approved by the school, LEA and SEA.

Changes: None.

Comments: Several commenters requested clarification regarding the requirements in § 200.21(e)(1) regarding the State's responsibilities for comprehensive support and improvement plan approval and monitoring, with some commenters recommending defining the term "periodically" as it applies to review of plan implementation to mean at least annually. Similarly, several commenters requested clarification regarding the requirement in § 200.22(d) regarding the LEA's responsibilities for plan approval, in particular what it means to review and approve a targeted support and improvement plan "in a timely manner." Other commenters stated that the review of improvement plans should include input from State Advisory Panels in special education.

Discussion: We do not believe it is necessary to further define the terms "in a timely manner" or "periodically" in these regulations, as we believe both States and LEAs should have discretion, consistent with the ESEA, as amended by the ESSA, to develop timelines related the development and implementation of comprehensive and targeted support and improvement plans, respectively, that reflect their needs and circumstances. We also note that these timelines will naturally be driven, in part, by the implementation timelines specified in these final regulations (i.e., plans must be fully implemented no later than the first day of school in the year immediately following a planning year/the year for which identified).

Changes: None.

Exit Criteria: Comprehensive Support and Improvement Plans

Comments: Several commenters generally supported the requirements in § 200.21(f) for exit criteria for schools implementing comprehensive support and improvement plans. Several other commenters, however, opposed the proposed regulations on exit criteria, contending that the Department does not have the authority to promulgate those regulations, that the regulation violates the provision in section 1111(e)(1)(B)(iii)(VII) of the ESEA, as amended by the ESSA, which states that the Secretary may not prescribe exit criteria established by the State, and that the determination of appropriate exit criteria, as well as the actions that an LEA with a school that does not meet the exit criteria must take, should be determined by the State. More specifically, several commenters objected to the regulations on the basis that they would prevent a State from establishing exit criteria based on measures other than test scores or graduation rates. One commenter expressed concern that the exit criteria parameters in the proposed regulations were not sufficiently rigorous. Finally, a number of commenters requested that the Department remain silent on the State-established timeline for exit criteria.

Discussion: The Department appreciates the support for the requirements related to exit criteria. In response to the comments suggesting that the States should be permitted to determine exit criteria, the Department notes that the regulations in § 200.21(f) allow a State to establish its own exit criteria, requiring only that those exit criteria fall within two parameters: (1) That they require improvements in student outcomes; and (2) that a school that meets the exit criteria no longer meets the criteria for identification as a comprehensive support and improvement school.

Under these regulations, "student outcomes" are not limited to outcomes on statewide assessments. Accordingly, a State may establish exit criteria that are based on measures in addition to or other than test scores, such as, for example, improvements on any indicator in the accountability system, including a School Quality or Student Success indicator. States also have flexibility to determine what constitutes "improvement" on an indicator, and the Department encourages States in establishing these parameters to consider whether a school has sustained improvements and is likely to not be re-identified. We also believe that the regulations strike the proper balance between setting safeguards to ensure meaningful exit criteria and providing each State with ample flexibility to establish the exit criteria most appropriate for its State context. Further, we believe the regulations are consistent with section 1111(e)(1)(B)(iii)(VII) of the ESEA, as amended by the ESSA, because they do not prescribe exit criteria. Rather, the regulations set broad parameters around exit criteria to ensure that the criteria are linked with improved schools as opposed to, for example, arbitrary measures unrelated to student outcomes. A State may establish whatever exit criteria it believes are appropriate within those parameters such as, for example, improved performance on the School Quality or Student Success indicator or improvements in other student outcomes, as required under section 1111(d)(3) of the ESEA, as amended by the ESSA. Additionally, we believe that the regulations fall within the scope of, and are necessary to ensure compliance with, the requirements in section 1111(d)(3)(A)(i) of the

ESEA, which requires exit criteria be designed to ensure continued progress to improve student academic achievement and school success in the State. As such, we believe these requirements constitute a proper exercise of the Department's rulemaking authority under GEPA, the DEOA, and section 1601(a) of the ESEA, and do not violate section 1111(e) of the ESEA, as amended by the ESSA.

Additionally, given the balance struck by the regulations, the Department declines to specify more rigorous parameters for exit criteria in the final regulations. Further, we note that the regulatory provision specifying that the State-determined timeline for meeting the exit criteria may not exceed four years merely restates the statutory provision in section 1111(d)(3)(A)(i)(I) of the ESEA, as amended by the ESSA.

Changes: None.

Comments: None.

Discussion: We have determined that the regulations could provide greater clarity regarding how a State determines that a school no longer meets the criteria for identification under § 200.19(a). Specifically, we believe that it is necessary to clarify that a State's exit criteria must ensure that a school no longer meets the specific criterion or criteria under which the school was identified, rather than all of the criteria under § 200.19(a) (e.g., if a school was identified because it was among the lowest-performing five percent of title I schools in the State, the exit criteria need not require that the school improve its graduation rate).

Changes: We have modified the language in § 200.21(f)(1)(ii) to specify that a State's exit criteria must require that a school no longer meet the specific criteria under which the school was identified as a comprehensive support and improvement school.

Comments: One commenter expressed support for the requirement, in § 299.17(c)(2) of the proposed regulations, that a State make publicly available the exit criteria it establishes under § 200.21(f).

Discussion: The Department appreciates the support for this requirement, and believes it would be helpful to further clarify this requirement by adding it to § 200.21 in the final regulations; we believe a similar clarification is also helpful in § 200.22(f)(1) with regard to title I schools with low-performing subgroups of students identified for targeted support and improvement.

Changes: We have modified the language in §§ 200.21(f)(1) and 200.22(f)(1) to reiterate the requirement in § 299.17(c)(2) and (5) that a State must make publicly available its exit criteria for schools identified for comprehensive support and improvement and for schools with low-performing subgroups of students identified for targeted support and improvement.

Comments: One commenter noted that the term "exit criteria" could be called "success criteria" instead.

Discussion: We retain the proposed terminology in the final regulations for consistency with the ESEA, as amended by the ESSA, but note that a State may use whatever term it deems appropriate for its exit criteria as long as the criteria meet the requirements in § 200.21(f).

Changes: None.

Comments: One commenter asked for clarification on how the requirements in the regulations with respect to timeline for exiting interact with the timeline for schools currently implementing interventions under ESEA flexibility as well as what types of support and monitoring a State must provide to an LEA with a school that does not meet the exit criteria.

Discussion: The Department agrees that clarification on the issues raised by the commenter would be helpful, but intends to address both issues in non-regulatory guidance rather than the final regulations.

Changes: None.

Comments: Several commenters requested that the Department eliminate the requirement that an LEA conduct a new needs assessment for a school implementing a comprehensive support and improvement plan that does not meet the exit criteria within the State-determined number of years. Those commenters claimed that the requirement is duplicative, burdensome, and inconsistent with the statute.

Discussion: The Department believes that a new, high-quality needs assessment, conducted in partnership with stakeholders, is an essential foundation for the development and successful implementation of the amended comprehensive support and improvement plan required by § 200.21(f)(3). Additionally, the requirement is necessary to reasonably ensure compliance with sections 1111(d)(1)(B)(iii) and 1111(d)(3) of the ESEA, as amended by the ESSA, because an amended needs assessment is essential to identifying areas for which improvement is needed in a school that has failed, after a State-determined number of years, to meet the State-established exit criteria. For these reasons, we believe the regulation falls squarely within the scope of section 1111(d) of the ESEA, as amended by the ESSA, consistent with section 1111(e), and our rulemaking authority under GEPA, the DEOA, and section 1601(a) of the ESEA, as amended by the ESSA, and, thus, decline to eliminate this requirement.

Changes: None.

Comments: A number of commenters suggested changes to § 200.21(f)(3) with respect to the actions an LEA must take if a school identified for comprehensive support and improvement does not meet the exit criteria within a State-determined number of years. Specifically, these commenters requested clarification that the additional interventions that the LEA must implement in the school may replace or supplement the existing interventions and that the additional interventions must address the needs identified by the new needs assessment, regardless of the level of evidence supporting those interventions. Some of these commenters were concerned that the requirement in § 200.21(f)(3)(iii)(B) appeared to require all of the additional interventions in the amended plan to be supported by strong or moderate evidence. Finally, one commenter suggested requiring annual State review of the implementation of the amended comprehensive support and improvement plan.

Discussion: We agree with the suggestions to clarify that not all the additional interventions that an LEA implements as part of an amended comprehensive support and improvement plan for a school that fails to meet exit criteria must be evidence-based interventions supported by strong or moderate evidence and is revising the regulation to reflect this clarification. The Department believes that interventions with stronger evidence are more likely to lead to success and, therefore, will maintain the requirement that at least one of the interventions be supported by strong or moderate evidence. We further agree that an LEA may either replace or supplement existing interventions, as determined by the State, and that an LEA should, as part of its new needs assessment, carefully review whether the existing interventions have been successful at improving the achievement of its students, but believe the regulations already are clear on this point. Finally, the Department declines to amend the regulations to include annual State review of the implementation of amended comprehensive support and improvement plans because it believes that the need for additional monitoring and support for such schools is adequately addressed by the requirement in § 200.21(f)(5)(ii).

Changes: The Department has amended § 200.21(f)(3)(iii)(B) to require that the additional interventions that an LEA with a school identified for comprehensive support and improvement that does not meet exit criteria must implement include one or more evidence-based interventions that are supported by strong or moderate evidence, but clarify that the amended plan may also include other rigorous interventions that are not supported by strong or moderate evidence.

Exit Criteria: Targeted Support and Improvement Plans

Comments: Several commenters supported generally the requirements in § 200.22(e) for exit criteria, including one who specifically supported the requirement that an LEA make the exit criteria publicly available. Several other commenters asserted that the Department does not have authority to set parameters around exit criteria or that either the exit criteria or the actions required for a school that does not meet the exit criteria should be determined by the State or LEA.

Discussion: The Department appreciates the support for the requirements related to exit criteria in the proposed regulations. We believe that these requirements fall squarely within the scope of, and are necessary to reasonably ensure compliance with the requirements in section 1111(d)(2)(B) of the ESEA, as amended by the ESSA, that schools identified for targeted support and improvement implement plans that improve student outcomes and that such plans result in additional action following unsuccessful implementation after a number of years. As such, we believe these requirements constitute a proper exercise of the Secretary's rulemaking authority under GEPA, the DEOA, and section 1601(a) of the ESEA, as amended by the ESSA, and do not violate section 1111(e) (see discussion of the Department's general rulemaking authority under the heading Cross-Cutting Issues). Further, the regulations reserve appropriate discretion for LEAs to determine their specific exit criteria for schools implementing targeted support and improvement plans.

Changes: None.

Comments: One commenter suggested requiring annual State review of the implementation of amended targeted support and improvement plans.

Discussion: The Department believes that requiring annual State review of the implementation of amended targeted support and improvement plans would be inconsistent with the ESEA, as amended by the ESSA, which gives LEAs primary responsibility for ensuring the effective implementation of targeted support and improvement plans. We also believes that the requirement in § 200.22(e)(2)(iii) that the LEA increase monitoring and support for school implementing amended targeted support and improvement plans partly addresses the commenter's concerns.

Changes: None.

Comments: A number of commenters recommended that the Department impose a maximum timeline for exit criteria for schools identified for targeted support and improvement due to one or more consistently underperforming subgroups. Two commenters suggested aligning the maximum timeline with the requirement that exit criteria for comprehensive support and improvement schools not exceed four years; another suggested requiring a cap of two years, noting that the exit criteria should be based on the school's progress against benchmark goals; and one commenter suggested that, if, after three years, a school has not met the exit criteria for targeted support and

155

improvement, the State be required to identify it for comprehensive support and improvement.

Discussion: The Department appreciates the recommendations of the commenters, each of which is aimed at ensuring that LEAs and States take meaningful action, over time, to improve outcomes for students in consistently underperforming subgroups. However, the Department believes that these recommendations generally are not consistent with the requirements of the ESEA, as amended by the ESSA, which reserve significant discretion to LEAs in the development and implementation of targeted support and improvement plans. The Department also believes that because the ESEA, as amended by the ESSA, specifies the types of schools that must be identified for comprehensive support and improvement, it would not be appropriate to expand this definition to include schools identified for targeted support and improvement due to one or more consistently underperforming subgroups that fail to meet exit criteria. For these reasons, we believe that the regulations strike the proper balance between establishing safeguards to ensure meaningful exit criteria and providing each LEA with flexibility to establish the exit criteria most appropriate for its specific context, as well as more rigorous consequences for failure to meet those criteria.

Changes: None.

Comments: A number of commenters recommended that the Department require that States, rather than LEAs, establish exit criteria or otherwise eliminate the LEA's control over the exit criteria for schools identified for targeted support and improvement based on one or more consistently underperforming subgroups. These commenters were concerned that the LEA-established exit criteria may conflict with State policies, including the State's criteria for identifying consistently underperforming subgroups, may be inconsistent across the State, and may create burden for LEAs.

Discussion: The Department appreciates commenters' interest in having States establish exit criteria for this type of school. The regulation, however, is consistent with the statute, which specifically grants authority to establish exit criteria for these schools to LEAs (section 1111(d)(2)(B)(v) of the ESEA). We note that States have authority to issue rules, regulations, and policies related to title I of the ESEA, and may exercise that authority in accordance with the requirements in section 1603 of the statute. A State may use that authority to issue rules, regulations, or policies that establish parameters around LEA-established exit criteria.

Changes: None.

Comments: Several commenters recommended requiring a school identified for targeted support and improvement that does not meet its exit criteria to conduct a needs assessment.

Discussion: While we encourage States and LEAs to require a needs assessment as a prerequisite for all school improvement plans—whether initial or amended—we decline to add such a requirement to the final regulations because the ESEA, as amended by the ESSA, requires such needs assessments only for schools identified for comprehensive support and improvement.

Changes: None.

State Discretion for Certain High Schools

Comments: Several commenters supported proposed § 200.21(g)(1), under which a State may permit differentiated improvement activities as part of comprehensive support and improvement plan for certain high schools identified due to low graduation rates. A number of commenters recommended various clarifications, including specific terms used in the provision, such as "differentiated improvement activities;" the specific schools eligible for differentiated treatment; and the extent of the permitted differentiation, including examples of appropriate interventions. Another commenter suggested that holding high schools serving significant populations of over-age and credit-deficient student accountable for meeting targets based on extended-time graduation rates would better serve these schools and their families than a different set of labels or interventions. One commenter recommended requiring States to provide a plan for how accountability will be maintained in these schools, including the calculation of extended-year adjusted cohort graduation rate for up to 7 years.

Discussion: We appreciate the support of some commenters for proposed § 200.21(g)(1) permitting differentiated activities in certain high schools identified for comprehensive support and improvement, and agree that additional clarity is needed regarding this flexibility. The intent of proposed § 200.21(g)(1) was to permit States discretion, consistent with section 1111(d)(1)(C)(i) of the ESEA, as amended by the ESSA, to allow differentiated improvement strategies in its comprehensive support and improvement plans for high schools with low graduation rates that predominantly serve students (1) returning to education after having exited secondary school without a regular high school diploma, or (2) who, based on their grade or age, are significantly off track to accumulate sufficient academic credits to meet high school graduation requirements, and not to simply forego implementation of improvement activities or otherwise reduce accountability in such schools, as is allowed for small high schools under proposed § 200.21(g)(2). We also note that LEAs may, and should, create differentiated improvement plans for such high schools identified for support and improvement that are based on the school's needs assessment and specifically designed to address identified needs. Other comments, such as concern about labels or recommendations for additional improvement plans, appear to overlook the fact that these schools are identified for comprehensive support and improvement and thus must develop and implement comprehensive support and improvement plans, though they may include differentiated improvement activities in such plans. We are revising §§ 200.21(d) and (g) to reflect these clarifications.

Changes: We have moved the language regarding differentiated improvement activities in any high school identified for comprehensive support and improvement due to a low graduation rate that predominantly serves students (1) returning to education after having exited secondary school without a regular high school diploma, or (2) who, based on their grade or age, are significantly off track to accumulate sufficient academic credits to meet high school graduation requirements from § 200.21(g)(1) to 200.21(d)(3)(vi).

Comments: Some commenters supported the provision in § 200.21(g)(2) allowing an SEA to exempt a high school that is identified for comprehensive support and improvement based on having a low graduation rate from implementing required improvement activities if it has a total enrollment of less than 100 students. Several commenters requested clarification about some of the terms in § 200.21(g)(2), such as "total enrollment" and "such a school". A few commenters recommended requiring a justification for such exemptions in annual LEA report cards, while others called for notifying parents when identified schools do not implement improvement plans. Two commenters recommended that the Department clarify in guidance that these LEAs are still subject to all other reporting requirements. Other commenters expressed concern about permitting such exemptions for extended periods of time or stated that this flexibility is inappropriate for certain schools, such as schools that predominantly serve students with disabilities or schools serving students in prison or juvenile justice facilities.

Discussion: We appreciate the support some commenters provided for State discretion for certain small high schools identified for comprehensive support and improvement due to low graduation rates. We agree that the regulations should be clarified to ensure that this flexibility is provided

157

only for small schools (with fewer than 100 students enrolled) that are identified for comprehensive support and improvement based on having a low graduation rate; small schools that are identified for other reasons must develop and implement a comprehensive support and improvement plan as required by the statute and regulations. However, we decline to include additional reporting and notice requirements in these final regulations, as the continued applicability of all reporting requirements in the statute and regulations will provide the transparency needed to promote accountability. We also believe that denying this flexibility to certain small schools, such as schools predominantly serving students with disabilities, would not be consistent with the ESEA, as amended by the ESSA, though we note that this flexibility may not be used to deprive these students of their rights under the IDEA, Section 504, and title II of the ADA.

Changes: We have revised § 200.21(g) to clarify that high schools identified for comprehensive support and improvement based on low graduation rate with a total enrollment of less than 100 students are the only high schools permitted to forgo implementation of improvement activities required by these regulations.

Public School Choice

Comments: Several commenters support the requirements in § 200.21(h) regarding public school choice, while others asserted that this subsection is not consistent with section 1111(d)(1)(D) of the ESEA, as amended by the ESSA. One of these commenters objected to requiring school districts that that are operating under a Federal desegregation order and wish to offer public school choice consistent with § 200.21(h) to obtain court approval for choice transfers, based on the belief that choice options should not interfere with the operation of desegregation plans. Another commenter objected to what the commenter appeared to believe is a requirement to offer public school choice, suggesting that such a requirement would negatively impact students that are homeless and/or transferring for a number of other reasons, including students that move mid-year and want to attend their new neighborhood school.

Discussion: An LEA is required to "obtain court approval" for transfers if it is unable to implement the choice provisions consistent with the desegregation plan, or where the governing orders specifically require authorization from the court. The Department anticipates that courts and responsible agencies will recognize the benefits of allowing students to transfer from schools identified as needing improvement and will grant amendments to desegregation orders permitting such transfers where they would not impede desegregation. We disagree with the commenter that believes the provision would have a negative impact on mobile students. An LEA may, but is not required to provide students with the option to transfer to another public school that is not identified for comprehensive improvement and support, and no student would be required to seek or accept such a transfer.

Changes: None.

Section 200.23   State Responsibilities To Support Continued Improvement

State Review of Available Resources

Comments: Several commenters strongly supported proposed § 200.23(a), which would require each State to periodically conduct a resource allocation review in each of its LEAs serving a significant number of schools identified for comprehensive support and improvement or targeted support and improvement. One commenter observed that resource inequities identified through such reviews could contribute to certain LEAs having a disproportionate number of schools identified for improvement, and that reducing such inequities could improve achievement for all students.

Discussion: The Department appreciates the support of these commenters for the proposed regulations and agrees that reducing inequitable resource allocation practices in LEAs and schools can help improve student achievement as well as other educational outcomes. Given the potential impact of these efforts, we are revising the final regulations to clarify that this periodic review considers the same resources that are reviewed by an LEA as part of comprehensive support and improvement plans for schools that are so identified. We are also revising the final regulations to further clarify that this periodic review considers "resources available" to emphasize that the review considers how allocation practices ultimately affect the availability of resources among LEAs and schools.

Changes: We have revised § 200.23(a) to require a State to periodically review "resources available" in LEAs with a significant number of percentage of schools identified for comprehensive or targeted support and improvement as compared to all other LEAs in the State, and in schools in those LEAs as compared to all other schools in the State, and to clarify that the resources included in this review must include the same resources an LEA reviews for purposes of a comprehensive support and improvement plan.

Comments: One commenter requested that the final regulations clarify the meaning of the term "significant number of schools" as used in proposed § 200.23. Another commenter recommended that the phrase be revised to read "significant number or percentage of schools" to avoid over-identification of large urban districts for additional State support.

Discussion: We decline to provide a more precise definition of the term "significant number of schools" because it may vary according to local circumstances, but we agree that adding "or percentage" to the term is a helpful clarification and are revising the final regulations accordingly.

Changes: We have revised the regulations to replace the term "significant number of schools" with the term "significant number or percentage of schools" throughout.

Comments: One commenter recommended requiring such reviews at least once every three years, rather than periodically, to encourage alignment of the reviews with needs assessments for schools identified for comprehensive support and improvement.

Discussion: We appreciate the commenter's intention of aligning resource reviews with school identification timelines, but decline to make the recommended change in recognition that States may need discretion to account for variations in State identification timelines as well as capacity to carry out required reviews.

Changes: None.

Comments: One commenter recommended that the Department provide more specific parameters around the resource allocation reviews required by proposed § 200.23(a), including the timeline for reviews, disaggregation of expenditures targeted to specific subgroups of students, an assessment of student needs, and the inclusion of all districts for comparison purposes. Another commenter recommended that in addition to examining resource allocation between LEAs and between schools, States also look at resource inequities between grades (e.g., between preschool and kindergarten).

Discussion: The Department appreciates commenters' desire for more granular data and information as part of resource reviews, as well as interest in expanding the comparison categories, but generally declines to include additional parameters in the final regulations to avoid increasing State and local burdens in conducting the reviews. We are, however, revising the language in § 200.23(a) to clarify the entities to be used for comparison purposes in the review of available resources.

Changes: We have revised § 200.23(a) to specify that each State must, with respect to each LEA in the State serving a significant number or percentage of schools identified for comprehensive support and improvement or targeted support and improvement, periodically review resources available between such LEAs and all other LEAs in the State and between schools in those LEAs and all other schools in the State.

Comments: One commenter recommended revising proposed § 200.23(a) to include a requirement that States evaluate schools implementing comprehensive support and improvement plans to determine whether such schools are improving more quickly than schools with a comparable student population.

Discussion: We believe that adding an evaluation requirement to the resource review requirements in the final regulations would impose significant burden on States unrelated to the resource reviews required under section 1111(d)(3)(A)(ii) of the ESEA, as amended by the ESSA.

Changes: None.

Comments: One commenter opposed the resource allocation reviews required by proposed § 200.23(a) because they would require States to review and potentially address teacher distribution issues related to disproportionate rates of ineffective, out-of-field, or inexperienced teachers in one or more LEAs or schools. The commenter also believes that the final regulations should not define "resources" for the purpose of the resource allocation reviews required by section 1111(d)(3)(A)(ii) of the ESEA, as amended by the ESSA.

Discussion: States, with respect to each LEA in the State serving a significant number or percentage of schools identified for comprehensive support and improvement or targeted support and improvement, will be required to review and take actions to address differences in rates of ineffective, out-of-field, or inexperienced teachers in LEAs and schools by § 299.18(c) of the final regulations and section 1111(g)(1)(B) of the ESEA, as amended by the ESSA; the resource reviews merely reinforce these actions by requiring States to periodically review educator data in the context of school improvement needs. We also believe that defining a minimum set of resources that must be reviewed supports effective State implementation of the required resource reviews while also reducing the burden of such reviews by highlighting readily available resource data collected in accordance with other requirements under the ESEA, as amended by the ESSA.

Changes: None.

Comments: One commenter opposed the resource allocation reviews required by proposed § 200.23(a) on grounds that such reviews could lead to SEA efforts to override the authority of local school districts over their own budgets. The commenter expressed further concern that such SEA actions might not take into account the local context for resource allocation decisions.

Discussion: The Department believes that the proposed language requiring State actions to address resource inequities "to the extent practicable," which is retained in the final regulations, will encourage a collaborative approach by States and LEAs in responding to any identified resource

160

inequities.

Changes: None.

Comments: One commenter opposed proposed § 200.23(a) because of what the commenter claimed to be the difficulty of disaggregating costs paid for with general categorical funding.

Discussion: The Department recognizes that disaggregating State and local expenditures may be challenging, but notes that States and LEAs must report per-pupil expenditures of Federal, State, and local funds annually under section 1111(h)(1)(C)(x) of the ESEA, as amended by the ESSA.

Changes: None.

State Technical Assistance

Comments: One commenter recommended that the final regulations include language encouraging States to include in the description of the technical assistance it will provide under proposed § 200.23(b) an explanation of how it will work with external partners with expertise in identifying or implementing school improvement strategies. The commenter believes that external organizations provide a ready resource that can help build State capacity to provide effective technical assistance to districts and schools. Another commenter similarly recommended the addition of language to proposed § 200.23(b)(3) regarding tools for implementing evidence-based interventions, including practices available through the Department's Regional Educational Laboratories and Comprehensive Assistance Centers.

Discussion: The Department agrees that external partners and resources can help States provide more effective technical assistance and other support to districts and schools, but declines to require or otherwise specify the use of such partners or resources in the final regulations. We will take these comments into consideration in developing non-regulatory guidance related to State-provided technical assistance.

Changes: None.

Comments: One commenter recommended revisions to proposed § 200.23(b) encouraging States to (1) provide guidance to districts on how to conduct a school-level needs assessment, with an emphasis on using assessment results to select evidence-based interventions; (2) promote the use of existing evidence-based intervention resources, including the Department's What Works Clearinghouse operated by the IES; and (3) develop a policy framework for sustainable school turnaround that includes additional resources, district-level reforms, tiered intervention strategies, stakeholder engagement, teacher and principal pipelines, and rigorous evaluation activities.

Discussion: The Department appreciates the commenter's interest in promoting more effective State support for school improvement, as well as the potential role of the What Works Clearinghouse in expanding the use of evidence-based interventions, but declines to require or otherwise specify additional State-level activities in this area in the final regulations. We will take these comments into consideration in developing non-regulatory guidance related to State-provided technical assistance.

Changes: None.

Comments: One commenter recommended revisions to proposed § 200.23(b) emphasizing that sustained school improvement requires (1) that evidence-based interventions selected by LEAs and schools are clearly connected to the findings of the needs assessment; (2) continuous monitoring of implementation, including through rapid-cycle impact evaluations; and (3) that States build the evidence base through piloting of interventions in areas where the evidence base is weak or no evidence exists.

Discussion: The Department appreciates the commenter's interest in promoting stronger State support for the use of evidence-based practices but declines to require or otherwise specify additional activities in this area in the final regulations. We believe it more appropriate to discuss these activities in non-regulatory guidance. We also note that § 200.21(d) requires a comprehensive support and improvement plan to include one or more evidence-based interventions that are supported, to the extent practicable, by the strongest level of evidence that is available and appropriate to meet the needs identified in the needs assessment.

Changes: None.

Additional State Improvement Actions

Comments: One commenter stated that proposed § 200.23(c)(1), which provides examples of additional school-level improvement actions that a State may take in LEAs with a significant number of schools identified for comprehensive support and improvement that are not meeting exit criteria or a significant number of schools identified for targeted support and improvement, is inconsistent with section 1111(e)(1)(B)(iii)(VI) of the ESEA, as amended by the ESSA, which provides that nothing in the statute authorizes the Secretary, as a condition of approval of the State plan, to prescribe any specific school support and improvement strategies for use by States or LEAs. Two commenters recommended moving the specified interventions to non-regulatory guidance.

Discussion: The list of interventions in proposed § 200.23(c)(1) is illustrative only, and is intended to provide examples of the types of meaningful actions a State may take to initiate additional improvement in any LEA, or in any authorized public chartering agency, in a school identified for comprehensive support and improvement or targeted support and improvement that has failed to respond to other interventions. For this reason, we believe it is appropriate to provide examples of such actions in regulation rather than in non-regulatory guidance. The final regulations, like the proposed regulations, do not require a State to take any of these actions and thus in no way prescribe any specific LEA or school support or improvement strategies. Therefore, § 200.23(c)(1)is not inconsistent with section 1111(e)(1)(B)(iii)(VI) of the ESEA, as amended by the ESSA. We further note that the additional improvement actions contemplated by the statue clearly include actions at both the LEA and school levels. Consequently, we are revising the final regulations to include examples of LEA-level improvement action (including reducing the LEA's operational or budgetary autonomy; removing one or more schools from the jurisdiction of the LEA; or restructuring the LEA, including changing its governance or initiating State takeover of the LEA), as well as action a State might take with regard to an authorized public chartering agency.

Changes: We have revised § 200.23(c)(1) to include examples of improvement actions a State may take at the LEA level and examples of improvement actions in an authorized public chartering agency.

Comments: One commenter recommended that the final regulations give States flexibility to determine the improvement activities to be carried out under proposed § 200.23(c)(1). Another commenter recommended removal of the list of interventions in proposed § 200.23(c)(1) because it believes that such a list may discourage the use of evidence-based interventions that would better address the improvement needs of the school identified through its needs assessment.

Discussion: The list of interventions in proposed § 200.23(c)(1) is intended to provide examples of the types of meaningful actions a State may take in a chronically low-performing school that has failed to respond to other interventions. The list is illustrative only, and we do not believe it will preclude or otherwise discourage States from considering other types of interventions in such schools, including evidence-based interventions that respond to schools' needs assessments. We are, however, revising the school leadership example to emphasize the importance of selecting new leadership with the skills and experience needed to turn around low-performing schools. We also are revising § 200.23(c) to clarify that a State may take the specified additional school improvement actions only to the extent that they are consistent with State law.

Changes: We have revised § 200.23(c) to clarify that the additional improvement actions taken by a State must be consistent with State law. We also have revised the replacing school leadership example in 200.23(c)(1) to emphasize the importance of replacing school leadership with leaders who are trained for, or have a record of, success in low-performing schools.

Comments: One commenter recommended revising proposed § 200.23(c)(1) to clarify that States may take additional improvement actions in LEAs with a significant number of schools that are both identified for targeted support and improvement and not meeting exit criteria. The commenter believes that, similar to the proposed parameters for LEAs with a significant number of schools identified for comprehensive support and improvement, LEAs with schools identified for targeted support and improvement should be given time for the schools to improve before State intervention may be triggered. Another commenter recommended that schools identified for targeted support and improvement not be subject to the interventions specified in proposed § 200.23(c)(1); this commenter believes that schools identified for targeted support and improvement that are not meeting exit criteria are addressed adequately by the requirement for amended improvement plans in proposed § 200.22(e)(2).

Discussion: We appreciate the first commenter's desire for consistent treatment of schools identified for comprehensive support and improvement and targeted support and improvement that may be subject to additional improvement action by the State under § 200.23(c)(1). However, the categories of schools to which additional improvement actions apply are specified by section 1111(d)(3)(B)(i) of the ESEA, as amended by the ESSA, and the Department does not have the discretion to modify these categories. Similar considerations apply to the concern expressed by the second commenter; schools identified for targeted support and improvement (in an LEA with a significant number of such schools) are potentially subject to additional improvement action under the ESEA, as amended by the ESSA, albeit at the discretion of the State.

Changes: None.

Comments: A few commenters opposed the language in proposed § 200.23(c)(1) authorizing a State to take additional improvement action in any authorized public chartering agency with a significant number of schools identified for comprehensive support and improvement that are not meeting exit criteria or a significant number of schools identified for targeted support and improvement. One commenter asserted that the proposed regulation confused the roles of charter authorizers and charter operators, noting that authorizers are limited to monitoring school performance and using their non-renewal and charter revocation authority to close low-performing schools, rather than providing support and intervention to such schools. The same commenter warned that the proposed regulation could encourage States to take actions regarding charter authorizers that are inconsistent with State charter school law. Another commenter emphasized that the statutory provision in section 1111(c)(5) of the ESEA, as amended by the ESSA, which requires ESEA accountability provisions to be implemented for charter schools in accordance with State charter school law, together with implementing regulations in proposed § 200.12, are sufficient to ensure strong accountability for public charter schools, and that proposed § 200.23(c)(1) would potentially lead to less rigorous accountability actions by subjecting low-performing public charter schools to improvement and intervention, rather than revocation and closure. This commenter further noted that the proposed regulations could create a disincentive for such agencies to serve high-need populations or restart low-performing traditional public schools for fear of reaching the "significant number" threshold that might trigger State intervention. Another commenter stated that the proposed application of additional State improvement actions to authorized public chartering agencies would not be consistent with the ESEA, as amended by the ESSA, which does not include any accountability provisions for such entities in part A of title I. One commenter expressed concern that the proposed regulations would encourage authorizing agencies to revoke the charters of any identified charter school in an LEA serving a significant number of identified schools, a decision that might not always be the best approach or consistent with the requirements of an individual charter.

Discussion: The Department appreciates the concerns expressed by these commenters, but continues to believe that authorized public chartering agencies should, consistent with State charter school law, be subject to the same improvement actions as similarly performing LEAs. However, we are revising the final regulations to emphasize that such actions must respect the unique status and structure of charter school arrangements under State charter school law.

Changes: We have revised § 200.23(c)(1) to clarify that any action to revoke or non-renew a school's charter must be taken in coordination with the applicable authorized public chartering agency and be consistent with the terms of the school's charter.

Comments: One commenter expressed concern that the language in proposed § 200.23(c)(1) regarding the revocation or non-renewal of a charter school's charter could be read as authorizing a closure of a charter school that would not be consistent with the school's charter. The commenter noted that, for example, the school's charter might call instead for restarting the schools under new governance or hiring a new charter school operator. For this reason the commenter recommended revised language emphasizing that any State-determined intervention under proposed § 200.23(c)(1) must be consistent with both the terms of the school's charter and State charter school law.

Discussion: We agree with the commenter's recommendation, and are revising the final regulations to clarify that any State-determined action in a charter school under § 200.23(c)(1) must respect the unique status and structure of charter school arrangements under both State charter school law and the terms of the school's charter.

Changes: We have revised § 200.23(c)(1) to clarify that any action to revoke or non-renew a school's charter must be taken in coordination with the applicable authorized public chartering agency and be consistent with both State charter school law and the terms of the school's charter.

Comments: One commenter recommended the addition of expanded learning time strategies to the list of school-level improvement actions in proposed § 200.23(c)(1).

Discussion: We recognize that the use of expanded learning time strategies may be an important component of a school improvement plan but decline to make additions to the list of actions in § 200.23(c)(1), which is intended to be illustrative only and does not constrain a State from taking other actions such as those recommended by the commenter.

Changes: None.

Comments: Three commenters opposed the provision in proposed § 200.23(c)(2) permitting a State to establish an exhaustive list of State-approved, evidenced-based interventions for use in schools implementing comprehensive support and improvement or targeted support and improvement plans. Two of these commenters stated that this provision would limit local innovation in identifying and implementing evidence-based interventions, and noted that there is no statutory basis for limiting the evidence-based interventions available to an LEA. These commenters did not oppose a non-exhaustive list of State-approved, evidence-based interventions, but maintained that districts should be permitted to select and implement evidence-based interventions without restriction. One commenter supported what it described as the flexibility for States to establish exhaustive or non-exhaustive lists of evidence-based interventions for use in identified schools. Another commenter stated that the terms "exhaustive" and "non-exhaustive" could be confusing to stakeholders; for example, an "exhaustive" list could suggest either a complete compilation of all evidence-based interventions or an exclusive list of State-approved interventions that must be used by districts and schools. This commenter also encouraged the Department to clarify whether a State may adopt existing lists of evidence-based interventions rather than develop their own lists.

Discussion: The Department appreciates the concerns expressed by these commenters, but continues to believe that States should have the discretion to establish (or adopt) and approve an exhaustive list (i.e., from which an LEA must choose) or a non-exhaustive list (i.e., from which an LEA may choose) of interventions for use in schools implementing comprehensive or targeted support and improvement. This is not contrary to the ESEA or other regulatory requirements because it is permissible for States to create any such list and still requires that each identified school implement evidence-based interventions, consistent with the definition of evidence-based in title VIII of the ESEA.

Changes: None.

Comments: One commenter recommended that the Department specify the inclusion of community schools and extended learning opportunities in State lists of evidence-based practices under proposed §§ 200.23(c)(2) and (3). Another commenter requested that the Department highlight dropout prevention and recovery strategies, while a third commenter recommended the addition of school leadership programs and interventions as examples of evidence-based State-determined interventions in the final regulations.

Discussion: We decline to add specific categories of possible evidence-based interventions or strategies to the final regulations beyond the broad category of "whole-school reform models." The purpose of the regulations in this area is to describe how States may create their own lists of evidence-based interventions or develop their own evidence-based interventions, and not to require or promote specific practices.

Changes: None.

Comments: One commenter recommended a range of changes to proposed § 200.23(c) aimed at supporting more effective use of evidence-based interventions, including requiring States to provide more information on the evidence associated with each State-approved intervention; periodic updates of State-approved lists of evidence-based interventions; and State-sponsored, rigorously evaluated pilots of interventions in areas for which there is no evidence base.

Discussion: The Department appreciates the commenter's interest in promoting more effective use of evidence-based practices but declines to require or otherwise specify additional State-level activities in this area in the final regulations. We believe such activities may be addressed more appropriately, taking into account varying needs and capacities across States, through non-regulatory guidance. (26)

Changes: None.

Comments: One commenter recommended replacing the term "intervention" with "strategies" when referring to whole-school improvement strategies in proposed § 200.23(c)(3).

Discussion: We believe these terms are largely interchangeable in the school improvement context and decline to make the recommended change.

Changes: None.

Comments: One commenter recommended revisions to proposed § 200.23 that would require that additional improvement actions, if taken by a State, in schools where students receive instruction primarily through a Native American language, including any State-approved evidence-based interventions and any State-determined, school-level improvement actions, be based on research in schools where the Native American language is the primary medium of education, be conducted in the school's particular Native American language of instruction, and not limit the preservation or use of Native American languages and their distinctive features.

Discussion: The Department appreciates the concerns of the commenter that any additional State improvement actions taken in a Native American language medium school reflect and respect the importance of the language of instruction in such schools. Although we agree that States should not take improvement action without taking into account the unique nature and characteristics of Native American language medium schools, we decline to add specific requirements for such schools to the final regulations. The regulations provide sufficient flexibility for States to take into consideration multiple factors. We also note that during the required State consultation with local tribes prior to submitting the State plan (see § 299.15), local tribes can provide input regarding these issues, and we hope that the State, LEA and local tribes will work together towards the best interests of the affected students.

Changes: None.

Comments: One commenter observed that the provisions regarding State-determined interventions and State-approved lists of evidence-based interventions in proposed § 200.23(c) appear inconsistent with other provisions in the ESEA, as amended by the ESSA, emphasizing local discretion to develop and implement improvement plans in schools identified for comprehensive support and improvement or targeted support and improvement.

Discussion: The final regulations, like the proposed regulations, reflect the additional actions that States may take under the ESEA, as amended by the ESSA, to support meaningful and effective school improvement, particularly in LEAs with significant numbers of identified schools, including schools identified for comprehensive support and improvement that are not meeting exit criteria. Section 1111(d)(3) of the ESEA, as amended by the ESSA, recognizes that in such circumstances, local discretion over school improvement may not be working and thus it may be appropriate for a State to take a stronger role. Further, section 1111(d)(3)(B)(ii) specifically permits a State to establish alternative evidence-based, State-determined strategies that can be used in schools identified for comprehensive support and improvement, consistent with State law. The regulations give States flexibility to "establish" such strategies or interventions either by creating lists of State-approved, evidence-based interventions or by developing their own State-determined interventions. We are revising § 200.23(c)(3) to clarify the difference between these

166

two approaches and to include the statutory authority for State-determined interventions.

Changes: We have revised § 200.23(c)(3) to clarify that this provision permits States to develop their own evidence-based interventions and to reference the authority for such action in section 1111(d)(3)(B)(ii) of the ESEA, as amended by the ESSA.

Comments: None.

Discussion: Proposed § 200.23(c)(4) allowed a State to request that LEAs submit to the State for review and approval the amended targeted support and improvement plan required for each school in the LEA that is identified for targeted support and improvement and not meeting exit criteria over an LEA-determined number of years. After further consideration, we determined that this language was confusing. If a State chooses to conduct this review, we believe the State should be able to require an LEA to submit an amended plan for review and approval.

Changes: We have revised § 200.23(c)(4) to permit a State to require, rather than request, that an LEA submit to the State for review and approval the amended targeted support and improvement plan for each school that is required to develop such a plan under 200.22(e)(2)(i).

Section 200.24   Resources To Support Continued Improvement

LEA Application

Comments: Several commenters expressed support for the LEA application requirements in proposed § 200.24(b). One commenter supported the requirement for an assurance that each school an LEA proposes to serve with section 1003 school improvement funds will receive all of the State and local funds it would have otherwise received; this commenter also requested clarification on accountability regarding the use of funds awarded under section 1003.

Discussion: The Department appreciates the commenters' support of the requirements for LEA applications for school improvement funds. We believe any further clarification on accountability regarding the use of funds under section 1003 is more appropriate for non-regulatory guidance or technical assistance.

Changes: None.

Comments: A few commenters expressed confusion regarding proposed § 200.24(b)(1)-(2), and asked the Department to clarify that an LEA would not have to determine the interventions it will implement in a school before conducting a needs assessment and developing a plan on the basis of that assessment.

Discussion: In order to submit an application that meets all requirements, an LEA will have to conduct its needs assessment and determine the evidence-based interventions that best address the needs identified before submitting its application. We acknowledge that, depending on the timing of a State's process for awarding section 1003 funds, it could be difficult for an LEA to complete the necessary processes prior to submitting its application. Given the various timelines and procedures in place in different States, however, we decline to modify the regulations to dictate a specific timeline for allocating section 1003 funds. States should consider the general school improvement requirements, including the requirements to complete a needs assessment and identify evidence-based interventions based on that assessment, and the application process and timeline for funds under section 1003.

Changes: None.

Comments: A number of commenters recommended revisions to the LEA application provisions in the proposed regulations, including requiring to describe that each school will implement one or more evidence-based interventions based on strong, moderate, or promising evidence; requiring a demonstration that selected interventions address the results of the school's needs assessment; requiring that interventions are based on the strongest evidence available; and requiring a description of how the LEA will conduct the needs assessment; and requiring a description of the qualifications of any external partners.

Discussion: We believe the application requirements in § 200.24(b), combined with the separate but related requirements for comprehensive support and improvement plans in § 200.21, largely address the concerns of commenters while also striking the right balance between ensuring appropriate accountability for the effective use of section 1003 funds and recognizing State and local discretion in developing school improvement processes that address local needs and circumstances. Consequently, we decline to include additional application requirements in these final regulations.

Changes: None.

Comments: One commenter suggested that we require a description of the rigorous review process an LEA will use for all external service providers, not just those with which the LEA will partner for school improvement activities. This commenter further recommended that LEAs include in their applications information on their timelines and metrics for evaluating external providers, and that the regulations permit pay-for-performance contracts with external providers.

Discussion: We believe it is beyond the scope of § 200.24 to expand the requirements for review of external providers to cover all external providers, and not just those supporting school improvement projects funded through section 1003 of the ESEA, as amended by the ESSA. We further believe that other requirements related to external providers proposed by commenters, including the use of pay-for-performance contracts, are best left to the discretion of States and LEAs, most of which already have similar requirements in place based on their experience in implementing the supplemental educational services requirements of the ESEA, as amended by the NCLB.

Changes: None.

Comments: One commenter requested that the regulations require a rigorous review process of the interventions to be implemented rather than of the external provider that may help carry out the activities. Another commenter suggested that the LEA's application should describe how it will support schools in the continuous monitoring, implementation, and evaluation of interventions to ensure that any necessary adjustments are made in a timely fashion.

Discussion: Under § 200.24(d)(1)(iii), States must evaluate the use of funds under section 1003, including the impact of evidence-based interventions on student outcomes or other related outcomes and must disseminate the results of these efforts. Additionally, in the LEA application, an LEA must describe its plan to monitor each school for which the LEA receives school improvement funds, which may include reviewing both the implementation and impact of the selected interventions. Given these requirements, the Department declines to make any changes in response to these comments.

Changes: None.

Allocation of School Improvement Funds to LEAs

Comments: Several commenters requested that the Department clarify that a State may distribute school improvement funds through a combination of formula and competitive grants. Another commenter, however, recommended that funding for school improvement be based on a formula designed with input from stakeholders, rather than through a competitive process.

Discussion: Section 1003(b)(1)(A) of the ESEA, as amended by the ESSA, expressly permits States to make school improvement grants to LEAs on a formula or competitive basis. Accordingly, there is no need for the regulations to clarify that school improvement funds may be distributed through a combination of formula and competitive grants, and the Department lacks the authority to remove this statutory flexibility. For States that elect to distribute school improvement funds solely through a formula, nothing in the statute or the final regulations prohibits them from seeking stakeholder input on that formula.

Changes: None.

Comments: A couple of commenters requested that the Department clarify whether the proposed minimum grant size in § 200.24(c)(2)(ii) is annual or cumulative for schools identified for comprehensive and targeted support and improvement.

Discussion: The recommended minimum grant sizes of $500,000 and $50,000 in the regulations for each school identified for comprehensive or targeted support and improvement, respectively, are annual. The Department does not believe that additional regulatory language is needed to clarify this point. We note, however, that while these are the recommended grant sizes, the general requirement is for States to make awards of sufficient size to help LEAs effectively implement all requirements of a support and improvement plan developed under § 200.21 or § 200.22 of the final regulations, including selected evidence-based interventions.

Changes: None.

Comments: A number of commenters provided feedback on the proposed minimum grant sizes for comprehensive and targeted support schools in § 200.24(c)(2)(ii). Many of these commenters opposed the proposed minimum grant size, or any specific minimum grant size, noting that the Department should leave it to the States to decide the size of the grant. Those commenters stated that the proposed minimum grant sizes in the regulations are arbitrary, reduce flexibility, result in inefficiency, and do not take into account student populations or the unique needs of each school.

Several commenters stated that the minimum grant sizes are inconsistent with the statutory provisions allowing the State to establish the method to allocate the funds and requiring the grants to be of sufficient size to enable an LEA to effectively implement improvement activities. One commenter stated that the minimum grant size requirement assumes that additional funding is the key to successful school improvement, while other commenters suggested that many low-performing or rural schools may struggle to spend such significant amounts of funding.

Several commenters also noted that for some States, requiring awards of at least $500,000 to schools identified for comprehensive support and improvement would make it impossible to serve all such schools, or to make any awards to schools identified for targeted support and improvement. On the other hand, one commenter suggested that the proposed $50,000 minimum award for targeted support and improvement schools might not be sufficient to prevent such schools from ultimately becoming comprehensive support and improvement schools. Another commenter recommended different minimum award sizes, suggesting $30,000 for targeted support schools and $100,000 for comprehensive support schools, and suggested that rather than requiring the LEA's application demonstrate that a smaller award is appropriate, that the LEA's application must demonstrate that a larger award is appropriate. A few commenters also opposed requiring LEAs to justify awards below the proposed minimum award sizes.

Finally, several commenters recommended alternatives to regulating minimum grant sizes, including allowing States to propose their own minimum grant sizes or to simply base award sizes on such factors as the school size, the needs of students, and the interventions to be implemented.

Discussion: The minimum grant sizes required for school improvement awards under section 1003 of the ESEA, as amended by the ESSA, are not intended to limit States and LEAs from recognizing differences among schools, but rather to ensure that the grants LEAs receive to support schools identified for comprehensive and targeted support and improvement are of sufficient size to support effective implementation of evidence-based interventions and improve student outcomes. For example, the much higher minimum grant size for comprehensive support schools is intended to support the broad, fundamental, whole-school reforms that are consistent with both the purpose and requirements of comprehensive support and improvement plans under the ESEA, as amended by the ESSA. The statute and regulations recognize diversity among schools by requiring each State to give priority in awarding funds to LEAs with the greatest need for such funds and the strongest commitment to using funds to improve student outcomes— priorities that permit States to take into account such factors as school size, student needs, and selected interventions when making section 1003 awards that exceed minimum grant sizes. We also believe that because the regulations already include flexibility for States to make smaller grants, there is no need to either modify the proposed minimum grant sizes or create alternative methods that States might use to determine section 1003 grant sizes. For these reasons, we are retaining minimum award sizes for section 1003 grants in the final regulations. However, we are revising the regulations to specifically incorporate some of the factors suggested by commenters that may justify awards below the $500,000 and $50,000 minimum grant sizes.

Changes: We have revised § 200.24(c)(2)(ii) to clarify that the characteristics a State must consider in choosing to award a grant that is less than the minimum grant size include enrollment, identified needs, selected evidence-based interventions, and other relevant factors described in the LEA's application on behalf of the school.

Comments: One commenter stated that, provided there is not an increase in title I funding and in the absence of a "hold harmless" provision for the school improvement fund set-aside taken by the SEA, many LEAs may actually see a decrease in the amount of funds they receive for school improvement. The commenter advocated for the use of all school improvement funds at the local level, rather than the SEA level, and recommended that all minimum grant sizes be removed so States can make adjustments to award sizes based on title I appropriations.

Discussion: This commenter appears to be concerned that in some cases, the larger State-level school improvement reservation required by section 1003(a) of the ESEA, as amended by the ESSA, could reduce an LEA's regular title I, part A allocation below the amount it received in the prior year. Further, the commenter appears to recommend that some portion of section 1003 funds (including the State share of school improvement funding), rather than being used to support school improvement, should be used to compensate or "restore" regular LEA title I, part A allocations. This recommendation is wholly inconsistent with the requirements of the ESEA, as amended by the ESSA, which requires section 1003 funds to be used solely for school improvement activities, and not to supplement regular title I, part A allocations.

Changes: None.

State Responsibilities: Greatest Need and Strongest Commitment; Requirement To Evaluate Efforts; Renewing Grants

Comments: A few commenters recommended that the Department eliminate proposed § 200.24(c)(4)(i), which requires that a State award funds to LEAs to serve schools identified for comprehensive support and improvement ahead of those identified for targeted support and improvement. Some of these commenters noted that section 1003 of the ESEA, as amended by the ESSA, does not distinguish between comprehensive and targeted support and improvement schools. Another commenter stated that the requirement to serve schools identified for comprehensive support and improvement before schools identified for targeted support and improvement unduly limits States' and LEAs' ability to allocate resources to best meet the needs of their schools. Several commenters stated that LEAs should determine which comprehensive or targeted support and improvement schools receive funding when there are insufficient funds to award a grant of sufficient size to each LEA that submits an approvable application. Commenters were particularly concerned that, under the proposed regulations, no targeted support and improvement schools would ever receive funding due to the minimum grant award requirements.

Discussion: The Department appreciates the commenters' concern that schools identified for targeted support and improvement may not always receive funding under section 1003 of the ESEA, as amended by the ESSA. However, section 1003 of the ESEA, as amended by the ESSA, requires States to identify schools with the greatest need. We believe that schools identified for comprehensive support and improvement are the schools with the greatest need because they are the lowest-performing schools in the State.

Although we strongly agree that schools with low-performing and consistently underperforming subgroups need additional support, including additional fiscal resources to do so, we recognize that resources under section 1003 are limited and are therefore requiring that States focus those funds on the lowest performing schools overall. While LEAs have the discretion to determine which comprehensive support and improvement schools they serve first, it would be inconsistent with the statute to serve targeted support schools first.

Changes: None.

Comments: One commenter stated that States should take into account the size and characteristics of the student population that will be served, in addition to "greatest need."

Discussion: Although the Department declines to make any changes in response to this comment, the required factors in proposed § 200.24(c)(4)(ii) are minimum requirements. Thus, a State may include additional factors when determining greatest need, such as the characteristics of the student population, to the extent they are consistent with the statute and regulations.

Changes: None.

Comments: One commenter recommended that States give preference to LEAs that have (1) invested their own resources in school improvement, (2) selected evidence-based interventions that best address their needs assessments, (3) plans to monitor and evaluate programs to promote continuous improvement, and (4) demonstrated a commitment to using evidence.

Discussion: We believe most of the factors recommended as priorities by the commenter reflect existing requirements for improvement plans under the ESEA, as amended by the ESSA, and thus would not support meaningful differentiation among applicants. The exception, which is the extent to which an LEA has invested its own resources in school improvement, potentially excludes many high-poverty LEAs with few resources of their own but great need for additional school improvement funding. Consequently, we decline to modify the priorities included in the final regulation, though we note that States may include additional factors beyond those in proposed § 200.24(c)(4), to the extent that they are consistent with the statute and regulations.

Changes: None.

Comments: A few commenters stated that the regulations establishing the factors a State must consider in determining which LEAs demonstrate the "greatest need" for school improvement funds and the "strongest commitment" to use those funds to improve academic achievement and student outcomes in the lowest-performing schools exceed the Department's authority, or impose an unnecessary burden on SEAs or LEAs. These commenters stated that these determinations should be left to States, and suggested including the factors listed in the regulations as examples, rather than requirements, of how a State might make these determinations. A couple of commenters opposed particular factors for consideration, including resource allocation among LEAs and current academic achievement, with a couple of these commenters asserting that the requirement to look at resource allocation is contrary to the statute. One of these commenters also asserted that, through these regulations, the Department was attempting to influence the allocation of State and local funds, which the commenter believed to be prohibited by section 8527(a) of the ESEA, as amended by the ESSA.

Discussion: We disagree with the comments asserting that these regulations exceed the Department's authority. Section 1003(f) of the ESEA, as amended by the ESSA, requires a State, in allocating section 1003 school improvement funds, to give priority to LEAs that "demonstrate the greatest need for such funds, as determined by the State" and that "demonstrate the strongest commitment to using [such] funds . . . to enable the lowest-performing schools to improve student achievement and student outcomes." The statute, however, does not clearly define the terms "greatest need" or "strongest commitment." We believe the regulations are necessary to clarify the statutory terms and to ensure that States meet these statutory requirements in a way that advances the purpose of section 1111(d)(1) and (2) as well as the overall purpose of title I—to improve student outcomes and close educational achievement gaps. As such, we believe these requirements fall squarely within the scope of title I, part A of the statute as well as the Secretary's rulemaking authority under GEPA, the DEOA, and section 1601(a) of the ESEA, as amended by the ESSA, and do not violate section 1111(e) (see discussion of the Department's rulemaking authority under the heading Cross-Cutting Issues). Further, we believe that the requirements strike the proper balance between ensuring compliance with these key provisions of the statute while maintaining States' authority to make determinations regarding the award of school improvement funds. We do not agree with commenters that these requirements add new or unnecessary burden to States and LEAs because States and LEAs must meet these requirements; the regulations clarify how they must do so.

Further, we disagree that the requirements in § 200.24(c)(4)(ii) violate section 8527 of the ESEA, as amended by the ESSA. That provision states that nothing in the ESEA authorizes an officer or employee of the Federal Government "to mandate, direct, or control" a State, LEA, or school's allocation of State or local resources. As the requirements in § 200.24(c)(4)(ii) simply establish the factors a State must consider in determining how to prioritize awards of Federal school improvement funds, it in no way "mandates, directs, or controls" the allocation of State or local resources.

Changes: None.

Comments: Several commenters supported the requirement that a State consider, in determining strongest commitment, the proposed use of evidence-based interventions supported by the strongest level of evidence. One commenter recommended giving priority to an LEA that maximizes the use of evidence-based interventions in all appropriate aspects of its improvement plan, while another commenter recommended that the State consider the degree to which the LEA maximizes the use of evidence-based interventions supported by evidence that is both rigorous and relevant to the problems to be addressed.

Discussion: We agree with commenters that it is not only the rigor of the evidence supporting interventions that should be considered, but also whether the interventions to be implemented address the full scope of problems to be addressed. Thus, we are revising § 200.24(c)(4)(iii)(A) to require that a State consider, in determining strongest commitment, the proposed use of evidence-based interventions and whether they are sufficient to support the school in making progress toward meeting the exit criteria under §§ 200.21 or 200.22.

Changes: We have revised § 200.24(c)(4)(iii)(A) to require that a State consider, in determining strongest commitment, not only the proposed use of evidence-based interventions that are supported by the strongest level of evidence available, but also whether the evidence-based interventions are sufficient to support the school in making progress toward meeting exit criteria under §§ 200.21 or 200.22.

Comments: One commenter opposed § 200.24(c)(4)(iii)(A), asserting that this provision requires levels of evidence not required by the statute and which may impose financial burdens on LEAs that must conduct their own studies to meet the required evidence levels.

Discussion: Section 200.24(c)(4)(iii)(A) is consistent with section 8101(21)(B) of the ESEA, as amended by the ESSA, which requires that the activities and strategies funded under section 1003 of the ESEA meet the requirements for strong, moderate, or promising evidence under section 8101(21)(A). Further, the regulations do not limit the award of section 1003 funds to an applicant implementing interventions at a specific evidence level, nor do they require LEAs to expend their own funds to conduct studies. States may support LEAs in conducting or reviewing existing studies, and States and LEAs may use existing sources of studies, including the What Works Clearinghouse.

Changes: None.

Comments: Several commenters supported the inclusion of family and community engagement in the proposed regulations as a factor a State must consider in determining strongest commitment. One commenter also encouraged a greater allocation of resources for family and community engagement.

Discussion: The Department appreciates the support of commenters for this provision. We note that LEAs have the flexibility to spend as much as is reasonable and necessary for family and community engagement under section 1003, and thus, decline to address this issue in the final regulations.

Changes: None.

Comments: One commenter suggested that the regulations include a commitment to delivering a well-rounded education for all students in proposed § 200.24(c)(4)(iii) as a factor to be considered in determining strongest commitment.

Discussion: The Department agrees that access to a well-rounded education is a key goal supported by the ESEA, as amended by the ESSA, but notes that an emphasis on a well-rounded education may not be consistent with the requirements of comprehensive and targeted support and improvement plans, which generally must focus on the specific academic needs of students that led to identification. For this reason, we decline to make changes in response to this comment.

Changes: None.

Comments: One commenter requested that the Department strike or clarify the requirement in § 200.24(d)(2)(ii) that if a State, using funds under section 1003, directly provides for school improvement activities or arranges for their provision through an external provider that such a provider have a "record of success."

Discussion: We believe it is essential that a State directly providing these services through an external provider ensure that such a provider has a record of success in helping LEAs and schools. We also believe that each State should have flexibility in determining whether a provider has a record of success, the criteria for which may vary depending on the services and assistance that the provider will offer, and decline to constrain this flexibility through any changes to the final regulations.

Changes: None.

Comments: A few commenters supported the focus in § 200.24(d) on the evaluation and dissemination of findings on the impact of evidence-based interventions funded with section 1003 funds. Several commenters encouraged the Department to expand this evaluation requirement to include studying the implementation of the evidence-based interventions, not just the impact of such interventions. Another commenter recommended revising proposed § 200.24(d)(1)(iii) to require that States disseminate results of their evaluation efforts not only to LEAs with schools identified under § 200.19, but also to all LEAs in the State.

Discussion: The Department appreciates commenters' support of the evaluation and dissemination provisions for evidence-based interventions funded by section 1003. These provisions are intended to strike a balance between the need to build the evidence base on school improvement interventions and the recognition that many States may have limited resources and capacity to carry out such work; consequently, we decline to add to these requirements.

Changes: None.

Comments: A few commenters objected to the regulations making annual renewal of section 1003 school improvement awards contingent on a determination that a funded school is making progress on a State's goals and indicators. One commenter suggested clarifying the definition of "progress" by looking at data from the School Improvement Grants program, while another recommended the addition of examples of leading indicators that might be used to demonstrate progress.

Discussion: The Department appreciates these comments and understands that the process of improvement in a low-performing school can take several years and requires a plan for sustainability, consistent with the statutory acknowledgement that schools may need a grant for up to four years. Under the statute and regulations, the State defines the long-term goals and measurements of progress and determines how much progress is sufficient to support renewing an LEA's school improvement grant. For example, the State could set growth goals on the indicator or measure that resulted in the schools' identification, either for the all students group or particular subgroups. We believe this flexibility, in combination with the regulations, strikes the right balance between providing appropriate support for school improvement efforts and ensuring accountability for the effective expenditure of taxpayer funds. Therefore, the Department declines to make changes in response to these comments, and believes that any further clarification would be provided more appropriately through non-regulatory guidance.

Changes: None.

Comments: None.

Discussion: In reviewing the proposed regulations, the Department believes it is helpful to clarify what States will be required to submit in their title I State plans under section 1111 of the ESEA, as amended by the ESSA, to ensure that States are fulfilling their responsibilities under § 200.24(d). While proposed § 200.12 required that each State plan must include information about the State's process for ensuring development and implementation of school improvement plans consistent with the requirements of § 200.24, it will be more helpful for States if greater specificity regarding the required information is described in § 200.24. As § 200.24(d) includes five specific State responsibilities regarding funds under section 1003 of the ESEA, as amended by the ESSA, we are revising the final regulations to specify that a State must describe how it will fulfill these responsibilities in its State plan.

Changes: We have revised § 200.24(d) to clarify that a State must describe how it will meet the requirements pertaining to State responsibilities for funds under section 1003 of the ESEA, as amended by the ESSA.

Eligibility for School Improvement Funds

Comments: One commenter stated that before the passage of the ESSA, States were able to identify schools for supports if they were title I eligible. However, the commenter stated that under the proposed regulations, States are no longer afforded that option. Similarly, another commenter stated that the regulations are not clear that any school identified for comprehensive or targeted support and improvement is eligible for school improvement funding, regardless of title I status. This commenter recommended including language in the regulations stating that any school that is identified for comprehensive or targeted support under section 1111(d) of the ESEA, as amended by the ESSA, should be eligible for funding under section 1003(a), regardless of whether such school participates, or is eligible to participate, under title I.

Discussion: The relationship between title I status and eligibility for school improvement support has changed under the ESEA, as amended by the ESSA, and section 1003(b)(1)(A) of the ESEA is requires that any school that is identified for comprehensive or targeted support and improvement is eligible for school improvement funding under section 1003. Section 200.19 of the regulations clearly identifies which schools must be identified for comprehensive or targeted support and improvement, clarifying which categories of schools include title I and non-title I schools. Section 200.24(a) reiterates the statutory requirement that any schools meeting the statutory definition of comprehensive or targeted support and improvement are eligible for funds under section 1003. Therefore, we decline to add additional regulatory language to § 200.24 to this point.

Changes: None.

Other Reporting Requirements

Comments: A few commenters recommended that each State make publicly available on its State report card a list of LEAs and schools eligible for school improvement funds that did not receive them, due to insufficient funds at the State level.

Discussion: While the information requested by commenters is available on State report cards (which must include all schools identified for comprehensive or targeted support and improvement—and thus eligible for school improvement funding—and those receiving school improvement funds), insufficient funding is not the only reason that some eligible schools might not receive funding. Any State that implements the statutory priorities for targeting school improvement funds, ensures that each grant is of sufficient size to support full and effective implementation of the evidence-based interventions selected by each grantee, and generally adheres to minimum grant size requirements is unlikely to have sufficient resources under section 1003 of the ESEA, as amended by the ESSA, to award a grant to each LEA such that every identified school receives funding. In addition, not every LEA with one or more eligible schools is likely to apply for section 1003 funds, particularly if the State implements a rigorous application process consistent with the requirements of the ESEA, as amended by the ESSA, and applicable regulations.

Changes: None.

Specific Uses of School Improvement Funds

Comments: Several commenters asked the Department to clarify that specific uses of funds are permissible under section 1003 of the ESEA, as amended by the ESSA, including: Expansion of access to high-quality, developmentally appropriate early education; the creation of new charter schools to serve students enrolled in schools identified for comprehensive support and improvement, and other students in the local community and low-performing schools; and summer learning and enrichment activities.

Discussion: The use of funds provided under section 1003 of the ESEA, as amended by the ESSA, generally is governed by the requirements for comprehensive or targeted support and improvement plans in §§ 200.21 and 200.22, as well as the evidence requirements in section 8101(21)(B) of the ESEA, as amended by the ESSA. Consequently, the uses of funds proposed by the commenters would be allowable only as part of such improvement plans, thus it would be potentially misleading and inconsistent with the ESEA, as amended by the ESSA, to specify particular uses of section 1003 funds outside of those plans.

Changes: None.

Comments: One commenter requested that the Department specify that Parent Training and Information Centers may be used as a resource for improvement activities.

Discussion: The Department believes that it would be more appropriate to identify the wide range of resources that States and LEAs could enlist in support of school improvement activities, including Parent Training and Information Centers, through non-regulatory guidance and other technical assistance than in these final regulations.

Changes: None.

Other Comments on School Improvement Funds

Comments: One commenter requested that the Department clarify whether several schools could share a single allocation of funds for comprehensive and targeted support and improvement if they have similar challenges and are willing to undertake collaborative projects to develop and implement intervention strategies. Similarly, another commenter requested allowing States to combine school-level allocations in a zone-approach to managing turnaround of two or more schools identified for improvement.

Discussion: The Department appreciates these comments and the creative approaches to effectively use limited funds. However, the Department's interpretation of section 1003 of the ESEA, as amended by the ESSA, is that a district must apply for funds on behalf of one or more specific schools to ensure that each application meets all of the requirements with respect to that school. Even though each application must be separate, schools and LEAs may choose to collaborate as they complete the applications and may determine that it is appropriate in some cases to share certain resources as they implement their interventions such as, for example, technical assistance providers, professional development resources, or instructional coaches. For these reasons, the Department declines to make any changes in response to these comments.

Changes: None.

Comments: One commenter expressed general opposition to the reporting requirements in proposed § 200.24(e) and recommended removing them because they generally opposed data collection and reporting.

Discussion: Subsection 200.24(e) merely incorporates into regulation the reporting requirements related to section 1003 funds found in section 1111(h)(1) of the ESEA, as amended by the ESSA.

Changes: None.

Comments: One commenter recommended adding a new provision to proposed § 200.24 that would require each State and LEA involved in the allocation of funds under section 1003(a) of the ESEA, as amended by the ESSA, to assure that LEA applications on behalf of schools, including charter schools, serving students primarily instructed through a Native Language instruction program include provisions that improvement support will be in the Native American language. The commenter also recommended that the LEA assure the selected interventions: (1) Include evidence-based interventions that are conducted through a Native American language and which are based on evidence that was obtained through research in a school conducted primarily through a Native American language; (2) do not limit the preservation or use of Native American languages; and (3) are specific to the specific Native American language of instruction and its distinctive features. Finally, the commenter recommended that the State and LEA assure that external partners of an LEA include staff fully proficient in the Native American language used in the school receiving support.

Discussion: The Department believes that the existing requirements for school improvement plans, including such elements as the needs assessment required for comprehensive support and improvement schools, stakeholder consultation requirements, and the selection of evidence-based interventions are sufficient to address the concerns of the commenter. For example, one consideration in selecting appropriate evidence-based interventions is determining whether the research supporting the effectiveness of the intervention was collected based on a population that overlaps with the population of students to be served in the identified school. For these reasons, the Department declines to make any changes in response to this comment.

177

Changes: None.

Comments: One commenter asked that the Department clarify that the term "intervention" is a reference to schoolwide improvement strategies for improving student outcomes, rather than individual-level student interventions.

Discussion: We believe that the term "intervention" reasonably means different things in different contexts. While "intervention" could refer to a whole-school reform strategy, it also could mean an activity focused on addressing a particular academic need for a low-performing subgroup or, in some cases, individual student-level interventions.

Changes: None.

Comments: One commenter suggested that the Department add "scheduling" to the list of operational flexibilities in proposed §§ 200.24(b)(7) and 200.24(d)(1)(v) that an SEA or LEA consider providing to support full and effective implementation of comprehensive and targeted support and improvement plans. This commenter stated that this addition is necessary to ensure that principals have autonomy to make critical school-level decisions regarding not only staffing and budgets, but also scheduling. In addition, this commenter recommended adding to proposed § 200.24(b)(8) an assurance that the new principal, if applicable, will be identified on a timeline that allows for meaningful participation in the planning activities so that new principals have sufficient time to plan before the school year begins.

Discussion: We agree with the commenter that there may be other areas of operational flexibility beyond budgeting and staffing, including scheduling, that States or LEAs should consider providing, as appropriate, to ensure full and effective implementation of school improvement plans. However, we believe that States and LEAs are best positioned to determine which areas of operational flexibility should be considered, and decline to add any further examples beyond those already included in the non-exhaustive list in the regulations.

Changes: None.

Comments: One commenter recommended requiring States to provide some type of support to targeted support and improvement schools that do not receive section 1003 funds.

Discussion: We agree that States should provide technical assistance and other support to all identified schools, including schools that do not benefit from section 1003 funds, and we note that States may use their 5 percent State-level set-aside under section 1003 for this purpose. However, we decline to require such support in the final regulations because it could conflict with other provisions in the ESEA, as amended by the ESSA, such as the requirement that States prioritize school improvement technical assistance and related support to LEAs with significant numbers or percentages of identified schools.

Changes: None.

Comments: One commenter stated that the way funding is allocated to support school improvement is unnecessary and extremely time consuming to document.

Discussion: The requirements and procedures for awarding section 1003 school improvement funds are closely tied to the requirements of the ESEA, as amended by the ESSA, and are designed to both ensure that school improvement funds are used effectively to support improved student outcomes in identified schools and to ensure appropriate accountability for taxpayer-provided funds. However, we appreciate that the term "allocate" may imply that States should provide detailed documentation about their fiscal allocation process; therefore, we are revising § 200.24(d)(1)(i) to clarify that the State must describe, in its State plan, its process to award grants to LEAs.

Changes: We have revised § 200.24(d)(1)(i) to clarify that each State must describe, in its State plan under section 1111 of the ESEA, as amended by the ESSA, the process to award grants to LEAs under section 1003.

Comments: One commenter supported the requirement making schools identified for targeted support and improvement due to low assessment participation rates ineligible for section 1003 school improvement. This commenter also requested clarification regarding whether schools that do not meet exit criteria after the initial award period can receive additional school improvement funding. This commenter stated that the regulations do not specify what occurs after the award period expires if the school has not met the defined exit criteria.

Discussion: We appreciate the commenter's support and further clarify that grants under section 1003 may be awarded for up to four years, and thus may be continued for schools that do not meet their exit criteria, provided that such schools take the actions required by either §§ 200.21(f) for schools identified for comprehensive support or 200.22(e) for schools identified for targeted support.

Changes: None.

Sections 200.30 and 200.31   Annual State and LEA Report Card

General

Comments: Several commenters expressed support for proposed regulations clarifying statutory requirements for the State and LEA report cards required by the ESEA, as amended by the ESSA, and highlighted increased transparency and disaggregation for many of the data elements as particularly helpful. Conversely, some commenters expressed general opposition to the proposed regulations, variously asserting that they exceed statutory requirements; would be burdensome to implement; and, based on past experience, would be unlikely to result in better student outcomes.

Discussion: The Department appreciates support for the State and LEA report card regulations and notes that they are consistent with sections 1111(h)(1)(C) and 1111(h)(2)(C) of the ESEA, as amended by the ESSA, which maintain a majority of the State and LEA report card requirements required by NCLB and add several new requirements.

The Department values transparency, consistent with the statute, and disagrees that efforts to support improvements in teaching and learning have not benefited from the State and LEA report card provisions under the ESEA, as amended by NCLB. With respect to LEA report cards in particular, there is evidence that when school quality information, including information about school accountability results, is provided to parents, they pay attention and respond. (27) Report cards can positively impact the extent to which parents engage in their children's education and, in turn, help to improve student outcomes. As such, we believe that any burden imposed by the report card requirements is outweighed by the resulting educational benefits.

In response to commenters who generally opposed the requirements on the ground that they exceed the statutory requirements, as discussed previously in the discussion of Cross-Cutting Issues, the Department has rulemaking authority under section 410 of GEPA, section 414 of the DEOA, and the section 1601(a) of the ESEA, as amended by the ESSA. Given that authority and that these regulations fall squarely within the scope of title I, part A of the statute, consistent with section 1111(e), the regulations need not be specifically authorized by the statute, nor is the Department limited to issuing regulations that merely restate the requirements in the statute.

Changes: None.

Development of Report Cards in Consultation With Parents

Comments: Many commenters supported proposed §§ 200.30(b)(1) and 200.31(b)(1), which require that State and LEA report cards be developed in consultation with parents. Some commenters requested that the language be expanded to require consultation with other stakeholders as well, including teachers, principals, other school leaders, specialized instructional support personnel, and special education teachers. Some commenters suggested that each State also be required to describe its consultation process. Additionally, one commenter asserted that the statute does not require parental consultation on the LEA report card and, therefore, such consultation would be more appropriately addressed through non-regulatory guidance.

Discussion: We appreciate the support from many commenters who share our belief that it is essential that the perspectives of parents—who are among the primary consumers of State and LEA report cards—be solicited, considered, and incorporated into the report card development process. We also believe that while the ESEA, as amended by the ESSA, does not specifically require consultation with parents in the development of LEA report cards, requiring such consultation falls within the scope of and is consistent with the statutory consultation requirement for State report cards, consistent with section 1111(e) of the ESEA, as amended by the ESSA. Moreover, we believe parental consultation on LEA report cards is particularly important given that these report cards typically contain the school- and district-level information that is most relevant and useful to parents. In addition, as discussed previously in the section on Cross-Cutting Issues, the Department's rulemaking authority under section 410 of GEPA, section 414 of the DEOA, and section 1601(a) of the ESEA, as amended by the ESSA, allows it to issue regulatory provisions not specifically authorized by statute.

States and LEAs have discretion to include other stakeholders in the development of their report cards and we believe they are likely to include many of the individuals suggested by commenters. As noted previously, however, the emphasis of the regulations on parental consultation is based on the requirements of the ESEA, as amended by the ESSA. For these reasons, we decline to specify additional stakeholders in the final regulations.

Changes: None.

Accessibility of Notices, Documentation, and Information

Comments: Many commenters remarked on the requirements that appear in several sections of the proposed regulations (including proposed §§ 200.30(c), 200.30(d)(1)(i), 200.31(c), 200.31(d)(1), 200.31(d)(2), 200.32(b), 299.13(f), and 299.18(c)(4)(v)), regarding the use of Web sites to disseminate required information including, for example, annual State and LEA report cards and a State's consolidated State plan or individual program State plan. Further, while proposed § 200.21(b) does not explicitly mention posting of the notice that an LEA must provide to parents of students in schools identified for comprehensive or targeted support and improvement on a Web site, some commenters suggested that a Web site may be the vehicle through which LEAs meet this requirement.

While a small number of commenters supported the accessibility requirements generally, several commenters asserted that the requirements do not sufficiently ensure that parents and other stakeholders are able to access the documentation and information discussed in the proposed requirements. Specifically, many commenters expressed concern regarding the accessibility for individuals with disabilities, and requested that we strengthen the requirements. For example, commenters recommended requiring that Web sites conform with the World Wide Web Consortium's Web Content Accessibility Guidelines (WCAG) 2.0 Level AA and the Web Accessibility Initiative Accessible Rich Internet Applications Suite (WAI-ARIA) 1.0 for web content. In addition, some commenters recommended that States and LEAs ensure that parents without home access to the Internet are provided with the information included on State and LEA report cards.

Further, many commenters suggested that the Department strengthen the provisions to accommodate parents with limited English proficiency by, for example, requiring that such documentation and information be available in the most populous languages in the State or LEA, as applicable, or that the Department define certain terms in the proposed accessibility requirements (e.g., "to the extent practicable"). Finally, several commenters suggested that the Department require States to provide information included on State report cards in an easily accessible manner that is publicly downloadable by all visitors to a State's Web site without restrictions, necessary permissions, or fees.

Discussion: We agree that all parents and other stakeholders, including those with disabilities and those who have limited English proficiency, must have meaningful access to documentation and information that States and LEAs disseminate. Such access is critical in order to understand State, LEA, and school performance and progress, meaningfully engage in reform efforts, and help to ensure that all children have an opportunity to meet a State's academic standards.

Although the ESEA, as amended by the ESSA, and its implementing regulations require that certain information on State or LEA Web sites be "accessible," the requirement that Web sites be accessible to individuals with disabilities is also based on the Federal civil rights requirements of Section 504 of the Rehabilitation Act, 29 U.S.C. 794, title II of the Americans with Disabilities Act, 42 U.S.C. 12131 et seq., and their implementing regulations, all of which are enforced against SEAs and LEAs by the Department's Office for Civil Rights (OCR).

Although the Department does not currently require States and LEAs to use specific Web site accessibility standards, under the ESEA, as amended by the ESSA, and Federal civil rights laws and regulations, States and LEAs must ensure that information provided through electronic and information technology, such as on Web sites, is accessible to individuals with disabilities. In OCR's enforcement experience, where a State or LEA provides required information through Web sites, it may be difficult to ensure compliance with accessibility requirements without adherence to modern standards such as the WCAG 2.0 Level AA standard, which includes criteria that provide comprehensive Web accessibility to individuals with disabilities—including those with visual, auditory, physical, speech, cognitive, developmental, learning, and neurological disabilities. Accordingly, we strongly encourage States and LEAs that disseminate information via Web sites to consider that standard as they take steps to ensure that their Web sites comply with requirements of these regulations and with Federal civil rights laws. WCAG 2.0 has been designed to be technology neutral to provide Web developers more flexibility to address accessibility of current as well as future Web technologies; in addition, Level AA conformance is widely used, indicating that it is generally feasible for Web developers to implement. The developers of WCAG

2.0 have made an array of technical resources available on the W3C Web site at no cost to assist entities in implementing the standard. For more information, see www.w3.org/WAI/.

Similarly, the Department expects that States and LEAs will provide access for parents who may not have online access, such as by providing online access at their local school or LEA administrative office. Regarding requests to add accessibility requirements to ensure that parents with limited English proficiency can access documentation and information, including by defining certain terms in the proposed accessibility requirements (e.g., "to the extent practicable"), please see additional discussion in § 200.21(b)(2).

Finally, with respect to making SEA and LEA report card data available to be downloaded, while the Department encourages States and LEAs to make available the information included on report cards in easily accessible, downloadable formats that are freely open to the public, the Department declines to impose additional potentially burdensome requirements on States and LEAS given the extent of information required by the statute for inclusion on report cards.

Changes: None.

Recommendations To Include Additional Information on State and LEA Report Cards

Comments: Many commenters recommended that the Department add additional requirements, data elements, or other information to State and/or LEA report cards. Specifically, several commenters recommended that the Department require that report cards provide for comparability of all State and LEA report card data at the State, LEA, and school levels, and that data be presented such that it can be easily compared across LEAs. Some of these commenters further requested that the Department specify certain parameters for States choosing to meet the cross-tabulation assurance under section 1111(g)(2)(N) of the ESEA, as amended by the ESSA, via their State report cards, including that the data be in certain file formats to ensure that it can be easily downloaded and analyzed.

Several commenters requested that the Department require additional data elements or information not required by the statute be included on State and LEA report cards, including, for example, disaggregation by additional subgroups such as justice-involved youth and American Indians; further disaggregation within subgroups currently required including Asian American/Pacific Islanders, English learners, and students with disabilities; indication of subgroups too small for reporting; reporting on whether an LEA chooses the exemption under § 200.21(g) for a high school identified for comprehensive support and improvement and, if so, the reason for such exemption; more prominent information on subgroups whose performance declined so that school-level declines are not attributed to any one subgroup; data on access to technology resources; data on access to the arts in high- versus low-poverty schools; and information on how LEAs will use funds under title I and elsewhere to support activities that coordinate and integrate before- and after-school programs.

One commenter appreciated the Department indicating that States and LEAs can add information related to the number and percentage of students attaining career and technical proficiencies. Finally, two commenters requested additional information, including student achievement data on subject areas in addition to reading/language arts and mathematics (report cards also require results of the State's science assessments) and results on the indicators in a State's accountability system for all schools, including those that have not been identified as comprehensive or targeted support and improvement schools.

Discussion: The ESEA, as amended by the ESSA, maintains the majority of the State and LEA report card provisions required under the ESEA, as amended by NCLB, and adds several additional reporting requirements. For example, LEA report cards must continue to include information on how the academic achievement of students in the LEA compares to that of students in the State as a whole and, at the school level, how the academic achievement of students in the school compares to that of students in the LEA and the State, respectively, in reading/language arts, mathematics, and science. Further, the ESEA, as amended by the ESSA, requires that LEA report cards include, for all schools (not solely schools identified for comprehensive or targeted support and improvement), results on the indicators in a State's accountability system including, for example, information on the performance on the other academic indicator under section 1111(c)(4)(B)(ii) of the ESEA, as amended by the ESSA, used by the State in the State accountability system for public elementary schools and secondary schools that are not high schools; high school graduation rates; and information on the performance on the other indicator or indicators of School Quality or Student Success under section 1111(c)(4)(B)(v) of the ESEA, as amended by the ESSA, used by the State in the State accountability system, etcetera.

With respect to additional requirements that commenters recommended the Department add to the State and LEA report card regulations, while we agree that States and LEAs should strive to develop report cards that convey data and information in ways that maximize use by parents and others, we believe that the requirements for State and LEA report cards under section 1111(h)of the ESEA, as amended by the ESSA, and §§ 200.30 through 200.37 sufficiently ensure that State and LEA report cards will be transparent and maximally useful to parents and other stakeholders. Further, States and LEAs can, if they choose to do so, display graphically, or in other ways, comparisons of State, LEA, and school performance on data elements other than student academic achievement on the assessments required under section 1111(b)(2). States choosing to meet the cross-tabulation assurance under section 1111(g)(2)(N) of the ESEA, as amended by the ESSA, via their State report cards, can provide the data—as well as other data reported on report cards— in certain file formats to ensure that it can be easily downloaded and analyzed. The Department believes that doing so would facilitate use by a wide range of consumers of report cards, including people who may use the data to identify trends that may be of use to States, LEAs, and schools in engaging in data driven decision making. However, we are not requiring States to do so, as this may impose additional burden for some States.

With respect to requiring additional information on State and LEA report cards that is not required under section 1111(h)(1)-(2) of the ESEA, as amended by the ESSA, and proposed §§ 200.30-200.37, given the extent of information that is required for inclusion on State and LEA report cards, the Department declines to require additional information. However, sections 1111(h)(1)(C)(xiv) and (h)(2)(C)(iii) of the ESEA, as amended by the ESSA, provide for both States and LEAs, at their discretion, to include additional information that they believe will help parents and other stakeholders understand State, LEA, and school performance and progress. Such additional information could include any or all of the data elements that commenters noted above. In particular, in light of the student demographics in particular States, LEAs, or schools, States or LEAs may wish to report on the performance of additional student subgroups not required under the ESEA, as amended by the ESSA, or further disaggregate required reporting elements by subgroups that are not required under the ESEA. For example, States and LEAs may wish to disaggregate data by subgroups, such as justice-involved youth or American Indians, that are not required under the ESSA, as amended by the ESSA. Doing so may help to better identify the needs of students in these subgroups and support State, LEA, and school efforts to improve teaching and learning for these students.

In general, States and LEAs have flexibility to go beyond what section 1111(h)(1)(C), (2)(C) and §§ 200.30 through 200.37 require regarding presentation and information required on State and

LEA report cards. For example, States and LEAs can provide report card data in formats that can be easily downloaded, add additional information unique to their State and local contexts, and include additional comparative data or provide mechanisms for the public to generate such comparisons. The Department supports State and LEA report cards that both align with the requirements in the ESEA, as amended by the ESSA, and are tailored to the unique composition and needs of States and LEAs.

Changes: None.

State and LEA Report Card Overview

Comments: Some commenters supported the overview section in proposed §§ 200.30(b)(2) and 200.31(b)(2) on either or both the State and LEA report cards, explaining that such a section will help ensure that parents and other stakeholders encounter key metrics about State, LEA, and school performance as the first information when they review report cards.

Conversely, some commenters opposed the overview section requirements on either or both the State and LEA report card. Some commenters asserted that the overview requirements extend beyond what is required for State and/or LEA report cards under sections 1111(h)(1)-(2) of the ESEA, as amended by the ESSA. Others asserted that the parameters were too prescriptive and decisions of content and format for the overview sections would best be left to States and LEAs or addressed in non-regulatory guidance. A few commenters specified that States should be able to decide, in particular, whether or not to include a school's summative rating on the LEA report card overview for each school served by the LEA. One commenter recommended that the Department allow for States to differentiate the content of the State and LEA report card overview sections so that these sections can be tailored to what parents need to know most given the particular State and LEA context. One commenter suggested that providing disaggregated data for some subgroups but not others on the report card overview section could be confusing.

Specific to the format of the LEA report card overview for each school served by the LEA, several commenters contended that the required information would not fit on a single sheet of paper as required in proposed § 200.31(b)(3). Others suggested that the Department be mindful of the need to ensure that the font size on the LEA report card overview for each school served by the LEA be of sufficient size to be able to effectively communicate information. One commenter suggested that the page length of the LEA report card overview for each school served by the LEA cannot be appropriately determined until a State finalizes the elements of its accountability system. Finally, other commenters requested clarification regarding what exactly constitutes a single sheet of paper.

Discussion: We appreciate the comments that support the State and LEA report card overview section, and concur that the overview section will help parents and the public more effectively access and consider data in engaging in State, LEA, and school reform efforts. Particularly given the amount of information that State and LEA report cards must include under the ESEA, as amended by the ESSA, the overview section serves to highlight certain data elements in order to quickly convey State, LEA, and school performance and progress. With the flexibility States are given to include extensive accountability system indicators in evaluating the performance and progress of schools, a school's determination is an important piece of summary information that will help provide a holistic picture of school performance and progress. The information to be included on the State and LEA overviews can help to provide context for reviewing the full data elements on State and LEA report cards.

The State and LEA report card overviews align with the requirement in sections 1111(h)(1)(B) and 1111(h)(2)(B) of the ESEA, as amended by the ESSA, that report cards be concise and presented in an understandable and uniform format. In particular, the overview sections serve to succinctly convey State, LEA, and school performance and progress while not abandoning minimum statutory report card requirements related to transparent and accurate presentation of a broad range of data and therefore fall squarely within the scope of section 1111(h) of the ESEA, as amended by the ESSA, consistent with section 1111(e). As discussed previously in the discussion of Cross-Cutting Issues, the Department has rulemaking authority under section 410 of GEPA, section 414 of the DEOA, and the section 1601(a) of the ESEA, as amended by the ESSA. Given that authority, it is not necessary for the statute to specifically authorize the Secretary to issue a particular regulatory provision.

Regarding the subgroups included on the overview section, States and LEAs have discretion as to whether to include all disaggregated subgroups required under section 1111(c)(2) of the ESEA, as amended by the ESSA, and § 200.16(a), while including, at a minimum, the subgroups a State uses for accountability purposes consistent with § 200.16. While the Department believes that it is critical to identify the needs of all subgroups for which the statute requires disaggregated reporting, gathering an understanding of the performance that led to a school's accountability determination can help frame school performance overall and provide context for the further disaggregation that will be provided in the full State and LEA report cards.

Further, the Department agrees with several commenters that the LEA overview section for each school served by the LEA must be of sufficient length and font size to meet the goal of providing critical information to help parents and other stakeholders understand key metrics of State, LEA, and school performance. We also agree that additional flexibility is needed to do so. To help determine the most appropriate length and font size of the LEA overview for each school served by the LEA, LEAs should include discussion of this LEA report card section when they consult with parents in the development of the LEA report cards as required under § 200.31(b)(1).

Finally, given the concern regarding length of the overview section, rather than prescribe a particular length, we are deleting the requirement for that the LEA report card overview for each school served by the LEA be limited to a single piece of paper. Thus, the regulations need not clarify what constitutes a single sheet of paper.

Changes: We revised § 200.31(b)(3) to remove the requirement that the LEA overview for each school served by the LEA be on a single sheet of paper.

Dissemination of LEA Report Card School-Level Overviews

Comments: Some commenters addressed the requirement in proposed § 200.31(d)(3)(i) regarding dissemination of the LEA report card overview for each school served by the LEA. One commenter commended the Department for including a requirement to provide such overview to parents of each student enrolled in the LEA by either mail or email. However, some commenters asked for clarification of the proposed dissemination requirement. In addition, one commenter expressed opposition to what the commenter perceived as a requirement to provide parents with hard copies of the LEA report card overview for each school. Another commenter opposed the requirement to disseminate the LEA report card overview to parents of each enrolled student in each school via either mail or email, asserting that this requirement extends beyond what section 1111(h)(2)(B)(iii) of the ESEA, as amended by the ESSA, requires.

Discussion: We appreciate support for the requirement in § 200.31(d)(3)(i) to disseminate the LEA overview section for each school served by the LEA directly to parents. This provision offers regular mail and email as examples of how this requirement could be met. Hard copy dissemination is not required. As suggested by one commenter, methods such as providing the overview at parent-teacher conferences, at parent nights, or with students to take home would also be sufficient to meet this requirement.

Regardless of the method selected for providing this information to parents, we believe that, consistent with the dissemination and accessibility requirements under section 1111(h)(2)(A) and (B)(iii) of the ESEA, as amended by the ESSA, key information about school performance must reach parents directly and in a timely fashion so that they have relevant information to work effectively with educators and local school officials during the school year. Moreover, as discussed previously in the discussion of Cross-Cutting Issues, the Department has rulemaking authority under section 410 of GEPA, section 414 of the DEOA, and the section 1601(a) of the ESEA, as amended by the ESSA. Given that rulemaking authority and that these regulations fall within the scope of section 1111(h) of the ESEA, as amended by the ESSA, consistent with section 1111(e), it is not necessary for the statute to specifically authorize the Secretary to issue a particular regulatory provision.

Changes: We have revised § 200.31(d)(3)(i) to clarify that LEAs can disseminate the LEA report card overview for each school served by the LEA directly to parents by means such as email, mail, or other direct means of distribution.

Report Card Dissemination Timeline Generally

Comments: Several commenters expressed support for the annual December 31 deadline for States and LEAs to disseminate report cards under §§ 200.30(e) and 200.31(e), suggesting that an annual deadline would encourage States and LEAs to provide more timely information to parents and stakeholders. Many commenters opposed the annual deadline because of concerns related to additional administrative burden that would be caused by overlapping report card dissemination and Department reporting timelines. These commenters offered a number of alternative proposals, including the removal of the deadline for dissemination of report cards, an alternate deadline of March 31, and a State-determined deadline that would be included in a State consolidated plan. Some commenters suggested maintaining the December 31 deadline, but also allowing States and LEAs to update report cards after December 31 with data unavailable on December 31.

Some commenters also claimed that the ESEA, as amended by the ESSA, does not authorize the Department to require a specific deadline for dissemination of State and LEA report cards. These commenters argued that December 31 is an arbitrary reporting deadline not found in statute.

A few commenters cited challenges meeting the deadline specifically for reporting graduation rates, per pupil expenditures, and postsecondary enrollment. Responses to those comments are provided below in separate comment summaries specific to these data elements.

Discussion: We believe that timely report card dissemination, when combined with the report card overview section requirements in §§ 200.30 and 200.31, will help ensure parents and the public can more effectively access and use State-, LEA-, and school-level data to help address achievement, opportunity, and equity gaps during the school year.

We acknowledge that the newly required report card elements under the ESEA, as amended by the ESSA, may, initially, be more difficult for States and LEAs to implement. For this reason, §§ 200.30 and 200.31 include a one-time, one-year extension for those reporting elements.

Although we decline to extend the general report card dissemination deadline, as discussed below, we have revised §§ 200.30(e) and 200.31(e) to permit States and LEAs to delay inclusion of data on per-pupil expenditures on annual State and LEA report cards until no later than June 30 following the December 31 deadline, provided that the report cards otherwise meet the December 31 dissemination deadline and include a description of when per-pupil expenditure data will be made available. We note that specific comments related to the timeline for reporting graduation rates, per pupil expenditures, and postsecondary enrollment are discussed more fully below.

In response to commenters who questioned our authority in this area, as discussed previously in the discussion of Cross-Cutting Issues, the Department has rulemaking authority under section 410 of GEPA, section 414 of the DEOA, and the section 1601(a) of the ESEA, as amended by the ESSA. Given that rulemaking authority and given that these regulations fall within the scope of title I, part A of the statute, consistent with section 1111(e), it is not necessary for the statute to specifically authorize the Secretary to issue a particular regulatory provision. The Department believes that December 31 provides States with sufficient time to report on the required data elements, while maintaining the goal of timeliness such that parents, teacher, principals, and other stakeholders can consider the information in helping to focus school improvement efforts. The December 31 date is purposefully chosen to balance the needs of States and LEAs in ensuring accurate data while providing such data in as timely a manner as possible.

Changes: None.

Graduation Rates Reporting Timeline

Comments: Several commenters opposed the December 31 deadline for reporting prior year adjusted cohort graduation rates on State and LEA report cards. Commenters cited several reasons for their opposition. Some commented that it is an unreasonable timeline because of the inclusion of summer graduates, and because States use the October 1 enrollment count to determine whether students have dropped out. Others indicated a preference for continuing to allow States to lag graduation rates for report card purposes. One commenter suggested that to report prior year graduation rate data on the report card, it would be necessary to move the deadline to March 31 or later every year. One commenter noted that the deadline would require system changes that would be difficult or impossible to perform without significant additional resources.

Discussion: We believe that it is important that graduation rate data is as timely as possible to give stakeholders, including parents, access to information that is still relevant for their decision making and to accurately describe the success of a school in the most recent school year. We understand that some State processes to review and audit graduation rate data are on a timeline that does not currently allow for a December release of graduation rate data and this provision will require some States to adapt their systems to meet the December 31 timeline. However, we do not agree with commenters that indicated that releasing prior year graduation rate data by December 31 is unreasonable. By December of 2018, States will have had seven years to refine their process for producing adjusted cohort graduation rate data (since the requirements went into effect in 2008 for reporting on the 2010-11 school year). Even with the inclusion of summer graduates, States should have sufficient time to review and release their data without the need for significant additional resources.

We also disagree with commenters suggesting that a State should be permitted to lag its graduation rate data. Data are most useful and meaningful when they represent the most recent year. If a State reports lagged data in 2018, then it would be reporting 2016-17 graduation rates in December of the 2018-19 school year, meaning that the data available to parents would be a year and a half old. This delay will have an adverse impact on the utility of the data for decision making and transparency, which is one of the primary purposes of making timely data available on State and LEA report cards.

Changes: None.

Per-Pupil Expenditures Reporting Timeline—Annual Reporting

Comments: Many commenters requested that, for reporting per-pupil expenditures under proposed § 200.35, the Department allow additional flexibility beyond the one-time, one-year extension a State may request under proposed §§ 200.30(e)(2) and 200.31(e)(2) if the State or its LEAs cannot meet the December 31, 2018, deadline for reporting newly requested information, such as per-pupil expenditures, on report cards. These commenters stated that reporting per-pupil expenditures annually by December 31 is an unreasonable timeline because of possible auditor shortages, inconsistencies with single audit requirements for Federal grantees, incompatible LEA expenditure reporting timelines, which in some cases are established in State law, and the increased likelihood of inaccurate data production if States must publish report cards with per-pupil expenditure data shortly after receiving unverified LEA expenditure reports.

A majority of these commenters requested that we change the annual per-pupil expenditure reporting deadline to June 30 annually. Other commenters suggested extending the deadline to March 31, while some recommended using a State-determined date for publishing per-pupil expenditure data on report cards. One commenter supported the December 31 annual deadline for per-pupil expenditures and two additional commenters generally supported the December 31 annual deadline for disseminating report cards, although they did not specifically mention per-pupil expenditures.

Discussion: We agree with commenters that States and LEAs should report per-pupil expenditure data that is accurate, has been thoroughly reviewed, and clearly reflects how resources are allocated in schools. We also agree with commenters that an annual reporting deadline of June 30 would provide the appropriate amount of time for States and LEAs to ensure high-quality data is publicly available.

Therefore, we have added new §§ 200.30(e)(2) and 200.31(e)(2), which permit a State or LEA that is unable to include per-pupil expenditures on report cards by the December 31 deadline to update its report card with such data no later than the following June 30. Additionally, the Department will provide technical assistance and support to States and LEAs in implementing the per-pupil expenditure reporting requirement.

Changes: We have revised §§ 200.30(e) and 200.31(e) to clarify when newly required information must be included on State and LEA report cards and to permit States and LEAs to delay inclusion of data on per-pupil expenditures on annual State and LEA report cards until no later than June 30, provided that the report cards otherwise meet the December 31 dissemination deadline and include a brief description of when per-pupil expenditure data will be made available.

Per-Pupil Expenditures Reporting Timeline—First Time Reporting of These Data

Comments: Several commenters noted that some State and LEA data collection systems may be unable to collect and report school year 2017-2018 per-pupil expenditure data. Some commenters

188

indicated that SEAs have invested in sophisticated data systems that focus on student achievement over the past few years, but have not invested in comparable fiscal tracking systems. Commenters also stated that maintaining the statutory implementation timelines would mean fewer SEA resources could be devoted to the development and implementation of new accountability systems. These commenters requested that the Department allow flexibility for States and LEAs that do not have the capacity to implement the per-pupil expenditure reporting requirement by the December 31, 2018, deadline proposed in the regulations.

Discussion: To accommodate potential challenges in implementing new report card requirements, States and their LEAs may request a one-time, one-year extension to build technical capacity, where necessary. We believe that this flexibility, in addition to the option to defer annual reporting of per-pupil expenditures from December 31, 2018, to the following June 30, provides States a sufficient amount of time for State fiscal collection and reporting systems to be aligned with statutory and regulatory requirements. As a result of this additional flexibility, if a State is unable to report per-pupil expenditures in school year 2017-2018 by June 30, 2019, and is granted a one-time, one-year extension their plan and timeline would outline how the State will include school year 2018-2019 per-pupil expenditure information on State and local report cards by June 30, 2020.

Changes: None.

Postsecondary Enrollment Reporting Timeline

Comments: Some commenters expressed concerns with timelines for postsecondary enrollment reporting. Two commenters indicated that due to processing time or collection timelines, States may not be able to report postsecondary data on the immediately preceding school year by December 31. One commenter provided data that indicated that seven percent of all students and 11 percent of low income, high minority students would not be captured in the calculation if data on the immediately preceding school year are required by December 31. Instead, commenters recommended that States be allowed to lag their postsecondary enrollment data. One commenter indicated that the requirement to begin reporting in 2017 is too ambitious and suggested that States establish their own reporting timeline following consultation with stakeholders. Another commenter recommended that we allow for a delay between graduation and postsecondary actions for reporting this metric if the student was unable to enroll due to health problems or some other circumstance.

Discussion: We appreciate commenters that noted the challenges of reporting data on the immediately preceding school year by December 31 due to collection and processing timelines. While the statute specifies that the postsecondary enrollment metric must be defined in such a way that it captures students who enrolled in the first academic year that follows their graduation (or the immediately following academic year), the Department does not believe that the language implies that States are expected to include the data representing the graduating class from the immediately preceding school year on their report cards. We recognize that the academic year could include students that enroll in the fall, spring, or summer following their graduation from high school. Since report cards are due before the completion of the full academic year, it would not be possible for States to include complete postsecondary data on their report cards. As such, the Department's expectation is that postsecondary enrollment will be lagged (i.e., the report card produced in December of 2018 will contain data on the graduating class from the 2016-17 school year instead of the 2017-18 school year). While we recognize that reporting on this new metric by the time report cards for the 2017-2018 school year must be disseminated may be challenging for some States and LEAs, we note that under §§ 200.30(e)(2) and 200.31(e)(2) a State may request a one-time, one-year extension for reporting on some or all of the new information, including postsecondary enrollment data, that must be included on State and LEA report cards.

We also recognize that there are circumstances that prevent students from immediately enrolling in programs of postsecondary education, but the time frame in which students can be included in this metric is also in the statute, which specifies that it must be in the first academic year that follows the student's graduation. However, we believe that the first academic year can include students that first enroll in the fall, spring, or summer, which allows for the inclusions of students that may be unable to enroll by the fall.

Changes: None.

Additional Statutory Subgroups Generally

Comments: Some commenters submitted general comments related to three new subgroups on which States must disaggregate certain information on report cards as required under section 1111(h)(1)(C)(ii) of the ESEA, as amended by the ESSA: Children who are homeless, children in foster care, and children with parents who are members of the Armed Forces. A few commenters indicated their support for the definitions included in the regulations, which would require States to use definitions consistent with other Federal laws for these subgroups to ensure consistency in reporting across States. Some commenters noted that reporting data on these new subgroups would create privacy concerns or other sensitive issues, since there will be small numbers of students in each group, particularly at the LEA and school levels.

Discussion: We appreciate comments supporting the definitions for the new subgroups required under the ESEA, as amended by the ESSA. We believe that these definitions will not only help ensure consistency across States but also align with definitions currently used for other programs supporting these populations, which will help our understanding of the outcomes of these students across programs. We agree with commenters that these populations may be small and that it is important to protect the privacy of small subgroups of students. In this regard, section 1111(i) of the ESEA, as amended by the ESSA, clearly addresses privacy of student data by requiring data to be collected and disseminated in a manner that protects the privacy of individual students, consistent with section 444 of GEPA (commonly known as the Family Educational Rights and Privacy Act (FERPA)). Section 1111(i) further states that disaggregation shall not be required if the n-size is small enough to reveal personally identifiable information or information that is not statistically sound. The Department has reinforced this requirement by including it in §§ 200.30(f)(2) and 200.31(f) of the regulations.

Changes: None.

Status as a Child in Foster Care

Comments: Some commenters noted that some States use a more expansive definition of children in foster care, which includes not just children living in 24-hour substitute care, but also children who may not yet have been removed from their homes but for whom the Title IV-E agency has placement responsibility. They requested that the requirements allow a State with an expanded definition to include these students in its status as a child in foster care subgroup.

Discussion: We do not agree with the recommendation that a State with an expanded definition of students in foster care should be permitted to use this definition for the purposes of reporting on this subgroup in title I report cards. Children who are placed in foster care and children who are allowed to remain at home under State custody represent two distinct populations; thus we believe it is important to preserve the subgroup being reported as those students who are placed in foster care. We believe that requiring disaggregation for the students placed in foster care will help States, State child welfare agencies, and other stakeholders gain a better understanding of the educational outcomes of a highly mobile population and the impact that being removed from home has on a child's ability to learn. As such, we believe that it is important to collect data only on those children who are placed in traditional out-of-home foster care. These data will be most useful to stakeholders if all children are reported using the same definition of children in foster care, and using an existing definition is the cleanest approach to implementing this new requirement. Further, this definition is consistent with the definition used in the non-regulatory guidance that we issued jointly with the Department of Health and Human Services, "Ensuring Educational Stability for Children in Foster Care" (Children in Foster Care Guidance) which helps to ensure consistency across program requirements. The Foster Care Guidance can be found at: http://www2.ed.gov/policy/elsec/leg/essa/edhhsfostercarenonregulatorguide.pdf.

Changes: None.

Status as a Military-Connected Student

Comments: Several commenters supported the requirement in proposed § 200.30 to report academic results for students with a parent who is a member of the Armed Forces on active duty. Several commenters suggested proposed § 200.30 should also require identifiers for students with parents serving in the Reserve components of the military services or full or part-time National Guard. They argued that regardless of the specific military connection, parental deployment impacts children in the same manner. Two commenters suggested the identifier should also be extended to military-connected students who are eligible for special education services under the IDEA.

Two commenters requested the Department expand the definition of parent to include caretakers such as legal guardians, custodians, State-determined definitions of the legal guardians and custodians, and stepparents. These commenters also requested the Department specify at what time during the school year service by a military-connected parent is to be counted for purposes of identification.

One commenter asked the Department to explain the definition of all active duty and whether it includes deployed military parents only or also full-time military who are not deployed. One commenter asked why Congress included this identifier under the ESEA, as amended by the ESSA, and if there is evidence of delayed academic progress for children of parents in the military. One commenter argued the military-connected identifier will result in an unlawful violation of privacy.

One commenter requested that the Impact Aid regulatory requirements and these regulations be aligned, where possible, to limit administrative burden for LEAs, and that the Department gather feedback from LEAs that educate a significant number of military-connected students to ensure effective implementation of the new requirement. One commenter requested that the military-connected identifier be aligned with the reporting requirements under 20 U.S.C. 7703 (i.e., the Impact Aid program).

Discussion: We agree with commenters that students with parents serving full-time in the National Guard face the same challenges as students with parents on active duty in the Armed Forces. We also recognize that, as part of the process for developing proposed assessment regulations under title I, part A, the negotiated rulemaking committee reached consensus on regulations in which the issue of disaggregating achievement data for students with parents on active duty in the Armed Forces or on full-time National Guard duty is addressed. The negotiated rulemaking committee, relying on the same rationale as commenters, recommended that the Department require that State assessment systems be able to disaggregate assessment results for military-connected students to include those with parents on full-time National Guard duty. This recommendation is reflected in the Department's proposed assessment regulations, which require that State assessment systems enable results to be disaggregated within each State, LEA, and school by students with a parent who is a member of the Armed Forces on active duty or serves on full-time National Guard duty, where "armed forces," "active duty," and "full-time National Guard duty" have the same meanings given them in 10 U.S.C. 101(a)(4), 101(d)(1), and 101(d)(5). Additionally, because section 1111(h)(1)(C)(ii) of the ESEA, as amended by the ESSA, (which we have clarified in § 200.30(f)(iv)) cross-references the statutory definition of "full-time National Guard duty" in 10 U.S.C. 101(d)(5), it is unclear if Congress intended to extend the military connected identifier to include student with parents on "full-time National Guard duty." Given these considerations, the Department agrees with commenters that in disaggregating information on student achievement on the State's academic assessments based a student's military-connected status, States and LEAs should be required to include students with a parent who is a member of the Armed Forces on active duty as well as students with a parent who serves on full-time National Guard duty in the subgroup of students with a parent who is a member of the Armed Forces on active duty.

We recognize the importance of service in the Reserve components of the military services and part-time National Guard. We note, however, that the statute focuses on full-time and active duty service in the military. As such, the Department declines to further extend the requirement regarding disaggregation by military-connected status.

We appreciate requests for additional clarification related to legal guardian status and when service by a military connected parent are to be counted for purposes of identification, but believes these questions are best addressed in non-regulatory guidance. We note though, that section 8101(38) defines a parent to include a legal guardian. With respect to the meaning of active duty, the term is clearly defined in the § 200.30(f)(iv)(B) consistent with the statutory definition in 10 U.S.C. 101(d)(1) and, as a result, the Department does not believe additional clarification is needed. However, the Department will consider providing additional information regarding this term in non-regulatory guidance.

The Department is unable to provide additional clarity related to the intent of Congress in requiring States and LEAs to disaggregate student achievement based on military-connected status. Nor is the Department able to provide evidence of delayed academic progress for children of parents in the military, primarily because the requirement to track academic performance of this subgroup of students did not exist prior to the enactment of the ESSA. The Department respects the concerns a commenter raised about student privacy, particularly of military-connected students, but is comforted by strong privacy protections under the ESEA, as amended by the ESSA, FERPA, and § 200.30, which it expects will be faithfully implemented by States and LEAs.

Although the Department declines to require States and LEAs to further disaggregate the military-connected student subgroup to distinguish between military connected students who utilize special education services under the IDEA and those that do not, the Department encourages State and LEAs to include reporting on additional subgroups, as appropriate. Further, we remind commenters that under section 1111(g)(2)(N) of the ESEA, as amended by the ESSA, States are able to provide cross-tabulated information by additional subgroups beyond the minimum requirements, which include major racial and ethnic group, gender, English proficiency status, and children with or without disabilities.

While the Department seeks to create consistency across program requirements where possible, there is a misalignment of military-connected statutory definitions between 20 U.S.C. 7703 (i.e., the Impact Aid program) and definitions under the ESEA that reference 10 U.S.C. 101. Under Impact Aid, students are identified if they have a parent on active duty in the uniformed services (as defined in 37 U.S.C. 101) that do or do not reside on Federal property, while title I of the ESEA, as amended by the ESSA, references definitions of member of the Armed Forces on active duty or who serves on full-time National Guard duty (as defined in 10 U.S.C. 101). Further, the procedures for counting military students under the Impact Aid statute are more specific than military subgroup reporting requirements under the ESEA, as amended by the ESSA. Lastly, the Department will take into consideration the request to gather feedback from LEAs that educate a significant number of military-connected students and encourages SEAs to complete the same type of outreach as part of their required consolidated State plan consultation activities.

Changes: We have revised § 200.30(f)(iv) to clarify that, for purposes of reporting data on State and LEA report cards by military-connected status, a parent who is a member of the Armed Forces on active duty includes a parent on full-time National Guard duty. In so doing, we have further defined "full-time National Guard duty" consistent with 10 U.S.C. 101(d)(5). In addition, we made conforming edits in § 200.33(a)(3)(ii)(F).

Section 200.30   Annual State Report Card

Demographic and Achievement Data for Charter School Students by Charter School Authorizer

Comments: Many commenters supported the proposed requirement in § 200.30(a)(2)(ii) that State report cards include certain information for each authorized public chartering agency in the State, explaining that reporting this information would increase transparency and accountability for charter school authorizers. Other commenters, however, opposed this requirement, including some who suggested striking the requirement. Some commenters asserted the Department lacks the authority to require this information to be included on report cards because the statute does not require it. Other commenters indicated that it would be complicated and burdensome for States to identify the required comparison group, and that this complexity could undermine the goal of transparency. Some commenters suggested that the Department remove the comparison group component of the provisions and instead require States to report solely on the demographic composition and achievement of students in charter schools organized by charter authorizer.

Discussion: We appreciate the support for this provision from some commenters. With respect to the Department's authority to issue this requirement, as discussed previously in the discussion of Cross-Cutting Issues, the Department has rulemaking authority under section 410 of GEPA, section 414 of the DEOA, and the section 1601(a) of the ESEA, as amended by the ESSA. Given that rulemaking authority, it is not necessary for the statute to specifically authorize the Secretary to issue a particular regulatory provision. Moreover, the Department believes that transparency regarding the demographic composition and student achievement of charter school students, as compared to that of the relevant LEA or LEAs, falls within the scope of title I, part A of the statute, consistent with section 1111(e) and is necessary to advance the overall purpose of title I, which is "to provide all children significant opportunity to receive a fair, equitable, and high quality education and to close educational achievement gaps." We note that providing this information by authorizer is particularly important given that authorizers generally have a significant oversight role with respect to the charter schools they authorize, and parents and other stakeholders may not be able to easily access this information by authorizer absent this requirement.

With respect to the comments regarding the potential difficulties associated with identifying an appropriate comparison group, the regulations provide flexibility for a State to determine the appropriate comparison, which may include the LEA or LEAs from which the charter school draws a significant portion of its students or a more specific, State-determined geographic community within an LEA. To ensure they are able to determine the appropriate comparison, we encourage States to consult with the charter school community, including authorized public chartering agencies. Further, we believe the benefits that will result from this reporting requirement in terms of increased transparency and accountability for this growing segment of public schools outweigh any burden it might impose on a State.

Changes: None.

Section 200.32   Description and Results of a State's Accountability System

General Comments

Comments: A few commenters expressed support for the requirements in proposed § 200.32 that State and LEA report cards include information on and results from a States' accountability system, including the requirement in proposed § 200.32(c)(2) and (c)(3) that LEA report cards include the reason that led to a school's identification as a comprehensive or targeted support and improvement school. One commenter noted that requiring the reason for identification will help LEA and school staff target school needs.

However, some commenters opposed the requirement that State and LEA report cards include a school's identification as a comprehensive or targeted support and improvement school and the reason that led to such identification, suggesting that these particular requirements extend beyond what sections 1111(h)(1)(C) and (h)(2)(C) of the ESEA, as amended by the ESSA, require. Another commenter suggested that proposed § 200.32(c)(2) and (c)(3) be expanded to require that LEA report cards include additional information regarding a school's identification as a comprehensive or targeted support and improvement school, specifically "any missed targets." A few commenters requested that State and LEA report cards include additional information related to a State's minimum n-size for accountability, such as the number and percentage of all students and students in each subgroup for whose results schools in the LEA are not held accountable in the State's system of meaningful differentiation.

Two commenters supported the option in proposed § 200.32(b) for State and LEA report cards to provide the Web address or URL of, or a direct link to, the State's State plan or other location on the SEA's Web site where one can access the required description of a State's accountability system. Finally, one commenter requested that the Department replace the term "rating" with the term "determination."

Discussion: We appreciate the support of some commenters for various provisions in § 200.32. Sections 1111(h)(1)(C)(i)(V) and (h)(2)(C) of the ESEA, as amended by the ESSA, require that State and LEA report cards include the names of all schools identified by the State for comprehensive support and improvement or implementing targeted support and improvement plans. Further, we believe that, in conjunction with the identification of a school as a comprehensive or targeted support and improvement school, it is important for State and LEA report cards to indicate the reason that led to a school's identification in order to help focus school, parent, and community efforts to improve teaching and learning for all students and particularly for historically underperforming subgroups of students. As discussed previously in the discussion of Cross-Cutting Issues, the Department has rulemaking authority under section 410 of GEPA, section 414 of the DEOA, and the section 1601(a) of the ESEA, as amended by the ESSA. Given that rulemaking authority and that these regulations fall squarely within the scope of section 1111(h) of the ESEA, as amended by the ESSA, consistent with section 1111(e), it is not necessary for the statute to specifically authorize the Secretary to issue a particular regulatory provision.

We decline to require additional information on State and LEA report cards related specifically to schools identified as comprehensive or targeted support and improvement or implications of a State's minimum n-size beyond what section 1111(h)(1)(C)(i) of the ESEA, as amended by the ESSA, and § 200.32 require. However, States and LEAs may include any additional information that they believe will provide parents and other stakeholders with important information about school performance and progress. Further, with respect to one commenter's request for additional information regarding a State's minimum n-size, we note that § 299.17(b)(4) requires States to provide additional detail related to their minimum n-size in either their consolidated State plan or individual title I plan. Thus, because § 299.13(f) requires the State plan to be published on a State's Web site, such information will be publicly available.

We concur with the commenters who supported the option to allow States and LEAs to provide the Web address or URL of, or a direct link to, the State's State plan or other location on the State's Web site where one can access the description of a State's accountability system required under section 1111(h)(1)(C)(i), (h)(2) of the ESEA, as amended by the ESSA, and § 200.32. Given the amount of information on State and LEA report cards, we recognize that a detailed description of some of the accountability system elements may not add significantly to parents' or other stakeholders' understanding of school performance and progress and thus believe it is appropriate to allow the State or LEA to provide a Web address for, or direct link to, the State plan or another location on the SEA's Web site for detailed information on the accountability system. We do encourage States and LEAs, in developing report cards, to consider the amount of information needed to help parents and other stakeholders engage in and understand the State accountability system. Finally, the Department is replacing the term "rating" with "determination" for the same reasons as we discussed previously in § 200.18.

Changes: We have removed the term summative "rating" in final § 200.32(c)(4) and replaced it with "determination.".

Section 200.33   Calculations for Reporting on Student Achievement and Progress Toward Meeting Long-Term Goals

Reporting on Achievement

Comments: Two commenters supported the requirement in § 200.33(a)(3)(iii) for calculating and reporting the results of students at each level of achievement, while others opposed it. A few commenters requested that States be able to report information on student achievement using something other than percent proficient, including scale scores or a performance index. Other commenters suggested that it could be confusing to provide two different calculations for percent proficient, with some commenters elaborating that reporting both percentage of students tested and not tested in addition to proficiency based on valid test scores would be sufficient to reach appropriate conclusions regarding State, LEA, and school achievement information. Finally, some commenters requested that the Department add a requirement that States either notify parents of students in schools with differences in proficiency rates or explain on State and LEA report cards the difference between the two different proficiency calculations.

Discussion: We appreciate commenters who supported the requirement in § 200.33(a)(3)(iii). Section 1111(c)(4)(E)(ii) of the ESEA, as amended by the ESSA, requires that States measure, calculate, and report on the Academic Achievement indicator under section 1111(c)(4)(B)(i), in a manner in which the denominator includes the greater of either 95 percent of all such students, or 95 percent of all such students in the subgroup, as the case may be; or the number of students participating in the assessments. Thus, with respect to this indicator of a State's accountability system, a school's performance will be based on this calculation. Because States will use this calculation for accountability purposes, we believe it is important to provide States, LEAs, and schools with information on student achievement on the reading/language arts, mathematics, and science academic assessments described under section 1111(b)(2) that is based on this calculation. However, we also believe that it is important to provide information on student achievement based on the number of valid test scores, as that represents the achievement of students that actually took the assessment. Together, these two calculations will help ensure that parents, teachers, principals, and other key stakeholders have access to a more nuanced picture of State, LEA, and school performance on the assessments required under the ESEA, as amended by the ESSA.

With respect to reporting on student achievement using a metric other than percent proficient, sections 1111(h)(1)(C)(xiv) and (h)(2)(C)(2)(iii) of the ESEA, as amended by the ESSA, provide for States and LEAs to include on report cards any additional information they believe will best provide parents, students, and other members of the public with information regarding the progress of each of the State's public elementary and secondary schools. This could include additional metrics of school, LEA, and State performance.

Changes: None.

Reporting Overall and by Grade

Comments: None.

Discussion: We wish to clarify that, in addition to State and LEA report cards including the percentage of students performing at each level of achievement under section 1111(b)(1)(A) of the ESEA, as amended by the ESSA, on the academic assessments under section 1111(b)(2) by grade, State and LEA report cards must include such information overall. In doing so, report cards will convey student achievement for all students at each grade-level tested and also for the State, LEA, and school as a whole. Thus, parents and other stakeholders will have a targeted, as well as more holistic, understanding of student achievement and be able to identify trends by grade and overall. Requiring reporting of these results overall is particularly important for LEA report cards that include information for each school served by the LEA, as small schools may not have enough students by grade in order to meet a State's minimum n-size for reporting but may have enough students overall by school.

Changes: We have revised § 200.33(a)(1) to require reporting overall and by grade.

Section 200.34   High School Graduation Rate

General

Comments: A few commenters generally supported the requirements for calculating the four-year adjusted cohort graduation rate in proposed § 200.34, while another commenter noted that they were little changed from the requirements under the previous regulations. One commenter objected to the four-year graduation rate because some students may need less time and some may need more time to graduate. Another commenter recommended attaching more value to a high school diploma.

Discussion: We appreciate support from commenters for regulations supporting on the calculation and reporting of meaningful four-year cohort graduation rates, and agree that they are very similar to the previous regulations. One important change, however, is that States and LEAs now may include in the numerator of the calculation students with the most significant cognitive disabilities who were assessed using the alternate assessment aligned to alternate academic achievement standards and receive State-defined alternate diplomas. We believe that the four-year adjusted cohort rate is an appropriate measure because it reflects the typical amount of time required to obtain a high school diploma, but we note that the regulations permit States to implement an extended-year graduation rate. Finally, the significant role of graduation rates for high schools in statewide accountability systems demonstrates the high value attached to a high school diploma as an essential outcome for all students under the ESEA, as amended by the ESSA.

Changes: None.

Comments: A few commenters raised technical considerations related to the adjusted cohort graduation rate, including the need to accurately track students that move between schools, business rules that may be necessary to account for different types of diplomas or alternative schools, and the importance of defining a ninth-grade cohort early in the school year.

Discussion: We believe that the requirements in the final regulations for calculating the adjusted cohort graduation rate, combined with State experience in implementing these requirements, generally provide both the guidance and flexibility that States need to address the technical concerns noted by the commenters. The adjusted cohort graduation rate accounts for many of the issues identified by commenters in its design. For example, as reflected in § 200.34(b), LEAs and schools are required to track students throughout their time in the cohort. Moreover, to remove a student from a cohort, schools and LEAs must confirm in writing the basis for such removal. Additionally, § 200.34(a)(2), consistent with section 8101(25)(A)(i) and (23)(A)(i) of the ESEA, as amended by the ESSA, includes language that will ensure that the cohort is formed early enough in the year that it can account for most attrition, since it requires that a new cohort of students is formed no later than the date by which student membership data is collected by States for submission to NCES, which is typically near October 1. States should establish clear business rules and internal controls so that graduation rates information is tracked accurately at the school, LEA, and State levels.

Changes: None.

Comments: Some commenters suggested alternative metrics to replace or to report in addition to the adjusted cohort graduation rate, such as a completion indicator for students who finish high school using alternate pathways and timelines or a one-year graduation rate for certain schools designed to reengage students who are over age. Another commenter asserted that States should be permitted to select or define their own graduation rate measure.

Discussion: The regulations are consistent with section 1111(h)(1)(C)(iii)(II) and (h)(2)(C) of the ESEA, as amended by the ESSA, which require that a State and its LEAs calculate and report a four-year adjusted cohort graduation rate. A State may also calculate and report, at its discretion, one or more extended-year adjusted cohort graduation rates. Completer rates and other metrics that do not track students through their high school career mask critical information about student outcomes, such as students who drop out earlier in their high school career or students who take an extended period of time to graduate. While not required, States may include additional metrics that provide supplemental information about students completing high school through alternative routes or programs.

Changes: None.

Comments: One commenter requested clarification in the regulations about the inclusion of summer graduates in the four-year adjusted cohort graduation rate.

Discussion: Section 8101(23) and (25) of the ESEA, as amended by the ESSA, provides for students to be included as graduates in the numerator if they earn a regular high school diploma, or State-defined alternate diploma for students with the most significant cognitive disabilities, before, during, or at the conclusion of their fourth year of high school or a summer session immediately following the fourth year of high school. This permits, but does not require, a State to include summer graduates. If a State chooses not to include summer graduates in the numerator, those students still must be included in the denominator if they are part of the original cohort for that class.

Changes: None.

Regular High School Diploma Definition

Comments: Many commenters provided input on the definition of the term "regular high school diploma" under proposed § 200.34(c)(2), particularly insofar as the definition provides that it may not include a diploma based on meeting IEP goals that are not fully aligned with the State's grade-level academic content standards. Although one commenter supported this language, the remaining commenters opposed some or all of the language around the IEP diploma. Some commenters asserted that the Department should not add to the plain language of the statute, but the majority of commenters opposed the language because of the potential unintended consequences of allowing an IEP diploma that is based on grade-level standards to be treated as equivalent to a regular high school diploma.

Discussion: We agree with the majority of commenters that a regular high school diploma should not include a diploma based on meeting IEP goals, regardless of whether those goals are fully aligned with a State's grade-level academic content standards. Under 34 CFR 300.320(a)(2), each child's IEP must include a statement of measurable annual goals designed to meet the child's needs that result from the child's disability to enable the child to be involved and make progress in the general education curriculum and to meet each of the child's other educational needs that result from the child's disability. Although the use of standards-based IEPs has greatly expanded, IEP goals cannot serve as a proxy for determining whether a student has met a State's grade-level academic content standards. Therefore, a diploma based on meeting IEP goals will not provide a sufficient basis for determining that the student has met a State's grade-level academic content standards; rather, it will only demonstrate that the student has attained his or her IEP goals during the annual period covered by the IEP. Therefore, a diploma based on attainment of IEP goals, regardless of whether the IEP goals are fully aligned with a State's grade-level content standards, should not be treated as a regular high school diploma, and we are revising the final regulations to clarify this point. Finally, as discussed previously in the section on Cross-Cutting Issues, the Department's rulemaking authority under section 410 of GEPA, section 414 of the DEOA, and section 1601(a) of the ESEA, as amended by the ESSA, allows it to issue regulatory provisions not specifically authorized by statute, and we appropriately exercise that authority here given that the regulations fall squarely within, and are reasonably necessary to ensure compliance with, section 1111(h) of the ESEA, as amended by the ESSA, consistent with section 1111(e).

Changes: We have revised proposed § 200.34(c)(2) to remove the language "that are not fully aligned with the State's grade level academic content standards" following "such as a diploma based on meeting IEP goals."

State-Defined Alternate Diplomas

Comments: Some commenters supported proposed § 200.34(a)(1)(ii), which requires students receiving a State-defined alternate diploma to be counted in the numerator of the four-year adjusted cohort graduation rate. However, other commenters opposed the retroactive reporting requirements in proposed § 200.34(e)(ii)(4) for students who take longer than 4 years to earn an alternate diploma. These commenters opposed the proposed method of including students with the most significant cognitive disabilities who earn a State-defined alternate diploma in the adjusted cohort graduation rate only through retroactive reporting. These commenters recommended revising the final regulations to allow students to be included in the year that they graduate (instead of tying them to their original cohort and including them retroactively once they graduate). Commenters also recommended requiring disaggregation of the number and percentage of students with disabilities reported in the adjusted cohort graduation rate by (1) students receiving a regular high school diploma and (2) students receiving a State-defined alternate diploma.

Discussion: We appreciate the comments supporting the inclusion of students receiving a State-defined alternate diploma in graduation rate calculations. We also agree with commenters who recommended including such students in the four-year adjusted cohort graduation rate calculation in the year in which they graduate, while still ensuring that they are accounted for in a cohort, and are revising the final regulations accordingly. The final regulations will require a State to keep such a student in his or her original cohort until grade 12 and, at which time the IEP team can evaluate if the student is eligible and on track to receive the State-defined alternate diploma within the time period for which the State ensures the availability of FAPE. The final regulations ensure that a student removed from the cohort in grade 12 will be reassigned to the four-year graduation cohort of the year of exit, regardless of how the student exits. Additionally, the language allows for a meaningful way to include students with the most significant cognitive disabilities in extended-year graduation rates, if such rates are adopted by the State, by including such students in the extended-year rates associated with their new cohort (i.e., in the subsequent years following their inclusion in the four-year graduation rate). Finally, the change allows for students with the most significant disabilities to be meaningfully included in measuring school and LEA performance under a State's accountability system.

We decline to require States to disaggregate graduation rates for students with disabilities those receiving a regular high school diploma and the State-defined alternate diploma, in part because we believe minimum n-size requirements would limit meaningful reporting of students receiving the alternate diploma in most districts. While States have discretion to include such disaggregated graduation rate data for students with disabilities on their report cards, they must comply with applicable local, State, and Federal privacy protections.

Changes: We have revised § 200.34(e)(4) by removing the language that required States to retroactively update the adjusted cohort graduation rate annually for students with the most significant cognitive disabilities receiving the State-defined alternate diploma. We have also added § 200.34(b)(5) regarding adjusting the cohort for students with the most significant cognitive disabilities who receive a State-defined alternate diploma.

Comments: One commenter requested that the Department clearly state that a State-defined alternate diploma received by a student with the most significant cognitive disabilities should not be treated as a regular high school diploma for the purposes of determining the termination of services under IDEA.

Discussion: Consistent with the definition of "regular high school diploma" in section 8101(43) of the ESEA, as amended by the ESSA, a regular high school diploma must be fully aligned with State standards, and may not be aligned with the alternate academic achievement standards described in section 1111(b)(1)(E) of the ESEA. We agree with commenters that graduation from high school with a State-defined alternate diploma does not terminate a student's entitlement to FAPE under IDEA, provided that the student continues to meet the definition of "child with a disability" in section 602(3) of the IDEA and is within the State's mandated age range for the provision of FAPE.

Entitlement to FAPE under IDEA could last until an eligible student's 22nd birthday, depending on State law or practice. However, under 34 CFR 300.102(a)(3)(i) a State's obligation to make FAPE available to all children with disabilities does not apply with respect to children with disabilities who have graduated from high school with a regular high school diploma. However, § 300.102(a)(3)(ii) clarifies that this exception does not apply to children with disabilities who have not graduated from high school with a regular high school diploma. Because a State-defined alternate diploma for students with the most significant cognitive disabilities does not align with the definition of a regular high school diploma, graduation from high school with such a diploma does not terminate the obligation of a State and its public agencies to make FAPE available until students awarded such a diploma are appropriately exited from special education and related services in accordance with § 300.305(e)(1) of the IDEA Part B regulations or exceed the age of eligibility for the provision of FAPE under State law. Because the IDEA regulations already address this obligation, no further clarification in these final regulations is needed.

Changes: None.

Extended-Year Graduation Rate

Comments: Several commenters opposed the requirement in proposed § 200.34(d) that would limit an extended-year graduation rate to seven years, and recommended that the Department change the proposed number of years from seven to eight years. Commenters argued that this more closely corresponds with the time period for which States are required to offer a FAPE under the IDEA. One commenter opposed any limitation on the grounds that a State should be allowed to include a student in an extended-year rate, regardless of how long it has taken the student to graduate. Another commenter did not specifically address the limitation, but opposed the requirement that four-year and extended-year graduation rates must be reported separately, asserting that it was not aligned with accountability provisions for alternative schools. Another commenter recommended that the Department provide guidance encouraging States to report extended-year graduation rates in order to capture students that typically take longer than four years to graduate.

Discussion: The Department initially proposed to limit extended-year graduation rates to seven years because it is consistent with the time period in which most States ensure the availability of FAPE and no State currently calculates an extended year rate longer than seven years. We acknowledge, however, that some States provide FAPE for a longer period. In light of such differences across States, the Department is removing the limitation on extended-year graduation rates.

Although we are removing the limitation on extended-year rates, we nonetheless believe that most students not graduating after four years will graduate in five or six years. Further, students with the most significant cognitive disabilities receiving a State-defined alternate diploma within the time period in which most States ensure the availability of FAPE can be included in both the four-year and extended-year graduation rates. For these reasons, the Department encourages States to limit extended-year rates to five or six years in order to capture the most meaningful information about student graduation outcomes for use in reporting and accountability systems.

With respect to the recommendation that States and LEAs not be required to report the four-year and extended-year rates separately, and that instead States and LEAs should be able to report only one, we note that section 1111(h)(1)(C)(iii)(II) of the ESEA, as amended by the ESSA, specifically requires reporting on four-year graduation rates and, if adopted by the State, extended-year graduation rates. If a State chooses to implement an extended-year graduation rate, such information is most useful if reported separately from the four-year rate so that stakeholders can see the differences in graduation rate outcomes in the additional years beyond the four-year rate. Consequently, the Department believes that it is important that those rates be reported separately.

We appreciate suggestions from commenters about topics for potential guidance on this issue. Should we determine that further guidance is needed related to this issue, we will take these comments into consideration.

Changes: The Department has revised § 200.34(d)(2) to remove the requirement that an extended-year graduation rate cannot be for a period longer than seven years.

Standard Criteria for Including Certain Subgroups

Comments: Many commenters responded to the Department's directed question seeking input on whether to create standard criteria for including children with disabilities, English learners, children who are homeless, and children who are in foster care in their corresponding subgroups within the adjusted cohort graduation rate calculation. A number of commenters supported standardizing the criteria for including students within these subgroups in the graduation rate calculation. Commenters generally addressed only one or two of the subgroups identified in the question, and, together, the comments offered different recommendations for different subgroups (e.g., different recommendations for English Learners than students in foster care). A number of commenters submitted comments assuming the Department was suggesting standardizing all students in the directed question.

Some commenters focused generally on standard criteria for all four subgroups identified in the directed question. Several of these commenters supported basing a student's inclusion in a subgroup on being part of that subgroup at any time during the cohort period. Several commenters supported creating standard criteria, but suggested either different criteria based on the specific characteristics of the subgroup, or getting input from stakeholders, such as States and advocates, about the appropriate criteria for each subgroup.

Several commenters opposed requiring standard criteria, specifying that the decision should be left to States. Of these, two commenters included recommendations for the Department to consider if it decided to require standard criteria. One commenter recommended including students in the subgroup if they were part of that subgroup at any time during the cohort period. The other recommended that the Department consider current practices of States and align the requirements to the method used by a majority of States.

Many commenters addressed children with disabilities specifically. The majority of commenters supporting standardization suggested including children with disabilities if (1) they were a member of the subgroup at graduation and (2) they had spent the majority of their time in high school in the subgroup. The rest of the supporting commenters suggested varied approaches for standardization (e.g., at any time, at the time of graduation).

Some commenters addressed English learners specifically. One commenter requested special criteria and additional disaggregation for students who are English learners and have been part of Native American Language Schools and Programs for at least six years. Other commenters supported requiring standard criteria, but suggested different approaches for determining those criteria. Commenters suggested: Basing a student's membership in a cohort if they were part of that subgroup at any time during the cohort period; requiring standard criteria appropriate to the characteristics of the subgroups; and aligning the criteria with other definitions associated with English learners (e.g., aligning with long term English learners or including former English learners).

Many other commenters addressed concerns related to students who are homeless and students who are in foster care specifically and supported requiring standard criteria. All commenters supporting standard criteria for these groups suggested basing a student's membership in a cohort on whether they were part of that subgroup at any time during the cohort period and emphasized that this is particularly important for these groups since they may move in and out of that subgroup multiple times while they are in school and point in time counts would underrepresent the population. A subset of these commenters suggested that graduation rates should be reported both for students that were part of that subgroup at any time during the cohort period and students who were part of that subgroup at the time of graduation. Commenters indicated that if only one rate for these groups was possible, their preference was for the former. One commenter requested additional clarity regarding the assignment of students to particular subgroups. The commenter requested clarity as to whether a student could be assigned to multiple subgroups (e.g., the English learner subgroup and the children with disabilities subgroup), or if a student could only be assigned to one. If the latter, the commenter requested information on which group would take precedence.

Discussion: We agree that requiring standard criteria for the inclusion of specific subgroups in the graduation rate calculation will make the data more useful. One of the key reasons for requiring an adjusted cohort graduation rate is to ensure that all States use a consistent graduation rate calculation, which allows data to be compared across States. While differences in graduation rate requirements mean that there will continue to be some limitations to the comparability of the data, we believe that any step that improves the comparability of the data will improve the ability of parents and other stakeholders to use the data as intended. We note that this standard criteria is solely for the purpose of calculating and reporting on graduation rate data.

We disagree with the recommended approach of those commenters that supported standardizing the criteria for how children with disabilities are included in the cohort graduation rate calculation. The commenters suggested including children with disabilities if (1) they were a member of the subgroup at graduation and (2) they had spent the majority of their time in high school in the

202

subgroup. The Department is unaware of any State that currently uses this approach when including children with disabilities in the cohort. Moreover, the Department believes that States, LEAs, and schools should be able to count children with disabilities if such children remain in that subgroup throughout high school or if they successfully exit from special education services in high school, as the data represent the long-term effort by States, LEAs, and schools to serve these students. The Department is also concerned that following the suggested approach could encourage States to unnecessarily retain some higher functioning students with disabilities in special education services in order to count these students in the disability subgroup. Additionally, we note that, under § 299.14(c)(5), each State must assure that it has policies and procedures in place regarding the appropriate identification of children with disabilities consistent with the child find evaluation requirements in section 612(a)(3) and (a)(7) of the IDEA. We feel confident that this will mitigate against the risk of students being inappropriately identified.

In response to commenters indicating that a student should be included in the English learners subgroup for purposes of reporting the adjusted cohort graduation rate if he or she was part of that subgroup at any time during the cohort period, we are revising § 200.34(e)(2) to require this practice for the limited purpose of reporting the adjusted cohort graduation rate under the ESEA. As with students with disabilities, this approach under the ESEA recognizes the long-term effort by States, LEAs, and schools to serve these students even if they are not English learners at the time they graduate.

We agree with commenters indicating that students who are homeless and students who are in foster care should be included in those subgroups for purposes of reporting the adjusted cohort graduation rate if they were part of the subgroup at any time during the cohort period. We agree that these students will move in and out of these subgroups depending on their current situation and that only capturing these students at the time of graduation would risk significantly underreporting these students.

On balance, the Department believes that the final regulations will create more consistency in graduation rate reporting for specific subgroups, which is an important improvement to current reporting practices which have made it difficult to compare certain subgroups across States. We believe that the long term benefits of increasing the comparability across States outweigh the interruption of the longitudinal data and the one-time effort to change business rules. Further, it seems appropriate to use this opportunity to require this approach for subgroups newly required for purposes of reporting adjusted cohort graduation rates under the ESEA, as amended by the ESSA, (i.e., students who are homeless and students in foster care) to ensure that students in these groups are appropriately and consistently captured in graduation rates.

We note that a number of commenters indicated that further disaggregation of certain subgroups would provide the most useful information for understanding student graduation outcomes. While we understand that this information may be useful, the statute includes a specific list of subgroups for which disaggregation is required. As such, the Department will not require further disaggregation; however, States and LEAs are free to add further information to their report cards if they believe that further detail will convey useful context for their stakeholders.

Additionally, the Department notes that a commenter requested further clarification about subgroup inclusion. In this regard, we note that students can be included in multiple subgroups, and we expect that an individual student will be counted in any subgroup that applies to that student. For example, a student with a disability who is also an English learner would be counted in both subgroups.

Changes: We have added § 200.34(e)(2), which requires a State to include children with disabilities, English learners, children who are homeless, and children who are in foster care in the respective subgroup for the limited purpose of reporting the adjusted cohort graduation rate under the ESEA, if such students were identified as a member of the subgroup at any time during the cohort period.

Transfers to Prisons or Juvenile Facilities

Comments: A number of commenters supported the Department's clarification related to cohort removal for students transferring to prison or juvenile facilities, and the requirement under proposed § 200.34(b)(3)(iii) that these students can be removed from the cohort only if they participate in a program that culminates in the award of a diploma aligned to the statutory requirements. These commenters also suggested revisions to the requirement, including revising it to align with the statute, which defines "transferred out" as having transferred to an educational program "from which the student is expected to receive" a regular high school diploma or State-defined alternate diploma, as opposed to the proposed regulation, which focused on a student's transfer to a program "that culminates in the award of" a regular or State-defined alternate high school diploma. Many commenters also requested that the Department clarify that a student can be removed from the cohort only if he or she has been adjudicated as delinquent, and one commenter further suggested that the student must also be enrolled in an educational program in a prison or juvenile facility for at least one year.

Many commenters suggested further clarifying the requirement in a number of other ways, including by specifying that, to be removed from a sending school's cohort, a student must be "meaningfully participating" in an education program while in a prison or juvenile facility, that documentation of the transfer must include written confirmation of the student's enrollment in an educational program from which he or she can expect to receive a regular high school diploma, and that the provisions related to partial enrollment also apply to students in prison or juvenile facilities. A few commenters recommended adding a requirement to disaggregate graduation rate data for students who are in the juvenile justice system.

Two commenters opposed the proposed requirement, indicating that States may have trouble complying because they may lack authority over juvenile facilities and students in those facilities. One commenter noted that it would not be possible to produce consistent data across States.

Several commenters requested further guidance from the Department about responsibilities for educating students in juvenile facilities. Most of these commenters requested that the Department address the timing for transferring a student from the sending school, the process for transferring a student from a prison or juvenile facility back into a school, and requirements for oversight and accountability of schools in these facilities. One commenter requested further clarification on which LEA is responsible for a student that enters a prison or juvenile facility that does not award the applicable diploma types.

Discussion: We appreciate the comments noting that certain proposed regulatory language differed from the statutory language, and agree that it is more appropriate to use the statutory language. We also agree with commenters who suggested that a student must be adjudicated as delinquent, and that it must be clear that the student will be enrolled in a program from which he or she can expect to receive a regular high school diploma or State-defined alternate diploma, before the student can be removed from the sending school's cohort. Students who are awaiting hearings and who have not yet been adjudicated as delinquent may end up in a different facility, may transfer to another school, or may be released and return to their sending school. As such, the result of the adjudication and the student's placement should be clear before the student is removed from the cohort.

We also agree that a student should not be removed from a cohort unless the student will be in a facility long enough that he or she can expect to receive a regular high school diploma or, if applicable, a State-defined alternate diploma for students with the most significant cognitive disabilities from the facility. While the Department does not agree with comments suggesting that a student must remain in the facility for at least a year before being removed the sending school's cohort, the Department does believe that it is reasonable to clarify that a student should be in a facility long enough to receive a diploma from that facility. Otherwise, the student should remain in the cohort of the sending school, since the student would be expected to transfer back to the sending school before the time of his or her graduation. Further, upon a student's release from a prison or juvenile facility, it is critical for the LEA or school that the student previously attended to re-engage with the student to ensure a positive and supportive transition that provides a pathway to a regular or State-approved alternative high school diploma. The Department encourages LEAs and schools to maintain an open line of communication with prisons and juvenile facilities to help ensure that students who are assigned to, and ultimately released from, such facilities receive an appropriate education and do not disappear from a graduation cohort.

The Department appreciates the suggestion that a student must "meaningfully participate" in an education program in a prison or juvenile facility, but, given the inherent challenge in defining that term, we decline to add it to the regulation. We do, however, encourage States to implement procedures to ensure that educational programs in prisons and juvenile facilities are of high quality.

The Department does not believe that it is necessary to revise the language on partial enrollment to clarify that the requirements related to reporting on students partially enrolled also apply to students in juvenile facilities. The Department believes that the language as written will apply to those facilities, and that adding specific language to that section will not clarify the requirement, but will instead create confusion.

The Department notes that some commenters have indicated that disaggregating data for students in juvenile justice facilities will provide useful information for understanding their graduation outcomes. While we understand that this information may be useful, we decline to expand the statutory list of subgroups for which disaggregation is required. We note, however, that States are free to add to their report cards information that they believe will be useful for their stakeholders.

We appreciate suggestions from commenters about topics for potential guidance on this issue. Should we determine that further guidance is needed related to this issue, we will take these comments into consideration.

Changes: We have revised § 200.34(b)(3)(iii) to align with statutory language by replacing the phrase "culminates in the award of" with the phrase "expected to receive" a diploma. The Department has further revised § 200.34(b)(3)(iii) to clarify that, in order for students that transfer to a prison or juvenile facility to be removed from a cohort, there must first be an adjudication of delinquency and the student must be expected to receive a regular high school diploma or State-defined alternate diploma during the period in which the student is assigned to the prison or juvenile facility.

Cross Reference to the Assessment Regulation

Comments: None.

Discussion: In defining "alternate diploma" under proposed § 200.34(c), the Department cross-referenced a proposed requirement in § 200.6(d)(1) related to assessment requirements under title I, part A, of the ESEA, as amended by the ESSA, that was subject to negotiated rulemaking under the ESSA and on which the negotiated rulemaking committee reached consensus. This proposed requirement, included in a notice of proposed rulemaking published in the Federal Register on July 11, 2016, would require a State to adopt guidelines for IEP teams to use when determining which students with the most significant cognitive disabilities should take an alternate assessment aligned with alternate academic achievement standards, including a State definition of students with the most significant cognitive disabilities. These proposed requirements have not been finalized and, as a result, the Department is removing this language from the final regulations.

Changes: We have revised § 200.34(c)(3) to remove references to proposed § 200.6(d)(1).

Section 200.35   Per-Pupil Expenditures

Student Count Procedure

Comments: One commenter supported the use of an October 1 membership count as the uniform denominator used in per-pupil expenditure calculations. Several commenters, however, noted that many States define student counts for State-determined school finance formulas using a date other than October 1 and, as a result, States could be required to collect additional enrollment count data to comply with the requirements in proposed § 200.35(c)(2). Several commenters recommended that we revise the requirement to provide States greater flexibility, by, for example, requiring States to specify a uniform statewide definition of student count, requiring a State and its LEAs to use the same student count for per-pupil expenditures as is used for State funding allocations, or allowing States to select either the October 1 count or the student count the State uses for State funding allocations.

Discussion: We acknowledge that States use various methods to measure student enrollment for use in State-determined school finance formulas. However, all States annually report to NCES, by LEA and school for every grade that is offered, a uniform membership count (i.e., enrollment) of all students to whom each LEA provides a free public education on or about October 1. This measure is a count of the number of students for whom the reporting LEA is financially responsible and is collected annually by NCES through Common Core of Data (CCD) collection. This information is then used to calculate per-pupil expenditures by LEA and State, as reported by NCES through the National Public Education Financial, LEA Finance (F-33) surveys, and by school, as reported to NCES through the pilot School-Level Finance survey. We recognize that SEAs also report average daily attendance (ADA) data to NCES to determine the average State Per Pupil Expenditure (SPPE) for elementary and secondary education. But because ADA data is not comparable across States, we elect to follow the NCES convention of using membership data to calculate and report expenditures per pupil for public reporting purposes. Further, by establishing minimum requirements that align with existing data collections we are limiting the burden on States and LEAs for complying with this new statutory requirement.

Therefore, to encourage consistent, fair, and aligned reporting practices across States and LEAs, we decline to change the manner in which the number of students is determined for purposes of calculating per-pupil expenditures. We are, however, modifying the regulation to clarify that the NCES CCD enrollment count data that is used to calculate per-pupil expenditures for annual report card purposes must reflect enrollment data from "on or about" October 1.

206

Changes: We have revised § 200.35(c)(2) to clarify that the denominator used for purposes of calculating per-pupil expenditures must use the student count data from "on or about" October 1, consistent with the figure reported to NCES.

Comments: Several commenters asked if the per-pupil expenditure denominator should include preschool students and if preschool students are included in the membership count collected by NCES.

Discussion: The CCD collection includes an annual count of students, which includes students in the group or classes that are part of a public school program that is taught in the year or years preceding kindergarten. Therefore, the expenditure denominator should include preschool students.

Changes: We have revised § 200.35(c)(2) to clarify that the denominator used for purposes of calculating per-pupil expenditures must include preschool enrollment, consistent with the universe portion of the school CCD collection student membership definition.

Account Code Definitions

Comments: Many commenters requested that the Department specify account code definitions to enable States to calculate per-pupil expenditures. For example, one commenter supported the proposed rule because it would ensure all schools have fair and equitable access to funds and would broaden public knowledge of resource disparities, but requested that the Department require States and LEAs to implement a uniform chart of accounts that identifies additional categories of expenditures to increase transparency. A number of other commenters stated that proposed § 200.35 is ambiguous about the definition of private funds. One commenter proposed a different set of expenditure categories to include on report cards than those in the proposed regulations.

Discussion: We agree with commenters that definitions should be clear for all entities calculating and reporting per-pupil expenditures. We also believe, where feasible, calculations should be uniform across States and consistent with existing data collections, so that the public can easily compare and contrast school system spending patterns. To this end, the final regulations clearly specify the composition of the numerator and denominator for the calculation, including the types of expenditures that must be included. Additionally, to the extent possible, § 200.35 aligns current expenditure reporting requirements with existing NCES collection procedures.

However, we do not specify or require the use of particular account codes because we believe that States should have flexibility to develop and implement the uniform statewide procedures for calculating and reporting per-pupil expenditures that work best for the unique configurations and capacities of their LEAs and schools. Nevertheless, we encourage States to adopt statewide account code definitions aligned with those found in the NCES Financial Accounting for Local and State School Systems handbook (NCES handbook, available at: http://nces.ed.gov/pubs2015/2015347.pdf), in recognition of the fact that States already use these definitions for existing NCES data collections and their adoption for the purpose of calculating per-pupil expenditures thus would minimum the administrative burden of meeting the new reporting requirements.

Changes: None.

Classification of Expenditures

Comments: Many commenters requested clarification as to whether local funds should include local revenue from rent/royalties and fees collected and expressed concern that the proposed regulation does not account for other Federal funds that are similar to Impact Aid. Another commenter requested guidance on how to report final Impact Aid payments made during the preceding fiscal year.

Discussion: We generally believe that States have both the discretion and the responsibility to clarify the composition of local revenues as well as other revenue classifications as part of developing their statewide procedures for calculating LEA- and school-level expenditures per pupil. As noted previously, we encourage States to adopt NCES handbook account code definitions, but decline to prescribe additional requirements in these final regulations. However, we do believe that funding from other Federal programs designed offset losses in local tax revenues should be counted as State and local funds, and we are revising the final regulations accordingly. The Department will consider providing additional information on these types of Federal programs, along with suggestions on how to report final Impact Aid payments made during the preceding fiscal year, in non-regulatory guidance.

Changes: We have revised § 200.35(a) and (b) to clarify that State and LEA report cards must, when reporting per-pupil expenditures, include with State and local funds all Federal funds intended to replace local tax revenues.

Implementation Concerns

Comments: Several commenters expressed concern that States and LEAs lack sufficiently detailed data or accounting systems to collect and report school-level expenditures, making the proposed requirements costly, impractical, burdensome, and likely to yield little useful information. One commenter stated that the regulations would force LEAs to invest significant resources to report school-level expenditures that ultimately will not provide a meaningful measure of expenditure reporting.

Discussion: We disagree with the concerns that school-level reporting of expenditures may not provide valuable insight to local administrators and agree with other commenters who have asserted that these data will be an important source of information for administrators, parents, and local stakeholders.

Changes: None.

Comments: One commenter suggested the Department require only personnel costs to be reported at the school level because of the difficulty of reporting other types of expenditures that are shared by schools within an LEA. Many commenters stated specifically that centrally managed support services, such as food service or transportation, are not easily disaggregated or reported at the school level. Two commenters suggested that the Department adopt more detailed requirements for expenditure reporting at the school and LEA levels.

Many commenters requested further clarification of the requirements, including, for example, specifying a uniform standard procedure for allocating expenditures at the school level or even requiring LEAs to assign all expenditures to the school level.

One commenter stated that the ESEA, as amended by the ESSA, allows central office expenditures to be excluded from school-level reporting and that assigning expenditures to individual schools would be complicated by different LEA accounting methodologies, resulting in data quality issues.

One commenter suggested the Department add requirements that LEAs report the comparison between LEA average expenditures and individual schools and the percentage of LEA expenditures on administration and shared services. One commenter expressed concern over the reporting procedures for State payments to private preschool providers. One commenter recommended that the Department not specify an order of operation for calculating per-pupil expenditures, stating that some States are capable of calculating school-level expenditures without LEA reports.

Discussion: We appreciate the varied suggestions offered by commenters, which collectively demonstrate both the importance and difficulty of producing uniform and clear per-pupil expenditure data at the school and LEA levels. We also acknowledge the decision to report certain types of expenditures only at the LEA level requires serious deliberation that considers the merits of alternative reporting approaches. However, we also believe such decisions are best made by States, with input from local stakeholders. For this reason § 200.35 requires States to develop and clearly describe the statewide uniform procedures that delineate which expenditures are reported at the school and LEA levels, including how school-level expenditures are reported as they relate to LEA expenditures.

Based on the comments received, it also appears some commenters may have misinterpreted the proposed regulations. Although States will determine which expenditures are reported at the school level, under proposed § 200.35 it is up to States to determine if expenditures such as superintendent salaries or food service costs are excluded from school-level reporting and only reported at the LEA level.

In addition, we believe that the establishment of national uniform school-level reporting procedures could stifle innovative approaches to reporting per-pupil expenditures and would fail to take into account local considerations and State laws. Because the statewide approaches will be uniformly applied within a State, implementation of proposed § 200.35 preserves the ability of within and cross-LEA comparisons of per-pupil expenditures.

Changes: None.

Comment: One commenter asked the Department to clarify the meaning of expenditures not allocated to public schools and whether school-level expenditures in aggregate equal total LEA expenditures.

Discussion: We believe it is necessary to clarify how current expenditures not reported at the school level are reported and are revising the final regulations accordingly.

Changes: We have revised § 200.35(a)(2) and (b)(2) to clarify that State and LEA report cards must report the total current expenditures that were not reported in school-level per-pupil expenditure figures.

Comment: One commenter stated that reporting school-level expenditures would cause the increased use of pull-out models of instruction for students.

Discussion: We disagree with the concerns that school-level reporting of expenditures could cause increased use of pull-out models of instruction for students and are unaware of research demonstrating a link between school-level expenditure reporting and commensurate shifts in the use of pull-out instruction for students.

Changes: None.

Reporting Exemptions

Comments: Several commenters requested an exemption for small and rural LEAs from the per-pupil expenditure reporting requirement, suggesting such an exemption would be consistent with similar exemptions under other title I provisions.

Discussion: While the ESEA, as amended by the ESSA, includes special provisions for rural and small LEAs in a number of areas, there is no such provision related to the reporting requirement for per-pupil expenditures under section 1111(h)(C)(x). Moreover, advocates for rural and small LEAs have long expressed concerns about funding equity and other resource challenges faced by such LEAs, and reporting on per-pupil expenditures will support greater transparency and analysis around such concerns. Identifying resource disparities among LEAs of all types is a key goal of the new per-pupil expenditures reporting requirement, and we do not believe excluding the one-third to one-half of all LEAs that are small and/or rural from the new requirement would be consistent with this goal.

Changes: None.

Comments: A number of commenters addressed the inclusion of expenditures from private sources in per-pupil expenditure reporting, with some commenters requesting clarification on the exclusion of private funds, others recommending that the final regulations require that they be included, and one commenter asking the Department to encourage States and LEAs to include them voluntarily.

Discussion: Under section 1111(h)(1)(C)(x) of the ESEA, as amended by the ESSA, States and LEAs must report per-pupil expenditures of Federal, State, and local funds. Funds from private sources do not fall within any of these three categories, which encompass only public funds. Therefore, § 200.35 requires the exclusion of private funds from per-pupil expenditure reporting. We nonetheless encourage States and LEAs to consider improving transparency around education finances by including the reporting on the use of private funds for public educational purposes.

Changes: None.

Disaggregating Per-Pupil Expenditure Data

Comments: Some commenters supported the requirement in proposed § 200.35(a)(1)(i)(B) and (b)(1)(i)(B) that per-pupil expenditures must be disaggregated by (1) Federal and (2) State/local funds. One commenter claimed, however, that the ESEA, as amended by the ESSA, requires that per-pupil expenditures be disaggregated separately for Federal, State, and local funds and requested that proposed § 200.35 be revised to also require disaggregation of State and local funds. Another commenter recommended further disaggregating per-pupil expenditures by grade level.

Discussion: We appreciate the commenters support for the method of disaggregating Federal, State, and local funds in § 200.35(a)(1)(i)(B) and (b)(1)(i)(B). The Department disagrees with the commenter claiming the ESEA, as amended by the ESSA, requires that Federal, State, and local funds be separately disaggregated. Although the section 1111(h)(1)(C)(x) of the ESEA, as amended by the ESSA, requires that per-pupil expenditures be disaggregated by source of funds, it does not specify the level at which such disaggregation must occur. Thus, § 200.35(a)(1)(i) and (b)(1)(i) clarify that a State and its LEAs are required to report per-pupil expenditures in total (i.e., including all Federal, State, and local funds) and disaggregated by (1) Federal funds, and (2) State and local funds. Because typical LEA accounting procedures do not require State and local funds to be separately tracked, implementation of the commenter's proposal would be impractical, complicated, and would likely result in the dissemination of inaccurate fiscal data to the public. Further, States with more sophisticated accounting systems that are able to disaggregate per-pupil expenditure reporting by Federal, State, and local funds are not precluded from including such data on their report cards. Similarly, States are welcome to include disaggregated per-pupil expenditure data by grade level on annual State and LEA report cards, but it is not required under the ESEA, as amended by the ESSA.

Changes: None.

Uniform Statewide Procedure

Comments: Many commenters supported the regulations proposed § 200.35, arguing that the regulations will increase transparency in a manner that will allow the public to identify and address financial inequities within a State. Several commenters strongly supported the requirement in proposed § 200.35(c) that States develop a single statewide procedure for LEA and State use, arguing implementation of these regulations will allow the public to hold States, LEAs, and school leaders accountable for ensuring that schools and LEAs serving traditionally underserved populations are provided the resources they need to succeed academically. Commenters also stated the uniform procedure requirement will allow for consistent presentation of financial data that can be used to evaluate how investments impact student outcomes, which will result in more informed budgetary decisions by local policymakers. Several commenters recommended removing the uniform statewide procedure requirement to allow States and LEAs to calculate per-pupil expenditures in the manner they determine appropriate.

Discussion: The Department appreciates the support of commenters, including the specific support for the uniform procedures requirement in § 200.35(c). The Department disagrees with the commenter regarding the removal of this provision. We agree the commenters in support of this requirement that absent standard definitions and a statewide procedure for calculating expenditures, per-pupil expenditure data would not be comparable and would not support meaningful analysis of resource inequities between and within LEAs and schools across a State.

Changes: None.

Alignment With Existing Data Collection Requirements

Comments: Several commenters suggested the development of a statewide school finance reporting system that is able to comply with proposed § 200.35 requirements would be onerous and recommended that States report in a uniform manner as determined by the State. One commenter asked if the Department will align with NCES's fiscal collection requirements and whether NCES will cease publishing fiscal collection results once per-pupil expenditures are disseminated through annual State and LEA report cards. One commenter argued a universal per-pupil expenditure reporting requirement is incongruous with the recent increase of the single-audit expenditure threshold for non-Federal entities from $500,000 to $750,000.

Discussion: In clarifying the per-pupil expenditure reporting requirements under the ESEA, as amended by the ESSA, the Department sought to align these requirements, to the extent practicable, with the requirements of the NCES National Public Education Financial Survey, the LEA Finance survey (F-33), and the School-Level Finance pilot survey. We believe this approach will allow for more efficient administration of new collection and reporting processes. We note, however, that the new ESEA reporting requirements will not replace NCES reporting of national expenditure survey data, which will continue to be of use to education researchers, policymakers, and the public because they allow for precise comparisons of LEA and SEA spending patterns over time. Further, existing NCES collections are not as timely as State and LEA report cards and do not report on school-level expenditures.

Regarding the comment referencing the Uniform Administrative Requirements, Cost Principals, and Audit Requirements in part 200 of title 2 of the Code of Federal Regulations, the Department disagrees with claims that single audit requirements are misaligned with per-pupil expenditure requirements, as these separate requirements are in place for different purposes under different regulations. The administration of a single audit ensures that Federal funds are expended properly, while universal per-pupil reporting requirements ensure the public has access to comparable fiscal data.

Changes: None.

Data Interpretation

Comments: Two commenters questioned the value of reporting per-pupil expenditures, arguing such reporting can be misleading depending on local factors such as cost-of living.

Discussion: Under section 1111(h)(1)(C)(x) of the ESEA, as amended by the ESSA, States and LEAs must report per-pupil expenditures of Federal, State, and local funds. The Department agrees that the per-pupil expenditure data collected and reported under § 200.35 must be presented and analyzed with care, taking into account within-State variations based on multiple factors, including differences in the cost of education. However, we anticipate that States will include such context, where appropriate, in their presentation of per-pupil expenditure data on State and local report cards. For example, a State could choose to also provide cost-of-living adjusted data on its report card if it determined this would be valuable for accurate cross-district comparisons.

Changes: None.

General Opposition

Comments: A numbered of commenters expressed opposition to proposed § 200.35, variously claiming that its provisions are not required or are inconsistent with the requirements of the ESEA, as amended by the ESSA; that the proposed regulations exceed the Department's authority; that requiring uniform procedures for calculating per-pupil expenditures could limit SEA and LEA flexibility to meet local needs; that reporting per-pupil expenditures could lead to pressure to equalize education funding, including for charter schools; and that it is not clear how such reporting will affect compliance with the title I, part A supplement not supplant or comparability requirements. In response to such concerns, commenters generally recommended either striking the provisions of the proposed regulations that are not explicitly required under the ESEA, as amended by the ESSA; making such provisions permissive; or replacing most of proposed § 200.35 with non-regulatory guidance.

Discussion: Section 200.35 clarifies reporting requirements established by section 1111(h)(1)(C)(x) of the ESEA, as amended by the ESSA, so that local policymakers, parents, and the public can easily understand how public education funds are distributed across LEAs and schools. The regulations establish minimum requirements to ensure timely access to comparable spending data, but do not mandate equal per-pupil funding at the LEA or school level, prescribe how such data should be used in implementing supplement not supplant or comparability requirements, or require reporting of additional information to the Department beyond that required by statute. Further, as discussed previously under Cross-Cutting Issues, the Department has rulemaking authority under section 410 of GEPA, section 414 of the DEOA, and the section 1601(a) of the ESEA, as amended by the ESSA. Given that rulemaking authority and that the regulations fall squarely within the scope of title I, part A of the statute, consistent with section 1111(e), it is not necessary for the statute to specifically authorize the Secretary to issue a particular regulatory provision.

Changes: None.

Section 200.36   Postsecondary Enrollment

Definition of Programs of Postsecondary Education

Comments: Two commenters supported the proposal in § 200.36(a)(2) to define "programs of postsecondary education" in the same manner as "institution of higher education" as that term is defined under the Higher Education Act of 1965, as amended (HEA). One commenter expressed concern about the definition, indicating that it was unclear how it would accommodate programs specific to children with disabilities that grant certificates instead of degrees. One commenter disagreed with the rationale for using the HEA definition (to promote consistency in data reporting and allow users to compare across States), indicating that the use of this definition would not create comparability across States due to different sizes and structures of postsecondary systems across States.

Discussion: We agree with the comments supporting the proposal to define the term "programs of postsecondary education" to align with the definition of "institution of higher education" used in the HEA. We believe that it is important that States report on enrollment in accredited two- and four-year institutions, as specified in the existing HEA definition. With respect to the concerns raised about comparability across States, we acknowledge that this definition does present limitations for cross-State comparisons due to the differences in postsecondary structures across States. Nonetheless, we believe that requiring the use of the HEA definition will promote consistency in data reporting, since all States will be including postsecondary institutions based on the same parameters.

We do not agree that the definition should accommodate students with disabilities who receive certificates of completion. This metric is intended to capture postsecondary enrollment of students earning diploma types consistent with the graduation rate requirements in § 200.34. States are able to include additional metrics of postsecondary actions if they wish to provide more robust information to parents and other stakeholders.

Changes: None.

Postsecondary Indicators

Comments: Some commenters requested adding further indicators related to postsecondary activities to the regulations. Some commenters noted that the postsecondary indicators were solely focused on entry into education programs and suggested that they be expanded to include other postsecondary actions such as community-based roles, the military, job training programs, or service organizations. Two commenters recommended including language indicating that postsecondary enrollment includes additional metrics, such as the number of courses taken without the need for remediation and postsecondary completion. One commenter requested disaggregation of postsecondary enrollment data by students receiving a regular high school diploma and students receiving an alternate diploma; and another commenter requested disaggregation by two- and four-year institutions. This commenter also requested that the Department require additional information on numbers of students receiving scholarships or grants.

Discussion: We appreciate commenters who indicated that there are important postsecondary metrics, including metrics beyond enrollment in programs of postsecondary education, that provide a more comprehensive picture of student actions after high school. We agree that there are many important postsecondary indicators that would provide parents and other stakeholders with useful information.

However, the Department is cognizant of the many reporting requirements already included in the State report card, as well as the particular challenge involved in linking secondary and postsecondary information. As such, the Department declines to impose additional burden on States by requiring additional postsecondary measures on State and LEA report cards. We note, however, that at its discretion a State may choose to include additional information on report cards.

Changes: None.

Providing Information "Where Available"

Comments: Several commenters expressed support for the language in § 200.36(c) clarifying that postsecondary enrollment data is "available" and therefore must be reported under proposed § 200.36(a) if a State is obtaining it or if it is obtainable, and that States that cannot meet the reporting requirement must include on report cards the year in which they expect complete data to be available. Of these, one commenter specifically expressed support for part of the Department's rationale, which stated that at least 47 States can currently produce high school feedback reports, and encouraged the Department to consider guidance on making data as transparent and accessible as possible. Two commenters expressed concern with the requirement, indicating that there would be an ongoing cost associated with meeting the requirement. One commenter additionally detailed the current challenges and burden of obtaining data from postsecondary institutions due to privacy legislation, necessity to work with multiple entities, data quality issues, and the challenge in capturing students in private and out-of-State institutions. One commenter suggested that the Department should consider a funding mechanism that would enable the use of National Student Clearinghouse data for all States.

Discussion: We appreciate comments supporting the requirement to clarify the meaning of "available." As noted by one commenter, many States already have the capacity to report on at least some postsecondary enrollment data, indicating that most States should be able to meet the requirement to track some, if not all, students in a graduating class. This requirement is intended to ensure that as many States as possible make postsecondary enrollment information available so that parents and stakeholders have access to information about how successfully each public high school is in graduating students who go on to enroll in postsecondary programs. Additionally, reporting publicly on when data will be available if they are not already available will encourage States not currently able to meet the requirements to obtain and make available this information.

We recognize that linking secondary and postsecondary data systems is challenging and requires an investment in new system infrastructure and processes. States are free to obtain the data from any source available to them, and States currently linking their systems approach this in a number of ways. Some States use the National Student Clearinghouse, which houses the most comprehensive information on postsecondary actions, but also requires an ongoing investment. States are not required to use this source, and some States are developing other innovative ways of obtaining data, including data sharing agreements or memoranda of understanding with other agencies. States engaging in data sharing agreements may contribute data to centralized repositories (centralized model), or store data separately and link data on demand (federated model). Acknowledging the added challenge of obtaining data on private or out-of-State institutions, Congress specifically differentiated requirements for those institution types compared to public, in-State institutions by adding "to the extent practicable" to the statutory requirements. The Department understands that new data elements, particularly those that involve the complexity of navigating multiple systems, will have data quality challenges; however, we believe that States need to continue to proactively develop the necessary processes to report these metrics in order for critical information on postsecondary actions to improve. States should clearly document limitations in their reported data to ensure that it is interpreted appropriately.

The Department also understands that data-sharing agreements can create privacy concerns and encourages States to use the Department's Privacy Technical Assistance Center, which provides resources on best practices for ensuring the confidentiality and security of personally identifiable information.

Changes: None.

Other

Comments: One commenter indicated that students should only be counted in the numerator as enrolling in a program of postsecondary education if they have enrolled in credit-bearing coursework without the need for remediation.

Discussion: We appreciate the desire to ensure that the postsecondary enrollment metric is a meaningful measure of college-readiness. However, the Department also believes that adding further parameters to the requirement creates added burden and many States are still in the early stages of linking their data systems. As such, the Department does not agree that additional parameters should be added to the metric.

Changes: None.

Comments: Two commenters recommended specific topics for guidance. One commenter suggested guidance on building internal capacity within States to establish linkages between K-12 and postsecondary data systems. The commenter further suggested guidance regarding the establishment of governance structure to advise on the management of these systems. One commenter requested guidance about how to treat students who take a gap between their graduation and their enrollment in a postsecondary institution into the postsecondary enrollment calculation.

Discussion: We appreciate suggestions from commenters about topics for potential guidance on these issues. Should we determine that further guidance is needed related to these issues, we will take these comments into consideration.

Changes: None.

Comments: Some commenters expressed concern about the burden associated with the regulations. One commenter indicated general concerns with the burden of new reporting requirements, and noted that postsecondary enrollment data was an example of a new burdensome requirement. They suggested that the final regulations should clarify statutory requirements rather than create new requirements in order to maintain State flexibility to meet statutory requirements. One commenter specifically noted concerns regarding the burden associated with the requirement to disaggregate by subgroup.

Discussion: The statute adds the requirement to collect postsecondary enrollment data and to disaggregate data by subgroup. While commenters are correct that postsecondary enrollment is newly added to statutory reporting requirements, many States have been reporting on postsecondary enrollment under ESEA flexibility. As such, this is a continued requirement for most States, not a new requirement. The Department believes that the regulations clarify statutory requirements by ensuring consistency and maximizing the utility of data reported, but still allowing States the flexibility to determine how to meet the reporting requirement (e.g., the source to use for postsecondary information).

Changes: None.

Section 200.37   Educator Qualifications

Definitions

Comments: Several commenters expressed concerns and some offered suggestions regarding the uniform definitions and requirements in § 200.37. Specifically, several commenters requested that the regulations include additional text to the effect that a State's definitions under proposed § 200.37(b)(1) and (2), as applied to charter schools, must defer to State charter school law. Some commenters requested that the Department require that State and LEA report cards use specific definitions for the term "inexperienced," and the phrase "not teaching in the subject or field for which the teacher is certified or licensed," rather than allowing States to adopt their own statewide definition for use on State and LEA report cards. In addition, some commenters expressed concern with the definition of high- and low-poverty schools in § 200.37, with a few commenters elaborating that these definitions are arbitrary. One of these commenters requested that the Department allow States to define what constitutes a high- and low-poverty school; one commenter suggested defining high- and low-poverty schools based on the percentage of economically disadvantaged students in a school; and one commenter suggested that the definition of high- and low-poverty school reflect title I eligible schools or schools with a specific threshold of students with free and reduced lunch that would warrant title I eligibility.

One commenter indicated that the requirements for educator qualification definitions in §§ 200.37 and 299.18(c)(2) extend beyond that which the statute requires, and, in addition, the different reporting timelines in these sections would be problematic. Another commenter suggested that the timeline for implementing the ESEA, as amended by the ESSA, is overly aggressive and does not provide States with sufficient time to make necessary changes to State law regarding educator qualification definitions. This same commenter further contended that the statute prohibits the Department from mandating that States define certain terms as required in §§ 200.37 and 299.18(c)(2). In a related sentiment, one commenter requested that the Department add text to § 200.37(b) to indicate that States can use definitions for the terms "inexperienced" and "not teaching in the subject or field for which the teacher is certified or licensed" that may already exist in State law. Another commenter asserted that the requirement in § 299.18(c)(2)(ii) and (iii) that States use the same definitions of "out-of-field teacher" and "inexperienced teacher" as States adopt under proposed § 200.37(b) will necessitate a change in LEA hiring practices and will preclude them from hiring novice teachers and novice teachers from teaching in a school of their choice.

Discussion: We appreciate suggestions related to the uniform definitions and requirements in § 200.37(b). However, we decline to either add additional requirements related to the definitions of "inexperienced" and the phrase "not teaching in the subject or field for which the teacher is certified or licensed" as applied to charter schools or to include specific definitions of these terms. Further, we decline to remove or otherwise revise the requirements for these definitions in § 200.37(b).

We believe that standardized statewide definitions of "inexperienced" and "not teaching in the subject or field for which the teacher is certified or licensed," adopted by each State and used consistently in reporting teacher qualification data on State and LEA report cards, will ensure transparency and increase understanding of staffing needs in high-poverty and difficult-to-staff schools. Furthermore, we believe that uncovering such needs may encourage States to target efforts to recruit, support, and retain excellent educators in these schools. However, given variation in State laws and contexts, we believe States are best positioned to select the required statewide definitions of "inexperienced" and "not teaching in the subject or field for which the teacher is certified or licensed" and therefore decline to require use of a particular definition as require under § 200.37.

With respect to defining what constitutes a high- and low-poverty school, we disagree that the definitions are arbitrary as they are consistent with the definitions of these terms under the ESEA, as amended by NCLB. This ensures that States can continue to use the same definition of these schools that they have used since they began reporting teacher qualification data disaggregated by high- and low-poverty schools. At the State and LEA levels, parents and other stakeholders will be familiar with disaggregated teacher qualification data based on these definitions and better able to consider implications of the information. In light of the benefits of statewide definitions of teacher qualification definitions, the Department believes the requirements in § 200.37(b) align with section 1111(h)(1)(B) and 1111(h)(2)(B) of the ESEA, as amended by the ESSA, to develop State and LEA report cards in an understandable and uniform format.

With respect to commenters asserting that the Department does not have the authority to require definitions of certain teacher qualification terms required under §§ 200.37(b) and 299.18(c)(2) and that the ESEA, as amended by the ESSA, prohibits requirements for such definitions, please see discussion below in § 299.18 in response to other similar comments on this topic. With respect to commenters' concerns that the existing State laws regarding definitions of "inexperienced" and "not teaching in the subject or field for which the teacher is certified or licensed" would need to be revised, as long as current definitions for these terms meet the requirements under §§ 200.37(b) and 299.18(c)(2), States can, in fact, use them to meet the requirements in §§ 200.37(b) and 299.18(c)(2). As to the impact of the required definitions of these terms being the same in §§ 200.37(b) and 299.18(c)(2), LEAs need not necessarily revise their hiring policies, and could instead implement other strategies, such as modifying teacher recruitment and retention policies and procedures. Nevertheless, regardless of the strategies that an LEA elects to implement, it must report and, as necessary, address any differences in rates.

Finally, regarding the timelines for reporting the information required in § 200.37 not being sufficient for States to meet the requirements, States have been reporting on teachers teaching with emergency or provisional credentials as required under the ESEA, as amended by NCLB. With respect to the teacher qualification reporting requirements new under the ESEA, as amended by the ESSA, as noted previously, States and LEAs can request a one-year, one-time extension of such new requirements. Further, States and LEAs can choose to align the reporting timelines for information reported under § 299.18(c)(2) with the December 31 deadline for State and LEA report cards.

Changes: None.

Other Comments Related to § 200.37

Comments: Some commenters supported the requirements in § 200.37 generally, while others requested additional regulatory text or opposed various provisions. Specifically, a few commenters suggested requiring additional disaggregation of educator qualification data, including by schools with high concentrations of students of color, English learners, and students with disabilities or grade level. One commenter requested that the Department provide guidance to clarify that the categories of teachers reported under proposed § 200.37 are not mutually exclusive. One commenter requested that § 200.37 specifically include as inexperienced teachers those teachers of Native students who do not have experience with Native culture and language. Finally, one commenter expressed concern regarding the elimination of the highly-qualified teacher requirements under the ESEA, as amended by NCLB, and questioned how that interacts with teacher qualification reporting requirements.

Discussion: The Department appreciates support for the requirements in § 200.37. While States and LEAs can calculate and report on teacher qualification data disaggregated by categories in addition to high- and low-poverty schools, the Department declines to require additional disaggregation given the extent of information included on State and LEA report cards required by the ESEA, as amended by the ESSA. Section 1111(h)(1)(C)(xiv) and 1111(h)(2)(C)(2)(iii) provide for States and LEAs to include on report cards any additional information they believe will best provide parents, students, and other members of the public with information regarding the progress of each of the State's public elementary and secondary schools. The Department will take into consideration one commenter's question on the reporting categories under § 200.37 as we consider guidance to support States and LEAs on the implementation of the reporting requirements under the ESEA, as amended by the ESSA. We decline to add regulatory requirements around the term "inexperienced" teachers; while we agree with the comment concerning the value of having teachers of Native American students who have experience with native culture or language, States may add these type of requirements if they choose to do so. Finally, regarding highly-qualified teacher requirements, the ESEA, as amended by the ESSA, eliminates the highly-qualified teacher requirements under the ESEA, as amended by the ESSA. (28) Under title I of the ESEA, as amended by the ESSA, the SEA is required to ensure that all teachers and paraprofessionals working in a program supported with funds under title I meet applicable State certification and licensure requirements, including any requirements or certification obtained through alternative routes to certification.

Changes: None.

Other Data—Civil Rights Data Collection Data

Comments: Some commenters requested that the Department specify the data elements that States must report under sections 1111(h)(1)(C)(viii) and 1111(h)(2)(C) of the ESEA, as amended by the ESSA. Specifically, some commenters requested that we clarify in regulations what States must report regarding, for example, the number and percentage of students enrolled in preschool programs, data on chronic absenteeism, and data on incidents of violence.

Discussion: The Department appreciates these comments requesting clarification the information that States need to implement the provisions under section 1111(h)(1)(C)(viii) and 1111(h)(2)(C) of the ESEA, as amended by the ESSA. These provisions require State and LEA report cards to include information as reported under the Civil Rights Data Collection (CRDC) in categories including measures of school quality, climate, and safety, including rates of in-school suspensions, out-of-school suspensions, expulsions, school-related arrests, and referrals to law enforcement; chronic absenteeism (including both excused and unexcused absences); incidences of violence, including bullying and harassment; number and percentage of students enrolled in preschool programs; and the number and percentage of students enrolled in accelerated coursework to earn postsecondary credit while still in high school. We wish to allow States and LEAs flexibility regarding the particular data elements they use to report information on these categories. We will consider providing additional information about how States and LEAs can meet these requirements as we consider guidance to support States and LEAs on the implementation of the reporting requirements under the ESEA, as amended by the ESSA.

Sections 299.13-299.19   Cross-Cutting Issues

Accessibility of Notices, Documentation, and Information

Comments: Many commenters remarked on the requirements that appear in § 299.13(f) and proposed § 299.18(c)(4)(v), which specifically reference the use of Web sites to publish required information including a consolidated State plan or individual program State plan, and information regarding educator equity. These sections include specific language designed to maximize access to the required information by individuals with disabilities and individuals with limited English proficiency. While a small number of commenters supported the proposed accessibility requirements generally, several of the commenters expressed concern that the requirements do not sufficiently ensure that parents and other stakeholders are able to access the information regarding the consolidated State plan or individual program State plan or the information regarding educator equity. Of the commenters expressing concern, many discussed the accessibility of notices, documentation, and information provided on SEA and LEA Web sites, particularly for individuals with disabilities or individuals with limited English proficiency.

Discussion: The Department agrees with the commenters regarding the necessity of ensuring that all parents and other stakeholders, including those with disabilities and those with limited English proficiency, have meaningful access to the information disseminated under these provisions. Such access is critical to ensure transparency to parents, educators and the public on State plans and educator equity data. Regarding additional regulatory language to ensure that individuals with limited English proficiency can access notices and documentation and information, please see discussion in § 200.21(b)(2). Regarding additional regulatory language to ensure that individuals with disabilities can access the information regarding a State's consolidated State plan or individual program State plan and information regarding educator equity, please see discussion in § 200.30(c). In every instance in § 299.13 where an SEA is required to publish information or data, we are aligning the language throughout the section.

Changes: We have aligned the language in § 299.13(b)(1), (b)(2), (c)(1)(iii)(E), and (f) to require the information to be published "on the SEA's Web site in a format and language, to the extent practicable, that the public can access and understand in compliance with the requirements under § 200.21(b)(1) through (3)."

Section 299.13   Overview of State Plan Requirements

Proposed Removal of All Plan Requirements

Comments: Several commenters recommended removing §§ 299.13-299.19 from the final regulations. These commenters argued that States should be permitted to establish State plan procedures and timelines. Additionally, commenters stated that the Department lacks authority to require a State to provide the specific information detailed in §§ 299.13-299.14.

Discussion: Whether a State submits consolidated State plans or individual program plans, the statute provides the Secretary with authority to establish procedures and timelines for submission. For example the individual program State plans in title II, part A, are generally to be submitted "at such time and in such manner as the Secretary may reasonably require" under section 2101(d)(1) of the ESEA, as amended by the ESSA. In regards to consolidated State plans, section 8302(a)(1) of the ESEA, as amended by the ESSA, indicates that the Secretary "shall establish procedures and criteria under which, after consultation with the Governor, a State educational agency may submit a consolidated State plan or a consolidated State application meeting the requirements of this section." Additionally, section 410 of GEPA, 20 U.S.C. 1221e-3, authorizes the Secretary, "in order to carry out functions otherwise vested in the Secretary by law or by delegation of authority pursuant to law, . . . to make, promulgate, issue, rescind, and amend rules and regulations governing the manner of operations of, and governing the applicable programs administered by, the Department." Moreover, section 414 of the DEOA similarly authorizes the Secretary to prescribe such rules and regulations as the Secretary determines necessary or appropriate to administer and manage the functions of the Secretary or the Department. 20 U.S.C. 3474.

The regulatory provisions in §§ 299.13-299.19 specify that the State plan requirements are being issued in accordance with the authority granted to the Secretary by GEPA, DEOA, and section 8302 of the ESEA, as amended by the ESSA. With respect to the commenter's specific concern that States should be allowed the discretion to establish State plan procedures and timelines, §§ 299.13-299.19 are not inconsistent with individual program State plan requirements or the consolidated State plan requirements in section 8302 because the Secretary has the authority to establish the time and manner for submission of individual program State plans and establish the procedures and criteria for a consolidated State plan under section 8302.

Changes: None.

Additional Assurances

Comments: Several commenters noted that section 8302(b)(3) of the ESEA, as amended by the ESSA, requires the Department to explicitly include an assurance regarding the equitable participation of private school students and teachers because it is, according to the commenters, absolutely necessary for the consideration of the consolidated State plan. This assurance was not, however, included in the proposed regulations, and the commenters recommend that § 299.13(c) be amended to include it.

Additionally, one commenter requested that States provide the assurances in section 1111(g) of the ESEA, as amended by the ESSA, specifically emphasizing that the Committee of Practitioners has been involved in the development of the State plan.

Discussion: We agree, in part, with these commenters. Section 8302(b)(3) of the ESEA, as amended by the ESSA, contemplates that the consolidated State plan include an assurance of compliance with applicable provisions regarding participation by private school children and teachers. Therefore, we agree with the commenters that this assurance is a necessary part of the consolidated State plan. We are adding § 299.14(c), a new section on consolidated State plan assurances, to include an assurance regarding participation by private school children and teachers.

However, the Department declines to include an additional assurance regarding the Committee of Practitioners. All statutory assurances for covered programs are generally applicable under section 8304(a) of the ESEA, as amended by the ESSA, which requires that each SEA assure that each program covered by the State plan be administered in accordance with all applicable statutes, regulations, program plans and applications. Furthermore, section 8302(b)(3) of the ESEA, as amended by the ESSA, requires the Secretary to include only assurances that are absolutely necessary for the consideration of consolidated State plans. Therefore, we do not think it is necessary to include a specific assurance regarding the Committee of Practitioners.

Changes: We have revised § 299.14 to include a new § 299.14(c) on consolidated State plan assurances, which includes a new assurance regarding State compliance with sections 8501 and 1117 of the ESEA, as amended by the ESSA, regarding participation by private school children and teachers.

Section 299.13(k)   Individual Program State Plan Requirements for Title I, Part C

Comments: None.

Discussion: Based on further internal review, the Department is clarifying in final § 299.13(k)(2) that SEAs who choose to submit individual program State plans for title I, part C, must also meet the consolidated State plan requirements in § 299.19(b)(2) in order to address sections 1303(f)(2), 1304(d), and 1306(b)(1) of the ESEA, as amended by the ESSA. The specific requirements are related to the proper identification and recruitment of eligible migratory children and their unique educational needs, consultation, measureable program objectives, and uses of funds. It is essential for all title I, part C State plans, whether submitted as an individual title I, part C State plan or consolidated State plan to address these requirements as they provide necessary information for each SEA and the Department in addressing statutory requirements included in title I, part C of the ESEA, as amended by the ESSA.

Changes: We have added § 299.13(k)(2) to include the specific requirements in § 299.19(b)(2) for title I, part C that a State must also include if it submits an individual title I, part C State plan.

Section 299.13(b)   Timely and Meaningful Consultation

Comments: Many commenters supported the Department's proposed requirements for timely and meaningful consultation in § 299.13(b). Commenters appreciated that the requirements emphasized consultation with a variety of stakeholders at various stages of State plan development, including an explanation of how input was taken into consideration. A number of commenters requested that the Department align the requirements with the Secretary's Dear Colleague letter issued on June 23, 2016, regarding stakeholder engagement (Stakeholder Engagement DCL). Many commenters also requested that the Department provide further guidance consistent with the requirements in § 299.13(b) for other ESEA programs. One commenter suggested that the Department consider providing more specific resources for ensuring meaningful stakeholder engagement. Another commenter suggested that the Department provide guidance clarifying that meaningful engagement means engagement in ways that are culturally and linguistically responsive.

Discussion: The Department appreciates the extensive support for the timely and meaningful consultation requirements in § 299.13(b). In order to ensure that States implement ESEA with fidelity, the Department strongly encourages States to consult and engage with stakeholders consistent with the best practices identified in the Stakeholder Engagement DCL, which is available at: http://www2.ed.gov/policy/elsec/guid/secletter/160622.html. In addition to ensuring the specific requirements in § 299.13(b) are met during the design and development of the SEA's plan, prior to initial submission of the plan, and prior to any revisions or amendments of the approved plans, the Department encourages States to consider applying the timely and meaningful consultation requirements throughout its implementation of the ESEA, as amended by the ESSA. Where relevant, we will consider issuing additional ESEA non-regulatory guidance regarding timely and meaningful consultation in the future, including guidance on culturally and linguistically responsive engagement.

Changes: None.

Comments: While commenters generally supported the requirements for timely and meaningful consultation in § 299.13(b), several recommended changes or additions to the proposed requirements. Some commenters asked that the regulations require not only consultation during preparation of the State plan, but also throughout implementation of the plan. Other commenters asked that language be added requiring States to describe their systems and structures for ensuring that meaningful and continuous stakeholder engagement occurs.

Additional commenters asked that the regulation be amended to require States to: (1) Provide 60 days public notice of the draft State plan; (2) provide written agendas prior to meetings and written responses to public comments; and (3) ensure high quality two-way communications between the State and stakeholders about the State plan. In particular, some commenters asked that two-way communication be required with teachers, and with parents and families. Another commenter suggested that the final regulations require that stakeholder engagement include meetings that educators can attend, which one commenter specifically provided should be through the provision of flexible leave to school employees for attendance at such meetings.

Discussion: The Department appreciates the comments suggesting additional requirements for timely and meaningful consultation but declines to add the requested requirements, which are, for the most part, already addressed in the regulations. We are requiring SEAs in the performance management requirements in § 299.15(b)(2)(i) to "collect and use data and information, which may include input from stakeholders and data collected and reported under section 1111(h), to assess the quality of SEA and LEA implementation." In regards to requiring descriptions of systems and structures for consultation and requiring two-way communication about the plan, § 299.13(b) details a process that States must follow to satisfy the requirement for timely and meaningful consultation, including a requirement in § 299.13(b)(3) that the State "[d]escribe how the consultation and public comment were taken into account in the consolidated State plan or individual program State plan." Therefore, we believe that States will provide valuable information on how the communication was a two-way dialogue. In addition, the provisions in § 299.15(b)(2)(i) encourage each SEA to continue to meaningfully engage with stakeholders to collect data on implementation of SEA and LEA plans. In regards to requiring two-way consultation specifically with teachers, and with parents and families, these two groups are among those already listed in § 299.15(a) with whom the State must ". . . [engage] in timely and meaningful consultations consistent with § 299.13(b)." We encourage all States to specifically ensure that timely and meaningful consultation occurs during hours that parents, families, and current educators can participate and identified this as a best practice in the Stakeholder Engagement DCL.

In response to the comments requesting that we extend the public notice period from 30 days to 60 days, the Department encourages all States to provide as much time for public notice and outreach as possible. However, since section 1111(a)(8) of the ESEA, as amended by the ESSA, on which this requirement is based, only requires a State to make the State plan available for "not less than 30 days," the Department declines to make this change. With regard to adding language requiring agendas and written follow up to comments, the Department encourages States to provide this sort of feedback to stakeholders, whenever possible, but finds making this a requirement would be unduly burdensome. Given the volume of comments received indicating that the consolidated State plan requirements, as drafted, are overly burdensome, the Department will not add the additional requirements to the consolidated State plan.

Changes: None.

Comments: Several commenters suggested that the regulations should require States to engage with Tribal governments above and beyond stakeholder engagement. Commenters recommended that the Department use Executive Order 13175 as a guide for ensuring that the regulations properly outline tribal consultation in the regulations. Commenters suggested that including a requirement in § 299.13(b) for SEAs to consult with tribes using agendas that are agreed upon in advance, and requiring SEAs to follow up in writing with stakeholders would help ensure that consultation is meaningful, and is respectful of the trust responsibility. Finally, one commenter urged the Department to condition State plan approval upon proof of meaningful consultation with Tribal nations.

Discussion: The commenter correctly notes that the Department has a government-to-government relationship with tribes, and that the consultation between the Department and tribes is outlined in Executive Order 13175. However, the Federal trust responsibility does not extend to SEAs. Therefore, the Department declines to add language to § 299.13(b) regarding additional requirements for tribal consultation. As noted previously, the Department encourages SEAs to provide agendas and written follow-up to stakeholders, whenever possible, but finds making this a requirement unduly burdensome.

In response to the commenter who asked that State plan approval be conditioned upon proof of meaningful consultation with Tribal nations, § 299.13(b)(3) requires States to describe how consultation and public comment were taken into account in the consolidated or individual State plan. We believe that this requirement addresses the commenter's concerns. Therefore, we decline to add additional language.

Changes: None.

Comments: Several commenters expressed satisfaction with the required processes for how States should engage in timely and meaningful consultation with stakeholders in formulating the State plan. Commenters asked that § 299.13(b) be amended to require LEAs to use the same timely and meaningful consultation processes in formulating LEA plans.

Discussion: The Department declines to add the requested requirement as it is outside of the scope of the regulations, which address only State plan requirements, not requirements for LEA plans. Additionally, if States choose to allow LEAs to submit consolidated LEA plans, section 8305(c) of the ESEA, as amended by the ESSA, makes clear that procedures for submission of the plans are not set by the Department noting, "a State educational agency, in consultation with the Governor, shall collaborate with local educational agencies in the State in establishing procedures for the submission of the consolidated State plans or consolidated State applications under this section." If the State decides to use individual program applications rather than a consolidated local plan, individual applications for most covered programs already include consultation requirements. However, because we believe that timely and meaningful consultation is important and that ESEA implementation must be transparent, we encourage States to consider including the timely and meaningful consultation requirements at the local level.

Changes: None.

Comments: A few commenters commended the Department for including consultation with the Governor under section 8540 of the ESEA, as amended by the ESSA, in the requirements for timely and meaningful consultation in § 299.13(b). Two commenters requested that the Department require States to describe how they are meeting this requirement, including how the SEA engaged with the Governor by describing, among other things, the frequency of meetings and the extent of collaborative planning.

Discussion: Although the Department believes that SEA consultation with the Governor is important, the Department declines to require an additional description regarding how the SEA completed this consultation. Section 299.15 requires an SEA to describe how it engaged in timely and meaningful consultation consistent with § 299.13(b), including the Governor's consultation requirement in § 299.13(b)(4). An SEA must already describe in its consolidated State plan how it met the requirements of section 8540 of the ESEA, as amended by the ESSA. Therefore, we do not believe that requiring an additional description is necessary. Furthermore, in order to limit burden associated with submitting a consolidated State plan, the Department declines to add an additional requirement that an SEA, when describing how it consulted with the Governor, describe the frequency of meetings and the extent of collaborative planning.

Changes: None.

Foster Care Requirements

Comments: Many commenters expressed concern about the proposed assurance in § 299.13(c)(1)(ii) that required SEAs to ensure that LEAs receiving funds under title I, part A of the ESEA, as amended by the ESSA, would provide children in foster care with transportation to and from their schools of origin even if the LEA and local child welfare agency did not agree on which agency or agencies would pay the additional costs incurred to provide such transportation. Many commenters indicated that the assurance appeared inconsistent with section 1112(c)(5)(B) of the ESEA, as amended by the ESSA, and expressed concern that it would undermine the collaborative process anticipated by the ESEA. Other commenters expressed concern that the regulations would impose a significant financial burden on LEAs.

Many commenters praised the Department for including the protections for children in foster care in the State plan requirements, but many also proposed that the final regulations mirror the statutory requirements for collaboration. Other commenters suggested that the regulations require the procedures developed by the LEA and child welfare agency to include a dispute resolution process. Some commenters specified that it should be the child welfare agency that pays the additional costs of transportation, and others asked that the regulations require the LEA and child welfare agency to automatically split the costs if the agencies cannot reach agreement. A number of commenters requested that the regulations require both the SEA and the State child welfare agencies to ensure that the LEAs and local child welfare agencies collaborate to develop and implement clear written transportation procedures. Some commenters also requested that the regulations be amended to clarify that the LEA must provide or arrange for adequate and appropriate transportation to and from the school of origin while any disputes are being resolved. Other commenters expressed concern that requiring the LEA to provide transportation while disputes were being resolved would cause child welfare agencies to initiate a dispute process in order to avoid paying for transportation.

Discussion: The Department appreciates the concerns expressed by commenters that the proposed regulations may undermine that collaborative process by defaulting to the LEA as the responsible party for paying any additional transportation costs. Likewise, the Department believes that defaulting to the child welfare agency as the sole agency responsible for paying any additional costs associated with providing transportation would undermine the collaborative nature of the statute. As noted in the Department's non-regulatory guidance entitled Ensuring Educational Stability for Children in Foster Care, children in foster care are a particularly vulnerable subgroup of students. We believe these students have a right to educational stability, including transportation services as needed, to maintain them in their school of origin when in their best interest. Therefore, the Department believes that the final assurance in § 299.13(c)(1)(ii) should clarify the joint obligations for educational and child welfare agencies to ensure that transportation is provided to maintain educational stability.

The Department likewise recognizes that there may be circumstances where a dispute resolution process is required if an LEA and child welfare agency are unable to reach agreement as to which agency or agencies will pay any additional costs that may be associated with providing transportation to children in foster care to and from their schools of origin. However, the Department does not believe it is necessary to mandate a specific dispute resolution process as the statute clearly requires that LEAs collaborate with child welfare agencies to develop procedures that ensure that children in foster care needing transportation promptly receive such transportation.

In order to ensure this statutory requirement is met, the Department is clarifying that the SEA must assure that an LEA receiving funds under title I, part A has developed procedures that describe how such transportation will be provided and funded if the agencies cannot reach agreement, whether through a dispute resolution process or through default cost sharing. An SEA's assurance here means that the SEA must take a leading and active role to ensure that LEAs collaborate with State and local child welfare agencies to develop clear and written procedures regarding how children in foster care will receive transportation, as necessary, to their school of origin when determined to be in their best interest.

We appreciate commenters' concerns about children in foster care continuing to receive transportation to the schools of origin while disputes are pending, along with concerns about which agency or agencies should be responsible for providing this transportation, and are clarifying that the written procedures must also describe which agency or agencies will initially pay the additional costs incurred in providing transportation so that transportation is provided promptly during the pendency of the dispute. We believe that the appropriate agency or agencies responsible for initially paying the additional costs incurred may vary depending on the individual child's circumstances. The LEA and local child welfare agency should explore a variety of options that consider such circumstances. For example, for one child, the foster parent may be willing to transport the child to the child's school of origin; for another child, there may existing

225

transportation readily available; and there may be instances that necessitate the child's transportation being funded.

Changes: We have revised § 299.13(c)(1)(ii) to remove the language requiring the LEA to provide transportation to children in foster care if the LEA and child welfare agency do not agree on which agency or agencies will pay any additional costs incurred to provide such transportation. We have also added language to clarify that the written procedures developed by the LEA and State or local child welfare agency must address how the transportation requirements will be met in the event of a dispute over which agency or agencies will pay any additional costs incurred in providing transportation and indicate which agency or agencies will initially pay the additional costs so that transportation is provided promptly during the pendency of the dispute.

Comments: Several commenters wrote to express views on the best interest determination, school of origin, the timing of implementation of the new educational stability provisions, the foster care point of contact, the timing of the best interest determination, and other related issues concerning the educational stability of children in foster care.

Discussion: We agree that the educational stability of children in foster care is an important issue and appreciate the feedback on this issue. The proposed regulations, however, only addressed the topic of which agency or agencies should pay any additional costs associated with providing transportation to children in foster care to and from their schools of origin. Comments on related issues—such as the best interest determination, school of origin, and concerns about timing—are therefore outside the scope of the regulations. Furthermore, these topics are addressed in the Department's non-regulatory guidance entitled Ensuring Educational Stability for Children in Foster Care. For clarity on the statutory requirements in Sections 1111(g)(1)(E) and 1112(c)(5) of the ESEA, as amended by the ESSA, we refer commenters to this non-regulatory guidance document.

Changes: None.

Plan Submission Process

Comments: Several commenters remarked on the proposed plan submission dates of March 6, 2017, or July 5, 2017. Many of these commenters indicated that the proposed timeline for submission did not allow sufficient time for consultation; of particular concern was States' ability to adequately consult on a new accountability system prior to having the system ready to implement in the 2017-2018 school year. Some commenters expressed concern that the proposed submission dates would require that States begin to implement their accountability systems in school year 2017-2018 before their plans could be approved by the Secretary. Other commenters felt that the proposed submission deadlines were too late to ensure that SEAs had an approved plan in place in time to identify comprehensive and targeted support schools for the 2017-2018 school year and asked that the submission date be moved up to December 2016; two of these commenters also recommended that the Department's review timeline be shortened from 120 to 60 days to ensure that plan approval occurs prior to the beginning of the 2017-2018 school year. Other commenters suggested that the Department allow SEAs to submit portions of the plan in a staggered fashion to allow additional time for consultation.

Discussion: Given that the Department has revised § 200.19(d) to permit States to delay full implementation of their accountability systems until the 2018-2019 school year and to allow SEAs additional time for timely and meaningful consultation, the Department has determined it is appropriate to adjust plan submission timelines and offer later submission dates. Accordingly, the

Department will adjust the submission deadlines to April 3, 2017, or September 18, 2017.

The Department declines to move submission timelines up to December 2016 because doing so would not allow sufficient time for each SEA to engage in timely and meaningful consultation consistent with § 299.13(b). The Department also declines to reduce its time to review plans from 120 to 60 days; sections 1111(a)(4)(A)(v) and 8451 of the ESEA, as amended by the ESSA, allow 120 days for review and the Department believes that a 60-day review period allows inadequate time for the required peer review. While the Department appreciates the idea of allowing SEAs to submit their plans in parts, the Department believes that the entire consolidated State plan must be submitted at one time to ensure fully coordinated strategies.

Changes: None.

Comments: One commenter requested clarification on § 299.13(e) regarding the process for submitting revisions of consolidated State plans during the period for Secretarial review under sections 1111(a)(4)(A)(v) or 8451 of the ESEA, as amended by the ESSA. This commenter also requested that the Department streamline the process for review.

Discussion: The Department appreciates the opportunity to clarify the requirements in § 299.13(e). During the period of Secretarial review, an SEA may revise its initial plan in response to a preliminary written determination by the Secretary. When submitting revisions to the plan the SEA originally submitted, the SEA must resubmit the entire revised State plan, not just the parts that contain the additional revisions. The Department intends to provide additional information on the timing, format, and process for submitting and reviewing consolidated and individual program State plans in the near future.

Additionally, proposed § 299.13(b)(2)(iii) required timely and meaningful consultation prior to the submission of any significant revisions or amendments to the consolidated State plan. In order to distinguish the requirements for revising an initial State plan from the timely and meaningful consultation requirements for an approved State plan, the Department is clarifying the language in § 299.13(b)(2)(iii) to apply to an approved consolidated State plan or individual program State plan rather than an initial consolidated State plan.

Changes: The Department has revised § 299.13(e) to indicate that an SEA, when resubmitting its initial consolidated State plan, must resubmit the entire State plan, which includes its revisions. We have also clarified that the timely and meaningful consultation requirements in § 299.13(b)(2)(iii) apply to an approved consolidated State plan or individual program State plan and not to the process for revising initial consolidated State plans under § 299.13(e).

Comments: None.

Discussion: Under § 299.13(d)(i), the Department described the process for submitting an initial consolidated State plan or individual program State plan. In the proposed regulation § 299.13(d), we indicated that an SEA must submit the plan to the Department on a date and time to be established by the Secretary. The Department is clarifying that the Secretary will, at a future date, also establish the manner (e.g., electronic or paper) by which an SEA must submit its State plan. Under proposed § 299.13(d)(ii), the Department detailed when a consolidated State plan or individual program State plan was considered to be submitted by the Secretary if it was received prior to an established deadline. We are clarifying that any State plan received prior to the deadline established by the Secretary is considered to be submitted on the date of the established deadline (rather than the date received) for the purposes of the 120 day period of Secretarial review under sections 1111(a)(4)(A)(v) or 8451 of the ESEA, as amended by the ESSA.

Changes: The Department has revised § 299.13(d)(i) to indicate that an SEA must submit its consolidated State plan or individual program State plan in the manner (e.g., paper or electronic) to be established by the Secretary. The Department has also revised § 299.13(d)(ii) to indicate that the provision regarding State plans received prior to an established deadline is for the purposes of tolling the period of Secretarial review under sections 1111(a)(4)(A)(v) or 8451 of the ESEA, as amended by the ESSA.

Extension for Reporting Student-Level Data

Comments: As discussed later in this document under § 299.18(c), a few commenters noted that the requirement to provide educator equity data at the student level is burdensome. Commenters expressed concern as to whether the Department could prescribe any date at which the reporting of student-level data is required.

Discussion: While a few commenters suggested removing the student-level data requirement altogether, as discussed later in this document under § 299.18(c), we believe the requirement to provide educator equity data at the student level is critical. However, we understand that some States may not currently have the capacity to collect or report data at the student level. In light of the fact that the requirement may be burdensome for certain States and districts that have not yet begun collecting or using student-level data, the Department is adding an additional year to the extension that an SEA may request, detailed in § 299.13(d)(3). An SEA requesting a three-year extension for providing educator equity data at the student level must, during the three-year extension, publish and provide those data in its State plan at the school level, consistent with § 299.13(d)(3)(ii).

Changes: We have revised § 299.13(d)(3) to allow an SEA to request an extension for three years if it provides the information and data required under § 299.18(c) at the school level and submits a detailed plan and timeline to provide those data at the student level within three years of the date of submission of its title I, part A State plan or consolidated State plan.

Section 299.14   Requirements for the Consolidated State Plan

Content of the Consolidated State Plan—Burden and Authority

Comments: While a small number of commenters appreciated the integrated and comprehensive nature of the proposed consolidated State plan requirements, several commenters objected to the volume of proposed consolidated State plan requirements. The commenters asserted that the Department has the statutory authority, under section 8302 of the ESEA, as amended by the ESSA, to require an SEA to provide "only descriptions, information, assurances . . . and other materials that are absolutely necessary for the consideration of the consolidated State plan." Some commenters stated that the requirements would result in cumbersome and complicated plans that stakeholders would find difficult to review and understand. Other commenters asserted that the requirements promoted certain education policies not explicitly required in the statute and would allow the Department to implement a peer review process that further promoted those policies. Some commenters recommended that the Department condense and streamline the consolidated State plan requirements, but did not make specific recommendations for requirements to remove. Others recommended that the Department reduce specific consolidated State plan requirements including the performance management requirements in proposed § 299.14, assessment requirements in proposed § 299.16, teacher quality and equity requirements in proposed § 299.18, and the well-rounded and supportive education for all students requirements in proposed § 299.19.

Discussion: Section 8302(a)(1) of the ESEA, as amended by the ESSA, indicates that the Secretary "shall establish procedures and criteria under which, after consultation with the Governor, [an SEA] may submit a consolidated State plan or a consolidated State application meeting the requirements of this section." Additionally, section 410 of GEPA, 20 U.S.C. 1221e-3, authorizes the Secretary, "in order to carry out functions otherwise vested in the Secretary by law or by delegation of authority pursuant to law, . . . to make, promulgate, issue, rescind, and amend rules and regulations governing the manner of operations of, and governing the applicable programs administered by, the Department." Moreover, section 414 of the DEOA similarly authorizes the Secretary to prescribe such rules and regulations as the Secretary determines necessary or appropriate to administer and manage the functions of the Secretary or the Department. 20 U.S.C. 3474. The requirements for a consolidated State plan in §§ 299.14-299.19 are being issued in accordance with the authority granted to the Secretary by GEPA, DEOA, and section 8302 of the ESEA, as amended by the ESSA. With respect to the commenters' concerns that the Secretary does not have the authority to include some of the required descriptions or information because it is not "absolutely necessary for consideration of the consolidated State plan," all of the descriptions, information and assurances included in §§ 299.14-299.19 have been determined by the Secretary to be absolutely necessary and consistent with the authority in section 8302 of the ESEA, as amended by the ESSA. The consolidated State plans must provide sufficient detail across the included programs in order to ensure transparency for all stakeholders, proper administration of Federal funds and allow the Secretary to consider whether such plan is consistent with the ESEA, as amended by the ESSA, and applicable regulations. Additionally, consistent with the purpose of the consolidated State plan, we believe that the regulations would significantly reduce burden on each SEA choosing to submit a consolidated State plan rather than individual program State plans. Furthermore, the Secretary believes that all requirements of the consolidated State plan have a statutory basis in the covered program provisions throughout the ESEA, as amended by the ESSA, and other applicable regulations.

In response to the concern that the Department may be promoting specific education policies through the peer review process for the consolidated State plan, the Department is required under section 8452 of the ESEA, as amended by the ESSA, to ensure that any portion of a consolidated State plan that is related to title I, part A is subject to the peer review process described in section 1111(a)(4) of the ESEA, as amended by the ESSA. The Department intends to administer a peer review of consolidated State plans consistent with the purpose of the peer review under section 1111(a)(4)(B) to "maximize collaboration with each State; promote effective implementation of challenging State standards through State and local innovation; and provide transparent, timely, and objective feedback to States designed to strengthen the technical and overall quality of the State plans."

However, given the concerns expressed by several commenters and the Department's desire to eliminate unnecessary burden from State plans, we believe that some of the requirements within and across the consolidated State plan regulations can be further consolidated. Therefore, in an effort to reduce additional burden on States, we are changing some previously required descriptions into either an optional description or an assurance, and removing some previously required descriptions entirely from the consolidated State plan. Additionally, in an effort to streamline the requirements, we are reorganizing the structure of the consolidated State plan to place all cross cutting requirements in § 299.15, including required descriptions on consultation and performance management. For performance management, each SEA would only have to discuss these cross-cutting requirements once rather than under each component as proposed in § 299.14(c). Furthermore, we also believe that some of the requirements were not clear and therefore were interpreted to be more burdensome than intended. As a result, we are clarifying some consolidated State plan requirements to address those instances where a lack of clarity in the regulatory language resulted in an increase in perceived burden. The discussion of the exact changes to reduce burden in §§ 299.16-299.19 of the consolidated State plan are discussed below in the specific section where the changes were made.

Changes: We have moved the requirement in proposed § 299.14(c) regarding performance management to § 299.15(b) and revised it so that an SEA describes its system of performance management for implementation of SEA and LEA plans once rather than separately for each of the components required under §§ 299.16 through 299.19. With the exception of § 299.18(c), we have streamlined the required descriptions throughout §§ 299.15 through 299.19 by removing the requirement to identify specific strategies and timelines in each required description. We have also revised proposed § 299.14(c)(1) and (2)(i) to make certain descriptive details optional rather than required regarding how the SEA's plan approval process is aligned to the strategies identified in the consolidated State plan and whether to consider specific data collected and reported under section 1111(h) of the ESEA, as amended by the ESSA, and specific input from stakeholders when assessing the quality of SEA and LEA implementation. The changes are reflected in final § 299.15(b)(1) and (2). As a result of those changes, we have removed the requirement in proposed § 299.19(a)(3)(A)-(D) regarding a review of data and information on resource equity, and revised final § 299.15(b)(2) to indicate that each SEA may consider such information broadly as part of review and approval of LEA plans under the revised requirements for an SEA's system of performance management. We have also removed the requirement in proposed § 299.15(b) for each State to describe how it will coordinate across Federal laws impacting education and included this requirement as an assurance in the new section on consolidated State plan assurances in final § 299.14(c). We have further removed some previously required descriptions and streamlined other requirements in §§ 299.16 through 299.19 including by changing previously required descriptions into assurances and only requiring certain descriptions if a State intends to use Federal funds for that purpose.

Comments: Some commenters suggested that additional State plan requirements be added to proposed § 299.14. Specifically, one commenter asked that proposed § 299.14(c) be augmented to include a requirement that SEAs ensure data transparency by describing their plans for preparing and disseminating State report cards, and for ensuring that LEAs prepare and disseminate local report cards. Other commenters asked that proposed § 299.14(c) be amended to require that SEAs provide additional information about their strategies and timelines for ensuring continuous improvement so that States continuously improve all strategies, not just strategies that do not lead to satisfactory progress.

Discussion: The Department agrees with the commenters that data transparency and promotion of continuous improvement are important goals. To that end, we have already included in final § 299.15(b) requirements that consolidated State plans address continuous improvement strategies and the use of data in the consolidated State plan. We have also established in §§ 200.30 and 200.31 requirements to ensure that State and local report cards contain all elements required by the statute, including that these report cards be presented in an understandable and uniform format. However, given the comments received indicating that the consolidated State plan requirements, as drafted, are overly burdensome, the Department will not add additional requirements to the consolidated State plan. The Department believes that existing statutory and regulatory requirements for report cards are sufficient to ensure data transparency. We agree with the comment on proposed § 299.14(c) that SEAs should review all strategies for continuous improvement and not only those strategies that are not improving outcomes and are revising final § 299.15(b)(2)(iii) to ensure that SEAs review all SEA and LEA plans and implementation of those plans for continuous improvement.

Changes: We have revised § 299.15(b)(2)(iii) to require that an SEA describe its plan to continuously improve implementation of all SEA and LEA plans.

Integrated Nature of the State Plan

Comments: Several commenters supported the Department's proposal that SEAs develop consolidated State plans that address: Consultation and coordination; challenging academic standards and assessments; accountability, support, and improvement for schools; supporting excellent educators; and supporting all students in a truly consolidated manner across all covered programs. One commenter expressed concern that the State plan structure is insufficiently integrated and will reinforce traditional silos in the education system; this commenter recommended that the regulations require SEAs to articulate a vision or theory of action that ties the five components of the consolidated State plan together.

Discussion: We appreciate commenters' support for the proposed regulations. With regard to a requirement that SEAs articulate an overall vision or theory of action, while we encourage SEAs to do this, we believe that requirement would unnecessarily increase burden on States.

Changes: None.

Section 299.15   Consultation and Coordination

Stakeholder Engagement

Comments: Many commenters recommended that the Department strengthen the requirements related to SEAs' consultation with stakeholders during the design and development of the consolidated State plan. Specifically, commenters requested that the Department ensure that the voices of stakeholders are heard. Another commenter suggested that the Department ensure that teachers are in control of the education system. Additionally, one commenter suggested that the process for revising the consolidated State plan should be vetted by a wide range of stakeholders. An additional commenter suggested that the Department define the term "to be developed in partnership with stakeholders" to mean that the process must be proactive and inclusive, and that partners must have all of the same information and the assistance needed to fully understand it, the time to develop responses, and the vehicles for responding.

In contrast, two commenters suggested that the consultation requirements be removed from the consolidated State plan regulations to permit States additional flexibility to establish State plan procedures and timelines.

Discussion: The Department appreciates the comments on ways to strengthen engagement, as well as the comments on the importance of State flexibility in regard to these requirements. Just as we believe that meaningful stakeholder engagement is critical to the consolidated State plan development and implementation process, we also believe that discrete decisions about the specific process for engagement are best made at the local level.

We appreciate the best practices in consultation and stakeholder engagement highlighted by many of the commenters, including information sharing and providing vehicles for responding, as well as the proposed definition that one commenter provided for the phrase "to be developed in partnership with stakeholders." We encourage the use of these best practices throughout the consultation process. We further appreciate that many commenters emphasized that their voice should be honored and not undermined, and we believe the final regulations will help ensure that a wide range of stakeholders will be consulted throughout the process of consolidated State plan development and implementation. See § 299.13 for a discussion of additional comments related to timely and meaningful consultation.

Changes: None.

Comments: Multiple commenters recommended that the Department require each SEA to consult with additional stakeholder groups in developing its consolidated State plan, including: Representatives of private school students, representatives of non-government school students and teachers, and non-government school students and teachers; early childhood educators and leaders; parent and teacher advisory groups and parents; representatives of teachers' unions; practicing and current K-12 teachers; organization members who specifically represent students with disabilities; civil rights organizations, including those who represent lesbian, gay, bisexual, and transgender (LGBT) students; tribal elected or appointed representatives; specialized instructional support personnel; school psychologists; community representatives; Alaska Native corporations; school librarians; local government; individuals knowledgeable about how to meet the needs of specific subgroups of students; entities that serve and support some of the most vulnerable students, including students involved in child welfare, homeless students, juvenile justice-involved youth, and workforce development staff, providers, and advocates; employers; and families of traditionally underserved students, including low-income children, minority children; and English learners. Commenters recommended that we require SEAs to consult with these specific groups because of their unique voices, as well as the specialized needs of the populations that these groups represent. Specifically with respect to tribal elected or appointed representatives, the commenter noted while the inclusion of "representatives of Indian tribes located in the State" is important, representatives should not be named as surrogates for tribal government representation.

Discussion: The final regulations include a broad group of required stakeholders with whom each SEA must consult when developing its consolidated State plan. This group includes each of the groups prescribed by the statute, as well as additional stakeholder groups that have the potential to bring important and varied perspectives to a State's work to develop and implement a consolidated State plan. Additionally, the required group of stakeholders in the regulations includes a number of the stakeholder groups specifically requested by commenters, including: Civil rights organizations, including those representing students with disabilities, English learners, and other historically underserved students; teachers, principals, other school leaders, paraprofessionals, specialized instructional support personnel, and organizations representing such individuals; community-based organizations; employers; and parents and families. For these reasons, we generally decline to add additional required stakeholder groups, as requested by commenters.

However, we note that commenters highlighted two critical stakeholder groups that were not included in § 299.15(a) of the proposed regulations and have unique perspectives to provide to a State in its development of its consolidated State plan: Representatives of private school students, and early childhood educators and leaders. We find particularly compelling commenters' arguments that consolidated State plans may not sufficiently reflect the interests of these two stakeholder groups-representatives of private school students, and early childhood educators and leaders-without the explicit inclusion of these groups in the required list of stakeholders with whom a State must consult in developing and implementing its consolidated State plan. Therefore, we are expanding the list of required stakeholder groups to explicitly include these two stakeholder groups. Additionally, in order to address the concerns of commenters who did not see their particular constituency represented in the required list of stakeholders with whom a State must consult on its consolidated State plan, we are clarifying in the final regulations that the required group of stakeholders with whom a State must consult is a mandatory, but non-exhaustive list, and may be supplemented by States as appropriate, based on local context and need.

232

Changes: We have revised § 299.15(a) to add the following to the required list of stakeholders with whom a State must consult on its consolidated State plan: Representatives of private school students, and early childhood educators and leaders. We have clarified in § 299.15(a) that the required stakeholder groups represent minimum requirements and may be supplemented at each SEA's discretion.

Coordination

Comments: A few commenters expressed support regarding the requirements for the Department's efforts to increase coordination across related program plans. One commenter also suggested we add the WIOA and career and technical educational programs to the list of required programs for plan coordination.

Discussion: We appreciate the commenters' support for ensuring that SEAs coordinate the work they are conducting under their consolidated State plan with other programs in the State. The proposed regulations in § 299.15(b), as well as the final regulations in § 299.14(c), include required coordination between the consolidated State plan and an extensive group of plans from additional programs, including under the WIOA and the Carl D. Perkins Career and Technical Education Act of 2006.

Changes: None.

Section 299.16   Challenging Academic Standards and Academic Assessments

Challenging Academic Standards and Academic Assessments in General

Comments: Many commenters expressed concern regarding proposed § 299.16(a)(1) that requires an SEA to provide evidence at such time and in such manner specified by the Secretary that the State has adopted challenging academic content standards. Some commenters indicated that the Department should only require an SEA to provide an assurance that the State adopted challenging academic content standards consistent with 1111(b)(1) of the ESEA, as amended by the ESSA.

Discussion: As some commenters noted, section 1111(b)(1)(A) of the ESEA, as amended by the ESSA, requires each State, in its title I, part A State plan, to provide an assurance that the State has adopted challenging academic content standards and aligned academic achievement standards that will be used to carry out title I, part A. At the same time, section 1111(b)(1)(D) of the ESEA requires a State to "demonstrate" that those challenging State academic standards are aligned with entrance requirements for credit-bearing coursework in the system of public higher education in the State and relevant State career and technical education standards. Similarly, section 1111(b)(1)(E) of the ESEA, as amended by the ESSA, permits a State to adopt alternate academic achievement standards but only if those standards meet specific statutory requirements and section 1111(b)(1)(F) of the ESEA requires a State to "demonstrate" that the State has adopted ELP standards that meet certain statutory requirements. Moreover, section 1111(b)(2) of the ESEA requires a State to "demonstrate" that it has implemented a set of high-quality academic assessments in at least mathematics, reading/language arts, and science. The Department is committed to ensuring that all States meet the statutory requirements in sections 1111(b)(1) and (b)(2) of the ESEA, as amended by the ESSA, including through peer review consistent with section 1111(a)(4).

In order to avoid any confusion that proposed § 299.16(a)(1) may have raised, the Department is removing the provisions in § 299.16 related to section 1111(b)(1) and replacing them with a general assurance of compliance with relevant statutory and regulatory provisions regarding standards and assessments in final § 299.14(c)(2). Because the statutory language is clear, we do not believe that further regulatory efforts in the consolidated State plan are necessary other than a general assurance that a State will comply with the standards and assessment requirements in sections 1111(b)(1)(A)-(F) and 1111(b)(2) of the ESEA, as amended by the ESSA, and applicable regulations.

Changes: We have removed the requirements in proposed § 299.16(a), (b)(1)-(2), (4)-(5), and (6) and replaced them with an assurance in § 299.14(c)(2) that the State will meet the standards and assessments requirements of sections 1111(b)(1)(A)-(F) and 1111(b)(2) of the ESEA, as amended by the ESSA, and applicable regulations.

Comments: Some commenters praised the coherence of the State plan regulations, including § 299.16, while other commenters suggested that the requirements were burdensome and recommended removing § 299.16 entirely. A number of commenters urged the Department to expand local control over standards and assessments, or generally to reduce the requirements to use standardized tests. A few commenters suggested that testing should happen less frequently, such as once in each of several grade spans, instead of annually.

Discussion: The Department appreciates the diversity of opinions with regard to the structure of § 299.16. Section 1111(b)(1)(B) of the ESEA, as amended by the ESSA, requires each State to establish the challenging academic content and academic achievement standards that apply to all public schools and public school students in the State, except in certain narrow circumstances also described in statute. Section 1111(b)(2) of the ESEA, as amended by the ESSA, enumerates State responsibilities for statewide academic assessments using the same assessments, except in certain cases. The statute clearly requires continued use of statewide academic assessments annually in grades three through eight and once in high school, regardless of the specific reference to such responsibilities in this regulation. However, in an effort to streamline the requirements in this section and reduce burden for States, the Department is no longer asking each State to describe in its consolidated State plan each of the requirements previously proposed in § 299.16 that will be reviewed as part of the peer review process. States remain responsible for implementing challenging academic standards and assessments consistent with the statute and applicable regulations. Additionally, in an effort to reduce the overall burden associated with submitting the consolidated State plan, we are removing the required description of how the State will use formula grant funds under section 1201 of the ESEA, as amended by the ESSA, and removing this program from the programs included in the consolidated State plan under § 299.13(j)(2).

Changes: As previously described, we have removed the proposed requirements in proposed § 299.16(a) and replaced them with an assurance in final § 299.14(c)(2) that the State will meet the standards and assessments requirements of sections 1111(b)(1)(A)-(F) of the ESEA, as amended by the ESSA. Additionally, we have removed the proposed requirements in § 299.16(b)(1)-(2) and (4)-(5) and replaced them with an assurance of compliance with section 1111(b)(2) of the ESEA, as amended by the ESSA, and applicable regulations. Finally, we removed the proposed requirement in § 299.16(b)(7) to describe how a State will use formula grant funds awarded under section 1201 of the ESEA, as amended by the ESSA, and have removed this program from the programs included in the consolidated State plan under § 299.13(j)(2).

Comments: A number of commenters proposed specific changes regarding the substance of the assessments as required under section 1111(b)(2) of the ESEA, as amended by the ESSA, including by reflecting on challenges experienced by military students who must adjust to various

State policies and tests; underscoring that alternate assessments be aligned with grade-level academic content standards for the grade in which the student is enrolled; proposing that alternate assessments for students impacted by trauma be created to measure success in schools that serve large populations of such students; requesting that States be allowed to assess some students with significant cognitive disabilities who do not meet the criteria for students with the most significant cognitive disabilities using assessments based on academic standards for a grade other than the student's enrolled grade; proposing that States coordinate with the Head Start community regarding academic standards; requesting an assessment pause during the transition to the ESEA, as amended by the ESSA; suggesting that additional focus be applied to the needs of students with disabilities and English learners with respect to test accommodations; asking that ELP not impede English learners from passing standardized tests required for graduation; emphasizing that ELP tests should be subject to assessment peer review; requesting that students receiving instruction primarily in a Native American language be explicitly allowed to take assessments in that language; urging that social studies assessments be required; recommending that protections generally be made clearer for English learners who receive instruction primarily in a Native American language school or program; and suggesting that English learners be exempt from taking academic content assessments if those students are taking ELP assessments.

Discussion: The proposed consolidated State plan requirements in §§ 299.14 and 299.16 address the information and assurances that a State must submit to the Department in order to receive Federal funds, including information and assurances regarding a State's compliance with section 1111(b)(2) of the ESEA, as amended by the ESSA. In March and April 2016, the Department engaged in negotiated rulemaking regarding the substance of the assessment requirements, including how a State complies with section 1111(b)(2) of the ESEA, as amended by the ESSA. As a result, any comment received in response to this NPRM regarding assessment requirements that were subject to negotiated rulemaking are considered outside the scope of these regulations. The Department will consider any comments on the assessment regulations received in response to this NPRM when responding to comments received on the notice of proposed rulemaking for title I, improving academic achievement of the disadvantaged, Academic Assessments published in the Federal Register on July 11, 2016 (81 FR 44927) (Assessments NPRM).

Changes: None.

Mathematics Exception for Students in Advanced Courses in Eighth Grade in States That Use End-of-Course Mathematics Assessments in High School

Comments: A few commenters objected to proposed § 299.16(b)(3), which would require an SEA to describe its strategies in the consolidated State plan to provide all students in the State the opportunity to be prepared for and to take advanced mathematics coursework in middle school consistent with section 1111(b)(2)(C) of the ESEA, as amended by the ESSA, and applicable regulations. The commenters noted that the final consensus-based language from negotiated rulemaking, on which this proposed requirement was based, would only require an SEA to describe its strategies if the State administers end-of-course mathematics assessments to high school students to meet the requirements under section 1111(b)(2)(B)(v)(I)(bb) of the ESEA, as amended by the ESSA, and uses the exception for students in eighth grade to take such assessments under section 1111(b)(2)(C). As written, however, commenters noted that the requirement would apply to all States.

Discussion: The Department agrees with the commenters. The final consensus-based language from negotiated rulemaking and the proposed regulations in the Assessments NPRM would only require an SEA to describe its strategies to provide all students in the State the opportunity to be prepared for and to take advanced mathematics coursework in middle school if the State administers end-of-course mathematics assessments to high school students to meet the requirements under section 1111(b)(2)(B)(v)(I)(bb) of the ESEA, as amended by the ESSA, and uses the exception for students in eighth grade to take such assessments under section 1111(b)(2)(C) of the ESEA, as amended by the ESSA.

Changes: We have revised § 299.16(a) to indicate that an SEA would only be required to describe its strategies in the consolidated State plan to provide all students in the State the opportunity to be prepared for and to take advanced mathematics coursework in middle school if the State administers end-of-course mathematics assessments to high school students to meet the requirements under section 1111(b)(2)(B)(v)(I)(bb) of the ESEA, as amended by the ESSA, and uses the exception for students in eighth grade to take such assessments under section 1111(b)(2)(C) of the ESEA, as amended by the ESSA.

Section 299.17   Accountability, Support, and Improvement for Schools

§ 299.17(b)(8)   Including All Public Schools in the State Accountability System

Comments: A few commenters sought clarification regarding whether a State may use a different methodology for accountability for schools serving special populations than the methodology used for all public schools. One commenter noted that the list of schools for which a State may describe a different methodology from the methodology used for all public schools only appeared in the consolidated State plan requirements and did not appear in the accountability regulations. Specifically, commenters recommended that a State be able to use a different methodology for certain accountability indicators for alternative schools, schools in the juvenile justice system, schools serving reengaged children and youth, credit-recovery schools, and schools serving over-age students. Some commenters stated that one such modification to the methodology would be to identify schools and require interventions based not on a low four-year graduation rate but that a State should be able to identify and require interventions in these types of schools based on an extended-year graduation rate.

Discussion: The Department agrees that it was unclear to include a list of schools for which a State may use a different methodology for accountability in the consolidated State plan requirements but not in the accountability regulations. Placing this list in the consolidated State plan section gave the incorrect impression that a State might not be able to use a different methodology to identify schools for support and improvement that serve special populations of students if it completed an individual title I, part A State plan. We intended to permit a State to use a different methodology for specific types of schools, regardless of whether it submits a consolidated State plan or an individual title I, part A State plan. See the previous discussion regarding Other Requirements in Annual Meaningful Differentiation of Schools in this preamble for a discussion of changes to the types of schools included in the list.

Changes: We have revised § 299.17 by removing from the consolidated State plan requirements the list of schools for which an SEA may describe an accountability methodology that is different from its statewide methodology. We have included the list of schools in the final regulation at § 200.18(d)(1)(iii) within the context of a State's system of annual meaningful differentiation.

§ 299.17(d) and (e)—Burden Reduction

Comments: A number of commenters generally objected to the volume of proposed consolidated State plan requirements, including those requirements in proposed § 299.17(d) and (e). Some commenters contest whether such requirements were absolutely necessary for the consideration of the consolidated State plan.

Discussion: The Department agrees that some of the requirements within and across the consolidated State plan regulations can be further streamlined. In an effort to reduce burden across all of the consolidated State plan requirements, we reconsidered which of the proposed descriptions were absolutely necessary for ensuring each State is in compliance with the statute and applicable regulations. Given that accountability systems under the ESEA, as amended by the ESSA, will be significantly different from accountability systems under the ESEA, as amended by NCLB, we are preserving many of the consolidated State plan requirements regarding each State's new accountability system under the ESEA, as amended by the ESSA. In examining the proposed requirements related to State support and improvement and performance management and technical assistance for low-performing schools, we are streamlining the required descriptions and converting one proposed description into a required assurance. Under proposed § 299.17(e)(3), an SEA was asked to describe additional improvement actions the State may take in an LEA with a significant number of identified schools. This description is similar to the description required under proposed § 299.17(e)(2) regarding technical assistance to LEAs with a significant number of identified schools. This description may have also overlapped with an SEA response to proposed § 299.17(d)(5) in which a State would identify other strategies to improve low-performing schools. An SEA could include a description of additional improvement actions or other strategies to improve low-performing schools in its description of technical assistance. Therefore, we are consolidating the descriptions related to these provisions into a single required description. We believe that the response an SEA might have provided in the proposed descriptions at §§ 299.17(e)(2) and (d)(5) may be captured in the remaining required descriptions. In addition, to further reduce burden in this component of the consolidated State plan, we converted the proposed description in § 299.17(e)(1) to an assurance in the new consolidated State plan assurance section in § 299.14. Final § 299.14(c)(3) requires each SEA to assure that it will approve, monitor, and periodically review LEA comprehensive support and improvement plans consistent with requirements in section 1111(d)(1)(B)(v) and (vi) of the ESEA and § 200.21(e). The Department believes this assurance is absolutely necessary for the consideration of consolidated State plans to ensure compliance with statutory requirements under section 1111(d)(1) of the ESEA, as amended by the ESSA.

Changes: We have revised § 299.17 by deleting proposed (d)(5) and (e)(2).

Cross-Cutting Changes

Comments: A few commenters recommended we strike or amend specific consolidated State plan requirements because they objected to the requirements, or they had suggested changes to the accountability requirements, which would necessitate conforming changes to the State plan requirements. Commenters recommended that we strike or amend consolidated State plan requirements related to, for example, summative ratings, comprehensive support and improvement plans, and the needs assessment.

Discussion: Each State plan requirement on accountability directly relates to the accountability requirements as described in the ESEA, as amended by the ESSA, and in the regulations. In response to comments, we have made a change or declined to make changes to the accountability, support, and improvement requirements as described in the sections of this preamble under

§§ 200.12 through 200.24. When an accountability requirement changed, we made a corresponding change to the consolidated State plan requirement, as described in § 299.17. For a discussion of comments related to the summative rating, see discussion under the section titled Summative Ratings; for a discussion of comments related to targeted support and improvement plans, see the discussion under the section titled Comprehensive and Targeted Support and Improvement Plans: In General; and for a discussion of comments related to needs assessments, see the discussion under the section titled Needs Assessment: Comprehensive Support and Improvement.

Changes: We have revised the consolidated State plan requirements related to accountability, support, and improvement for schools in §§ 299.17(b)(3)(ii), (b)(5)(i), (b)(5)(ii), (b)(5)(iii), (b)(5)(iv), (b)(7), (b)(8), (c)(3), (c)(4), (c)(5), (d)(2), (d)(4), and (d)(5) to conform with changes made in these final regulations.

Comments: None.

Discussion: In the course of reviewing the proposed regulations, the Department identified opportunities to clarify the regulations and strengthen the connections between the accountability regulations and the consolidated State plan requirements related to accountability. Therefore, we are clarifying multiple requirements in the accountability section of the consolidated State plan. There are two types of clarifications: (1) Adding or modifying a citation to align to the corresponding accountability requirement; and (2) modifying language to align with the accountability requirement and specify what would be requested in a consolidated State plan.

Changes: We have revised § 299.17(b)(1), (b)(3)(i),(b)(3)(ii), (d)(1), (d)(2), (d)(4) to ensure the consolidated State plan requirements align with the requirements in the final accountability regulations.

Section 299.18   Supporting Excellent Educators

§ 299.18(a)   Systems of Educator Development, Retention, and Advancement

Comments: Multiple commenters expressed support for § 299.18(a) regarding a comprehensive approach to systems of educator development, retention, and advancement. Commenters also recommended a variety of changes, including the addition of teachers of students with disabilities and early childhood educators to § 299.18(a)(2), an emphasis on evidence-based strategies" where appropriate, and replacing the word "adequate" in § 299.18(a)(2) with the term "high-quality." Another commenter advised the Department to clarify that each SEA should describe the efforts it is making in regard to each of the requirements in § 299.18(a), in addition to describing how it is ensuring that each LEA implements a comprehensive system of professional growth and improvement for educators that encompasses these efforts. Finally, one commenter asserted that the inclusion of State plan requirements related to systems of professional growth and improvement is not consistent with the statute and exceeds the Department's statutory authority.

Discussion: The Department appreciates commenters' general support for the requirements in proposed § 299.18(a), as well as their recommendations for strengthening the final regulations. However, because State systems and strategies for educator development, retention, and advancement may vary substantially, the Department declines to expand the requirements in this area. In addition, we anticipate that in response to State and local needs and circumstances many

238

SEAs will, for example, address additional categories of educators or include evidence-based strategies in their plans. We also note that on September 27, 2016, the Department recently published non-regulatory guidance for title II, part A: Building Systems of Support for Excellent Teaching and Leading available at: http://www2.ed.gov/policy/elsec/leg/essa/essatitleiipartaguidance.pdf (Title II, Part A Guidance). Furthermore, the Department will consider additional guidance and technical assistance regarding how SEAs can help ensure that their systems of educator development, retention, and advancement are supporting all educators.

We agree with the commenter's concern that the term "adequate preparation" was insufficiently rigorous, and are revising § 299.18(a)(2) to better reflect our expectations for educator preparation programs, including by clarifying that the description should describe State strategies to improve teacher preparation programs rather than a system of preparation.

As noted in the regulatory language itself, we believe that proposed § 299.18(a) is consistent with sections 2101 and 2102 of the ESEA, as amended by the ESSA, and is not outside of the Department's statutory authority in section 8302 of the ESEA, as amended by the ESSA, to establish the process and criteria for submitting a consolidated State plan. Additionally, given that the Secretary has general rulemaking authority under GEPA and DEOA, it is not necessary for the ESEA, as amended by the ESSA, to specifically authorize the Secretary to issue a particular regulatory provision. However, we agree that it is important for the final regulations to be clear about where uses of funds were permissive, rather than mandatory. For this reason and in response to the comments regarding the overall burden associated with submitting a consolidated State plan, we are revising the language in § 299.18(a) to provide that the required descriptions are applicable only to SEAs who intend to use funds under one or more of the covered programs for the activities in § 299.18(a)(1)-(3). Additionally, we are revising § 299.18(a)(3) to further clarify that an SEA is permitted, but not required, to include a description of how it will work with LEAs in the State to develop or implement State or local teacher, principal, or other school leader evaluation and support systems.

Changes: We have revised § 299.18(a) to clarify that it applies to each SEA that intends to use funds under one or more of the included programs for the activities in § 299.18(a)(1)-(3). We have revised § 299.18(a)(2) to reflect that we expect State plans to include strategies to improve educator preparation programs. Finally, we have revised § 299.18(a)(3) to clarify that an SEA's plan may, but is not required to, include a description of how it will work with LEAs in the State to develop or implement State or local teacher, principal, or other school leader evaluation and support systems.

Comments: Multiple commenters recommended adding requirements related to teacher certification and preparation, including how SEAs will ensure that all teachers and paraprofessionals working in title I programs meet applicable State certification and licensure requirements, incorporating teacher certification into the educator equity requirements in § 299.18(c), clarifying the definition of certification, requiring specific coursework in teacher preparation programs, reporting on teacher preparation programs, and publicly reporting the demographics of certified teachers.

Discussion: We appreciate commenters' interest in clarifying and strengthening requirements related to teacher certification and preparation in the final regulations. However, the ESEA, as amended by the ESSA, recognizes State discretion in determining requirements and definitions related to teacher preparation and certification, and we decline to limit that discretion in these final regulations.

We also note that requirements related to teacher preparation programs generally are governed by the Higher Education Act of 1965, as amended (HEA), rather than the ESEA. The Department recently finalized regulations regarding teacher preparation under, available at: http://www.ed.gov/news/press-releases/education-department-releases-final-teacher-preparation-regulations.

Changes: None.

Comments: A number of commenters recommended clarifying in § 299.18 that professional development in the consolidated State plan should be consistent with the definition provided in section 8101(42) of the ESEA, as amended by the ESSA. Commenters also urged the Department to add guardrails around the rigor or professional development provided by LEAs, to link teacher and leader development to school improvement strategies in State plans, and to promote measuring the quality of professional development as part of statewide accountability systems. Other commenters encouraged the Department to promote a wide range of particular professional development activities in the final regulations; including, for example, an emphasis on bilingual instruction, involving the Committee of Practitioners in setting priorities for professional development, and training on the use of strategies to create safe, healthy, and affirming school environments.

Discussion: We agree that the final regulations would be strengthened by incorporating the definition of professional development in section 8101(42) of the ESEA, as amended by the ESSA, and are revising § 299.18(a)(3) accordingly. However, because we believe that specific decisions regarding the design and implementation of professional development and learning opportunities are best made at the State and local level, we decline to highlight particular types of professional development or related activities in the final regulations. We further note that the Department issued non-regulatory Title II, Part A Guidance on the use of title II, part A funds that addresses some of the concerns expressed by commenters.

Changes: We have revised § 299.18(a)(3) to incorporate the definition of "professional development" in section 8101(42) of the ESEA, as amended by the ESSA.

Comment: One commenter recommended adding a requirement for an SEA to describe how it will use title II, part A funds and English learner set-aside funds to develop teachers to lead bilingual and dual language classrooms.

Discussion: We appreciate the suggestion to add a description regarding how an SEA will use funds to develop teachers to lead bilingual and dual language classrooms. As written, the regulations provide an SEA with flexibility to describe how it will use funds to meet the purpose of title II, part A of the ESEA, as amended by the ESSA, which could include developing teachers to lead bilingual and dual language classrooms. Because of the general comments regarding reducing burden on SEAs submitting a consolidated State plan, we decline to prescribe this as a requirement for all SEAs.

Changes: None.

§ 299.18(b)   Support for Educators

Comments: A number of commenters expressed support for the provisions in § 299.18(b) aimed at improving instruction by increasing the number of effective teachers and school leaders. Commenters also recommended the inclusion of strategies to improve educators' capacity to create safe and inclusive school environments and to address the impact of adversity and stress on students' readiness to learn. Other commenters requested a stronger emphasis on evidence-based strategies. One commenter urged the Department to maintain the proposed language under § 299.18(b) to ensure that each State describes how it will work with LEAs to develop or implement teacher, principal, and other school leader evaluation and support systems. One commenter also recommended that the strategies in § 299.18(b)(1)(iv) be designed to provide low-income and minority students with "equitable" rather than "greater" access to effective teachers, principals, and other school leaders. Finally, one commenter requested clarification that the use of Federal funds to improve educator evaluation systems is allowable, rather than required.

Discussion: We appreciate the general support for the proposed consolidated State plan requirements related to improving support for educators. However, we believe that States should have significant discretion in determining the specific focus of their efforts to support educators and we decline to include the additional requirements suggested by commenters. We also appreciate the lack of a robust evidence base in the area of professional development, a factor that could make new evidence requirements in this area both burdensome and ineffectual. We believe that providing "greater" access to effective educators is consistent with the statutory purpose of title II in section 2001 of the ESEA, as amended by the ESSA, and we note that proposed § 299.18(b)(2)(ii) is clear that an SEA must describe efforts to support LEAs in developing or implementing educator evaluation systems only if Federal funds are used for this purpose.

However, consistent with commenters' suggestions to clarify the connection between Federal funds and certain activities, we have moved the requirements that were originally found at proposed § 299.18(b)(ii) and (iii) to § 299.18(a)(3), where it is clear that such activities must be included in State plans only to the extent that they are supported with Federal funds.

Changes: We have revised the final regulations by moving the provisions in proposed 299.18(b)(2)(ii) and (iii) regarding educator evaluation and support systems and educator preparation programs, respectively, to § 299.18(a)(3).

Comments: Several commenters suggested that we revise proposed § 299.18(b)(1)(iv) to add students with disabilities to the groups for which SEAs must describe strategies for providing greater access to effective teachers, principals, and other school leaders; other commenters recommended including the full list of underserved subgroups of students addressed by the ESEA, as amended by the ESSA.

Discussion: The Department agrees that all students should have access to effective teachers, principals, and other school leaders. However, § 299.18(b)(1)(iv) is based on section 2001 of the ESEA, as amended by the ESSA, which focuses teacher equity requirements on low-income and minority students. We also note that many, if not most, of the students in the other subgroups mentioned by commenters also are low-income and minority students. For these reasons, and because adding subgroups of students beyond those specified by the statute would add considerable burden to the State plan requirements, we decline to include additional subgroups of students in the final regulations. However, we note that the regulations provide an SEA with the discretion to specifically highlight specific subgroups of students including students with disabilities, English Learners, migratory children, and children and youth in foster care.

Changes: None.

Comments: A number of commenters recommended expanding the list of subgroups of students in proposed § 299.18(b)(2)(i) for which an SEA must describe how it will improve the skills of teachers, principals, and other school leaders in identifying students with specific learning needs in order to improve instruction based on those needs. However, two commenters recommended limiting the list of subgroups to those described in section 2101(d)(2)(J) of the ESEA, as amended by the ESSA: Children with disabilities, English learners, students who are gifted and talented, and students with low literacy levels. Other commenters stated that the requirement in proposed § 299.18(b)(2)(i) was unnecessary and overly burdensome.

Discussion: We appreciate the different perspectives provided by the commenters. After weighing these perspectives, and, in particular, in recognition of potential burden of requiring SEAs to address a large, one-size-fits-all list of subgroups of students in describing their plans for improving the skills of teachers and leaders, we are removing the list of student subgroups from this section of the final regulations. We believe States should have flexibility, in developing their consolidated State plans, to determine the subgroups of students with the greatest need for specialized instruction and related school leadership.

Changes: We have revised § 299.18(b)(2)(i) by removing the list of specific subgroups of students.

Comments: Several commenters requested that we specify subgroups of teachers and related personnel that an SEA must address in its work to support excellent educators, including early childhood educators; educators in mediums of instruction other than English; community-based educators, such as elders or native and cultural artisans and practitioners; and National Board Certified Teachers. One commenter noted the importance of including specialized instructional support personnel in State systems of professional growth and improvement.

Discussion: While the Department recognizes the value of a diverse education workforce, we decline to prescribe subgroups of educators that an SEA must address in its work to support excellent educators. The proposed regulations require an SEA describe its strategies to support teachers, principals and other school leaders and permit an SEA to include educators such as early childhood educators, community-based educators, educators in mediums of instruction other than English, and SISPs, when discussing its strategies to support educators in its State. The consolidated State plan requirements are consistent with sections 2101 and 2102 of the ESEA, as amended by the ESSA. An SEA may, at its discretion and in response to State and local needs, include other educators in its consolidated State plan, but we decline to add additional requirements in this area.

Changes: None.

Comments: One commenter recommended that the use of the term "school leader" align with the definition of school leader in section 8101(44) of the ESEA, as amended by the ESSA. Another commenter suggested using the word "and" instead of "or" when referring to "teachers and principals or other school leaders." Another commenter recommended that we revise § 299.18(a)(2) to clarify that teachers, principals, and other school leaders are included in the State's system to ensure adequate preparation of new educators.

Discussion: We agree that the phrase "teachers, principals, and other school leaders" better captures the role of teachers and other school leaders. Therefore, with the exception of § 299.18(b)(2) which directly incorporates the statutory requirement in section 2101(d)(2)(J), we are revising the final regulations to incorporate the phrase "teachers, principals, and other school leaders" consistently throughout § 299.18(b). Additionally, we note that school leaders is defined in section 8101(44) of the ESEA, as amended by the ESSA, to include both principals and other types of school leaders. Moreover, we believe it is unnecessary to further specify in § 299.18(a)(2) that the preparation programs address teachers, principals, and other school leaders because the requirement to describe educator preparation programs includes such individuals.

Changes: We have revised § 299.18(b)(1) to refer to "teachers, principals, and other school leaders."

Educator Evaluation

Comments: A number of commenters stated that teacher evaluations should not be tied to student test scores. Other commenters expressed their support for ending the requirement to link evaluation and test scores. A few commenters expressed support for continuing to provide teachers with fair evaluations, using test scores, and improving teacher assessments.

Discussion: The final regulations, like the proposed regulations, do not include any requirements related to the use of student assessment results in educator evaluation systems. However, the Department released non-regulatory Title II, Part A Guidance that clarifies the statutory requirements for educator evaluation systems that are supported by title II, part A funds including the requirements in sections 2101(c)(4)(B)(ii) and 2103(b)(3)(A) of the ESEA, as amended by the ESSA, that such systems be based in part on evidence of student achievement, which may include student growth; include multiple measures of educator performance, such as high-quality classroom observations; and provide clear, timely and useful feedback to educators.

Changes: None.

Section 299.18(c)   Educator Equity

Comments: Many commenters expressed support for the requirements in § 299.18(c) regarding educator equity. In particular, commenters appreciated the inclusion of the educator equity provisions within the consolidated State plan, the definitions of teacher quality indicators in § 299.18(c) and § 200.37, and the clarification of the State's authority to ensure that title II, part A funds are used to address inequities.

Discussion: The Department appreciates the expressions of support from commenters.

Changes: None.

Comment: One commenter noted the impact that an effective school leader can have on the effectiveness, satisfaction, and retention of teachers. The commenter suggested that we revise the educator equity regulations in § 299.18(c) to include language that would allow, but not require, an SEA to track the equitable distribution of effective and experienced principals and school leaders.

Discussion: The educator equity requirements in § 299.18(c) require an SEA to describe whether low-income and minority students are taught at different rates by ineffective, out-of-field, or inexperienced teachers consistent with sections 1111(g)(1)(B) of the ESEA, as amended by the ESSA. We believe further revisions to § 299.18(c)(2) are unnecessary because under § 299.18(c)(2)(vi), an SEA may, at its discretion and in response to State and local needs, include other educators in this description by identifying other definitions and key terms it will use for the purpose of meeting this requirement.

Changes: None.

Comments: One commenter advised that the Department's use of the term "demonstrate" in place of the statutory term "describe" in proposed § 299.18(c) represented a higher standard of review for the consolidated State plan, and therefore increased the burden associated with the consolidated State plan, as compared to individual program plans.

Discussion: The Department appreciates the commenter's concern and is modifying the text of this section to align with the statutory terms in section 1111(g)(1)(B) of the ESEA, as amended by the ESSA. In response to the comment regarding the burden associated with meeting this consolidated State plan requirement, we note that § 299.13(k)(1)(i) requires an SEA that files an individual title I, part A State plan to provide the same description that is required under § 299.18(c). Therefore, the burden associated with meeting the requirements of section 1111(g)(1)(B) is the same whether an SEA submits a consolidated State plan or an individual title I, part A State plan under § 299.13(k).

Changes: We have revised § 299.18(c)(1) and (3) by replacing the term "demonstrate" with the term "describe."

Comments: A number of commenters requested explicit definitions and clear guidelines around the terms "disproportionality" and "disproportionate rates" in the final regulations, with some commenters recommending that the Department include this information in § 200.37 and incorporate it by reference in § 299.18(c)(2)(vi). Other commenters specifically recommended defining disproportionality as any non-zero difference between the rates at which student subgroups are served by ineffective, inexperienced, or out-of-field teachers.

Discussion: We agree that without additional clarification, it would be difficult for SEAs to ensure they are meeting the requirements of § 299.18(c)(1); for this reason we are revising the final regulations to make clear that throughout § 299.18(c), "disproportionality" refers to the "differences in rates." We are also revising § 299.18(c)(5), as renumbered in the final regulations, to clarify that different rates mean higher rates, defined as greater than zero.

Changes: We have revised § 299.18(c) to clarify that disproportionality refers to the "differences in rates." We have also renumbered and revised § 299.18(c)(5) to define disproportionate rates as higher rates, defined as greater than zero.

Section 299.18(c)(2)   Educator Equity Definitions

Comments: Some commenters supported having a definition of "ineffective teacher" and provided suggestions for ways to strengthen the definition. However, several commenters asked that the Department remove the requirement that an SEA establish a statewide definition of ineffective teacher. Some of these commenters indicated that requiring a definition would result in Federal interference with evaluation systems. Other commenters raised concerns that requiring the definition would violate statutory prohibitions regarding teacher evaluation systems.

Discussion: Section 1111(g)(1)(B) and (2)(A) of the ESEA, as amended by the ESSA, requires each SEA to describe how low-income and minority children enrolled in title I schools are not served at disproportionate rates by, among other teachers, "ineffective teachers" and to make public the methods or criteria the State is using to measure teacher effectiveness for the purpose of meeting this educator equity requirement. The requirements that an SEA provide its definition of "ineffective teacher," or its guidelines for LEA definitions of "ineffective teacher," and that the definition or guidelines differentiate between categories of teachers and provide useful information about educator equity, are essential for ensuring compliance with this statutory requirement. Without a definition or guidelines for local definitions of "ineffective teachers," the related data, inequities, and strategies to address inequities described by an SEA would be meaningless to the public and to policy makers. Accordingly, these requirements constitute a proper exercise of the Department's rulemaking authority under GEPA, the DEOA, and section 8302 of the ESEA, as amended by the ESSA. With respect to comments that this requirement violates specific provisions of the statute, section 1111(e)(1)(B)(iii)(IX) and (X) of the ESEA, as amended by the ESSA, provides that "nothing in this Act shall be construed to authorize or permit the Secretary . . . to prescribe (IX) any aspect or parameter of a teacher, principal, or other school leader evaluation system within a State or LEA, or (X) indicators or specific measures of teacher, principal, or other school leader effectiveness or quality." However, requiring a statewide definition of, or statewide guidelines for LEA definitions of, "ineffective teacher" in no way constitutes prescribing an aspect or parameter of an evaluation system, nor the indicators or specific measures of effectiveness or quality.

With respect to the specific suggestions regarding what should be addressed in the definitions of "ineffective," we believe that the regulations appropriately ensure that these definitions are developed at the State and local level. We further note that the final regulations ensure that each SEA determine and make public a definition, or provide statewide guidelines to its LEAs to determine a definition of "ineffective." Local context and discretion is important, and we believe it is critical that States and districts are the ones to define the term "ineffective." Therefore, we decline to include these recommendations in the regulations.

Changes: None.

Comments: Several commenters recommended changes to the requirements in the proposed regulations for defining an "out-of-field" teacher, including aligning those requirements with the definition used in § 200.37, creating a uniform definition that all States must use, and providing flexibility for States to adopt a definition that differs from that used for § 200.37.

Discussion: We note that the requirements for defining an "out-of-field teacher" in § 299.18(c)(2)(ii) are aligned with requirements of § 200.37 in both the proposed and final regulations. We further note that while there may be some benefits to a uniform definition that is comparable across all States and districts, we believe that SEAs should have flexibility to develop a statewide definition that reflects State and local needs and circumstances. However, we are concerned that permitting different definitions under §§ 200.37 and 299.18 could result in masking the number of "out-of-field" teachers that are teaching in high-need subjects and schools with chronic teacher shortages, increasing data collection and reporting burdens for SEAs and LEAs, and reducing transparency for educators and the public alike.

Changes: None.

Comments: A number of commenters recommended specific definitions of "inexperienced teacher" in § 299.18(c)(2)(iii), including alignment with the requirements of § 200.37 and uniformity across a State.

Discussion: Similar to the requirements for defining an "out-of-field" teacher, we note that the requirements for defining an "inexperienced" teacher in § 299.18(c)(2)(iii) are aligned with the requirements of § 200.37 in both the proposed and final regulations. While we appreciate the specific definitions recommended by commenters, we believe that SEAs should have flexibility to develop or adopt definitions that reflect State and local needs and circumstances. We agree with commenters that further guidance on the definitions required by § 299.18(c) may be helpful and will consider providing such guidance at a future time.

Changes: None.

Comments: None.

Discussion: After review of proposed § 299.18(c)(2), which required the educator equity definitions "to provide useful information about educator equity and disproportionality rates," we determined that the placement of the phrase was too broad and potentially confusing to SEAs. As a result, we are clarifying that the phrase "to provide useful information about educator equity and disproportionality rates" was only intended to apply to the three teacher characteristics.

Changes: We have revised § 299.18(c)(2)(i)-(iii) by adding the phrase "and provides useful information about educator equity" to all three required teacher characteristic definitions.

Comments: Several commenters supported the use of "distinct criteria" in establishing the definitions required by § 299.18(c)(2), with some commenters also recommending various options for strengthening this requirement, including, for example, limiting the measures that may be used to define each term or allowing definitions to share certain criteria.

Discussion: We appreciate the support of commenters, as well as their interest in strengthening the final regulations. However, we note that section 1111(e)(1)(B)(iii)(X) of the ESEA, as amended by the ESSA, prohibits the Secretary from prescribing indicators or specific measures of teacher, principal, or other school leader effectiveness or quality. In light of this prohibition, we decline to further specify or limit the measures that may be used by an SEA in establishing the definitions required by § 299.18(c)(2).

We further clarify that the regulations are intended to ensure that each definition is be wholly unique and based on entirely different criteria. That is, an SEA may not use part of any definition for each of the terms "ineffective," "inexperienced," or "out-of-field" in defining each of the other terms. We believe that this requirement is necessary and appropriate to ensure that each of these terms is defined in a manner that reflects the statutory intent of providing three unique pieces of information on teacher characteristics related to ensuring equitable access to effective teaching. Additionally, allowing an SEA to use a part of a definition for one particular term in the definition of another term is likely to impact the ability of the data to provide useful information about educator equity.

Changes: None.

Comments: A number of commenters recommended that we revise the proposed regulation in § 299.18(c), which requires SEAs to determine the differences in rates at which low-income and minority students are taught by ineffective, out-of-field, or inexperienced teachers, to include additional student subgroups, including children with disabilities, English learners, and rural students. One commenter recommended that we also revise § 299.18(c)(3)(ii), which permits an SEA to calculate and report the rates at which students represented by other key terms are taught by ineffective, out-of-field, and inexperienced teachers, to clarify that "students represented by any other key terms" may include children with disabilities, English learners, and rural students.

Discussion: The Department recognizes that, in some cases, other subgroups of students are being taught at disproportionate rates by ineffective, out-of-field, or inexperienced teachers, and § 299.18(c)(2)(vi) and (3)(ii) permit an SEA to include other subgroups of students when calculating such rates. However, requiring, rather than permitting, such analyses for other subgroups of students would not be consistent with section 1111(g)(1)(B) of the ESEA, as amended by the ESSA, which focuses solely on low-income and minority children.

Changes: None.

Section 299.18(c)(3) Educator Equity Rates and Student-Level Data Requirement

Comments: Some commenters expressed general support for student-level data requirements in proposed § 299.18(c)(3)(i) to report the rates described in § 299.18(c)(1) "based on student-level data." Commenters stressed the importance of evaluating within-school inequities in students' access to effective teaching, in addition to between school inequities, and that such an analysis requires the collection of student-level data. However, a few commenters suggested removing the student-level data requirement stating that the requirement is burdensome and not justified in the ESEA, as amended by the ESSA. Commenters also requested clarification on what constitutes student-level analysis.

Discussion: We appreciate commenters' support for requiring the collection and reporting of student-level data to meet the educator equity requirements of section 1111(g)(1)(B) of the ESEA, as amended by the ESSA. Student-level data are necessary to evaluate inequities within schools and to determine the relationship between specific student and teacher characteristics.

One study (29) examined how a sample of districts with high low-income, minority populations implemented policies for distributing effective teachers equitably. This two-year study found that a low-income student was more than twice as likely to have a less effective teacher as a higher income peer, and 66 percent more likely to have a less effective math teacher. The patterns were even more pronounced for students of color, with Latino and African-American students two to three times more likely (in math and reading/language arts, respectively) to have bottom-quartile teachers than their white and Asian peers.

Another multi-site, multi-year study (30) conducted by RAND Corporation found that when policies for distributing effective teachers equitably were implemented in a sample of districts with high low-income minority (LIM) populations, effective teachers were generally more likely to be assigned to those schools with higher proportions of low-income and minority students than other schools, but, within a school, effective teachers were generally less likely to be assigned to classes with higher proportions of low-income minority students than to other classes. That is, the most-effective teachers were placed in schools with high percentages of low-income minority students, but they were not placed in high-LIM classrooms within those schools. This suggests that improving low-income minority students' access to effective teachers requires efforts to ensure within-school access to effective teachers in addition to between-school access.

Though some commenters suggested removing the student-level data requirement altogether, the Department has determined that requiring student-level data is not only justified, but indeed, necessary to ensure compliance with the statutory requirement in section 1111(g)(1)(B) of the ESEA, as amended by the ESSA, that an SEA describe how low-income and minority children enrolled in schools assisted under title I, part A are not served at disproportionate rates than other children in the State by ineffective, out-of-field and inexperienced teachers. Because the required analysis is of the rates at which particular groups of children are served by teachers, and not the rates at which particular schools are served by teachers, requiring SEAs to use student-level data to inform the required description in order to ensure that they meet the statutory requirement constitutes a proper exercise of the Department's rulemaking authority.

We appreciate commenters' suggestions regarding clarification of how to implement the student-level data requirement and note that the Department plans to provide technical assistance and other support in this area, building in part on best practices from States already collecting and reporting student-level data.

Changes: None.

Comments: A few commenters recommended aligning the language in the requirement in § 299.18(c)(3)(ii) regarding the use of student-level data by SEAs who choose to examine differences in rates for other student groups, with the student-level data requirement in § 299.18(c)(3)(i) for required student groups.

Discussion: We decline to align the language because section 1111(g)(1)(B) only requires an SEA to provide educator equity data for low-income and minority students. If an SEA chooses to examine differences in rates for other student groups, an SEA has flexibility in determining the level of data to use in that analysis.

Changes: None.

Comments: Some commenters questioned whether the student-level data requirement, including the option of a two-year extension for the reporting of student-level data under proposed § 299.13(d)(3), conflicts with section 2104(a) of the ESEA, as amended by the ESSA, which prohibits the Department from requiring the collection and reporting of any data on the retention rates of effective teachers that was not available on the day before ESSA was enacted.

Discussion: We do not believe that the proposed regulations implementing section 1111(g)(1)(B) of the ESEA, as amended by the ESSA, conflict with section 2104(a) of the ESEA. More specifically, the rule of construction in section 2104(a)(4) of the ESEA, as amended by the ESSA, which limits the collection of data on the retention rates of ineffective and effective teachers to data elements collected prior to enactment of the ESSA, applies only to the title II, part A, reporting requirement regarding teacher retention, and there is no similar rule applicable to section 1111(g)(1)(B) of the ESEA, as amended by the ESSA.

Changes: None.

Comments: Several commenters expressed that the proposed comparison of rates—between low-income and minority students enrolled in schools receiving title I, part A funds and non-low-income and non-minority students enrolled in schools not receiving title I, part A funds—would yield little useful information in a State where the majority of schools receive title I, part A funds. Some commenters also asserted that the statutory language requires that low-income students and minority students at schools receiving title I, part A funds be compared to all non-low-income students and non-minority students at any school, regardless of that school's receipt or non-receipt of title I, part A funds, and recommended revising the final regulations consistent with this interpretation of the statute. Other commenters cited what they described as the inconsistency of proposed in § 299.18(c) with the report card requirement in § 200.37, which calls for disaggregation of teacher qualification data between high- and low-poverty schools. Similarly, one commenter suggested revising the proposed comparison groups to focus on high- and low-poverty schools (using the § 200.37 definition) and high- and low-minority schools (defined as schools in the top and bottom quartile for minority student enrollment). Finally, several commenters expressed concern that the proposed comparison groups would not help identify or address between-school or within-school inequities.

Discussion: Section 1111(g)(1)(B) of the ESEA, as amended by the ESSA, specifically requires that SEAs describe how low-income and minority children "enrolled in schools assisted under this part" are not served at disproportionate rates by certain teachers. Based on this language, we proposed comparison groups that we believe will be most likely to illuminate inequities with respect to the students identified by the statute. Although we appreciate the difficulties of making this comparison in a State or an LEA in which the majority of schools receive title I, part A funds, we believe that an alternative comparison group comprised of all schools in the State would be inconsistent with the statutory language prescribing the groups of students for whom disproportionate rates must be described. Further, such a comparison group would mask the differences in rates at which low-income and minority students enrolled in schools receiving title I, part A funds and their peers are taught by certain teachers. Requiring a comparison between high-poverty and low-poverty schools identified for purposes of compliance with § 200.37 would likewise be inconsistent with the statutory requirement in section 1111(g)(1)(B) of the ESEA, as amended by the ESSA, because a State's high-poverty school quartile does not necessarily include all of a State's title I, part A schools. Accordingly, we have maintained the proposed comparison groups in these final regulations.

With respect to commenters' concern that the selected comparison group would not sufficiently illuminate between-school or within-school inequities, as discussed above in the Student-level Data Requirement discussion and below in the Section 299.18(c)(5) Causes of and Strategies to Address Differences in Educator Equity Rates discussion, we have retained the student-level data requirement in § 299.18(c)(3)(i) and amended § 299.18(c)(5)(i) to replace root cause analysis with "likely causes" including an analysis of within-school differences in rates to ensure that between-school or within-school inequities are considered.

Changes: None.

Section 299.18(c)(5)   Causes of and Strategies To Address Differences in Educator Equity Rates

Comments: Multiple commenters stated that the requirement that SEAs conduct a "root cause analysis" in proposed § 299.18(c)(6)(i) is confusing, unnecessary, and overly prescriptive, with some commenters recommending that determinations regarding the appropriate level and method of analysis be left to SEAs. Another commenter recommended that the Department specifically require that an SEA analyze the extent to which disparities between LEAs within the State, between schools within LEAs, and within schools contribute to any statewide disparity, and then examine the causes of any disparity at each level.

Discussion: While the Department believes that it is necessary and appropriate for SEAs to determine the likely causes of the identified differences in the rates at which certain subgroups of students are taught by teachers with certain characteristics, our inclusion of the term "root cause analysis" was not intended to specify a particular methodology for determining such causes, and we are revising the final regulations to eliminate this term. We also are revising the language in the renumbered § 299.18(c)(5)(i) to clarify that an SEA must determine the likely causes of the most significant differences in the rates at which certain subgroups of students are taught by teachers with certain characteristics. To provide further clarity, we added examples of such causes. We have also aligned the language in § 299.18(c)(5)(i) with the Department's May 2015 non-regulatory guidance regarding State Plans to Ensure Equitable Access to Excellent Educators so that the regulations now incorporate language with which SEAs are familiar. In so doing, we have clarified the requirement and minimized the burden it imposes on SEAs by incorporating the guidance language that SEAs previously relied upon when developing educator equity plans in 2015.

We also agree with the commenter who advised that, to maximize the benefits associated with student-level data, the Department require that an SEA analyze the extent to which disparities at different levels contribute to the statewide differences in rates, and the causes of the disparities at each of those levels. As discussed in the student-level data discussion above, the benefits associated with calculating and reporting student-level data statewide are substantial because it illuminates within-school disparities; accordingly, we have amended this portion of the regulation to take advantage of the student-level data requirement in § 299.18(c)(3).

Changes: We have revised and renumbered § 299.18(c)(5)(i) to replace the phrase "root cause analysis" with "identify the likely causes" and clarified that SEAs need only identify the likely causes of the most significant differences in rates.

We have further revised § 299.18(c)(5)(i) to clarify that an SEA must identify whether the differences in rates at which certain student subgroups are taught by teachers with certain characteristics reflect differences between districts, within districts, and within schools, as well as the likely causes of those differences in rates, for example: Teacher shortages, working conditions, school leadership, compensation, or other factors.

Comments: Some commenters expressed support for the requirement that SEAs prioritize efforts aimed at reducing the extent to which low-income and minority students are taught at disproportionate rates by ineffective, out-of-field, or inexperienced teachers in schools identified for comprehensive or targeted support and improvement.

Other commenters recommended allowing States to prioritize strategies focused on the teacher attribute with the most negative effects on student outcomes; for example, if State data showed that student performance suffered the most from inexperienced teachers, an SEA could elect to focus its efforts on reducing students' disproportionate exposure to inexperienced teachers.

Discussion: We appreciate commenters' support for the requirement that SEAs prioritize efforts aimed at eliminating disproportionalities in schools identified for comprehensive or targeted support. Further, we appreciate commenters' recommendation to include additional options for prioritization. We agree that this may be an important approach to lessening the differences in rates and are revising the regulatory language to allow an SEA additional flexibility to provide in its State plan strategies for the most significant differences in rates as described by the SEA.

Changes: We have revised § 299.18(c)(5) to allow SEAs to prioritize strategies to address the most significant differences in rates as identified by the SEA.

Comments: One commenter supported the proposed requirement that an SEA include in its State plan the timelines and funding sources for its strategies to address inequitable access to excellent educators.

Discussion: We agree with the commenter that an SEA must provide timelines and funding sources to ensure successful implementation of its strategies to address inequitable access to effective educators and are retaining this requirement in the final regulations. Additionally, we are clarifying that an SEA must describe whether Federal or non-federal funds will support the identified strategies.

Changes: We have clarified § 299.18(c)(5)(ii) to require each SEA to describe whether Federal or non-federal funds will support its educator equity strategies.

Progress Targets and Monitoring

Comments: Some commenters requested additional detail in proposed § 299.18(c)(6) on how each SEA planned to monitor its progress in eliminating any disproportionate rates at which low-income and minority children are served by ineffective, out-of-field, or inexperienced teachers. Commenters encouraged the Department to define "progress" and require clear goals, timelines, and progress targets. Commenters also suggested requiring SEAs to describe the manner in which the State will monitor and support LEA efforts to eliminate such disparities.

Discussion: Section 1111(g)(1)(B) of the ESEA, as amended by the ESSA, requires each SEA to describe how low-income and minority children enrolled in title I, part A schools will not be served at disproportionate rates by ineffective, out-of-field, or inexperienced teachers. Therefore, if an SEA identifies any difference in rates, the SEA must work to eliminate the difference in rates. Consequently, we agree with commenters that to effectively eliminate a difference in rates, it is important to establish clear goals towards eliminating any differences in rates and report progress towards those goals, and we are revising the final regulations accordingly.

Changes: In renumbered § 299.18(c)(5)(iii), we have added a requirement for each SEA to describe timelines and targets for eliminating any differences in rates at which low-income and minority students enrolled in title I, part A schools served by inexperienced, out-of-field, and ineffective teachers.

Other Educator Equity Issues

Comments: Some commenters asserted that the phrase "or statewide guidelines for district definitions of ineffective teacher" in § 299.18(c)(2)(i) effectively permits States where districts do not provide teacher appraisal data to the State, or where the provision of such data is prohibited by State law, to comply with the statute.

Other commenters claimed that requiring SEAs to define and report on "ineffective teachers" inherently requires State evaluations that include an indicator for effectiveness, which commenters assert is prohibited in the ESEA, as amended by the ESSA.

Other commenters asserted that the requirements in § 299.18(c)(2)(v) must not violate individual privacy rights of teachers. Commenters noted that educator evaluation data are protected by law in some States, and claimed that reporting information required by the proposed regulation is prohibited. Commenters recommended that publication of data must be consistent with State and Federal privacy laws and principles, in addition to any other policies regarding the confidentiality of personnel information, and should not allow publication of data that is personally identifiable of individual teachers.

Discussion: The phrase "or Statewide guidelines for LEA definitions of ineffective teacher" in § 299.18(c)(2)(i) does not provide an exception to the requirement for reporting uniform teacher effectiveness data to the State; rather, this phrase gives SEAs the flexibility to allow variance in LEA definitions of "ineffective teacher" so long as each LEA complies with the statewide guidelines. Although commenters asserted that certain State laws prohibit local entities from providing teacher appraisal data to the State entity, an SEA receiving title I, part A funds is required to report on ineffective, out of field, or inexperienced teachers in order to comply with section 1111(g)(1)(B) of the ESEA, as amended by the ESSA. Further, to meet the requirements in § 299.18(c) an LEA may report aggregate numbers without any personally identifying information.

As discussed earlier, we do not agree that requiring each SEA to define and report on ineffective teachers is prohibited by the ESEA, as amended by the ESSA, because it is necessary for meeting the requirements of section 1111(g)(1)(B) of the ESEA. Further, consistent with the statutory provision in section 1111(e)(1)(B)(iii)(X), the final regulations, like the proposed regulations, require SEAs to establish their own definitions of "ineffective teacher" and do not prescribe the use of any specific definition.

We agree with commenters that the requirements in § 299.18(c)(2)(v) must not violate individual privacy rights of teachers. Section 1111(i)(1) of the ESEA, as amended by the ESSA, specifies that "information shall be collected and disseminated in a manner that protects the privacy of individuals consistent with section 444 of GEPA (20 U.S.C. 1223g, commonly known as [FERPA]) and this Act." Consistent with these requirements, we are revising the final regulations to clarify that reporting under § 299.18(c) must be consistent with FERPA. Commenters noted that evaluation data are protected by law in some States, and claimed that reporting information required by the proposed regulation is prohibited. However, this is not the case because there is no requirement that any of these data be personally identifiable.

Changes: We have revised § 299.18(c)(4) by adding a provision clarifying that when publishing and reporting educator equity information in § 299.13(c)(1)(iii), SEAs must comply with FERPA, 20 U.S.C. 1232g, and applicable regulations.

Comments: One commenter asked that the Department include a savings clause which would allow collective bargaining agreements and State laws that already define the statutory terms in § 299.18(c) to remain intact and enforceable even given the requirements in § 299.18(c).

Discussion: The Department does not believe that a savings clause to accommodate collective bargaining agreements or State laws is necessary because an SEA has discretion in defining the statutory terms related to ineffective, inexperienced, or out-of-field teachers, consistent with § 299.18(c). Accordingly, an SEA should have sufficient flexibility to define these terms consistent with State law and in ways that do not violate collective bargaining agreements.

Changes: None.

Comments: Several commenters requested that the Department protect charter school autonomy by preserving the ability of charter schools to hire teachers that meet the needs of their students, consistent with State charter school law. These commenters recommended the final regulations clarify that State definitions of ineffective, inexperienced, or out-of-field teachers, as they apply to charter schools, must defer to State charter school law. Furthermore, commenters asked that the Department include language clarifying that SEAs must carry out the requirements under § 299.18(c) and § 200.37, as they affect teachers in charter schools, in a manner consistent with State charter schools law and all other State laws and regulations governing public school teacher evaluation.

Discussion: As a condition of receiving title I, part A funds, an SEA must ensure compliance with all applicable statutory and regulatory requirements, including the requirements in section 1111(g)(1)(B) of the ESEA, as amended by the ESSA, and § 299.18(c) of these final regulations. We note that under the final regulations, each SEA and, in the case of the term "ineffective teachers" in States that elect to provide LEAs with statewide guidelines for defining this term in lieu of providing a statewide definition, districts, have substantial latitude in defining the terms ineffective, inexperienced, and out-of-field in a manner that is consistent with State charter schools law and all other State laws and regulations governing public school teacher evaluation.

Changes: None.

Section 299.18(c)(6)   State Authority To Deny LEA Plans and Direct LEA Use of Title II, Part A Funds

Comments: Two commenters expressed strong support for the Department's proposal to permit an SEA to direct an LEA to use a portion of its title II, part A funds to provide low-income and minority students greater access to effective teachers and to require an LEA to describe in its title II, part A plan how it will use such funds to address any differences in rates at which certain subgroups of students are taught by teachers with certain characteristics and to deny approval of the plan if an LEA fails to do so.

Discussion: The Department appreciates commenters support for these provisions.

Changes: None.

Section 299.19   Supporting All Students

Ensuring All Students Have the Opportunity To Meet State Standards

Comments: Some commenters expressed support for the requirement in proposed § 299.19(a) that each SEA describe how it will ensure that all students have a significant opportunity to meet its challenging State academic standards and career and technical education standards, as applicable. Some of these commenters requested that the Department require each SEA to describe how it will incorporate additional, specific strategies in its efforts to support students in meeting such standards, including personalized learning, expanded learning time, and early developmental and behavioral screening. Further, one commenter requested that the Department extend the continuum of a student's education covered under § 299.18 college and career.

Other commenters suggested that the Department include additional requirements in § 299.19, such as consultation requirements specific to this section; efforts to engage families of traditionally underserved students; and reporting on equitable access to a well-rounded coursework.

Other commenters stated that the proposed requirements in § 299.19(a) were overly burdensome and were not necessary to consider a consolidated State plan under section 8302 of the ESEA, as amended by the ESSA.

Discussion: The Department appreciates commenters' support of the requirements in proposed § 299.19(a). However, to streamline and reduce burden in the preparation of consolidated State plans, we are revising the requirements in § 299.19(a) to focus on the use of funds for title IV, part A and other included programs to support the continuum of a student's education and provide equitable access to a well-rounded education and rigorous coursework. We also are revising § 299.19(a)(1) to ensure that each SEA supports LEAs doing this work, as well the remaining subsections in § 299.19(a) to require descriptions of the SEA's strategies for school conditions, technology, and parent engagement to the extent that an SEA intends to use Federal funds for such purposes which may have significant benefit to students.

Consistent with this effort to streamline requirements in § 299.18(a), we also decline to include additional strategies in the required descriptions of SEA activities and plans or to extend the continuum of education covered by such plans beyond grade 12. However, we note that § 299.19(a)(1)(i) continues to require an SEA to describe how it will support a student's transition beyond high school. We also believe that consultation related to § 299.19(a) is adequately addressed by the consultation requirements in § 299.15(a) that requires that each SEA to consult with stakeholders on each component of the consolidated State plan. Further, the Stakeholder DCL provides recommendations on how States can meaningfully engage with stakeholders, including strategies to ensure engagement with parents of students from socioeconomically diverse backgrounds, parents of students from subgroups identified by the ESEA, as amended by the ESSA, and parents of students with disabilities. The Stakeholder DCL is available at http://www2.ed.gov/policy/elsec/guid/secletter/160622.html. Similarly, existing reporting requirements in section 1111(h)(1)(viii) and (2)(C) of the ESEA, as amended by the ESSA, address some aspects of equitable access to coursework and we decline to expand those requirements in the final regulations.

Changes: We have revised § 299.19(a)(1) to focus on the use of funds provided under title IV, part A and other included programs to support the continuum of a student's education and provide equitable access to a well-rounded education and rigorous coursework. We also have revised § 299.19(a)(2) to require an SEA to provide descriptions of its strategies only if it intends to use funds from title IV, part A funds or included programs for the specific activities detailed in paragraph (a)(2).

Arts

Comments: Many commenters requested that the Department include "arts" in the list of subjects described under proposed § 299.19(a)(1)(ii) regarding equitable access to a well-rounded education and rigorous coursework.

Discussion: The proposed regulations inadvertently omitted "arts" from the list of subjects in § 299.19(a)(1)(ii). We are revising the final regulations to correct this omission.

Changes: We have revised § 299.19(a)(1)(ii) to include "arts" in the list of subjects included in a well-rounded education.

School Conditions

Comments: Many commenters requested that the Department expand and further define the requirements in proposed § 299.19(a)(1)(iii) regarding school conditions for student learning, including, for example, a definition for the "overuse" of discipline practices and "aversive behavioral interventions, " adding examples of such interventions, and describing strategies to create safe, healthy, and affirming school environments inclusive of all students.

Discussion: The requirement in § 299.19(a)(1)(iii) is consistent with section 1111(g)(1)(C) of the ESEA, as amended by the ESSA. We appreciate the suggestions and underscore the importance of ensuring that all students have access to a safe and healthy learning environment. In recent years, the Department has released guidance and numerous resources that describe best practices to improve school climate and school discipline, as well as guidance on how schools can meet their obligations under Federal law to administer student discipline without discriminating on the basis of race, color, or national origin (for example, see http://www2.ed.gov/policy/gen/guid/school-discipline/fedefforts.html) . We believe this requirement will ensure that an SEA works with its LEAs to implement locally designed activities to promote school conditions for student learning. We also agree that specific strategies related to safe, healthy, and affirming school environments for all students are essential to improve school conditions and are revising this regulation accordingly.

Changes: We have revised § 299.19(a)(2)(i) to require each SEA using funds for this purpose to describe strategies to improve school conditions that create safe, healthy, and affirming school environments inclusive of all students.

Effective Use of Technology

Comments: A few commenters recommended that the Department ensure that all students, including for students with disabilities, have access to computers and broadband internet connections because many jobs in the future will have a science, technology, engineering, and mathematics (STEM) component. Another commenter noted that the statute only requires SEAs to describe how they will support LEAs, rather than requiring an SEA to describe its strategies. The commenter recommended that we revise the language in proposed § 299.19(a)(1)(iv) to more closely reflect the statutory language.

Discussion: We agree that access to the computers and the internet is an important part of a high-quality education and supports STEM education for all students. We also agree that the final regulations should be more closely aligned with statutory requirements. For these reasons, we are revising the final regulations to require an SEA to describe how it will support LEAs to effectively use technology only if the SEA is proposing to use funds under one or more of the included programs for that purpose. We also are revising § 299.19(a) to focus on SEA support for LEA efforts to use technology effectively.

Changes: We have revised § 299.19(a)(2) to require an SEA to describe its strategies to support LEAs to effectively use technology to improve academic achievement only if the State is proposing to use funds under one or more of the included programs for that purpose.

Accurate Identification of Children With Disabilities and English Learners

Comments: One commenter noted the importance of identifying disabilities early in a child's educational experience. The commenter recommended that we revise proposed § 299.19(a)(1)(vi) to add that the identification of children with disabilities includes the early identification of children with disabilities.

Discussion: We agree with the commenter that the early identification of students with disabilities is critical and results in the provision of required special education and related services to eligible children as early as possible in the course of their education. However, because the importance of, and timely and accurate identification of eligible children with disabilities is already addressed in the IDEA and its implementing regulations, the Department has determined that including similar requirements in these final regulations would be unnecessarily duplicative and burdensome. Consequently, the final regulations would instead require an assurance in § 299.14(c)(5) that the SEA has policies and procedures in effect regarding the appropriate identification of children with disabilities consistent with the child find and evaluation requirements in section 612(a)(3) and (a)(7) of the IDEA, respectively. This assurance is necessary to ensure the purpose of section 1001 of the ESEA, as amended by the ESSA, is met "to provide all children a significant opportunity to receive a fair, equitable and high quality education" and to coordinate title I, part A activities under section 1111(a)(1)(B) with federal programs, including Part B of the IDEA.

The appropriate identification of students with disabilities is addressed in the IDEA and its implementing regulations in sections 612(a)(3) and (a)(7) and 614(a)-(c) and 34 CFR 300.111, 300.122, and 300.300-300.311. In order to be eligible for an IDEA Part B grant, a State is required to submit a plan that provides assurances that the State has in effect policies and procedures to ensure that the State meets specific conditions prescribed in section 612 of the IDEA, including that all children with disabilities residing in the State, regardless of the severity of their disabilities, and who are in need of special education and related services, are identified, located, and evaluated in accordance with applicable IDEA Part B requirements. These requirements are designed to ensure that eligible children are appropriately identified and provided required special education and related services in a timely manner.

Proposed § 299.19(a)(1)(vi) also required the accurate identification of English learners which unnecessarily duplicated other statutory and regulatory requirements, including section 3113(b)(2) of the ESEA, as amended by the ESSA, and § 299.13(c)(2) of these final regulations.

Changes: We have revised § 299.19(a)(1) by removing the requirement that each SEA address the accurate identification of children with disabilities and English learners. We have added an assurance in § 299.14(c)(5) regarding the appropriate identification of children with disabilities.

Subgroups of Students Whom States Must Address

Comments: Several commenters supported the inclusion of particular subgroups in proposed § 299.19(a)(2)(i), such as students in foster care, homeless children and youth, and children with disabilities, while others recommended the addition of other groups of vulnerable students, including those aligned with eligible in-school youth definitions under WIOA and students taught primarily through Native American languages. However, other commenters expressed concern about the burden associated with addressing the needs of the required subgroups in State plans.

Discussion: We appreciate the commenters' support for proposed § 299.19(a)(2)(i). While an SEA may choose to address the needs of additional subgroups of students in its State plan, we decline to include additional subgroups in the final regulations, in part because we believe most, if not all, of the students in the additional subgroups proposed by commenters are likely to be captured by one or more of the existing subgroups in final § 299.19(a)(1)(iii). In response to concerns about administrative burden, we note that while an SEA must address the needs of each subgroup in § 299.19(a)(1)(iii), it does not have to address each subgroup of students individually; for example, it may use a single strategy to address the needs of multiple subgroups.

Changes: None.

Physical Education

Comments: One commenter recommended that the Department provide guidance regarding use of title IV, part A funds to support physical education.

Discussion: The Department will be issuing guidance on allowable uses of title IV, part A funds, including use of these funds to support physical education.

Changes: None.

Title I, Part C   Priority for Services Requirements

Comments: None.

Discussion: Based on further internal review, we have determined that the proposed requirement in § 299.19(c)(2)(v) for each SEA to describe its processes and procedures when implementing priority for services for migratory students under section 1304(d) of the ESEA, as amended by the ESSA, would place an unnecessary burden on SEAs. Under the final regulations, each SEA must describe the measures and data sources used in making priority for services determinations, as well as when and how such determinations will be communicated on a statewide basis, but it will not be required to describe how it will delegate responsibilities for documenting such determinations and the provision of services. Finally, the Department is aligning the requirement in § 299.19(b)(2)(v) to the statutory requirement in section 1304(b)(4) of the ESEA, as amended by the ESSA. The description in final § 299.19(b)(2)(v) is more limited because the SEA is required to only describe its priorities for the use of title I, part C funds related to the needs of migratory children with "priority for services."

Changes: We have revised § 299.19(b)(2)(v) to require each SEA to describe only its priorities for the use of title I, part C funds related to the needs of migratory children with "priority for services," including (1) the measures and sources of data the SEA, and if applicable, its local operating agencies (LOAs), which may include LEAs, will use to identify which migratory children are a priority for services; and (2) when and how the SEA will communicate those determinations to all LOAs in the State.

Title III, Part A   Standardized Entrance and Exit Procedures for English Learners

Comments: Some commenters generally supported proposed § 299.13(c)(3), including the requirement that criteria to determine a student's placement in or exit from English learner status be applied consistently across LEAs in a State. While supporting proposed § 299.13(c)(3) generally, other commenters requested clarification of some of the provisions in proposed § 299.13(c)(3), including their application to both entrance and exit criteria, assurances related to criteria other than ELP assessment results, the input of local educators on exit decisions, and continued eligibility for services following exit from English learner status.

Finally, some commenters expressed various concerns. Specifically, one commenter opposed the requirement to include criteria and not just procedures in proposed § 299.19(c)(3), asserting that the statute does not require criteria but only procedures; another expressed concern that proposed § 299.19(c)(3) does not allow for locally administered assessments as part of an SEA's exit criteria, and one questioned the need for proposed § 299.19(c)(3)(iv), which references civil rights obligations, given that proposed § 299.13(c)(2) appears to address the requirement.

Discussion: We appreciate commenters' general support for proposed § 299.19(c)(3). Under proposed § 299.19(c)(3), an SEA's standardized entrance and exit procedures must include valid, reliable, and objective criteria that are applied consistently across the State. We agree that it is important for an SEA to consistently apply both entrance and exit criteria and that the criteria that an SEA selects, in addition to results on an SEA's ELP assessment, must be narrowly defined such that they can be consistently applied in LEAs across the State. However, we believe that final § 299.19(b)(4) sufficiently ensures these parameters around entrance and exit criteria.

With regard to including local input in an SEA's exit criteria, under proposed § 299.19(c)(3), which is moved to § 299.19(b)(4) in the final regulations, an SEA may incorporate local input that is valid, reliable, objective, and applied and weighted the same way across the State. For example, an SEA's exit criteria may include local input such as the use of an observational protocol or rubric-graded portfolio, as long as such input is applied and weighted consistently across the State. Thus, the regulations permit a local team to recommend continuing a student in English learner status even if the student scores proficient on the State's ELP assessment.

We also note that a student may continue to receive English language support with local or State funds even after exiting from English learner status. Furthermore, we will consider reemphasizing this in guidance.

Regarding concern over the requirement that an SEA's standardized entrance and exit procedures must also include criteria, as discussed earlier, under GEPA and DEOA, the Secretary has general rulemaking authority. Therefore, it is not necessary for the Act to specifically authorize the Secretary to issue a particular regulatory provision. Given the title III, part A requirement to describe statewide entrance and exit procedures under section 3113(b)(2) of the ESEA, as amended by the ESSA, we believe it is within our regulatory authority to ensure that the procedures include criteria that will ensure the purposes of title III, part A are met, including to ensure that English learners attain ELP and develop high levels of academic achievement in English. With respect to the use of locally administered assessments, the Department believes that final § 299.19(b)(4) appropriately precludes use of locally administered ELP assessments as part of its exit criteria, as local assessments, by definition, are not standard across the State. However, local assessments may be used to help identify the needs of and appropriate instructional supports for English learners so that they can attain English proficiency. Finally, we agree with the commenter regarding proposed § 299.19(c)(3)(iv) on civil rights obligations, and are moving that provision to § 299.13(c)(2).

Changes: We have removed proposed § 299.19(c)(3)(iv) and added necessary text to § 299.13(c)(2) requiring an SEA to provide an assurance that its exit procedures as well as its entrance procedures are consistent with civil rights obligations.

Title III, Part A   Exit Procedures for English Learners

Comments: Some commenters supported proposed § 299.19(c)(3), which restricts the use of content area assessments as part of an SEA's standardized exit criteria, with one commenter explaining that content area assessments are neither designed nor intended to measure a student's ELP and thus should not be used as a criterion in deciding to continue a student in or exit a student from English learner status. This same commenter, however, asserted that an SEA can and should use results of content area assessments to set academic achievement standards (i.e., "cut scores") on the SEA's ELP assessment, particularly to help mitigate against cut scores that result in students prematurely exiting English learner status.

Commenters who opposed the restriction generally sought greater flexibility in using the results of content area assessments to inform decisions on both continuing a student in or exiting a student from English learner status. For example, some commenters stated that it may be appropriate to use the results of content assessments to continue a student's English learner status if the ELP assessment is not fully aligned with a State's academic content standards or the cut scores on the ELP assessment have not been set at appropriate levels and thus could result in a student prematurely exiting English learner status (and potentially violating a student's civil rights). Among commenters who supported using the results of content assessments to exit students from English learner status, one commenter asserted that a student who scores proficient on the State's reading/language arts assessment, but just below a score of proficient on the State's ELP assessment, should be permitted to exit English learner status, and that such flexibility could help account for error in ELP assessments. Finally, one commenter requested clarification as to what academic content assessments means under proposed § 299.19(c)(3).

Discussion: Under proposed § 299.19(c)(3), an SEA's standardized entrance and exit procedures must not include performance on an academic content assessment. Academic content assessments in this context means any academic content assessments, including the statewide assessments in reading/language arts, mathematics, or science used for accountability purposes, as well as other assessments.

The Department continues to believe that while performance on content area assessments may be affected by a student's level of ELP, such assessments are not valid and reliable measures of ELP and, if used to continue a student's status as an English learner, may do so inappropriately (i.e., when a student is proficient in English) and lead to negative academic outcomes for an individual student. We are aware that some SEAs and LEAs have entered into resolution agreements or consent decrees with Federal agencies that contain provisions relating to exit criteria for English learners. We encourage those SEAs and LEAs to contact the Department so that we may, together with the U.S. Department of Justice, assist those SEAs and LEAs with the requirements under both these regulations and the applicable resolution agreement or consent decree.

It would be equally inappropriate use a proficient score on the reading/language arts assessment to exit a student whose ELP assessment results are close to the cut score. The reading/language arts assessment typically does not assess all four domains (reading, writing, listening, and speaking); consequently, using results on such an assessment as part of exit criteria may result in a student exiting who is not able to succeed in a classroom in which listening and speaking in English are crucial skills. Finally, we agree that using the results on content area assessments to help establish cut scores on an ELP assessment may contribute to more meaningful cut scores on the English language proficiency assessment, and we note that the final regulations do not restrict the use of content area assessment results for this purpose.

Changes: None.

Comments: Some commenters expressed support for the requirement in proposed § 299.13(c)(3) that an SEA's standardized exit criteria for English learners must include a score of proficient on the State's ELP assessment as one criterion to exit a student from English learner status. However, one of these commenters recommended prohibiting SEAs from using the results of the ELP assessment as its sole criterion for determining English learner status. Other commenters opposed § 299.13(c)(3), with some expressing concern that English learners who are also students with disabilities might never be able to exit English learner status and others questioning how a student whose parents opt their children out of all State standardized testing would be able to exit English learner status without an ELP score.

Discussion: We believe that, consistent with the January 7, 2015 Dear Colleague Letter on serving English learners, including those with disabilities, which was jointly signed by the U.S. Department of Justice and OCR, a score of proficient on the State's ELP assessment is critical to ensuring that a student is appropriately exited from English learner status (see http://www2.ed.gov/about/offices/list/ocr/letters/colleague-el-201501.pdf). Such exit must, at a minimum, be based on a valid and reliable measure that demonstrates sufficient student performance across the required domains in order to consider an English learner to have attained proficiency in English, i.e., a State's ELP assessment. While States have flexibility under the final regulations to use objective criteria related to English language proficiency in addition to a proficient score on the State ELP assessment to determine English learner status, we decline to require the use of multiple criteria.

259

With respect to a student whose parents may have chosen to opt the student out of all State standardized testing, a high-quality assessment system, including State standardized tests, helps parents, teachers, and other stakeholders to understand and address the needs of individual and groups of students. A State's ELP assessment, along with other indicators of a student's performance and progress at achieving ELP, can focus efforts on areas where students most need support to help ensure their academic success, attainment of a regular high school diploma, and pursuance of postsecondary education or a career of their own choosing.

Changes: None.

McKinney-Vento Education for Homeless Children and Youths (McKinney-Vento) Program

Comments: We received one comment supporting the inclusion of the McKinney-Vento program in the consolidated State plan. We received another comment, submitted with multiple signatories, expressing concern that several key elements of the State plan required in the McKinney-Vento Homeless Assistance Act, as amended by the ESSA, were omitted from the program-specific requirements under § 299.19(c)(5) and recommending the addition of certain requirements to the final regulations. The commenters expressed concern that without the inclusion of these requirements in the consolidated State plan, each SEA may not provide adequate attention to them when implementing the McKinney-Vento Homeless Assistance Act, as amended by the ESSA. The commenters also noted that because the SEA's plan for addressing these critical elements would not be included in the consolidated State plan, stakeholders and the public would not have a formal opportunity to provide comments on them, as required by the consultation requirements in § 299.13.

Discussion: We appreciate the comments supporting the inclusion of the McKinney-Vento program in the consolidated State plan. We note that under § 299.13(c), all SEAs, whether submitting an individual or consolidated State plan, must submit a single set of section 8304(a)(1) assurances, applicable to each program for which the plan or application is submitted, that provides that each such program will be administered in accordance with all applicable statutes, regulations, program plans, and applications. These assurances are consistent with the purpose of the consolidated State plan requirements under Section 8302 of the ESEA, as amended by the ESSA, which aims to simplify application requirements and which requires the Secretary to require only descriptions, information, assurances, and other materials that are absolutely necessary for the consideration of the consolidated State plan. The consolidated State plan requirements for the McKinney-Vento program contain those requirements that we have determined are absolutely necessary for the consideration of the consolidated State plan, and we decline to add any additional requirements beyond those that are absolutely necessary. We also note that these areas are covered in depth in the updated non-regulatory guidance the Department released on July 27, 2016, (available at http://www2.ed.gov/policy/elsec/leg/essa/160240ehcyguidance072716.pdf).

Changes: None.

Program-Specific Requirements for Title I, Part D

Comments: A number of commenters expressed concern that there was not more specific mention of title I, part D requirements in the NPRM. Several of these commenters expressed a desire for more emphasis in the regulations on transition services for students moving between correctional facilities and locally operated programs, and several commenters requested more focus in the final regulations on how States plan to assess the effectiveness of their title I, part D programs in improving the academic, career, and technical skills of children in the program. Some commenters also requested regulatory changes to provide clear instructions for monitoring. Finally, one commenter asked that the Department define "at-risk" in the regulations.

Discussion: We agree with the commenters that title I, part D should be addressed in the consolidated State plan requirements and are adding title I, part D requirements in § 299.19(c)(3). Consistent with Section 8302 of the ESEA, as amended by the ESSA, we are adding only those requirements that we have determined are absolutely necessary for the consideration of the consolidated State plan. Regarding monitoring, the SEA is expected to meet the requirements outlined in title I, part D, and the Department declines to add any additional monitoring requirements. Similarly, section 1432(2) of the ESEA, as amended by the ESSA, already includes a definition of the term "at-risk."

Changes: We have revised § 299.19(c)(3) to include title I, part D consolidated State plan requirements.

Executive Orders 12866 and 13563

Regulatory Impact Analysis

Under Executive Order 12866, the Office of Management and Budget (OMB) must determine whether this regulatory action is significant and, therefore, subject to the requirements of the Executive order and subject to review by OMB. Section 3(f) of Executive Order 12866 defines "significant regulatory action" as an action likely to result in a rule that may—

(1) Have an annual effect on the economy of $100 million or more, or adversely affect a sector of the economy, productivity, competition, jobs, the environment, public health or safety, or State, local, or tribal governments or communities in a material way (also referred to as an "economically significant" rule);

(2) Create serious inconsistency or otherwise interfere with an action taken or planned by another agency;

(3) Materially alter the budgetary impacts of entitlement grants, user fees, or loan programs or the rights and obligations of recipients thereof; or

(4) Raise novel legal or policy issues arising out of legal mandates, the President's priorities, or the principles stated in the Executive order.

This final regulatory action is an economically significant regulatory action subject to review by OMB under section 3(f) of Executive Order 12866.

We have also reviewed these regulations under Executive Order 13563, which supplements and explicitly reaffirms the principles, structures, and definitions governing regulatory review established in Executive Order 12866. To the extent permitted by law, Executive Order 13563 requires that an agency—

(1) Propose or adopt regulations only upon a reasoned determination that their benefits justify their costs (recognizing that some benefits and costs are difficult to quantify);

(2) Tailor its regulations to impose the least burden on society, consistent with obtaining regulatory objectives and taking into account, among other things and to the extent practicable, the costs of cumulative regulations;

(3) In choosing among alternative regulatory approaches, select those approaches that maximize net benefits (including potential economic, environmental, public health and safety, and other advantages; distributive impacts; and equity);

(4) To the extent feasible, specify performance objectives, rather than the behavior or manner of compliance a regulated entity must adopt; and

(5) Identify and assess available alternatives to direct regulation, including economic incentives such as user fees or marketable permits, to encourage the desired behavior, or provide information that enables the public to make choices.

Executive Order 13563 also requires an agency "to use the best available techniques to quantify anticipated present and future benefits and costs as accurately as possible." The Office of Information and Regulatory Affairs of OMB has emphasized that these techniques may include "identifying changing future compliance costs that might result from technological innovation or anticipated behavioral changes."

We are issuing these final regulations only on a reasoned determination that their benefits justify their costs. In choosing among alternative regulatory approaches, we selected those approaches that maximize net benefits. Based on the analysis that follows, the Department believes that these final regulations are consistent with the principles in Executive Order 13563.

We have also determined that this regulatory action will not unduly interfere with State, local, and tribal governments in the exercise of their governmental functions.

We have assessed the costs and benefits of this regulatory action. The costs associated with the final regulations are those resulting from statutory requirements and those we have determined as necessary for administering these programs effectively and efficiently. Elsewhere in this section under Paperwork Reduction Act of 1995, we identify and explain burdens specifically associated with information collection requirements.

In assessing the costs and benefits—both quantitative and qualitative—of these final regulations, we have determined that the benefits justify the costs.

Discussion of Costs and Benefits

The Department believes that the majority of the changes in these final regulations will not impose significant costs on States, LEAs, or other entities that participate in programs addressed by this regulatory action. Other changes will impose costs, but in many cases they are one-time or initial costs that will not recur, and the Department believes that the benefits resulting from the regulations will exceed the costs by a significant margin. We also note that while the Department received over 20,000 public comments on the proposed regulations, only four commenters addressed the Regulatory Impact Analysis, with one commenter supporting the cost estimates in the NPRM and three commenters asserting that the estimates did not fully reflect the costs of implementation. We believe that this relatively low level of concern about administrative burdens and costs confirms our view, as expressed in the NPRM, that the regulatory framework in these regulations for State accountability systems based on the ESEA, as amended by the ESSA, closely parallels current State systems, which include long-term goals and measurements of interim progress; multiple indicators, including indicators of Academic Achievement, Graduation Rates, and other academic measures selected by the State; annual differentiation of school performance; the identification of low-performing schools; and the implementation of improvement plans for identified schools.

In addition, the final regulations, consistent with the requirements of the ESEA, as amended by the ESSA, provide considerable flexibility to States and LEAs in determining the specific approaches to meeting new requirements, including the rigor of long-term goals and measurements of interim progress, the timeline for meeting those goals, the selection and weighting of indicators of student and school progress, the criteria for identification of schools for improvement, and the development and implementation of improvement plans. This flexibility allows States and LEAs to build on existing measures, systems, and interventions rather than creating new ones, and to determine the most cost-efficient and least burdensome means of meeting proposed regulatory requirements, instead of a standardized set of prescriptive requirements. For all of these reasons, this final cost-benefit analysis generally is consistent with the Department's original estimates.

One commenter asserted that virtually the entire reduced burden in the proposed regulations resulted from statutory rather than regulatory changes, implying that the cost-benefit analysis improperly attributed burden reduction to the regulations. The commenter also asserted that in reducing flexibility for States compared to statutory requirements, the proposed regulations would likely increase costs for States due to the additional administrative burdens of meeting new requirements. In response, we note that, consistent with OMB requirements, our cost-benefit analysis in the final regulations, as in the proposed regulations, takes into account the estimated costs of both statutory and regulatory changes compared to previous statutory and regulatory requirements.

Accordingly, we identify certain statutory changes to the accountability systems and school improvement requirements of the ESEA, as amended by the ESSA, which would result in a significant reduction in costs and administrative burdens for States and LEAs. First, the previous regulations, which are based on the core goal of ensuring 100 percent proficiency in reading and mathematics for all students and all subgroups, potentially result in the identification of the overwhelming majority of participating title I schools for improvement, corrective action, or restructuring. Such an outcome would produce unsustainable demands on State and local capacity to develop, fund, implement, and monitor school improvement plans and related school improvement supports. It was the prospect of this outcome that drove the development of, and rapid voluntary requests for, waivers of certain accountability and school improvement requirements under ESEA flexibility prior to enactment of the ESSA. The final accountability regulations instead will require, consistent with the requirements of the ESEA, as amended by the ESSA, more flexible, targeted, largely State-determined systems of differentiated accountability and school improvement focused on the lowest-performing schools in each State, including the bottom five percent of title I schools based on the performance of all students, as well as other schools identified for consistently underperforming subgroups. Based on the experience of ESEA flexibility, the Department estimates that States will identify a total of 10,000-15,000 schools for school improvement nationwide—of which the Department estimates 4,000 will be identified for comprehensive support and improvement—compared with as many as 50,000 under the previous regulations in the absence of waivers. While the costs of carrying out required school improvement activities under the previous regulations varied considerably across schools, LEAs, and States depending on a combination of factors, including the stage of improvement and locally selected interventions, it is clear that the final regulations will dramatically decrease potential school improvement burdens for most States and LEAs.

Second, under the final regulations, LEAs will not be required to make available supplemental educational services (SES) to students from low-income families who attend schools identified for improvement. This means that States will not be required to develop and maintain lists of approved SES providers, review provider performance, monitor LEA implementation of SES requirements, or set aside substantial amounts of title I, part A funding for SES. States and LEAs also will no longer be required to report on either student participation or expenditures related to public school choice or SES. While States participating in ESEA flexibility generally already have benefited from waivers of the statutory and regulatory requirements related to public school choice and SES, the final regulations will extend this relief to all States and LEAs without the additional burden of seeking waivers.

Third, the final regulations will eliminate requirements for State identification of LEAs for improvement and the development and implementation of LEA improvement and corrective action plans. As would be the case for schools, the current regulations would require such plans for virtually all participating title I LEAs; the final regulations will not require States to identify any LEAs for improvement.

While most of the elements and requirements of State accountability systems required by the final regulations involve minimal or even significantly reduced costs compared to the requirements of the previous regulations, there are certain proposed changes that could entail additional costs, as described below.

Goals and Indicators

Section 200.13 requires States to establish a uniform procedure for setting long-term goals and measurements of interim progress for English learners that can be applied consistently and equitably to all students and schools for accountability purposes and that consider individual student characteristics (e.g., grade level, English language proficiency level) in determining the most appropriate timeline and goals for attaining English language proficiency for each English learner. We estimate that each State will, on average, require 80 hours of staff time to develop the required uniform procedure. Assuming a cost of $40 per hour for State staff, the final regulations will result in a one-time cost, across 50 States, the District of Columbia, and Puerto Rico, of $166,400. We believe that the development of a uniform, statewide procedure will minimize additional costs and administrative burdens at the LEA level, and that any additional modest costs will be outweighed by the benefits of the final regulations, which will allow differentiation of goals for an English learners based on their language and educational backgrounds, thereby recognizing the varied needs of the English learner population. Setting the same long-term goals and measurements of interim progress for all English learners in the State would fail to account for these differences in the English learner population and would result in goals that are inappropriate for at least some students and schools.

Under § 200.14(b)(5), States will be required to develop at least one indicator of School Quality or Student Success that measures such factors as student access to and completion of advanced coursework, postsecondary readiness, school climate and safety, student engagement, educator engagement, or any other measure the State chooses. Section 200.14(c) specifies that measures within School Quality or Student Success indicators must, among other requirements, be valid, reliable, and comparable across all LEAs in the State and support meaningful differentiation of performance among schools. We recognize that the development and implementation of new

School Quality or Student Success indicators, which may include the development of instruments to collect and report data on one or more such measures, could impose significant additional costs on a State that elects to develop an entirely new measure. However, the Department also believes, based in part on its experience in reviewing waiver requests under ESEA flexibility, that all States currently collect data on one or more measures that may be suitable as an indicator of School Quality or Student Success consistent with the requirements of § 200.14(b)(5). Consequently, we believe that all, or nearly all, States will choose to adapt a current measure to the purposes of § 200.14(b)(5), rather than developing an entirely new measure, and thus that the final regulations will not impose significant new costs or administrative burdens on States and LEAs.

Participation Rate

Section 200.15(b)(2)(iv) provides flexibility for a State to develop and submit for approval—as part of either a consolidated State plan or a title I, part A State plan—a State-determined action or set of actions for factoring the 95 percent participation rate requirement into its system of annual meaningful differentiation of schools that is sufficiently rigorous to improve a school's assessment participation rate so that it meets the 95 percent participation rate requirement. We note that a State may avoid the administrative burden and cost of developing its own State-determined action, or set of actions, by adopting one or more of the alternative actions provided in § 200.15(b)(2)(i)-(iii). Nevertheless, we estimate that 26 States will take advantage of this flexibility and incur the one-time costs of developing or adopting and submitting for approval to the Department a State-determined action or set of actions for schools that miss the 95 percent participation rate. The Department further estimates that these 26 States would need, on average, 32 hours to develop or adopt and submit for peer review and approval such a State-determined action. At $40 per hour, the average cost per State would be $1,280, resulting in total costs of $33,280 for the estimated 26 States. We expect that States generally would use Federal education funds they reserve for State administration under title I, part A to cover these one-time costs.

In addition, § 200.15(c)(2) requires an LEA with a significant number of schools that fail to assess at least 95 percent of all students or 95 percent of students in any subgroup to develop and implement an improvement plan that includes support for school-level plans to improve participation rates that must be developed under § 200.15(c)(1). Section 200.15(c)(2) further requires States to review and approve these LEA plans.

These improvement plan requirements are similar to previous regulations that required States to: Annually review the progress of each LEA in making AYP; identify for improvement any LEA that fails to make AYP for two consecutive years, including any LEA that fails to make AYP as a result of not assessing 95 percent of all students or each subgroup of students; and provide technical assistance and other support related to the development and implementation of LEA improvement plans. Current regulations also require States to take certain corrective actions in LEAs that miss AYP for four or more consecutive years, including LEAs that miss AYP due to not assessing 95 percent of all students or each subgroup of students. As noted previously, the final regulations no longer require annual State review of LEA progress; State identification of LEAs for improvement; or the development, preparation, or implementation of LEA improvement or corrective action plans. This significant reduction in State burden more than offsets the burden in the final regulations related to both the potential one-time cost of developing a State-determined action for schools that miss the 95 percent participation rate and reviewing and approving LEA plans to address low assessment participation rates in their schools. In addition, State discretion to define the threshold for "a significant number of schools" that would trigger the requirement for LEA plans related to missing the 95 percent participation rate will provide States a measure of control over the burden of complying with the final regulations. Consequently, the Department believes that the final regulations related to the 95 percent participation rate will not increase costs or administrative burdens significantly for States, as compared to the current regulations. Moreover, we believe that these requirements will have the significant benefit of helping to ensure that the plans include effective interventions that will improve participation in assessments, facilitate transparent information for families and educators on student progress, and assist schools in supporting high-quality instruction and meeting the demonstrated educational needs of all students.

School Improvement Process

The school improvement requirements in the final regulations generally are similar to those required under the current regulations. The previous regulations required identification of schools for multiple improvement categories, State and LEA notification of identified schools, the development and implementation of improvement plans with stakeholder involvement, State support for implementation of improvement plans, LEA provision of public school choice and SES options (the latter of which also imposes significant administrative burdens on States), and more rigorous actions for schools that do not improve over time. In addition, the previous regulations included a prescriptive timeline under which schools that do not improve must advance to the next stage of improvement, typically only after a year or two of implementation at the previous stage (e.g., a school is given only one year for corrective action to prove successful before being identified for restructuring). The previous regulations also generally did not allow for a planning year prior to implementation of the required improvement plans (with the exception of the penultimate restructuring phase). The final regulations, consistent with the statute, provide more flexibility around the timeline for identifying schools (e.g., once every three years for comprehensive support and improvement schools), up to a full year to develop comprehensive support and improvement and targeted support and improvement plans, and more time for full and effective implementation of improvement plans based on State- and LEA-determined timelines for meeting improvement benchmarks. The final regulations also eliminate the public school choice and SES requirements, which impose substantial administrative costs and burdens on LEAs that are not directly related to turning around low-performing schools. We believe that the final regulations will result in a significant reduction in the administrative burdens and costs imposed by key school improvement requirements by the previous regulations.

The final regulations also clarify certain elements of the school improvement process required by the ESEA, as amended by the ESSA, including the needs assessment for schools identified for comprehensive support and improvement, the use of evidence-based interventions in schools identified for both comprehensive support and improvement and targeted support and improvement, and the review of resource inequities required for schools identified for comprehensive support and improvement as well as for schools with low-performing subgroups identified for targeted support and improvement under § 200.19(b)(2). Section 200.21 requires an LEA with such a school to carry out, in partnership with stakeholders, a comprehensive needs assessment that takes into account, at a minimum, the school's performance on all indicators used by the State's accountability system and the reason(s) the school was identified. The final regulations also require the LEA to develop a comprehensive support and improvement plan that is based on the needs assessment and that includes one or more evidence-based interventions. These requirements are similar to the requirements in the previous regulations, under which LEAs with schools identified for improvement must develop improvement plans that include consultation with stakeholders. Thus we believe that the final regulations related to conducting a needs assessment and the use of evidence-based interventions will not increase costs or administrative burdens significantly for LEAs, as compared to the previous statutory and regulatory requirements. Moreover, we believe that these requirements will have the significant benefit of helping to ensure that the required improvement plans include effective interventions that meet the demonstrated educational needs of students in identified schools, and ultimately improve outcomes for those students.

Section 200.21 also requires LEAs with schools identified for comprehensive support and improvement, as well as schools with low-performing subgroups identified for targeted support and improvement that also must receive additional targeted support under § 200.19(b)(2), to identify and address resource inequities, including any disproportionate assignment of ineffective, out-of-field, or inexperienced teachers and possible inequities related to the per-pupil expenditures of Federal, State, and local funds. These requirements involve an additional use of data and methods that LEAs would be required to develop and apply to meet other statutory and regulatory requirements in the final regulations, including requirements related to ensuring that low-income and minority students are not taught at disproportionate rates by ineffective, out-of-field, or inexperienced teachers, the inclusion of per-pupil expenditure data on State and LEA report cards, and the use of per-pupil expenditure data to meet the title I supplement not supplant requirement. In addition, the final regulations do not specify how an LEA must address any resource inequities identified through its review. We believe it is critically important to ensure equitable access to effective teachers, and that the fair and equitable allocation of other educational resources is essential to ensuring that all students, particularly the low-achieving, disadvantaged, and minority students who are the focus of ESEA programs, have equitable access to the full range of courses, instructional materials, educational technology, and programs that help ensure positive educational outcomes. (31) Consequently, we believe that the benefits of the required review of resource inequities outweigh the minimal additional costs that may be imposed by the final regulations.

Section 200.21 establishes a new requirement for State review and approval of each comprehensive support and improvement plan developed by LEAs with one or more schools identified for comprehensive support and improvement, as well as proposed amendments to previously approved plans. This requirement potentially imposes additional costs compared to the previous regulations. One commenter noted that while cost estimates in the NPRM captured a portion of the costs of these plans, the estimates did not recognize other start-up costs, such as preparing for the collection and review of plans and training LEAs on plan requirements, as well as ongoing costs related to monitoring comprehensive support and improvement plans and revising plans when necessary. The commenter further noted that States would likely have to engage both LEAs and schools to ensure the development and implementation of effective improvement plans. The Department agrees that its initial estimates likely understated the average costs that States would incur in creating an application process, training LEA staff, collecting applications, and reviewing and approving comprehensive support and improvement plans for the estimated 4,000 schools that will be identified for comprehensive support and improvement under the final regulations. Consequently, we are increasing the number of hours that we estimate these activities would take, on average, for each identified school from 20 hours to 30 hours, representing the addition of 5 hours for training and 5 hours for administrative processing of each application. Assuming a cost of $40 per hour for State staff, the total estimated State costs related to comprehensive support and improvement plans rises from $3,200,000 in the NPRM to $4,800,000 in these final regulations. States are expected to incur these costs just once over the course of the four-year authorization of the law due to the delayed timeline for identification of the initial cohort of comprehensive support and improvement schools, which under the final regulations will take place at the beginning of the 2018-2019 school year. We also note that this cost represents less than 3 percent of the funds that States are authorized to reserve annually for State-level administrative and school improvement activities under part A of title I of the ESEA, as amended by the ESSA. Given the critical importance of ensuring that LEAs implement rigorous improvement plans in their lowest-performing comprehensive support and improvement schools, and that a significant proportion of the approximately $1 billion that States will reserve annually under section 1003 of the ESEA, as amended by the ESSA, will be used to support effective implementation of these plans, we believe that the potential benefits of a robust State review and approval role will far outweigh the costs. Moreover, those costs would be fully paid for with formula grant funds made available through the ESEA, as amended by the ESSA, including the 1 percent administrative reservation under title I, part A and the 5 percent State-level share of section 1003 school improvement funds.

We further note that the analysis in the NPRM did account for the requirement that the State monitor and periodically review each LEA's implementation of approved comprehensive support and improvement plans. As described in the NRPM, these activities are essentially the same as those carried out under the previous statute and regulations for schools identified for improvement, corrective action, and restructuring, as well as State-level monitoring requirements under the School Improvement Grants program, and thus do not represent new burden or costs for States. In addition, section 1003 of the ESEA, as amended by the ESSA, which requires States to reserve a total of approximately $1 billion annually to support implementation of comprehensive support and improvement and targeted support and improvement plans, permits States to use up to 5 percent of these funds for State-level activities, including "monitoring and evaluating the use of funds" by LEAs using section 1003 funds for comprehensive support and improvement plans. For these reasons, we believe that the requirement in the final regulations to monitor and periodically review each LEA's implementation of approved comprehensive support and improvement plans would impose few, if any, additional costs compared to previous regulatory requirements, and that any increased costs would be paid for with Federal funding provided for this purpose.

The final regulations also require States to establish exit criteria for schools implementing comprehensive support and improvement plans and for certain schools with low-performing subgroups identified for targeted support and improvement that also must receive additional targeted support under § 200.19(b)(2) and implement enhanced targeted support and improvement plans. In both cases, the final regulations require that the exit criteria established by the State ensure that a school (1) has improved student outcomes and (2) no longer meets the criteria for identification. Schools that do not meet exit criteria following a State-determined number of years will be identified for additional improvement actions (as outlined by an amended comprehensive support and improvement plan for schools already implementing such plans, and a comprehensive support and improvement plan for schools previously identified for targeted support and improvement due to low-performing subgroups that also receive additional targeted support). We believe that these additional requirements will be minimally burdensome and entail few, if any, additional costs for States. Moreover, most States already have developed similar exit criteria for their priority and focus schools under ESEA flexibility, and likely will be able to adapt existing criteria for use under the final regulations. Rigorous exit criteria linked to additional improvement actions are essential for ensuring that low-performing schools, and, more importantly, the students who attend them, do not continue to underperform for years without meaningful and effective interventions. Moreover, the additional improvement actions primarily involve revision of existing improvement plans, which will be less burdensome than, for example, moving from corrective action to restructuring under current regulations, which requires the creation of an entirely new plan involving significantly different interventions. For these reasons, we believe that the benefits of the final regulations will outweigh the costs.

In addition to requiring States to review and approve comprehensive support and improvement plans, monitor implementation of those plans, and establish exit criteria, the final regulations require States to provide technical assistance and other support to LEAs serving a significant number of schools identified either for comprehensive support and improvement or targeted support and improvement.

Section 200.23 requires each State to periodically review available resources between LEAs and between schools. The final regulations also require each State to take action, to the extent practicable, to address any resource inequities identified during its review. These reviews generally will not require the collection of new data and, in many cases, will involve re-examining information and analyses provided to States by LEAs during the process of reviewing and approving comprehensive support and improvement plans and meeting title I requirements regarding disproportionate assignment of low-income and minority students to ineffective, out-of-field, or inexperienced teachers. In addition, the final regulations give States flexibility to identify the LEAs targeted for resource reviews. Consequently, we believe that the final regulations regarding State resource reviews will be minimally burdensome and entail few if any new costs, while contributing to the development of statewide strategies for addressing resource inequities that can help improve outcomes for students served under ESEA programs.

Similarly, § 200.23(b) of the final regulations requires each State to describe in its State plan the technical assistance it will provide to each of its LEAs serving a significant number of schools identified for either comprehensive support and improvement or targeted support and improvement. The final regulations also specify minimum requirements for such technical assistance, including how the State will assist LEAs in developing and implementing comprehensive support and improvement plans and targeted support and improvement plans, conducting school-level needs assessments, selecting evidence-based interventions, and reviewing and addressing resource inequities. We believe that these requirements related to State-provided technical assistance to certain LEAs will be better differentiated, more reflective of State capacity limits, and significantly less burdensome and costly than previous regulatory requirements related to LEA improvement and corrective action and the operation of statewide systems of support for schools and LEAs identified for improvement. Moreover, given the schools that would be targeted for technical assistance, most costs could be paid for with the State share of funds reserved for school improvement under section 1003 of the ESEA, as amended by the ESSA.

Data Reporting

The ESEA, as amended by the ESSA, expanded reporting requirements for States and LEAs in order to provide parents, practitioners, policy makers, and public officials at the Federal, State, and local levels with actionable data and information on key aspects of our education system and the students served by that system, but in particular those students served by ESEA programs. The final regulations implement these requirements primarily by clarifying definitions and, where possible, streamlining and simplifying reporting requirements consistent with the purposes of the ESEA. Although the regulatory changes in §§ 200.30 through 200.37 involve new requirements that entail additional costs for States and LEAs, we believe the costs are reasonable in view of the potential benefits, which include a more comprehensive picture of the structure and performance of our education system under the new law. Importantly, the ESEA, as amended by the ESSA, gives States and LEAs considerable new flexibility to develop and implement innovative, evidence-based approaches to addressing local educational needs, and the final regulations help ensure that the comprehensive data reporting requirements of the ESEA, as amended by the ESSA, capture the shape and results of that innovation without imposing unreasonable burdens on program participants.

The Department estimates that the new data reporting requirements impose a one-time increased burden of 230 hours per State. Assuming an average cost of $40 an hour for State staff, we estimate a total one-time cost of $478,400 for meeting the new State report card requirements. The Department further estimates that the preparation and dissemination of LEA report cards will require a new one-time average burden of 80 hours per respondent in the first year and annual burden of 10 hours per respondent, resulting in a one-time total burden across 16,970 LEAs of 1,357,600 hours and annual burden of 169,700 hours per LEA. (32) Assuming an average cost of

$35 an hour for LEA staff, we estimate the one-time total cost to be $47,516,000 and a total annual cost of $5,939,500. The annual burden on LEAs for creating and publishing their report cards remains unchanged at 16 hours per LEA, posing no additional costs relative to the costs associated with the previous statutory and regulatory requirements. The Department believes these additional costs are reasonable for collecting essential information regarding the students, teachers, schools, and LEAs served through Federal programs authorized by the ESEA, as amended by the ESSA, that currently award more than $23 billion annually to States and LEAs.

A key challenge faced by States in meeting current report card requirements has been developing clear, effective formats for the timely delivery of complex information to a wide range of customers. Sections 200.30 and 200.31 specify requirements intended to promote improvements in this area, including a required overview aimed at ensuring essential information is provided to parents in a manageable, easy-to-understand format; definitions for key elements; dissemination options; accessible formats; and deadlines for publication. We believe the benefits of the final regulations are significant and include transparency, timeliness, and wide accessibility of data to inform educational improvement and accountability.

Section 200.32 streamlines reporting requirements related to State and local accountability systems by permitting States and LEAs to meet those requirements by referencing or obtaining data from other existing documents and descriptions created to meet other requirements in the final regulations. For example, § 200.32 allows States and LEAs to meet the requirement relating to a description of State accountability systems through a link to a Web address, rather than trying to condense a complex, lengthy description of a statewide accountability system into an accessible, easy-to-understand "report card" format. Section 200.33 clarifies calculations and reporting of data on student achievement and other measures of progress, primarily through modifications to existing measures and calculations. These changes help ensure that State and local report cards serve their intended purpose of providing the public with information on a variety of measures in a State's accountability system that conveys a complete picture of school, LEA, and State performance. The final regulations have a key benefit of requiring all LEA report cards to include results from all State accountability system indicators for all schools served by the LEA to ensure that parents, teachers, and other key stakeholders have access to the information for which schools are held accountable.

A critical new requirement in the ESEA, as amended by the ESSA, is the collection and reporting of per-pupil expenditures. Section 200.35 includes requirements and definitions aimed at helping States and LEAs collect and report reliable, accurate, and comparable data on these expenditures. We believe that these data will be essential in helping districts meet their obligations under the supplement not supplant requirement in title I-A, which requires districts to develop a methodology demonstrating that Federal funds are used to supplement State and local education funding. In addition, making such data widely available has tremendous potential to highlight disparities in resource allocations that can have a significant impact on both the effective use of Federal program funds and educational opportunity and outcomes for the students served by ESEA programs. Broader knowledge and understanding of such disparities among educators, parents, and the public can lead to a more informed conversation about how to improve the performance of our education system, and the ESEA, as amended by the ESSA, highlights the importance of resource allocation considerations by making them a key component of school improvement plans, and ultimately improve educational outcomes.

Section 200.36 provides specifications for the newly required collection of information on student enrollment in postsecondary education, including definitions of key data elements. Sections 200.34 and 200.37 clarify guidelines for calculating graduation rates and reporting on educator qualifications, respectively, and reflect a change to existing reporting requirements in current regulations rather than new items (e.g., requirements related to the reporting of "highly qualified teachers," a term that no longer exists in the ESEA, as amended by the ESSA).

Optional Consolidated State Plans

We believe that the final State plan regulations in §§ 299.13 to 299.19 generally do not impose significant costs on States. As discussed in the Paperwork Reduction Act of 1995 section of this document, we estimate that, over a three-year period, States will need on average 1,109 additional hours to carry out the requirements in the State plan regulations. At $40 per hour, the average additional State cost associated with these requirements is accordingly an estimated $44,358, resulting in a total cost across 52 States of $2,306,640. We expect that States will generally use the Federal education program funds they reserve for State administration to cover these costs, and that any costs not met with Federal funds will generally be minimal.

Moreover, the final regulations implement statutory provisions expressly intended to reduce burden on States by simplifying the process for applying for Federal education program funds. Section 8302 of the ESEA, as amended by the ESSA, allows States to submit a consolidated State plan in lieu of multiple State plans for individual covered programs. The Department anticipates, based on previous experience, that all States will take advantage of the option in § 299.13 to submit a consolidated State plan, and we believe that the content areas and requirements for those plans in §§ 299.14 to 299.19 are appropriately limited to those needed to ensure that States and their LEAs provide all children significant opportunity to receive a fair, equitable, and high-quality education and close achievement gaps, consistent with the purpose of title I of the ESEA, as amended by the ESSA. As discussed in detail elsewhere in this notice, in these final regulations we have revised certain provisions from proposed §§ 299.14 to 299.19 to ensure a limited burden on States submitting a consolidated State plan, including by eliminating certain proposed requirements and reducing the amount of information that a State must provide under other requirements.

Section 8302(a)(1) of the ESEA, as amended by the ESSA, permits the Department to designate programs for inclusion in consolidated State plans in addition to those covered by the statute. In § 299.13, the Department has added to the covered programs the Grants for State Assessments and Related Activities in section 1201 of title I, part B of the ESEA, as amended by the ESSA, and the Education for Homeless Children and Youths program in subpart B of title VII of the McKinney-Vento Homeless Assistance Act. Inclusion of these programs in a consolidated State plan will further reduce the burden on States in applying for Federal education program funds.

In general, the Department believes that the costs of the final State plan regulations (which are discussed in more detail in the following paragraphs) are clearly outweighed by their benefits, which include, in addition to reduced burden on States: Increased flexibility in State planning, improved stakeholder engagement in plan development and implementation, better coordination in the use of Federal education program funds and elimination of funding "silos," and a sustained focus on activities critical to providing all students with equitable access to a high-quality education.

Section 299.13 establishes the procedures and timelines for State plan submission and revision, including requirements for timely and meaningful consultation with stakeholders that are based on requirements in titles I, II, and III of the ESEA, as amended by the ESSA. The Department does not believe that the consultation requirements impose significant costs on States. We expect that, as part of carrying out their general education responsibilities, States will have already developed procedures for notifying the public and for conducting outreach to, and soliciting input from, stakeholders, as the regulations require. In the Department's estimation, States will not incur significant costs in implementing those procedures for the State plans.

Sections 299.14 to 299.19 establish requirements for the content of consolidated State plans (i.e., the "necessary materials" discussed in section 8302(b)(3) of the ESEA, as amended by the ESSA). Section 299.14 establishes five content areas of consolidated State plans, including: Consultation and performance management (the requirements for which are specified in § 299.15); challenging academic assessments (§ 299.16); accountability, support, and improvement for schools (§ 299.17); supporting excellent educators (§ 299.18); and supporting all students (§ 299.19). We believe that, in general, the requirements for these content areas minimize burden on States insofar as they consolidate duplicative requirements and eliminate unnecessary requirements from State plans for individual covered programs.

Section 299.15 requires States to describe how they engaged in timely and meaningful consultation with specified stakeholder groups in consolidated State plan development. We estimate that the costs of complying with the requirements in this section are minimal.

Section 299.16 requires States to describe how they are complying with requirements related to assessments in languages other than English, consistent with section 1111(b)(2)(F) of the ESEA, as amended by the ESSA. In addition, for a State that exempts an eighth-grade student from taking the mathematics assessment the State typically administers in eighth grade because the student takes an end-of-course mathematics assessment that is used by the State to meet high school assessment requirements, § 299.16 requires the State to describe how the State is complying with the requirements of section 1111(b)(2)(c) of the ESEA, as amended by the ESSA, and applicable regulations. The Department believes that the costs to States of complying with these requirements are likewise minimal.

The Department believes that the requirements in §§ 299.17 and 299.18 similarly do not involve significant new costs for most States. Section 299.17 establishes consolidated State plan requirements for describing the State's long-term goals, statewide accountability system, school identifications, and support for low-performing schools, consistent with the requirements in section 1111(c) and (d) of the ESEA, as amended by the ESSA. Section 299.18 requires a State to describe, consistent with requirements in sections 1111(g), 2101, and 2102 of the ESEA, as amended by the ESSA: Educator development, retention, and advancement practices in the State, if the State intends to use Federal education program funds to support such practices; how the State will use Federal education program funds for State-level activities to improve educator quality and effectiveness; and whether low-income and minority students in title I-participating schools are taught at higher rates by ineffective, out-of-field, or inexperienced teachers compared to their peers, including the likely causes of any differences in rates and strategies to eliminate those differences. The Department anticipates that, in complying with §§ 299.17 and 299.18, States will rely to a significant degree on existing State ESEA flexibility requests and Educator Equity Plans. Accordingly, the final regulations should generally not result in significant new costs for States.

Finally, § 299.19 requires States to describe how they will use Federal education program funds to provide all students equitable access to a well-rounded and supportive education, and includes program-specific requirements necessary to ensure that such access is provided to particularly vulnerable student groups, including migratory students, neglected and delinquent children and youths, English learners, and homeless children and youths. We believe that the requirements in this section would accomplish this purpose with minimal burden on, and cost to, States, consistent with section 8302(b)(3) of the ESEA, as amended by the ESSA.

The major benefit of these regulations, taken in their totality, is a more flexible, less complex, and costly accountability framework for the implementation of the ESEA that respects State and local decision-making while continuing to ensure that States and LEAs use ESEA funds to ensure that all students have significant opportunity to receive a fair, equitable, and high-quality education, and to close educational achievement gaps.

Accounting Statement

As required by OMB Circular A-4 (available at www.whitehouse.gov/sites/default/files/omb/assets/omb/circulars/a004/a-4.pdf), in the following table we have prepared an accounting statement showing the classification of the expenditures associated with the provisions of these final regulations. This table provides our best estimate of the changes in annual monetized costs and benefits as a result of the final regulations. The transfers reflect appropriations for the affected programs. We note that the regulatory baselines differ within the table; the cost estimates are increments over and above what would be spent under the ESEA if it had not been amended by the ESSA, whereas the transfers (appropriations) are totals, rather than increments relative to the ESEA. We further note that, although we refer to appropriations amounts as transfers, where they pay for new activities they would appropriately be categorized as costs.

Accounting Statement Classification of Estimated Expenditures

Category	Benefits
More flexible and less complex and costly accountability framework with uniform procedures	Not Quantified.
More transparency and actionable data and information with uniform definitions, all of which provide a more comprehensive picture of performance and other key measures	Not Quantified.
Less burden on States through simplified process for applying and planning for Federal education program funds	Not Quantified
Category	Costs (over 4-year authorization).
Uniform procedure for setting long-term goals and measurements of interim progress for English learners	$166,400.
Review and approval of LEA comprehensive support and improvement plans	4,800,000.
State Report Cards	478,400.
LEA Report Cards	65,334,500.
Consolidated State Plans	2,306,640.
Category	Transfers (over 4-year authorization; based on FY 2016 appropriations).
Title I, part A: Improving Basic Programs Operated by State and Local Educational Agencies	59,639,208,000.
Title I, part B: Grants for State Assessments	1,512,000,000.
Title I, part C: Education of Migratory Children	1,499,004,000.
Title I, part D: Prevention and Intervention Programs for Children and Youth Who Are Neglected, Delinquent, or At-Risk	190,456,000.
Title II, part A: Supporting Effective Instruction	9,399,320,000.
Title III, part A: Language Instruction for English Learners and Immigrant Students	2,949,600,000.
Title IV, part A: Student Support and Academic Enrichment Grants	6,450,000,000 (no FY 2016 funding; reflects authorization of appropriations).
Title IV, part B: 21st Century Community Learning Centers	4,666,692,000.
Title V, part B, subpart 2: Rural and Low-Income School Program	351,680,000.
Education for Homeless Children and Youths program under subtitle B of title VII of the McKinney-Vento Homeless Assistance Act	280,000,000.

Unfunded Mandates Reform Act

Under the Unfunded Mandates Reform Act (UMRA) (2 U.S.C. 1531), an agency must assess the effects of its regulatory actions on State, local, and tribal governments. The Department has set forth that assessment in the Regulatory Impact Analysis section of this document. Section 1532 of the UMRA also requires that an agency provide a written statement regarding any regulation that would involve a Federal mandate. These final regulations do not involve a Federal mandate as defined in section 658 of UMRA because the duties imposed upon State, local, or tribal governments in these regulations are a condition of those governments' receipt of Federal formula grant funds under the ESEA.

Regulatory Flexibility Act Certification

The Secretary certifies that these final requirements would not have a significant economic impact on a substantial number of small entities. Under the U.S. Small Business Administration's Size Standards, small entities include small governmental jurisdictions such as cities, towns, or school districts (LEAs) with a population of less than 50,000. Although the majority of LEAs that receive ESEA funds qualify as small entities under this definition, the requirements established in this document would not have a significant economic impact on these small LEAs because the costs of implementing these requirements would be covered by funding received by these small LEAs under ESEA formula grant programs, including programs that provide funds largely for such small LEAs (e.g., the Rural and Low-Income School program authorized under subpart 2 of part B of title V). The Department believes the benefits provided under this final regulatory action outweigh the burdens on these small LEAs of complying with the final requirements. However, one commenter disagreed that that the final regulations would not have significant economic impact on small entities. This commenter specifically cited the requirement for assessment rate improvement plans in § 200.15(c)(1) for schools that do not meet the 95 percent participation rate requirement, claiming that such plans may be costly to develop and implement while acknowledging that Federal program funds are available to pay such costs. In addition to the fact that Federal funds may be used to pay any costs associated with assessment rate improvement plans, we note that such costs typically would be commensurate with the size and enrollment of an LEA, and thus reasonably would be expected to be lower for small entities. Further, the costs and other burdens associated with assessment rate improvement plans are likely to be significantly lower than the costs of Federal or State compliance remedies that otherwise could be required for small LEAs that do not meet the 95 percent participation rate requirements in section 1111(c)(4)(E) of the ESEA, as amended by the ESSA. Consequently, the final requirements, including § 200.15, would help ensure that State plans for using ESEA formula grant funds, as well as State-provided technical assistance and other support intended to promote the effective and coordinated use of Federal, State, and local resources in ensuring that all students meet challenging State standards and graduate high school college- and career-ready, reflect the unique needs and circumstances of small LEAs and ensure the provision of educational resources that otherwise may not be available to small and often geographically isolated LEAs.

Paperwork Reduction Act of 1995

Sections 200.21, 200.22, 200.24, 200.30, 200.31, 200.32, 200.33, 200.34, 200.35, 200.36, 200.37, 299.13, 299.14, 299.15, 299.16, 299.17, 299.18, and 299.19 of the final regulations contain information collection requirements that will impact the burden and costs associated with two currently approved information collections, 1810-0581 and 1810-0576. Under the Paperwork Reduction Act of 1995 (PRA) the Department submitted a copy of these sections to OMB for its review.

These changes were described in the NPRM and subject to comments at that time. One commenter acknowledged that the proposed regulations affected the information collections, and agreed that the proposed regulations would reduce some existing burden. A second commenter indicated that the burden estimates were too low, but did not provide specific suggestions for improving the estimates. We continue to believe these burden hour estimates to be accurate, and in the absence of specific feedback, decline to make changes. Another commenter specifically noted that the estimated reporting burden of 230 hours for State report cards was too low. We agree with this commenter that the burden on States for preparing report cards is higher than 230 hours. When describing the burden hours in the NPRM, we described these hours in relation to the current approved burden under the relevant information collections, and we estimated an increase of 230 burden hours, in addition to the already approved burden hours. For clarity, we describe the total estimated burden below.

Collection of Information From SEAs—Report Cards; Collection of Information From LEAs—Report Cards and Public Reporting

Section 1111(h) of the ESEA, as amended by the ESSA, requires States and LEAs to prepare and disseminate annual report cards; these report cards provide essential information to school communities regarding activities under title I of the ESEA. Sections 200.30-200.37 of the final regulations further require States and LEAs to include specific elements on the report cards. These information collection requirements will impact the burden and costs associated with information collection 1810-0581, State Educational Agency, Local Educational Agency, and School Data Collection and Reporting Under ESEA, Title I, Part A, under which the Department is approved to require States and LEAs to collect and disseminate information. The estimated burden for this collection remains unchanged from the NPRM.

Under §§ 200.30 through 200.37, States are required to annually prepare and disseminate a State report card, including specific elements. Among other things, each State must describe its accountability system in the report card, create and publish a report card overview, and ensure that the report cards are accessible. To ensure that States can report on all required elements, States will be required to adjust their data systems, and some States may need to submit a plan requesting an extension of the deadline to include certain date elements.

On an annual basis, we continue to estimate that each State will devote 370 hours to preparing and disseminating the State report card, and making it accessible; across all States, this will result in an annual burden of 19,240 hours. We anticipate that each State will devote 80 hours to creating and preparing a State report card overview, one time. During the three-year information collection period, this will result in an annual burden of 26.67 hours for each State; across all States, this will result in an annual burden of 1,387 hours. We expect that 15 States may need to request an extension to report certain required data elements on behalf of the State or its LEAs, and that such request will take 50 hours to prepare. Over the three-year information collection period, this will result in an annual burden of 16.66 hours for each affected State, resulting in an annual burden of 250 hours across all States. Each State must annually include a description of its accountability system in the report card; we anticipate that this will result in an annual burden of 10 hours for each State, resulting in an annual burden of 520 hours across all States. Finally, we anticipate that each State will have to make a one-time adjustment to its data collection system, to report on required data elements under §§ 200.32 through 200.37. We expect that this adjustment will require 120 hours for each State; over the three-year information collection period, this will result in an annual burden of 40 hours, and a total burden for all States of 2080 hours.

Annual Collection of Information From SEAs: Report Cards

Citation	Description	Respondents	Average hours per respondent	Total hours	Total cost (total hours × $40)
Section 1111(h)(1); § 200.24(e); § 200.30	Prepare and disseminate the State report card, and make it accessible. This includes posting the report card on the Web site alongside the annual report to the Secretary required in § 200.30(d)(ii)(B). Except as described below, this includes all requirements under section 1111(h) of the ESEA and all pre-existing requirements.	52	370	19,240	$769,600
§ 200.30(b)(2)	Create and publish a State report card overview	52	26.67	1,386.67	55,467
§§ 200.30(e)(3); 200.31(e)(3)	Request an extension	15	16.67	250	10,000
§§ 200.32(a); 200.32(b)	Describe the accountability system in the report card	52	10.00	520	20,800
§§ 200.32(c); 200.33; 200.34; 200.35; 200.36; 200.37	Describe the accountability system results in the report card, and adjust the data system to report on all of the elements required under these sections of the regulations	52	40.00	2,080	83,200
Total				23,476.67	939,067

Similarly, we have not adjusted the estimated burden arising from the development and release of the LEA report card, or the estimated burden for LEAs with schools identified for comprehensive or targeted support and improvement to notify parents of the identification, or make publicly available plans for improvement. We continue to estimate that each LEA, on average, will devote 30 hours across the three-year information collection period, or 10 hours annually, to notifying parents that schools have been identified, and to make publically available the resulting plans. In total, for 16,970 LEAs, this results in an annual burden of 169,700 hours. We expect that each LEA will devote 16 hours to preparing and disseminating the LEA report card each year, for a total burden of 271,520 hours across all LEAs. We anticipate that each LEA will devote 80 hours to creating and preparing an LEA report card overview, one time. During the three-year information collection period, this will result in an annual burden of 26.67 hours for each LEA; across all LEAs, this will result in an annual burden of 452,533 hours. Finally, all LEAs will be required to revise their report cards to report on new elements required under the ESEA, as amended by the ESSA, as well as the regulations in §§ 200.30 through 200.37. However, we expect that these adjustments will be addressed through modifications to the State data collection systems, and therefore do not expect these changes to impose additional burden hours on LEAs.

Annual Collection of Information From LEAs: Report Cards and Public Reporting

Citation	Description	Respondents	Average hours per respondent	Total hours	Total cost (total hours × $35)
§§ 200.21(b); 200.21(d)(6); 200.22(b); 200.22(d)(2)	LEAs with schools identified for comprehensive or targeted support and improvement must make publicly available the resulting plans and any amendments to these plans, and notify parents of the identification	16,970	10	169,700	$5,939,500
Section 1111(h)(2); § 200.31	Prepare and disseminate the LEA report card, and make it accessible. Except as described below, this includes all requirements under section 1111(h) of the ESEA and all pre-existing requirements	16,970	16	271,520	9,503,200
§ 200.31(b)(2)	Create and publish the LEA report card overview	16,970	26.67	452,533	15,838,667
§§ 200.32; 200.33; 200.34; 200.35; 200.36; 200.37	Describe the accountability system and				

results on the LEA report card | 16,970 | 0 | 0 | 0 |
| Total | | | | 893,753.33 | 31,281,367 |

Consolidated State Application

Under information collection 1810-0576, Consolidated State Application, the Department is currently approved to collect information from States. As proposed in the NPRM, we will replace the previously authorized consolidated State application with the consolidated State plan, authorized under section 8302 of the ESEA, as amended by the ESSA. The consolidated State plan seeks to encourage greater cross-program coordination, planning, and service delivery; enhance program integration; and provide greater flexibility, and reduce burden, for States. We will use the information from the consolidated State plan as the basis for approving funding under the covered programs.

Section 299.13 permits a State to submit a consolidated State plan, instead of individual program applications. States may choose not to submit consolidated State plans; however, for purposes of estimating the burden, we assume all States will choose to submit consolidated State plans. Each consolidated State plan must meet the requirements described in §§ 299.14 to 299.19. In the NPRM, we estimated the total annual burden for the collection of information through the submission of consolidated State plans to be 23,200 hours. Based upon revisions to the requirements of the consolidated State plan, and efforts to reduce burden on States, we now revise the estimates as detailed below.

Each State submitting a consolidated State plan will be required to describe consultation with stakeholders; provide assurances; report on performance management and technical assistance; describe how the State is complying with requirements relating to assessments in languages other than English; report on accountability, support, and improvement for schools; report on supporting excellent educators; and report on equitable access and support for schools. In total, over the three-year information collection period, we anticipate that each State will devote 993 hours to the preparation and submission of these plans, resulting in a total annual burden of 17,212 hours.

Additionally, we estimate that each State, on average, will amend its request once during the three-year information collection period, and will devote 60 hours to preparing this amendment. This amendment process will result in a total annual burden of 1,040 hours, across all States.

We further expect that 16 States will submit plans to apply for extensions for the required educator equity student-level data calculation, and that each State submitting a plan and extension request will devote 60 hours to this process. Over the three-year information collection period, we expect that this will result in an annual burden of 20 hours for 16 States, or 320 total burden hours.

Finally, certain States will be required to describe their strategies for middle school math equity. We estimate that 26 States will be required to address these strategies, and will devote 75 hours to describing these strategies in the State plan. Over the three-year information collection period, we expect that this will result in an annual burden of 25 hours for 25 States, or 650 total burden hours.

Annual Collection of Information from SEAs: Consolidated State Plan
| Citation | Description | Respondents | Hours per respondent | Total hours | Total cost (total hours × $40) |
| §§ 299.13(a); 299.13(d)(2); 299.13(e); 299.13(h); 299.13(k) | Submit consolidated State plan or

individual program State plans; submit optional revisions to State plans | 52 | 10 | 520 | 20,800 |
§§ 299.13(a); 299.13(b); 299.14(b); 299.15(a)	Report on meaningful consultation with stakeholders, including public comment	52	40	2080	83,200
§§ 299.13(a); 299.13(c); 299.13(d)(1); 299.14(c)	Provide assurances	52	1	52	2,080
§§ 299.13(a); 299.13(g)	Submit amendments and significant changes, as well as revisions, as appropriate	52	20	1040	41,600
§§ 299.13(a); 299.13(d)(3)	Submit a plan to apply for an extension for the educator equity student-level data calculation	16	20	320	12,800
§ 299.13(f)	Publish approved consolidated State plan or individual program State plans on State website	52	5	260	10,400
§§ 299.13(a); 299.13(d)(2); 299.15(b)	Report on performance management and technical assistance	52	50	2600	104,000
§§ 299.13(a); 299.16(a)	Describe strategies for middle school math equity	26	25	650	26,000
§§ 299.13(a); 299.16(b)	Describe how the State is complying with the requirements related to assessments in languages other than English	52	25	1300	52,000
§§ 299.13(a); 299.14(b)(3); 299.17	Report on accountability support and improvement for schools	52	150	7800	312,000
§§ 299.13(a); 299.14(b)(4); 299.18	Report on supporting excellent educators	52	25	1300	52,000
§§ 299.13(a); 299.14(b)(5); 299.19	Report on equitable access and support for students	52	25	1300	52,000
Total				19222	768,880

The PRA does not require you to respond to a collection of information unless it displays a valid OMB control number. We display the valid OMB control number assigned to the collections of information in these final regulations at the end of the affected section of the regulations.

Intergovernmental Review

This program is not subject to Executive Order 12372 and the regulations in 34 CFR part 79.

Assessment of Educational Impact

In the NPRM we requested comments on whether the proposed regulations would require transmission of information that any other agency or authority of the United States gathers or makes available.

Based on the response to the NPRM and on our review, we have determined that these final regulations do not require transmission of information that any other agency or authority of the United States gathers or makes available.

Accessible Format: Individuals with disabilities can obtain this document in an accessible format (e.g., Braille, large print, or electronic format) on request to the person listed under FOR FURTHER INFORMATION CONTACT.

Electronic Access to This Document: The official version of this document is the document published in the Federal Register. Free Internet access to the official edition of the Federal Register and the Code of Federal Regulations is available via the Federal Digital System at:

www.gpo.gov/fdsys. At this site you can view this document, as well as all other documents of this Department published in the Federal Register, in text or Portable Document Format (PDF). To use PDF you must have Adobe Acrobat Reader, which is available free at the site.

You may also access documents of the Department published in the Federal Register by using the article search feature at: www.federalregister.gov. Specifically, through the advanced search feature at this site, you can limit your search to documents published by the Department. (Catalog of Federal Domestic Assistance Number does not apply.)

LIST OF SUBJECTS

Elementary and secondary education, Grant programs—education, Indians—education, Infants and children, Juvenile delinquency, Migrant labor, Private schools, Reporting and recordkeeping requirements.

Administrative practice and procedure, Elementary and secondary education, Grant programs—education, Private schools, Reporting and recordkeeping requirements.

Dated: November 16, 2016.
John B. King, Jr.,
Secretary of Education.
For the reasons discussed in the preamble, the Secretary of Education amends parts 200 and 299 of title 34 of the Code of Federal Regulations as follows:

PART 200 TITLE I IMPROVING THE ACADEMIC ACHIEVEMENT OF THE DISADVANTAGED

REGULATORY TEXT

1. The authority citation for part 200 is revised to read as follows:

Authority:

20 U.S.C. 6301 through 6376, unless otherwise noted.

§ 200.7
[Removed and Reserved]

REGULATORY TEXT

2. Remove and reserve § 200.7.

3. Section 200.12 is revised to read as follows:

§ 200.12 Single statewide accountability system.

(a)(1) Each State must describe in its State plan under section 1111 of the Act that the State has developed and will implement a single, statewide accountability system that meets all requirements under paragraph (b) of this section in order to improve student academic achievement and school success among all public elementary and secondary schools, including public charter schools.

(2) A State that submits an individual program State plan for subpart A of this part under § 299.13(j) must meet all application requirements in § 299.17.

(b) The State's accountability system must—

(1) Be based on the challenging State academic standards under section 1111(b)(1) of the Act and academic assessments under section 1111(b)(2) of the Act;

(2) Be informed by the State's ambitious long-term goals and measurements of interim progress under § 200.13;

(3) Include all indicators under § 200.14;

(4) Take into account the achievement of all public elementary and secondary school students, consistent with §§ 200.15 through 200.17 and 200.20;

(5) Be the same accountability system the State uses to annually meaningfully differentiate all public schools, including public charter schools, in the State under § 200.18, and to identify schools for comprehensive and targeted support and improvement under § 200.19; and

(6) Include the process the State will use to ensure effective development and implementation of school support and improvement plans, including evidence-based interventions, to hold all public schools, including public charter schools, accountable for student academic achievement and school success consistent with §§ 200.21 through 200.24.

(c)(1) The accountability provisions under this section must be overseen for public charter schools in accordance with State charter school law.

(2) In meeting the requirements of this section, if an authorized public chartering agency, consistent with State charter school law, acts to decline to renew or to revoke a charter for a particular charter school, the decision of the agency to do so supersedes any notification from the State that such a school must implement a comprehensive support and improvement plan or targeted support and improvement plan under §§ 200.21 or 200.22, respectively.

4. Remove the undesignated center heading "Adequate Yearly Progress (AYP)" following § 200.12.

5. Section 200.13 is revised to read as follows:

§ 200.13 Long-term goals and measurements of interim progress.

In designing its statewide accountability system under § 200.12, each State must establish long-term goals and measurements of interim progress that use the same multi-year timeline to achieve those goals for all students and for each subgroup of students, except that goals for Progress in Achieving English language proficiency must only be established for the English learner subgroup. The long-term goals and measurements of interim progress must include, at a minimum, each of the following:

(a) Academic achievement. (1) Each State must, in its State plan under section 1111 of the Act—

(i) Identify its ambitious State-designed long-term goals and measurements of interim progress for improved academic achievement, as measured by the percentage of students attaining grade-level proficiency on the annual assessments required under section 1111(b)(2)(B)(v)(I) of the Act, for all students and separately for each subgroup of students described in § 200.16(a)(2); and

(ii) Describe how it established those goals and measurements of interim progress.

(2) In establishing the long-term goals and measurements of interim progress under paragraph (a)(1) of this section, a State must—

(i) Apply the same academic achievement standards consistent with section 1111(b)(1) of the Act to all public school students in the State, except as provided for students with the most significant cognitive disabilities, whose performance under subpart A of this part may be assessed against alternate academic achievement standards defined by the State consistent with section 1111(b)(1)(E) of the Act;

(ii) Measure achievement separately for reading/language arts and for mathematics; and

(iii) Take into account the improvement necessary for each subgroup of students described in § 200.16(a)(2) to make significant progress in closing statewide proficiency gaps, such that the State's measurements of interim progress require greater rates of improvement for subgroups of students that are lower-achieving.

(b) Graduation rates. (1) Each State must, in its State plan under section 1111 of the Act—

(i) Identify its ambitious State-designed long-term goals and measurements of interim progress for improved graduation rates for all students and separately for each subgroup of students described in § 200.16(a)(2); and

(ii) Describe how it established those goals and measurements of interim progress.

(2) A State's long-term goals and measurements of interim progress under paragraph (b)(1) of this section must be based on—

(i) The four-year adjusted cohort graduation rate consistent with § 200.34(a); and

(ii) If a State chooses to use an extended-year adjusted cohort graduation rate as part of its Graduation Rate indicator under § 200.14(b)(3), the extended-year adjusted cohort graduation rate consistent with § 200.34(d), except that a State must set more rigorous long-term goals and measurements of interim progress for each such graduation rate, as compared to the long-term goals and measurements of interim progress for the four-year adjusted cohort graduation rate.

(3) In establishing the long-term goals and measurements of interim progress under paragraph (b)(1) of this section, a State must take into account the improvement necessary for each subgroup of students described in § 200.16(a)(2) to make significant progress in closing statewide graduation rate gaps, such that a State's measurements of interim progress require greater rates of improvement for subgroups that graduate high school at lower rates.

(c) English language proficiency. (1) Each State must, in its State plan under section 1111 of the Act—

(i) Identify its ambitious State-designed long-term goals and measurements of interim progress for increases in the percentage of all English learners in the State making annual progress toward attaining English language proficiency, as measured by the English language proficiency assessment required in section 1111(b)(2)(G) of the Act; and

(ii) Describe how it established those goals and measurements of interim progress.

(2) Each State must describe in its State plan under section 1111 of the Act a uniform procedure, applied to all English learners in the State in a consistent manner, to establish research-based student-level targets on which the goals and measurements of interim progress under paragraph (c)(1) of this section are based. The State-developed uniform procedure must—

(i) Take into consideration, at the time of a student's identification as an English learner, the student's English language proficiency level, and may take into consideration, at a State's discretion, one or more of the following student characteristics:

(A) Time in language instruction educational programs.

(B) Grade level.

(C) Age.

(D) Native language proficiency level.

(E) Limited or interrupted formal education, if any;

(ii) Based on the selected student characteristics under paragraph (c)(2)(i) of this section, determine the applicable timeline, up to a State-determined maximum number of years, for English learners sharing particular characteristics under paragraph (c)(2)(i) of this section to attain English language proficiency after a student's identification as an English learner; and

(iii) Establish student-level targets, based on the applicable timelines under paragraph (c)(2)(ii) of this section, that set the expectation for all English learners to make annual progress toward attaining English language proficiency within the applicable timelines for such students.

(3) The description under paragraph (c)(2) of this section must include a rationale for how the State determined the overall maximum number of years for English learners to attain English language proficiency in its uniform procedure for setting research-based student-level targets, and

282

the applicable timelines over which English learners sharing particular characteristics under paragraph (c)(2)(i) of this section would be expected to attain English language proficiency within such State-determined maximum number of years.

(4) An English learner who does not attain English language proficiency within the timeline under paragraph (c)(2)(ii) of this section must not be exited from English learner services or status prior to attaining English language proficiency.

6. Section 200.14 is revised to read as follows:

§ 200.14 Accountability indicators.

(a) In its statewide accountability system under § 200.12, each State must, at a minimum, include four distinct indicators for each school that—

(1) Except for the indicator under paragraph (b)(4) of this section, measure performance for all students and separately for each subgroup of students described in § 200.16(a)(2); and

(2) Use the same measures within each indicator for all schools in the State, except as provided in paragraph (c)(2) of this section.

(b) A State must annually measure the following indicators consistent with paragraph (a) of this section:

(1) For all schools, based on the long-term goals established under § 200.13(a), an Academic Achievement indicator, which—

(i) Must include the following:

(A) A measure of student performance on the annual reading/language arts and mathematics assessments required under section 1111(b)(2)(B)(v)(I) of the Act at the proficient level on the State's grade-level academic achievement standards consistent with section 1111(b)(1) of the Act, except that students with the most significant cognitive disabilities may be assessed in those subjects against alternate academic achievement standards defined by the State consistent with section 1111(b)(1)(E) of the Act; and

(B) The performance of at least 95 percent of all students and 95 percent of all students in each subgroup consistent with § 200.15(b)(1); and

(ii) May include the following:

(A) In addition to a measure of student performance under paragraph (b)(2)(i)(A) of this section, measures of student performance on such assessments above or below the proficient level on such achievement standards so long as—

(1) A school receives less credit for the performance of a student who is not yet proficient than for the performance of a student who has reached or exceeded proficiency; and

(2) The credit the school receives from the performance of a student exceeding the proficient level does not fully compensate for the performance of a student who is not yet proficient in the school;

and

(B) For high schools, student growth based on the reading/language arts and mathematics assessments required under section 1111(b)(2)(B)(v)(I) of the Act.

(2) For elementary and secondary schools that are not high schools, an Academic Progress indicator, which must include either—

(i) A measure of student growth based on the annual assessments required under section 1111(b)(2)(B)(v)(I) of the Act; or

(ii) Another academic measure that meets the requirements of paragraph (c) of this section.

(3) For high schools, based on the long-term goals established under § 200.13(b), a Graduation Rate indicator, which—

(i) Must measure the four-year adjusted cohort graduation rate consistent with § 200.34(a); and

(ii) May measure, at the State's discretion, the extended-year adjusted cohort graduation rate consistent with § 200.34(d).

(4) For all schools, a Progress in Achieving English Language Proficiency indicator, based on English learner performance on the annual English language proficiency assessment required under section 1111(b)(2)(G) of the Act in at least each of grades 3 through 8 and in grades for which English learners are otherwise assessed under section 1111(b)(2)(B)(v)(I)(bb) of the Act, that—

(i) Uses objective and valid measures of student progress on the assessment, comparing results from the current school year to results from the previous school year, such as student growth percentiles;

(ii) Is aligned with the applicable timelines, within the State-determined maximum number of years, under § 200.13(c)(2) for each English learner to attain English language proficiency after the student's identification as an English learner; and

(iii) May also include a measure of proficiency (e.g., an increase in the percentage of English learners scoring proficient on the English language proficiency assessment required under section 1111(b)(2)(G) of the Act compared to the prior year).

(5) One or more indicators of School Quality or Student Success that meets the requirements of paragraph (c) of this section, which may vary by each grade span and may include one or more of the following:

(i) Student access to and completion of advanced coursework.

(ii) Postsecondary readiness.

(iii) School climate and safety.

(iv) Student engagement.

(v) Educator engagement.

(vi) Any other indicator the State chooses that meets the requirements of paragraph (c) of this section.

(c) A State must demonstrate in its State plan under section 1111 of the Act that each measure it selects to include within any indicator under this section—

(1) Is valid, reliable, and comparable across all LEAs in the State;

(2) Is calculated in the same way for all schools across the State, except that measures within the indicator of Academic Progress and within any indicator of School Quality or Student Success may vary by each grade span; and

(3) For all indicators except the Progress in Achieving English Language Proficiency indicator, is able to be disaggregated for each subgroup of students described in § 200.16(a)(2).

(d) A State must demonstrate in its State plan under section 1111 of the Act that each measure it selects to include within the indicators of Academic Progress and School Quality or Student Success is supported by research that high performance or improvement on such measure is likely to increase student learning (e.g., grade point average, credit accumulation, performance in advanced coursework), or, for a measure within indicators at the high school level, graduation rates, postsecondary enrollment, postsecondary persistence or completion, or career readiness.

(e) A State must demonstrate in its State plan under section 1111 of the Act that each measure it selects to include within the indicators of Academic Progress and School Quality or Student Success aids in the meaningful differentiation of schools under § 200.18 by demonstrating varied results across schools in the State.

7. Section 200.15 is revised to read as follows:

§ 200.15 Participation in assessments and annual measurement of achievement.

(a)(1) To meet the requirements for academic assessments under section 1111(b)(2) of the Act, each State must administer the academic assessments required under section 1111(b)(2)(B)(v) of the Act to all public elementary school and secondary school students in the State and provide for the participation of all such students in those assessments.

(2) For purposes of the statewide accountability system under section 1111(c) of the Act, each State must annually measure the achievement of at least 95 percent of all students, and 95 percent of all students in each subgroup of students described in § 200.16(a)(2), who are enrolled in each public school on the assessments required under section 1111(b)(2)(B)(v)(I) of the Act.

(3) Each State must measure participation rates under paragraph (a)(2) of this section separately in reading/language arts and mathematics.

(b) For purposes of annual meaningful differentiation under § 200.18 and identification of schools under § 200.19, a State must—

(1) Annually calculate any measure in the Academic Achievement indicator under § 200.14(b)(1)

so that the denominator of such measure, for all students and for all students in each subgroup, includes the greater of—

(i) 95 percent of all such students in the grades assessed who are enrolled in the school; or

(ii) The number of all such students enrolled in the school who participated in the assessments required under section 1111(b)(2)(B)(v)(I) of the Act; and

(2) Factor the requirement for 95 percent student participation in assessments under paragraph (a)(2) of this section into its system of annual meaningful differentiation so that missing such requirement, for all students or for any subgroup of students in a school, results in at least one of the following actions:

(i) A lower summative determination in the State's system of annual meaningful differentiation under § 200.18(a)(4).

(ii) The lowest performance level on the Academic Achievement indicator in the State's system of annual meaningful differentiation under § 200.18(a)(2).

(iii) Identification for, and implementation of, a targeted support and improvement plan consistent with the requirements under § 200.22.

(iv) Another State-determined action or set of actions described in its State plan under section 1111 of the Act that is sufficiently rigorous to improve the school's participation rate so that the school meets the requirements under paragraph (a) of this section.

(c) To support the State in meeting the requirements of paragraph (a) of this section—

(1) A school that fails to assess at least 95 percent of all students or 95 percent of each subgroup of students in any year must develop and implement an improvement plan that—

(i) Is developed in partnership with stakeholders (including principals and other school leaders; teachers; and parents and, as appropriate, students);

(ii) Includes one or more strategies to address the reason or reasons for low participation rates in the school and improve participation rates in subsequent years;

(iii) Is reviewed and approved by the LEA prior to implementation; and

(iv) Is monitored, upon submission and implementation, by the LEA; and

(2) An LEA with a significant number or percentage of schools that fail to assess at least 95 percent of all students or 95 percent of each subgroup of students in any year must develop and implement an improvement plan that includes additional actions to support effective implementation of the school-level plans developed under paragraph (c)(1) of this section and that is reviewed and approved by the State.

(3) If a State chooses to identify a school for, and require implementation of, a targeted support and improvement plan under paragraph (b)(2)(iii) of this section, the requirement for such a school to develop and implement a targeted support and improvement plan consistent with § 200.22 fulfills the requirements of this paragraph.

(d)(1) A State must provide a clear and understandable explanation of how it has met the requirements of paragraph (b) of this section in its State plan under section 1111 of the Act and in its description of the State's system for annual meaningful differentiation of schools on its State report card pursuant to section 1111(h)(1)(C)(i)(IV) of the Act.

(2) A State, LEA, or school may not systematically exclude students, including any subgroup of students described in § 200.16(a), from participating in the assessments required under section 1111(b)(2)(B)(v) of the Act.

(3) To count a student who is assessed based on alternate academic achievement standards described in section 1111(b)(1)(E) of the Act as a participant for purposes of meeting the requirements of this section, the State must have guidelines that meet the requirements described in section 1111(b)(2)(D)(ii) of the Act and must ensure that its LEAs adhere to such guidelines.

(4) Consistent with § 200.16(c)(3)(i)(A), a State may count a recently arrived English learner as defined in section 1111(b)(3)(A) of the Act as a participant in the State assessment in reading/language arts for purposes of meeting the requirements in paragraph (a) of this section if he or she takes either the State's English language proficiency assessment under section 1111(b)(2)(G) of the Act or reading/language arts assessment under section 1111(b)(2)(B)(v)(I) of the Act.

8. Section 200.16 is revised to read as follows:

§ 200.16 Subgroups of students.

(a) In general. In establishing long-term goals and measurements of interim progress under § 200.13, measuring performance on each indicator under § 200.14, annually meaningfully differentiating schools under § 200.18, and identifying schools under § 200.19, each State must include the following categories of students consistent with the State's minimum number of students under § 200.17(a)(1):

(1) All public school students.

(2) Each of the following subgroups of students, separately:

(i) Economically disadvantaged students.

(ii) Students from each major racial and ethnic group.

(iii) Children with disabilities, as defined in section 8101(4) of the Act.

(iv) English learners, as defined in section 8101(20) of the Act.

(b) Children with disabilities. With respect to a student previously identified as a child with a disability who has exited special education services as determined by the student's individualized education program (IEP) team, a State may include such a student's performance within the children with disabilities subgroup under paragraph (a)(2)(iii) of this section for not more than two years after the student ceases to be identified as a child with a disability (i.e., the two school years following the year in which the student exits special education services) for purposes of calculating any indicator under § 200.14(b) that uses data from State assessments under section 1111(b)(2)(B)(v)(I) of the Act, provided that the State develops a uniform statewide procedure for

287

doing so that includes all such students and includes them—

(1) For the same State-determined period of time; and

(2) For purposes of determining if a school meets the State's minimum number of students under § 200.17(a)(1) for the children with disabilities subgroup when calculating performance on any such indicator.

(c) English learners. (1) With respect to a student previously identified as an English learner who has achieved English language proficiency consistent with the standardized, statewide exit procedures in section 3113(b)(2) of the Act, a State may include such a student's performance within the English learner subgroup under paragraph (a)(2)(iv) of this section for not more than four years after the student ceases to be identified as an English learner (i.e., the four years following the year in which the student meets the statewide exit criteria, consistent with § 299.19(b)(4)) for purposes of calculating any indicator under § 200.14(b) that uses data from State assessments under section 1111(b)(2)(B)(v)(I) of the Act, if the State develops a uniform statewide procedure for doing so that includes all such students and includes them—

(i) For the same State-determined period of time; and

(ii) For purpose of determining if a school meets the State's minimum number of students under § 200.17(a)(1) for the English learner subgroup when calculating performance on any such indicator.

(2) With respect to an English learner with a disability that precludes assessment of the student in one or more domains of the English language proficiency assessment required under section 1111(b)(2)(G) of the Act such that there are no appropriate accommodations for the affected domain(s) (e.g., a non-verbal English learner who because of an identified disability cannot take the speaking portion of the assessment), as determined, on an individualized basis, by the student's IEP team, 504 team, or individual or team designated by the LEA to make these decisions under Title II of the Americans with Disabilities Act, a State must, in measuring performance against the Progress in Achieving English Language Proficiency indicator, include such a student's performance on the English language proficiency assessment based on the remaining domains in which it is possible to assess the student.

(3) With respect to a recently arrived English learner as defined in section 1111(b)(3)(A) of the Act, a State must include such an English learner's results on the assessments under section 1111(b)(2)(B)(v)(I) of the Act upon enrollment in a school in one of the 50 States or the District of Columbia (hereafter "a school in the United States") in calculating long-term goals and measurements of interim progress under § 200.13(a), annually meaningfully differentiating schools under § 200.18, and identifying schools under § 200.19, except that the State may either—

(i)(A) Exempt such an English learner from the first administration of the reading/language arts assessment;

(B) Exclude such an English learner's results on the assessments under section 1111(b)(2)(B)(v)(I) and 1111(b)(2)(G) of the Act in calculating the Academic Achievement and Progress in Achieving English Language Proficiency indicators in the first year of such an English learner's enrollment in a school in the United States; and

(C) Include such an English learner's results on the assessments under section 1111(b)(2)(B)(v)(I) and 1111(b)(2)(G) of the Act in calculating the Academic Achievement and Progress in Achieving English Language Proficiency indicators in the second year of such an English learner's enrollment in a school in the United States and every year of enrollment thereafter; or

(ii)(A) Assess, and report the performance of, such an English learner on the assessments under section 1111(b)(2)(B)(v)(I) of the Act in each year of such an English learner's enrollment in a school in the United States;

(B) Exclude such an English learner's results on the assessments under section 1111(b)(2)(B)(v)(I) of the Act in calculating the Academic Achievement indicator in the first year of such an English learner's enrollment in a school in the United States;

(C) Include a measure of such an English learner's growth on the assessments under section 1111(b)(2)(B)(v)(I) of the Act in calculating either the Academic Progress indicator or the Academic Achievement indicator in the second year of such an English learner's enrollment in a school in the United States; and

(D) Include a measure of such an English learner's proficiency on the assessments under section 1111(b)(2)(B)(v)(I) of the Act in calculating the Academic Achievement indicator in the third year of such an English learner's enrollment in a school in the United States and every year of enrollment thereafter.

(4) A State may choose one of the exceptions described in paragraphs (c)(3)(i) or (ii) of this section for recently arrived English learners and must—

(i)(A) Apply the same exception to all recently arrived English learners in the State; or

(B) Develop and consistently implement a uniform statewide procedure for all recently arrived English learners that considers students' English language proficiency level at the time of the their identification as English learners and that may, at a State's discretion, consider one or more of the student characteristics under § 200.13(c)(2)(i)(B) through (E) in order to determine whether such an exception applies to an English learner; and

(ii) Report on State and LEA report cards under section 1111(h) of the Act the number and percentage of recently arrived English learners who are exempted from taking such assessments or whose results on such assessments are excluded from any indicator under § 200.14 on the basis of each exception described in paragraphs (c)(3)(i) and (ii) of this section.

(d) Limitations. A State may not include former children with disabilities or former English learners within the applicable subgroups under paragraph (a)(2) of this section for—

(1) Any purpose in the accountability system, except as described in paragraphs (b) and (c)(1) of this section with respect to an indicator that uses data from State assessments under section 1111(b)(2)(B)(v)(I) of the Act and as described in § 200.34(e) with respect to calculating the four-year adjusted cohort graduation rate; or

(2) Purposes of reporting information on State and LEA report cards under section 1111(h) of the Act, except for providing information on the performance of the school, including a school's level of performance under § 200.18(b)(3), on any indicator that uses data from State assessments under section 1111(b)(2)(B)(v)(I) of the Act and for calculating the four-year adjusted cohort graduation rate consistent with § 200.34(e).

(e) State plan. Each State must describe in its State plan under section 1111 of the Act how it has met the requirements of this section, including by describing any subgroups of students used in the accountability system in addition to those in paragraph (a)(2) of this section, its uniform procedure for including former children with disabilities under paragraph (b) of this section and former English learners under paragraph (c)(1) of this section, and its uniform procedure for including recently arrived English learners under paragraph (c)(4) of this section, if applicable.

9. Section 200.17 is revised to read as follows:

§ 200.17 Disaggregation of data.

(a) Statistically sound and reliable information. (1) Based on sound statistical methodology, each State must determine the minimum number of students sufficient to—

(i) Yield statistically reliable information for each purpose for which disaggregated data are used, including purposes of reporting information under section 1111(h) of the Act or purposes of the statewide accountability system under section 1111(c) of the Act; and

(ii) Ensure that, to the maximum extent practicable, each subgroup of students described in § 200.16(a)(2) is included at the school level for annual meaningful differentiation and identification of schools under §§ 200.18 and 200.19.

(2) Such number—

(i) Must be the same number for all students and for each subgroup of students in the State described in § 200.16(a)(2);

(ii) Must be the same number for all purposes of the statewide accountability system under section 1111(c) of the Act, including measuring school performance for each indicator under § 200.14;

(iii) Must not exceed 30 students, unless the State provides a justification for doing so in its State plan under section 1111 of the Act consistent with paragraph (a)(3)(v) of this section; and

(iv) May be a lower number for purposes of reporting under section 1111(h) under the Act than for purposes of the statewide accountability system under section 1111(c) of the Act so long as such number for reporting meets the requirements of paragraph (a)(2)(i) of this section.

(3) A State must include in its State plan under section 1111 of the Act—

(i) A description of how the State's minimum number of students meets the requirements of paragraphs (a)(1) and (2) of this section;

(ii) An explanation of how other components of the statewide accountability system, such as the State's uniform procedure for averaging data under § 200.20(a), interact with the State's minimum number of students to affect the statistical reliability and soundness of accountability data and to ensure the maximum inclusion of all students and each subgroup of students described in § 200.16(a)(2);

(iii) A description of the strategies the State uses to protect the privacy of individual students for each purpose for which disaggregated data is required, including reporting under section 1111(h) of the Act and the statewide accountability system under section 1111(c) of the Act, as required in paragraph (b) of this section;

(iv) Information regarding the number and percentage of all students and students in each subgroup described in § 200.16(a)(2) for whose results schools would not be held accountable in the system of annual meaningful differentiation under § 200.18; and

(v) For a State proposing a minimum number of students exceeding 30, a justification that explains how a minimum number of students exceeding 30 promotes sound, reliable accountability determinations, including data on the number and percentage of schools in the State that would not be held accountable in the system of annual meaningful differentiation under § 200.18 for the results of students in each subgroup described in § 200.16(a)(2) under the minimum number proposed by the State compared to the data on the number and percentage of schools in the State that would not be held accountable for the results of students in each subgroup if the minimum number of students were 30.

(b) Personally identifiable information. (1) A State may not use disaggregated data for one or more subgroups described in § 200.16(a) to report required information under section 1111(h) of the Act if the results would reveal personally identifiable information about an individual student, teacher, principal, or other school leader.

(2) To determine whether the collection and dissemination of disaggregated information would reveal personally identifiable information about an individual student, teacher, principal, or other school leader, a State must apply the requirements under section 444 of the General Education Provisions Act (the Family Educational Rights and Privacy Act of 1974).

(3) Nothing in paragraph (b)(1) or (2) of this section may be construed to abrogate the responsibility of a State to implement the requirements of section 1111(c) of the Act to annually meaningfully differentiate among all public schools in the State on the basis of the performance of all students and each subgroup of students described in section 1111(c)(2) of the Act on all indicators under section 1111(c)(4)(B) of the Act.

(4) Each State and LEA must implement appropriate strategies to protect the privacy of individual students in reporting information under section 1111(h) of the Act and in establishing annual meaningful differentiation of schools in its statewide accountability system under section 1111(c) of the Act on the basis of disaggregated subgroup information.

(c) Inclusion of subgroups in assessments. If a subgroup described in § 200.16(a) is not of sufficient size to produce statistically sound and reliable results, a State must still include students in that subgroup in its State assessments under section 1111(b)(2)(B)(i) of the Act.

(d) Disaggregation at the LEA and State. If the number of students in a subgroup is not statistically sound and reliable at the school level, a State must include those students in disaggregated information at each level for which the number of students is statistically sound and reliable (e.g., the LEA or State level).

10. Section 200.18 is revised to read as follows:

§ 200.18 Annual meaningful differentiation of school performance: Performance levels, data dashboards, summative determinations, and indicator weighting.

(a) Each State must establish a system for annual meaningful differentiation for all public schools, including public charter schools, that—

(1) Includes the performance of all students and each subgroup of students in a school, consistent with §§ 200.16, 200.17, and 200.20(b), on each of the indicators described in § 200.14;

(2) Includes, for each indicator, at least three distinct and discrete levels of school performance that are consistent with attainment of the long-term goals and measurements of interim progress under § 200.13, if applicable, and that are clear and understandable to the public;

(3) Provides information on a school's level of performance (e.g., through a data dashboard) on each indicator described in § 200.14, separately, as part of the description of the State's system for annual meaningful differentiation of schools on LEA report cards under § 200.32;

(4) Results in a single summative determination from among at least three distinct categories for each school, which must meaningfully differentiate between schools based on differing levels of performance on the indicators and which may include the two categories of schools described in § 200.19(a) and (b), to describe a school's overall performance in a clear and understandable manner as part of the description of the State's system for annual meaningful differentiation on LEA report cards under §§ 200.31 and 200.32;

(5) Meets the requirements of § 200.15 to annually measure the achievement of at least 95 percent of all students and 95 percent of all students in each subgroup of students on the assessments described in section 1111(b)(2)(B)(v)(I) of the Act; and

(6) Informs the State's methodology described in § 200.19 for identifying schools for comprehensive support and improvement and for targeted support and improvement, including differentiation of schools with consistently underperforming subgroups of students consistent with paragraph (c) of this section and § 200.19(c).

(b) In providing annual meaningful differentiation among all public schools in the State, including providing a single summative determination for each school under paragraph (a)(4) of this section, a State must—

(1) Afford substantial weight to each of the following indicators, as applicable, under § 200.14:

(i) Academic Achievement indicator.

(ii) Academic Progress indicator.

(iii) Graduation Rate indicator.

(iv) Progress in Achieving English Language Proficiency indicator;

(2) Afford, in the aggregate, much greater weight to the indicators in paragraph (b)(1) of this section than to the indicator or indicators of School Quality or Student Success under § 200.14(b)(5), in the aggregate; and

(3) Within each grade span, afford the same relative weight to each indicator among all schools consistent with paragraph (d)(3) of this section.

(c) To show that its system of annual meaningful differentiation meets the requirements of paragraphs (a) and (b) of this section, a State must—

(1) In identifying schools for comprehensive support and improvement under § 200.19(a), demonstrate that performance on the indicator or indicators of School Quality or Student Success may not be used to change the identity of schools that would otherwise be identified for comprehensive support and improvement without such indicators, unless such a school has made significant progress in the prior year as determined by the State, for all students consistent with § 200.16(a)(1), on at least one of the indicators described in paragraph (b)(1)(i) through (iii) of this section;

(2) In identifying schools for targeted support and improvement under § 200.19(b), demonstrate that performance on the indicator or indicators of School Quality or Student Success may not be used to change the identity of schools that would otherwise be identified for targeted support and improvement without such indicators, unless such a school has made significant progress in the prior year as determined by the State, for each consistently underperforming or low-performing subgroup of students, on at least one of the indicators described in paragraph (b)(1) of this section; and

(3) Demonstrate that a school with a consistently underperforming subgroup of students under § 200.19(c) receives a lower summative determination under paragraph (a)(4) of this section than it would have otherwise received if it did not have any consistently underperforming subgroups of students; and

(d)(1) A State must demonstrate in its State plan under section 1111 of the Act how it has met the requirements of this section, including a description of—

(i) How a State calculates the performance levels on each indicator and a summative determination for each school under paragraph (a) of this section;

(ii) How the State's methodology under this section and § 200.19, including the weighting of indicators under paragraphs (b) and (c) of this section, will ensure that schools with low performance on the indicators described in paragraph (b)(1) of this section are more likely to be identified for comprehensive support and improvement or targeted support and improvement; and

(iii) Any different methodology, if a State chooses to develop such methodology, that the State uses to include all public schools in its system of annual meaningful differentiation consistent with paragraph (a) of this section, such as—

(A) Schools in which no grade level is assessed under the State's academic assessment system (e.g., P-2 schools), although the State is not required to administer a standardized assessment to meet this requirement;

(B) Schools with variant grade configurations (e.g., P-12 schools);

(C) Small schools in which the total number of students who can be included in any indicator under § 200.14 is less than the minimum number of students established by the State under § 200.17(a)(1), consistent with a State's uniform procedures for averaging data under § 200.20(a), if applicable;

(D) Schools that are designed to serve special populations (e.g., students receiving alternative programming in alternative educational settings; students living in local institutions for neglected or delinquent children, including juvenile justice facilities; students enrolled in State public schools for the deaf or blind; and recently arrived English learners enrolled in public schools for newcomer students); and

(E) Newly opened schools that do not have multiple years of data, consistent with a State's uniform procedure for averaging data under § 200.20(a), if applicable, for at least one indicator (e.g., a newly opened high school that has not yet graduated its first cohort for students).

(2) In meeting the requirement in paragraph (b)(1) of this section to afford substantial weight to certain indicators, a State is not required to afford each such indicator the same substantial weight.

(3) If a school does not meet the State's minimum number of students under § 200.17(a)(1) for the English learner subgroup, a State must—

(i) Exclude the Progress in Achieving English Language Proficiency indicator from the annual meaningful differentiation for such a school under paragraph (a) of this section; and

(ii) Afford the Academic Achievement, Academic Progress, Graduation Rate, and School Quality or Student Success indicators the same relative weights in such a school as are afforded to such indicators in a school that meets the State's minimum number of students for the English learner subgroup.

11. Section 200.19 is revised to read as follows:

§ 200.19 Identification of schools.

(a) Schools identified for comprehensive support and improvement. Based on its system for annual meaningful differentiation under § 200.18, each State must establish and describe in its State plan under section 1111 of the Act a methodology, including a timeline consistent with paragraph (d) of this section, to identify one statewide category of schools for comprehensive support and improvement under § 200.21, which must include the following three types of schools:

(1) Lowest-performing. Not less than the lowest-performing five percent of all schools in the State participating under subpart A of this part, consistent with the requirements of § 200.18(a)(4).

(2) Low high school graduation rate. Any public high school in the State with a four-year adjusted cohort graduation rate, as calculated under § 200.34(a), at or below 67 percent, or below a higher percentage selected by the State.

(3) Chronically low-performing subgroup. Any school participating under subpart A of this part and identified pursuant to paragraph (b)(2) of this section that has not improved, as defined by the State, after implementing a targeted support and improvement plan over a State-determined number of years consistent with paragraph (d)(1)(i) of this section.

(b) Schools identified for targeted support and improvement. Based on its system for annual meaningful differentiation under § 200.18, each State must establish and describe in its State plan under section 1111 of the Act a methodology to identify schools for targeted support and improvement under § 200.22, which must include the following two types of schools:

(1) Consistently underperforming subgroup. Any school that is not identified under paragraph (a) of this section with one or more consistently underperforming subgroups of students, as defined in paragraph (c) of this section and consistent with §§ 200.16 and 200.17.

(2) Low-performing subgroup. Any school that is not identified under paragraph (a) of this section in which one or more subgroups of students is performing, using the State's methodology for identifying the lowest-performing schools under paragraph (a)(1) of this section, at or below the performance of all students in any school identified under paragraph (a)(1) of this section. Schools identified under this paragraph must receive additional targeted support in accordance with section 1111(d)(2)(C) of the Act.

(c) Methodology to identify consistently underperforming subgroups. The description required by paragraph (b)(1) of this section must demonstrate that the State's methodology to identify schools with one or more consistently underperforming subgroups of students under paragraph (b)(1) of this section—

(1) Considers each school's performance among each subgroup of students in the school consistent with §§ 200.16 and 200.17, over no more than two years, unless the State demonstrates that a longer timeframe will better support low-performing subgroups of students to make significant progress in achieving the State's long-term goals and measurements of interim progress in order to close statewide proficiency and graduation rate gaps, consistent with section 1111(c)(4)(A)(i)(III) of the Act and § 200.13;

(2) Is based on all indicators under § 200.14 used for annual meaningful differentiation under § 200.18 consistent with the requirements for weighting of indicators described in § 200.18(b); and

(3) Defines a consistently underperforming subgroup of students in a uniform manner across all LEAs in the State, which must include—

(i) A subgroup of students that is not meeting at least one of the State's measurements of interim progress or is not on track to meet at least one of the State-designed long-term goals under § 200.13 or is performing below a State-determined threshold on an indicator for which the State is not required to establish long-term goals under § 200.13; or

(ii) Another State-determined definition.

(d) Timeline. (1) A State must identify—

(i) Each type of school for comprehensive support and improvement under paragraphs (a)(1) through (3) of this section at least once every three years, beginning with identification for the 2018-2019 school year, except that identification of schools with chronically low-performing subgroups under paragraph (a)(3) of this section is not required for the 2018-2019 school year;

(ii) Schools with one or more consistently underperforming subgroups of students for targeted support and improvement under paragraph (b) of this section annually, beginning with identification for the 2019-2020 school year; and

(iii) Schools with one or more low-performing subgroups of students for targeted support and improvement under paragraph (b)(2) of this section—

(A) Beginning with identification for the 2018-2019 school year;

(B) At least once every three years; and

(C) With such identification occurring in each year, consistent with paragraph (d)(1)(i) of this section, in which the State identifies schools for comprehensive support and improvement.

(2) Each year for which a State must identify schools for comprehensive or targeted support and improvement, it must—

(i) Make such identification as soon as possible, but no later than the beginning of each school year; and

(ii) For purposes of identifying schools under this section, use data from the preceding school year (e.g., data from the 2017-2018 school year inform identification for the 2018-2019 school year), and, at the State's discretion, data from earlier school years, consistent with § 200.20(a), except that a State is not required to use adjusted cohort graduation rate data from the preceding school year if the State uses data from the school year immediately prior to the preceding school year (e.g., data from the 2016-2017 school year inform identification for the 2018-2019 school year).

| Types of schools | Description | Statutory provision | Regulatory provision | Timeline for identification | Initial year of identification |

Category: Comprehensive Support and Improvement					
Lowest-Performing	Lowest-performing five percent of schools in the State participating in Title I	1111(c)(4)(D)(i)(I)	§ 200.19(a)(1)	At least once every three years	2018-2019.
Low High School Graduation Rate	Any public high school in the State with a four-year adjusted cohort graduation rate at or below 67 percent, or below a higher percentage selected by the State, over no more than three years	Section 1111(c)(4)(D)(i)(II)	§ 200.19(a)(2)	At least once every three years	2018-2019.
Chronically Low-Performing Subgroup	Any school participating in Title I that (a) was identified for targeted support and improvement because it had a subgroup of students performing at or below the performance of all students in the lowest-performing schools and (b) did not improve after implementing a targeted support and improvement plan over a State-determined number of years	Section 1111(c)(4)(D)(i)(III), 1111(d)(3)(A)(i)(II)	§ 200.19(a)(3)	At least once every three years	State-determined.
Category: Targeted Support and Improvement					
Consistently Underperforming Subgroup	Any school with one or more consistently underperforming subgroups	Section 1111(c)(4)(C)(iii), 1111(d)(2)(A)(i)	§ 200.19(b)(1), (c)	Annually	2019-2020.
Low-Performing Subgroup	Any school in which one or more subgroups of students is performing at or below the performance of all students in the lowest-performing schools. These schools must receive additional targeted support under the law	Section 1111(d)(2)(D)	§ 200.19(b)(2)	At least once every three years	2018-2019.
	If this type of school is a Title I school that does not improve after implementing a targeted support and improvement plan over a State-determined number of years, it becomes a school that has a chronically low-performing subgroup and is identified for comprehensive support and improvement				

12. Section § 200.20 is revised to read as follows:

§ 200.20 Data procedures for annual meaningful differentiation and identification of schools.

(a) Averaging data. For the purposes of calculating the indicators under § 200.14 that are used for annual meaningful differentiation under § 200.18, meeting the requirement under § 200.15(b)(2), and identifying high schools with low graduation rates under § 200.19(a)(2), a State may establish a uniform procedure for averaging school-level data that includes one or both of the following:

(1) Combining data across school years. (i) A State may combine data across up to three school years.

(ii) If a State combines data across school years for these purposes, the State must—

(A) Use the same uniform procedure for combining data from the school year for which the identification is made with data from one or two school years immediately preceding that school year for all public schools, including by summing the total number of students in each subgroup of students described in § 200.16(a)(2) across all school years when calculating a school's performance on each indicator under § 200.14 and determining whether the subgroup meets the State's minimum number of students described in § 200.17(a)(1);

(B) Report data for a single school year, without combining, on report cards under section 1111(h) of the Act; and

(C) Explain its uniform procedure for combining data in its State plan under section 1111 of the Act and specify that such procedure is used in its description of the indicators used for annual meaningful differentiation on the State report card pursuant to section 1111(h)(1)(C)(i)(III) of the Act.

(2) Combining data across grades. (i) A State may combine data across grades in a school.

(ii) If a State combines data across grades for these purposes, the State must—

(A) Use the same uniform procedure for combining data for all public schools;

(B) Report data for each grade in the school on report cards under section 1111(h) of the Act; and

(C) Explain its uniform procedure for combining data in its State plan under section 1111 of the Act, and specify that such procedure is used in its description of the indicators used for annual meaningful differentiation in its accountability system on the State report card pursuant to section 1111(h)(1)(C)(i)(III) of the Act.

(b) Partial enrollment. (1) In calculating school performance on each of the indicators for the purposes of annual meaningful differentiation under § 200.18 and identification of schools under § 200.19, a State must include all students who were enrolled in the same school within an LEA for at least half of the academic year.

(2) A State may not use the performance of a student who has been enrolled in the same school within an LEA for less than half of the academic year in its system of annual meaningful differentiation and identification of schools, except that—

(i) An LEA must include such student in calculating the Graduation Rate indicator under § 200.14(b)(3), if applicable;

(ii) If such student exited a high school without receiving a regular high school diploma and without transferring to another high school that grants a regular high school diploma during such school year, the LEA must assign such student, for purposes of calculating the Graduation Rate indicator and consistent with the approach established by the State under § 200.34, to either—

(A) The high school in which such student was enrolled for the greatest proportion of school days while enrolled in grades 9 through 12; or

(B) The high school in which the student was most recently enrolled; and

(iii) All students, regardless of their length of enrollment in a school within an LEA during the academic year, must be included for purposes of reporting on the State and LEA report cards under section 1111(h) of the Act for such school year.

13. Section 200.21 is revised to read as follows:

§ 200.21 Comprehensive support and improvement.

(a) In general. A State must notify each LEA in the State that serves one or more schools identified for comprehensive support and improvement under § 200.19(a) of such identification as soon as possible, but no later than the beginning of the school year for which such school is identified.

(b) Notice. Upon receiving the notification from the State under paragraph (a) of this section, an LEA must promptly notify the parents of each student enrolled in the school of the school's identification for comprehensive support and improvement, including, at a minimum, the reason or reasons for the identification under § 200.19(a) (e.g., low performance of all students, low graduation rate, chronically low-performing subgroup), and an explanation of how parents can become involved in the needs assessment under paragraph (c) of this section and in developing and implementing the comprehensive support and improvement plan described in paragraph (d) of this section. Such notice must—

(1) Be in an understandable and uniform format;

(2) Be, to the extent practicable, written in a language that parents can understand or, if it is not practicable to provide written translations to a parent with limited English proficiency, be orally translated for such parent; and

(3) Be, upon request by a parent who is an individual with a disability as defined by the Americans with Disabilities Act, 42 U.S.C. 12102, provided in an alternative format accessible to that parent.

(c) Needs assessment. For each identified school, an LEA must conduct, in partnership with stakeholders (including principals and other school leaders, teachers, and parents), a comprehensive needs assessment that examines, at a minimum—

(1) Academic achievement data on each of the assessments required under section 1111(b)(2)(B)(v) of the Act for all students in the school, including for each subgroup of students described in § 200.16(a)(2);

(2) The school's performance, including among subgroups of students described in § 200.16(a)(2), on the long-term goals and measurements of interim progress and indicators described in §§ 200.13 and 200.14;

(3) The reason or reasons the school was identified for comprehensive support and improvement

under § 200.19(a);

(4) The school's unmet needs, including those with respect to—

(i) Students (e.g., wrap-around support);

(ii) School leadership and instructional staff (e.g., professional development, working conditions, time for planning, career ladder, and leadership opportunities);

(iii) Quality of the instructional program;

(iv) Family and community involvement;

(v) School climate; and

(vi) Distribution of resources (e.g., based on the State periodic review of resources under § 200.23(a)); and

(5) At the LEA's discretion, the school's performance on additional, locally selected measures that are not included in the State's system of annual meaningful differentiation under § 200.18 and that affect student outcomes in the identified school.

(d) Comprehensive support and improvement plan. Each LEA must, with respect to each school identified by the State for comprehensive support and improvement, develop and implement a comprehensive support and improvement plan for the school to improve student outcomes that—

(1) Is developed in partnership with stakeholders (including principals and other school leaders; teachers; parents and, as appropriate, students; and, for LEAs affected by section 8538 of the Act, Indian tribes), as demonstrated, at a minimum, by describing in the plan how—

(i) Early stakeholder input was solicited and taken into account in the development of the plan, including any changes made as a result of such input; and

(ii) Stakeholders will participate in an ongoing manner in the plan's implementation;

(2) Includes and is based on the results of the needs assessment described in paragraph (c) of this section;

(3) Includes one or more interventions (e.g., increasing access to effective teachers or adopting incentives to recruit and retain effective teachers; increasing or redesigning instructional time; interventions based on data from early warning indicator systems; reorganizing the school to implement a new instructional model; strategies designed to increase diversity by attracting and retaining students from varying socioeconomic, racial, and ethnic backgrounds; replacing school leadership with leaders who are trained for or have a record of success in low-performing schools; increasing access to high-quality preschool (in the case of an elementary school); converting the school to a public charter school; changing school governance; closing the school; and, in the case of a public charter school, working in coordination with the applicable authorized public chartering agency, revoking or non-renewing the school's charter by its authorized public chartering agency consistent with State charter school law and the terms of such a school's charter) to improve student outcomes in the school that—

(i) Meet the definition of "evidence-based" under section 8101(21) of the Act;

(ii) Are supported, to the extent practicable, by evidence from a sample population or setting that overlaps with the population or setting of the school to be served;

(iii) Are supported, to the extent practicable, by the strongest level of evidence that is available and appropriate to meet the needs identified in the needs assessment under paragraph (c) of this section;

(iv) May be selected from a non-exhaustive list of evidence-based interventions if such a list is established by the State, and must be selected from an exhaustive list of evidence-based interventions if such a list is established by the State, consistent with § 200.23(c)(2);

(v) May be an evidence-based intervention determined by the State, consistent with State law, as described in section 1111(d)(1)(3)(B)(ii) of the Act and § 200.23(c)(3); and

(vi) May include differentiated improvement activities that utilize interventions that meet the definition of "evidence-based" under section 8101(21) of the Act in any high school identified under § 200.19(a)(2) that predominantly serves students—

(A) Returning to education after having exited secondary school without a regular high school diploma; or

(B) Who, based on their grade or age, are significantly off track to accumulate sufficient academic credits to meet high school graduation requirements, as established by the State;

(4) Identifies and addresses resource inequities, by—

(i) Including a review of LEA- and school-level resources among schools and, as applicable, within schools with respect to—

(A) Differences in rates at which low-income and minority students are taught by ineffective, out-of-field, or inexperienced teachers identified by the State and LEA consistent with sections 1111(g)(1)(B) and 1112(b)(2) of the Act;

(B) Access to advanced coursework, including accelerated coursework as reported annually consistent with section 1111(h)(1)(C)(viii) of the Act;

(C) Access in elementary schools to full-day kindergarten programs and to preschool programs as reported annually consistent with section 1111(h)(1)(C)(viii) of the Act;

(D) Access to specialized instructional support personnel, as defined in section 8101(47) of the Act, including school counselors, school social workers, school psychologists, other qualified professional personnel, and school librarians; and

(E) Per-pupil expenditures of Federal, State, and local funds required to be reported annually consistent with section 1111(h)(1)(C)(x) of the Act; and

(ii) Including, at the LEA's discretion, a review of LEA- and school-level budgeting and resource allocation with respect to resources described in paragraph (d)(4)(i) of this section and the availability and access to any other resource provided by the LEA or school, such as instructional materials and technology;

(5) Must be fully implemented in the school year for which such school is identified, except that an LEA may have a planning year during which the LEA must carry out the needs assessment

required under paragraph (c) of this section and develop the comprehensive support and improvement plan to prepare for successful implementation of interventions required under the plan during the planning year or, at the latest, the first full day of the school year following the school year for which the school was identified;

(6) Must be made publicly available by the LEA, including to parents consistent with the requirements under paragraphs (b)(1) through (3) of this section; and

(7) Must be approved by the school identified for comprehensive support and improvement, the LEA, and the State.

(e) Plan approval and monitoring. The State must, upon receipt from an LEA of a comprehensive support and improvement plan under paragraph (d) of this section—

(1) Review such plan against the requirements of this section and approve the plan in a timely manner, as determined by the State, taking all actions necessary to ensure that the school and LEA are able to meet all of the requirements of paragraphs (a) through (d) of this section to develop and implement the plan within the required timeframe; and

(2) Monitor and periodically review each LEA's implementation of such plan.

(f) Exit criteria. (1) To ensure continued progress to improve student academic achievement and school success, the State must establish, make publicly available, and describe in its State plan under section 1111 of the Act, uniform statewide exit criteria for each school implementing a comprehensive support and improvement plan under this section. Such exit criteria must, at a minimum, require that the school—

(i) Improve student outcomes; and

(ii) No longer meet the criteria under which the school was identified under § 200.19(a) within a State-determined number of years (not to exceed four years).

(2) If a school does not meet the exit criteria established under paragraph (f)(1) of this section within the State-determined number of years, the State must, at a minimum, require the LEA to conduct a new comprehensive needs assessment that meets the requirements under paragraph (c) of this section.

(3) Based on the results of the new needs assessment, the LEA must, with respect to each school that does not meet the exit criteria, amend its comprehensive support and improvement plan described in paragraph (d) of this section, in partnership with stakeholders consistent with the requirements in paragraph (d)(1) of this section, to—

(i) Address the reasons the school did not meet the exit criteria, including whether the school implemented the interventions with fidelity and sufficient intensity, and the results of the new needs assessment;

(ii) Update how it will continue to address previously identified resource inequities and to identify and address any newly identified resource inequities consistent with the requirements in paragraph (d)(4) of this section; and

(iii) Include implementation of additional interventions in the school that may address school-level operations (which may include staffing, budgeting, and changes to the school day and year) and that must—

(A) Be determined by the State, which may include requiring an intervention from among any State-established evidence-based interventions or a State-approved list of evidence-based interventions, consistent with State law and § 200.23(c)(2) and (3);

(B) Be more rigorous, including one or more evidence-based interventions in the plan that are supported by strong or moderate evidence, consistent with section 8101(21)(A) of the Act;

(C) Be supported, to the extent practicable, by evidence from a sample population or setting that overlaps with the population or setting of the school to be served; and

(D) Must be described in its State plan under section 1111 of the Act.

(4) Each LEA must—

(i) Make the amended comprehensive support and improvement plan described in paragraph (f)(3) of this section publicly available, including to parents consistent with paragraphs (b)(1) through (3) of this section; and

(ii) Submit the amended plan to the State in a timely manner, as determined by the State.

(5) After the LEA submits the amended plan to the State, the State must—

(i) Review and approve the amended plan, and any additional amendments to the plan, consistent with the review process required under paragraph (e)(1) of this section; and

(ii) Increase its monitoring, support, and periodic review of each LEA's implementation of such plan.

(g) State discretion for small high schools. With respect to any high school in the State identified for comprehensive support and improvement under § 200.19(a)(2), the State may, in the case of such a school that has a total enrollment of less than 100 students, permit the LEA to forego development or implementation of a school support and improvement plan or any implementation of improvement activities required under this section.

(h) Public school choice. Consistent with section 1111(d)(1)(D) of the Act, an LEA may provide all students enrolled in a school identified by the State for comprehensive support and improvement under § 200.19(a) with the option to transfer to another public school that is served by the LEA and that is not identified for comprehensive support and improvement under § 200.19(a), unless such an option is prohibited by State law or inconsistent with a Federal desegregation order, in which case the LEA must petition and obtain court approval for such transfers.

(Approved by the Office of Management and Budget under control number 1810-0581)

(Authority: 20 U.S.C. 6311(d); 20 U.S.C. 6571(a); 20 U.S.C. 1221e-3; 20 U.S.C. 3474; 42 U.S.C. 12102)

14. Section 200.22 is revised to read as follows:

§ 200.22 Targeted support and improvement.

(a) In general. With respect to each school that the State identifies under § 200.19(b) or, as applicable, under § 200.15(b)(2)(iii), as a school requiring targeted support and improvement, each State must—

(1) Notify as soon as possible, but no later than the beginning of the school year for which such school is identified, each LEA serving such school of the identification; and

(2) Ensure such LEA provides notification to each school identified for targeted support and improvement, including the reason for identification (i.e., the subgroup or subgroups described in § 200.16(a)(2) that are identified as consistently underperforming under § 200.19(b)(1), the subgroup or subgroups that are low-performing under § 200.19(b)(2) and will receive additional targeted support, and, at the State's discretion, the subgroup or subgroups that are identified under § 200.15(b)(2)(iii)), no later than the beginning of the school year for which such school is identified.

(b) Notice. (1) Upon receiving the notification from the State under paragraph (a)(1) of this section, the LEA must promptly notify the parents of each student enrolled in the school of the school's identification for targeted support and improvement, consistent with the requirements under § 200.21(b)(1) through (3).

(2) The notice must include—

(i) The reason or reasons for the identification (i.e., which subgroup or subgroups are consistently underperforming under § 200.19(b)(1), which subgroup or subgroups are low-performing under § 200.19(b)(2) and will receive additional targeted support, and any subgroup or subgroups identified under § 200.15(b)(2)(iii) if the State chooses to require such schools to implement targeted support and improvement plans); and

(ii) An explanation of how parents can become involved in developing and implementing the targeted support and improvement plan described in paragraph (c) of this section.

(c) Targeted support and improvement plan. Upon receiving the notification from the LEA under paragraph (a)(2) of this section, each school must develop and implement a school-level targeted support and improvement plan to address the reason or reasons for identification and improve student outcomes for the lowest-performing students in the school that—

(1) Is developed in partnership with stakeholders (including principals and other school leaders; teachers; and parents and, as appropriate, students) as demonstrated by, at a minimum, describing in the plan how—

(i) Early stakeholder input was solicited and taken into account in the development of each component of the plan, including any changes made as a result of such input; and

(ii) Stakeholders will have an opportunity to participate in an ongoing manner in such plan's implementation;

(2) Is designed to improve student performance for the lowest-performing students on each of the indicators under § 200.14 that led to the identification of the school for targeted support and improvement or, in the case of schools implementing targeted support and improvement plans consistent with § 200.15(b)(2)(iii), to improve student participation in the assessments required

under section 1111(b)(2)(B)(v)(I) of the Act;

(3) Takes into consideration—

(i) The school's performance on the long-term goals and measurements of interim progress and the indicators described in §§ 200.13 and 200.14, including student academic achievement on each of the assessments required under section 1111(b)(2)(B)(v) of the Act; and

(ii) At the school's discretion, the school's performance on additional, locally selected measures that are not included in the State's system of annual meaningful differentiation under § 200.18 and that affect student outcomes in the identified school;

(4) Includes one or more interventions to address the reason or reasons for identification and improve student outcomes for the lowest-performing students in the school that—

(i) Meet the definition of "evidence-based" under section 8101(21) of the Act;

(ii) Are supported, to the extent practicable, by evidence from a sample population or setting that overlaps with the population or setting of the school to be served;

(iii) Are supported, to the extent practicable, by the strongest level of evidence that is available and appropriate to improve student outcomes for the lowest-performing students in the school; and

(iv) May be selected from a non-exhaustive list of evidence-based interventions if such a list is established by the State, and must be selected from an exhaustive list of evidence-based interventions if such a list is established by the State, consistent with § 200.23(c)(2);

(5) Must be fully implemented in the school year for which such school is identified, except that a school identified under § 200.19(b) may have a planning year during which the school must develop the targeted support and improvement plan and complete other activities necessary to prepare for successful implementation of interventions required under the plan during the planning year or, at the latest, the first full day of the school year following the school year for which the school was identified;

(6) Is submitted to the LEA for approval, pursuant to paragraph (d) of this section;

(7) In the case of a school with low-performing subgroups as described in § 200.19(b)(2), and to ensure such school receives additional targeted support as required under section 1111(d)(2)(C) of the Act, identifies and addresses resource inequities by—

(i) Including a review of LEA- and school-level resources among schools and, as applicable, within schools with respect to—

(A) Differences in rates at which low-income and minority students are taught by ineffective, out-of-field, or inexperienced teachers identified by the State and LEA consistent with sections 1111(g)(1)(B) and 1112(b)(2) of the Act;

(B) Access to advanced coursework, including accelerated coursework as reported annually consistent with section 1111(h)(1)(C)(viii) of the Act;

(C) Access in elementary schools to full-day kindergarten programs and to preschool programs as reported annually consistent with section 1111(h)(1)(C)(viii) of the Act;

(D) Access to specialized instructional support personnel, as defined in section 8101(47) of the Act, including school counselors, school social workers, school psychologists, other qualified professional personnel, and school librarians; and

(E) Per-pupil expenditures of Federal, State, and local funds required to be reported annually consistent with section 1111(h)(1)(C)(x) of the Act; and

(ii) Including, at the school's discretion, a review of LEA- and school-level budgeting and resource allocation with respect to resources described in paragraph (c)(7)(i) of this section and the availability and access to any other resource provided by the LEA or school, such as instructional materials and technology; and

(8) For any school operating a schoolwide program under section 1114 of the Act, addresses the needs identified by the needs assessment required under section 1114(b)(6) of the Act.

(d) Plan approval and monitoring. The LEA must, upon receipt of a targeted support and improvement plan under paragraph (c) of this section from a school—

(1) Review each plan against the requirements of this section and approve such plan in a timely manner, taking all actions necessary to ensure that each school is able to meet all of the requirements under paragraph (c) of this section within the required timeframe;

(2) Make the approved plan, and any amendments to the plan, publicly available, including to parents consistent with the requirements under § 200.21(b)(1) through (3); and

(3) Monitor the school's implementation of the plan.

(e) Exit criteria. Except with respect to schools described in paragraph (f) of this section, the LEA must establish and make publicly available, including to parents consistent with the requirements under § 200.21(b)(1) through (3), uniform exit criteria for schools identified by the State under § 200.19(b) and, as applicable, § 200.15(b)(2)(iii), and use such criteria to make one of the following determinations with respect to each such school after a number of years as determined by the LEA:

(1) The school has successfully implemented its targeted support and improvement plan such that it no longer meets the criteria for identification and has improved student outcomes for its lowest-performing students, including each subgroup of students that was identified as consistently underperforming under § 200.19(b)(1) or low-performing under § 200.19(b)(2), or, in the case of a school implementing a targeted support and improvement plan consistent with § 200.15(b)(2)(iii), has met the requirement under § 200.15(a)(2) for student participation in the assessments required under section 1111(b)(2)(B)(v)(I) of the Act, and will exit targeted support and improvement status.

(2) The school has unsuccessfully implemented its targeted support and improvement plan such that it has not improved student outcomes for its lowest-performing students, including each subgroup of students that was identified as consistently underperforming under § 200.19(b)(1) or low-performing under § 200.19(b)(2), or, in the case of a school implementing a targeted support and improvement plan consistent with § 200.15(b)(2)(iii), has failed to meet the requirement under § 200.15(a)(2) for student participation in the assessments required under section 1111(b)(2)(B)(v)(I) of the Act, in which case the LEA must subsequently—

(i) Require the school to amend its targeted support and improvement plan to include additional actions that continue to meet all requirements under paragraph (c) of this section and address the reasons the school did not meet the exit criteria, and encourage interventions that either meet a higher level of evidence under paragraph (c)(4) of this section than the interventions included in the school's original plan or increase the intensity of effective interventions in the school's original plan;

(ii) Review and approve the school's amended plan consistent with the review process required under paragraph (d)(1) of this section; and

(iii) Increase its monitoring and support of such school's implementation of the plan.

(f) Special rule for schools with low-performing subgroups. (1) With respect to any school participating under subpart A of this part that has one or more low-performing subgroups as described in § 200.19(b)(2), the State must establish, make publicly available, and describe in its State plan under section 1111 of the Act, uniform statewide exit criteria that, at a minimum, ensure each such school—

(i) Improves student outcomes for its lowest-performing students, including each subgroup of students identified as low-performing under § 200.19(b)(2); and

(ii) No longer meets the criteria for identification under § 200.19(b)(2).

(2) If a school does not satisfy the exit criteria established under paragraph (f)(1) of this section within a State-determined timeline, the State must identify the school for comprehensive support and improvement under § 200.19(a)(3), consistent with § 200.19(d)(1)(i).

(Approved by the Office of Management and Budget under control number 1810-0581)

(Authority: 20 U.S.C. 6311(d); 20 U.S.C. 6571(a); 20 U.S.C. 1221e-3; 20 U.S.C. 3474)

15. Add § 200.23 to read as follows:

§ 200.23 State responsibilities to support continued improvement.

(a) State support. Each State must include in its State plan under section 1111 of the Act a description of how it will, with respect to each LEA in the State serving a significant number or percentage of schools identified for comprehensive or targeted support and improvement under § 200.19, periodically review resources, including the resources listed in § 200.21(d)(4)(i)(A) through (E), available in such LEAs as compared to all other LEAs in the State and in schools in those LEAs as compared to all other schools in the State, consider any inequities identified under §§ 200.21(d)(4) and 200.22(c)(7), and, to the extent practicable, address any identified inequities in resources.

(b) State technical assistance. Each State must include in its State plan under section 1111 of the Act a description of technical assistance it will provide to each LEA in the State serving a significant number or percentage of schools identified for comprehensive or targeted support and improvement, including, at a minimum, a description of how it will provide technical assistance to LEAs to ensure the effective implementation of evidence-based interventions and support and increase their capacity to successfully—

(1) Develop and implement comprehensive support and improvement plans that meet the requirements of § 200.21;

(2) Ensure schools develop and implement targeted support and improvement plans that meet the requirements of § 200.22; and

(3) Develop or use tools related to—

(i) Conducting a school-level needs assessment consistent with § 200.21(c);

(ii) Selecting evidence-based interventions consistent with §§ 200.21(d)(3) and 200.22(c)(4); and

(iii) Reviewing resource allocation and identifying strategies for addressing any identified resource inequities consistent with §§ 200.21(d)(4) and 200.22(c)(7).

(c) Additional improvement actions. Consistent with State law, the State may—

(1) Take action to initiate additional improvement in any LEA, or in any authorized public chartering agency consistent with State charter school law, that serves a significant number or percentage of schools that are identified for comprehensive support and improvement under § 200.19(a) and are not meeting exit criteria established under § 200.21(f) or a significant number or percentage of schools identified for targeted support and improvement under § 200.19(b), which may include—

(i) LEA-level actions such as reducing the LEA's operational or budgetary autonomy; removing one or more schools from the jurisdiction of the LEA; or restructuring the LEA, including changing its governance or initiating State takeover of the LEA;

(ii) In the case of an authorized public chartering agency, monitoring, limiting, or revoking the authority of the agency to issue, renew, and revoke school charters; and

(iii) School-level actions such as reorganizing a school to implement a new instructional model; replacing school leadership with leaders who are trained for or have a record of success in low-performing schools; converting a school to a public charter school; changing school governance; closing a school; or, in the case of a public charter school, working in coordination with the applicable authorized public chartering agency, revoking or non-renewing the school's charter consistent with State charter school law and the terms of the school's charter;

(2) Establish and approve an exhaustive or non-exhaustive list of evidence-based interventions consistent with the definition of evidenced-based under section 8101(21) of the Act for use in schools implementing comprehensive support and improvement or targeted support and improvement plans under § 200.21 or § 200.22;

(3) Develop one or more evidence-based, State-determined interventions consistent with section 1111(d)(3)(B)(ii) of the Act that can be used by LEAs in a school identified for comprehensive support and improvement under § 200.19(a), such as whole-school reform models; and

(4) Require that LEAs submit to the State for review and approval, in a timely manner, the amended targeted support and improvement plan for each school in the LEA described in § 200.22(e)(2)(i) prior to the approval of such plan by the LEA.

16. Add § 200.24 to read as follows:

§ 200.24 Resources to support continued improvement.

(a) In general. (1) A State must allocate school improvement funds that it reserves under section 1003(a) of the Act to LEAs to serve schools implementing comprehensive or targeted support and improvement plans under §§ 200.21 or 200.22, except that such funds may not be used to serve schools implementing targeted support and improvement plans consistent with § 200.15(b)(2)(iii).

(2) An LEA may apply for school improvement funds if—

(i) It has one or more schools identified for comprehensive support and improvement under § 200.19(a) or targeted support and improvement under § 200.19(b) consistent with paragraph (a)(1) of this section; and

(ii) It applies to serve each school in the LEA identified for comprehensive support and improvement that it has sufficient capacity to serve before applying to serve any school in the LEA identified for targeted support and improvement.

(b) LEA application. To receive school improvement funds under paragraph (a) of this section, an LEA must submit an application to the State to serve one or more schools identified for comprehensive or targeted support and improvement. In addition to any other information that the State may require, such an application must include each of the following:

(1) A description of one or more evidence-based interventions that are based on strong, moderate, or promising evidence as defined under section 8101(21)(A) of the Act and that will be implemented in each school the LEA proposes to serve.

(2) A description of how the LEA will carry out its responsibilities under §§ 200.21 and 200.22 for schools it will serve with funds under this section, including how the LEA will—

(i) Develop and implement a comprehensive support and improvement plan that meets the requirements of § 200.21 for each school identified under § 200.19(a), for which the LEA receives school improvement funds to serve; and

(ii) Support each school identified under § 200.19(b), for which the LEA receives school improvement funds to serve, in developing and implementing a targeted support and improvement plan that meets the requirements of § 200.22.

(3) A budget indicating how it will allocate school improvement funds among schools identified for comprehensive support and improvement and targeted support and improvement that it proposes to serve.

(4) The LEA's plan to monitor schools for which the LEA receives school improvement funds, including the LEA's plan to increase monitoring of a school that does not meet the exit criteria consistent with §§ 200.21(f), 200.22(e), or 200.22(f).

(5) A description of the rigorous review process the LEA will use to recruit, screen, select, and evaluate any external partners with which the LEA will partner in carrying out activities supported with school improvement funds.

(6) A description of how the LEA will align other Federal, State, and local resources to carry out the activities supported with school improvement funds.

(7) A description of how the LEA will sustain effective activities in schools after funding under this section is complete.

(8) As appropriate, a description of how the LEA will modify practices and policies to provide operational flexibility, including with respect to school budgeting and staffing, that enables full and effective implementation of comprehensive support and improvement and targeted support and improvement plans.

(9) For any LEA that plans to use the first year of its school improvement funds for planning activities in a school that it will serve, a description of the activities that will be supported with school improvement funds, the timeline for implementing those activities, how such timeline will ensure full implementation of the comprehensive or targeted support and improvement plan consistent with §§ 200.21(d)(5) and 200.22(c)(5), and how those activities will support successful implementation of comprehensive or targeted support and improvement plans.

(10) An assurance that each school the LEA proposes to serve will receive all of the State and local funds it would have received in the absence of funds received under this section.

(c) Allocation of school improvement funds to LEAs. (1) A State must review, in a timely manner, an LEA application for school improvement funds that meets the requirements of this section.

(2) In awarding school improvement funds under this section, a State must—

(i) Award the funds on a competitive or formula basis;

(ii) Make each award of sufficient size, with a minimum award of $500,000 per year for each school identified for comprehensive support and improvement to be served and a minimum award of $50,000 per year for each school identified for targeted support and improvement to be served, to support the LEA to effectively implement all requirements for a support and improvement plan under § 200.21 or § 200.22, as applicable, including selected evidence-based interventions, except that a State may determine that an award of less than the minimum award amount is appropriate if, based on each school's enrollment, identified needs, selected evidence-based interventions, and other relevant factors described in the LEA's application on behalf of the school, that such lesser amount will be sufficient to support effective implementation of such plan; and

(iii) Make awards not to exceed four years, which may include a planning year consistent with paragraph (b)(9) of this section during which the LEA must plan to carry out activities that will be supported with school improvement funds by, at the latest, the beginning of the school year following the school year for which the school was identified, and that will support the successful implementation of interventions required under §§ 200.21 or 200.22, as applicable.

(3) If a State permits an LEA to have a planning year for a school under paragraph (c)(2)(iii) of this section, prior to renewing the LEA's school improvement award with respect to such school, the State must review the performance of the LEA in supporting such school during the planning year against the LEA's approved application and determine that the LEA will be able to ensure such school fully implements the activities and interventions that will be supported with school improvement funds by the beginning of the school year following the planning year.

(4) If a State has insufficient school improvement funds to award a grant of sufficient size to each LEA that submits an approvable application consistent with paragraph (c)(1) of this section, the

State must, whether awarding funds through a formula or competition—

(i) Award funds to an LEA to serve a school identified for comprehensive support and improvement before awarding funds to an LEA to serve a school identified for targeted support and improvement;

(ii) Give priority in funding to an LEA that demonstrates the greatest need for such funds, as determined by the State, and based, at a minimum, on—

(A) The number or percentage of elementary and secondary schools in the LEA implementing plans under §§ 200.21 or 200.22;

(B) The State's review of resources available among and within LEAs under § 200.23(a); and

(C) Current academic achievement and student outcomes in the school or schools the LEA is proposing to serve.

(iii) Give priority in funding to an LEA that demonstrates the strongest commitment to use such funds to enable the lowest-performing schools to improve academic achievement and student outcomes, taking into consideration, with respect to the school or schools to be served—

(A) The proposed use of evidence-based interventions that are supported by the strongest level of evidence available and sufficient to support the school in making progress toward meeting exit criteria under § 200.21 or § 200.22; and

(B) Commitment to family and community engagement.

(iv) Take into consideration geographic diversity within the State.

(d) State responsibilities. (1) In its State plan under section 1111 of the Act, each State must describe how it will—

(i) Award school improvement funds to LEAs, consistent with paragraph (c) of this section;

(ii) Monitor the use of funds by LEAs receiving school improvement funds;

(iii) Evaluate the use of school improvement funds by LEAs receiving such funds including by, at a minimum—

(A) Engaging in ongoing efforts to analyze the impact of the evidence-based interventions implemented using funds allocated under this section on student outcomes or other relevant outcomes; and

(B) Disseminating on a regular basis the State's findings on the impact of the evidence-based interventions to LEAs with schools identified under § 200.19;

(iv) Prior to renewing an LEA's award of school improvement funds with respect to a particular school each year and consistent with paragraph (c)(2)(ii) of this section, determine that—

(A) The school is making progress on the State's long-term goals and measurements of interim progress and accountability indicators under §§ 200.13 and 200.14; and

(B) The school is implementing evidence-based interventions with fidelity to the LEA's application and the requirements under §§ 200.21 or 200.22, as applicable; and

(v) As appropriate, reduce barriers and provide operational flexibility for each school in an LEA receiving funds under this section, including flexibility around school budgeting and staffing.

(2) A State may—

(i) Set aside up to five percent of the school improvement funds the State reserves under section 1003(a) of the Act to carry out the activities under paragraph (d)(1) of this section; and

(ii) Directly provide for school improvement activities funded under this section or arrange for their provision in a school through external partners such as school support teams, educational service agencies, or nonprofit or for-profit entities with expertise and a record of success in implementing evidence-based strategies to improve student achievement, instruction, and schools if the State has the authority under State law to take over the school or, if the State does not have such authority, with LEA approval with respect to each such school, and—

(A) The State undertakes a rigorous review process in recruiting, screening, selecting, and evaluating any external partner the State uses to carry out activities directly with school improvement funds; and

(B) The external provider has demonstrated success implementing the evidence-based intervention or interventions that are based on strong, moderate, or promising evidence consistent with section 8101(21)(A) of the Act that it will implement.

(e) Reporting. The State must include on its State report card required under section 1111(h)(1) of the Act a list of all LEAs, and schools served by such LEAs, that received funds under this section, including the amount of funds each LEA received to serve each such school and the types of interventions implemented in each such school with the funds.

(Approved by the Office of Management and Budget under control number 1810-0581)

(Authority: 20 U.S.C. 6303; 20 U.S.C. 6311(d); 20 U.S.C. 6571(a); 20 U.S.C. 1221e-3; 20 U.S.C. 3474)

17. Revise the undesignated center heading following § 200.29 to read as follows:

State and LEA Report Cards

18. Section 200.30 is revised to read as follows:

§ 200.30 Annual State report card.

(a) State report cards in general. (1) A State that receives funds under subpart A of this part must prepare and disseminate widely to the public, consistent with paragraph (d) of this section, an annual State report card for the State as a whole that meets the requirements of this section.

(2) Each State report card must include, at a minimum—

(i) The information required under section 1111(h)(1)(C) of the Act;

(ii) As applicable, for each authorized public chartering agency in the State—

(A) A comparison between the percentage of students in each subgroup defined in section 1111(c)(2) of the Act for each charter school authorized by such agency and such percentage for the LEA or LEAs from which the charter school draws a significant portion of its students, or the geographic community within the LEA in which the charter school is located, as determined by the State; and

(B) A comparison between the academic achievement under § 200.30(b)(2)(i)(A) for students in each charter school authorized by such agency and the academic achievement for students in the LEA or LEAs from which the charter school draws a significant portion of its students, or the geographic community within the LEA in which the charter school is located, as determined by the State; and

(iii) Any additional information that the State believes will best inform parents, students, and other members of the public regarding the progress of each of the State's public elementary schools and secondary schools, which may include the number and percentage of students requiring remediation in postsecondary education and the number and percentage of students attaining career and technical proficiencies.

(3) A State may meet its cross-tabulation requirements under section 1111(g) of the Act through its State report cards.

(b) Format. (1) The State report card must be concise and presented in an understandable and uniform format that is developed in consultation with parents.

(2) The State report card must begin with a clearly labeled overview section that is prominently displayed and includes the following statewide information for the most recent school year:

(i) For all students and disaggregated, at a minimum, for each subgroup of students described in § 200.16(a)(2), results on—

(A) Each of the academic assessments in reading/language arts, mathematics, and science under section 1111(b)(2) of the Act, including the number and percentage of students at each level of achievement;

(B) Each measure included within the Academic Progress indicator under § 200.14(b)(2) for students in public elementary schools and secondary schools that are not high schools;

(C) The four-year adjusted cohort graduation rate and, if adopted by the State, any extended-year adjusted cohort graduation rate consistent with § 200.34; and

(D) Each measure included within the School Quality or Student Success indicator(s) under § 200.14(b)(5).

(ii) The number and percentage of English learners achieving English language proficiency, as measured by the English language proficiency assessments under section 1111(b)(2)(G) of the Act.

(3) If the overview section required under paragraph (b)(2) of this section does not include disaggregated data for each subgroup required under section 1111(h)(1)(C) of the Act, a State

312

must ensure that the disaggregated data not included in the overview section are otherwise included on the State report card.

(c) Accessibility. Each State report card must be in a format and language, to the extent practicable, that parents can understand in compliance with the requirements under § 200.21(b)(1) through (3).

(d) Dissemination and availability. A State must—

(1) Disseminate widely to the public the State report card by, at a minimum, making it available on a single Web page of the SEA's Web site; and

(2) Include on the SEA's Web site—

(i) The report card required under § 200.31 for each LEA in the State; and

(ii) The annual report to the Secretary required under section 1111(h)(5) of the Act.

(e) Timing of report card dissemination. (1) Beginning with the State report card based on information from the 2017-2018 school year, a State must annually disseminate the State report card for the preceding school year no later than December 31.

(2) In meeting the deadline under paragraph (e)(1) of this section, a State may delay inclusion of per-pupil expenditure data required under § 200.35 until no later than the following June 30, provided the State report card includes a brief description of when such data will be publicly available.

(3) If a State cannot meet the December 31, 2018, deadline for reporting some or all of the newly required information under section 1111(h)(1)(C) of the Act for the 2017-2018 school year, the State may request from the Secretary a one-time, one-year extension for reporting on those elements. To receive an extension, a State must submit to the Secretary, by July 1, 2018—

(i) Evidence satisfactory to the Secretary demonstrating that the State cannot meet the deadline in paragraph (e)(1) of this section; and

(ii) A plan and timeline addressing the steps the State will take to disseminate the State report card for the 2018-2019 school year consistent with this section.

(f) Disaggregation of data. (1) For the purpose of reporting disaggregated data under section 1111(h) of the Act, the following definitions apply:

(i) The term "migrant status" means status as a "migratory child" as defined in section 1309(3) of the Act, which means a child or youth who made a qualifying move in the preceding 36 months—

(A) As a migratory agricultural worker or a migratory fisher; or

(B) With, or to join, a parent or spouse who is a migratory agricultural worker or a migratory fisher.

(ii) The term "homeless status" means status as "homeless children and youths" as defined in section 725 of the McKinney-Vento Homeless Assistance Act, as amended, which means individuals who lack a fixed, regular, and adequate nighttime residence (within the meaning of section 103(a)(1) of the McKinney-Vento Homeless Assistance Act) and includes—

(A) Children and youths who are—

(1) Sharing the housing of other persons due to loss of housing, economic hardship, or a similar reason;

(2) Living in motels, hotels, trailer parks, or camping grounds due to the lack of alternative adequate accommodations;

(3) Living in emergency or transitional shelters; or

(4) Abandoned in hospitals;

(B) Children and youths who have a primary nighttime residence that is a public or private place not designed for or ordinarily used as a regular sleeping accommodation for human beings (within the meaning of section 103(a)(2)(C) of the McKinney-Vento Homeless Assistance Act);

(C) Children and youths who are living in cars, parks, public spaces, abandoned buildings, substandard housing, bus or train stations, or similar settings; and

(D) Migratory children (as defined in this paragraph) who qualify as homeless for the purposes of this section because they are living in circumstances described in paragraph (f)(1)(ii)(A) through (C) of this section.

(iii) With respect to the term "status as a child in foster care," the term "foster care" has the same meaning as defined in 45 CFR 1355(a), which means 24-hour substitute care for children placed away from their parents and for whom the title IV-E agency has placement and care responsibility. This includes, but is not limited to, placements in foster family homes, foster homes of relatives, group homes, emergency shelters, residential facilities, child care institutions, and preadoptive homes. A child is in foster care in accordance with this definition regardless of whether the foster care facility is licensed and payments are made by the State, tribal, or local agency for the care of the child, whether adoption subsidy payments are being made prior to the finalization of an adoption, or whether there is Federal matching of any payments that are made.

(iv) With respect to the term "student with a parent who is a member of the Armed Forces on active duty," such term includes a parent on full-time National Guard duty. The terms "Armed Forces," "active duty," and "full-time National Guard duty" have the same meanings as defined in 10 U.S.C. 101(a)(4), 101(d)(1), and 101(d)(5):

(A) "Armed Forces" means the Army, Navy, Air Force, Marine Corps, and Coast Guard.

(B) "Active duty" means full-time duty in the active military service of the United States, including full-time training duty, annual training duty, and attendance, while in the active military service, at a school designated as a service school by law or by the Secretary of the military department concerned. Such term does not include full-time National Guard duty.

(C) "Full-time National Guard duty" means training or other duty, other than inactive duty, performed by a member of the Army National Guard of the United States or the Air National Guard of the United States in the member's status as a member of the National Guard of a State or territory, the Commonwealth of Puerto Rico, or the District of Columbia under section 316, 502, 503, 504, or 505 of title 32 for which the member is entitled to pay from the United States or for which the member has waived pay from the United States.

(2) A State is not required to report disaggregated data for information required on the State report card under section 1111(h) of the Act if the number of students in the subgroup is insufficient to yield statistically sound and reliable information or the results would reveal personally identifiable information about an individual student, consistent with § 200.17.

(Approved by the Office of Management and Budget under control number 1810-0581)

(Authority: 20 U.S.C. 1221e-3; 20 U.S.C. 3474; 20 U.S.C. 6301; 20 U.S.C. 6311(h); 20 U.S.C. 6571(a))

19. Section § 200.31 is revised to read as follows:

§ 200.31 Annual LEA report card.

(a) LEA report card in general. (1) An LEA that receives funds under subpart A of this part must prepare and disseminate to the public, consistent with paragraph (d) of this section, an annual LEA report card that meets the requirements of this section and includes information on the LEA as a whole and each school served by the LEA.

(2) Each LEA report card must include, at a minimum, the information required under section 1111(h)(2)(C) of the Act.

(b) Format. (1) The LEA report card must be concise and presented in an understandable and uniform format that is developed in consultation with parents.

(2) Each LEA report card must begin with, for the LEA as a whole and for each school served by the LEA, a clearly labeled overview section that is prominently displayed and includes the following information for the most recent school year:

(i) For all students and disaggregated, at a minimum, for each subgroup of students required described in § 200.16(a)(2)—

(A) All information required under § 200.30(b)(2);

(B) For the LEA, how academic achievement under § 200.30(b)(2)(i)(A) compares to that for students in the State as a whole; and

(C) For each school, how academic achievement under § 200.30(b)(2)(i)(A) compares to that for students in the LEA and the State as a whole.

(ii) For each school—

(A) The summative determination of the school consistent with § 200.18(a)(4);

(B) Whether the school is identified for comprehensive support and improvement under § 200.19(a) and, if so, the reason for such identification (i.e., lowest-performing school, low graduation rates, or school with a chronically low-performing subgroup(s)); and

(C) Whether the school is identified for targeted support and improvement under § 200.19(b) or § 200.15(b)(2)(iii) and, if so, each subgroup for which it is identified (i.e., subgroup or subgroups who are consistently underperforming or low-performing or, as applicable, who have missed the requirement for 95 percent student participation in assessments).

(iii) Identifying information, including, but not limited to, the name, address, phone number, email, student membership count, and status as a participating Title I school.

(3) Each LEA must ensure that the overview section required under paragraph (b)(2) of this section for each school served by the LEA can be distributed to parents, consistent with paragraph (d)(3)(i) of this section.

(4) If the overview section required under paragraph (b)(2) of this section does not include disaggregated data for each subgroup required under section 1111(h)(1)(C)(ii) of the Act, an LEA must ensure that the disaggregated data not included in the overview section are otherwise included on the LEA report card.

(c) Accessibility. Each LEA report card must be in a format and language, to the extent practicable, that parents can understand in compliance with the requirements under § 200.21(b)(1) through (3).

(d) Dissemination and availability. (1) An LEA report card must be accessible to the public.

(2) At a minimum the LEA report card must be made available on the LEA's Web site, except that an LEA that does not operate a Web site may provide the information to the public in another manner determined by the LEA.

(3) An LEA must provide, for each school served by the LEA, the information described in paragraph (b)(2) of this section to the parents of each student enrolled in the school—

(i) Directly to parents, through such means as regular mail, email, or other direct means of distribution; and

(ii) In a timely manner, consistent with the requirements under paragraph (e) of this section.

(e) Timing of LEA report card dissemination. (1) Beginning with the LEA report card based on information from the 2017-2018 school year, an LEA must annually disseminate its report card for the preceding school year no later than December 31.

(2) In meeting the deadline under paragraph (e)(1) of this section, an LEA may delay inclusion of per-pupil expenditure data required under § 200.35 until no later than the following June 30, provided the report card includes a brief description of when such data will be publicly available.

(3) If an LEA cannot meet the December 31, 2018, deadline for reporting some or all of the newly required information under section 1111(h)(2)(C) of the Act for the 2017-2018 school year, a State may request from the Secretary a one-time, one-year extension for reporting on those elements on behalf of the LEA consistent with the requirements under § 200.30(e)(3).

(f) Disaggregation of data. For the purpose of reporting disaggregated data under section 1111(h)(2)(C) of the Act, the requirements under § 200.30(f) apply to LEA report cards.

(Approved by the Office of Management and Budget under control number 1810-0581)

(Authority: 20 U.S.C. 1221e-3; 20 U.S.C. 3474; 20 U.S.C. 6571(a); 20 U.S.C. 6311(h))

20. Section 200.32 is revised to read as follows:

§ 200.32 Description and results of a State's accountability system.

(a) Accountability system description. Each State and LEA report card must include a clear and concise description of the State's current accountability system under §§ 200.12 to 200.24. Each accountability system description must include—

(1) The minimum number of students that the State establishes under § 200.17(a) for use in the accountability system;

(2) The long-term goals and measurements of interim progress that the State establishes under § 200.13 for all students and for each subgroup of students described in § 200.16(a)(2);

(3) The indicators used by the State under § 200.14 to annually meaningfully differentiate among all public schools, including, if applicable, the State's uniform procedure for averaging data across years or grades consistent with § 200.20(a);

(4) The State's system for annually meaningfully differentiating all public schools in the State under § 200.18, including—

(i) The specific weight, consistent with § 200.18(b) and (c), of each indicator described in § 200.14(b) in such differentiation;

(ii) The way in which the State factors the requirement for 95 percent student participation in assessments under § 200.15(a)(2) into its system of annual meaningful differentiation described in §§ 200.15(b) and 200.18(a)(5);

(iii) The methodology by which the State differentiates all such schools under § 200.18(a), including information on the performance levels and summative determinations provided by the State consistent with § 200.18(a)(3) and (4);

(iv) The methodology by which the State identifies a school for comprehensive support and improvement as described in § 200.19(a); and

(v) The methodology by which the State identifies a school for targeted support and improvement as described in § 200.19(b) and (c), including the definition and time period used by the State to determine consistently underperforming subgroups of students; and

(5) The exit criteria established by the State under §§ 200.21(f) and 200.22(f), including the number of years by which a school must meet the exit criteria.

(b) Reference to State plan. To the extent that a State plan or another location on the SEA's Web site provides a description of the accountability system elements required in paragraph (a)(1) through (5) of this section that complies with the requirements under § 200.21(b)(1) through (3), a State or LEA may provide the Web address or URL of, or a direct link to, such State plan or location on the SEA's Web site to meet the reporting requirement for such accountability system elements.

317

(c) Accountability system results. (1) Each State and LEA report card must include, as applicable, the number and names of each public school in the State or LEA identified by the State for—

(i) Comprehensive support and improvement under § 200.19(a); or

(ii) Targeted support and improvement under § 200.19(b).

(2) For each school identified by the State for comprehensive support and improvement under § 200.19(a), the State and LEA report card must indicate which of the following reasons led to such identification:

(i) Lowest-performing school under § 200.19(a)(1).

(ii) Low graduation rates under § 200.19(a)(2).

(iii) One or more chronically low-performing subgroups under § 200.19(a)(3), including the subgroup or subgroups that led to such identification.

(3) For each school identified by the State for targeted support and improvement under § 200.19(b) or § 200.15(b)(2)(iii), the State and LEA report card must indicate—

(i) Which subgroup or subgroups led to the school's identification; and

(ii) Whether the school has one or more subgroups who are consistently underperforming or low-performing or, as applicable, who have missed the requirement for 95 percent student participation in assessments.

(4) Each LEA report card must include, for each school served by the LEA, the school's performance level consistent with § 200.18(a)(2) and (3) on each indicator in § 200.14(b) and the school's summative determination consistent with § 200.18(a)(4).

(5) If a State includes more than one measure within any indicator under § 200.14(b), the LEA report card must include each school's results on each individual measure and the single performance level for the indicator overall, across all such measures.

(Approved by the Office of Management and Budget under control number 1810-0581)

(Authority: 20 U.S.C. 1221e-3; 20 U.S.C. 3474; 20 U.S.C. 6311(c), (h); 20 U.S.C. 6571(a))

21. Section 200.33 is revised to read as follows:

§ 200.33 Calculations for reporting on student achievement and progress toward meeting long-term goals.

(a) Calculations for reporting student achievement results. (1) Consistent with paragraph (a)(3) of this section, each State and LEA report card must include the percentage of students performing at each level of achievement under section 1111(b)(1)(A) of the Act (e.g., proficient, advanced) on the academic assessments under section 1111(b)(2) of the Act, overall and by grade.

(2) Consistent with paragraph (a)(3) of this section, each LEA report card must also—

(i) Compare the results under paragraph (a)(1) of this section for students served by the LEA with students in the State as a whole; and

(ii) For each school served by the LEA, compare the results under paragraph (a)(1) of this section for students enrolled in the school with students served by the LEA and students in the State as a whole.

(3) Each State and LEA report card must include, with respect to each reporting requirement under paragraphs (a)(1) and (2) of this section—

(i) Information for all students;

(ii) Information disaggregated by—

(A) Each subgroup of students described in § 200.16(a)(2);

(B) Migrant status;

(C) Gender;

(D) Homeless status;

(E) Status as a child in foster care; and

(F) Status as a student with a parent who is a member of the Armed Forces on active duty or serves on full-time National Guard duty; and

(iii) Results based on both—

(A) The percentage of students at each level of achievement, in which the denominator includes the greater of—

(1) 95 percent of all students, or 95 percent of each subgroup of students, who are enrolled in the school, LEA, or State, respectively; or

(2) The number of all such students enrolled in the school, LEA, or State, respectively, who participate in the assessments required under section 1111(b)(2)(B)(v) of the Act; and

(B) The percentage of students at each level of achievement, in which the denominator includes all students with a valid test score.

(b) Calculation for reporting on the progress of all students and each subgroup of students toward meeting the State-designed long-term academic achievement goals. (1) Each State and LEA report card must indicate whether all students and each subgroup of students described in § 200.16(a)(2) met or did not meet the State measurements of interim progress for academic achievement under § 200.13(a).

(2) To meet the requirements of paragraph (b)(1) of this section, each State and LEA must calculate the percentage of students who are proficient and above on the State assessments

required under section 1111(b)(2)(B)(v)(I) of the Act based on a denominator that includes the greater of—

(i) 95 percent of all students, and 95 percent of each subgroup of students, who are enrolled in the school, LEA, or State, respectively; or

(ii) The number of all such students enrolled in the school, LEA, or State, respectively who participate in the assessments required under section 1111(b)(2)(B)(v)(I) of the Act.

(c) Calculation for reporting the percentage of students assessed and not assessed. (1) Each State and LEA report card must include the percentage of all students, and the percentage of students disaggregated by each subgroup of students described in § 200.16(a)(2), gender, and migrant status, assessed and not assessed on each of the assessments required under section 1111(b)(2)(B)(v) of the Act.

(2) To meet the requirements of paragraph (c)(1) of this section, each State and LEA must include in the denominator of the calculation all students enrolled in the school, LEA, or State, respectively, at the time of testing.

(Approved by the Office of Management and Budget under control number 1810-0581)

(Authority: 20 U.S.C. 1221e-3; 20 U.S.C. 3474; 20 U.S.C. 6311(c), (h); 20 U.S.C. 6571(a))

22. Section 200.34 is revised to read as follows:

§ 200.34 High school graduation rate.

(a) Four-year adjusted cohort graduation rate. A State must calculate a four-year adjusted cohort graduation rate for each public high school in the State in the following manner:

(1) The numerator must consist of the sum of—

(i) All students who graduate in four years with a regular high school diploma; and

(ii) All students with the most significant cognitive disabilities in the cohort, assessed using an alternate assessment aligned to alternate academic achievement standards under section 1111(b)(2)(D) of the Act and awarded a State-defined alternate diploma.

(2) The denominator must consist of the number of students who form the adjusted cohort of entering first-time students in grade 9 enrolled in the high school no later than the date by which student membership data is collected annually by the State for submission to the National Center for Education Statistics.

(3) For those high schools that start after grade 9, the cohort must be calculated based on the earliest high school grade students attend.

(b) Adjusting the cohort. (1) "Adjusted cohort" means the students who enter grade 9 (or the earliest high school grade) plus any students who transfer into the cohort in grades 9 through 12, and minus any students removed from the cohort.

(2) "Students who transfer into the cohort" means the students who enroll after the beginning of the date of the determination of the cohort, up to and including in grade 12.

(3) To remove a student from the cohort, a school or LEA must confirm in writing that the student—

(i) Transferred out, such that the school or LEA has official written documentation that the student enrolled in another school or educational program from which the student is expected to receive a regular high school diploma, or a State-defined alternate diploma for students with the most significant cognitive disabilities;

(ii) Emigrated to another country;

(iii) Transferred to a prison or juvenile facility after an adjudication of delinquency, and is enrolled in an educational program from which the student is expected to receive a regular high school diploma, or a State-defined alternate diploma for students with the most significant cognitive disabilities, during the period in which the student is assigned to the prison or juvenile facility; or

(iv) Is deceased.

(4) A student who is retained in grade, enrolls in a general equivalency diploma program or other alternative education program that does not issue or provide credit toward the issuance of a regular high school diploma or a State-defined alternate diploma, or leaves school for any reason other than those described in paragraph (b)(3) of this section may not be counted as having transferred out for the purpose of calculating the graduation rate and must remain in the adjusted cohort.

(5) For students with the most significant cognitive disabilities assessed using an alternate assessment aligned to alternate academic achievement standards under section 1111(b)(2)(D) of the Act and who are eligible for a State-defined alternate diploma under § 200.34(c)(3), an LEA or school must—

(i) Assign the student to the cohort of entering first-time students in grade 9 and ensure that the student remains in that cohort through grade 12.

(ii) Remove such a student from the original cohort if the student does not graduate after four years but continues to be enrolled in the school or LEA and is expected to receive a State-defined alternate diploma that meets the requirements of paragraph (c)(3) of this section;

(iii) Reassign such a student who graduates with a State-defined alternate diploma after more than four years to the cohort of students graduating in that year and include the student in the numerator and denominator of the graduation rate calculation—

(A) For the four-year adjusted cohort graduation rate for the year in which the student graduates; and

(B) For an extended-year adjusted cohort graduation rate under paragraph (d) of this section for one or more subsequent years, if the State has adopted such a rate.

(iv) Reassign such a student who after more than four years does not graduate with a State-defined alternate diploma that meets the requirements of paragraph (c)(3) of this section to the cohort of students graduating in the year in which the student exits high school and include the student in the denominator of the graduation rate calculation—

(A) For the four-year adjusted cohort graduation rate for the year in which the student exits high school; and

(B) For an extended-year adjusted cohort graduation rate under paragraph (d) of this section for one or more subsequent years, if the State has adopted such a rate.

(c) Definition of terms. For the purposes of calculating an adjusted cohort graduation rate under this section—

(1) "Students who graduate in four years" means students who earn a regular high school diploma before, during, or at the conclusion of their fourth year, or during a summer session immediately following their fourth year.

(2) "Regular high school diploma" means the standard high school diploma awarded to the preponderance of students in the State that is fully aligned with State standards, or a higher diploma. A regular high school diploma does not include—

(i) A diploma aligned to the alternate academic achievement standards described in section 1111(b)(1)(E) of the ESEA, as amended by the ESSA; or

(ii) A general equivalency diploma, certificate of completion, certificate of attendance, or any similar or lesser credential, such as a diploma based on meeting individualized education program (IEP) goals.

(3) "Alternate diploma" means a diploma for students with the most significant cognitive disabilities, as defined by the State, who are assessed with a State's alternate assessments aligned to alternate academic achievement standards under section 1111(b)(2)(D) of the Act and is—

(i) Standards-based;

(ii) Aligned with the State's requirements for a regular high school diploma; and

(iii) Obtained within the time period for which the State ensures the availability of a free appropriate public education under section 612(a)(1) of the Individuals with Disabilities Education Act (20 U.S.C. 1412(a)(1)).

(d) Extended-year adjusted cohort graduation rate. In addition to calculating a four-year adjusted cohort graduation rate, a State may calculate and report an extended-year adjusted cohort graduation rate.

(1) "Extended-year adjusted cohort graduation rate" means the number of students who graduate in four years, plus the number of students who graduate in one or more additional years beyond the fourth year of high school with a regular high school diploma or a State-defined alternate diploma, divided by the number of students who form the adjusted cohort for the four-year adjusted cohort graduation rate, provided that the adjustments account for any students who transfer into the cohort by the end of the year of graduation being considered minus the number of students who transfer out, emigrate to another country, transfer to a prison or juvenile facility, or are deceased, as described in paragraph (b)(3) of this section.

(2) A State may calculate one or more extended-year adjusted cohort graduation rates.

(e) Reporting on State and LEA report cards. (1) A State and LEA report card must include, at the school, LEA, and State levels—

(i) Four-year adjusted cohort graduation rates and, if adopted by the State, extended-year adjusted cohort graduation rates for all students and disaggregated by each subgroup of students described in § 200.16(a)(2), homeless status, and status as a child in foster care.

(ii) Whether all students and each subgroup of students described in § 200.16(a)(2) met or did not meet the State measurements of interim progress for graduation rates under § 200.13(b); and

(2) In reporting graduation rates disaggregated by each subgroup of students described in § 200.16(a)(2), homeless status, and status as a child in foster care, a State and its LEAs must include students who were children with disabilities, English learners, children who are homeless (as defined in § 200.30(f)(1)(ii)), or children who are in foster care (as defined in § 200.30(f)(1)(iii)) at any time during the cohort period.

(3) A State and its LEAs must report the four-year adjusted cohort graduation rate and, if adopted by the State, extended-year adjusted cohort graduation rate that reflects results of the immediately preceding school year.

(4) If a State adopts an extended-year adjusted cohort graduation rate, the State and its LEAs must report the extended-year adjusted cohort graduation rate separately from the four-year adjusted cohort graduation rate.

(f) Partial school enrollment. Each State must apply the same approach in all LEAs to determine whether students who are enrolled in the same school for less than half of the academic year as described in § 200.20(b) who exit high school without a regular high school diploma and do not transfer into another high school that grants a regular high school diploma are counted in the denominator for reporting the adjusted cohort graduation rate—

(1) At the school in which such student was enrolled for the greatest proportion of school days while enrolled in grades 9 through 12; or

(2) At the school in which the student was most recently enrolled.

(Approved by the Office of Management and Budget under control number 1810-0581)

(Authority: 20 U.S.C. 1221e-3; 20 U.S.C. 3474; 20 U.S.C. 6311(h); 20 U.S.C. 6571(a); 20 U.S.C. 7801(23), (25))

23. Section 200.35 is revised to read as follows:

§ 200.35 Per-pupil expenditures.

(a) State report card requirements. (1) Each State report card must include the following:

(i) Current expenditures per pupil from Federal, State, and local funds, for the preceding fiscal year, consistent with the timeline in § 200.30(e), for each LEA in the State, and for each school served by each LEA—

(A) In the aggregate; and

(B) Disaggregated by source of funds, including—

(1) Federal funds; and

(2) State and local funds combined plus Federal funds intended to replace local tax revenues, which may not include funds received from private sources.

(ii) The Web address or URL of, or direct link to, a description of the uniform procedure required under paragraph (c) of this section that complies with the requirements under § 200.21(b)(1) through (3).

(2) Each State report card must also separately include, for each LEA, the amount of current expenditures per pupil that were not included in school-level per-pupil expenditure data for public schools in the LEA.

(b) LEA report card requirements. (1) Each LEA report card must include the following:

(i) Current expenditures per pupil from Federal, State, and local funds, for the preceding fiscal year, consistent with the timeline in § 200.31(e), for the LEA and each school served by the LEA—

(A) In the aggregate; and

(B) Disaggregated by source of funds, including—

(1) Federal funds; and

(2) State and local funds combined plus Federal funds intended to replace local tax revenues, which may not include funds received from private sources.

(ii) The Web address or URL of, or direct link to, a description of the uniform procedure required under paragraph (c) of this section.

(2) Each LEA report card must also separately include the amount of current expenditures per pupil that were not included in school-level per-pupil expenditure data for public schools in the LEA.

(c) Uniform procedures. A State must develop a single statewide procedure to calculate LEA current expenditures per pupil and a single statewide procedure to calculate school-level current expenditures per pupil, such that—

(1) The numerator consists of current expenditures, which means actual personnel costs (including actual staff salaries) and actual non-personnel expenditures of Federal, State, and local funds, used for public education—

(i) Including, but not limited to, expenditures for administration, instruction, instructional support, student support services, pupil transportation services, operation and maintenance of plant, fixed charges, preschool, and net expenditures to cover deficits for food services and student body activities; but

(ii) Not including expenditures for community services, capital outlay, and debt service; and

(2) The denominator consists of the aggregate number of students enrolled in preschool through

grade 12 to whom the State and LEA provide free public education on or about October 1, consistent with the student membership data collected annually by the State for submission to the National Center for Education Statistics.

(Approved by the Office of Management and Budget under control number 1810-0581)

(Authority: 20 U.S.C. 1221e-3; 20 U.S.C. 3474; 20 U.S.C. 6571(a); 20 U.S.C. 6311(h))

24. Section 200.36 is revised to read as follows:

§ 200.36 Postsecondary enrollment.

(a) Reporting information on postsecondary enrollment. (1) Each State and LEA report card must include the information at the SEA, LEA and high school level on postsecondary enrollment required under section 1111(h)(1)(C)(xiii) of the Act, where available, consistent with paragraph (c) of this section. This information must include, for each high school in the State (in the case of a State report card) and for each high school in the LEA (in the case of an LEA report card), the cohort rate (for all students and each subgroup of students described in section § 200.16(a)(2)) at which students who graduate from high school enroll in programs of postsecondary education, including—

(i) Programs of public postsecondary education in the State; and

(ii) If data are available and to the extent practicable, programs of private postsecondary education in the State or public and private programs of postsecondary education outside the State.

(2) For the purposes of this section, "programs of postsecondary education" has the same meaning as the term "institution of higher education" under section 101(a) of the Higher Education Act of 1965, as amended.

(b) Calculating postsecondary enrollment. To meet the requirements of paragraph (a) of this section, each State and LEA must calculate the cohort rate in the following manner:

(1) The numerator must consist of the number of students who enroll in a program of postsecondary education in the academic year following the students' high school graduation.

(2) The denominator must consist of the number of students who graduated with a regular high school diploma or a State-defined alternate diploma from each high school in the State, in accordance with § 200.34, in the immediately preceding school year.

(c) Information availability. (1) For the purpose of paragraph (a) of this section, information is "available" if either—

(i) The State is routinely obtaining the information; or

(ii) The information is obtainable by the State on a routine basis.

(2) If the postsecondary enrollment information described in paragraph (a) of this section is not available or is partially available, the State and LEA report cards must include the school year in which such information is expected to be fully available.

(Approved by the Office of Management and Budget under control number 1810-0581)

(Authority: 20 U.S.C. 1001(a); 20 U.S.C. 6571(a); 20 U.S.C. 1221e-3; 20 U.S.C. 3474; 6311(h))

25. Section 200.37 is revised to read as follows:

§ 200.37 Educator qualifications.

(a) Professional qualifications of educators in the State. Each State and LEA report card must include, in the aggregate and disaggregated by high-poverty and low-poverty schools, the number and percentage of the following:

(1) Inexperienced teachers, principals, and other school leaders;

(2) Teachers teaching with emergency or provisional credentials; and

(3) Teachers who are not teaching in the subject or field for which the teacher is certified or licensed.

(b) Uniform definitions. For purposes of paragraph (a) of this section, the following definitions apply:

(1) "High-poverty schools" means schools in the top quartile of poverty in the State;

(2) "Low-poverty schools" means schools in the bottom quartile of poverty in the State; and

(3) Each State must adopt, and the State and each LEA in the State must use, a statewide definition of the term "inexperienced" and of the phrase "not teaching in the subject or field for which the teacher is certified or licensed."

(Approved by the Office of Management and Budget under control number 1810-0581)

(Authority: 20 U.S.C. 1221e-3; 20 U.S.C. 3474; 20 U.S.C. 6571(a); 20 U.S.C. 6311(h))

§§ 200.38 through 200.42
[Removed and Reserved]

REGULATORY TEXT

26. Remove and reserve §§ 200.38 through 200.42.

27. Add an undesignated center heading following reserved § 200.42 to read as follows:

Other State Plan Provisions

§ 200.43

[Removed]

REGULATORY TEXT

28. Remove § 200.43.

§ 200.58 [Redesignated as § 200.43]

29. Redesignate § 200.58 as § 200.43.

§§ 200.44 through 200.47
[Removed and Reserved]

REGULATORY TEXT

30. Remove and reserve §§ 200.44 through 200.47.

31. Add an undesignated center heading following reserved § 200.47 to read as follows:

Local Educational Agency Plans

§ 200.48
[Removed]

REGULATORY TEXT

32. Remove § 200.48.

§ 200.61
[Redesignated as 200.48]

REGULATORY TEXT

33. Redesignate § 200.61 as § 200.48.

§§ 200.49 through 200.53
[Removed and Reserved]

REGULATORY TEXT

34. Remove and reserve §§ 200.49 through 200.53.

35. Add an undesignated center heading following reserved § 200.54 to read as follows:

Participation of Eligible Children in Private Schools

§§ 200.55 through 200.57
[Removed and Reserved]

REGULATORY TEXT

36. Remove §§ 200.55 through 200.57.

§§ 200.62 through 200.64
[Redesignated as §§ 200.55 through 200.57]

REGULATORY TEXT

37. Redesignate §§ 200.62 through 200.64 as §§ 200.55 through 200.57.

§§ 200.58 through 200.60 [Removed]

38. Remove §§ 200.58 through 200.60.

§ 200.65
[Redesignated as § 200.58]

REGULATORY TEXT

39. Redesignate § 200.65 as § 200.58.

§§ 200.66 through 200.67 [Redesignated as §§ 200.59 through 200.60]

40. Redesignate §§ 200.66 through 200.67 as §§ 200.59 through 200.60.

§ 200.61
[Reserved]

REGULATORY TEXT

41. Add reserved §§ 200.61.

§ 200.62
[Removed and Reserved]

REGULATORY TEXT

42. Remove and reserve § 200.62.

43. Add an undesignated center heading following reserved § 200.62 to read as follows:

Allocations to LEAs

§§ 200.63 through 200.67
[Removed]

REGULATORY TEXT

44. Remove §§ 200.63 through 200.67.

§§ 200.70 through 200.75
[Redesignated as §§ 200.63 through 200.68]

REGULATORY TEXT

45. Redesignate §§ 200.70 through 200.75 as §§ 200.63 through 200.68.

46. Add an undesignated center heading following reserved § 200.69 to read as follows:

Procedures for the Within-District Allocation of LEA Program Funds

§§ 200.77 and 200.78
[Redesignated as §§ 200.70 and 200.71]

REGULATORY TEXT

47. Redesignate §§ 200.77 and 200.78 as §§ 200.70 and 200.71.

48. Add an undesignated center heading following § 200.71 to read as follows:

Fiscal Requirements

§ 200.79
[Redesignated as § 200.73

REGULATORY TEXT

49. Redesignate § 200.79 as § 200.73.

§ 200.79
[Reserved]

REGULATORY TEXT

50. Add reserved § 200.79.

PART 299 GENERAL PROVISIONS

REGULATORY TEXT

51. The authority citation for part 299 is revised to read as follows:

§ 299.1
[Amended]

REGULATORY TEXT

52. In § 299.1 revise paragraph (a) to read as follows:

§ 299.1 What are the purpose and scope of these regulations?

(a) This part establishes uniform administrative rules for programs in titles I through XII of the Elementary and Secondary Education Act of 1965, as amended (ESEA or the Act). As indicated in particular sections of this part, certain provisions apply only to a specific group of programs.

* * * * *

53. Add Subpart G to read as follows:

Subpart G—State Plans

Subpart G—State Plans

§ 299.13
Overview of State plan requirements.

(a) In general. In order to receive a grant under a program identified in paragraph (j) of this section, an SEA must submit a State plan that meets the requirements in this section and:

(1) Consolidated State plan requirements detailed in §§ 299.14 to 299.19; or

(2) Individual program application requirements under the Act (hereinafter "individual program State plan") as detailed in paragraph (k) of this section.

(b) Timely and meaningful consultation. In developing an initial consolidated State plan or an individual program State plan, or revising or amending an approved consolidated State plan or an individual program State plan, an SEA must engage in timely and meaningful consultation with stakeholders. To satisfy its consultation obligations under this paragraph, each SEA must—

(1) Provide public notice, in a format and language, to the extent practicable, that the public can access and understand in compliance with the requirements under § 200.21(b)(1) through (3), of the SEA's processes and procedures for developing and adopting its consolidated State plan or individual program State plan.

(2) Conduct outreach to, and solicit input from, the individuals and entities listed in § 299.15(a) for submission of a consolidated State plan or the individuals and entities listed in the applicable statutes for submission of an individual program State plan, in a format and language, to the extent practicable, that the public can access and understand in compliance with the requirements under § 200.21(b)(1) through (3)—

(i) During the design and development of the SEA's plan to implement the programs included in paragraph (j) of this section;

(ii) At a minimum, prior to initial submission of the consolidated State plan or individual program State plan by making the plan available for public comment for a period of not less than 30 days; and

(iii) Prior to the submission of any revisions or amendments to the approved consolidated State plan or individual program State plan.

(3) Describe how the consultation and public comment were taken into account in the consolidated State plan or individual program State plan submitted for approval, including—

(i) How the SEA addressed the issues and concerns raised through consultation and public comment; and

(ii) Any changes made as a result of consultation and public comment.

(4) Meet the requirements under section 8540 of the Act regarding consultation with the Governor, or appropriate officials from the Governor's office, including—

(i) Consultation during the development of a consolidated State plan or individual title I or title II State plan and prior to submission of such plan to the Secretary; and

(ii) Procedures regarding the signature of such plan.

(c) Assurances. An SEA that submits either a consolidated State plan or an individual program State plan must submit to the Secretary the assurances included in section 8304 of the Act. An SEA also must include the following assurances when submitting either a consolidated State plan or an individual program State plan for the following programs:

(1) Title I, part A. (i) In applying the same approach in all LEAs to determine whether students who are enrolled in the same school for less than half of the academic year as described in § 200.20(b), the SEA will assure that students who exit high school without a regular high school diploma and do not transfer into another high school that grants a regular high school diploma are counted in the denominator for reporting the adjusted cohort graduation rate using one of the following:

(A) At the school in which such student was enrolled for the greatest proportion of school days while enrolled in grades 9 through 12; or

(B) At the school in which the student was most recently enrolled.

(ii) To ensure that children in foster care promptly receive transportation, as necessary, to and from their schools of origin when in their best interest under section 1112(c)(5)(B) of the Act, the SEA must ensure that an LEA receiving funds under title I, part A of the Act will collaborate with State and local child welfare agencies to develop and implement clear written procedures that describe:

(A) How the requirements of section 1112(c)(5)(B) of the Act will be met in the event of a dispute over which agency or agencies will pay any additional costs incurred in providing transportation; and

(B) Which agency or agencies will initially pay the additional costs so that transportation is provided promptly during the pendency of the dispute.

(iii) The SEA must assure, under section 1111(g)(1)(B) of the Act, that it will publish and annually update—

(A) The statewide differences in rates required under § 299.18(c)(3);

(B) The percentage of teachers categorized in each LEA at each effectiveness level established as part of the definition of "ineffective teacher" under § 299.18(c)(2)(i), consistent with applicable State privacy policies;

(C) The percentage of teachers categorized as out-of-field teachers consistent with § 200.37; and

(D) The percentage of teachers categorized as inexperienced teachers consistent with § 200.37.

(E) The information required under paragraphs (c)(1)(iii)(A) through (D) of this section in a format and language, to the extent practicable, that the public can access and understand in compliance with the requirements under § 200.21(b)(1) through (3) and available at least on a Web site.

(2) Title III, part A. (i) In establishing the statewide entrance procedures required under section 3113(b)(2) of the Act, the SEA must ensure that:

(A) All students who may be English learners are assessed for such status using a valid and reliable instrument within 30 days after enrollment in a school in the State;

(B) It has established procedures for the timely identification of English learners after the initial identification period for students who were enrolled at that time but were not previously identified; and

(C) It has established procedures for removing the English learner designation from any student who was erroneously identified as an English learner, which must be consistent with Federal civil rights obligations.

(ii) In establishing the statewide entrance and exit procedures required under section 3113(b)(2) of the Act and § 299.19(b)(4), the SEA will ensure that the criteria are consistent with Federal civil rights obligations.

(3) Title V, part b, subpart 2. The SEA will assure that, no later than March of each year, it will submit data to the Secretary on the number of students in average daily attendance for the preceding school year in kindergarten through grade 12 for LEAs eligible for funding under the Rural and Low-Income School program, as described under section 5231 of the Act.

(d) Process for submitting an initial consolidated State plan or individual program State plan. When submitting an initial consolidated State plan or an individual program State plan, an SEA must adhere to the following timeline and process.

(1) Assurances. In order to receive Federal allocations for the programs included in paragraph (j) of this section, each SEA must submit the required assurances described in paragraph (c) of this section, and if submitting a consolidated State plan, the required assurances under § 299.14(c), on a date, time, and manner (e.g., electronic or paper) established by the Secretary.

(2) Submission deadlines. (i) Each SEA must submit to the Department either a consolidated State plan or individual program State plan for each program in paragraph (j) of this section on a date, time, and manner (e.g., electronic or paper) established by the Secretary.

(ii) For the purposes of the period for Secretarial review under sections 1111(a)(4)(A)(v) or 8451 of the Act, a consolidated State plan or an individual program State plan is considered to be submitted on the date and time established by the Secretary if it is received by the Secretary on or prior to that date and time and addresses all of the required components in § 299.14 for a consolidated State plan or all statutory and regulatory application requirements for an individual program State plan.

(iii) Each SEA must submit either a consolidated State plan or an individual program State plan for all of the programs in paragraph (j) in a single submission on the date, time, and manner (e.g., electronic or paper) established by the Secretary consistent with paragraph (d)(2)(i) of this section.

(3) Extension for educator equity student-level data calculation. If an SEA cannot calculate and report the data required under paragraph § 299.18(c)(3)(i) when submitting its initial consolidated State plan or individual title I, part A State plan, the SEA may request a three-year extension from the Secretary.

(i) To receive an extension, the SEA must indicate in its initial consolidated State plan or individual title I, part A State plan that it will calculate the statewide rates described under paragraph § 299.18(c)(3)(i) using school-level data and provide a detailed plan and timeline addressing the steps it will take to calculate and report, as expeditiously as possible but no later than three years from the date it submits its initial consolidated State plan or individual title I, part A program State plan, the data required under § 299.18(c)(3)(i) at the student level.

(ii) An SEA that receives an extension under this paragraph (d)(3) must, when it submits either its initial consolidated State plan or individual title I, part A program State plan, still calculate and report the differences in rates based on school-level data consistent with § 299.18(c).

(e) Opportunity to revise initial State plan. An SEA may revise its initial consolidated State plan or its individual program State plan in response to a preliminary written determination by the Secretary. The period for Secretarial review of a consolidated State plan or an individual program State plan under sections 1111(a)(4)(A)(v) or 8451 of the Act is suspended while the SEA revises its plan. If an SEA fails to resubmit a revised plan within 45 days of receipt of the preliminary written determination, the Secretary may issue a final written determination under sections 1111(a)(4)(A)(v) or 8451 of the Act.

(f) Publication of State plan. After the Secretary approves a consolidated State plan or an individual program State plan, an SEA must publish its approved consolidated State plan or individual program State plan on the SEA's Web site in a format and language, to the extent practicable, that the public can access and understand in compliance with the requirements under § 200.21(b)(1) through (3).

(g) Amendments and Significant Changes. If an SEA makes significant changes to its approved consolidated State plan or individual program State plan at any time, consistent with section 1111(a)(6)(B) of the Act, such information must be submitted to the Secretary in the form of an amendment to its State plan for review and approval. Prior to submitting an amendment to its consolidated State plan or individual program State plan, the SEA must engage in timely and meaningful consultation, consistent with paragraph (b) of this section.

(h) Revisions. At least once every four years, an SEA must review and revise its approved consolidated State plan or individual program State plans. The SEA must submit its revisions to the Secretary for review and approval. When reviewing and revising its consolidated State plan or individual program State plan, each SEA must engage in timely and meaningful consultation, consistent with paragraph (b) of this section.

(i) Optional consolidated State plan. An SEA may submit either a consolidated State plan or an individual program State plan for any program identified in paragraph (j) of this section. An SEA that submits a consolidated State plan is not required to submit an individual program State plan for any of the programs to which the consolidated State plan applies.

(j) Programs that may be included in a consolidated State plan. (1) Under section 8302 of the Act, an SEA may include in a consolidated State plan any programs authorized by—

(i) Title I, part A: Improving Basic Programs Operated by State and Local Educational Agencies;

(ii) Title I, part C: Education of Migratory Children;

(iii) Title I, part D: Prevention and Intervention Programs for Children and Youth Who Are Neglected, Delinquent, or At-Risk;

(iv) Title II, part A: Supporting Effective Instruction;

(v) Title III, part A: Language Instruction for English Learners and Immigrant Students;

(vi) Title IV, part A: Student Support and Academic Enrichment Grants;

(vii) Title IV, part B: 21st Century Community Learning Centers; and

(viii) Title V, part B, subpart 2: Rural and Low-Income School Program.

(2) In addition to the programs identified in paragraph (j)(1) of this section, under section 8302(a)(1)(B) of the Act, an SEA may also include in the consolidated State plan, as designated by the Secretary, the Education for Homeless Children and Youths program under subtitle B of title VII of the McKinney-Vento Homeless Assistance Act, as amended by the ESSA.

(k) Individual program State plan requirements. An SEA that submits an individual program State plan for one or more of the programs listed in paragraph (j) of this section must address all State plan or application requirements applicable to such programs as contained in the Act and applicable regulations, including all required statutory and programmatic assurances. In addition to addressing the statutory and regulatory plan or application requirements for each individual program, an SEA that submits an individual program State plan—

(1) For title I, part A, must:

(i) Meet the educator equity requirements in § 299.18(c) in order to address section 1111(g)(1)(B) of the Act; and

(ii) Meet the schoolwide waiver requirements in § 299.19(c)(1) in order to implement section 1114(a)(1)(B) of the Act;

(2) For title I, part C, must meet the education of migratory children requirements in § 299.19(b)(2) in order to address sections 1303(f)(2), 1304(d), and 1306(b)(1)of the Act; and

(3) For title III, must meet the English learner requirements in § 299.19(b)(4) in order to address section 3113(b)(2) of the Act.

(l) Compliance with program requirements. Each SEA must administer all programs in accordance with all applicable statutes, regulations, program plans, and approved applications, and maintain documentation of this compliance.

(Approved by the Office of Management and Budget under control number 1810-0576)

(Authority: 20 U.S.C. 1221e-3, 3474, 6571(a), 7801(11), 7842, 7844, 7871)

§ 299.14
Requirements for the consolidated State plan.
(a) Purpose. Pursuant to section 8302 of the Act, the Department defines the procedures under which an SEA may submit a consolidated State plan for any or all of the programs listed in § 299.13(j).

(b) Framework for the consolidated State plan. Each consolidated State plan must address the requirements in §§ 299.15 through 299.19 for the following five components and their corresponding elements:

(1) Consultation and performance management.

(2) Academic assessments.

(3) Accountability, support, and improvement for schools.

(4) Supporting excellent educators.

(5) Supporting all students.

(c) Assurances. In addition to the assurances in § 299.13(c), an SEA must include the following assurances on a date, time, and manner (e.g., electronic or paper) established by the Secretary as part of its consolidated State plan:

(1) Coordination. The SEA must assure that it coordinated its plans for administering the included programs, other programs authorized under the ESEA, as amended by the ESSA, and the Individuals with Disabilities Education Act (IDEA), the Rehabilitation Act, the Carl D. Perkins Career and Technical Education Act of 2006, the Workforce Innovation and Opportunity Act, the Head Start Act, the Child Care and Development Block Grant Act of 1990, the Education Sciences Reform Act of 2002, the Education Technical Assistance Act of 2002, the National Assessment of Educational Progress Authorization Act, and the Adult Education and Family Literacy Act.

(2) Challenging academic standards and academic assessments. The SEA must assure that the State will meet the standards and assessments requirements of sections 1111(b)(1)(A) through (F) and 1111(b)(2) of the Act and applicable regulations.

(3) State support and improvement for low-performing schools. The SEA must assure that it will approve, monitor, and periodically review LEA comprehensive support and improvement plans consistent with requirements in section 1111(d)(1)(B)(v) and (vi) of the Act and § 200.21(e).

(4) Participation by private school children and teachers. The SEA must assure that it will meet the requirements of sections 1117 and 8501 of the Act regarding the participation of private school children and teachers.

(5) Appropriate identification of children with disabilities. The SEA must assure that it has

policies and procedures in effect regarding the appropriate identification of children with disabilities consistent with the child find and evaluation requirements in section 612(a)(3) and (a)(7) of the IDEA, respectively.

(Approved by the Office of Management and Budget under control number 1810-0576)

(Authority: 20 U.S.C. 1221e-3, 3474, 7842)

§ 299.15
Consultation and performance management.
(a) Consultation. In its consolidated State plan, each SEA must describe how it engaged in timely and meaningful consultation consistent with § 299.13(b) with stakeholders in the development of the four components identified in §§ 299.16 through 299.19 of its consolidated plan. The stakeholders must include, at a minimum, the following individuals and entities and must reflect the geographic diversity of the State:

(1) The Governor, or appropriate officials from the Governor's office;

(2) Members of the State legislature;

(3) Members of the State board of education (if applicable);

(4) LEAs, including LEAs in rural areas;

(5) Representatives of Indian tribes located in the State;

(6) Teachers, principals, other school leaders, paraprofessionals, specialized instructional support personnel, and organizations representing such individuals;

(7) Charter school leaders, if applicable;

(8) Parents and families;

(9) Community-based organizations;

(10) Civil rights organizations, including those representing students with disabilities, English learners, and other historically underserved students;

(11) Institutions of higher education (IHEs);

(12) Employers;

(13) Representatives of private school students;

(14) Early childhood educators and leaders; and

(15) The public.

(b) Performance management and technical assistance. In its consolidated State plan, each SEA must describe its system of performance management of SEA and LEA plans consistent with its consolidated State plan. This description must include—

(1) The SEA's process for supporting the development, review, and approval of the activities in

337

LEA plans in accordance with statutory and regulatory requirements, which should address how the SEA will determine if LEA activities are aligned with the specific needs of the LEA and the SEA's strategies described in its consolidated State plan.

(2) The SEA's plan to—

(i) Collect and use data and information, which may include input from stakeholders and data collected and reported under section 1111(h) of the Act, to assess the quality of SEA and LEA implementation of strategies and progress toward meeting the desired program outcomes;

(ii) Monitor SEA and LEA implementation of included programs using the data in paragraph (b)(2)(i) of this section to ensure compliance with statutory and regulatory requirements; and

(iii) Continuously improve SEA and LEA plans and implementation; and

(3) The SEA's plan to provide differentiated technical assistance to LEAs and schools to support effective implementation of SEA, LEA, and other subgrantee strategies.

(Approved by the Office of Management and Budget under control number 1810-0576)

(Authority: 20 U.S.C. 1221e-3, 3474, 7842)

§ 299.16
Academic assessments.
(a) In its consolidated State plan, if the State administers end-of-course mathematics assessments to high school students to meet the requirements under section 1111(b)(2)(B)(v)(I)(bb) of the Act and uses the exception for students in eighth grade to take such assessments under section 1111(b)(2)(C) of the Act, describe how the State is complying with the requirements of section 1111(b)(2)(C) and applicable regulations; and

(b) In its consolidated State plan, each SEA must describe how the State is complying with the requirements related to assessments in languages other than English consistent with section 1111(b)(2)(F) of the Act and applicable regulations.

(Approved by the Office of Management and Budget under control number 1810-0576)

(Authority: 20 U.S.C. 1221e-3, 3474, 7842)

§ 299.17
Accountability, support, and improvement for schools.
(a) Long-term goals. In its consolidated State plan, each SEA must provide its baseline, measurements of interim progress, and long-term goals and describe how it established its ambitious long-term goals and measurements of interim progress, for academic achievement, graduation rates, and English language proficiency, and its State-determined timeline for attaining such goals, consistent with the requirements in section 1111(c)(4)(A) of the Act and § 200.13.

(b) Accountability system. In its consolidated State plan, each SEA must describe its statewide accountability system consistent with the requirements of section 1111(c) of the Act and § 200.12, including—

(1) The measures included in each of the indicators under § 200.14(b) and how those measures meet the requirements described in section 1111(c)(4)(B) of the Act and § 200.14;

338

(2) The subgroups of students from each major racial and ethnic group, consistent with § 200.16(a)(2), and any additional subgroups of students used in the accountability system;

(3) If applicable, the statewide uniform procedures for:

(i) Former children with disabilities in the children with disabilities subgroup consistent with § 200.16(b);

(ii) Former English learners in the English learner subgroup consistent with § 200.16(c)(1); and

(iii) Recently arrived English learners in the State to determine if an exception applies to an English learner consistent with section 1111(b)(3) of the Act and § 200.16(c)(3) and (4);

(4) The minimum number of students that the State determines are necessary to be included in each of the subgroups of students consistent with § 200.17(a)(2) and (3);

(5) The State's system for meaningfully differentiating all public schools in the State, including public charter schools, consistent with the requirements of section 1111(c)(4)(C) of the Act and § 200.18, including—

(i) The distinct and discrete levels of school performance, and how they are calculated, under § 200.18(a)(2) on each indicator in the statewide accountability system;

(ii) The weighting of each indicator, including how certain indicators receive substantial weight individually and much greater weight in the aggregate, consistent with § 200.18(b) and (c)(1) and (2);

(iii) The summative determinations, including how they are calculated, that are provided to schools under § 200.18(a)(4); and

(iv) How the system for meaningful differentiation and the methodology for identifying schools under § 200.19 will ensure that schools with low performance on substantially weighted indicators are more likely to be identified for comprehensive support and improvement or targeted support and improvement, consistent with § 200.18(c)(3) and (d)(1)(ii);

(6) How the State is factoring the requirement for 95 percent student participation in assessments into its system of annual meaningful differentiation of schools consistent with the requirements of § 200.15;

(7) The State's uniform procedure for averaging data, including combining data across school years, combining data across grades, or both, as defined in § 200.20(a), if applicable;

(8) If applicable, how the State includes all public schools in the State in its accountability system if it is different from the methodology described in paragraph (b)(5), consistent with § 200.18(d)(1)(iii).

(c) Identification of schools. In its consolidated State plan, each SEA must describe—

(1) The methodologies, including the timeline, by which the State identifies schools for comprehensive support and improvement under section 1111(c)(4)(D)(i) of the Act and § 200.19(a), including:

(i) Lowest-performing schools;

(ii) Schools with low high school graduation rates; and

(iii) Schools with chronically low-performing subgroups;

(2) The uniform statewide exit criteria for schools identified for comprehensive support and improvement established by the State, including the number of years over which schools are expected to meet such criteria, under section 1111(d)(3)(A)(i) of the Act and consistent with the requirements in § 200.21(f)(1);

(3) The State's methodology for identifying any school with a "consistently underperforming" subgroup of students, including the definition and time period used by the State to determine consistent underperformance, under § 200.19(b)(1) and (c);

(4) The State's methodology, including the timeline, for identifying schools with low-performing subgroups of students under § 200.19(b)(2) and (d) that must receive additional targeted support in accordance with section 1111(d)(2)(C) of the Act; and

(5) The uniform exit criteria, established by the SEA, for schools participating under title I, part A with low-performing subgroups of students established by the State, including the number of years over which schools are expected to meet such criteria, consistent with the requirements in § 200.22(f).

(d) State support and improvement for low-performing schools. In its consolidated State plan, each SEA must describe—

(1) How the SEA will meet its responsibilities, consistent with the requirements described in § 200.24(d) under section 1003 of the Act, including the process to award school improvement funds to LEAs and monitoring and evaluating the use of funds by LEAs;

(2) The technical assistance it will provide to each LEA in the State serving a significant number or percentage of schools identified for comprehensive or targeted support and improvement, including how it will provide technical assistance to LEAs to ensure the effective implementation of evidence-based interventions, consistent with § 200.23(b), and, if applicable, the list of State-approved, evidence-based interventions for use in schools implementing comprehensive or targeted support and improvement plans consistent with § 200.23(c)(2) and (3);

(3) The more rigorous interventions required for schools identified for comprehensive support and improvement that fail to meet the State's exit criteria within a State-determined number of years consistent with section 1111(d)(3)(A)(i) of the Act and § 200.21(f)(3)(iii); and

(4) How the SEA will periodically review, identify, and, to the extent practicable, address any identified inequities in resources to ensure sufficient support for school improvement in each LEA in the State serving a significant number or percentage of schools identified for comprehensive or targeted support and improvement consistent with the requirements in section 1111(d)(3)(A)(ii) of the Act and § 200.23(a).

(Approved by the Office of Management and Budget under control number 1810-0576)

(Authority: 20 U.S.C. 1221e-3, 3747, 7842)

§ 299.18
Supporting excellent educators.

(a) Educator development, retention, and advancement. In its consolidated State plan, consistent with sections 2101 and 2102 of the Act, if an SEA intends to use funds under one or more of the included programs for this purpose, the SEA must describe—

(1) The State's system of certification and licensing of teachers and principals or other school leaders;

(2) The State's strategies to improve educator preparation programs consistent with section 2101(d)(2)(M) of the Act, particularly for educators of low-income and minority students; and

(3) The State's systems of professional growth and improvement, for educators that addresses induction, development, consistent with the definition of professional development in section 8101(42) of the Act, compensation, and advancement for teachers, principals, and other school leaders which may also include how the SEA will work with LEAs in the State to develop or implement systems of professional growth and improvement, consistent with 2102(b)(2)(B) of the Act, or State or local teacher, principal, or other school leader evaluation and support systems consistent with section 2101(c)(4)(B)(ii) of the Act.

(b) Support for educators. (1) In its consolidated State plan, each SEA must describe how it will use title II, part A funds and funds from other included programs, consistent with allowable uses of funds provided under those programs, to support State-level strategies designed to:

(i) Increase student achievement consistent with the challenging State academic standards;

(ii) Improve the quality and effectiveness of teachers, principals, and other school leaders;

(iii) Increase the number of teachers, principals, and other school leaders who are effective in improving student academic achievement in schools; and

(iv) Provide low-income and minority students greater access to effective teachers, principals, and other school leaders consistent with the provisions described in paragraph (c) of this section.

(2) In its consolidated State plan, each SEA must describe how the SEA will improve the skills of teachers, principals, or other school leaders in identifying students with specific learning needs and providing instruction based on the needs of such students consistent with section 2101(d)(2)(J) of the Act.

(c) Educator equity. (1) Each SEA must describe, consistent with section 1111(g)(1)(B) of the Act, whether low-income and minority students enrolled in schools that receive funds under title I, part A of the Act are taught at different rates by ineffective, out-of-field, or inexperienced teachers compared to non-low-income and non-minority students enrolled in schools not receiving funds under title I, part A of the Act in accordance with paragraph (c)(3) of this section.

(2) For the purposes of this section, each SEA must establish and provide in its State plan a different definition, using distinct criteria, for each of the terms included in paragraphs (c)(2)(i) through (vi) of this section—

(i) A statewide definition of "ineffective teacher", or statewide guidelines for LEA definitions of "ineffective teacher", that differentiates between categories of teachers and provides useful information about educator equity;

(ii) A statewide definition of "out-of-field teacher" consistent with § 200.37 that provides useful information about educator equity;

341

(iii) A statewide definition of "inexperienced teacher" consistent with § 200.37 that provides useful information about educator equity;

(iv) A statewide definition of "low-income student";

(v) A statewide definition of "minority student" that includes, at a minimum, race, color, and national origin, consistent with title VI of the Civil Rights Act of 1964; and

(vi) Such other definitions for any other key terms that a State elects to define and use for the purpose of meeting the requirements in paragraph (c)(1) of this section.

(3) For the purpose of the required description under paragraph (c)(1) of this section—

(i) Rates. Each SEA must annually calculate, using student-level data, except as permitted under § 299.13(d)(3), the statewide rates at which—

(A) Low-income students enrolled in schools receiving funds under title I, part A of the Act, are taught by—

(1) Ineffective teachers;

(2) Out-of-field teachers; and

(3) Inexperienced teachers; and

(B) Non-low-income students enrolled in schools not receiving funds under title I, part A of the Act, are taught by—

(1) Ineffective teachers;

(2) Out-of-field teachers; and

(3) Inexperienced teachers; and

(C) Minority students enrolled in schools receiving funds under title I, part A of the Act are taught by—

(1) Ineffective teachers;

(2) Out-of-field teachers; and

(3) Inexperienced teachers; and

(D) Non-minority students enrolled in schools not receiving funds under title I, part A of the Act are taught by—

(1) Ineffective teachers;

(2) Out-of-field teachers; and

(3) Inexperienced teachers.

(ii) Other rates. Each SEA may annually calculate and report statewide at the student level, except as permitted under § 299.13(d)(3), the rates at which students represented by any other key terms that a State elects to define and use for the purpose of this section are taught by ineffective teachers, out-of-field teachers, and inexperienced teachers.

(iii) Statewide differences in rates. Each SEA must calculate the differences, if any, between the rates calculated in paragraph (c)(3)(i)(A) and (B), and between the rates calculated in paragraph (c)(3)(i)(C) and (D) of this section.

(4) Each SEA must provide the Web address or URL of or a direct link to where it will publish and annually update the rates and differences in rates calculated under paragraph (c)(3) of this section and report on the rates and differences in rates in the manner described in § 299.13(c)(1)(iii), consistent with the Family Educational Rights and Privacy Act, 20 U.S.C. 1232g, and applicable regulations.

(5) Each SEA that describes, under paragraph (c)(1) of this section, that low-income or minority students enrolled in schools receiving funds under title I, part A of this Act are taught at higher rates, which are rates where any of the statewide differences in rates calculated under paragraph (c)(3)(iii) is greater than zero, by ineffective, out-of-field, or inexperienced teachers must—

(i) Describe the likely causes (e.g., teacher shortages, working conditions, school leadership, compensation, or other causes), which may vary across districts or schools, of the most significant statewide differences in rates described in paragraph (c)(1) of this section including by identifying whether those differences in rates reflect gaps between districts, within districts, and within schools;

(ii) Provide its strategies, including timelines and Federal or non-Federal funding sources, that are—

(A) Designed to address the likely causes of the most significant differences in rates identified under paragraph (c)(5)(i) of this section; and

(B) Prioritized to address the most significant differences in rates identified under paragraph (c)(1) of this section as identified by the SEA, including by prioritizing strategies to support any schools identified for comprehensive or targeted support and improvement under § 200.19 that are contributing to those differences in rates; and

(iii) Describe its timelines and interim targets for eliminating all differences in rates identified under paragraph (c)(1).

(6) To meet the requirements of section 1111(g)(1)(B) of the Act, an SEA may—

(i) Direct an LEA, including an LEA that contributes to the differences in rates described by the SEA in paragraph (c)(1) of this section, to use a portion of its title II, part A, funds in a manner that is consistent with allowable activities identified in section 2103(b) of the Act to provide low-income and minority students greater access to effective teachers, principals, and other school leaders; and

(ii) Require an LEA to describe in its title II, part A plan or consolidated local plan how it will use title II, part A funds to address differences in rates described by the SEA in paragraph (c)(1) of this section and deny an LEA's application for title II, part A funds if an LEA fails to describe how it will address such differences in rates or fails to meet other local application requirements applicable to title II, part A.

(Approved by the Office of Management and Budget under control number 1810-0576)

(Authority: 20 U.S.C. 1221e-3, 3474, 7842)

§ 299.19
Supporting all students.
(a) Well-rounded and supportive education for students. (1) In its consolidated State plan, each SEA must describe how it will use title IV, part A funds and funds from other included programs, consistent with allowable uses of funds provided under those programs, to support State-level strategies and LEA use of funds designed to ensure that all children have a significant opportunity to meet challenging State academic standards and career and technical standards, as applicable, and attain, at a minimum, a regular high school diploma consistent with § 200.34. This description must:

(i) Address the State's strategies and how it will support LEAs to support the continuum of a student's education from preschool through grade 12, including transitions from early childhood education to elementary school, elementary school to middle school, middle school to high school, and high school to post-secondary education and careers, in order to support appropriate promotion practices and decrease the risk of students dropping out;

(ii) Address the State's strategies and how it will support LEAs to provide equitable access to a well-rounded education and rigorous coursework in subjects in which female students, minority students, English learners, children with disabilities, or low-income students are underrepresented, such as English, reading/language arts, writing, science, technology, engineering, mathematics, foreign languages, civics and government, economics, arts, history, geography, computer science, music, career and technical education, health, or physical education; and

(iii) Describe how, when developing its State strategies in paragraph (1) and, as applicable, paragraph (2), the SEA considered the academic and non-academic needs of the subgroups of students in its State including:

(A) Low-income students.

(B) Lowest-achieving students.

(C) English learners.

(D) Children with disabilities.

(E) Children and youth in foster care.

(F) Migratory children, including preschool migratory children and migratory children who have dropped out of school.

(G) Homeless children and youths.

(H) Neglected, delinquent, and at-risk students identified under title I, part D of the Act, including students in juvenile justice facilities.

(I) Immigrant children and youth.

(J) Students in LEAs eligible for grants under the Rural and Low-Income School program under section 5221 of the Act.

(K) American Indian and Alaska Native students.

(2) If an SEA intends to use title IV, part A funds or funds from other included programs for the activities that follow, the description must address how the State strategies in this paragraph support the State-level strategies in paragraph (a)(1) of this section to:

(i) Support LEAs to improve school conditions for student learning, including activities that create safe, healthy, and affirming school environments inclusive of all students to reduce—

(A) Incidents of bullying and harassment;

(B) The overuse of discipline practices that remove students from the classroom, such as out-of-school suspensions and expulsions; and

(C) The use of aversive behavioral interventions that compromise student health and safety;

(ii) Support LEAs to effectively use technology to improve the academic achievement and digital literacy of all students; and

(iii) Support LEAs to engage parents, families, and communities.

(b) Program-specific requirements—(1) Title I, part A. Each SEA must describe the process and criteria it will use to waive the 40 percent schoolwide poverty threshold under section 1114(a)(1)(B) of the Act submitted by an LEA on behalf of a school, including how the SEA will ensure that the schoolwide program will best serve the needs of the lowest-achieving students in the school.

(2) Title I, part C. Each SEA must describe—

(i) How the SEA and its local operating agencies (which may include LEAs) will—

(A) Establish and implement a system for the proper identification and recruitment of eligible migratory children on a statewide basis, including the identification and recruitment of preschool migratory children and migratory children who have dropped out of school, and how the SEA will verify and document the number of eligible migratory children aged 3 through 21 residing in the State on an annual basis;

(B) Identify the unique educational needs of migratory children, including preschool migratory children and migratory children who have dropped out of school, and other needs that must be met in order for migratory children to participate effectively in school;

(C) Ensure that the unique educational needs of migratory children, including preschool migratory children and migratory children who have dropped out of school, and other needs that must be met in order for migratory children to participate effectively in school, are addressed through the full range of services that are available for migratory children from appropriate local, State, and Federal educational programs; and

(D) Use funds received under title I, part C to promote interstate and intrastate coordination of services for migratory children, including how the State will provide for educational continuity through the timely transfer of pertinent school records, including information on health, when children move from one school to another, whether or not such move occurs during the regular school year (i.e., use of the Migrant Student Information Exchange (MSIX), among other vehicles);

(ii) The unique educational needs of the State's migratory children, including preschool migratory children and migratory children who have dropped out of school, and other needs that must be met in order for migratory children to participate effectively in school, based on the State's most recent comprehensive needs assessment;

(iii) The current measurable program objectives and outcomes for title I, part C, and the strategies the SEA will pursue on a statewide basis to achieve such objectives and outcomes;

(iv) How it will ensure there is consultation with parents of migratory children, including parent advisory councils, at both the State and local level, in the planning and operation of title I, part C programs that span not less than one school year in duration, consistent with section 1304(c)(3) of the Act;

(v) Its priorities for the use of title I, part C funds, specifically related to the needs of migratory children with "priority for services" under 1304(d) of the Act, including:

(A) What measures and sources of data the SEA, and if applicable, its local operating agencies, which may include LEAs, will use to identify those migratory children who are a priority for services; and

(B) When and how the SEA will communicate those determinations to all local operating agencies, which may include LEAs, in the State.

(3) Title I, part D. In its consolidated State plan, each SEA must include:

(i) A plan for assisting in the transition of children and youth between correctional facilities and locally operated programs; and

(ii) A description of the program objectives and outcomes established by the State that will be used to assess the effectiveness of the program in improving the academic, career, and technical skills of children in the program, including the knowledge and skills needed to earn a regular high school diploma and make a successful transition to postsecondary education, career and technical education, or employment.

(4) Title III, part A. (i) Each SEA must describe its standardized entrance and exit procedures for English learners, consistent with section 3113(b)(2) of the Act. These procedures must include valid and reliable, objective criteria that are applied consistently across the State.

(ii) At a minimum, the standardized exit criteria must—

(A) Include a score of proficient on the State's annual English language proficiency assessment;

(B) Be the same criteria used for exiting students from the English learner subgroup for title I reporting and accountability purposes; and

(C) Not include performance on an academic content assessment.

(5) Title IV, part B. In its consolidated State plan, each SEA must describe, consistent with the strategies identified in (a)(1) of this section and to the extent permitted under applicable law and regulations:

(i) How it will use title IV, part B funds, and other Federal funds to support State-level strategies and

(ii) The processes, procedures, and priorities used to award subgrants.

(6) Title V, part B, subpart 2. In its consolidated State plan, each SEA must provide its specific measurable program objectives and outcomes related to activities under the Rural and Low-Income School program, if applicable.

(7) McKinney-Vento Education for Homeless Children and Youths program. In its consolidated State plan, each SEA must describe—

(i) The procedures it will use to identify homeless children and youths in the State and assess their needs;

(ii) Programs for school personnel (including liaisons designated under section 722(g)(1)(J)(ii) of the McKinney-Vento Homeless Assistance Act, as amended, principals and other school leaders, attendance officers, teachers, enrollment personnel, and specialized instructional support personnel) to heighten the awareness of such school personnel of the specific needs of homeless children and youths, including such children and youths who are runaway and homeless youths;

(iii) Its procedures to ensure that—

(A) Disputes regarding the educational placement of homeless children and youths are promptly resolved;

(B) Youths described in section 725(2) of the McKinney-Vento Homeless Assistance Act, as amended, and youths separated from the public schools are identified and accorded equal access to appropriate secondary education and support services, including by identifying and removing barriers that prevent youths described in this paragraph from receiving appropriate credit for full or partial coursework satisfactorily completed while attending a prior school, in accordance with State, local, and school policies;

(C) Homeless children and youths have access to public preschool programs, administered by the SEA or LEA, as provided to other children in the State;

(D) Homeless children and youths who meet the relevant eligibility criteria do not face barriers to accessing academic and extracurricular activities; and

(E) Homeless children and youths who meet the relevant eligibility criteria are able to participate in Federal, State, and local nutrition programs; and

(iv) Its strategies to address problems with respect to the education of homeless children and youths, including problems resulting from enrollment delays and retention, consistent with sections 722(g)(1)(H) and (I) of the McKinney-Vento Homeless Assistance Act, as amended.

(Approved by the Office of Management and Budget under control number 1810-0576)

(Authority: 20 U.S.C. 1221e-3, 3474, 7842)

[FR Doc. 2016-27985 Filed 11-28-16; 8:45 am]
BILLING CODE 4000-01-P

FOOTNOTES

(1) For more information, including resources and links to research, on providing high-quality instruction and supports for English learners, please see the Department's non-regulatory guidance on English Learners and Title III of the ESEA, as amended by the ESSA, found here: http://www2.ed.gov/policy/elsec/leg/essa/essatitleiiiiguidenglishlearners92016.pdf.

(2) See, for example, Hakuta, K., Goto Butler, Y., & Witt, D. (2000). "How long does it take English learners to attain proficiency?" University of California Linguistic Minority Research Institute Policy Report 2000-1; MacSwan, J., & Pray, L. (2005). "Learning English bilingually: Age of onset of exposure and rate of acquisition among English language learners in a bilingual education program." Bilingual Research Journal, 29(3), 653-678; Motamedi, J.G. (2015). "Time to reclassification: How long does it take English language learners in the Washington Road Map school districts to develop English proficiency?" U.S. Department of Education, Institute of Education Sciences; and Slavin, R.E., Madden, N.A., Calderón, M.E., Chamberlain, A., & Hennessy, M. (2011). "Reading and language outcomes of a five-year randomized evaluation of transitional bilingual education." Educational Evaluation and Policy Analysis, 33 (1), 47-58.

(3) See, for example, the Department's non-regulatory guidance on English Learners and Title III of the ESEA, as amended by the ESSA, found here: http://www2.ed.gov/policy/elsec/leg/essa/essatitleiiiiguidenglishlearners92016.pdf. Please also see the 2016 policy issued by the U.S. Department of Health and Human Services and U.S. Department of Education Policy Statement on Supporting the Development of Children who are Dual Language Learners in Early Childhood Programs which addresses bilingualism and nurturing the native and home languages of our youngest learners. The statement and its recommendations can be found here: https://www.acf.hhs.gov/sites/default/files/ecd/dll_policy_statement_final.pdf.

(4) See: 81 FR 34540, 34544 notes 1 and 2 (May 31, 2016).

(5) See: http://www2.ed.gov/policy/elsec/guid/secletter/160622.html.

(6) See: 73 FR 64335, 64441-64442 (October 29, 2008).

(7) Cardichon, J. (2016). "Ensuring equity in ESSA: The role of n-size in subgroup accountability." Alliance for Excellence in Education. http://all4ed.org/reports-factsheets/n-size/.

(8) Cardichon, J. (2016). "Ensuring equity in ESSA: The role of n-size in subgroup accountability." Alliance for Excellence in Education. http://all4ed.org/reports-factsheets/n-size/.

(9) U.S. Department of Education. Institute of Education Sciences, National Center for Education Statistics (2010). "Statistical Methods for Protecting Personally Identifiable Information in Aggregate Reporting." Brief 3, NCES 2011-603. https://nces.ed.gov/pubsearch/pubsinfo.asp?pubid=2011603.

(10) Harr-Robins, J., Song, M., Hurlburt, S., Pruce, C., Danielson, L., & Garet, M. (2013). "The inclusion of students with disabilities in school accountability systems: An update (NCEE 2013-4017)." Washington, DC: National Center for Education Evaluation and Regional Assistance, Institute of Education Sciences, U.S. Department of Education, pp. 24-26.

(11) Hough, H., & Witte, J. (2016). "Making students visible: Comparing different student

subgroup sizes for accountability." CORE-PACE Research Partnership, Policy Memo, 16-2.

(12) Simpson, M. A., Gong, B., & Marion, S. (2006). "Effect of minimum cell sizes and confidence interval sizes for special education subgroups on school-level AYP determinations." Council of Chief State School Officers; Synthesis Report 61. National Center on Educational Outcomes, University of Minnesota.

(13) Cardichon, J. (2016). "Ensuring equity in ESSA: the role of n-size in subgroup accountability." Alliance for Excellence in Education. http://all4ed.org/reports-factsheets/n-size/.

(14) In the last two years alone, sixteen States and the California CORE districts lowered their n-size for either reporting or accountability purposes: Alaska from 26 to 5; Arizona from 40 to 30; Connecticut from 40 to 20. California's CORE districts from 100 to 20; Florida from 30 to 10; Georgia from 30 to 15; Idaho from 34 to 25; Illinois from 45 to 10; Maine from 20 to 10. Minnesota from 40 to 10 for reporting, and to 20 for accountability; Mississippi from 30 to 10; Nevada from 25 to 10; North Carolina from 40 to 30; Pennsylvania from 30 to 11; Rhode Island from 45 to 20; South Carolina from 40 to 30; and Texas from 50 to 25.

(15) See, for example: https://education.ohio.gov/getattachment/Topics/Every-Student-Succeeds-Act-ESSA/Nsize-Topic-Discussion-Guide.pdf.aspx.

(16) U.S. Department of Education. Institute of Education Sciences, National Center for Education Statistics (2010). "Statistical Methods for Protecting Personally Identifiable Information in Aggregate Reporting." Brief 3, NCES 2011-603. https://nces.ed.gov/pubsearch/pubsinfo.asp?pubid=2011603.

(17) ESEA Flexibility refers to the set of waivers from certain provisions of the ESEA, as amended by the NCLB, that the Department offered to States from the 2011-2012 through 2015-2016 school years. Given the overdue reauthorization of the ESEA, as amended by the NCLB, President Obama announced in September 2011 that the Department would grant these waivers to qualified States—those adopting college- and career-ready expectations for all students; creating differentiated accountability systems that target the lowest-performing schools, schools with the largest achievement gaps, and other schools that are not meeting targets for at-risk students; and developing and implementing teacher and principal evaluation and support systems that take into account student growth, among multiple measures, and are used to help teachers and principals improve their practices. In total, 43 States, the District of Columbia, and Puerto Rico were awarded ESEA Flexibility. For more information, see: http://www2.ed.gov/policy/elsec/guid/esea-flexibility/index.html.

(18) See: http://mclaughlinonline.com/pols/wp-content/uploads/2014/05/NATL-CSS-X-TABS-PRIMARY-4-18-14.pdf.

(19) See, for example, Dee, Thomas S., & Jacob, B. (May 2011). "The impact of No Child Left Behind on student achievement." Journal of Policy Analysis and Management, 30(3), 418-446; Carnoy, Martin, & Loeb, S. (2002). "Does external accountability affect student outcomes? A cross-state analysis." Educational Evaluation and Policy Analysis, 24(4), 305-31; Ahn, T., & Vigdor, J.L. (September 2014). "The impact of No Child Left Behind's accountability sanctions on school performance: Regression discontinuity evidence from North Carolina." NBER Working Paper No. w20511; Hanushek, Eric A., & Raymond, M.E. (2005). "Does school accountability lead to improved student performance?" Journal of Policy Analysis and Management, 24(2), 297-327; Winters, Marcus A. (2016). "Grading Schools Promotes Accountability and Improvement: Evidence from New York City, 2013-2015." Manhattan Institute; Burgess, Simon, Wilson, D., and Worth J. (2013); and "A natural experiment in school accountability: The impact of school

performance information on pupil progress." Journal of Public Economics, 106(C), 57-67.

(20) See, for example, Lipnevich, A.A., and Smith, J.K. (June 2008). "Response to assessment feedback: The effects of grades, praise, and source of information." Princeton, NJ: ETS; National Research Council. Incentives and Test-Based Accountability in Education. Washington, DC: The National Academies Press, 2011. doi:10.17226/12521; and the Oklahoma Center for Education Policy and the Center for Educational Research and Evaluation. (January 2013). "An Examination of the Oklahoma State Department of Education's A-F Report Card."

(21) See, for example, Winters, Marcus A. (2016). "Grading Schools Promotes Accountability and Improvement: Evidence from New York City, 2013-2015." Manhattan Institute; Rockoff, Jonah and Turner, Lesley J. (2010). "Short-Run Impacts of Accountability on School Quality." American Economic Journal: Economic Policy, 2(4): 119-47; Winters, M.A., and Cowen, J.M. (2012). Grading New York accountability and student proficiency in America's largest school district. Educational Evaluation and Policy Analysis, 34(3), 313-327; Rouse, C.E., Hannaway, J., Goldhaber D., and Figlio D. (2013). "Feeling the Florida Heat? How Low-Performing Schools Respond to Voucher and Accountability Pressure." American Economic Journal: Economic Policy, 5(2): 251-81; Figlio, David N. and Rouse, Cecilia Elena. (2006). "Do accountability and voucher threats improve low-performing schools?" Journal of Public Economics, 90(1-2):239-255; and Chiang, Hanley. (2009). "How accountability pressure on failing schools affects student achievement." Journal of Public Economics, 93(9-10):1045-1057.

(22) This chart provides a summary description only; please refer to the regulatory text for a complete description of the schools in these categories.

(23) Section numbers refer to sections of the ESEA, as amended by the ESSA.

(24) For more information on agencies' civil rights obligations to Limited English Proficient parents, see the Joint Dear Colleague Letter of Jan. 7, 2015, at Section J. (http://www2.ed.gov/about/offices/list/ocr/letters/colleague-el-201501.pdf).

(25) See: http://www2.ed.gov/policy/elsec/leg/essa/guidanceuseseinvestment.pdf. Non-Regulatory Guidance: Using Evidence to Strengthen Education Investments.

(26) See: http://www2.ed.gov/policy/elsec/leg/essa/guidanceuseseinvestment.pdf. Non-Regulatory Guidance: Using Evidence to Strengthen Education Investments.

(27) Black, S.E. (1999). "Do better schools matter? Parental valuation of elementary education." Quarterly Journal of Economics, 114 (2): 577-99.

Charbonneau, E., & Van Ryzin, G.G. (2012). "Performance measures and parental satisfaction with New York City Schools." American Review of Public Administration, 42 (1): 54-65.

Figlio, D.N. & Lucas, M.E. (2004). "What's in a grade? School report cards and the housing market." American Economic Review, 94 (3): 591-604.

Hastings, J.S. & Weinstein, J.M. (2008). "Information, school choice, and academic achievement: Evidence from two experiments." Quarterly Journal of Economics, 123 (4): 1373-414.

Jacobsen, R. & Saultz, A. (2013). "Do good grades matter? Public accountability data and perceptions of school quality." In The Infrastructure of Accountability, ed. Anagnostopoulos, D., Rutledge, S.A., & Jacobsen, R. Cambridge, MA: Harvard Education Press.

Jacobsen, R., Saultz, A. & Snyder, J.W. (2013). "When accountability strategies collide: Do policy changes that raise accountability standards also erode public satisfaction?" Educational Policy, 27 (2): 360-89.

Koning, P. & Wiel, K.V.D. (2013). "Ranking the Schools: How school-quality information affects school choice in the Netherlands." Journal of the European Economic Association, 11 (2): 466-493.

Nunes, L.C., Reis. A.B., & Seabra, C. (2015). "The publication of school rankings: A step toward increased accountability?" Economics of Education Review, 49 (December): 15-23.

Rockoff, J.E. & Turner, L.J. (2008). Short run impacts of accountability on school quality. Working Paper 14564, National Bureau of Economic Research, http://www.nber.org/papers/w14564.

(28) The ESSA also amended the IDEA by removing the definition of "highly qualified" in section 602(10) and the requirement in section 612(a)(14)(C) that special education teachers be "highly qualified" by the deadline established in section 1119(a)(2) of the ESEA, as amended by NCLB. However, Section 9214(d)(2) of the ESSA amended section 612(a)(14)(C) of the IDEA by incorporating the requirement previously in section 602(10)(B) that a person employed as a special education teacher in elementary school, middle school, or secondary school must: (1) Have obtained full certification as a special education teacher (including certification obtained through alternative routes to certification), or passed the State special education teacher licensing examination and hold a license to teach in the State as a special education teacher, except that a special education teacher teaching in a public charter school must meet the requirements set forth in the State's public charter school law; (2) not have had special education certification or licensure requirements waived on an emergency, temporary, or provisional basis; and (3) hold at least a bachelor's degree.

(29) Learning Denied: The Case for Equitable Access to Effective Teaching in California's Largest School District. Oakland, CA: The Education Trust West, 2012. http://edtrust.org/wp-content/uploads/2013/10/ETW-Learning-Denied-Report_0.pdf.

(30) Baird, Matthew D., John Engberg, Gerald Hunter and Benjamin Master. Trends in Access to Effective Teaching: The Intensive Partnerships for Effective Teaching Through 2013-2014. Santa Monica, CA: RAND Corporation, 2016. http://www.rand.org/pubs/research_briefs/RB9907.html.

(31) See, for example, U.S. Department of Education, Office for Civil Rights Dear Colleague Letter, Resource Comparability, October 1, 2014. http://www.ed.gov/ocr/letters/colleague-resourcecomp-201410.pdf.

(32) 16,790 is, according to NCES data, the total number of operating school districts of all types, except supervisory unions and regional education service agencies; including these types would result in double-counting. We note that the number of LEAs fluctuates annually.

Made in the USA
Monee, IL
28 August 2019